"The wonderful thing about Ed Cray's *Ramblin' Man* is that it puts aside the legend and the myth and gives us the man, without tearing him apart in the process."   —*The Globe and Mail*

"This biography resonates."   —Carlo Wolff, *Fort Worth Star-Telegram*

"[*Ramblin' Man* is] the best thing ever written about [Guthrie]. And it reminds us, just in time, of the things he stood for."
                                    —Dan Hayes, *Statesman Journal*, Oregon

"Guthrie was never really so authentic, as Ed Cray shows in *Ramblin' Man*. [This is] the first notable Guthrie biography since Joe Klein's."
                                    — David Hadju, *The New Yorker*

"By the time you close the covers, you'll likely see both Guthrie's legacy and his life in a new light."   —Jeffe Lindholm, *Dirty Linen*

"It's been left to American folklorist Ed Cray to come up with . . . the most comprehensive story of the man himself. . . . Highly recommended."
                                    —Jim Marshall, *The Folk Diary*

"It's an amazing story, never less than well-told here, on occasion considerably more."   —*St. Louis Post-Gazette*

"This surely will be the definitive biography of a legend whose songs continue to inspire millions of listeners, young and old."
                                    —Mike Nobles, *Book Scene*

"Cray's biography does much good work. It shows us, ably but without overdoing the point, just how political—and just how talented—Guthrie was."   —Gregory McNamee, *The Hollywood Reporter*

"This book is a gold mine of information."
                                    — Les Coles, *The Daily Yomiuri*, Tokyo

"*Ramblin' Man* documents Guthrie's life in a highly readable, factual manner and provides greater details of the darker side of his character than has been done in previous biographical efforts."　—Mike Nobles, *Book World*

"*Ramblin' Man* is easily the most factual and well-written biography of a little man who made a big impression around the world."

—Sandi Davis, *Oklahoman*

"*Ramblin' Man* reads with all the passion and drama of the novel but is a solid factual review of Woody Guthrie's inherently fascinating life and times."　—*Bookwatch*

"More than a dozen writers have tried to chronicle the vagabond life of Woody Guthrie, but none brought him alive quite like Ed Cray, not even Guthrie himself."　—John Rogers, Associated Press

"A compelling look of this legendary champion of the underdog."

—Bruce Bostick, *People's Weekly World Newspaper*

"Cray magnificently brings Guthrie and his times vividly alive." —John McTernan, *Scotland on Sunday*

"With unprecedented access to Guthrie's personal letters, Cray illuminates all areas of a short but important life."　—London *Sunday Times*

"Cray separates the man from the myth. . . . A monumental work."

—Geoff Ward, *Western Daily Press*

"Cray's tome is a fine read, both in terms of his subject and the America of the times."　—Michael Clifford, *Sunday Tribune*

"Cray eloquently sums up [Guthrie's] sorrowful life."　—*Booklist*

"Cray makes few assumptions; rather, he follows close on Guthrie's heels, letting the actions speak for themselves. . . . A jam-packed life, unfolded with an artful blend of perspective and admiration."　—*Kirkus Reviews*

"Cray contributes a valuable picture of the American West."

—*West Palm Beach Post*

Also by Ed Cray

Ramblin' Man

THE LIFE AND TIMES

OF WOODY GUTHRIE

Ed Cray

W. W. NORTON & COMPANY | NEW YORK LONDON

Frontispiece: Woody Guthrie, ca. 1943–44. Woody Guthrie Foundation and Archives.

Since this page cannot legibly accommodate all the copyright notices, pages 467–70
constitute an extension of the copyright page.

For information about permission to reproduce selections from this book, write to Permissions,
W. W. Norton & Company, Inc., 500 Fifth Avenue, New York, NY 10110

Manufacturing by Maple-Vail Book Manufacturing Group
Production manager: Julia Druskin

Library of Congress Cataloging-in-Publication Data
Cray, Ed.
  Ramblin' man : the life and times of Woody Guthrie / Ed Cray.— 1st ed.
       p. cm.
Includes bibliographical references and index.
  ISBN 0-393-04759-8 (hardcover)
 1. Guthrie, Woody, 1912–1967. 2. Folk singers—United States—Biography. I. Title.
ML419.G852 C73 2004
 782.42162'13'0092—dc22

                                                          2003021071

                        ISBN-13: 978-0-393-32736-1 pbk.
                        ISBN-10: 0-393-32736-1 pbk.

W. W. Norton & Company, Inc., 500 Fifth Avenue, New York, N.Y. 10110
                        www.wwnorton.com

W. W. Norton & Company Ltd., Castle House, 75/76 Wells Street, London W1T 3QT

  2 3 4 5 6 7 8 9 0

This book is dedicated to

Emily and Tessa

by their grandfather

CONTENTS

About all a human being is, anyway,

is just a hoping machine.

—WOODY GUTHRIE

IN ALL CASES I have used the names of people as they were known at
the time. Thus Marianne Robinson of 2003 is "Jolly" Smollens of 1948,
and so on.

Furthermore, I have attempted to replicate Woody Guthrie's writings
here as faithfully as possible, without correcting his deliberately idiosyncratic spellings or grammar. As the perceptive reader will soon realize,
Woodrow Wilson Guthrie was a well-read autodidact; he deliberately
adopted misspellings and grammatical "lapses" for effect.

ACKNOWLEDGMENTS

A BOOK OF THIS nature would not be possible without the contributions of many, first among whom is my wife, Diane Kovacs. She was, in the words of the late Dean Acheson, present at the creation, and she taught me much I needed to know to understand the complex man who was Woody Guthrie.

It is important too to acknowledge five people who trod this path before me and generously allowed me unlimited access to their research: the late Richard Reuss, whose wife JoAnne opened Reuss's invaluable files at Indiana University; E. Victor and Judy Wolfenstein, who thought to write a biography of Guthrie but were stolen away by the tantalizing Malcolm X; Bill Murlin, who has devoted himself to documenting Guthrie's Bonneville Dam song cycle; and Barry Ollman, who shared what is probably the largest collection of Guthrieana in private hands.

Their papers amplify or complement those held by the Woody Guthrie Archives, whose holdings are reflected on every page of this book. I was granted access to this trove—the first biographer to work in the West 57th Street quarters—by Nora Guthrie and Harold Leventhal, a man who defines the Yiddish meaning of the word *mensch*. May his tribe increase.

In one sense it does. At Leventhal's instruction, Jorge Arevalo, Amy Danielian, Jennifer Gotwals, Felicia Katz, and Michael Smith—Guthrie archivists all—patiently located documents and tape recordings for me. I am grateful.

Various people read portions of the manuscript: Harold Leventhal and Pete Seeger read the introduction and various chapters; Guy Logsdon read the first two chapters; Mary Jennings Guthrie Boyle read the third chapter; and stalwart Bess Lomax Hawes read the chapters on the Almanac years. Any errors that remain there or elsewhere are the sole property of the author.

Others helped, each in fondly remembered ways: Rachel Adams and Jon Connolly, Greta Walker and Bob Witten, all offered the hospitality of New

York City; and Mary Jo Guthrie Edgmon and Ann Guthrie provided spirited Oklahoma welcomes.

Others provided documents or specialists' information, including Bill Aldacushion; the late Bernard Asbell; Matt Barton, archivist at the Alan Lomax Archive; Thelma Bray; Anna Lomax Chairetakis, Alan Lomax Archive; Norm Cohen; Ronald Cohen, aka Folk Music Central; Brad Cook at the Indiana University Archives; Margie Crawford and Amy Davis of the Southern Folklife Collection, University of North Carolina; Bill Deverell of CalTech, whose passion for Woody Guthrie is exceeded only by his interest in California history; Christina Gallagher; Judith Gray, American Folklife Center, Library of Congress; Sylvia Grider, of Pampa and Texas A&M; David Gustafson; Frank Hamilton; Marc Igler; Davis Joyce; Kaori Maeyama; Marc Magoni, Annenberg School for Communication, University of Southern California, who dubbed tapes for me; Guy Mason, owner-editor of the *Okemah News Leader*, for introductions in that town; Evelyn Matzat, of the Long Beach, California, Public Library; Judy McCulloh; Carol Moskowitz, for her paper on Marjorie Guthrie; Joe Mozingo; Donna Munker; Sybilla Nash; Jeff Place of Folkways/Smithsonian; Gerald Porter; Morton Robbin; June Shelley; Nick Spitzer, host of Public Radio International's *American Routes*; Bernard "Bert" Somers; Ellen Stekert; Ron Taylor; Stacy Tidmore; and Betty Zulani, of the Orange County, California, Genealogical Society.

Needless to say, I am also grateful to the people who allowed me to record their memories of Woody, sometimes happy recollections, often sad or painful. I acknowledge them here, and list their names in the succeeding pages.

Finally, I would thank Woody Guthrie's three surviving children, Arlo, Joady, and Nora. They set no conditions, no limits on this project. They have not asked to read the manuscript, implicitly seeking only an honest portrayal of their father.

I have sought to honor that commission.

Ed Cray
January 2003

Studs Terkel

*W*OODY GUTHRIE WAS, *is*, America's balladeer. During the epoch of our deepest despair, the Great Depression, his were the songs that lifted the lowly spirits of the "ordinary," the millions of the dispossessed. They may have lacked for bread, but he offered them something else: self-esteem, hope, and a laugh or two along the way. Who was this bard?

Woody Guthrie, a tough, skinny, wind-blown, freckled, curly-headed Huck Finn. A little piece of leather. A dirt-road, hard-pavement, dank-box-car, cold-city, hot-desert gamin. Coast-to-coast poet and minstrel. Plus shoe shine boy, spittoon washer, hoer of fields, picker of mustang grapes, carpenter's helper, well-digger's assistant, sign painter, merchant mariner, fortune-teller, radio entertainer, street singer. The only thing I'm sure he hadn't been was a lawyer. I guess he'd never been a banker, either.

In 1912, the *Titanic* sank. In 1912, Woodrow Wilson was elected president. In 1912, Woodrow Wilson Guthrie was born. Fate sings its own kind of poetry. The day was July 14, Bastille Day in Paris, France; Woody's Day in Okemah, Oklahoma. On that day, the French "ordinary" sang their anthem, "La Marseillaise." In America, we sing ours, "This Land Is Your Land." It has nothing to do with bombs bursting in air nor with sanctimonious blessing. It has to do with what this country is all about.

> *This land is your land, this land is my land,*
> *From California to the New York Island,*
> *From the redwood forest to the Gulf Stream waters,*
> *This land was made for you and me.*

Nobody knows the exact number of songs written by Woody. Take a thousand, a good, round, conservative figure. The odds are better than even that there are more, many more, written on the spot, any old spot: the wayside inn, the gas station, the greasy spoon, the ma and pa tavern, the hamburger heaven, the subway bench, the jungle camp, the friendly davenport; been-here-and-gone pieces. How many of these were lost, bartered for a bologna sandwich or a pint of muscatel, or casually slipped away—not even Woody had the slightest idea.

I remember the summer of '41. Woody and three singing colleagues were in transit and spent a few days and nights in our jam-packed Chicago flat.* At four in the morning, my dream was interrupted by the click, click of my portable typewriter, my Royal. It was Woody, who had just ambled home, touch-typing like crazy. I turned over and slept dreamlessly. A few hours later as Woody snored softly, innocently in the adjoining room, I was picking sheets of paper from out of the wastebasket. There must have been at least thirty pages, single-spaced. Verse, prose, fragments of songs, impressions, wild, vivid images of his night at a South Side tavern. They danced off the pages. The remembered words of barflies, their lost-in-the-fog look, and the cock-eyed, tangential wisdom poured forth from the mumbo-jumbo of beer, the whiskey shot, the false-bottom glass, and the wino's muscatel. "I cannot help but learn the most from you who count yourself least," wrote the bantam bard on another occasion. "But I feel my best with you that need me most. I never did exactly know why this is, but that's just the way we're built."

Dust bowl songs, hobo songs, children's songs, work songs, loafing songs, union songs, river songs, lonesome turtledove songs; songs infinite in their variety, celebrating the wonder of man. For what is man to Woody? "Just a hoping machine, a working machine. The human race will sing this way as long as there is a human race. The human race is a pretty old place."

The men of the Bonneville Power Administration sensed the strength and poetry of Woody's ways. They commissioned him in 1941 to write songs celebrating the building of the Coulee and Bonneville Dams, of the Columbia River Project that was changing the whole face of our Northwest. With pencil stub, pen, battered portable, or whatever he could lay his hands on, he wrote twenty-six such ballads in thirty days. The impact of these rolling, sweeping songs on all who hears was inestimable. A Washington State senator said that any one of these Woody songs was worth a dozen legislative speeches in getting things done. Getting things done. Affecting people. Touching them where they live, moving them up a little higher. This was Woody.

Studs Terkel

---

* One was Pete Seeger, a skinny, gangly kid of nineteen with a bobbing Adam's apple; another was Lee Hays, a mountain of a man from Arkansas; the third was Millard Lampell, a writer.

Feathers from a Pillow

*T*HEY WERE NERVOUS. The advance sale had been slow, but then it always was for the hootenannies they had staged at Pythian Hall for the past four years. And the inexperienced promoter Harold Leventhal worried anyway, right up to the moment a concert began. Suppose you got hit with a sudden storm; rain could wash out any walk-up sale.

They had advertised in the *National Guardian* and the *New York Post* to reach out to the scattered remnants of the Old Left. And they put up a few posters where folk music records sold, to tap the young people who had taken up guitars and banjos in the postwar years. That was their core crowd.

Perhaps the hall was too big. It was not easy singing to a half-empty house. But twelve hundred seats with a five-dollar top would give the children's fund a good start, and there really wasn't much else to choose from. Better the well-maintained Pythian Hall just off Central Park West than one of the smaller, grimy union halls like Woody's own National Maritime Union or the Furriers'. Not many other auditoriums were available to radicals.

Then there was the basic concept of the program, a tribute to a vague, almost legendary figure. A whole evening of songs by one man, songs rich in poetry and symbolism, but songs so musically simple, wouldn't they all sound the same, some had wondered.

The script too was troublesome. Millard Lampell was an experienced radio writer, true enough, but the story of the fiery death of Guthrie's older sister was so sad, and so near the end of the show. Pete Seeger fretted that people would leave the theater depressed. Mill hardly reassured him, no matter how often he told Seeger, "Trust me, it would work just fine."

Then there were the kids, seventeen of Marjorie Mazia Guthrie's dance students at her Sheepshead Bay studio. No one would really get angry if they messed up the pantomime to the children's songs. They were kids, after all. But so near the finale, it could be embarrassing and keep the entire program from peaking.

Backstage, the Kossoy twins shifted anxiously among the singers and giggling dancers. Queens girls, they had become interested in folk music after listening to the first Weavers' recordings just a few years earlier. Like many of the younger folk-song fans, Irene and Ellen had sung on Sunday afternoons during jam sessions at Washington Square in the Village; unlike most of their folkie friends, the twins had visited Guthrie at the hospital. This was the first time they would sing on the same program as Seeger and Lee Hays, two of the founding members of the Weavers. That alone left the twins both excited and anxious.

It would help if they would settle on a program too. "So Long" was in. And "Bound for Glory." "Go to Sleep My Little Hobo" was out, replaced by "Rambling, 'Round Your Country." That would send them off to huddle in a corner, heads together, to quietly rehearse.

Out front, the doors opened and the audience began to straggle in. Soon enough his friends backstage would learn if the name "Woody Guthrie" meant anything.

Woody himself presented no problem. Marjorie and Al Addeo, her new husband, would not bring him into the building until just before the curtain. Once prickly proud and fiercely independent, a figure larger than life, now he seemed shrunken, even emaciated, his wiry hair graying at forty-four, his face weathered by wind, sun, and tragedy. The voice was all but mute. Fire had seared his right arm, the angry skin drawn red and taut, the elbow cocked so he no longer could play an instrument or lift a pen.

And all the while the illness had crept over him insidiously, tugging on his arms or canting his head to one shoulder. Though his speech was slurred—people had often thought he was drunk—his mind seemed clear. He would be okay with Al Addeo in the first box at stage right; the two men, Marjorie's second and third husbands, got on well together.

Nearby sat Woody and Marjorie's three children, Arlo, the oldest at nine; Joady, seven; and Nora, six. They saw their father on weekends, sometimes visiting him at the state mental hospital in Montclair, New Jersey, occasionally taking him home to Brooklyn.

The hall on West 70th Street filled slowly. It always did when there was a big walk-up sale. Which meant they would start late, another worry for Leventhal. The show was long and he didn't want to go into overtime. Every penny that went to the union stagehands was a penny that didn't go to the newly created Guthrie Children's Trust Fund.

The program on that Saturday night in March 1956 included thirty of Guthrie's most popular songs. Most he had written in a span of five years while living in California, or while traveling "over that 66 enough to run it up to 6666."* They began with the traditional gospel song Guthrie had learned at some revival meeting, a song that had given him the title of his autobiography, "Bound for Glory." Then narrator Lee Hays's rolling bass voice took up the story:

> His name is Woodrow Wilson Guthrie . . . a bit of information which may come as kind of a surprise. Most people don't know he's got any other name but just Woody. He started out from Oklahoma, and he traveled all of the forty-eight states and most of the seven seas. And wherever he went he made music.

There were songs Woody had learned from his mother and from his fiddling Uncle Jeff, songs like "Gypsy Davy" and "Going Down the Road Feeling Bad." There were his dust bowl ballads, the sardonic "Do-Re-Mi" and the proud "Pastures of Plenty." There were the songs he had written praising the Columbia River dams, "Seven Wonders" and "Roll on, Columbia." There were some of his union songs and some of the songs he had tossed off to spur morale during the war.

In the first box stage right, Woody Guthrie sat quietly. An arm muscle tensed unbidden. A hand twitched. But his eyes stayed fixed on the stage as he listened to the songs he had dashed off and the stories of raucous Okemah and hard traveling, of California's fertile valleys and scant wages, stories he had typed late into the night, then thrown forgotten on the floor.

> I don't know what this stuff called time is made out of. Don't even know where it boils up and steams up from, don't even know where time rolls back to. I don't know what I, my own self, am made out of, because just about every day I find out that I'm made out of something new, like time its own self is.

> You could just take a handful of these things you call days and weeks, and things you say are months, and hold them in your hand like this, and blow them up into the air like a feather out of old Aunt Rhody's Pillow, and you'd find me out there back in Oklahoma, out on my Grandma's farm paying a visit.

---

* Notes to the sources of quoted material follow the text.

Seeger came downstage to the solitary microphone, the longneck banjo cocked across his lanky body. Of them all, Pete had been the closest to Woody. A Harvard dropout, a barely twenty-one-year-old at once naive and grave, Seeger had sung his way across the country and back with Guthrie. Woody and the road had taught Pete an understanding of American grit he could never have learned in school.

Sixteen years after first meeting Guthrie, sixteen years of singing folk songs learned from records in the Library of Congress and protest songs they had quickly crafted for strikes and picket lines, dark years of surveillance by the Federal Bureau of Investigation and lies by paid informers, hopeful years of doggedly touring colleges and churches to sing down the Red Menace and McCarthyism, sixteen years later Pete Seeger would repay a debt to his friend.

The first four notes, by now a familiar phrase, marched up the scale then repeated the fourth: "This land is your land."

No other song so embodied Guthrie the man, his optimism, his love of the nation and its people: "This land is my land."

Guthrie had written the lines while hitchhiking in the wintry February of 1940. For weeks the sometime dust bowl refugee and ever restless Okie had listened to the jukeboxes and Kate Smith booming the saccharine "God Bless America." Maybe the Almighty had or would sometime in the future, but so far He had missed the America Guthrie knew, the sharecroppers, the boomers, the kids living in ditches alongside California's rural roads. There was something too pat, too smug about Irving Berlin's patriotic plea. Responding to the song, Guthrie snarled:

> *One bright sunny morning in the shadow of the steeple*
> *By the Relief Office I saw my people-*
> *As they stood hungry, I stood there wondering if*
> *God blessed America for me.*

He would later rework the text, scratching that verse, leeching the bitterness from the words and restoring the sense of optimism his father Charley had imbued in the Guthrie children four decades earlier.

> *From the redwood forest to the Gulf Stream waters,*
> *This land was made for you and me.*

People across the country were singing the song now—at hoots and sing-a-longs and, better still, in public schools. Often the kids didn't know who wrote it, didn't care even. No matter, the skinny man in the oversized sport jacket sitting in the box at stage right had never bothered to copyright his thousand or more songs. He just wrote them, sang them, then wrote some more. If someone learned one of his songs and sang it, Woody figured he did him a favor.

> *When the sun came shining, then I was strolling*
> *The wheat fields waving, and the dust clouds rolling,*
> *A voice was chanting as the fog was lifting:*
> *This land was made for you and me.*

The applause spilled down on the cast strung across the stage. A spotlight beam slashed across the hall to settle on the first box stage right and the slight figure of Woody Guthrie. On stage, Seeger pointed toward the box. Swaying slightly, Guthrie stood up to take the salute, a cigarette pack clutched in his hand. He smiled faintly.

"There's Woody" rippled through the auditorium. The vanished man had returned, a legend made real.

As the applause rose, Guthrie waved slowly, tentatively. Earl Robinson turned to Seeger on the stage. "Sing the last chorus over again."

Seeger sang with tears in his eyes as the audience joined in the tribute.

> *This land is your land, this land is my land,*

Old members of the Movement, veterans of picket lines and protest rallies, sang.

> *From California to the New York Island.*

The youngsters new to folk music, only vaguely aware of the political struggles of that earlier generation, sang a song they had taken as their own.

> *From the redwood forest to the Gulf Stream waters,*
> *This land was made for you and me.*

They sang. And Woodrow Wilson Guthrie, Woody, on that Saturday night in March 1956 became a part of the American myth.

Ramblin' Man

CHAPTER ONE

The Guthries of Okemah

*T*HE LAND SLIPS EASTERLY from the High Plains and south from the Kansas line, toward the Mississippi and the Gulf of Mexico, the softly eroded hills of this geologic red-bed country cut by pecan-lined creeks and shallow washes flowing into the Deep Fork and Canadian Rivers. In the rolling fields, the corn and cotton struggle from the spare topsoil, a rich loam once, but now worn thin by spring rains and autumn winds howling from the north and west.

Between the Deep Fork and the north fork of the Canadian River, the town of Okemah, Oklahoma, sits at the end of a string of sandstone hills that run north toward Jayhawker country. Newly incorporated on "surplus" land once set aside for the Creek Indian Nation, Okemah boasted as much promise as any clapboard town thrown up along the Fort Smith and Western Railroad tracks. Okemah—variously the "city on a hill" in the Creek tongue or the name of a Kickapoo "high man"—was the county seat of Okfuskee County in the new state of Oklahoma.

To this town clinging to the hardscrabble land, newly elected district court clerk Charley Guthrie took his wife and two young children in April 1907. The local paper welcomed him as a man of "irreproachable private life" who "stands unusually high with all who enjoy his acquaintance." Okemah welcomed optimistic go-getters like Charley Edward Guthrie.

Charley had acquired both ambition and determination from his father, formally Jeremiah Pearsall Guthrie, but "Jerry P." to the people of his native Bell County in South Texas. Restless Jerry P. had moved his family, including then-eighteen-year-old Charley, from the cattle and cotton country of Bell County north across the state to Indian Territory in 1897. The federal government was awarding land grants as large as 160 acres to anyone with Indian blood; Jerry P.'s second wife, Charley's stepmother, was one-eighth Creek. It was enough to qualify.

Charley, one of eight children, had grown to be a wiry young man on his father's ranch, herding cattle by day, studying correspondence courses by night. While he never went beyond the seventh grade, he taught himself bookkeeping and, because bookkeepers were required to write a fine hand, Creamer Method penmanship. (He risked that fine hand by also taking up boxing, learned from yet another correspondence course.) Before long, family legend has it, the son was advising the father on business matters dealing with the ranch—and giving penmanship lessons.

Cowboying held little promise for enterprising Charley, and farming less still after Jerry P. decided to sell out and return to ranching in the Chisos Mountains along the Texas-Mexico border shortly after the turn of the century. Instead, Charley elected to stay in the territory, drifting from store to ranch to store, until he eventually landed in the small town of Castle in 1902.

Charley Guthrie was twenty-three, clerking in J. B. Wilson's dry general store, when he met Nora Belle Tanner. She was the daughter of one of the first log-cabin schoolteachers in Okfuskee County, Mary Sherman Tanner, and if Kansas-born Nora was not the prettiest girl, she was among the most spunky.* Inevitably people judged fourteen-year-old Nora something of a tomboy because of her spirited attitude. How else would she assert herself in a house with three brothers and sisters, and three half-brothers?

Nora and her new beau Charley had shared interests. They liked to ride horses together—it was said Nora, sitting sidesaddle, rode as fast as any man—and they enjoyed music. Jerry P. had been a fiddler; his son was a sometime guitar and banjo picker, a sturdy bass in the choir at the Baptist church. Nora sang the old songs, hymns and sentimental ballads learned from her mother, songs Nora accompanied with great blocks of chords on the Price and Deeple piano in the parlor of the seven-room home Lee and Mary Tanner had built on their ranch outside Castle.

Charley and Nora made a handsome couple. Charley was well dressed, and if not quite handsome, he carried himself with a certain athletic grace. With younger half-brothers Gid and Claude, he played for the local baseball team against clubs from neighboring towns. Charley was a pitcher with a wicked curveball and "a pretty good hitter," Claude said.

---

* Nora was born in 1888 to George Sherman and Mary Mahoney Sherman, who were then living in Kansas. The Shermans moved to the vicinity of Welty, Oklahoma, and there Sherman, then twenty-seven, drowned while fording a stream on horseback. His widow, left with four children, eventually married a prosperous cattleman, Lee Tanner. They had three sons: Warren, Leonard, and Lawrence, Nora's half-brothers. Daughter Mary Jo Edgmon said her mother Nora used her stepfather's name.

"He had a lot of pride," Charley's youngest daughter would recall years later, pride in his accomplishments, pride in his family. They were Scots-Irish, MacGuthries in a distant past, more recently settled in Tennessee. The Guthries had migrated to Texas in covered wagons after the War Between the States, fervent Confederates still. It was no accident that Charley had a younger half-brother named Jefferson Davis Guthrie.

Nora and Charley were a good match. He was brimming with energy and ideas; she was strongminded and a steadying hand on his enthusiasms. For the next eighteen months Charley was a frequent visitor to the Tanner home on the road between Castle and Welty, welcomed by schoolteacher Mary for his love of books and by father Lee for his humorous yarns. In time the visits became a courtship. Nora was barely sixteen when her parents consented to the marriage.

Married on Valentine's Day in 1904, Nora and Charley moved into a small house in Castle. When their first child, Clara Edna, was born in November 1904, ambitious family man Charley Guthrie began to read law. He also plunged into Democratic Party politics and the related task of shaping a new state from the red clay of the Indian territories.

With statehood in the offing, Charley Guthrie, a solid Democrat, ran for election as district court clerk and won on September 18, 1907—after 395 votes from all-Negro and heavily Republican precincts were arbitrarily thrown out on the pretext that their ballot boxes had been stuffed.

The new district court clerk moved five miles from Castle to Okemah, a town "partly western in its optimism and quick acceptance of outsiders, and partly southern, in the soft accents of its inhabitants, its prejudice against blacks, and its tolerance of booze, sidewalk fights, and public drunkenness."

He gave up clerking in J. B. Wilson's general store for something more ambitious, more enterprising. Real estate was just the ticket for a man like Charley Guthrie in this new and bustling county seat. As an up-and-comer, he joined Masonic Lodge No. 139 and the First Methodist Church; as a dedicated Democrat, he began giving speeches about the looming peril of Eugene Debs and the Socialist Party.

Charley Guthrie prospered in Okemah. "Our house was full of the smells of big leather law books, and the poems of pomp and high dignity that he memorized and performed over us," his middle son would write later. Charley did well enough to buy the first automobile in Okemah, a Chalmers, and took it on a trip over unpaved roads in 1909 to Kansas City; there Nora visited with relatives.

While Charley prospered, others fared poorly. For all its brave talk, Oklahoma was a troubled land in these early years of the twentieth century. Once set aside for the Five Civilized Tribes—the Choctaw, Chickasaw, Cherokee, Creek, and Seminole—after 1889 the Indian territories had been opened to land-poor and often desperate outsiders seeking 160-acre quarter sections to farm. As many as 125,000 families made their way to this "Promised Land" to take part in the land rush; they hoped to forge a new start on the two million virgin acres opened to the boomers. The sharpers and speculators quickly followed.

Here on the nation's last frontier was "the greatest wheat country in the world," boosters crowed, "with corn bigger than saw logs and watermelons bigger than whales." For good workers, there was also coal, lead, and zinc to be mined from the hills around Henryetta, east of Okemah.

The territories sat empty, a sea of bluestem grass stretching to the horizons, turning ochre, then purple, then copper as season succeeded season. In late fall and winter, the cold northers ripped down the Great Plains; in spring and early summer the winds blew southerly and warm from the Gulf of Mexico. With spring, the rains came too, turning dry washes into deadly rivers, the storms often accompanied by vicious tornadoes that capriciously dipped down to shatter houses and barns, stores and business blocks.

The sodbusters, even the experienced farmers among them, found the going tough. Wheat growers in the northern and western parts of the new state could not operate economically on small acreage; in time they would sell out to the speculators, and the speculators, in turn, would sell to well-financed corporations capable of purchasing labor-saving combines and harvesters.

In the red-bed country around Okemah, cotton was the dominant crop. In cotton-picking time, the farmers lined up fifteen deep, waiting their turn at the six gins. But the small farmers of Okfuskee County had little better luck than those farther west.

In hard times, the small farmer turned to the banks, borrowing at 10 percent interest rates and putting up the farm as collateral. When they could not meet the payments, Oklahoma and neighboring Texas became "the earthly paradise of the grasping banker."

One by one, then by the tens and hundreds, farmers went broke and sold out, unable to pay off their debts. More galling still, once-independent farmers found themselves renting back from speculators and banks the very acreage they had owned the year before. By 1915, half of Oklahoma's farmers were poverty-ridden renters, victims of "tooth-and-claw" capitalism. One frustrated tenant, speaking for a thousand like himself, blamed greedy landlords, who told him what to raise, and impersonal bankers, who set high interest rates. "I am a small farmer and a renter in Okfuskee County where you can hardly rent enough land to plant feed stock. . . . Everything is cotton."

The new pattern of landownership fostered a parallel myth of a "farm ladder of success." Newspaper editorials and Sunday sermons advised young men to begin their careers as hired hands, to frugally put aside money to buy the livestock and feed they would need to set up as renters. Then, as renters, they and their pennywise "helpmates" would save each year to buy their own farms, raise their families, and prosper.

Few succeeded. Cyclic drought, unpredictable weather, and perennially low farm prices shattered that meager dream. "The $25.00 a bale rent you pay the landlord would buy lots of biscuits and calico for the wife," fumed the *Madill Socialist-Herald*, "but then it enables the landlord's wife to wear silk and ride in an automobile, and no matter if your wife does walk."

Walk she would. The farm tenant's life was miserable. He provided the labor and the farm animals and paid rents of one-third of all corn and one-fourth of his cotton harvest. At that he earned no more than a bare living from the poor land. He worked twice the hours of sharecroppers in Mississippi and Louisiana, yet his yields were less. His children as young as three might be drafted to pick cotton, and still it was never enough. The *Oklahoma Farmer-Stockman* in 1913 estimated that the cost of production on cotton tenant farms was twice the market price of cotton.

Frustration and hard times bred desperate men—to the point that insurance companies canceled policies protecting banks from losses to robbers. They had good reason. Henry Starr, the first bank robber to use an automobile, robbed banks for six years in eastern Oklahoma and Arkansas while neighbors looked on benignly. As Starr blandly explained, the banks he had held up were in the "robbery business too."

By the time Oklahoma entered the union in 1907, corporate business interests, particularly in agriculture and livestock, controlled the state's economy. For the next decade, these economically powerful forces, guiding a southern wing of the Democratic Party, vied with agrarian reformers, populists, itinerant Industrial Workers of the World organizers, and Eugene Debs Socialists.

Up-and-coming Charley Guthrie knew where he stood: four square with the other "hard hittin', fist-fightin' Democrats." The Democrats were all for an enterprising man, a man like Charley Guthrie, making his own way.

He and Nora began building a six-room house with a wide screened-in porch on South Sixth Street, a home to easily accommodate not only Charley and his wife, but Clara, going on five, and little Roy, two and a half. Their home was completed at a cost of $800, and the Guthries moved in during the fall of 1909.

A month later, it burned to the ground. Sparks from a fire in neighbor W. H. Fields's kitchen ignited the Guthrie house. While they were able to save many of their possessions, Charley's law books among them, the splendid yellow house on Sixth Street was no more.

It was a serious setback. Charley had insured the home for just $300 of its $800 cost, "leaving him a pretty heavy loser," a local newspaper reported.

Nora grieved the loss of her yellow house on the hill; Charley Guthrie simply moved his family into the vacant Bewley property, determined to restore the family fortunes.

Early the next year, Charley announced for reelection as court clerk. Endorsed by the *Okemah Ledger* as "one of the most satisfactory and popular of our county officers," he faced no serious opposition. Any threat the Republicans might have posed had been cut down by a new literacy law.

Oklahoma in politics was a southern state, its constitutional convention and its first legislatures dominated by southern Democrats. The Negro, proclaimed the president of the constitutional convention, "Alfalfa Bill" Murray, was incapable of becoming "the equal of the white man in the professions or becoming an equal citizen to grapple with public questions." Charley Guthrie, "hot-headed Democrat" in the words of his half-brother Claude, was a strong Murray booster.

Jim Crow ruled. Oklahoma's Democratic legislature in its first sessions legally embraced segregation and a voters' literary test. The one assured they would keep the Negro in his place, the other that the Democrats would stay in office. The literacy test effectively barred Negroes—who tended to vote Republican—from voting at all. (A precautionary grandfather clause virtually exempted whites, the majority of whom were Democrats, from challenge.) Okfuskee County promptly struck a third of its voters from the precinct rolls.*

---

* Okfuskee County also perpetuated Jim Crow's ultimate threat, the lynching. On May 25, 1911, a mob intent on avenging the murder of a policeman summarily hung Laura Nelson, thirty-five, and her fourteen-year-old son, Lawrence, from the newly constructed railroad bridge over the Canadian River. A picture postcard of the hanging bodies was sold as a souvenir; that postcard later was one of sixty pictures of lynchings exhibited at New York City's Roth Horowitz Gallery in January and February 2000.

One threat, a growing one at that, remained to Democratic hegemony in Okfuskee County and Oklahoma: Eugene Debs and the surprisingly popular Socialist Party. Long before Jerry P. had moved to the territory, poverty on the Great Plains had given birth to radical sentiment and radical spokesmen. First came the prairie populists, raging against the railroads, the banks, the gold standard, and high tariffs. Then came Debs, in Oklahoma advocating an idealistic Christian socialism that fused old-time religious teachings with turn-of-the-century political action.

There were, in fact, two forms of socialism. One was the orthodox dogma imported from Europe, atheist, rigidly Marxist in its demand that the land and engines of production be held in common. The other was a peculiarly American hybrid, one that blended the apocalyptic Protestant beliefs of small-town America with the Marxist principle of shared wealth.

Protestantism ran deep on the western frontier, "an enveloping ideology that gave meaning to the world of the country folk," wrote historian Garin Burbank. It succored the poor in their misery and celebrated the rich in their success, explained good and evil as God's mysterious way, and comforted both rich and poor in dark times.

Many prairie socialists found it hard to entirely throw over the old faith for the atheistic new. Instead they melded the two, arguing that socialist reform would lead to the Kingdom of Christ. Did not Leviticus 25:23 thunder, "The land shall not be sold forever: for the land *is* mine; and ye *are* strangers and sojourners with me"?

Socialism in Oklahoma became "the primitive gospel of applied Christianity." Onetime Presbyterian elder O. E. Enfield, a recent convert to socialism, assured readers of the *Ellis County Socialist* that he wanted to be called "comrade." "There is only one title at the sound of which my heart throbs with greater joy, and that is the word Christian."

The threat of socialism seeped even to Okemah when the *Sledge Hammer* opened offices in town. Each week, that avowedly Socialist paper published the Rev. E. F. McClanahan's fierce arguments linking Christianity and socialism. "Under socialism," he argued, "you might find it much easier to put your religious belief into practice."

Unwavering Democrat that he was, Charley watched the rise of the Socialist Party in Oklahoma with concern. The Socialist vote had steadily grown until Oklahoma had the largest membership of any state in the union. In Okfuskee County, the socialists had skimmed off 15 percent of the votes in the 1908 presidential election.

Looking ahead to the 1912 elections, Democrats like Charley Guthrie fretted that Debs would steal enough votes from their nominee, Woodrow Wilson, to hand victory to the Republicans. For their part, the Socialists dismissed the stiff-necked Wilson as no better than the Republican contenders, ex-President Theodore Roosevelt and President William Howard Taft. The Democratic Party in Oklahoma, they proclaimed, was nothing but "a political tool of the banker-ginner-merchant-landlord class"—the tool of men like Charley Guthrie, lately taken to land trades when he was not serving as district court clerk.

Guthrie's response, characteristically, was to fight back. He began a series of essays on October 4, 1911, for the *Okemah Ledger*, raking the "Kumrids" doctrine by doctrine.

Each week, Guthrie turned in to the editor of the *Ledger* his fulminations, set out in the steel-pen hand of the Creamer Method. "Free Love the Fixed Aim of Socialism," his first sally charged. His next announced, "Socialism the Enemy of Christian Religion."

By the third week, with "Socialism Guards Secret Philosophy," Charley Guthrie was out on the front page of the *Ledger*. And there he stayed for the next five months, through "More Evidence of Socialist Free Love" and "Is It True Socialists Never Do Graft?" to the final blow, "Socialism Urges Negro Equality."

Charley's pointed essays provoked sharp responses, both from the *Sledge Hammer* and from Socialist Party headquarters in Oklahoma City. Near the end of the year, he began a series of debates with a Socialist spokesman who made the mistake of directly challenging Charley: "While charging free love on the socialists, do you deny you are a practical free lover?" According to Charley's younger half-brother Jeff, a furious Guthrie knocked his opponent through a bank window on Broadway. (As half-brother Claude remembered a similar incident, Charley "once hit a guy who hit his head on a cornerstone and Charley was in a tough scrape for a while.")

In March 1912, Charley gathered his articles into an eighty-nine-page booklet entitled "Kumrids." He asserted in an introduction to the reprint that for more than seven years he had "been an earnest, patient and faithful student of socialism. . . ." While he conceded there were "existing, evil conditions" upon the land, socialism was not the answer. His "little book," the distillation of many dollars' worth of socialist writings, was intended to alert the reader to "the poisonous and dangerous fangs of the tempting serpent which is lurking behind the advance claims of socialism."

Six months later, Charley compiled a second anthology, "Procrastination Is the Thief of Time," in which he argued that earlier socialistic communities inevitably had to fail. "The less industrious had sought incessantly
to exploit the more industrious, with the natural result that the industrious
found themselves working, not only for their own support, but also those
who were work-shy. . . ."

If Charley the pamphleteer thought his battle against the Socialists
would be rewarded by the Democratic Party, he was to be disappointed.
When the incumbent state representative, J. J. Roland, hinted he might not
run again, Charley allowed as how he was interested in the seat. The *Ledger*
promptly offered its endorsement, assuring readers, "He wants the rate of
taxation as low as possible."

Roland, however, reversed himself and promptly received the party's
endorsement. A chastened Charley Guthrie quietly withdrew, to run
instead for county assessor, a post where his taxation policy would have
more immediate affect.

Charley campaigned for the assessor's office through the spring of
1912 and the last months of Nora's third pregnancy. In the end he would
be unrewarded for his party loyalty. The election returns sent him home a
loser to the incumbent, Tom Hall.

On July 2, 1912, after forty-six ballots, the Democrats nominated the
governor of New Jersey, Woodrow Wilson, to be their presidential nominee.
When, twelve days later, Nora delivered her third child and second son,
Charley insisted the eight-pound boy be named after the Democratic candidate.

Charley was overjoyed, "as happy as a lobster." He announced his son's
birth in the *Ledger* with a fulsome notice asserting he had found the best
definition of a baby after searching "many volumes of the latest and most
up to date works. . . . 'A baby—a tiny feather from the wing of love dropped
into the sacred lap of motherhood; an inhabitant of lapland; a padlock on
the chains of life . . . the morning caller, noonday crawler, midnight bawler;
the latest edition of humanity of which every couple think they possess the
finest copy.' "

Woodrow Wilson Guthrie was, by all accounts, a happy child, with blue
eyes and brown hair, "bubbly and bouncy," his younger sister recalled.
From his earliest days, music captivated the boy they called Woody.

Virtually the child's first memory was the sight and sound of a "Negro
minstrel jazzy band blowing and tooting and pounding drums up and
down our street." As the boy grown to manhood remembered it, that

medicine show jazz band inspired him to march back and forth across the front porch of his home, "and sing out the first song I ever made up by my own self":

> Listen to the music, music, music.
> Listen to the music, music band.

Even if an infant's recollection might be doubted, music *was* important in the Guthrie household. Charley and Nora sang often to the child, his father booming square-dance calls and blues learned from black laborers. Nora disliked performing in front of visitors, but at home "she had a sort of a tender heart, made that way by suffering a lot of things, and by carrying big loads, and she went deeper, and tried to tell the 'story' or the 'thought' that is so rich in these old Hill Country songs."

Nora favored the moralistic parlor ballads so popular in the last decades of the nineteenth century, "The Dream of a Miner's Child," "A Picture from Life's Other Side," and "A Story I Know Too Well":

> The weeks and days I watched her, watched by the side of
>   her bed
> Till death had closed her eyelids and Nelly, my daughter,
>   was dead.
> Six weeks from the day I laid her in her graveyard plot,
> Her mother's body was taken to the quiet churchyard lot.

Nora also sang the far older Scots-Irish ballads of her parents' parents, tales of outlaws and demon lovers, border raids, and seafaring heroes.

> It was late last night when my lord got home.
> He was asking about his lady
> And the only answer that he got:
> "She's gone with a Gypsy Davy.
> She's gone with a Gypsy Dave."

The family was close knit. The oldest child, Clara Edna, not only shared the initials "C. E." with her father; she was a tomboy who took to the boxing gloves, Indian clubs, and iron-spring expanders Charley Edward brought home. Two years younger than his sister, Roy too "worked out pretty fair with his fists, but in our family, it was always Clara that tamed

. . . every boy up and down Sixth Street and finally worked her way up and down Seventh Street. . . ."

To Clara, almost eight years old when her youngest brother was born, fell much of the burden of looking out for the energetic Woody. Mother Nora seemed distracted at times, as if preoccupied. Woody's older brother Roy recalled going off to school in the morning, leaving his mother at the steaming washtub, only to return in the afternoon and find the forgotten clothes still soaking in cold water.

From the Bewley place, the Guthries moved to one house then another, finally settling in the fall of 1913 in the old London house on South First Street. Built over a stone foundation against a hillside, the six-room house looked down on the dirt track leading toward brick-paved Broadway.

As the boy grown to a man remembered the London place, Mama and Clara thought this "mean ol' house" frightening. Roy disliked telling people he lived in the once-abandoned home with the rock-walled cellar full of cobwebs and empty snuff tins. But young Woody was unconcerned. From the back porch, he could watch the loaded wagons creaking to Okemah's cotton gins and hear the engine whistles from the Fort Smith and Western depot. The parade a hundred feet below his dangling legs fascinated him, especially later, after oil was discovered at Spring Hill, just nine miles east of town. Then came the boomers, turning quiet Okemah into the "drinkingest, yellingest, preachingest . . . bleedingest, gamblingest, gun, club, and razor carryingest of our ranch and farm towns. . . ."

Charley Guthrie fit right in. "Papa was a man of brimstone and hot fire in his mind and in his fists, and was known all over that section of the state," Woody said later. Despite their reputation and feisty nature, Charley and Nora would sing hymns and spirituals together as they rode the seven miles to and from Grandmother Tanner's farm out toward the Deep Fork.

For his mother, Woody held a "deep devotion," a former neighbor recalled. Out of devotion the boy sought to protect her, especially as she began to sing "the hurt songs in a wilder way" and "our singing got the saddest." Nora was particularly anxious about Charley; she wanted him to find a new line of work.

No longer the court clerk, Charley Guthrie had plunged into the real estate business, shrewdly trading properties, keeping some as rentals and selling others. It was a good time for an ambitious man.

First there was Oklahoma's oil boom, begun in 1910, bringing spasms of prosperity and a tide of boomchasers who drifted from company town to company town. Sand Springs, Slick City, Garrison, wherever the boomers migrated, local merchants and real estate operators made money. In 1918, the boom reached Okfuskee County, and Charley Guthrie began to share in the bounty.

Prices were high—for food and housing, for drugs, for prostitutes, for alcohol. The boomtowns ran wide open. Local law enforcement authorities either owned the whorehouses and saloons or, amply bribed, looked the other way. Money the boomers earned in Sand Springs or Seminole or Healdton stayed in Sand Springs, Seminole, and Healdton.

By World War I, Oklahoma was the nation's largest oil-producing state. The huge Midcontinent field—with Okfuskee County sucking up its share—sprouted thirty thousand wooden derricks pumping easily refined "sweet" crude. The Midcontinent by 1916 was annually siphoning $139 million into the coffers of the Standard, Royal Dutch Shell, Sun, and Gulf Oil companies.

The state's small farmers were not so fortunate.

By the beginning of the Great War, Oklahoma's tenant farmers had their backs to the wall. Annually they shifted from tenant farm to tenant farm, hoping always for a little better land, better weather, and better crops. Their first moves were short, usually within the county; soon enough these "boll weevils" were abandoning their worn farms entirely to look for work on the bigger wheat, corn, or cotton ranges, in the oil fields, or in the boomtowns of eastern Oklahoma.

Wherever they went, the work was hard, the summer heat exhausting. "Fat men were few in the fields," wrote historian Nigel Anthony Sellars.

Food was poor, a steady diet of "the four B's" of beans, bacon, biscuits, and bullgravy. They slept wherever they could find a flophouse, a farmer's barn, or a toolshed; if none was available, they slept on the ground.

The work was dangerous for onetime farmers unfamiliar with oil rigs or railroads or with the great harvesting combines that did a day's work in an hour. A reaper could take a hand or a foot. An oil field fire or a burst boiler would leave an oil rigger or a hay binder scalded or dead.

The states had few safety laws and those went largely unenforced. Travel from town to town was often hazardous. Riding the rods was risky; if a bindle stiff was not injured trying to clamber aboard, he might be thrown off a moving freight by callous railroad guards.

And always there were too many men for too few jobs. The skilled hands—riggers, drillers, tool-dressers, and pipefitters—quickly found work. Until the wells were brought in and the pipelines laid. Meanwhile, the increasingly desperate boll weevils, the displaced farmers and the unskilled farm workers, scratched for what little work was left.

They labored twelve-hour days, seven days a week, then they moved on, unwanted. "In most towns all over the country," the young Woody was to learn, "it's a jailhouse offense to be unemployed." If the migrants were not arrested on vagrancy charges, they were often run out of town by deputies or roving bands of vigilantes.

Mounting anger and the frustration of the state's small farmers erupted in the wartime summer of 1917. Members of a small, radical tenant farmers' organization, the Working Class Union, began an implausible, even absurd march to Washington. Once there, they intended to protest "Big Slick" Woodrow Wilson's war and the newly adopted draft act. This was a "rich man's war, poor man's fight" and they wanted none of it.

On August 3, a ragtag band of these armed tenant farmers and farmworkers gathered some thirty-five miles south of Okemah. They provisioned themselves with green corn stolen from the fields and set off through the sandhills bound for the faraway capital. Marching along the dirt track, they randomly burned bridges and farm buildings until challenged by a heavily armed posse. A handful of shots sailed harmlessly past the two groups, and the marchers fled. With that, organized protest ended.

The "Green Corn Rebellion" was a last spasm of prairie radicalism. Eventually, 150 of the hapless marchers were convicted of riotous crimes; half would serve prison terms, most a year and a day, some for as long as six years.

Meanwhile, World War I doomed the Socialist Party. As patriotic fervor rose, buoyed by higher farm prices, the Socialist vote fell. From a peak in 1914 when some rural areas in Oklahoma delivered half of the vote to the Socialists, the party's tally steadily dropped. Okfuskee County, which had given 31 percent of the vote to the Socialists in 1912, mustered a scant 3 percent six years later.

With higher farm prices, business picked up in Charley Guthrie's real estate office above Citizen's National Bank. His family's complaints—the schoolmates had taken to teasing the Guthrie children for living in such a spooky place—prompted Charley to move them to a small three-room house on South Twelfth Street.

They would live there only a short time. A tornado swooped down on Okemah, taking with it the roof of their wood-frame home. Charley was able to move Nora and the three children crosstown to a house on the even more fashionable North Ninth Street.

Fire seemed to dog them. On October 5, 1916, the *Ledger* reported the Guthrie residence "had been set on fire by an oil stove." Only prompt work by neighbors and the volunteer fire department put out the fire before it seriously damaged the house. "Of course," the *Ledger* continued, "Charley had insurance, being an agent himself."

Real estate and insurance agent, Charley Guthrie was counted a successful businessman, holding as many as thirty pieces of rental property. On Saturdays Charley would load the children into "our big new black buggy in behind our fast pacer team, old Red Bess and Big White Tom, for the ride to Grandma Tanny's house." There older brother Roy and five-year-old Woody mounted attacks against imaginary Huns on the sweeping front lawn.

Golden-haired Clara meanwhile would be off tending to her dolls. At fourteen she was just at "that ripe and tender time in a young girl's life when she loves to walk around with her eyes about half shut and sing some song about the moon coming up and the moon going down."

Nora, pregnant with her fourth child, would sit at the upright piano in her mother's parlor, accompanying her old ballads of children lost in the wood, and ships that never returned, while son Woodrow stood behind her, brushing her waist-length hair. When Nora's bumptious half-brothers hooted and yelped from the rose bushes outside the open windows, the three Guthrie children chased them away. Mama's music was special.

It was an idyllic summer and fall for young Woodrow, that year of the Great War, 1917. "Papa went to town," the boy grown to man recalled,

and made real-estate deals with other people, and he brought their money home. Mama could sign a check for any amount, buy every little thing that her eyes liked the looks of. Roy and Clara could stop off in any store in Okemah and buy new clothes to fit the weather, new things to eat to make you healthy, and Papa was proud because we could all have anything we saw.

At least some of the neighbors thought the Guthries were *too* generous. Charley was easy with a dollar while Nora was sometimes so lost in her own thoughts she did not pay attention to the children. "The children always had expensive toys," one sniffed, "but necessities were scarce."

Nora Guthrie's ever more curious behavior attracted the neighbors' attention. She often seemed distracted. Or monumentally angry. "One day, when she was mad at Charley, she took all the furniture out of their house and piled it up in the front yard," one neighbor recalled.

Madison Jones, who lived across Ninth Street, suggested Charley have

Nora looked at, or maybe committed to the state asylum—like her older brother Jess. Charley refused. The asylum had not helped Jess, who had died there in 1912. Furthermore, Nora was the one who kept the family together, Charley insisted.

In February 1918, Nora delivered her fourth child and third son in the house on Ninth Street. At his sister's insistence, he was named George Gwynn; "Woodblock," as Nora called Woodrow, now would have to share his sister's time with the baby.

Charley, a man of great pride, hired a part-time maid to keep the house clean. He himself would be too busy running for state representative to do a proper job of managing the house.

Once more Charley Guthrie was directly challenging the local Democratic Party machine. Defeated in 1912 for county assessor, Charley had bounced back three years later to be elected justice of the peace. If the post was of little importance, it offered stature enough to run for the legislature.

It would be a tough campaign. Charley was not only taking on the local Democratic Party, but the incumbent, W. N. Barry, the party's boss in Okfuskee County. With Clara, Roy, and Woody for company, Charley campaigned across the county, delivering speeches from the back of hay wagons and shaking hands at crossroads. Nora feared her husband would attempt to settle political disputes with fisticuffs, but never objected enough to prevent the children from traveling with their father.

The campaign grew bitter as Charley and W. N. Barry exchanged charges of pilfering from county funds. Return Barry to the state legislature, Charley thundered, and "he will want to amend that certain one of the Ten Commandments which says 'Thou shalt not steal,' so as to read 'Thou shalt not steal on a small scale.'"

On election night, August 6, 1918, Charley scored a surprising victory, 529 to 499, with a third candidate gathering 164 votes. Barry challenged the results, and a recount a few days later summarily reversed the outcome—after numbers of ballot boxes had been tampered with in the county courthouse. The new total gave the election to Barry by a scant twenty-two votes. Even the staunchly Democratic *Okemah Ledger* editorially grumbled this was the "first indication of crooked election work since the organization of the county."

An appeal to the state election board was fruitless; Barry was a power in the legislature. Charley the two-fisted is said to have gained some measure of satisfaction by soundly thrashing one of Barry's lieutenants, but that would have been cold comfort.

The election behind him, Charley had other things to worry about, in particular, his wife's odd behavior. More and more she was acting like her older brother Jess, giving silly orders, behaving strangely or not paying attention, then finally just slipping off into a private world.

Clara came home from school one day to discover her infant brother swaddled in newspapers—and hidden in the oven. Nora began going to the Crystal Theater, taking Woody with her each day, she to watch the flickers, he to admire the silver stars painted on the ceiling. She wandered aimlessly about town, poking through trash in Okemah's alleys, or made arbitrary demands of the children and Charley.

One day in late May 1919, Nora ordered Clara to stay home from school; she needed help with the ironing. As strong willed as her mother, Clara insisted she had to take a final exam that day. The test would determine if she passed from the seventh to the eighth grade.

Their next-door neighbors heard the arguments, back and forth in the kitchen, mother and daughter each refusing to yield. They were too much alike, each rigid when she thought some principle at stake. Finally the furious Clara spilled kerosene on her dress, struck a match, and set it on fire.

"I put the coal oil on my clothes and was going to burn them a little to scare mother," Clara apologetically explained later. Instead, her dress burst into flame, the girl racing from the house in terror, Nora haplessly running after. Alarmed by Clara's screams, neighbors dashed over to smother the flames with a blanket.

The fire whistle's blasts signaled the ward, summoning Charley from his office over the bank and Woody from Grandma Tanner's. Clara was severely burned from her neck to her knees, her long, curly hair singed black.

The nerves of her skin literally seared off, the girl felt no pain. "Why are you crying, Daddy? I'm all right," she bravely assured Charley.

Laid on her bed, Clara remained cheerful, unaware how badly she had been burned. When Woody made his way through the crowd of clucking neighbors to Clara's bedside, she made him promise "not to cry like old Papa and like Mama setting there by her bed."

There was no need for tears, the tomboy turned young woman said. "I'm gonna jump out of this bed and start singing and dancing in about two minutes and a half," Clara assured her younger brother. "You go in there and tell your Papa and your Mama what I said and make your Mama and Roy quit their carrying on."

Woody promised.

She was contrite. "Oh, papa," Clara worried, "I know I won't get to take the examination now."

School friends and teachers visited Clara that night as the fretful girl lay in bed, swathed in bandages. Would she pass? Clara weakly asked her teacher.

"Yes, you passed," Mrs. Johnston assured her.

Moments later, Clara died.

Mindful of his promise, Woody held back the tears, running desperately around the house, until he fell into his father's arms. He cried a second time, at Clara's funeral, where his once-golden sister lay in a coffin under the canvas tent of an itinerant preacher conveniently in town.

Clara, the tomboy who had nicknamed him "Woodblock," who gave him piggyback rides right into the Deep Fork River, had instructed him not to cry. Not to be like Roy, and Papa, and Mama. "Laugh like me," she had said. "Be like me. Smile like I smile."

He was not yet seven years old. And he would not cry again.

CHAPTER TWO

Jig Dance in a Minor Key

*T*HE GUTHRIES REFUSED to talk about Clara's death. Charley, who would carry the girl's picture and a lock of her hair in his wallet the rest of his life, bore his bereavement in stoic silence.

For Nora there was an abiding sense of guilt. "If I'd not kept her here at home she'd be alive right this minute," she told her family.

Her husband and two oldest sons—Roy was thirteen, Woody not yet seven—repeatedly sought to comfort her, but failed to ease her guilt. "She never could shake the picture of Clara burnt to death . . ." Woody decided. "And all this got to eating its way into Mama's mind."

Woody found his own comfort. He would ever after deny that Clara had deliberately set herself on fire.

First he insisted that "a coal oil stove blew up and caught her dress on fire. . . . Her dress was all soaked with kerosene from filling the stove to heat her irons."

Later he would write simply that Clara was "ironing on an oil stove and it exploded."

Okemah's gossips were more cruel. Clara had committed suicide "to spite her mother," ran one story. The neighbors recalled the earlier fire that had destroyed the new yellow house on Sixth Street; there was craziness in the Sherman family, Nora's kin, the gossips hissed with knowing nods. Their children were cruel in other ways. "Did she do it," they asked the young Woody, "because she hated the crazier things that [his father] was doing to make a lot of money?"

There were too many memories in the house on Ninth Street for the Guthries to bear. Charley moved his family to a farm he owned two miles north of town where he raised prize Poland China hogs. He and Roy repaired the small farmhouse—Woody remembered it as about the size of a boxcar—lathing and plastering against the shrill winds of the Oklahoma winter.

Each day Charley went to his office on Broadway, ready to buy, sell, or trade properties around the county. It was a good time to make money.

The oil prospectors had descended upon Okemah, transforming a sedate agricultural center into a lively boomtown almost overnight. Though Okemah itself had no oil, it did have the railroad depot that would serve the fields at nearby Spring Hill, Garrison, and Cromwell. In just weeks, Okemah's population jumped from 1,500 to 5,000.

Housing was in short supply and money plentiful. Charley rented his vacant homes and scrambled to buy more, paying high prices and charging higher rents.

Young Woody reveled in the raucous excitement. Not even a left arm broken in a fall from a horse and badly reset could keep him from the tumult. Often he would leave his mother at the box office of the Crystal Theater, preferring to run off with his friends and provoke rock fights with the children of the newly arrived boomchasers.

Quiet Okemah fussed, torn between go-getter capitalism and newspaper stories of "crooked gamblers, pimps, whores, dope fiends, and peddlers, stray musicians and street singers, preachers cussing about love and begging for tips on street corners. . . ." Boomers and their children alike were outsiders, and newly prosperous, self-conscious Okemah was wary of these temporary residents with their brazen immorality and radical ways.

In the aftermath of the Great War, the solid citizens of Oklahoma had transformed militant patriotism into fervent self-righteousness. Once the *Tulsa World* had urged citizens to "Get Out the Hemp," and "strangle the I.W.W.'s. Kill 'em just as you would kill any other snake." Now American Legionnaires and a newly revived Ku Klux Klan, nothing less than "an extralegal arm of the business community," took up vigilante enforcement of public morality. The Klan, particularly in boomtowns like Okemah, rallied support for Jim Crow and Prohibition, while decrying the new sexual freedom and those it deemed radicals, particularly union organizers.*

The oil boom fostered both racial and social tension in Okemah. With the exception of a handful of domestic servants, the town was virtually all white. Only three of School District 26's 732 children were "colored." Most blacks who worked in Okemah lived nine miles away in Boley, one of twenty-nine all-black rural communities in Oklahoma.

* As late as 1928, Okfuskee County officials barred Negroes from registering to vote in the presidential elections, the *Ledger* reported on October 30, 1928.

The oil boom, and its labor shortage, momentarily upset that division. Black, Indian, and white mingled on the streets and in the stores of crowded Okemah—though not on what young Woody later considered to be "equal terms. There's been a lot of shooting scrapes and fights. [The people of Okemah] have some crazy way of looking at the colored situation."

Crazy indeed. Even to an eight-, nine-, ten-year-old boy, who noted that before the oil boom, poor Indians could marry blacks but not whites, while after the boom, oil-rich Indians could marry whites but not blacks.*

The self-appointed guardians of racial segregation, Guthrie came to realize, "were almost as many but not as honest" as Okemah's church folks. Okemah's leading citizens demanded that politicians clean out the thieves, whores, and bootleggers who preyed on the "honest, hard-working, hard-fighting and hard-talking working people that usually hit town broke, worked to build the country up, and made the living for the above three other kinds of people."

Charley Guthrie, ever one of Okemah's more enterprising businessmen, rode the boom upward—and a postwar recession downward. The economic slump began in May 1920, when the federal government summarily ended support for the price of wheat. Farm prices began to fall, bottoming out in August and September 1921, when a bushel of corn or oats fetched just half the price of the year before.

Nora, never very comfortable with Charley's business risks, urged him to withdraw from farm speculation, but Nora's fears were easily dismissed. She was a woman, and not all that stable, "just a little bit wrong" in the head, Charley's visiting brother-in-law, Robert Boydstun, decided.

Six years of boom had left Charley overextended and unprepared for a business downturn. No one had celebrated more the postwar credo that "the finest game is business. The rewards are for everybody, and all can win. There are no favorites—Providence always crowns the career of the man who is worthy."

Charley would learn otherwise. When his farm tenants' annual payments fell short, he found himself unable to make his mortgage. Pressed in

---

* "Judge Lynch" reaffirmed the old order on the night of May 31, 1921, when a mob of whites thronged the Tulsa city jail seeking to hang a black shoeshine boy who had allegedly assaulted a young white woman in an elevator. A group of armed Negroes surrounded the building, barring the mob from its prey. The frustrated whites rampaged through "Little Africa," Tulsa's black community, for two days firing block after block of middle-class homes. The official death toll counted nine white and sixty-nine black victims of the violence; later estimates placed the black death toll in gutted Little Africa as high as 300. Tulsa had sent a message: Oklahoma would not tolerate black independence. The Negro would stay in his place; Oklahoma was to remain segregated.

turn by the banks, which had eagerly extended credit in the fat years, Charley was compelled to sell his properties at distress prices. First one, then another plot or house went to the bigger, more prosperous investors from the East who had followed the economic boom to Okemah.

Nothing seemed to stem the slide. Through the winter of 1920–21, Charley scrambled to retain what he could of his accumulated holdings. But each tenant's default compounded Charley's mounting debt to the bank, and eventually he failed. "I'm the only man in this world that's lost a farm a day for thirty days," he groaned. In all, he tearfully told his sons, he had lost fifty thousand dollars.*

He bought a tractor and sought contracts from the county to drag roads between towns. "Mr. Guthrie," wrote the ever supportive editor of the *Okemah Ledger*, "takes this work not only for the money that he secures from the work, but his pleasure at seeing good roads in the county, and expects to have the best dragged roads in Okfuskee County."

By the time the postwar depression eased, Charley had lost everything, including the farm on which they lived. The Guthries continued to live there, but paid bitter rent to the new owners.

The boxcar-sized house was even more crowded after February 1922, when Nora delivered her fifth child. They named the girl Mary Josephine, "Mary Jo" to everyone but nine-year-old Woody, who had decided to nickname her "Tinkin."

Charley was to make a last desperate bid for elected office this year. Blocked in Okfuskee County by the Democratic organization, he announced instead for statewide office, as Oklahoma's corporation commissioner. It was foolhardy. Without backing from the party or the powerful KKK, Charley was the sort of candidate politicians casually dismissed as "a self-starter."

Charley could afford to campaign only regionally, delivering speeches from the back of a hay wagon while Roy and Woody nailed up campaign posters on fences and walls. Charley also taught Woody "short speeches to say standing up in the wagon, cussing the Socialists, running the Republicans into the ground, and bragging on the Democrats."

It was a cute ploy, but hardly enough. Charley ran fifth in a field of

---

* Discussing his life with Alan Lomax in 1940, Guthrie described himself as "a little bit different" from the dust bowl migrants brought to public attention by John Steinbeck's *The Grapes of Wrath* in 1939. "We wasn't in that class that John Steinbeck called the Okies because my dad was worth $35,000 to $40,000 and everything was hunky-dory an' he started havin' a little bit of bad luck. . . . I don't know if it's worth talking about much. I never do talk it much." Quoted from Woody Guthrie, *Library of Congress Recordings*, Rounder CD 1041, Track 5.

eight, some sixty thousand votes behind the winner. (The KKK's candidates were elected United States senator and governor.)

Charley had suffered a demoralizing blow. As Woody later summarized it, his father "had played the rich real estate game, making a young fortune, losing it to bigger politicians." Then he had made a doomed bid for elective office and had spent even more money. "When he lost, it really broke him."

For another year Charley sought to recoup his real estate fortune, but land values in the wake of the boom times had put even meager farms beyond his reach. Each day he went to his office on West Broadway, Charley Edward Guthrie, dealer in real estate, land leases, royalties, deeds, and titles. At night he went home to a crowded house filled with noisy children, and to an often distracted wife.

He was forty-three, a man scraping by while others skimmed the quick riches any boom proffered. For the first time he felt like an old man. Arthritis gripped his hands. Too many fistfights had broken too many bones.

Each night his three boys massaged Charley's hands, seeking to ease the tension as his fingers curled ever tighter into his palms, the nails slowly growing, eventually to dig into the flesh. At least twice he had operations to relieve the pain. According to Woody, "He had to have the finger muscles split several times to keep them from cutting into the bone." The treatment was no help. "The doctor cut one or two fingers off when the other fingers drawed down so tight they cut holes in the palms of both hands."

First the oil boom, then a war boom had come to Okemah, but passed over the Guthries. "We got the grease," Woody said later with a rueful laugh.

In mid-1923, Nora's younger half-brother, Leonard Tanner, offered Charley a job as business manager of a new motorcycle distributorship that Tanner planned to open. Doughboy Leonard had learned to ride motorcycles in France and had successfully taken up daredevil riding when he returned home. To capitalize on his growing fame, the newly organized Ace Motorcycle Company had proposed that he become Ace's statewide sales agent; Leonard was offering Charley the handsome sum of two hundred dollars a month if he would move to Oklahoma City and handle the business side of things.

On Woody's eleventh birthday, the Guthries loaded a Model-T truck with their four children and their household goods and rattled the seventy-five miles to Oklahoma City. They moved their furniture into "the shackiest house there was to be found out on West Twenty Eighth Street."

The day before he was to meet Leonard and close the deal, Charley read

in the newspaper that his brother-in-law had been killed in a traffic accident. Leonard had rammed his motorcycle into a sedan in the small town
of Chickasha, forty miles from Oklahoma City. He sustained a fractured
skull and died instantly.

Without Leonard, the Ace Motorcycle Company withdrew its offer. The
Guthries would spend the next year in the shackiest house in Oklahoma
City. "We never did get a rug laid down on the bare floors in the Oklahoma
City house," Woody recalled. "No paint outside nor inside. Our stuff stayed
packed in little boxes like we were camping inside the old house."

Charley delivered groceries for a dollar's worth of trade each day. He
took up peddling fire extinguishers door to door; who better than he knew
the value of a good fire extinguisher in a home? Roy found work in a service station on busy Classen Boulevard, while Woody, small for his age, wiry
rather than muscular, delivered milk. As pugnacious as his father had once
been, Woody found himself in "lots of fistfights with the kids, and it was
here that I was the boomchaser, instead of the hometowner, and found out
the odds that are against you."

They could not make a go of it. A year after arriving, the Guthries
loaded their Model-T truck once more and returned to Okemah, to "the
rottenest and wormiest and the dirtiest, dustiest house in the whole town,
the old Jim Cain house." It was a measure of just how far Charley Guthrie
had fallen. The Cain house was on Okemah's east end, where folks were
"too poor to paint, too proud to whitewash."

Okemah was bustling once again. Drillers had brought in a major field
in Cromwell, just thirteen miles southwest of the county seat. The population jumped to 15,000, the streets crowded with riggers and drillers, timber haulers and mule skinners.

Twelve-year-old Woody once more reveled in the hurly-burly. He ran
with a gang of town boys, a bantam cock picking more than his share of
fights with the children of boomers, as if by his heart, if not his size, he
might win approval.

His teacher that year remembered Woody, set back a grade in school for
the time lost in Oklahoma City, "a little fellow, [with] black, curly hair all
over his head. . . . He always sat on the front seat on the left hand side,
because he was so small."

There was little music in the classroom, Mrs. Nelle E. Bras remembered.
Instead, the boy made his own. "He would get something in his hand like a
ball or something and just kept [it] going constantly. . . . It looked like he had
rhythm in his hands."

He seemed brighter than his average grades suggested. "You could see sometimes he was not paying attention to what was going on. When you asked him, he would cooperate and come up with some clever answers."

Charley meanwhile sought the success of old. He returned to the trading and swapping game, as his son put it, "but never got a new toehold." With a partner, he bought three thousand fire-damaged shoes, cleaned and dyed them, then sold them for a dollar a pair. He took odd jobs as a carpenter, a painter, and a paperhanger; friends teased him about his different jobs, but Charley stayed employed.

Eventually, he secured a job recording automobile registrations for the state—in all likelihood a bit of patronage for past services to the Democratic Party. The job paid fifty cents per registration, enough to scrape by but not enough to rekindle his spirits. Charley's songs, Woody decided, were now intended more to cheer his children than himself.*

Always there was Nora's strange behavior, behavior that made her sons wary of coming home each afternoon after school. She was afraid, afraid most of all of fire, and particularly nervous about matches. "Maybe you don't even halfway guess the misery that goes through my mind every time I hold a match in my hand," she scolded Woody.

The big house she had furnished with nice furniture, the part-time maid, the automobile, all these were gone. With no one else to blame, she turned on her husband, her raging complaints loud enough for the neighbors to hear.

The anger abated on the days when Nora seemed to withdraw into herself. When she left the moldering Cain house unattended, Roy and Woody would straighten up as best they could, but seedy turned to shabby. Washing and sewing went unheeded.

Worst of all were the bizarre spasms in her arms and legs, and the punishing convulsions that hurled her to the floor. "She would be all right for a while and treat us kids as good as any mother, and all at once it would start in—something bad and awful—something would come over her, and it come by slow degrees. Her face would twitch and her lips would snarl and her teeth would show."

Hunched over, spit dribbling from her mouth, talking as loud as she

---

* In the 1924–25 fiscal year, Charley registered 1,888 vehicles from his office at the W. E. McKinney Motor Company at First and Broadway. The $944 he thus earned fell short of a laborer's $1,200 annual income, a steel worker's $1,500 per year, or a slaughterhouse worker's $1,600.

could, "she turned into another person, it looked like, standing right there before Roy and me."

At night, thirteen-year-old Woody would dream away the twitches and spasms, his mother once more like "other kids' mamas. But when I woke up it would still be all wrong."

Even in the good times her behavior grew ever more strange. Mary Jo recalled her brother telling her, "Mama would throw her food in the yard."

She also could be "hard on her children," meting out undeserved punishment to Woody and George, a rear-fence neighbor recalled. Mrs. R. G. Potter remembered the two boys at a bedroom window tearfully complaining they had been sent to bed without supper. "She sneaked them food on one or two occasions with the admonition that they were never to tell that they had gotten it or who from."

Nora alternated unpredictably between forgetfulness and blinding anger. She would stand in the yard, oblivious of the rain, staring at distant horizons. She failed to heat water for a bath, but forced George to bathe in the chilled tub anyway. Another time, she chased George around the house with a butcher knife, he later told his younger sister.

Charley arranged to have the infant Mary Jo spend more time at Grandma Tanner's, where she could get the attention a child not yet two needed. But lightening Nora's burden could not lift her dark moods nor fix her wandering attention.

As much as he sought to dismiss his wife's behavior merely as "a case of nerves," Charley was finally forced to take action. Mary Jo, just three years old, was left to wander alone down Broadway while her mother sat in the dark of the Crystal Theater watching a motion picture.

Nora "was incapable of being a mother," certainly not responsible enough to raise a three-year-old girl. Worse, "mama was not safe to be around," the family concluded.

Charley bundled the child's clothes into a paper bag, put her in the family's Model-T, and drove Mary Jo to the small town of Panhandle, Texas, in the oil- and wheat-rich high plains 260 miles west of Okemah. She was to stay with Charley's younger sister, Maude, and Maude's husband, Robert Boydstun, a "big, old, loveable kitty cat" of a man.

A year later, with the close of school in June 1926, George followed by train. At eight, he was old enough to travel alone, bravely decked out in clean overalls and a new straw hat.

Woody first attributed his mother's odd behavior to the death of her half-brother, Leonard. Then he ascribed it to the tumult of Okemah, "our

little farm town turning into an Oil and Money Rush. It was too much of a
load on my Mother's quieter nerves. She commenced to sing the sadder
songs in a loster voice, to gaze out our window and to follow her songs out
and up and over and away from it all, away over yonder in the minor keys."

Absorbed in her private songs, Nora left Woody free to roam Okemah
and the dusty farms that ringed the town. Charley was preoccupied with
Nora, and Roy with work. Woody went where curiosity led.

As Guthrie later told the story, he was almost fourteen, in this summer
after the eighth grade, when he first heard the keening harmonica of the
"big ol' colored boy," George, who shined shoes sitting on a bench in front
of Jigg's barbershop.

"That's undoubtedly the lonesomest music I ever run on to in my life,"
Woody told the black youth. What was the name of the piece?

"Railroad Blues," George replied. Then he sucked a blue note out of the
harmonica and played the tune once more.

And again. But each time he played it a bit differently.

> *I'm a-walkin' down the track,*
> *I got tears in my eyes,*
> *Tryin' to read the letter from my home;*
> *If that train runs right,*
> *I'll see my woman Saturday night,*
> *'Cause I'm nine hundred miles from my home.*
> *An' I hate to hear that lonesome whistle blow.*

Woody was enthralled. Daily he returned to the barbershop to listen to
George's harmonica. George played "The Fox and the Hounds," a musical
depiction of a hunt—complete with baying dogs. He played another he
called "Raincrow," explaining, "That's a big bird that gets out in the timber
and hollers when it's going to rain. Then he hollers while it's raining. Then
he hollers after it quits."

Woody had to have a "French harp." He saved nickels and dimes,
scrounged soda bottles to redeem at Moomaw's Drug Store, "missed a
lunch or two," but eventually had saved enough. Fifteen years later, Woody
recalled the sunny afternoon when he first sat on the scarred bench in the
alley behind the Creek Trading Company and played "The Fox and the
Hounds" alongside "George the shine boy . . . calling up all of the long-
eared hounds, getting ready for a big, fast-running coon hunt."

The boy "brought up . . . to push Negroes off the sidewalk" had made a friend. "It was a pretty empty-looking town when George lost his job at the shop," then moved away with his family. But in the short months of that summer, Woody had discovered black people, despite all he had been told, "to be full of jokes and wisdom."

Music and music making captured his imagination. When traveling musicians came through town, playing on Okemah's newly paved sidewalks for loose change, Woody was there, perched on a car fender, listening. (The imp in him also left his initials indelibly scribed in wet cement at two locations on West Broadway.) When medicine shows pulled into town, Woody was on hand to watch the perfunctory performances and listen to the hoary jokes and tired patter. He also absorbed the fiddle tunes and banjo showpieces. It was probably from one of these companies—with their loutish Rufus and Rastus comedy acts—that he learned to "jig dance" and play the bones.*

Woody doted on the "ear players," local musicians who made violins from old oil cans, or the grotesque war veteran rattling a tin cup while blowing a harmonica through a shrapnel hole in his throat. He also listened to the ballad singers, men and women like his mother, who taught him the old songs about Bold Turpin, the English highwayman, and Stewball, the Irish racehorse.

If he came upon a radio, he could also listen to KVOO, "The Voice of Oklahoma" broadcasting from Bristow, "where the oil flows and the cotton grows." The station thirty miles north of Okemah boasted live broadcasts by local performers, including Jimmie Wilson and the Catfish String Band, and Otto Gray and his Oklahoma Cowboy Band. Both groups mixed folk music with popular songs in their daily shows.

Music, or more important, *performing* seized him. When they needed money for school functions, former students recalled, Guthrie would sing and dance on the sidewalks, while classmates passed the hat. "He was a little showman, a natural performer."

He teamed with classmate Frank Streetman to perform "Let Me Call You Sweetheart" on the sidewalks, Streetman bowing a musical saw, Woody playing the mouth harp. Another time they blackened their faces to mount a curbside minstrel show.

---

* Woody's "jig" was probably something close to an Appalachian clog dance. The bones, earlier used by nineteenth-century minstrel players, were beef rib bones. The marrow was either drilled out, or the bones left for two days on an anthill, after which the white bones were hardened in an oven, according to Texas musician George Hamlin. The bones were played as rhythm instruments by rapping them against each other.

He took part in school productions, playing in front of the curtain between acts or during scenery changes. "The teacher never had to tell Woody what to do," said another classmate. "He'd just get up and begin to sing and dance." And whatever he did, Woody "would make people laugh."

Guthrie thought little of it; it came to him too easily. "I jig danced and cracked jokes between the acts. I never took part in a play, but always worked in front of the curtain. I seldom knew what I was going to do or say till the curtain rolled down behind me, and then I'd commence messing around and talking and the people would get tickled at that [and] clap for more."

The applause nourished him. It was a momentary substitute for the attention unavailable at home. There his mother seemed ever more distracted, or angry, uninterested in *him*. His father meanwhile was consumed with earning a living by day and soothing Nora by night.

In a last gesture to preserve memories of the free-spirited girl he had courted, Charley hid the truth of just what happened on Saturday afternoon, June 25, 1927. He dismissed it as merely "an accident." According to one account, he lay dozing, startled awake by the kerosene splashed across his chest, his shirt on fire and his wife standing over him, numbly watching the flames.*

Charley dashed from the house, slapping at the flames and rolling on the ground. A neighbor helped to smother the fire, but too late. Charley had been severely burned, his torso a welter of blackened, peeling flesh from his collarbone to his navel.

Perhaps for the first time in his life, he despaired. "He wanted to die," Charley confessed to Woody the next morning, "and to go the same way that sister Clara had gone."

Word quickly circulated around Okemah that Nora, seized by a fit of rage, had thrown a kerosene lamp at her husband. Even if the story was not true, she was plainly unhinged, Charley's Masonic brothers decided. With the permission of Grandma Tanner and Nora's half-brother Warren, they arranged for her immediate commitment to the Central State Hospital for the Insane in Norman on Monday, June 27.

Like his father, Woody would never acknowledge publicly just what

---

* Later Charley told daughter Mary Jo two different versions of "the accident": in the first he was underneath an automobile, unaware gasoline had dripped on him, then had lit a cigarette. In a second tale, he was sleeping in a sick bed when somebody set the bed clothes afire with a cigarette. She was unconvinced. "I really do think that mama set him on fire," she said in an interview on November 23, 1999.

happened. In one autobiographical essay he forged a half-truth: "My mother and father were hurt in a fire."

When he did elaborate the story of the family breakup, he always had his mother taken off to the state hospital *before* Charley burned himself. To explain Charley's burns, he wrote, "Papa went to sleep on a bed with his clothes soaked full of kerosene from an old stove he'd been fixing up to use. He had a big stack of Sunday's funny papers up on the bed with him when the cigarette fell down out of his mouth and onto his mattress."

Whatever the story offered, Woody too protected the memory of his mother, her mind gone "way over yonder in a minor key."

Charley was still in desperate pain from the burns when he was carried on a stretcher to the Fort Smith and Western depot on Columbia Street and lifted aboard the westbound train. Robert and Maude Boydstun had agreed to open their home in Panhandle, Texas, to Maude's half-brother. The Boydstuns had "hit rock bottom . . . but Daddy would do without" to take care of them all, daughter Geneva Boydstun Adkins explained.

Charley would spend the next eighteen months recuperating, flat on his back. All the while, Maude tended the half-inch-high welts seared across his torso, faithfully applying a poultice of sheep droppings gathered in the pasture of their bleak farm, then scorched in the oven.

Their father gone, Woody and Roy were left to fend for themselves in Okemah. Roy found a good job as a clerk in a market; they would have food, at least. For a while, Woody and a friend scavenged scrap metal along Okemah's alleys, hauling it on a wagon they pulled to Mark's Junk Yard. Then he found a job polishing brass spittoons in exchange for rent on a shoe-shine stand he opened in Meador's Hotel.

That lasted "only the few short months when the Indians had oil money and classy boots," he wrote. "My luck went bad as soon as the lawyers drained the oil from the land and the cash from the Indians."

He began to wash dishes at the chili palace, paid seventy-five cents a day, and charged twenty-five cents a meal. Like Oklahoma's tenant farmers, he ended up broke. "I put in one whole cotton season there and still owed the[m] nine dollars."

A later effort to pick cotton fared no better; he was, after all, a town boy, not a farmer. "I owed more for my sacks than I had coming."

He discovered Bull Durham tobacco and what he called "hard liquor," which in that era of Prohibition meant illegal corn whiskey, the local variety of "moonshine" peddled in Mason jars. Virtually unsupervised, hustling coins when he could—he made seven dollars dancing and playing the harmonica on one memorable night—Woody slept wherever he could find shelter.

It was, Guthrie's sister Mary Jo conceded, a "brief period in his life when people called him a tramp." Woody was indifferent; he scuffed about Okemah, dismissing his critics with a sing-song, "So long, it's been good to know you."

"Woody was a mess," one neighbor said. "He used to come to my back door, and sing a song. We'd have coffee or tea together." Other times Mrs. V. K. Chowning fed him sandwiches in exchange for a harmonica tune.

Woody scrounged home-cooked meals where he could. His friend Colonel Martin invited him home often enough; Guthrie would live with the Martin family for three months. He moved in with the Price family, quarreled, and moved out. For a week he slept in an unheated packing case converted into a hillside gang clubhouse until two members of his gang, brothers Casper and Floyd Moore, pleaded with their parents to let Woody live with them. Tom and Nora Moore agreed and Woody moved in, with a wardrobe of two shirts and a pair of mended overalls.

The Moore home was full of laughter, full of music. Tom Moore played violin and sang "a beautiful tenor voice," his youngest daughter recalled. Woody, who "could make up a song faster than anyone I ever knew, on the spur of the moment, about any subject," played a five-cent harmonica, a Jew's harp, and "could get more music out of an ordinary comb covered with tissue paper than many people could from a fine musical instrument," Gladys Moore Gordon added. Four decades later, she vividly recalled the imitation of a freight train whistle that Woody wrung from the harmonica. "The lonely wail of the sound remains with me to this day."

Woody lived with the Moores, but remained fiercely independent. Gladys remembered one evening the young man bringing home sixty dollars in coins, his share of the "kitty" for playing harmonica and jig-dancing at the Elks Club or American Legion.

Tom Moore suggested Woody take the money and "buy you some underwear."

"No need to," Woody replied. "I wouldn't wear it." The money instead went for treats for the Moore children.

For all his friendly nature, fifteen-year-old Woody Guthrie was often moody. "Woody had different ways," mother Nora Moore explained. "Sometimes he was sad and didn't talk much. . . . He often sat for long periods as if he were in a deep study. . . . Then again when he was with the gang of boys he was lively. He seldom laughed and if he did, it was short and quick, but he was witty and smart."

Woody was to stay with the Moores for most of 1927, welcomed into that raucous family, until Tom Moore packed his barbering tools, pomades, and powders into their Ford touring car and moved his family to Arizona. After four years, Okemah's oil boom had petered out; riggers, drillers, and roustabouts had moved on. Tom the barber, his wife, and four children followed late in the year.

Woody yearned to go with the Moores, and Nora Moore, fond of the young man, wanted to take him. Woody's older brother, Roy, refused; he did not want Woody so far from the family. Woody would stay in Okemah.

Before leaving, Tom and his wife fulfilled a promise to take Woody to visit his mother. With their daughter Gladys for company, the four of them drove the hard-packed roads of central Oklahoma to Norman and Central State Hospital for the Insane.

There Nora sat in a locked ward, her limbs jerking spasmodically, a shrunken hulk who stared blankly at her visitors. Woody sought to talk to her, but she did not respond. Only at the end, as they were leaving, did she dredge a name from her memory. "You're Woody, aren't you?" she asked vaguely.

She had markedly deteriorated in the past year, doctors told the young man. They held out little hope for either a recovery or her return home.

Woody was crushed. Nora had barely recognized him; the image of the tiny figure, his mother, twitching dumbly beside her bed, rather than anything the doctor had said, pressed on him. His mother was utterly lost to herself, to him.

The Moores' leaving was painful in a different way. Woody would lose close friends, the brothers he had nicknamed "Tuba" and "Booger Red." And he would lose once more the sense of family closeness—Tom Moore's stern guidance, and Mama "Nonie's" outlandish stories from her Tennessee girlhood about hoopsnakes that rolled tail-to-mouth downhill after her.

Guthrie was restless, without a steady job or even a place to stay when school closed in June 1928. With his friend Colonel Martin, he hitchhiked to Groom, Texas, and the new Boydstun home; they were two almost-sixteen-year-olds on a lark, "and every time we left a town we sang, 'So Long, It's Been Good to Know You.'"

They stayed with the Boydstuns until Martin returned to Okemah, and Woody set off on a trip south to the Gulf of Mexico. In part he planned to visit grandfather Jerry P. and Guthrie relatives, in part he wanted to satisfy an ever-widening curiosity. He hitchhiked through Houston, then on to Galveston and the Gulf Coast, working his way eastward along dirt roads that linked small town with fishing village and lumber camp.

The trip to East Texas affirmed the hard lessons learned in Okemah. Guthrie scrambled for whatever odd jobs he could in service stations, or hauling wood, picking mustang grapes, and helping carpenters and cement workers. He played his harmonica and sang for nickels and dimes at fish fries along the bayous, in railroad stations and hotel lobbies. In the timber towns he invariably found his way to the whorehouses, where "this old gal house song" would earn him a quarter.

> *It's hard and it's hard, ain't it hard,*
> *To love one that never did love you.*
> *And it's hard and it's hard, ain't it hard, great God,*
> *To love one that never will be true.*

He was learning "ear music," as he called it, and "all the tricks of strings and music." He learned from blacks, from Cajuns, from cowboys and ranchers, wherever there was a singer to be heard.

> I followed the religious street singers up and down the sidewalk and learnt all of the songs they sung. I never did learn how to make tips oft of religious folks because the best ones are always broke, but some of the best songs I ever heard and some of the best feelings I ever had was when I catch some girl's eye beating on a skin drum tambourine singing high hallelujah.

In East Texas too he saw poverty and disease, malaria from mosquitoes and pellagra from poor diets, "all caused by no good water, no good houses, no good work. . . ." It might have been the teenage youth's first political insight.

Until now Woody's fortunes, and politics, had been those of Charley—up or down. Always there was the feeling that a hard-working man could make something for himself and his family. In East Texas, Woody came to understand that that was not necessarily true. Sometimes it seemed that "some are supposed to work pretty hard and some are supposed to coast through life some way or another."

For part of the summer he stayed with the Mosier family, people he had known in Okemah who were now hoping to scratch a living from a truck farm. Woody would hoe fig trees in exchange for room and board. Here in the community he called "Algoa" with a girl he dubbed "Dorothy Schultz," he first discovered an interest in the opposite sex. At night, he wrote, there was a smell in her heavy, wavy hair "with the wind whipping in somewhere off the salty Gulf waters—so that the fine, clean whiff of homemade dresses mixes just right with the unperfumed waves of a pretty girl's hair."

Woody made his way back to Okemah before school resumed and moved in with the Sam Smith family: mother, father, and eleven children. While there was not much money in the Smith household either—the children slept head-to-foot in bed—there was supervision.

The young man effectively became a ward of Okemah's more prosperous families. Because he was a burden to the Smiths, he shifted to the E. L. Price family home on Sixth Street. The Prices bought him clothes, shirts, and a suit, with accessories. In return, Woody was to care for the family's scuttle of chickens, a chore he disliked.

The opening of school in September 1928, Woody's freshman year at Okemah High, barely captured his attention. His attendance was dutiful. "My harmonica would be in my shirt pocket, and I knew I couldn't play it in class; so I'd just sort of sneak it out real easy, cup it in my hands, and look out across the willow grove at the bottom of the hill."

He was irrepressible, full of jokes and jigs, early to school in the morning to draw stick-figure cartoons on the study hall blackboard, eager for attention. He was "a clown," high school classmate Bertha Bryan recalled. "He liked to do things that would make people laugh. He wasn't doing anything that was destructive or anything."

While the regular algebra teacher tolerated his antics, a substitute did not, Bryan continued. "When Woody got up in class and started acting silly," the irritated substitute teacher "reached over and got a handful of his curls—he had the most beautiful curly hair—and just raised him above his seat and set him back down.

"And that embarrassed Woody so bad that he tried to shrug it off, shrugged his shoulders, but he set down the rest of the time."

Too short and undersized for football or basketball, Woody instead carried the water bucket for the team. J. O. Smith, who would have little good to say about Guthrie the adult, remembered his schoolmate as "a little wiry haired fellow always under foot, always making some kind of music in the back of the classroom."

His appearance improved, if his marks in the tenth grade did not. "He didn't look like a ragged muffin, or anything like that," said Bertha Bryan, who sat behind him in class. "I understand he was living with some other folks, who kind of adopted him, maybe. He was dressed quite well. He was little, and like I say, he had these curls. I thought he was a very cute little fellow."

Though the girls did not take him seriously as a potential beau, he was popular. "I don't think anybody who ever knew Woody that didn't really like him and wasn't glad to be around him," said his boyhood chum, Colonel Martin, decades later.

Woody, a B-minus student at best, paid little attention to his school-work. In three years of English, he had managed a bare C average, though he did get a solid grounding in English fundamentals from the demanding Arthur "Ott" Harrison while in the ninth grade. If he excelled in anything, it was ninth-grade typing; not only did he earn an A, but he became an accomplished typist in the process. He was a member of the Boys Glee Club and the Publication Club. He served, appropriately enough, as joke editor of the school newspaper, the *Panther*. None of this was very taxing. He continued to work, selling newspapers, shining shoes, and later boasting he made from seven to thirteen dollars per week, "big money back in those days."

He spent some of his free hours in the new county library at the corner of Second and Birch Streets, reading voraciously, voluminously, without plan. He was educating himself. Other times he played harmonica or Jew's harp for the nickels passersby threw to him in front of the Creek Trading Company building at the corner of Second and Broadway.

Woody rattled aimlessly about Okemah until he received a letter from his father, inviting the young man to join him in Texas. Eighteen months after Charley Guthrie was carried aboard the Fort Smith and Western coach, his burns were healed—Charley would never *mend*—and it was time to reunite the family. (Roy, well established as a grocery store clerk, chose to remain in Oklahoma rather than chase another of his father's money-making dreams.)

The Boydstuns, Charley wrote, were moving to Pampa, about twenty-five miles northeast of the farm. Oil had been discovered in the region, and Pampa was booming. The town offered plenty of opportunity for a man with Charley Guthrie's get-up-and-go.

At the end of the school year in June 1929, Woody packed his few clothes into a single suitcase, shoved his harmonica and his wooden bones into a shirt pocket, and walked out to the county road south of town. He turned westward and put up his thumb.

CHAPTER THREE

The Oil Patch

*T*HIS WAS THE high country of the Texas Panhandle. Once it was unfenced cattle range owned by great syndicates. More lately the rolling plateaus had been quartered into wheat farms that stretched beyond arid horizons. The vast sweep of the Staked Plain rose forty-seven hundred feet above sea level, so high that the cold winds blowing down the Great Plains from Canada had blasted the land bare of trees. It was a harsh alkaline, red-clay landscape, with scant rain or runoff.

Through good years and bad, the wheat farmers had hung on, their bank debt rising and falling with the rain. Then suddenly, unexpectedly, the stubble fields of Gray County, Texas, sprouted wooden oil derricks, and the boom was on.

Pampa—so named by its well-traveled founder, George Tyng, for a stark similarity to the Argentine *pampas*—was the principal town in Gray County. Built on land once owned by an English syndicate, the White Deer Land Company, Pampa, population 1,000, had dozed for three decades. "There wasn't much Pampa until the oil boom," one of the more enterprising merchants conceded.

The town rudely wakened in 1926 when No. 1 Worley-McReynolds came in five miles south of town. By the time Woody Guthrie arrived early in the summer of 1929, Pampa boasted two paved streets and a population of 22,000.

The Panhandle & Santa Fe Railway served the town, first carrying cattle, then wheat, now crude oil and carbon black to far-off markets. The old-timers lived north of Atchison Avenue and the depot, the boomers to the south. That part of town, dubbed "Little Juarez," ran full time and full blast, under the benign protection of Sheriff E. S. Graves.

Little Juarez was "so bad and mean. You could get your brains knocked out," barber Jess Turner insisted. "There were gamblers, bums, and every kind of disreputable person there." In Little Juarez, south of the tracks, Charley Guthrie managed Old Man Eldridge's block of shabby buildings. His primary responsibility was a flophouse that catered to oilfield roughnecks.

Charley's second son had just turned seventeen when he showed up in Pampa. Woody's facial features were his mother's; his physique resembled his father's. The young man stood a wiry five feet five inches tall, perhaps an inch shorter than his father, but at 120 pounds, stronger than the badly scarred and arthritic Charley.

"Three things hit the upper north plains of West Texas pretty hard in the year of 1929, the dust storms, the depression, and me," the young man later quipped. Woody had come to work, to help his father manage the 120-cot flophouse, and to reunite their family.

As night clerk, Woody's responsibility was to "see to it that you found the right bed at night and the right door out the next morning, and to clean up rooms, collect room rents, kill rats, and argue with roaches, bedbugs, fleas, and ants, bugs, termites of all kinds. . . . This was the hardest and the dirtiest and the best job that I had got ahold of so far."

The two-story cothouse on the east side of Cuyler Street offered an education, even to a young man who had fended for himself on the streets of Okemah and the highways of South Texas. Both the rooms and the girls upstairs were cheap: a quarter for the bed, two dollars for the woman.

"The beds made so much racket it sounded like some kind of a factory creaking. But there was a rhythm and a song in the scraping and the oil boom chasers called it 'the rusty bedspring blues.'"

The night clerk position provided a roof over his head and an occasional fifty-cent piece. (It also left him with a lifelong terror of venereal disease.) For spending money, Guthrie took a job at Art Huey's outdoor root beer stand. Most often the root beer was laced with a vile and sometimes lethal potion known as "jake," imported Jamaican ginger and pure grain alcohol. Woody lasted only long enough to sample the wares, get roaring drunk, and then be fired.

Guthrie found a second job as a nominal soda jerk in "Shorty" Harris's purported drugstore "in a rough part of town. . . . I mean right next to everything," Woody's uncle, Jeff Guthrie, insisted.

Sodas and patent medicines were the smallest part of Harris's trade;

once again Guthrie was selling jake, as well as pot liquor and Sterno, the "canned heat" dipped out of a can with a soda cracker.* The jake was legal, if one had a prescription from a friendly doctor, a syrupy curative diluted at the soda fountain in a Coca-Cola or a Nehi soda. "Cowhands, circus and carnival folks, showpeople, construction engineers, roughnecks, roustabouts, drillers, pipeliners, line walkers, fast talkers, wheat raisers, cattle grazers, and other kinds of boom chasers dropt in before breakfast to take on a little anti-freeze."

Guthrie worked on and off for Harris, a few hours a day, mostly in the afternoons. He occasionally fixed milkshakes and sundaes at the twelve-foot-long soda fountain while Harris, cigar stub in mouth, dispensed jake and corn liquor in the back room where he slept. Harris—no one called him by his given name, Carl—paid Guthrie fifty cents or a dollar a day, depending on the number of hours.

It was all very casual, Harris recalled. "Wages were cheap in those days." If business was slow, Harris would tend both the drugstore and the jake shop himself, not making much money, "but getting through."

They fell into a pattern. Guthrie would work for two or three months until Harris decided to "do it himself." He would loan the youngster a dollar here and there, allowing him to work it off, or he would find odd jobs for Guthrie, just to keep him and his harmonica around. The layoffs did not last long. "You couldn't help but like him," Harris explained.

Guthrie was a pretty good worker, "better than anybody I ever saw," Harris allowed. "He was kinda sharp to catch on to things."

If there was a problem with Guthrie, Harris said, it was that the young man "didn't care if he had ten cents or ten dollars in his pocket." Nor was he dependable. "He'd be working for you one day, and then some kind of notion would get him. Why, if he was standing by the railroad tracks and a train was leaving, he was just liable to get on a freight train." Without notifying anybody.

---

* While the extract of Jamaican ginger could be legally sold as a medicine, it was frequently fortified with denatured alcohol and sold for fifty cents a bottle. Adulterated batches could be lethal, or result in "jake leg," paralysis in the feet and legs. Guthrie would later write a "Jake Walk" blues that concluded:

> *Jamaica ginger in a cold root beer*
> *Make your eyes see double and your ear sound queer.*
> *It'll paralyze your dingdong too.*
> *I'm a jake walk Daddy with the jake walk blues.*

A text is in the Woody Guthrie Archive, Songs1, Box 2, Folder "J."

"I must have fired him a dozen times," Harris said with a chuckle, "and hire him back the next day." Guthrie was unfazed, "used to getting fired. It didn't bother him."

Once in a while, Harris might chew the young man out, "but it was hard to get him mad." The next day Guthrie would be back, ready to run errands or wash the dust from Harris's car or spell Shorty in the store.

Harris simply liked having Guthrie around, especially after Guthrie began painting signs for the drugstore windows: he drew an ice-cream cone running over, a frothy milkshake, and a snow-covered mountain in watercolor paints purchased at the Woolworth five-and-dime. With black-on-white oil paints he lettered "Harris Drug Store" on the brick front of the building, tucking "Woody" in the corner as a self-advertisement. (Often repainted, the names were to endure until sandblasted off in 1977.)

Guthrie the sign painter branched out to walk South Cuyler with his paintbrushes in a back pocket, soliciting business. He painted window signs for a grocery on Saturdays, earning another fifty cents or a dollar. He sketched passersby or Shorty Harris's customers. He took what they paid him—a drink, five cents, or five dollars. "It didn't make much difference," Shorty said.

It was in the back room of Shorty's that Woody discovered a guitar with rusted strings left by a long-forgotten customer. Once tuned, with his Uncle Jeff's help, "I thought it sounded pretty," the young man said.

Jefferson Davis Guthrie, Charley's younger half-brother Jeff, had come to town in 1928, to become a patrolman for the Pampa Police Department. At age twenty-seven, he was tall and physically imposing, the first requirement for a job that involved maintaining some semblance of order along South Cuyler. Beyond that, his major qualification was a certificate demonstrating he had passed a mail-order course in criminal identification from the University of Applied Science in Chicago. He proudly claimed to be the first fingerprint man in the northern part of the state.

Jeff's enthusiasm for law enforcement was tempered when he shot and killed a bootlegger who he thought was reaching for a pistol in a domino parlor. "When I pulled my pistol to shoot, I thought I'd shoot that pistol out of his hand," Jeff explained. Instead, the unarmed Blackie Landers, shot through the stomach, was killed.

Needing the job, Jeff stayed on as patrolman, skirting the corruption all about him in Pampa. "I had to go through a lot of struggles, of temptations," remaining silent, but taking no payoffs himself. He relished the memory of the night he and a partner hauled sixteen furious whores from a raucous rooming house.

Jeff had another, even more compelling reason to stay in the Pampa area. He had taken a fancy to the attractive seventeen-year-old daughter of his older half-sister Maude Boydstun. Mildred Allene—"high-headed, high-spirited, bright-eyed, shiny-haired, clear- and loud-talking"—was equally smitten with her affable uncle.

Friendship over time turned into courtship despite her family's head-shaking reservations. Jeff repeatedly traveled the twenty-five miles of dirt road from Pampa to the Boydstun farm outside Groom, Texas. The troubling blood relationship aside—Charley assured the family that European royalty often intermarried in similar fashion—Allene and Jeff seemed well matched.

Jeff, counted one of the best fiddle players in the entire Texas Panhandle, frequently considered a career as a performer. Allene—she hated "Mildred"—was dazzled by the notion. She could accompany him on the piano or with her new accordion. They might even do a magic show together.

Jeff had become adept at sleight-of-hand and card tricks learned through a correspondence course. When he staged impromptu shows for the gaggle of Boydstuns and Guthries sitting on the orange and apple crates in the crowded living room of the farm, Allene assisted with the props.

Whatever the family's misgivings of an uncle-niece union, Jeff and Allene were married in February 1929. They moved into an apartment in Pampa where, nine months later, Allene delivered her firstborn. It was there that Jeff, fiddler, guitar player, sometime piano tuner, showed his nephew Woody his first simple guitar chords.

Nat Lunsford, who later played banjo, guitar, and mandolin with Guthrie in local bands, watched the young man from those first fumbling efforts to follow Jeff's lead. Woody, "a natural musician," seemed to learn fast. He had talent, and he was willing to work at it. "It's gotta be in ya' an' dig it out," Lunsford insisted.

Guthrie dug it out. He characteristically made light of the long hours he spent woodshedding, listening to others and copying what he heard played. "After a while, I was rattling around with [Jeff], playing my way at the ranch and farm house dances. We worked our way up to playing inside of the city limits." In fact, he was to work at it harder than anything else he had taken up in his young life. Certainly harder than at school.

Already a year behind, and lacking sufficient credits, Guthrie enrolled as a sophomore at Pampa High School in the fall of 1929. An outsider, a boomer, Guthrie made little impression on his classmates and less on his teachers. He was "not a leader," one former student insisted. "No one you'd remember."

Socially and academically, he lagged behind. He "never had a date," said another schoolmate. And he spent his hours in study hall filling pages of notebook paper with antic sketches of cowboys and bucking broncos he handed to other students. Guthrie passed only his class in American history, barely scraping by with a mark of 70. He failed English III, Algebra II, and beginning Latin. He did marginally better in his second semester, passing history, successfully repeating the English and algebra classes he had earlier failed, but failing to pass Latin I for a second time.

No scholar, he was instead the class clown. As a reporter for an imaginary newspaper, Guthrie jokingly introduced himself to classmates as "Alonzo Zilch of Ballyhoo Magazine." The class clown wore a mask—borrowed from a continuing character in the then popular and somewhat risqué humor magazine *Captain Billy's Whiz Bang.*

The Pampa High School yearbook for 1930, *The Harvester*, noted that graduating senior Evelyn Carter "wills her store of witty remarks to Woody Guthrie." In a column of "More Harvester Hallucinations," the head of the history department asks, "Where was the Declaration of Independence signed?" And "Woodie" replies, "At the bottom, of course."

"He didn't seem to take life seriously and certainly didn't take much interest in school," said one classmate. He was "come easy, go easy. Eat when he can. Hair standing up like a mop," and unwashed too, snorted Hattie Holt, the barber's wife. He was "the ugliest thing," just "trash," she concluded.

At Pampa High that fall of 1929 Guthrie began an enduring friendship with Matt Jennings. The two young men had much in common. Jennings was also new to town, the son of a railroad worker turned furniture store salesman who had moved his family to Pampa a year earlier. Two years younger than Guthrie, Jennings too hailed from small-town Oklahoma and like Guthrie, was ill fitted for school. "I wasn't very much of a student," he acknowledged. So far as he knew, Guthrie "probably done as good or better 'n me 'cause algebra I never got ahold of."

If school failed to interest them, music did, Matt said. "That was the first thing we discovered." Both played the harmonica, though Guthrie held his twenty-five-cent Marine Band backwards, with the bass notes on the right.

"I couldn't get a tune out of it that way," Jennings said. "It'd be like turning a newspaper upside down."

The two young men played "things like the railroad wreck song," Matt explained, "and I would stay with the melody." Woody meanwhile played some licks he told Jennings he "had learned from a nigger who shined shoes in Okemah."

While Jennings conceded his harmonica playing "wasn't too bad," the sound of two twenty-five-cent harmonicas was uninspiring. Matt bought a fiddle out of hock for ten dollars at Frank's Pawn Shop, and after Jeff Guthrie finally tuned it—Woody had tried and failed repeatedly—Jennings haltingly scratched out Stephen Foster's "My Old Kentucky Home." Jeff gave Matt his first fiddling lessons and taught him a handful of traditional breakdowns as well as currently popular songs that Jeff played at local dances.

Meanwhile Woody was practicing guitar, Jennings said, trying to master "the Carter Family lick" shaped by Maybelle Carter on a series of RCA Victor shellac records. Because "he wanted to do all the runs," Jennings explained, Guthrie listened to the records repeatedly in Shorty Harris's drugstore, imitating what he heard. He listened, he imitated, he listened again, he imitated once more, learning by rote.

When Harris grew weary of the records played repeatedly, particularly the Carter Family's version of "Bury Me Beneath the Willow," Guthrie sang. His voice had hardened, the syllables and tones produced in the head rather than the chest. Like the young man himself, the voice had grown thin, wiry, and uncommonly intense.

A quality of toughness born of conviction and his improvised guitar accompaniments rescued even the most sentimental of his mother's parlor songs from the bathetic. Wandering about Pampa, he often sang a favorite about

> . . . *the scene of a gambler*
> *He'd lost all his money at play;*
> *Took his dead mother's ring from his finger*
> *That she wore on her wedding day.*
> *His last earthly treasure, he stakes it,*
> *Bows his head so his shame he might hide.*
> *When they lifted his head, they found he was dead*
> *It's a picture from life's other side.*

About four in the afternoon, Guthrie would wander across the street to the Holt brothers' barbershop, guitar slung over his shoulder. There, for as long as an hour when business was slow, he would play square-dance tunes, Sid Holt on fiddle or guitar, his brother Roy fiddling while Woody chorded rhythmic accompaniment and sang. Uncle Jeff would sit in occasionally, picking up a guitar or fiddle. As he grew more confident, Matt too would join in. The Holts were friendly, "just fine people" with a "nice shop," Jeff Guthrie said.

The guitar playing was simple musically, but Woody was absorbing an important lesson.

"Old champ fiddlers," he discovered, " . . . want the guitar to stay purely down on the bottom of the stack, and they make you pluck or pick it their way so as to ride in and out and down around on their fiddle bow [without] your banjo or your guitar ruining their fiddle piece." One even insisted he strum only one chord throughout the tune.

Caught up in music, bored in his classes, Guthrie was to drop out of school in the first semester of his fourth year, leaving behind a spotty academic career. What Woody could not get in the classroom, he sought in the Pampa Public Library. Two or three times a week he slipped away from the drugstore on South Cuyler to make his way to the library in the basement of Pampa City Hall.

He read constantly, Matt Jennings recalled. "We'd go to the library together and check out two or three books, and he'd recap them for me before I got through one book." Guthrie systematically worked his way through the shelves, concentrating on psychology, Western religions, and Eastern philosophies, what Jennings called "yogi stuff." Guthrie read and reread the newly published mystical parables of Lebanese-American poet Kahlil Gibran, *The Prophet*. "He just wanted to know something about everything in the world," Matt explained.

According to librarian Evelyn Todd, the young man seemed intrigued by hypnotism and believed in the power of suggestion. She recalled one incident when Guthrie told her he was going to help his anxious sister, Mary Jo, pass a junior high school math test. He intended to sit by Mary Jo's bed all night, hold her hand, and communicate his confidence she would pass the test. He was transmitting positive thoughts to her, he told Mrs. Todd.

Woody sat up the entire night, fixed on his sleeping sister. Days later, he reported to Mrs. Todd that Mary Jo had indeed passed the test.

In time, young Guthrie felt confident enough to write in his tight longhand a book about the fundamentals of psychology, then to stuff his notebook pages inside a salvaged cover from another book, and donate the volume to the library. Mrs. Todd catalogued the manuscript under "Guthrie, Woodrow Wilson," and put it on the shelves.*

Mrs. Todd remembered the curly-haired Guthrie with affection. "If he had had a better education and been guided a little differently, probably he could have gone places. He was a talented boy," she added. "He had lots of talent."

The young man, in turn, was fond of Mrs. Todd. When he learned she was originally from Illinois and a distant relative of Mary Todd Lincoln, the president's wife, Guthrie painted an oil portrait of the sixteenth president as a gift for her. She hung the framed portrait, "a good picture," in her office. Guthrie then painted a second for the library's reading room.

Night after night Guthrie would talk to Jennings about what he had read, or greater things beyond Pampa, "about life." Woody talked "a lot, but he didn't tell you that much about himself. He had a thousand opinions, but he didn't include himself," Matt said.

Once, just once, Jennings recalled, did eighteen-year-old Woody Guthrie open himself up. The two young men had come in late one night in September 1930, so Matt decided to stay at the cothouse with Woody rather than go home. As they lay in bed, Woody tonelessly offered:

"Had a letter last week that my mother's dead." Charley had gathered his three children together and read them the official notification; Nora Guthrie had died three months before in the state hospital at Norman.†

Until that moment, Woody had given no hint. And even now, he showed no emotion.

"He had known for three or four days and he chose that night, for some reason, to tell me about it," Jennings added. Perhaps the bootleg alcohol they had been drinking through the evening had melted his reserve.

The doctors had diagnosed Nora as suffering from a rare, unnamed disease. It was not simply the madness that sent most inmates to the state asylum. "This disease," Guthrie added, "it's hereditary. It can be passed on from mother to son."

As Matt recalled that brief moment, the threat seemed distant, remote from the darkened cothouse on South Cuyler, from Pampa, from the High Plains. "No way this could bother us," Matt said.

"That's about all they could figure out . . . at the time, that the people

---

* There it sat, apparently unread. Mrs. Todd's successor apparently threw out the manuscript in a purge that also caught up *Tom Sawyer* and *Moby-Dick*.
† Buried in an unmarked grave in June 1930, Nora Belle Sherman Guthrie lay, anonymous and unvisited, in Norman's IOOF Cemetary on Porter Street for seventy-two years. According to Rob Collins, then of the *Norman Transcript*, the gravesite was rediscovered by Evelyn Parker, chairman of the Cleveland County Genealogical Society's research committee, in January 2002.

were crazy," Matt continued. They were crazy, and eventually they died. And as everyone knew, madness ran in families.

Woody said nothing more about his mother. Guthries did not complain. "Papa, Roy, Woody, George didn't want to talk about the sorrowful things in life," sister Mary Jo explained. Father and sons "never would talk about Mama."

His sadness Woody buried under visits to the library and a flurry of correspondence courses: law, medicine, religion, literature, and "ologies of all sorts and kinds," courses he shared with his father.

There was no order, no plan in either his readings or the self-taught courses that periodically came through the mails. Guthrie was curious about all things and groping for direction. He was restless as only an eighteen-year-old can be.

He hung around the courthouse when Shorty Harris did not need him, and walked the beat with Uncle Jeff through "the tough end of town, the south side. I rode with the cops, and learnt how to make the rounds and vag the whores, fine the pimps every so often, and take the kale on the rail." Young Guthrie came to understand "that some people must like for things to be wrong."

He seemed untouched by any ambition. "You always had the feeling he would get by just as well with fifteen cents as well as fifteen dollars; money didn't seem to mean much to him," said schoolmate and later Gray County Sheriff Rufus Jordan.

Guthrie seemed to know everyone, a "go-easy guy who didn't worry about tomorrow," as onetime Pampa policeman Charlie Pipes remembered him. Aside from Matt Jennings, he had no close friends; he preferred to travel alone, his wanderings as aimless as his life.

Woody's prospects as either innkeeper or bartender hardly improved when Texas Rangers swept down on the town in July 1930, declared martial law, and rounded up those they deemed undesirable. Hundreds found themselves escorted to the edge of town, then summarily ordered to move on. The Rangers returned to the jail, arrested Sheriff E. S. Graves, and padlocked the cribs, jake joints, and remaining cothouses along South Cuyler that Graves had protected. For three days Pampa was quiet, until the Rangers left; the gamblers, bootleggers, and prostitutes crept back, more discreet now, but still offering the same pleasures.

In the fall of that year, the owner of the cothouse, Old Man Eldridge, died. Out of respect, Charley insisted they close on the afternoon of the funeral—a solemn occasion Woody marked by jig-dancing on the sidewalk in front of the cothouse as the hearse passed down South Cuyler.

Eldridge's heirs elected to close the cothouse and sell the property; Charley and his son abruptly found themselves simultaneously unemployed and homeless.

Jeff Guthrie was to arrange a job for his half-brother Charley from Sheriff Graves. Though Charley hobbled about hunched over, he could handle the duties of office deputy and desk sergeant in the Sheriff's Department. His florid penmanship would look good on the police blotter.

Son Woodrow was left to shift for himself, supported by his dollar a day from Shorty Harris and whatever he picked up from painting signs on the weekends. The cothouse shut down, he found a bed where he could, staying with his father on South Somerville, with Jeff, Allene, and the baby in their crowded apartment, then moving out to the Boydstun farm for a week.

"Woody would visit us fairly often," friend and neighbor Fern Dulaney recalled. "Everyone laughed when they were with him. He would ride the freight train within two miles of our house and come down the lane singing and playing his guitar.

"He helped Dad with the plowing, and one day Dad saw Woody just really making tracks to catch the tractor. Woody said he was seeing if it would go by itself. I think they had to do some fencing after that episode."

He spent time in less reputable quarters as well. "Forced by the fun of the thing and by the heat of my feelings," he lived for a month with a prostitute in an "old rotty shack" in Pampa. For one brief, passion-inspired moment he thought to rescue this woman with "proud kicky legs" from her "bed of chancred hate." Then as suddenly as it had seized him, his ardor gave way to shame, and Guthrie instead slipped away, relieved he "didn't catch any disease from you."

School held no attraction for him. He enrolled in the fall of 1930, with barely enough credits to be counted a junior. Signed up for two required make-up classes, he shortly withdrew. He would not complete the last two years of high school.

He was eighteen years old, emancipated, and adrift, just as hard times settled on the oil patch of Gray County, Texas.

CHAPTER FOUR

Starting the Panther

*H*E WAS EIGHTEEN years old in that summer of 1930, the year of the Great Depression falling across the nation. A high school dropout, he was rudderless, guided by whim or grounded by inertia.

Woody worked sporadically for Shorty Harris selling jake, or he wandered off for days on end, even to travel as far as Okemah to visit old friends. He boldly splashed window cards in calcimine paints to advertise the specials at the Č and C Market where Matt Jennings worked as a butcher. Relying on books and a correspondence course, he taught himself to paint with oils; sister Mary Jo recalled stacks of canvases he had carefully stretched, and her brother patiently preparing the white background before he laid on darker colors.

Other times he read library books, "pretty heavy stuff," according to Jennings. When he finished a book, he would summarize the contents for Matt; it was Guthrie's way to comprehension. "Woody believed in simplicity like people in the Bible Belt believe in their scripture," Matt Jennings said. "He worshipped *simplicity*."

Guthrie's spasms of energy alternated with days spent lying on the bed of his room, smoking handrolled cigarettes, bestirring himself only to paint a window placard that would pay for another sack of Bull Durham tobacco, and more days in the shabby room.

Ever mercurial, he flitted from dark mood to prankish impulse. At one moment he was somber and withdrawn; the next he was clowning around, retelling corny jokes he had read in tattered copies of *Captain Billy's Whiz Bang* at the barbershop, or pretending to be a ventriloquist with Mary Jo's best doll.

Still, he remained private, acknowledging he was never totally open with any one. His friend Matt, who probably spent more time with Guthrie than anyone else, could only shrug. "I wouldn't claim to know everything about him at all," Matt finally conceded.

Woody was different, more complicated than the kids in their gang—Fred, Matt, and Mary Jennings, the Baker brothers, Minnie Dittmeyer, Joe Adair, Evelyn Barnes, and Rosemary Hinckle. His years of living alone, scuffling on the streets of Okemah, had toughened him. "Some people get poor and they stay scared all their lives. It never scared Woody; he didn't give a damn," Matt said with a chuckle.

In an unpredictable life, there was one constant. More and more, making music consumed him. He spent hours listening to the black shoeshine man at the barbershop "who could really play a lot of blues on the guitar," boastful ballads like "Stagolee" or leering jibes like "Candy Man Blues."

As Matt remembered him, the black man "had great long fingers, like so many of them have; he could walk all over the neck of a guitar," pulling on the strings to raise the pitch microtonally. "Woody learned quite a bit from this shine boy."

By day he practiced guitar. By night he and Matt listened to records on the Jennings family's windup Victrola, particularly the Carter Family and Mother Maybelle Carter's melodic guitar. "Woody loved long bass runs; he loved those bass runs," Matt said.

Off by himself, he sang the old ballads learned from his mother, "The Dream of a Miner's Child," "Barbara Allen," and "The Drunkard's Dream," or his father's thumping gospel tunes. From the new radio stations in Amarillo and Pampa he picked up topical songs like "The Sherman Cyclone" and later "The Hindenburg Disaster." From Lew Childre broadcasting on WWL from New Orleans, he learned the gospel song, "This Train Is Bound for Glory."

The music was all about them. From records he copied Vernon Dahlhart's "Wreck of the Old 97," Frank Crumit's "The Gay Caballero," and Jimmie Rodgers's "California Blues" about a place where people could "sleep out every night" and drink water that tasted like cherry wine.

Like his mother before him, he favored the older sentimental songs—if he thought the sentiment was honest. "Goodbye to the Stepstone" Guthrie sang often, mainly to himself, Matt recalled, as if it were a private anthem.

Goodbye, dear old stepstone, goodbye to my home.
Now the wind rustles by with a moan.
I'll cherish your memories wherever I roam.
Goodbye, dear old stepstone, goodbye.

Eventually he began to write songs himself, once confessing to Matt "he hoped to write a song someday that a lot of people would know, and sing it."

His first song, or the first he kept, was a humorous ballad written in a mock country style popular among early radio performers.

I was in a buckboard wagon going down the old plank road
When I spied a Ford a-coming down my way.
I will tell you just what happened, how I lost my wagon load
When that old gray team of hosses ran away.

When at first they heard the rattle and the clatter of the car,
Me and Lindy Lou was a-setting side by side.
Well, she throwed her arms around me when the hosses jumped the tongue,
And here is what my sweet Melindy cried:

"Ain't there somethin' you can do to keep these horses standin' still?
What makes you set and stare the way you do?"
Well, I put my arms around her and I took her by the hand,
And I says, "Now, don't you fret, Melindy Lou!"

Well, them hosses was a-running and they fairly split the breeze.
I was a-hugging sweet Melindy with a smile.
I had always wanted to hug her, so I bowed my head and prayed
They would run a hundred thousand million miles.

At a standstill there I kissed her when at last the hosses fell,
Quite exhausted from the run that they had made,
And I married sweet Melindy, so I'm happy in my soul
That the old gray team of hosses ran away.

As poetry, Sweet Melindy's adventure scarcely merits attention. Yet it does have characteristics that would stand as the Guthrie hallmark. It tells a coherent story. It is simple, direct, and idiomatic.

If it spoofs a passing rural America, it also smacked of the outlandish "hillbilly" posturing of the comedians on such popular radio shows as "Grand Ole Opry." Guthrie was learning by imitation.

In time, he would become prolific, dashing off as many as one song per day, Jennings said. Sometimes Charley helped with a line or rhyme; his son took ideas where he found them, unconcerned about credits or authorship.

Woody was seemingly diffident about his apprenticeship. "About sixteen years back down my road," he later wrote, "I started making up little songs, true stories, wild tales, long and short hauls about things I saw happened to the oil people, cattle people, wheat folks, on the upper north plains of high Texas, where the wind and the dust was born.

"My dad and myself made up crazy songs just for the fun of it: 'Flapper Fanny's Last Ride,' 'Barbary Ellen's Likker Pot,' 'Windy River Blues,' 'Dust Pneumonia,' 'Talking' Dustbowl Blues.'"

For all his casual, almost dismissive attitude, Guthrie had begun to apply himself, to hone both musical skill and writing craft. On occasion, he wrote instrumental tunes to play on the mandolin. Guitarist James King, whose father managed the radio station in Amarillo, remembered, "One night at a barn dance, Woody played a 'Chinese Breakdown' on a mandolin, a piece he made up which sounded weird."

Almost inevitably in that music-rich locale, Guthrie began playing in a band. He and Matt, joined by a mutual acquaintance, Cluster Baker, formed "The Corncob Trio." As the more accomplished guitarist, Baker played that instrument while Woody shifted to the mandolin and Matt played fiddle. As a trio they practiced when they could—Matt got off work managing the butcher shop in the C and C Market at 9:00 P.M. Because they were all comparatively new to their instruments, "everybody suffered together," Matt wryly noted.

They hacked out hoedowns and minstrel show tunes, improving to the point where they felt confident enough to perform at weekend house parties in shabby south Pampa. Their "old timey" music was not all that welcome in the tonier clubs and hotels north of the railroad tracks, Minnie Dittmeyer recalled. "It was only popular with the poor." The wealthier, more established residents of Pampa favored the newer swing music; the Tommy Dorsey Orchestra, which played one night at the Shamrock, was particularly popular in town.

Under Uncle Jeff's leadership, the Guthries also formed a family trio. First at Jeff's home on North Russell, then at ranch dances around Pampa, Woody played guitar and mandolin with Jeff and Allene Guthrie.

Jeff, the well-regarded fiddler, was the leader and the big draw. Old-timers in the Panhandle turned out to hear Jeff launch into a square-dance tune with a stomp and a shout, "Let's get this panther started!" Nephew and wife—who "played a real sweet accordion," according to fellow musician George Hamlin—played supporting or backup roles. So too the barbering Holt brothers, Sid and Roy, when they sat in.

In his music as well, Woody sought to simplify. Instead of learning the more difficult fingering that would allow him to play in all the keys, Guthrie became "a clamper fiend." He used a capo, a spring-loaded clamp that enabled him to shorten the length of the strings, and thus raise the pitch, fret by fret, half-step by half-step.

"I couldn't help myself," he explained. "This clamper gave me a good chance to bluff my way along and to sound like I really knew my okra on the handle of my guitar. Otherwise I couldn't have stayed within nine miles of Jeff . . ." when he played a fiddle tune in A-flat or E major.*

The Friday and Saturday night barn dances were hard work. The breakdowns that accompanied square dances ran uninterrupted for as long as one-half hour to frolic through the sets. They alternated with slower fox trots and waltzes, mostly popular songs of the day, to give musicians and dancers a rest.

There was little money in it. According to local custom, the musicians took a percentage of the gate, "but we didn't make enough money to fill our bellies, nor gas tank, either one," Woody groused.

One memorable evening, uncle and nephew did cash in. Joe Bowers, a whiskey-dipped cowboy whose ranch was speckled with oil wells, hired Woody and Jeff to play "I Ride an Old Paint" again and again, until early morning. Each time they played it, the weepy cowboy threw another bill on the table. "Woody was so sick of that song," Matt Jennings snorted. "But Woody come home with some money that time."

With Jeff and Allene, Woody made his first unpaid radio broadcasts, on WDAG in Amarillo, then early in 1936 on tiny KPDN on the second floor of the Culbertson Building in Pampa. While the appearances on WDAG were sporadic, "two-by-four" KPDN offered Guthrie and the Corncob Trio more regular fifteen-minute bookings on "The Breakfast Club."

Considering the upcoming radio programs, Guthrie weighed abandoning the mandolin in favor of Cluster's brother playing it. Instead, as Alonzo M. Zilch, he would be an entertainer, someone like the late Will Rogers, the onetime vaudevillian and syndicated humorist whom Guthrie admired; he would play the part of a country lad come to town, delivering a daily lecture, "one of his rubbish sort."

* If the tune was in A-flat, Guthrie placed the capo behind the first fret on the fingerboard, and then fingered in G major. If it was in E major, he placed the capo behind the second fret, and played as if in D major. In time, he came to finger virtually everything in those two keys, Matt Jennings stated.

As it turned out, Guthrie both played the mandolin and delivered his "rubbish sort." The KPDN broadcasts, squeezed in before Matt went to work at the meat market, were informal. Despite rehearsals and a playlist, Guthrie as nominal leader of the Corncob Trio often scuttled their neatly laid plans in the middle of a show. He would begin an introduction to a song, then wander off into a barely related anecdote that stretched to fill most of their fifteen minutes before they signed off with the ditty Woody taught them: "So long, it's been good to know you." As long as Guthrie was entertaining the audience, KPDN's manager was content; as long as he was entertaining himself, Guthrie was happy.

In time, Guthrie became "a favorite there, on at least once a week," longtime Pampa resident John Gikas said.

On Friday and Saturday nights, Woody, Matt, and Cluster played at Flaherty's Barn, a club outside of town popular with those who still favored the "good old songs." The crowds grew so large, lifelong Pampa resident Minnie Dittmeyer said, that musicians and dancers were moved out of doors.

His confidence in his musicianship building, over the next years Guthrie sat in with other players—at dance clubs, at parties, and, with the repeal of Prohibition, on outdoor platforms clapped together in the parking lots of newly reopened saloons.

People who knew the Guthries, particularly the men who performed with Woody, came to think the young man a "born natural" musician. "Give him a French harp and he was an artist on it," Shorty Harris said of his on-again, off-again employee.

Sooner or later Guthrie learned to play virtually anything with strings—guitar, mandolin, violin—anything but George Hamlin's left-handed tenor banjo. "Woody would play the drums one night, the guitar the next," Hamlin recalled. "He came out with Hawaiian picks one time to play the washboard. He got a good effect too, just like a snare drum."

Guthrie "was fairly good on the guitar then, but had a poor quality instrument. He was too broke to own any good instrument," Hamlin added.

It was all unplanned. Whim-struck, Guthrie would show up, unannounced, at the Willard Club where Hamlin and his wife, the Lowry brothers, Ted Simmons, and Jack Rocher performed as the Haybalers. At first, they were reluctant to let him sit in. "Once you had your audience warmed up and attuned to you," George explained, "you were reluctant to upset the applecart." Equally important, it meant splitting their 60 percent of the gate with a seventh person.

In time, Guthrie proved himself. If he turned up without an instrument, Hamlin would ask, "Are you sitting out tonight, Woody?"

"No, I'll do something," Woody might reply, pulling bones or two spoons from his pocket. Then he would stand by the drums "and cut loose on the spoons and bones at once."

He was unpredictable, the band as curious as the crowd about what instrument Guthrie might play: mandolin, double bass, drums, bones, spoons, washboard, or he might spell Forrest Lowry on guitar. "He had music in his blood but there was no definite way he would put it out at a given moment."

He played both drums and guitar well enough to sit in when the band turned to popular music or to the Dixieland tunes that tenor banjo player Hamlin favored. Whatever the instrument, Hamlin said, Guthrie "never let them down."

With the washboard, he acted the deadpan clown. "He would get an old cigar in his mouth and chomp on it while he played, making odd faces. He would stick it way into his mouth," as if to swallow it, guitarist James King remembered. Yet for all his clowning, Guthrie conveyed the impression "he was a worried man," according to King.

Guthrie's joking went just so far. He refused to play bawdy songs or sing suggestive lyrics. "He never did worsen the outlook any," Hamlin allowed.

As Hamlin remembered the year-long engagement of the Haybalers during 1934, Woody was not a particular draw. Perhaps fifty couples turned out on any of the five nights a week they performed at the Willard. Guthrie was merely an additional member of the band. He sang sparingly, through a megaphone, but never more than two choruses of any song, Hamlin said.

Meanwhile, both Guthrie and Hamlin were writing songs in the popular "western swing" style of Bob Wills and the Light Crust Doughboys, whose Fort Worth broadcasts easily reached Pampa. Hamlin recalled laboring over one song, "Can't Be Easy No More," then showing it to Guthrie the day after it was finally finished. It was good, Guthrie allowed, then sat down and overnight wrote another just as good, Hamlin said.

The major influence on young Woody in this first half of the new decade was his gregarious Uncle Jeff, country fiddler, great dreamer in a family of dreamers, fingerprint man, parlor magician, and sometime faith healer.

Jeff was constantly on the lookout for ways to capitalize on his music, even to leave law enforcement permanently—particularly after losing his patrolman's job in 1930 to a friend of the newly elected sheriff, Lon

Blancett. It was Jeff who arranged their dates to play barn dances, and it was Jeff who spotted the advertisement in the *Pampa Times* seeking entertainers for a traveling show.

The whole idea was mad. A wealthy rancher from Hereford, Texas, intended to tour a tent show featuring his young wife, a former Kansas City chorine. Claude Taylor needed some acts to fill out the bill; he hired the Guthries, Woody, Jeff, and Allene: comic, magician, and magician's assistant, the three of them doubling as musicians.

They played what Jeff called "popular music," that is, "any piece that people liked, old or new." They played "Doodle-de-Doo" and "Kansas City Kate" for the chorine's dances and "Back Home on My Back Porch" for the audience.

Woody bought what he called a "Yankee farmer wig, some freckle pencil, and flesh-colored grease paint, and took the part of the stumbling comedian." His job was to fill the time while Jeff was rigging his next trick behind the curtain.

Woody on stage was "comical, very comical." He sang, danced, spun long yarns to keep the scant audiences in their seats, even drew cartoons. "He always could put in something," Robert Boydstun reminisced.

He told jokes born of minstrel and medicine shows a half-century earlier:

I stopped with a family that had two twin boys. One was named Pete and the other Repete. At another place they had two twin girls. One they called Kate and the other Duplicate.

I used to play the organ for a living, but I gave it up. The monkey died.

Like Will Rogers he favored regional humor:

There is a section of the country lying in the western part of Texas that is so dry the jack rabbits carry canteens.

And like the droll Will Rogers, his acolyte Woody Guthrie found stories that had a sting:

They have raised the price of meat until it's getting so a working man can't eat meat; the nearest thing he can come to eating meat is oxtail soup and beef tongue; that is the only way he can make both ends meet.

Their audiences were sparse, their reception lukewarm, but no matter. They would not be returning. The chorus girl ran off with the stage manager of a competing show, and Taylor decided to cut his losses. Woody was resigned.

"Our show folded because of the seasons and us, and nobody had any money, anyhow in 1931 and 2."

This was just another lost opportunity for a family of missed opportunities, of tales of riches just over the next rise. And dreams of capturing those riches.

Jeff never tired of talking about helping Emmett Dalton, last of the bank-robbing brothers, scour the banks of the creek at Dalton Springs for the $100,000 in loot supposedly buried there before their ill-fated attempt on the Coffeyville, Kansas, bank. Dalton had promised the Guthries, then living in the vicinity, half the money "'cause he stayed at our house, ate at our table, slept in our bedrooms," Jeff explained.

There was old Jerry P.'s patent on a locker for railway stations, a patent he had failed to develop. Others, more shrewd, quietly waited for the patent to expire and made fortunes.

There was Jerry P.'s abortive attempt to register Charley's half-brothers on the Indian rolls based on the fact that their mother, Josie Sands, was said to be one-eighth Creek Indian. That bid for what would be oil-rich lands was mired in the mud of bad roads outside Muskogee and their arrival at the government offices after the deadline had passed.

And there was the story of Jerry P.'s lost mine, eternally calling to Jeff, ever a disappointment but firmly embedded in Guthrie family lore. As the story was told, Jerry P. had stumbled on the mine while running cows in the barren Chisos Mountains of the Big Bend Country. He had tied up a horse to an outcropping of rock, or had picked up a rock kicked loose by a cow, and there was the silver vein, assaying out to twenty dollars a ton, according to Jerry P.'s son Claude, or to an even more astounding sixty-five dollars a ton, if you believed his half-brother Jeff. Even better, the assay was said to have revealed commercially profitable traces of gold, mercury, copper, and zinc.

There was little chance anyone else would stumble on the site; it was too remote, eighty-five miles south of Alpine, Texas, near the Mexican border, three miles up Rough Run Canyon, then along an old wagon trail to the lode at the head of the canyon. Still, to stake his claim, Jerry P. had scratched his initials on a rock and turned it over as a marker. He also sketched a map.

Before Jerry P. could exploit his silver mine, he moved to Oklahoma in the futile effort to claim Indian headrights for his children. When he eventually thought to locate his lode, he could not. Memory or a faulty map had betrayed him. With his death in 1927, Jerry P.'s mine became the family will-o'-the-wisp.

"When times was good in the oil fields, Jerry's story about the rich gold and silver mine that lay 900 miles south, well, it just didn't get much attention," grandson Woodrow noted. "Everybody worked. Made big wages. Drank good rotgut. Had fun. They didn't care about Jerry's long lost tale of the gold mine, or was it silver?"

By the summer of 1931, however, the boom had flattened. Unloosed by the Crash of October '29, the Great Depression crept finally to the oil fields of the High Plains.

It was Robert Boydstun, never a great success as a wheat farmer, who suggested they might seek his father-in-law's lost mine. If his wife Maude was skeptical, son-in-law Jeff, a man "who was always going to make that ship come in," was quick to pick up on the scheme.

With nothing better to do, and nothing to hold him in Pampa, Woody was eager to go. "I wanted to be the Guthrie to uncover that dangburn rockpile and find old Jerry P.'s fortune he wept and cried on his dying bed so much about, begging and pleading and asking all of us to believe him, to go down to the Chisos Mountains."

Jeff drove a 1922 Model-T truck and thereby became the leader of the expedition. He also provided the moonshine, siphoned off after a raid on bootleggers the year before. Charley and his two oldest sons, Roy and Woodrow, crowded into the truck, and headed southward, toward the border.*

They would camp out, the four of them sheltering among the crumbling walls of an abandoned adobe house. They tramped up Rough Run Canyon, fruitlessly. Woody spent a day by himself, wandering among the mesquite brush and piñon pines that stubbornly pried their roots into the barren rocks. These eroded yellow buttes in the Big Bend Country were the first mountains he had ever seen, and he was fascinated.

"This was a sandyland country, this Pecos County, here all around us. Sandy desert bushes. Sandy cactus of every kind, slim and long, fat and thick, wide and low, high and skinny, curly, twisty, knotty, stickery, thorny,

---

* As with so many stories Guthrie retold of his life, the details of this trip south were embroidered with half-truths. In one account, the four were first going north to "Canada's orcharding country that lay free and open to homesteaders" until "a frizzlin cold blizzard on our parting and our leaving nite did cause the nosey brassy radiator cap to turnaway." Quoted by Edith Fowke, "A Tribute to Woody Guthrie," *Little Sandy Review* 5 (ca. July 1960), p. 22.

daggery-knifed, razor sharp. . . . The feel and the breath of the air was all different, new, high, clear, clean and light. None of the smokes and carbons, none of the charcoal smells of the oil fields. None of the sooty oil-field fires."

They spent five futile days in the canyon. Though it was unsuccessful, perhaps *because* it was unsuccessful, the search for Jerry P.'s mine and the stark Big Bend Country itself gripped the imagination of Charley Guthrie's second son.

The Guthrie men found no mine, but for those few days Woody once again felt close to his taciturn older brother Roy and to his father. They were a family once more. As Woody interpreted it, his father agreed that the trip "has done my soul a world of good. . . . If I never lay my finger on my daddy's claimstake, and never touch as much as a grain of gold or an ounce of silver, my old paw Jerry's spirit in heaven will know that I did come here, and that I did try."

They returned to Pampa, Charley intent upon preserving the family. He had tried once before to bring Mary Jo from Maude's to live with him and Woody in a trailer court. He insisted Roy leave Okemah and join them. It had not worked out; not-yet-ten-year-old Mary Jo needed more attention than a crippled father trying to start a real estate business, a working brother, and a footloose brother could provide.

Still the notion persisted; Charley gradually realized he needed a woman to manage things, to be the center of the family as Nora had once been. He determined to marry again.

Just how Charley met Betty Jean McPherson he never made clear. Woody said they met through the lonelyhearts column of a ladies' romance magazine, but when Mary Jo asked her father about it, he just laughed it off.

They did know that in September 1931, Betty Jean stepped down off a train from Oklahoma City, carrying a suitcase and a past. She was about forty-five years old, "fleshy," in Robert Boydstun's phrase, taller than Charley too, "a big, squareheaded woman, a good seventy pounds bigger than anybody in the house," Woody wrote later. "Her hair was always a frazzle; she never could comb it nor brush it up to do much good."

She had been married once in the past and had two grown children, she told them, but she was alone now. She was from Springfield, Illinois, or Omaha, Nebraska—the stories varied—had been a nurse in California and had the stiffly starched white uniform to prove it. Beyond that, they knew little. "We didn't ask her all about herself, and she didn't bother to tell us. We welcomed her. She welcomed us," Woody wrote.

Charley Guthrie and Betty Jean McPherson took out a marriage license on Tuesday, September 26, 1931, and returned it two days later. The marriage came as a surprise to his sister, Maude Boydstun. "All of a sudden she was here and they were married."

The newlyweds set up housekeeping in the trailer court on South Somerville, Betty Jean taking responsibility for the two children still at home, George, now fifteen, and Mary Jo, nine. Accustomed to the easygoing Boydstun family, the children took a keen dislike to the coarse woman who had married their father.

"She was a very, very homely person, and my mother was a *beautiful* lady, I thought, the prettiest, you know, and I could be proud of her," Mary Jo insisted. When Betty Jean visited her school, "I was ashamed to tell people she was my mother.

"She smoked incessantly, a chain-smoker, to the extent that her fingers were orange." She rasped the discoloration from her fingers with a nail file, and to mask the acrid cigarette odor, she dabbed generous amounts of eucalyptus oil on her lips, between her breasts, and on her fingers. Soon enough the house reeked of stale cigarette smoke and eucalyptus.

With Charley struggling to get his real estate business restarted, money was short in the Guthrie home. Furthermore, "Charley was pretty easy going," so he did not interfere when Betty Jean set herself up as a fortuneteller a few months after they were married.

As a rather impressed Woody Guthrie remembered her, Betty Jean McPherson had come to Pampa well versed on "Religious Faith Healing, Mental Healing, Psychology, Creative Mind, Unity, Magnetic Healing, Hypnotism, and such similar sciences." She put these to work.

Though she was neither the first fortune-teller nor the first mind-reader to set up shop in Pampa, Betty Jean soon had a stream of customers finding their way to the trailer court.

Across town, Woody continued to work for Shorty Harris, or he did not, as the mood suited. At nights he played music, rarely returning to his flop house room until the early morning hours. He was unhappy about his past, unsettled about his future.

"Life was all right. Or was it? I doubt it," he decided.

The high school dropout who had been too shy, or too immature to date, had begun to take an interest in girls his own age. Shorty and Matt remembered him infatuated for a period with a daughter of boomers, Hazel Finlay.

Matt considered Hazel to be Woody's girlfriend. "They were crazy about each other," Harris insisted, but the relationship abruptly ended when the Finlays closed their laundry business and left town.

At a football rally for the Pampa High football team late in 1930, Matt and Woody bumped into Matt's younger sister, Mary, and her best friend, Minnie Dittmeyer. After the rally the four of them walked home together, Mary quiet, Woody clowning around, "a funny couple," in Minnie Dittmeyer's mind.

Mary, six months past her fourteenth birthday, was equally unimpressed with her brother's antic friend. Guthrie was then dating Pauline Furlong, whose five feet ten inches towered over him. Minnie and Mary could only wonder, "What in the world did she see in him?"

Not everyone agreed with the two girls. Many people around town found Woody funny, a real comic. Some of the girls judged him cute, with his helmet of tight curly hair capping a high forehead. He seemed sensitive, or sad, with his eyes drooping down from the bridge of his straight nose, his thin lips and cleft chin. If he didn't wear fancy clothes, he dressed like most of the young men in Pampa, in work pants and the khaki shirts oil men favored, a newsboy's cloth cap with a short bill clapped on those unruly curls.

Eighteen months younger than Matt, Mary had been born in Hydro, Oklahoma, on February 28, 1916. She had grown up the lone girl, with three brothers, in the home of boomer Harry and Esther Jennings. Hard times and her family's traditional values shaped Mary.

Born in Illinois, Harry Jennings had migrated to Oklahoma for his health—a dry climate supposedly would help his tuberculosis. As a sharecropper, he moved from farm to farm, year by year, scratching out a bare living for his wife and four children in western Oklahoma. He had tried railroad work, only to be let go when the Santa Fe replaced its Anglo-Irish track workers with cheap-labor Mexican immigrants. When the oil boom hit Pampa, oldest son Fred followed; relatives were boasting of five-dollars-a-day wages, and with the oil fields pumping round the clock, there was work for all.

It was a heady time for the Jennings family—until the boom sighed to a halt. Once more Harry Jennings was laid off; this time he found a job in a store that rented household furniture. No more the five dollars a day. The six Jenningses often scraped by on what Matt earned at the butcher shop.

Woody, in turn, was welcome at the Jennings home—"My dad was a pretty sociable Irishman," son Matt said—and Woody felt at home with the family. If one of Mary's parents walked into the room, Woody invariably broke into "When You Wore a Tulip," the Jenningses' favorite song.

Woody spent his free time at the Jennings home, playing music with Matt. Fourteen-year-old Mary was just there, the younger sister hanging around. Over a period of two years though, Mary blossomed as an adolescent, "a nice girl, not too good looking, but a good person," neighborhood gossip Violet Pipes stated.

Woody took notice of the flaxen-haired girl. Mary was soft-spoken and undemanding. Woody's Uncle Jeff finally concluded Mary "just didn't have a lot to say."

Like Woody, she was not very interested in school; she would drop out after completing her sophomore year. Focused on home and family, "I was a young girl not doing much of a whole lot," she concluded.

Some of Mary's attraction for Woody came with his desire for a family life. Mary embodied that, and a stable, loving family. As his uncle noted, "The Jennings were fine people, very up-and-up nice people, all of them."

For her part, Mary was impressed because Woody "was so damned confident. He was the leader of this group. He did the talking and the entertaining. He had the answers." He even typed out a little magazine for their group, filling it with humorous, teasing, gossipy items—half of them invented.

The gang gathered at different homes each week to talk, to plot their future with the help of a Ouija board, to play music and sing. During the torpid Texas summers they made ice cream and fanned themselves in the backyard, sitting in the dark, listening to crickets and cicadas. Gradually singles paired off, split up, and found new partners in informal courtships. They did not date, Minnie Dittmeyer offered, for none of them had any money; the most they might do was buy a hot dog at the Gikas family's hot-dog shop on Broadway.

Guthrie and the very attractive Deaun Heiskel sparked for a while, John Gikas recalled sixty years later. "Woody had an eye for beauty." Eventually, as Mary explained, she and Woody "sort of paired off, and I was Woody's girl."

She followed Woody to weekend barn dances, Woody's girl listening to the music, sipping soda pop. Once he decided he was seriously interested in Mary, "Woody said he did not like the idea of I go [sic] to dances and dance with somebody while he's playing."

He was jealous, Mary decided. He told her, "I'm not going to stay up there and entertain and have you out there on the floor dancing." Mary stopped tagging along when Woody played for dances.

Their courtship was casual. Woody said little about himself, and little about his family. "Before we were married, I didn't know his mother was in an insane institution," Mary said. "I only knew she was dead." Matt knew;

Mary only learned later. The deepening nature of their courtship came as a surprise to even those closest to them. "I was stunned when Mom said that Woody wants to marry Mary," Matt confessed. Years later he decided Woody sought out Mary to fill a deep need. "Woody not having a mother may have left him feeling like he'd been rejected by his mother."

Despite her youth, despite his constant jokes and music, Mary realized that Woody "was never totally happy." He was moody and sometimes depressed around her; it was a side of him Woody had allowed few others to see.

If Mary was an uncomplaining companion, she was not so dutiful that she lacked opinions. Opinions she was willing to stand by.

After one sharp spat, they separated. Spiteful Woody took up with one of Mary's cousins, then ended that relationship after "a very short time" to return sheepishly to Mary.

She also nurtured a streak of independence. Though warned to avoid South Cuyler and the red-light district, Mary, Minnie, and two girlfriends one time ventured there to look for Woody. Four teenage girls were daring the forbidden—in broad daylight. When he learned of her adventure, Mary's father whipped her, said Minnie.

Mary's parents opposed the marriage, her father so mad she wanted to marry a non-Catholic "that he wouldn't speak to me." Catholicism ran deep in the family; two of Harry Jennings's sisters were nuns. Furthermore, Guthrie was virtually unemployed, with no prospects to speak of. How was he going to support a wife, a girl barely sixteen at that? And what about children?

Despite their opposition, Mary was determined to follow her heart. Eventually she prevailed upon her mother to sign a consent form allowing the underage girl to be wed.

Woody and Mary were married in the rectory of the Catholic Church on Saturday morning, October 28, 1933, by the parish priest, Father Joseph Wonderly. Matt Jennings couldn't get off work. The witnesses were two friends of Mary who happened to be at the church that day.

Immediately after the ceremony Mary and Woody sat for their wedding photographs, in a cramped booth at the local dime store. They couldn't afford to go to a regular photo studio, they told Minnie Dittmeyer when they gave her one of the sepia-toned prints.

Mary's father was furious, so angry he refused to shake hands with Woody until two days afterward when the Guthries came to call. Charley

Guthrie and Harry Jennings decided to celebrate, Mary remembered, and "drank up all the home brew my dad had made."

Married in the depths of the depression—the legislation of Franklin D. Roosevelt's Hundred Days yet to have an impact on the far-off Texas Panhandle—Woody and Mary moved into an apartment on the east end of town. Financially, it was "bad, very, very bad," Mary recalled. "We had very little. When he wasn't working in the drug store, he was playing for dances."

Yet "as much as we had bad times, we had good times," she continued. "We had lots of good times, going out, going to homes, going to dances."

Then the good times disappeared.

CHAPTER FIVE

Black Blizzard

*I*N FAR-OFF WASHINGTON, on a gray Saturday morning in March 1933, the newly inaugurated president of the United States shuffled to the bank of microphones arrayed on the Capitol steps. Hatless in the cold wind, he gripped the podium with two hands as he began speaking on this "day of national consecration."

To the tens of thousands huddled in overcoats before the flag-draped platform, and to a vast nationwide audience hunched around living room radios, Franklin Delano Roosevelt recognized "this nation asks for action, and action now." After three and a half years of economic decline and enduring depression, he promised presidential leadership.

Cold winds snapped across the Capitol steps as the president laid out a bold initiative that redefined the role of the federal government in American life. He was extending a hand to the unemployed, to the hungry, to the desperate and the despairing. "Those suffering hardship from no fault of their own have a right to call upon the government for aid."

The greatest task was to put people to work, he continued, even by "direct recruiting by the Government itself." The nation would have to halt home and farm foreclosures, and consolidate fragmentary relief efforts, end the more adventurous speculations of banks, and most of all restore confidence in government.

To those tasks the president pledged himself and a nation "ready and willing to sacrifice for the good of a common discipline."

But urgency in Washington could not produce instant relief. In the southern cotton states and in the wheatfields of the Midwest, farmers and merchants waited fretfully for aid.

The Agricultural Adjustment Act paid farmers not to plant, on the theory that scarcity would push farm prices up, but it favored those with large holdings. Those with smaller farms had fewer acres to take out of production and received smaller government checks. Sharecroppers, who only rented the land they farmed, received nothing; the effect was to drive them from their farms as landowners put their acreage into the land bank.

Sharecropper families in eastern Oklahoma, never very far from poverty, ironically "didn't know it was a Depression," said Anna Gideon Guthrie. "We had always been poor." Guthrie, herself the daughter of a sharecropper, "picked my way out of the cotton patch" and moved into town to be a housekeeper.

They—and tens of thousands of other sharecroppers throughout the South—raised cotton and lived off a vegetable garden and the hog they slaughtered. Each year they mortgaged their mule to buy seed and start over, always hoping for better weather, a bigger crop, and higher prices.

But the good times never came. Through the 1920s, prices for southern short-staple cotton fell, driven down by superior Egyptian, Brazilian, and Indian imports. As prices fell, the sharecroppers abandoned worn-out farms to move westward; the migrant workers who hoed the rows and picked the cotton followed. By the end of the decade, only 35 percent of farm families owned their own homes; most farmers rented the land they worked.

Prosperity and hardship rubbed shoulders. In the wheat- and corn-growing heartland, Henry Ford's Fordson tractor made it possible to work larger holdings with fewer workers; inevitably the more successful bought out the less fortunate. A half-million farm families were turned from the land, to become itinerant "honk-honk hoboes" in the 1920s. Hundreds of thousands more followed as the Great Depression set in.

Fortified by its oil fields, Pampa held out against the economic decline until late in 1931. "Oil was being sold cheap, but it was being sold; wages were cheap, but they were wages," Deputy Sheriff Rufus Jordan said.

Even a year later, as solidly Democratic Pampa voted overwhelmingly for Franklin Roosevelt, "five dollars meant you were pretty well fixed," Jordan stated.

If you had five dollars. Pampa saw its first soup lines as the once bold wildcatters went broke, one by one, and one by one sold out to Sinclair Oil.

When the boom petered out, the boomers moved on, some to California's oil fields, some to return to untilled farms left long before, some to drift here or there looking for work, any kind of work that would feed wife and children. "The big swappers, lords, owners, bankers, and traders kept us down in debt and the sheriffs and deputies and Old Nick the Bankerman kept us on the move and go," Guthrie grumbled.

The new president inspired hope with his "Fireside Chats." Down-in-debt Pampans like Guthrie kept the faith.

> *You talked just like my*
> *blacksmith Uncle John*
> *plays his fiddle and*
> *he's done won fifty rough*
> *contests and had his*
> *six or seven kids and died last year.*

> *I say you and my uncle*
> *John's anvil and fiddle are*
> *two things I could go on*
> *and listen to for twenty*
> *more elections.*

Still the depression fell hard on Woodrow Guthrie, sometime musician, sometime drugstore clerk, and his young wife Mary. At best Woody "halfway made his living" painting store signs, brother-in-law Matt Jennings said.

Mary was undemanding, "a good, easy girl," Guthrie wrote in a notebook of random thoughts he began to keep. "She's about the only person in circulation that knows just exactly how to handle me."

Handling Guthrie meant leaving him free to do whatever he wanted when whim overtook him. "She very seldom ever complained, and she worked hard all of the time. She could straighten up a house almost as fast as I could litter it up with scrap paper."

Together they bought "the ricketiest of the oil town shacks" behind her parents' home at the corner of Russell and Craven. They agreed to pay $25 for the shotgun shack—"but never did pay the last $5," Guthrie acknowledged.

Furnishings of the three-room, whitewashed house were sparse; Mary's kitchen housed only a sink and a two-burner hot plate in a screened-in porch. They shared a bathroom and its flush toilet at the rear of the property with the Jenningses.

They had little money. In the first three years of their marriage, Woody brought home less than four dollars a week in wages, most of it earned selling liquor for Shorty Harris. "But we got by somehow," Woody wrote.

Somehow. "It was good times when he would or could work and we could buy a little groceries, something here or there, and there were times that there was practically nothing coming in," Mary recalled. "And that was when my dad, my good old dad, would say come on over and he'd shove me a few dollars. You could take $2 and buy groceries for a week."

Even with the birth of his daughter Gwendolyn in November 1935, Guthrie was an indifferent husband, "the least adapted to marriage of anyone who ever took the vow," said Matt.

Guthrie, who came and went as he pleased, seemed to think his daughter no more important than anyone else's kids, Matt said. Guthrie played with Gwen, but left the hard task of child rearing to Mary.

Arranging a radio program on KPDN in Pampa or playing a dance with Jeff and Allene, Guthrie was reliable, Mary acknowledged. But as a husband and father, Guthrie was responsible "until he lost interest and started something else."

Woody in khaki shirts two sizes too big for his slight frame, his shirttail hanging out, rolled home barefooted late at night, according to a neighbor on West Craven. At two in the morning "wushy-headed" Guthrie would careen toward his house across the street, baying at the moon, "So long, it's been good to know you." Mrs. Violet Pipes disapproved.

Mrs. Pipes was not alone in her criticism. Hattie Hamlin, the daughter of Guthrie's sometime musical companion George Hamlin, grumbled, "At first he was just a little boy and then in a couple of years he was a growed up man walking the streets with his guitar on his back and shirt-tail hanging out in old dirty clothes. His hair was long and shaggy," Hamlin complained of her father's "ornery" friend. "He was nothing but trash, the lowest kind of cheap trash."

Mary was more accepting, though she conceded, "Woody wasn't ever easy to live with. He always more or less did what he wanted to do, I think, all his life."

As long as they were married, Mary did not work but stayed at home. She kept house, no small chore when the dust blew under the tarpaper roof and around out-of-plumb doors. She visited her mother in the front house or cousins who lived up the street, and played with her daughter.

Gwendolyn was the first grandchild on either side of the family, Mary said, "and that child had devotion you wouldn't believe, on both sides." Mary herself was just eighteen, and so young in appearance that when she took Gwen to a school where Guthrie was singing, a girl asked if the baby were a doll. Mary could only shake her head in disbelief. "I was very young."

As neighbor Violet Pipes viewed the Guthries from across the street, they seemed a loving couple, but ill matched. "Mary was desperately in love with Woody. He loved her as much as anyone—besides himself and the road."

Guthrie worked when he could, but hard times had settled on the Guthries and their neighbors. The oil fields were pumping less while prices for High Plains wheat remained low. Worse still, the Panhandle was now locked in drought, drought that stunted crops across the High Plains and withered life itself.

The vast grasslands of the American Midwest, casually abused for generations, lay vulnerable to the eternal of wet and dry years. Where once wandering buffalo fed on native grasses, corporate cattlemen had allowed their huge herds to range freely. What cattle did not graze off, foraging sheep did. Then wheat farmers with disc plows sliced into the topsoil; steam combines and tractors on ever larger farms put more acreage under cultivation.

For centuries, droughts had come and gone in periodic cycles. In good years, when the rains came, crops grew lush and droughts were forgotten. In bad years like 1932, 1933, and 1934, midwesterners looked to the skies anxiously and offered prayers.

Three years of drought had brought down upon the Panhandle two- and three-hour windstorms, furies that sucked fertile topsoil high into the air to sift down in a fine grit two or three inches deep on road and roof. If the winds were from the Southwest deserts, the dust was tan or gray; if they blew off the rich farmlands of Kansas to the north, the dust clouds were black. And all the while, the biggest storms flattened hundred-mile fronts.

The people of the newly named dust bowl could only endure the "Oklahoma rain" with wry jokes. After all, "there was nothing between Pampa and the North Pole except a fence post."

Day after day they looked to the skies. Day after day they would be disappointed. Six decades, a lifetime later, they still remembered the dry years in those sandblasted lands. "A cloud would come up and everybody would hope this would be it, we'd get some rain, and then the clouds'd go over," Okemah resident Bertha Bryan Edmoundson recalled.

As bad as it was in Okemah, "we didn't live in the Panhandle where they had the dust bowl worst," she added. "The dust clouds would come blowin' through, and you could see them rollin' down from the north where it was worst."

The red-tinted dust storms rose in the western portion of Kansas and adjoining southeastern Colorado, in northeastern New Mexico, the Texas Panhandle, and the Oklahoma Panhandle. They blew south, and eastward as far as six hundred miles, leaving a thin coat of grit on furniture and automobiles, before dying out at sunset. Inevitably, the next day would dawn clear—and dry, always dry.*

In Pampa, Guthrie later wrote, the dust storms turned day to night "so dark you can't see a dime in your pocket, a shirt on your back, a meal on your table, or a dadgum thing. Only thing that is higher than that dust is your debts. Dust settles, but debts don't."

However bad the storms of years past, none compared to "Black Easter" of 1935. Even to those who recalled "Big Red" of 1923, this was different, awesome, so great as to make grown men quail. "We were too scared to pray and too scared to run," Reverend E. C. McKenzie of Pampa's First Church of Christ said. "We were more interested in breathing."

The dust storm heaved up without warning late in the afternoon of Palm Sunday. From Amarillo on the southwest across a seventy-mile front to tiny Miami, Texas, on the northeast, it suddenly loomed, towering three, four, five thousand feet into the sky, rolling steadily onward. The sky turned black, black as night, so black, Pampans remembered, "you couldn't see your hand in front of your face." Nothing was more frightening than that first half hour of darkness.

The cloud rolled in from the north, tumbling black earth swept up from the rich Kansas topsoil and the lighter red dust of the Texas Panhandle, "like the Red Sea closing in on the Israel children," Woody Guthrie wrote later.

He and Mary stuffed wet newspapers around doors and windows, then hunkered down in their shotgun shack on South Russell. They struggled to catch a good breath as the fine dust filtered through cracks until the naked electric light hanging on a cord from the ceiling glowed no brighter than a lighted cigarette.

---

* Four factors joined to link the dust storms and dust bowl with Oklahoma in the popular mind, historian Guy Logsdon noted, though that state escaped comparatively unscathed. The first factor was the Associated Press's initial story coining the phrase "dust bowl"; it was filed from Guymon in the westernmost portion of the narrow Panhandle. Second, Farm Security Administration photographer Arthur Rothstein prowled Cimarron County in the Panhandle, capturing the oft-reprinted image of the overalled farmer and his two children beating their way through a dust storm. Third, novelist John Steinbeck erroneously attributed to drought and dust storm the migration of his fictional Joads and the hundreds of thousands of other Oklahomans who fled the eastern part of the state looking for work. (In the main, these "Okies" were victims of poor farming practices and low farm prices. Sharecroppers, Logsdon pointed out, might wear out the land of three or four farms in their lifetimes.) Finally, the people who settled Oklahoma were boomers. By habit, they moved from farm to town to oilfield, internal migrants seeking work. When the depression fell on Oklahoma, these migratory folk were quick to pull up stakes and move on to greener pastures.

As the storm struck, people scrambled for shelter wherever they could. On South Cuyler, barber Jess Turner's wife saw the great cloud tinged with red and concluded, "Lord amercy, the whole country's on fire."

Across the street, Shorty Harris turned on his soda fountain so the half-dozen people who took refuge in his drugstore could wash out their mouths and noses. The wind literally tumbled a nine-year-old girl along the sidewalk until Harris snatched her to safety. The dust so thick they couldn't catch their breath, "everybody was a little scared, wondering how long it would last," and wondering too what was to come.

Later everyone in Pampa had stories to tell. High school teacher B. G. Gordon rode out the storm, stranded in his brand new Chevrolet, for thirty minutes unable to see his wife sitting on the front seat beside him.

John Gikas, hunting rabbits north of town, raced the black cloud to Pampa at sixty miles per hour. Overtaken by the storm, his car shorted out by static electricity, and Gikas groped his way the last block to home. He joined his family members, Pentecostal, religious, and fervent, in prayer. "They thought it was the end of the world, they surely did. 'Let's all gather around the bed, and pray to God for forgiveness of our sins.' We just knew that was the end of the world."

Violet Pipes, who would never be able to get the grit out from what had been her new white birthday dress, recalled an old woman "coming down the street when the duster hit. She tottered into the first open door in the half light, and found herself in the Empire Cafe and Bar." (The waitresses there "were pretty raunchy," as restaurant owner John Gikas put it.) "When she realized where she was, she fell to her knees and prayed, 'Don't let me die in here. I'm a devout old lady.' She thought the duster was the end of time."

The worst of the storm passed in about a half hour. The winds died finally about ten that night, but the dust lingered in the air for days after. On the windward side of barns, sand dunes reached to the eaves. Fences lay buried under dust as fine as face powder. The young wheat stalks in the fields stood blackened, crisped by arcing static electricity.

"It was a year of disaster for the farmer—drought, dust, then a plague of grasshoppers," Gikas said.

Pampans sardonically amended the town motto, "Where the wheat grows and the oil flows," to add "and the wind blows." Guthrie would amend it even further: "This Panhandle country is said to be the place where the oil flows, the wheat grows, the wind blows and the people owes."

Between dust storm and parched earth, Woody and Mary Guthrie scraped by. He worked sporadically; he spent his days painting and his nights playing music.

When Amarillo's legendary fiddler Eck Robertson turned up in Pampa for a fiddling contest, Guthrie became his guide to some of the town's "damper spots." The two men played together, the cowboy who had recorded his "trickery fiddle" in 1922 for RCA and the youngster who would just "plink a little ole lostoff chord or bluffynote on my guitar and my mandybox."

Meanwhile, "I learnt every single humanly trick he'd pull here on his talking fiddle as well as my own Uncle Jaffry's [*sic*]." Each fiddler tried to quiz him about the other's bowing or ornaments, to gain some tiny advantage in the contest to come. Guthrie kept his "sipper zipped," crowing, "I'm an old trickystealer out of your first ranks myself. All I have to do is to just listen to your trickest dern tune just one little short circling time and I steal her . . . and I'm gone." He was obviously pleased with himself; it was one of the few times that Guthrie, a far more accomplished musician than he let on, actually boasted about his abilities.

By 1935, he was talented enough to be invited by the Junior Chamber of Commerce to join a local string band to celebrate the Texas Centennial. Guthrie was to play the string bass, garbed in an outlandish cowboy costume no cowboy ever wore, fitted with a false mustache, and playing the clown.

The humor may have been more important than the musicianship, one critical listener decided. "He was a better entertainer" with his comic routines than with his music, said James King, who worked around Amarillo's radio station in these years. Musician or comic, it suited Guthrie well, sister Mary Jo recalled. "Most of the time he was jovial, bouncy. He loved to always be making music on something: forks, forks on glasses on the table or a set of dishes. He was just full of energy. He was just Woody."

At age twenty-three in 1935, he was starting to mature. On stage, Guthrie was a deadpan clown, like Charlie Chaplin, his humor suggesting something deeper, yet never quite stated. "It always seemed like he was covering up a worry," said Pampa musician George Hamlin. "We all had it then, though," he added.

Somewhere about this time, Guthrie was to forsake the cornpone jokes of the hayseed clown in favor of a new role, the country philosopher. As an entertainer, Matt Jennings said, "he modeled himself almost completely after Will Rogers. He wanted to be a character like Will Rogers."*

The droll humor and cracker-barrel philosophy nourished Guthrie. "He loved to make people laugh," Jennings added. "He said, 'If you keep them laughing, they won't throw anything at ya.'"

With the Junior Chamber's string band, Guthrie had an additional responsibility: he was to write songs, including one on the history of the state, with a stanza for each of the seven flags that had flown over Texas.

At least one of the songs written about this time was inspired by the great dust storm of April 1935. Minnie Dittmeyer watched as Guthrie sat scribbling on lined notebook paper a topical song he called "The Texas Dust Storms."

> On the fourteenth day of April,
> Of nineteen thirty-five,
> There struck the worst of dust storms
> That ever filled the sky.
> You could see that dust storm coming,
> It looked so awful black,
> And through our little city,
> It left a dreadful track.

When he finished the ballad, Guthrie wrote across the top of the page: "Here, Minnie. Keep this. Might mean something someday." He handed her the manuscript.

Woody's facility as a graphic artist blossomed as well. While he still tossed off cartoons to amuse his friends, he began to think more seriously about the artistic gift he seemed to possess. Unschooled and self-taught, he *could* draw freehand and letter signs for local businessmen, or paint sprightly store windows for merchants for fifty cents or a dollar, windows he invariably signed "Woody."

By 1935 he was copying portraits in oils; Abraham Lincoln and Jesus Christ were repeated subjects. His sister-in-law Ann remembered too copies of "Whistler's Mother" and "A Boy and His Dog" ("Blue Boy") in the house on South Russell.

One of the pictures was a large oil painting, copied from a picture bible,

---

* Rogers and fellow aviator Wiley Post were killed in a plane crash near Point Barrow, Alaska, on April 15, 1935, the day after Black Easter. The coincidental events seem to have had a sobering impact on Guthrie.

of a woman carrying a jug of water to a man plowing a field with a team of oxen. He painted a large portrait of Mary, and another of daughter Gwendolyn. All these he framed himself. He drew heads of Christ, sometimes in oils, sometimes in inked sketches he gave away as quickly as he dashed them off. He painted scenics and he continued to draw cartoons. "Woody was a wonderful artist," insisted Mary Geneva Boydstun, Allene's sister and Woody's cousin.

Neither art nor music could provide a living for Mary and their daughter in depression-era Pampa. Woody needed something more, something even the poorest townspeople were willing to pay for.

Guthrie's inspiration was to come from an unlikely source, his stepmother Betty Jean, and the rationale from a series of pamphlets his Uncle Jeff had ordered through the mail.

Like Betty Jean, Jeff Guthrie believed in faith healing, in the laying-on of hands. He had a special gift for what he thought of as "magnetic healing," but had never sought to capitalize on it.

"You have to learn how to handle your hands," he said to explain why he responded to a magazine ad for the first of a series of pamphlets entitled "The Secret of the Ages." Collectively, the seven pamphlets offered assurance that the "secret of all power, all success, all riches, is in first thinking powerful thoughts, successful thoughts, thoughts of wealth, of supply."

Positive thinking was the key. "Prayer is a realization of the god-power within you—of your right of domination over your own body, your environment, your business, your health, your prosperity."

Power flowed from the individual, and "therefore is under our own control," author Robert Collier stressed. His message came as reassurance to a people feeling powerless in the face of all-powerful economic engines and uncontrollable environmental forces.

Those who followed his creed, to let "the man inside you" take command, summoned great resources, Collier insisted. "If we will work in harmony with it, we can draw upon the Universal Mind for all power, all intelligence."

Positive thinking could even cure illness, Collier insisted. "Time and again patients given over by their doctors as doomed have made miraculous recoveries through the faith of some loved one."

The simplicity of "The Secret" appealed to Jeff, and later to Woody: To heal, they had only to instruct the ailing part of the body to rid itself of illness.

"To treat one who has already succumbed to the belief of sickness . . . put your hand upon the part affected," Collier advised. "Try to visualize that organ as it should be. See it functioning perfectly. BELIEVE that it IS working normally again!"

Collier's philosophy was a cross between positive thinking and Christian capitalism. He advised that the ambitious succeeded, while those who lacked singleness of purpose fell by the wayside. "Let me quote again the words of the Master, because there's nothing more important in this whole book. 'Therefore I say unto you, what things soever ye desire, when ye pray, *believe that ye receive them* and ye shall have them.' "

To Jeff Guthrie and his nephew Woody, Collier's thesis was comfortably familiar, the stuff of half a hundred Sunday sermons imploring the congregants to moral uplift, to self-improvement, to holiness. To Woody, son of Charley the eternal optimist, Collier's assertion "never [to] let discouragement hold you back" was nothing more or less than he had learned from his father.

The seven pamphlets galvanized Betty Jean. Already established as a fortune-teller, she took her nurse's uniform from the closet and took up faith healing as well. Her theme was simple: "God Almighty put you here not to be sick, [but] to be healthy, and to believe in God Almighty."

It was based on positive thinking, Jeff stressed. "To do anything, you make up you mind to do it."*

Betty Jean the healer promised much. She attempted to restore Old Blind Tommy's sight, and offered to remove fourteen-year-old Geneva Boydstun's infected tonsils. Betty Jean would rub her hands together, creating the healing heat, then lay them on the afflicted part.

"She had quite a few patients," Fritz Buzbee recalled. Taken in by the Guthries as a six-year-old when his own family fell apart, Fritz played outside with Mary Jo when townsfolk sought out Betty Jean's "magnetic massages."

Betty Jean had no set fee, but charged according to the patient's illness or ability to pay. Most scraped up a quarter or fifty cents; a few of the wealthy oilmen paid her in ten- and twenty-dollar bills. "Most of them seemed to be people who had gone to medical doctors, an' more or less gave up, [and] the elderly," Buzbee said.

As Buzbee remembered Betty Jean, "In her own mind she thought she

---

* Jeff did not advertise his healing powers and asked for no money when neighbors sought his help. He claimed successes, among them a waitress whose legs hurt so much she could not walk, and a woman whom a doctor's shots did not aid. His technique was to put his hands in water, rub them, then pass them over his patient, and brush his hands together as if to dust them off.

really had something unusual there. She had faith in herself." She claimed
to have learned of her unusual skills by accident, when her mother, who
suffered from migraines, said the pain eased when her daughter touched
her forehead.

Those whom she treated, Buzbee said, "acted like they were pretty well
satisfied." They returned to the trailer court often enough for the Guthrie
family to afford a new home, north of the Panhandle tracks at 417 North
Hill Street.

Betty Jean's success inspired Woody. He visited the house on North Hill
Street often, talking with his father's new wife well into the early hours of
the morning.

Even though Betty Jean did a lot of her healing for free, Guthrie wrote
later, "I still figured that she was making a lot better living than me at the
whiskey store." Nerving himself, after six months of talking about it, he
painted a large sign proclaiming: "Faith Healing, Mind Reading, No
Charge."

Woody was evasive about his plunge into "the superstition business"
and faith healing. He implied he became involved only by accident. "Hundreds of people got my name mixed up with papa's new wife, and come to
my house by mistake. Finally I hung out a sign telling them to come on in
and talk it over. I decided that faith was the main thing."

In fact, his involvement in the superstition business was more deliberate, and Woody less passive than he later portrayed. In the first issue of
"News Expose," a mimeographed "newspaper" he wrote and edited for
friends at the end of 1935, Guthrie announced "ALONZO M. ZILCH BECOMES
PSYCHOLOGICAL READER." Zilch, Guthrie's alter ego, had "turned to a strange
field of endeavor, that of psychology, philosophy, and things of the mental
realm." The white house on South Russell Street was now "The Guthrie
Institute for Psychical [*sic*] Research."

Guthrie urged his readers to "take your troubles to Zilch, he is an expert
worrier. The eyes of lots of people are on this man for good or bad."

In a town boasting half a dozen resident fortune-tellers as well as itinerant healers of all stripes, Guthrie confidently went into business. He repainted
the front door frame with a special paint to which he had added chips of mica;
at night the door frame glittered in the headlights of passing cars. He advertised in the *Pampa Daily News*, offering private lessons in psychology, telepathy, "strange powers of the mind," and dreams. Two weeks later, his private
lessons became "PSYCHIC READINGS, phenomena of clairvoyance, telepathy." He
was available day or night, his ad promised, with "results guaranteed."

In January 1936, he ran a daily notice in the paper's "miscellaneous want ads" offering free psychic readings. He claimed to have "helped many in love, work, business, troubles. Results guaranteed. Better than medicine for worries of the mind." Those who sought help were to pay what they could.

The frightened and the curious found their way to the Guthrie home on South Russell, past the six-foot-tall sign, through the Jenningses' yard to the little house behind, and up the steps into the front room where a fidgeting Guthrie waited. A velvet curtain separated a newly made "parlor" from the kitchen area.

They paid what they could afford. Nickels, dimes, one time an astounding five dollars, and if they had nothing, Guthrie's advice was free. Once he took a jar of pickled beets, another time an old red rooster; neither lasted long in the Guthrie household.

"A lot of people put a lot of faith in him," Mary's friend Minnie Dittmeyer recalled. When Minnie dropped by after her shift at the telephone company, Mary would caution her to silence with a finger to the lips; Woody was behind the curtain, telling someone's fortune.

Guthrie not only told fortunes; he counseled his visitors as well. Minnie remembered one forlorn woman, out of work and uncourted, who followed Guthrie's advice to move to California. There, he predicted, she would find both work and a husband, but would never have any children.

"That's how it turned out," Minnie added. "She told me afterwards."

The anxious people who made their way to 408 South Russell offered young Guthrie a sobering education. "Most everybody that come had just recently lost everything they had in the world. The others were fixing to lose it. This caused a lot of fights and feuds to break out between husband and wife, and caused sweethearts to haul off and quit. . . . The crops was all dried up and the banks was taking the place. . . . It looked like there wasn't no hope down here on earth."

Emboldened by *The Secret of the Ages*, Guthrie ventured into faith healing as well. As Matt Jennings explained it, "Woody felt there was some underlying physical force that was involved in the divine healing."

While Jennings's explanation says little—and Guthrie himself offered less—still some Pampans entrusted themselves to him. "People thought he helped them," his uncle Robert Boydstun suggested.

Minnie Dittmeyer recalled a palsied woman living in a rooming house who had once worked for the Federal Bureau of Investigation. After she visited Guthrie, her tremors lessened. As Dittmeyer told the story, the woman "said that if it hadn't been for Woody she would have laid down and died."

On a visit to Pampa, boyhood friend Frank Streetman saw Guthrie treat one elderly man suffering from arthritis. Woody, whose hair had grown to shoulder length, claimed he was helping the man, and several others as well.

Guthrie spent some seven months in Pampa as a fortune-teller and sometime faith healer. In that time, he scraped out a precarious living for a man with a wife and a year-old daughter; too many of his visitors could pay him only in gratitude.

Neither family nor faith healing were enough to hold Guthrie in Pampa though. By the summer of 1936, he was once again looking toward the highway, wondering what opportunity lay out there, somewhere just down the road.

CHAPTER SIX

On the Jericho Road

G UTHRIE WAS RESTLESS, always restless, his wife Mary insisted. Woody "was not one to do the same thing over and over. He was not an eight-to-five man, no way in the world." According to her husband, "that's a waste of life. He's got to do a little something different, got to learn a little something different every day."

Pampa offered nothing different and little opportunity to Guthrie, unless he wanted to go back to selling liquor for Shorty Harris. He cringed at the prospect. He wasn't like Matt Jennings, running the butcher shop at C and C Market, or his brother Roy, managing the Streetman's Food Mart in Konawa, Oklahoma, forty miles southwest of Okemah.

He was not like them. When Roy married in the spring of 1936, Woody introduced himself in a letter to his new sister-in-law, Ann, with a mock warning of stable Roy's faults. "From what I know of Roy—he can't save a cent. Just as quick as he gets ten saved up, why he lends it to me and is broke again." Then in a burst of unusual insight, Guthrie added, "Your new husband isn't impulsive and high strung like his brother me. He takes everything orderly, decently, and in polished order. He is making his life, and I am letting my life make me."

In the summer of 1936, Guthrie left Mary and the baby he called "Teeny" with the Jennings family to visit the big city of Houston. As Guthrie later told of the journey, he began wandering the Texas highways, first to Houston with the idea of supporting his family by faith healing. "But the more of it I saw, the more I decided it was worse than a waste of time."

From Houston, he made his way north to Kilgore, Texas, and the welcoming family of former Okemah barber Tom Moore. Flat broke when he arrived, Guthrie found a job in a grocery and feed store. He worked two weeks, trudging some three miles from the Moore home to the store and back each day. Walking home with his first pay stuffed in a pocket, he met an old man and struck up a conversation with him. Guthrie learned that the man was despondent, out of work and his wife very ill.

That evening, Guthrie confessed he was broke once more. "Mr. Tom, I got paid today but I don't have any money." He had handed over his pay envelope to the man he had met on the road.

Why the devil did you give it all to him? Tom Moore asked.

The Moores and he were working and eating, and doing all right, Guthrie replied. "I figured that old fellow needed it worse than I did."

With the Moores, he was once again the Woody of seven years before in Okemah. He drew constantly—on books, on newspapers, on scraps of writing paper, even on tablecloths. He had a quick temper, Tom's daughter Gladys recalled, "and a quick tongue if things did not go well for him." But he was never mean. Let Guthrie alone, to draw or to write, and he was content, "at least on the surface," she commented.

In the evenings, Guthrie often disappeared to stomp the railroad tracks, to swap songs with the men huddled in hobo jungles or listen to stories about a fearsome railroad detective known as East Texas Red. The next morning Guthrie would turn up on the Moore's back porch, grinning or larking about as Nora Moore good-naturedly cracked two more eggs and sliced another piece of bread.

He was to stay about two months with the Moores, Gladys recalled, "just until he got too restless and moved on again." Kilgore offered no more than Pampa had.

From Kilgore Guthrie made his way north to Okemah to visit his boyhood friend Colonel Martin and the Martin family. He talked his way into a string band he encountered in a bar, then traveled from roadhouse to tavern to nightclub, singing for tips across Oklahoma.

The Woody Guthrie of this hard summer of 1936 itched with an "odd and curious feeling about fancery houses, law offices, courthouses, jails." He discovered in himself

a great sympathy for folks along our roads that are all down and out. I had a crazy notion in me that I wanted to stay down and out for a good long spell, so's I could get to live with every different kind of a person I could, to learn about all kinds of jobs they do, and to live with them for a long enough time to find out it was time to move on.

Some sense of responsibility to Mary and their daughter pulled him back to Pampa, "to my wife and baby. [I] tried to make a go of it there, but the oil field was dying down, people pouring out down the highway, and I poured with them."

With his metal mandolin, an instrument loud enough to drill through the din of the darkest juke joint or gin mill, Guthrie headed west on Highway 66. On the road from Amarillo to Tucumcari, New Mexico, he met a guitar player, a good singer, and the two of them busked in raucous saloons and *tequilarias* south to Hobbs, Eunice, and Jal, New Mexico. To supplement what they scored at night, Guthrie hustled sign-painting jobs by day; he found few takers in the gritty towns of the harsh desert.

He earned less than fifty cents a day for what he acknowledged were several pretty tough months in the fall of 1936. "I slept in jails when my kitty didn't do so good, and in cheap hotels whenever I had money. I made everything and nothing: from one cent to fifty-four dollars one single night."

He hitchhiked on to El Paso with the notion of looking up a wealthy second cousin who owned oil and land, and a bank. Once there, he wrote, "I walked up and got a gander at their big house, setting all by itself on a big square block, and decided that it looked a little too confining from the human race, and turned around and walked off, catching rides to Pampa."

Freezing cold had settled on the high plains by the time the twenty-four-year-old Guthrie found his way back to Pampa. He got back home "so stove up . . . had to go to bed for several days to get thawed out."

Woody spent part of the fall of 1936 and the following winter as a section hand on the Panhandle and Santa Fe. He was lucky to get the job, once disdained by whites as punishing work with low pay, and best left to the Mexicans. But in the hard years of the depression, $1.50 a day was counted good wages, and the *gringos* replaced *los Tejanos* on track gangs. Because Guthrie was slight, and hundred-pound-to-the-foot rail heavy, Minnie Dittmeyer assumed he might have worked as a water boy or time keeper on the track gang. Certainly the railroads wanted bigger, beefier men to line rails or drive spikes.

Steady work made Pampa all the more confining and less attractive to Guthrie. Life with Mary, as much as he admired her, was stifling. Beyond frolicking with his daughter, he had little to do with Gwen. Guthrie's father Charley meanwhile was embroiled in arguments with his second wife, arguments that made visits to their house on North Hill Street awkward and unpleasant.

Not long before, Guthrie had hung about his father's house, building frames for his paintings in the garage, or just talking with Betty Jean late into the night about magnetic healing and fortune telling. No longer.

The more Betty Jean contributed financially to their income, the more demanding she became. Once an accommodating stepmother, she now insisted that the children—George, Mary Jo, and the boy born Lee Roy Buzbee, now dubbed Fritz Guthrie—call her "mother." When they refused, she whipped them.

"My stepmother would slip around and do mean and cruel things, and she'd put the fear of God into you if you told Papa," Mary Jo said. "She had been whipping me with the bristle side of a brush, and making me bleed on the legs. She would make me go wash my face so Papa couldn't tell I'd been cryin'."

Mary Jo's nominally adopted brother Fritz came in for more than his share of abuse. "I was spanked more often than I needed it," he said.

Alternatively Betty Jean tried to woo her stepchildren. First she favored George with treats and Mary Jo with dresses. Then she tried to divide them, lavishing gifts on him while denying her.

Through it all, Charley turned a blind eye, perhaps to keep his family together, perhaps because his wife had become the major breadwinner.

"Betty Jean had him buffaloed," George said later. "He didn't want to see the home broken up, but it finally got to the extent where he got to believing us, and we hated her."

She attempted to divide the family's loyalties, Woody wrote, "to make us kids worship her . . . partly by pointing out that papa wasn't working or making money, partly by giving us crazy sums of money to spend anyway we wanted to, partly by acting like she'd discovered some kind of gift or power inside her head that we hadn't found." Charley Guthrie, sharpening knives and scissors in his newly opened Guthrie Hone Shop, yielded to her; how else would the children eat?

"He made us respect our stepmother," Mary Jo Guthrie grumbled. "He loved peace."

All the while Betty Jean disparaged their relatives, George said. Uncle Robert Boydstun was a failed dirt farmer. Brother Woody was worse. Woody, Roy, their father, even the kindly Aunt Maude and Uncle Robert were bad influences. She discouraged the children from visiting the Boydstun farm, and once even forbade George a trip across town to see Woody.

Young Fritz was confused. As he remembered his older "brother," Woody was light-hearted. "I never seen him when he wasn't smiling. Just a big kid.

"He would come over and say, 'Let's go out and play some marbles.' And I'd think, 'This is a real guy here.'

"And he'd go out and make up different rules and regulations, and he was quite an entertainer that way too."

Other times Guthrie would throw a football to the youngster "for hours on end. His time was mine when he was over there."

Fritz occasionally visited Woody's house on Russell Street, a house "full of music-making things": drums, guitar, mandolin, banjo. There was even a saxophone, "but I don't think he got much out of it."

Often enough Woody would be at the kitchen table writing, oblivious of little Gwen's clamor or Mary's bustle. Then abruptly he would pick up an instrument, or begin to tap out a rhythm with a spoon against a glass. "Out of nothing he'd start making up a song that don't sound like it's made-up."

Buzbee recalled the first stanza of one of the thirty or forty songs Guthrie included in "a portfolio" he eventually gave to Fritz:

> *I'm an iceman in the city,*
> *And I climb the golden stairs,*
> *And my story I will now relate to you.*
> *I will tell you how I sell*
> *Ice to Jane and all the belles*
> *To Agnes, and to Sally, and to Lou.*

Perhaps for the first time in his life, Charley Guthrie was cowed. He made little money selling barber's hones or sharpening knives; Betty Jean meanwhile supported their family, serving her patients one way or another in the bedroom set aside for her.

"There wasn't very much space left in her mindreading room for Betty Jean and a customer, cash or trade," Woody wrote later. "I always did hear the chairs scoot back, the bed and bedslats rattle, the dresser wiggle, the whole house vibrate a few good shivers, before Betty and her customer could walk out."

Betty Jean insisted that they move to Borger, twenty-five miles to the west. Business was slowing down in Pampa, and the local doctors had begun to complain to the local prosecutor that she was practicing medicine without a license. It was then that Charley finally called an end to their marriage.

"Papa was shirking his responsibilities a little bit" when he left the children with Betty Jean in Borger, daughter Mary Jo conceded grudgingly. "Papa's first obligation was to his children and he shirked that duty to George and me."

Woody was to step in, "fighting Betty Jean like cats," George said. Woody wrote to older brother Roy in Konawa to suggest he hire George at the grocery store. George was strong and capable of carrying hundred-pound sacks of potatoes, Guthrie pointed out. Hiring George was like hiring a truck.

Family was family. Roy, the steady one, the son with both feet firmly on the ground, sent train fare. George packed his cardboard suitcase, took down his good straw hat, and said goodbye to a forlorn Mary Jo.

Intimidated by his ever more domineering second wife, Charley finally rallied. He asked Roy and his new wife Anna to take in Mary Jo as well. He had left her with Betty Jean only because he could not support her, Charley explained. The problem was that Betty Jean might prevent Mary Jo from leaving; she could be vindictive, Charley warned. Roy borrowed the Street-man family touring car, drove from Konawa to Borger with his Uncle Claude for company, intercepted an unsuspecting Mary Jo on her way home from school, and drove off.*

With Roy, George, and Mary Jo in Konawa, and Charley in Okemah talking about joining his brother Claude in Tulsa, the once tightly knit Guthrie family was now scattered across two states. Even the Boydstuns had moved to Borger. Woody was left alone in Pampa—ever more rootless and ever more discontented.†

The sense of abandonment, of emptiness pained Guthrie, more than he ever acknowledged. The disintegration of his family—the death of a beloved sister, the injury to his father, and the loss of an idealized mother—had "left its scars," Mary Guthrie came to understand.

Welcoming as they were, the Jenningses could not fill the void. Guthrie seemed indifferent to simple pleasures. He ate whatever was set in front of him, as fast as possible, as if eating were a chore. "At Thanksgiving, Mom would have that table all filled up, and Woody was likely to fill his plate with

---

* Ever after, Mary Jo Guthrie Edgmon termed this her "kidnapping." She was delighted to be out from under Betty Jean's thumb. "My stepmother was a witch. She practiced witchcraft and made us victims of it," she said in a 1971 interview with E. Victor and Judy Wolfenstein. Her erstwhile adopted brother, Roy "Fritz" Buzbee, confirmed that Betty Jean believed in voodoo, cast spells, and wore a conjure bag tucked in her brassiere.

† Charley Guthrie moved first to Okemah, then to Tulsa to work with his brother Gid in Gid's machine shop. Eager to be his own boss, he opened a real estate business in Wewoka, Oklahoma. Shortly before the beginning of World War II, he received a letter forwarded there from Betty Jean. She was on the tramp in eastern Arkansas and in need of money. Charley wired her twenty dollars and never heard from her again. See the June 1968 interview of Claude Guthrie in Tulsa by Richard Reuss and Guy Logsdon, a transcript of which is in the Reuss papers, Box 8, Folder 2.

the first dish passed to him. He cleaned that up, and just excused hisself, and just lay down in a corner."

For a while he became interested in the occult fad of the Ouija board. Jeff, Allene, and the Jennings family would crowd around the dining table, first one, then the other asking, "If there is a spirit in the house, please give a sign by beating on the wall." Had not Houdini, the great escape artist Jeff so admired, promised to send a signal from the Beyond?

No sign came, "but they would sit there two or three hours a night, the whole crowd," visiting Fritz Buzbee said. "Woody was right there. Mary was pretty well enthused with that Ouija board."

Woody visited his brothers and sister in Konawa early in 1937, paint brushes stuck in a hip pocket, a guitar hung over his shoulder. He turned up flat broke, brother George recalled, but then Woody "was always without money—and no clothes, other than what he was wearing—and, of course, *hungry.*" Roy put him to work, painting signs and writing fliers for the grocery store.

Broke or not, Woody remained the "the sparkplug of the entertainment. . . . If they were playing music, he'd get right in the middle of it." If there was no music, Guthrie provided it.

When Ann's family gathered for ice cream, her new brother-in-law "grabbed a broom and a mop and he began to dance and cut up, and to sing a few songs, and make up little songs. And he was just really clowning. And George was doing the same thing, following right in his footsteps. And my folks were flabbergasted," Ann said.

Woody stayed one or two nights, then gathered his paint brushes and guitar, and set off for the next town. "He was just the restless kind who couldn't stay put," brother George Guthrie concluded. "He might get up from the dinner table and not come back for three or four days."

For Woody, the traveling was important; he needed to see new places and meet new people. "He didn't want to stay put. He enjoyed travelin', hoboing it, riding on the railroad and hitchhiking. Anyway to get there." Anyway but bus. "He wouldn't buy a bus ticket," George insisted.

Woody made serious, if shortlived efforts to stay with Mary and Gwen, but he was simply inept around the house. He once offered to help Mary by wiping the dishes, but used one of Teeny's often-washed diapers for the task. Mary merely sighed in exasperation and rewashed the dishes.

For a while he sought solace or refuge in the exoticism of Omar Khayyám and the pieties of Kahlil Gibran. When his sister-in-law Ann gave birth, Woody, signing himself "The Soul Doctor," sent "A Few Kind Words" of solicitous, if gratuitous advice to the newborn Mary Ann: "We adults in our wise foolishness have reached the stage where we must become again as little children before we can know paradise." Life, he advised, "is a proposition of giving. Give and Live. Crave and die."

The Soul Doctor advised her to "see the non-reality of affliction and realize the allness of God. For God is Truth, Love."

She was to "obey truth at all times," he cautioned. Finally he wished that she "pass beyond the seventh veil and solve the riddle of human life and destiny." It was the life-affirming philosophy of a diluted Gibran.

But Gibran seemingly was not enough to Guthrie himself. Drawn by religious thought if not to organized religion, a youthful Guthrie had once toyed with the idea of converting to Catholicism and even taking orders. That notion had lasted only until his fiddling uncle, Jeff Guthrie, suggested Woody join him and Allene on a musical tour of neighboring towns.

But Guthrie was still searching five years later. As a boy in Okemah, he had occasionally attended the First Methodist Sunday school. In Pampa, he had gone along to tent revivals when those touring attractions came to town, but no one in his immediate family regularly attended church until eight-year-old Mary Jo was baptized at one of those fervid tent meetings.

Religion, at least Sunday go-to-meeting religion, did not appeal to Woody. As Mary Jo put it, her brother "was not affiliated with anything."

Not until he encountered the charismatic figure of the Reverend E. C. McKenzie, minister to the Francis Avenue Church of Christ. "Brother Mac" was a powerful preacher, 235 pounds of fundamentalist fire and brimstone, "a great guy, no doubt about it," according to Matt Jennings.

When Brother Mac got warmed up, he would slam his palm on the Bible and thunder, "Now listen, dear friends, you can argue with old Mac, because he's just a plain country boy, but *this* is the word of the Lord that you're gettin' in dispute with if you don't believe ev'ry word I tell you."

Intrigued by McKenzie, Guthrie became interested in the Church of Christ. Even though the church frowned on musical instruments, Jeff, Allene, and band leader George Hamlin were all members of the Francis Avenue congregation. When Guthrie asked him about the contradiction, Hamlin shrugged. "We're all offbeats." Even Mac McKenzie enjoyed a good tune; he and his wife often dropped by for the Sunday-evening music at Jeff and Allene's. No one sang the hymn "On that Jericho Road" any better than the preacher.

Guthrie was baptized at the Francis Avenue church by the Reverend McKenzie. Guthrie may have been influenced by the reverend, or he may simply have taken the path of least resistance. As his cousin, Geneva Boyd-stun, noted, "Woody felt like he ought to be saved, so he joined the church."

He would not stay long in the church or in Pampa. His membership was yet an another attempt "to find himself." Just as he had looked for safe harbor and solid anchor in his practice of faith healing and fortune-telling, in reading Rosicrucian tracts and Oriental philosophy, becoming a member of the Baptist church was a means of soul searching for Guthrie.

He was adrift. Even in the election year of 1936, with Franklin Roosevelt running for a second term—Pampa, all of Texas was solidly Democratic—politics was of little interest to Guthrie. If there was anything fixed at all in his mind, it was a growing awareness of social inequities, of disparities of wealth, of privileges for the rich and their toadies. As early as April 1935, while performing on Pampa's "little two-by-four bootleg radio station," Guthrie typed out on lined notebook paper the first of a stream of songbooks. Two of the fourteen songs in "Alonzo Zilch's Own Collection of Original Songs and Ballads" contained hints of a newly discovered social consciousness:

> *If I was President Roosevelt,*
> *I'd make the groceries free—*
> *I'd give away new Stetson hats,*
> *And let the whiskey be.*
> *I'd pass out suits of clothing*
> *At least three times a week—*
> *And shoot the first big oil man*
> *That killed the fishing creek.*

In a parody to a then-popular song, "Old Faithful," Guthrie lamented, "When the harvest days are over,/We'll turn the property over/To the bank."*

The following year, Matt Jennings prodded Guthrie to a keener sense of social justice. Each week, Jennings brought home from church the *Sunday Visitor*, the archdiocese newspaper then running a series on the evils of communism by Monseignor Fulton J. Sheen. Each week Jennings fumed, particularly incensed by editorials in praise of Spain's fascist rebellion led by General Francisco Franco.

---

* Guthrie noted in a self-mocking introduction that his songs were better on paper than "being warbled to you by means of my smuthe [*sic*], gentle voice which has got me where I am today—nowhere!"

Jennings conceded he was "a little teed off on things. . . . When you're working behind a meat counter selling hamburger for five and a half cents a pound and people can't buy enough to feed their kids—" Millions were going hungry; maybe the communists had some way to change that.

At first Guthrie was uninterested. Woody was involved with "that counseling service of his" and with his healing practice. But Jennings persevered until "it got him on the trail of looking into true socialism."

Guthrie read what little was available in Pampa's public library, discussing it with Jennings, the two of them posing questions about the way things were, of poor farmers and rich banks, of some children going hungry on flour gravy while others enjoyed ice-cream sundaes at Shorty Harris's soda fountain. "Woody was always saying, 'There must be a better system.'"

Money, Guthrie told Jennings, was a trap, "something you get rid of, like a varmint." He repeatedly sneered at those he claimed had "sold their soul for a plate of beans."

In the manner of young men, they dreamed grand schemes to remedy the injustices.

"Woody was far more an idealist, I suppose, really far out, back in the thirties. A lot of his ideas were unworkable," Jennings said.

Guthrie was receptive to these new ideas, Pampa librarian Evelyn Todd decided, because he was "always serious, interested in life and the underdog, because he had had a rough time of it. He was always thataway."

Out of deference to his father, Guthrie did not discuss his new interest in politics with Charley. Fifteen years before, Charley Guthrie had challenged the Democratic Party in Oklahoma and had been slapped down for his effrontery; he was now a party regular. Woody would also vote for Roosevelt; what else could he do in Pampa, where, as Matt Jennings put it, "Republicans were just about as powerful as the Vegetarians"?

Still, Woody had his own half-formed ideas, his politics based on emotion rather than cold logic. "He was always for the underdog . . . one hundred percent," said Fritz Buzbee. "Anyone who was low in income, he had his heart out to 'em." Mary Guthrie concurred; her husband, she said, was "sour" about a society that set so many on the road to seek work.

Restlessness and dissatisfaction overcame him once more. In December 1936, Guthrie drifted as far west as Santa Fe, New Mexico, where he visited a native pueblo. The mud-daubed, umber walls with their piñon *vegas* and wooden rain spouts captivated Guthrie. As he stood admiring the ageless two- and three-story structures, "an old lady told me the world is made of adobe, and I added, 'So is man.' "

If the trip west did anything, it was to convince Guthrie he could not stay in Pampa. "I knew I didn't want to sell whiskey any more," he wrote later in his notebooks. "So I walked the floor from the kitchen to the front door a lot and read the Bible."

Guthrie was twenty-five years old, married, with one child and another due in July. He had no prospects in Pampa, no future beyond painting sale signs for the C and C Market. It would hardly pay enough to feed his family and it certainly did not still the yearnings that stirred his gut.

Now and again he spoke wistfully of the opportunities California offered, of his ambition, of a need "to be somebody and great" as Buzbee put it. "He was just one of those people who was bound and determined to be somebody or do something."

Mary was reluctant to let her husband leave. "It's a pretty tough thing to have to be apart from your family so long at a time but sometimes you can't hardly do nothing else."

Woody and Mary had lived together long enough, Guthrie wrote, "to have no clothes, no money, no groceries and two children." And they still owed the Jenningses five dollars on the house.

They did not argue; Woody, in any event, would simply leave the house, sometimes to be gone for days if they had. Instead Mary agreed "that if he could go somewhere else and get strung out better it would be pretty hard for a while but it would be worth it."

If Guthrie was to find opportunity, to make money for Mary and the children, and to better himself, it would not be in dust-dry Pampa. Work and hope lay westward, in far-off California. His father's sister, Aunt Laura, and cousin "Jack" Guthrie were already there, two of thousands of Oklahomans who had migrated to the Golden State.

Sometime in February 1937, Guthrie walked over to the telephone office. He had a favor he wanted to ask of Minnie Dittmeyer. He had decided to go to California, where he had kinfolk. There was no future in Pampa; he would follow the other Okies westward, like them seeking work. Would Minnie move in with Mary, then some four months pregnant? There was some money saved from his work on the track gang to pay for Mary's expenses.

When Minnie agreed, Guthrie simply told his wife he was leaving. "He was going to try to go to California and make something better for us," he explained to Mary. He would send for them, he promised, when he found work.

Sometime in late February or early March 1937, Matt's older brother

Fred drove Guthrie in Jennings's beer delivery truck the twenty-five miles to the federal highway south of Pampa. Just outside Groom, Texas, Guthrie climbed down from the cab, stuffed his paint brushes in a hip pocket, slung his guitar over his shoulder, and put up his thumb. Out there, at the end of Route 66, lay California and opportunity.

CHAPTER SEVEN

West of the West

WINTERS ON THE HIGH PLAINS are often bitter, the temperatures pinned below freezing when the northern winds knife through the pale sunlight. Standing on the road outside Groom left Guthrie "colder than a well-digger in Montana," so he abandoned the federal highway, Route 66, with its westbound stream of dusty flivvers and wheezing trucks. He would move southerly instead, toward warmer weather.

From Amarillo, Guthrie made his way to Hereford through a gray, gritty storm of half blowing snow and half dust. He tramped the dusty shoulders of the thinly paved road out of the Panhandle, southwesterly to the New Mexican desert. In Roswell and Clovis, he painted signs when he could wrangle the work, then moved on. He hitchhiked into Alamogordo, "a nice little town" with its adobe shacks and houses of sun-dried brick, then turned west in Las Cruces, hitching rides to Deming and Lordsburg before he crossed into Arizona.

He kept moving, singing in honky-tonks for a beer and a sandwich, thumbing rides on the side of the highway by day, by night looking for a dead-headed freight or asking police to let him sleep in their warm jails if the boxcars rumbled through town without slowing. He was in a hurry. "You hate to just sleep all night and not get anywhere," Guthrie wrote later.

Guthrie pulled into the Tucson freight yards tired, dirty, and most of all, hungry, so hungry that for the first time in his life he turned to begging. Worn and shabby, he knocked on the back doors at churches, "offering to do some work for something to eat."

But church after church turned Guthrie down. At the Catholic church a priest said, "Sorry, son, but we're livin' on charity ourselves; there's nothing here for you."

At first humiliated because he had begged, Guthrie was finally embittered by the repeated rejection. "I looked up at the cathedral, every single rock in it cost ten dollars to lay and ten to chop out, and I thought, Boy, you're right—there's nothing here for me."

He would finally cadge a sandwich at the door of a grimy house near the Southern Pacific railroad tracks. Here he was among people who understood hunger, the families of gandy dancers and trackwalkers, of maimed brakemen and roundhouse greasers.

"This was my first time. I wasn't a virgin no more." A second housewife down the line packed four "great big juicy sandwiches" in a bag for him; he shared them with three other hoboes in the freight yard. "I felt like I had learnt the secret of all religion. To give away all of the stuff you can't use. All other baloney is bull."

Beyond Yuma Guthrie crossed into California, hitchhiking north on farm trucks through the already green lettuce and cotton fields of the Imperial Valley. "Coming out of the dustbowl, the colors so bright and smells so thick all around, that it seemed almost too good to be true. . . . My eyes had got sort of used to Oklahoma's beat-up look, but here, with this sight of fertile, rich, damp, sweet soil that smelled like the dew of a jungle, I was learning to love another, greener, part of life."

Like hundreds of thousands before him, Woody Guthrie had crossed the last divide; he was no longer in the West, but "West of the West," as a touring Theodore Roosevelt had noted thirty years earlier. The dream of California had become shimmering reality for Guthrie.

The blacktop highway skirted the north shore of the Salton Sea, bored through the unlikely groves of date palms outside Indio, and widened to become the main street in Banning and Beaumont.

North of Riverside he rejoined Route 66 and the steady trickle of westing migrants in their sagging cars and trucks. He hitchhiked the last leg of the journey in a '29 Ford coupé driven by a friendly "Japanese boy." As the young man touted the soil, the climate, the life in California, they drove west through the endless orange groves that lined Arrow Highway into Los Angeles.

It was dark when the Ford pulled up in front of the Plaza church, tucked between the office buildings of downtown Los Angeles and the city's Chinatown, across a muddy field from the railyards and "a block from everything in the world." Guthrie was awed by the city, its sheer size and noise, so much bigger and louder than even the biggest cities he had tramped through. Whatever thoughts he had of seeing the ocean or staying any longer than it took to get out of town fled. Instead he decided to head north immediately, to the farming community of Turlock, where his Aunt Laura had settled.

He was broke. His paint brushes and guitar were gone, the brushes stolen by four youths who had given him a ride in New Mexico, the guitar swapped for food long since. To earn his dinner he mopped the floor of a shabby restaurant run by an elderly couple and washed down the tables.

It was nearly midnight when Guthrie finished his chicken dinner. As he was about to leave, the old woman handed Guthrie a sack. "Here's something extra to take with you. Don't let John know about it," she whispered.

And as I walked out the door again, listening to the whistle of the trains getting ready to whang out, John walked over and handed me a quarter and said, "Here's somethin' ta he'p ye on down th' road. Don't let th' ol' lady know.

In the early morning hours of a foggy March morning, Guthrie pulled on his remaining wool sweater and clambered aboard a northbound freight. He hunkered under the forward bulkhead of an open gondola as the train lumbered over the 4,400-foot-high Grapevine, the fog growing cold, then turning into a slow rain.

At the summit of the Tehachapi Mountains that separated Southern California from the San Joaquin Valley, the freight drew onto a siding to allow a faster mail train to pass. Guthrie painfully climbed down to stretch his legs, "creaking like an eighty-year-old rocking chair," pulling his green sweater around him.

He was surprised when the train suddenly lurched forward and gathered speed. Guthrie stiffly scrambled along the ballast in the dark and barely managed to grab a rung of a ladder on a refrigerator car. The chill wind whipped at his clothes as he hung trapped between cars and the train rumbled through the icy night.

His fingers clutching the iron ladder turned blue. He struggled to wrap a handkerchief around his hands, after one slipped from the rung. Breathing into the cloth to warm them only made things worse; the moisture in his breath froze on the dirty rag.

Once again his fingers slipped. Terrified, Guthrie recalled the stories old railroaders told of unidentified bodies found lying mangled by the tracks. If he lost his grip, he would become one of those nameless 'boes sliced to pieces under the wheels of a freight.

"That was the closest to the 6x3 that I've ever been," he later wrote. "My mind ran back to millions of things—my whole life was brought up to date, and all of the people I knew, and all that they meant to me."

He concentrated on his unfeeling hands, willing them to hold onto the cold iron. His arms ached with a pain that paralyzed his shoulders and back.

The winter sun rose, pale and cold, offering faint hope. Guthrie clung with numb fingers for the last twenty miles into Bakersfield. As the slowing freight entered the yards, he unlocked his fingers, gingerly, one by one, and jumped to safety. Then he slumped against an empty brakeman's shack to fall asleep under a warming sky.

A second freight later that day carried a cheerier Guthrie through the green valley to Fresno, the air "sweet as could be, and like the faint smell of blossom honey." Wherever he traveled in California, it seemed, the dark soil offered rich harvests and a future.

The Southern Pacific freight rumbled northward through a heavy rain, with a sleeping Guthrie rolled in brown wrapping paper in the shelter of a boxcar. He awoke to the clamor of railroad guards and hoboes scrambling through the rainy night. Guthrie's freight had rumbled forty miles past the small farming community of Turlock without slowing. He was in Tracy, a town tough on hoboes.

Broke and hungry, Guthrie stumbled into a chili joint. He sold his green sweater for a dime to a patron too tall to wear it, and spent the coin on a bowl of chili. It was nearly two in the morning when Guthrie asked a beat cop if he and his momentary companions could seek shelter from the rain in the city jail.

"You might," the hard-eyed policeman sneered. The jailers would let them in—for thirty days. "Give you an awfully good chance to rest up on the country farm, and dry your clothes by a steam radiator every night."

The men huddled on the porch of the chili joint slipped away in the rain. Guthrie followed a half dozen back to the railyard and climbed through a window into a sandhouse. It was warm and dry inside. On a mound of sand, which steam engines laid on the tracks to provide traction, Guthrie fell asleep.

Three railroad bulls in black cowboy hats used long batons to roust the sleeping men. "Git on outta town," they bellowed, herding the men from the sandhouse into the cold rain. "Keep travelin'! Don't even look back!"

The bedraggled group, muddy clothes askew, some carrying boots snatched as they were pushed out the door, finally halted in a field. With the rain coming harder, they began laughing at themselves, running about in circles, and splashing in puddles. "There is a stage of hard luck that turns into fun, and a stage of poverty that turns into pride, and a place in laughing that turns into fight," Guthrie had discovered.

Defiantly, they made their way back to the warm sandhouse, two by two. Just across the street from the barbed wire fence surrounding the rail-yard, they were suddenly pinned in the headlights of a waiting police car.

"Come here, you!" a voice from behind the headlights barked at Guthrie. What was he doing in town?

Passing through, Guthrie answered. On his way to Turlock, where he had kin.

"Kinda work?"

"Painter. Signs. Pictures. Houses. Anything needs paintin'."

As long as he was looking for work, anxious to join his relatives forty miles down the road, why, the police officers were pleased to show Guthrie to the highway. They ordered him to start walking, and drove behind, herding him into the face of the storm as passengers in passing cars hooted.

A mile or more out of Tracy, the police car swung about and roared off. Guthrie was left standing in the dark beside the highway, rain-soaked and shivering. He trudged up the road until he came to a cement bridge over a river, slipped down the muddy bank, and ducked under the roadbed. As long as the creek did not rise, it was comparatively dry under the bridge.

In the darkness Guthrie could make out the forms of a dozen people, curled up under newspapers and bedrolls in pairs to sleep. He lay down on a piece of discarded wrapping paper, lying in the dark, his body shaking in the cold, until a stocky man tucked in a bedroll grumbled, "Don't you know your shiverin's keepin' everybody awake?"

When Guthrie stammered an apology, the man suggested Guthrie "c'mon over here an' den up with me."

Guthrie peeled off his muddy shoes and wet clothes, then crawled under the wool blanket, shaking so hard he could not talk.

"Cops walk you?" the stranger in the darkness asked. His back to the man, Guthrie merely nodded.

As for himself, the big man shrugged off the miserable weather. He was a lumberjack, on his way to Vancouver, where it was a lot colder, cold enough to freeze the balls off a brass bulldog. He was still talking when Guthrie drifted off.

The next morning Guthrie set off, hungry, wearing his clammy clothes. By the shoulder of the road he found the remains of a ham sandwich, some olives, and a crust of bread thrown out by a roadside drinking party. "I didn't pass it up."

Turlock was a thriving town of more than 4,000, surrounded by hundreds of small farms. Nurtured by a sprawling irrigation system that siphoned the glacier-fed Merced River, the rich alluvial loam produced alfalfa, watermelons, row crops, peaches, and apricots nine months of the year. Even though Guthrie limped into town in the last days of winter, there was work to be had in bustling Turlock.

"I can't tell you how pretty this country did look to me," Guthrie acknowledged. "I can't tell you how ugly the cops looked, nor how ugly the jails looked, the hobo jungles, the shacktowns up and down the rivers, how dirty the Hoovervilles looked on the rim of the city garbage dump."

Jobless, and with no prospects, Woody Guthrie unexpectedly turned up on his Aunt Laura's doorstep. Family would take him in: Aunt Laura was Charley Guthrie's sister, the oldest of the four children Jerry P. had by his first wife. Laura and her husband had picked up their four children and moved to Glendale, California, the year before, then moved on to Turlock. But the work had run out, and they were ready to return to Glendale.

Guthrie stayed only a few days with his aunt and her family before moving on. Turlock offered little work for a sign painter without brushes and he had no interest in farm work.

At Laura's suggestion, apparently, Guthrie visited the gold rush town of Sonora, fifty miles from Turlock, up a winding mountain road into the foothills of the Sierra Nevada. The weathered town with its narrow streets and the silent mines with their gray tailings fascinated him. Idly whittling with his pocketknife, he spent hours staring out at the pine forests growing over mountains that had disgorged the richest vein of the mother lode.

From Turlock Guthrie made his way north on U.S. 99, through Sacramento with its Hooverville on the fetid banks of the Sacramento River hard by the city dump, then on to the Redding area. The federal government was going to build a huge dam, the first step in a vast irrigation plan to water the central valley; there were said to be jobs for laborers there.

Guthrie was a boomer once more. As many as five thousand job seekers waiting for the government to begin hiring had camped in the sardonically named Happy Valley, a shantytown fifteen miles outside of Redding. He decided to move on.

In Redding he sang on street corners with a blind man; the two of them swapped songs, playing for whatever pennies and nickels they could milk from the thin crowds. Then Guthrie decided to retrace his steps southward, to follow his Aunt Laura's family to Glendale. He could stay with them until he found some work.*

Guthrie was a few months shy of twenty-five, the father of one child, his wife pregnant with another. He sent occasional, small money orders to Mary, who depended on her concerned parents most of the time. "I know it upset my dad a lot—my mother too," she said. "Woody wasn't doing the manly thing."

Worse still, Guthrie was unsure of his future, seemingly no better off in California than he had been in Texas. The best he could say was that he liked this new and bountiful country, but he was still broke and without work. His lack of purpose was an itch he couldn't scratch, and it left him vaguely frustrated.

An unexpected visit from cousin Leon would change things.

Only his mother called him Leon. To everyone else, he was "Jack" or "Oke," sometimes "Okie" or "Oklahoma" Guthrie. The son of Charley Guthrie's younger brother John, Jack and his family had moved from Oklahoma to Sacramento five years before. He was tall, attractive, and musically talented. His father John played the fiddle; his mother Ethel sang the old ballads and heart songs popular in the last century. Jack himself boasted a rich tenor voice and played guitar well. He had dreams of becoming a western star, but he was responsible for a wife and child.

Three years younger than his cousin Woodrow, Jack Guthrie was polished in ways that Woody was not, a careful dresser, an accomplished guitarist, and a smooth singer who had taught himself to yodel by listening to Gene Autry and Jimmie Rodgers records. He was also something of a show-off, whereas Woody was self-effacing and quiet. Jack had cowboyed in rodeos up and down the state until, thrown from a high-winding bronco, he injured his back. He turned to singing when and where he could make a few dollars, supplementing that with work on construction sites.

Most important, Jack Guthrie was as ambitious as his cousin Woody was directionless. And he had a suggestion.

Why not team up and see if they could make a go of it in Los Angeles? The big city would offer lots of opportunities the small towns of the central valley lacked.

---

* Guthrie's precise movements during the spring of 1937 are not known. Conceivably he visited his Uncle John and cousin Jack in Sacramento, and he may have hitchhiked over the Sierra Nevada to Reno. He was in the Los Angeles area in mid-May.

They made an unlikely pair. Jack was a western singer; his songs were heavily influenced by popular music. Woody was a country singer, his music born of an older oral tradition. In practice, they could neither sing nor play guitar together; indeed, Woody privately despised the treacly sentiment of Jack's sagebrush serenades. Jack the guitarist used the jazz-influenced chords of popular music and played up the neck of the instrument; Woody disdained chords beyond the minimal tonic, subdominant and dominant. His idea of playing up the neck of the guitar was to use a capo.

Still, they were cousins. The two agreed to work up some sort of act.

Sprawling Los Angeles—an ill-sorted patchwork of insular neighborhoods, orchards, and truck farms—swallowed them without notice. Jack found work on construction projects while Woody hustled "all kinds of loose jobs all up and down the west coast. I shingled houses. I mixed cement. I painted signs. I painted houses. I played my guitar around at saloons." He spent six weeks washing dishes at wrestling champion "Strangler" Lewis's Monterey Lounge on Brand Boulevard in Glendale, a few blocks from Aunt Laura's home. That job lasted until he used lye to clean a sink full of aluminum skillets; the resulting chemical reaction spewed a foul-smelling smoke that emptied the restaurant for the night and the kitchen permanently of Woodrow Wilson Guthrie.

Living in a quarter-a-night hotel on Los Angeles's Main Street, Guthrie eked out a living by singing for tips in the musty saloons of Skid Row. When his cousin Amalee protested, Guthrie merely shrugged. The men in the bars were friends, and they had stories to tell. Even better, when he was out of work, he could pitch his hat on the sidewalk in front of a bar and hustle tips with songs.

On May 12, 1937, Jack, with Woody in tow, dropped in on the family of Roy Crissman. Jack had worked with Crissman on construction jobs, and years before had dated the younger of the two Crissman daughters, Mary Ruth. Jack was charming and gregarious; Woody spent the evening quietly sitting in a corner.

The following night, they returned to the Crissman's Glendale home on West Magnolia, this time bringing a guitar. They started singing, Jack and Woody handing the guitar back and forth, the Crissman family joining in. Sometime during the evening, the Crissman's older daughter recalled, Woody and she joined in a duet—probably on one of the older "heart" songs of the nineteenth century like "Little Rosewood Casket" or "The Baggage Coach Ahead."

"And it was immediate," the musical effect electric, she said. With scarcely a thought, Maxine Crissman began singing in a low register, Woody adding a tight-knit harmony high above her melody line.

Maxine had what Guthrie described as "a low, tomboy-sounding voice," rough and husky, untrained, but sure of pitch. His voice no more cultivated, Guthrie sang a tenor harmony and played his driving "Southern E-chord guitar." Together they found what Guthrie would call "the crossnote"—for lack of a better term. The sum of their two voices was greater than the parts.

Maxine was twenty-two, three years younger than Woody, born in Henry County, Missouri, in the same farmhouse in which her father, Roy, had been born. When she was an infant, the Crissmans moved to nearby Creighton, Missouri, in "the flat grass grazing country around the Missouri Ozarks," and it was there that she grew up.

Music was everywhere in Creighton, Maxine recalled. She learned the old songs so popular in her fiddling grandfather's day, songs Woody Guthrie had also learned in Okemah. Offered grandfather Thomas Jefferson Crissman's fiddle, she declined, the left-handed girl unwilling to play it "backwards." Instead she insisted on playing the saxophone and would practice hymn tunes in the backyard. Neighbors would telephone, asking Maxine to play favorites: "Beulah Land," "Jesus Loves Me, This I Know," and "Whispering Hope."

"That was my start in broadcasting," she later joked.

The family moved about, following father Roy as he looked for work: to Kansas City where he was a streetcar conductor; to Quapaw, Oklahoma, where he worked in the zinc and lead mines; then back to Creighton and the family farm. Finally, in August 1932, Royal and Georgia Crissman moved with their two daughters to Glendale. Roy's sister had written earlier to assure them of the wonderful opportunities California offered.

Maxine would spend her senior year at Glendale High School, graduating in June 1933. Following her mother's example, she found a job in Los Angeles's garment district, sewing pockets on men's bathrobes. In short order, she found work with Lettie Lee, a custom dress and movie costume designer.

Maxine was doing fine needlework when her father, Roy Crissman, met Jack Guthrie and Guthrie's brother-in-law, Ted Adkins, on a construction job. The two younger men gravitated to the Crissman home and the two attractive Crissman girls; seventeen-year-old Jack began to date thirteen-year-old Mary Ruth.

Handsome blue-eyed Jack cut a glamorous figure. Caught up in the western music craze, he had bought himself a fancy cowboy suit, a white silk handkerchief—and a bullwhip. Intent on a career as a cowboy singer, he wanted to work up an act using the plaited whip to snap cigarettes from the lips of a stage partner. Maxine and Mary Ruth were the first to hold up pieces of paper and cigarettes with their hands—until Jack missed and cut Mary Ruth's wrist.

In the weeks after he first visited, Woody dropped by the house on West Magnolia frequently. Invariably there was singing, with everyone joining in, guitars, four-string banjo, and Georgia Guthrie's piano or organ playing along. If Jack was busy, drumming up singing engagements where he could find them, Woody came alone, riding the Pacific Electric's interurban from downtown Los Angeles. The elder Crissmans grew fond of him and doted on the older, familiar songs he sang with Maxine. Their affection was strong enough to suppress their irritation when Guthrie repeatedly dumped six teaspoons of sugar into his coffee, drizzled cold water into the brew, and drank the whole cup without bothering to stir the sugar.

Guthrie was equally fond of the Crissmans, particularly the woman he called "Mama," who played organ as his own mother had so long ago. Georgia would stand at the sink as she peeled peaches for canning, all the while cutting slices for Guthrie, who hated the feel of peach fuzz. He was like a grown-up child, Maxine Crissman recalled, and Georgia Crissman was like the mother he had lost ten years before.

Meanwhile Jack scouted for whatever paying appearances he could find. He and Woody swapped two loads of gravel—Woody did not reveal just how they came by the stones—for a battered Model-T truck. They sawed the roof off the cab and larked about the streets of Los Angeles, shouting at pedestrians, "How do you get out of here to the United States?" and "Is this where Betty Grapple lives? We come to gab with the Gables."

At a western music jamboree held in the Shrine Auditorium in Los Angeles, Jack wrangled an appearance for them at the Strand Theater in Long Beach. Between showings of the newly released *Waikiki Wedding* and the short subjects, Jack, Woody, and a popular local group, the Beverly Hill-billies, entertained on stage during the last week of June 1937.

Polished Jack Guthrie was the featured singer in their duo, Woody the comic sidekick playing his harmonica, his spoons, or his bones. They evenly divided their nine-dollar daily pay—five dollars for singing and four dollars for driving around town in their truck, bedecked with a sign proclaiming "Headed for the Strand."

On the first day they were to appear, Friday, June 25, Woody and Jack loaded the four Crissmans and assorted Guthrie relatives onto the back of the truck, drove the forty miles from Glendale to Long Beach, and bluffed their way past the usher at the side door.

The movie theater was crowded. Country and western music was popular; the added attraction of live entertainment was certain to draw a good house—even if the feature film was poor.

As Maxine recalled the billing, Jack and Woody were merely to play with the Beverly Hillbillies on stage. Instead, in the middle of the set, Jack stepped downstage and accompanying himself on guitar, sang Gene Autry's lugubrious cowboy ballad, "There's an Empty Cot in the Bunkhouse Tonight." Woody's musical contribution was solely to rap the oven-dried bones together—clop-clip-clop-clip-clop.

The audience was enthusiastic, enough so that the irate manager throttled his anger and paid the two of them their five-dollar fee. He did not, however, extend the booking.

"Oke" Guthrie was undeterred. In the next week he began talking about doing a radio show, even for free. "You see," he argued, "you can get more jobs at saloons, churches and markets if you've got a radio program every day." Publicity was everything; furthermore, the program would give them enough prestige to ask for a two-dollar guarantee for six hours of singing in saloons.

Jack, who "could sell ice cubes to Eskimos," as Maxine put it, had even picked out a station: KFVD. It was about the only radio station in Los Angeles that did not have a country-western program on its schedule.

Los Angeles in the summer of 1937 was awash in country-hillbilly-cowboy-western music. The Stuart Hamblen Gang was on KEHE, and busy Hamblen was also on KMTR. The Covered Wagon Jubilee and Beverly Hillbillies each had a show on KMPC, the Saddle Pals on KMTR and KMPC, Bronco Busters on KFWB, Saddle Tramps on KFOX, and the Sons of the Pioneers on KRKD. There was a *Hollywood Barn Dance*, and a *Hollywood Hillbillies*, a show that featured Cincinnati-born Leonard Slye, before he became Roy Rogers.*

---

* Slye-Rogers, who appeared in his first film the year Woody came to California, recalled his first auto trip in 1930 to depression-era California. One night he drew a small crowd to listen to him sing with his father and cousin. "They were people like us, camping out and mostly pretty hungry," Rogers told a reporter for the *Los Angeles Times*. "You could tell most of them hadn't smiled in a long, long time, But now they smiled, listening to the music. It made them happy; kept the dark away for a little bit. That's what I learned that night: I learned what music is for." Quoted from Rogers's obituary in the *Los Angeles Times*, July 7, 1998.

By tuning the dial every fifteen minutes, a listener could spend from five in the morning past midnight with country or western music in the air.

KFVD, on the other hand, offered everything from the Radio Poets Club to organ music to a Spanish-language program each morning and the "Editor of the Air" daily at noon. The owner of the station, a defiantly individualistic J. Frank Burke Sr., presided over the show.

A onetime Progressive, Burke had kept the reformer's faith. As other Progressives, including California's United States Senator Hiram Johnson, moved toward the center, then on to the right and eventually to the isolationist right, Burke continued to plug for social and political reform. He remained a determined and outspoken liberal.

In 1927, Burke had purchased the *Register*, the largest newspaper in Orange County, and for "an exciting eight years" he had railed against an increasingly conservative state Republican Party. Eventually he bolted and registered as a Democrat—out of step there too because of his staunch Prohibitionist sentiments.

Burke switched from newspapers to radio in 1935, when he bought KFVD, its powerful transmitter, and its easily remembered broadcast band, 1000 kilocycles. His radio audience was infinitely larger than the *Register*'s readership, and his potential influence on state politics that much greater.

As editor of the air, Burke was caught up in the welter of California's unusual politics. A leader in the state's newly reborn Democratic Party, he presided over a clangorous array of retirees seeking twenty-five- or thirty-dollars-a-week pensions, old-line socialists grubbing for a utopian community in the desert, technocrats and Upton Sinclair's End Poverty in California advocates with their rival schemes to end the hegemony of big business, the open shop, and the unchallenged sway of the *Los Angeles Times* in southern California. Confronted with an array of pressing social issues—including the recall of a corrupt mayor of Los Angeles—Burke left day-to-day management of the station to his son, Frank Junior.

On Thursday, July 15, the two cousins drove with Roy Crissman over the Hollywood Hills from Glendale to the KFVD studio housed in what had once been a grand mansion on Wilshire Boulevard. They were early, so the three men stretched out on a patch of grass across from the posh Ambassador Hotel.

Woody was in a pensive mood that evening. He wanted to make enough money to bring his wife and child to California, and reunite his family. Jack, of course, had bigger ambitions. Even if they weren't paid for singing on the radio, they could build their reputation and then command higher fees, and make their money in personal appearances. All the cowboys you heard on the radio worked that way.

The audition went well. Frank Burke Jr. was impressed. Jack was a polished entertainer, the sort of man who appealed to a younger audience, especially young women. Woody, on the other hand, would draw an older audience. It was a good mix.

Burke offered them a daily, fifteen-minute slot at 8:00 A.M. They could do the program and still make it to a construction site early enough to pick up at least a half-day's work. They could begin next Monday.

The Guthrie cousins accepted. They were radio performers.

CHAPTER EIGHT

Old Familiar Songs

*S*HORTLY BEFORE 8:00 on the morning of July 19, 1937, Woody Guthrie and his cousin Jack stepped up to the microphone in the cramped studio on the third floor of radio station KFVD. As the engineer's finger snapped in their direction, they began singing the theme song of the first *Oklahoma and Woody Show*. It was a song Woody had picked up somewhere east of California, a song widely known among the Okies, Arkies, and Texans who had made their way west.

> *I'm a-going down this road a-feeling bad,*
> *I'm a-going down this road a-feeling bad,*
> *I'm a-going down this road a-feeling bad,*
> *And I ain't gonna be treated this-a-way.*

Though it was called *The Oklahoma and Woody Show*, the program featured Jack, his big Washburn guitar, and the cowboy songs he favored. Because their musical styles were so different—the one slick, the other rough-hewn—the two men could not sing well together. Their joint repertoire essentially consisted of their theme song, "Lonesome Road Blues."

Jack generally sang solo, with Woody adding an occasional vocal harmony, a four-string banjo accompaniment, or a rhythmic punctuation on the bones. From time to time Woody played one of the harmonica showpieces he had learned in Okemah long before, sometimes with Jack Guthrie's accomplished fiddle chasing the fox or train along with him.

The Oklahoma and Woody Show was unsponsored; neither performer had a contract. They would remain on the air at the sufferance of young Frank Burke.

Despite the tenuous nature of the show, it was a big hit with the scattering of Guthries and Crissmans living in Glendale. Woody or Jack often slipped in dedications to one or another family member, but there was little talk and no banter between the two singers. As Maxine Crissman recalled, *The Oklahoma and Woody Show* was just another of "the run-of-the-mill cowboy shows of the day."

The fact that there were so many cowboy shows on the air, particularly in Los Angeles, was hardly accidental.

From the earliest days of silent films, former cowboys like Bronco Billy Anderson had turned out one—, two—, then four-reel flickers. Over the years, particularly after the invention of the talkie, the heroic cowboy of a legendary West gave way to singing cowboys in a West that existed only on Hollywood's back lots.

The introduction of the so-called singing cowboy came with Ken Maynard's *In Old Arizona*. The 1929 film was credited as the first musical western; Maynard's songs were as important as his rope tricks and gaudy costumes in the melodramatic story of good triumphant. By the time Woody Guthrie reached Los Angeles in 1937, the "horse operas" of Maynard and Gene Autry were Saturday matinee favorites.

Meanwhile, cowboy singers dressed in spangled attire that no working cowhand had ever worn proliferated on the airwaves and in recording studios. Initially reluctant, by the 1930s recording companies had added "western" or "cowboy" music to their "hillbilly" or "country" catalogues.*

Even in such urban areas as Philadelphia, New York, and Los Angeles, country or western music filled large blocks of airtime. The NBC network broadcast two country programs weekly, *National Barn Dance* from Chicago and *Grand Ole Opry* from Nashville. Gospel music and hymns crowded Sunday-morning broadcast schedules.

Not only was the music popular with listeners, it was inexpensive. Station managers and program directors had no trouble finding musicians like the Guthrie cousins willing to perform for free in the hope of building a following. With recognition, Jack Guthrie argued, they could cash in when they appeared in local nightclubs and bars.

But even a radio program did not guarantee fame or fortune. Jack Guthrie had only modest success when he sought paying bookings. He did sign them up for a musical contest to be held in conjunction with a rodeo in Los Angeles. The cash prize was an incentive for him to agree to the sponsor's one condition: contest participants had to take part in the rodeo's opening grand entrance—on horseback.

---

* So-called race records—that is, releases aimed at both urban and rural black audiences—remained segregated in catalogues.

Cowboy Jack knew how to ride. Not so his cousin. The seemingly docile horse Woody chose at the riding stable promptly threw him. Woody picked himself up, wincing at a badly skinned elbow, and remounted.

His equine troubles were not over; he lost control of his mount as the grand parade trotted onto the Gilmore Field auto-racing track and his horse bolted through a band of buckskin-clad Indians. The parade scattered as Woody clung frantically to the animal, then tumbled to the dirt-covered blacktop of the converted stadium. Maxine described the rodeo parade in pandemonium as "hilarious"; Woody would later embellish the story until he was "picking feathers out of himself for a while."

The guest appearances that Woody and Jack had hoped for were few. They hustled saloons for bookings, played the less selective Skid Row bars for tips or free beers, and made the rounds of the motion picture studios.

Together they scraped by, Jack ever torn between the need to feed his family and his desire to make a career as a cowboy singer. He vacillated, one day talking of quitting and going back to construction work, the next enthusing about the paying dates that were sure to come their way.

Woody chafed as "the sidekick," with little to do on the show. One day he suggested that Maxine come to the studio to harmonize with him on a song or two. Jack raised no objection.

Maxine spent the night gripped by stagefright. The butterflies in her stomach alternated with laryngitis, leaving her both hoarse and nervous when they departed for KFVD the next morning.

Woody and Maxine sang two songs together on the morning program, including Woody's adaptation of "Curly-Headed Baby."

She's my curly-headed baby,
Used to sit on daddy's knee.
She's my curly-headed baby,
Come from sunny Tennessee.

*   *   *   *

Every night and day that passes
We go playing in my dreams
And I dream that we're together
Down in sunny Tennessee.

The sentiment was cloying; the tune owed more than a little to George M. Cohan's "Yankee Doodle Dandy," but it put an end to Maxine's stage-fright.

Four nights later, Woody and Maxine appeared on the hour-long *Cowtown Program* broadcast over Glendale station KIEV. Their invitation was an extended-family affair. The hosts of the show were the Poe Brothers, whose sister was married to Aunt Laura's son Delbert.

To the tune of "The Martins and the Coys," the duo sang a song Woody had just written that had been inspired by headlines in the daily paper.*

The chorus and last verse apparently summed up public opinion of the war abroad:

> *Chorus:*
> *O' the Chinese and the Japs*
> *They was easy goin' chaps*
> *Till they got disputin' o'er th' bound'ry wall;*
> *Now they're marchin' and a-runnin'*
> *And a-shellin' and a-gunnin'*
> *And the air is full of sizzlin' cannon balls.*
>
> *We don't know just who will ever win the battle*
> *And as far as we're concerned we do not care*
> *If they bombard good old Tokio—*
> *Well, I guess that's okie dokio*
> *But let's pray they don't go droppin' 'em over here.*

Three days later, Maxine and Woody joined Jack at a "Frontier Day" celebration in Hermosa Beach. Jack, singing with yet another cowboy band, invited his cousin and Maxine up to the stage to sing. The two sang together, without Jack. The drive from Glendale to Hermosa Beach had been long, they earned nothing for their token appearance, but it gave Maxine increasing confidence.

The first two weeks of September were chaotic for the Guthrie cousins and Maxine Crissman. On the first day of the month, Burke Junior shifted their show from morning to 11 P.M. Jack at least could work construction

---

* On the pretext that their troops had been fired upon by Chinese soldiers near Beijing, the Japanese army in July seized a major foothold in the north of China. Within weeks, the Japanese navy had attacked Shanghai, had "accidentally" shelled the U.S. cruiser *Augusta*, and gone on to blockade the entire coast of China.

jobs by day. Two days later, Burke handed the morning slot to Woody. Guthrie asked Maxine to join him.

In the casual atmosphere of local radio, such program changes were constant. There was no audition, recalled Maxine. Woody simply introduced her on the air as "Lefty Lou from Old Mizzou"—"Lefty" a childhood nickname because she was left-handed, "Lou" simply because it rhymed with "Mizzou."

On September 7, Jack sang for the last time on the nighttime program; singing at night had cut down on his appearances in local saloons. He asked to return to the morning show with Woody.

Still Jack Guthrie vacillated between quitting KFVD entirely and trying to parlay the program into a show business living. Twice he threatened to leave, and twice changed his mind. Finally, on Monday, September 13, he quit for good.

Woody chose to stay at KFVD. "I thought it was better than nothing, could very easy turn into something, so I kept on," he explained.

The next morning Woody and Maxine, now Lefty Lou, took over the 8:00-to-8:30 show. On top of that, Burke offered them the nighttime slot as well.

Within days, the station began receiving letters for Woody and Lefty Lou, letters praising the "sweet singers" who offered songs the listeners remembered from their youth, songs that reminded them of distant homes, of Saturday-night church socials and Sunday-morning church services. Many wrote to request particular songs and hymns, requests Woody and Lefty Lou tried to fulfill.

Woody and Maxine were different from the cowboy singers who favored artificial "buckaroo ballads." Rather than sing of a West that never was, Woody preferred to re-create in song a West that had vanished, with ballads like the gritty "Sam Bass," learned in Pampa from his Uncle Jeff, or the hardbitten "Corinna, Corinna," picked up somewhere between Pampa and California.

At the same time, Woody's performances reflected influences of both nineteenth-century medicine and minstrel shows and twentieth-century vaudeville. He mixed cornpone humor borrowed from hoary stage routines and jokebooks with contemporary, sardonic observation.

Just twenty-five, Woody's singing style was evolving. The unusual two-part harmony with Maxine Crissman stemmed from the century-old church tradition of shape-note hymn books, with the male voice providing the tenor harmony above the alto carrying the melody. At the same time, he forsook the traditional, nasal, pinched-throat voice of the southern mountains; he sang with a harsh head tone, more of the West, a rasping voice at once old and new.

The programs were unrehearsed and virtually unplanned. Maxine learned Woody's songs, old or new, as they walked the mile from his Aunt Laura's house to the Crissman residence. They would stop passersby and try out the tune there on the sidewalk. It was as good a test of a new song as any.

Rehearsal was no more than singing as Maxine drove to the station in her father's automobile. (Woody was a poor driver who paid little attention to the road and less to traffic.) The songs they might play on any show were as casually chosen, Maxine recalled.

Guthrie had begun to compile a songbook by typing out the lyrics of songs and ballads that he knew, as well as those that he had written. "We would set it up on a rack in the studio and wherever it opened up, that's what we would sing," Maxine said. "If we started on a wrong note, we just stopped, and started over. It was never anything formal. It was exactly like Sunday-afternoon back-porch singing back home."

In mid-September, Woody wrote a new theme song, "Here Comes Woody and Lefty Lou." That was the single fixed element in the show. Most of the songs were duets, sung in improvised harmony. Guthrie would skewer his lighted cigarette on the end of a string wound round a peg, tilt his head back to keep the smoke from his squinting eyes, and start a guitar introduction. Maxine followed his lead.

At Woody's prodding, Maxine overcame her shyness enough to sing a solo on the air—something she refused to do in their public appearances. Woody might play a guitar or harmonica piece, or he might not. He read listeners' mail, told tall tales of upside-down cyclones and hoopsnakes, offered a "thought" for the day or simply chatted with Maxine, all in a slightly exaggerated Oklahoma drawl that turned "pardner," Woody's title of address for everyone, into "pahdna."

Despite his affable radio demeanor, Guthrie was still stiff with the prejudices of Okemah and Pampa. He casually referred to African-Americans as "niggers," and once after an unpleasant clash with blacks on the beach at Santa Monica Bay, he typed up a "Santa Monica Social Register Examine 'Er and Society Section" in which "De Beach Combin' Repo'tah" noted that "hit might in'rest you to know dat de 100 yd. dark record was broke fo'teen times in fifteen minutes las' nite at Santy Monica Beach."

His racism was unconscious and unexamined, a by-product of a boyhood spent not far from that part of Oklahoma known as "Little Dixie." (Both Matt Jennings and Woody's Uncle Jeff later remarked how they had to take pains not to use the word "nigger," though Matt, practicing Catholic that he was, ignored racial differences.)

One evening Gutherie introduced a harmonica solo by its traditional name, "Run, Nigger, Run." Shortly afterwards, he received a polite letter from a listener:

> I am a Negro, a young Negro in college and I certainly resented your remark. No person, or person of any intelligence uses that word over the radio today. . . .

> I don't know just how many Negroes listened to your program tonight, but I, for one, am letting you know that it was deeply resented.

Guthrie was shaken. He apologized on the air, declined to play the harmonica showpiece again—under that title—and from then on spoke of "colored men."

All the while, Guthrie remained largely indifferent to politics. Los Angeles was awash in rumors of a recall of its corrupt mayor—Burke Senior was an outspoken proponent on his daily radio show—but Guthrie paid no heed. On the air, he ignored political subjects, other than to tell stories of election-day fights and bloody noses in Oklahoma inspired by his father Charley's campaigns. His social commentary was slight and mostly confined to the ironic, as in a new song he had written to the tune of "Hang Out the Front Door Key":

Thousands of folks back east they say
Leavin' home every day,
Beatin' a hot and dusty way
To the California line.
O'er the desert sands they roll
Tryin' to get out of the old dust bowl.
They think they're a-comin' to a sugar bowl,
But here's what they find:

The police at the port of entry say:
"You're number 14,000 for today!" Oh!

If you ain't got the do-re-mi, folks,
If you ain't got the do-re-mi,
Better hang on in beautiful Texas,

Oklahoma, Kansas, Georgia, Tennessee.
California is a garden of Eden,
A paradise to live in or see,
But, believe it or not,
You won't find it so hot,
If you ain't got the do-re-mi.

The song was a warning to the naive, to those who believed western singer Jimmie Rodgers's assurance that "California's waters taste like cherry wine." "Do-Re-Mi" offered no solutions; it was wry, not angry. "Lefty Lou and me agrees that it ain't so much on poetry, but it tells a LOT of truth."

Similarly, the social commentary of another of Guthrie's most popular songs, "Philadelphia Lawyer," was implicit or indirect. Guthrie, inspired by a newspaper story forwarded by a listener, borrowed the tune and various stanzas of the traditional American murder ballad "The Jealous Lover" for the song he first called "Reno Blues."

Way out in Reno, Nevada,
Where romances bloom and fade,
There was a Philadelphia lawyer
In love with a Hollywood maid.

The maid, however, is Cowboy Bill's sweetheart. One night Bill creeps to the maiden's window and spies the "Philadelphia lawyer," slang for a sharpie or an ambulance chaser, wooing the lady.

"Your hands are too pretty and lovely,
Your form so rare and divine.
Come go back with me to the city
And leave this wild cowboy behind."

Tonight back in old Pennsylvania,
Among those beautiful pines,
There's one less Philadelphia lawyer
In old Philadelphia tonight!

With two shows a day, six days a week, with the time traveling in Roy Crissman's car to and from the station, Woody and Maxine spent most of their hours together. Between programs they would tramp the green slopes of Forest Lawn Cemetery a few miles from the Crissman home, or climb to the third-floor roof of KFVD and look down in silent envy on Wilshire Boulevard, "on all that wealth and everything" across the street, where behind a great green lawn stood the faux-Mediterranean Ambassador Hotel, costly and socially aloof. "Everybody didn't go in there," Maxine recalled.

After the morning program, they would return to Glendale. Woody spent hours at the Crissman home, hammering away on Maxine's typewriter, writing long, chatty letters to Mary, to Charley, to Matt Jennings, sometimes two a day, all stuffed with family anecdotes, comments about California, and reports of the success they were enjoying on the air.

To fill the programs, Guthrie culled his memory for songs he had learned in Oklahoma and Texas, which he taught to Maxine. He was simultaneously writing his own songs, inspired by a newspaper story, a sudden turn of phrase, or a fleeting impulse. Maxine vividly remembered him sitting on the back porch of the Crissman home on a September afternoon, idly playing his guitar when Eugene Bozart, a neighbor's five-year-old grandson, asked, "Where you from?"

"Those Oklahoma hills," Guthrie replied.

Moments later, he got up, came into the house for paper and pencil, and returned to the back porch. Fifteen or twenty minutes passed before Guthrie was back with a song.

The song, promptly sung that night on KFVD, was to become one of Guthrie's most popular:

> *Many years have come and gone*
> *Since I wandered from my home*
> *In those Oklahoma Hills where I was born.*
> *Many a page of life has turned,*
> *Many a lesson I have learned,*
> *And I feel like in those hills I still belong.*

> *Chorus:*
> *Way down yonder in my Indian Nation*
> *Ride my pony o'er the reservation,*
> *Make a cowboy's life my occupation*
> *In those Oklahoma Hills where I was born.**

---

* There is disagreement about the tune Guthrie adapted for the song: "The Girl I Loved in Sunny Tennessee," or "Bring It on Down to My House" by country singer Charlie Poole. See Guy Logsdon, "Woody Guthrie and His Oklahoma Hills," *Mid-America Folklore* 19 (1991), p. 69.

The free-form nature of *The Woody and Lefty Lou Show* led to difficulty. Woody was continually inviting his relatives to perform on the 11:00 P.M. program. "Woody had relatives all over the place, and most of them seemed to sing or play to boot," Maxine grumbled.

There were Woody's Uncle Jeff, pursuing another rainbow, and his accordion-playing wife, Allene, drawn to California by news of Woody's success in landing a radio show. Jack Guthrie's father and mother, he a fiddler, she a singer whose wailing voice sent shudders down Woody's spine, wanted to be on the program. Woody owed the Poe Brothers a reciprocal invitation. Then there was Possom Trot Bruce, a second cousin or some such—they never did work out the relationship—who played a good guitar.

Maxine and a fair number of listeners protested. The show was being diluted.

"You're selfish," Woody snapped.

It was about as mad as Woody ever got, Maxine explained many years later. "*This was not like Woody,*" she said, emphasizing each word. It led her to believe that the family was pressuring him. Guthrie was "between a rock and a hard place."

Maxine came to understand at least one source of the pressure. She and Woody were spending a considerable amount of time together, usually alone. While it was all innocent, whispers of a romance, a dalliance, something, got back to Mary in Pampa. The source, Maxine believed, was Jack Guthrie's older sister, Wava, who was jealous that talented Jack had given up the program while Woody, the mere comic sidekick and harmonica player, continued on the air.

When Maxine again protested, Woody's response was to summarily discontinue the nighttime program on which his family members appeared. (Bound to workaday jobs, the relatives could not make the morning show.)

Burke Junior was upset when they cancelled the 11:00 P.M. show on October 8. "You're out of your mind," he protested. "You're reaching people."

Their mail proved it. They were not only broadcasting locally, but because of the peculiarities of the frequency, KFVD's signal reached far beyond California. When atmospheric conditions were right, the nighttime program bounced off the cooling ionosphere as far as Hawaii to the west, and well into the Great Plains to the east. In Pampa, at 1:00 A.M., Mary Guthrie tuned to 1000 kilocycles on the dial to listen for the code words of love Woody had promised in his letters.

All the while, the morning program ran on as usual. Woody and Maxine sang, Woody fit in a harmonica or fiddle tune and continued to interject his tall stories. At Burke's urging, Woody agreed to resume the 11:00 P.M. program on October 27, 1937—without his relatives. "Old Burke," as Woody perversely had dubbed the son, argued that their nighttime show reached a broader audience. That, in turn, made sponsorship more likely.

Nothing meant more than sponsorship to the performers donating their time and talent to reach an audience. Sponsors guaranteed income for three months, the length of the contract. Sponsors meant they would not have to open markets, attend fairs, or enter contests to eke out a living. Sponsors meant they had taken the first step to fame, if not fortune.

Sponsors did not care how good you were, Crissman said. Instead, they asked, "How much mail do you get?"

Woody and Lefty Lou were getting a surprising number of letters, more than Jack and Woody had ever polled together. In October, despite a seventeen-day hiatus during which they had abandoned the nighttime show, Woody and Lefty Lou received 410 pieces of mail. The mail sacks bulked larger still during the first week of November. Here was ample proof of the show's popularity, so much so that Burke Junior offered them a year's contract on November 12.

According to the terms of the contract, they were to share a sustaining fee of twenty dollars a week whether they were sponsored or unsponsored. In addition, they would receive fifteen dollars each for every fifteen minutes sponsors bought.

These were riches. Neither was working, Maxine having long since given up her job at the couturiere's shop. KFVD's sustaining fee would at least pay for their meals. (Woody had already worked out deals whereby he would periodically mention nearby Henry's Service station in exchange for free repairs on Roy Crissman's weary automobile, and Polly Gasoline for a full tank. Guthrie also received complimentary tickets when he plugged a touring rodeo.)

Their first paycheck in hand, Woody and Maxine marched across Wilshire Boulevard to the branch bank in the snooty Ambassador Hotel where KFVD maintained an account. Woody, bearded, in hiking boots, khaki trousers, worn work shirt, his brown hair curling in all directions, presented himself to the teller and demanded they be paid in silver dollars.

Outside on the sidewalk, Woody and Maxine cavorted like children. They lagged the silver dollars against a crack in the sidewalk. They cackled and danced with their good fortune. They were on their way.

That evening, Guthrie called Mary in Pampa and asked her to bring their two daughters and join him in Glendale. He suggested that Matt drive them to California; Woody would send the ten-dollar gas money.

Mary and the girls, Teeny, three, and Sue, four months old, arrived with Matt in November. They temporarily crowded in with Aunt Laura on South Louise Avenue in Glendale, then moved with Woody's cousin Amalee, her husband "Chief," and their three children to a home nearby in a predominantly Mexican-American neighborhood. Matt followed.

Mary deemed the house at 4026 Baywood Street a delight, no matter how poor their neighbors. For the first time in the five years of their marriage, they had money to live on and the security of a steady income. They were once again a family.

Furthermore, in Amalee, Mary had someone with whom to talk. Griffith Park lay just across the Los Angeles River—they could hear the lions in the Los Angeles Zoo howling into the night. The two women often took the children to the park; at a nickel a ride, the merry-go-round was a special treat. The swings in the playground were free.

Woody was less pleased with the living arrangement. With Mary's arrival, his plan to "sail the seas and walk foreign lands" was overtaken by her dream of owning a ceramic shop; she would run the business, and Woody would paint.

Such domesticity was beyond Woody. "He just wasn't a nine-to-five man," Maxine said. He liked to work through the night, do their morning show, then return home to sleep during the day. With five children running through the house, that schedule was difficult to keep. He loved his two daughters and Mary, Maxine concluded, "but he just wanted to get away from them."

Guthrie often escaped to the Crissman home. "He spent a lot of time at our house," Maxine acknowledged. "Which caused a lot of problems." According to Maxine, Wava Guthrie wrote Mary insinuating that "there were things going on between Woody and me, which wasn't true at all. That caused her misery and it caused me unhappiness."

Woody may well have fantasized about a relationship with Maxine, this "Lefty Lou from Old Mizzou." She was attractive and comparatively sophisticated, unlike homespun Mary. And she was musical, as Mary was not.

After an argument with Mary, Guthrie suggested to Maxine, "If we were married, we'd be hitchhiking and singing our way across country."

Spying a string of empties in the freight yard along San Fernando Road, Guthrie suddenly brightened. "Hey, Lefty Lou, how'd you like to take a ride on a freight?"

Roy Crissman, who had ridden the rods as a younger man, instantly scotched the idea. How could Guthrie even suggest such a hare-brained scheme. Maxine didn't realize the risks; what was Woody thinking?

Outside, Woody expelled a long sigh. "Damn! I thought old Roy was going to take his belt to the both of us."

Maxine eventually talked with Mary, "a sweetheart" in Maxine's words. Her husband *was* spending a lot of time at the Crissman home, Maxine agreed. But Maxine, after all, had a typewriter. Woody would take the machine into the dinette off the kitchen where he would sit, typing and smoking, while Maxine's mother cooked. He would often type for hours, then abruptly stand, sidle into the living room, stretch out on the floor, face up, without a pillow, and go to sleep. The Crissmans simply walked around the sleeping form.

Woody came and went as he pleased. Maxine's mother left a pot of coffee on the stove for him; he left a litter of cups, spilled coffee, sugar, and milk for her to wipe up, and a note of thanks.

He could not behave that way at the house on Baywood Street. There were just too many people living in the house. Moreover, Mary realized that the Crissmans had come to represent a surrogate family for Woody. As Maxine explained, "Me, my dad and mom were very close," the Crissman home a haven for him. "For the first time in his life, Woody stayed put," she pointed out.

Maxine's talk with Mary helped to allay her suspicions. Still to keep the peace, Woody promised never to go on the air with a woman other than Maxine without Mary's approval.*

If Maxine was never stirred to romantic thoughts by her singing partner, Woody nonetheless had a big impact on her. Maxine's fashion-conscious mother, who made hats for stars like Mary Pickford, had long insisted her daughter dress well. From the time Maxine was eleven years old, she was never a barefoot girl, but a little adult in powder and lipstick. Until she met Guthrie, she "wouldn't open the door unless she had her make-up on."

But dresses and coiffures were unsuitable for the hot, cramped studios of KFVD, or the long drives from Glendale to the station and back. Furthermore, there were the hikes through the cemetery or dusty Griffith Park.

---

* Years later, Mary waved off rumors that her husband and Maxine had had an affair. Mary did say she suspected he had had a relationship with *some* woman in California prior to her arrival with the children.

Woody had had a terrible childhood, and hers had been cut short, Maxine said. "We were living our second childhood. . . . We were getting a childhood—acting crazy—that we didn't have when we were little."

Maxine put away her make-up, cut her hair, and began wearing old pants and a shirt to go to the station. "Everyone started wonderin' what had happened."

Woody had happened. "He was just like a little kid, a very intelligent little kid." Or perhaps she saw in him "an old child. He acted like an old child." And he taught her to play with him.

Guthrie also nurtured a little boy's lack of respect for titles, and less for stuffed shirts. Confronted with the self-important, the pompous, or the plainly foolish, he played the none-too-bright country boy. "He was a master [at the] put-on," Maxine said. "He would give the impression he just hopped off the turnip wagon, and all the time he was sitting there with those wise eyes looking at that person. He got a big kick out of that put-down."

Following one personal appearance, he deliberately set out to offend Mirandy, a soberly dignified singer who often appeared with the Beverly Hillbillies in churches and schools. At a drive-in restaurant, Guthrie filled a coffee cup to the brim, bellowed, "Sound your G!," and slurped his coffee. Mirandy was horrified at such manners. "That was the last time we went out with her," Maxine said.

Guthrie's indifference to authority extended even to those he respected. One day early in their career, Guthrie and Crissman encountered Frank Burke Sr. at the station. The older man with feigned displeasure protested, "I was the top mail-receiver here until you hillbillies came."

Guthrie cocked his head to one side and drawled, "Well, pardner, it looks like you're gonna have to find yourself another station."

Burke guffawed. "The Burkes really liked Woody," Maxine recalled. They liked him enough to give him an opportunity for popular success. Not once, but twice.

CHAPTER NINE

Guthrie's People

*T*HE OFFER CAME as a surprise. Doug Mack, the manager of the Sons of the Pioneers, had heard *The Woody and Lefty Lou Show* on KFVD. Impressed with the singing—and particularly Maxine's throaty alto, Mack suggested to booking agent Hal Horton that "he listen to these kids." The two singers would do well on Horton's radio station XELO.

Horton was both a booking agent and the sales manager on the West Coast for Consolidated Drug Company of Chicago. The pharmaceutical company peddled beauty supplies and an array of over-the-counter remedies with hard-sell radio commercials that barely skirted the outrageous and illegal.

Horton was as aggressive, as intense a salesman as his on-air commercials. He spoke with Woody on the telephone, praised the noontime program he had just heard, and proposed that Guthrie take the show to XELO with studios just across the border in Tia Juana. While Horton already had some performers under contract, he would make Guthrie responsible for the noon-to-11 P.M. slot. Horton was prepared to pay both Guthrie and Maxine seventy-five dollars a week. In addition, to the three musicians Horton already had under contract, Guthrie could pick three others to accompany them.

It was a tantalizing offer, but Guthrie insisted on one condition: he was to be completely in charge. As Maxine later commented, "Nobody spoke for Woody. NOBODY." Horton agreed.

The Horton offer was a great opportunity. The pay was more than twice what they were making at KFVD, and XELO's thunderous signal reached a huge audience day and night. Furthermore, Guthrie could put his Uncle

Jeff, Allene, and Jack on the payroll. They would each get fifty dollars a week with three months guaranteed.*

Scattered along the border, the "X-stations" like XELO were licensed by the Mexican government but maintained business offices across the border. The oldest of the stations, XER, built its transmitter and antenna in Villa Acuña, Coahuila, in 1930, across the Rio Grande from Del Rio, Texas. Free of the wattage limitations imposed by the Yankees' Federal Communications Commission, the signal of XER and its successor, XERA, blanketed the entire American Midwest well into Canada.

Broadcasting from Mexico also freed promoters from Federal Trade Commission restrictions. Consequently, patent medicine and snake oil salesmen prospered on these "border blasters," selling cure-alls for feminine ailments and unlikely concoctions like J. R. Brinkly's goat-gland extract for sexual impotence.

The stations were immensely profitable—to both owners and Mexican bureaucrats, who discovered requirements for all manner of local "license fees." In short order, there were a half dozen of these stations ranged along the Mexican border, from XEAW with a transmitter in Reynosa, Tamaulipas, on the Gulf Coast, west to XELO in Tia Juana, Baja California, on the Pacific.

Programming aimed at rural, less sophisticated audiences offered a stream of country and western singers, Pentecostal evangelists, and shrill commercials. "If one could endure the seemingly never ending advertising, he could occasionally hear a hillbilly song of the best quality," country music historian Bill Malone wrote.

The XELO deal was too good to pass up. When Maxine and Woody told the younger Burke they had Horton's offer, Burke released them from their contractual obligation to his station. "Okay, come back when you finish your contract" with Horton, he added. (Burke knew they were saleable. *The Woody and Lefty Lou Show* had had a succession of sponsors: the headache remedy had been replaced by Victor Clothing Company, which specialized in work clothes and uniforms, and by a local firm that sold inexpensive perfumes.)

A noisy caravan of crowded automobiles pulled into the auto court in the tiny town of Chula Vista, just over the border from Tia Juana, on January 25, 1938. Woody, Mary, and their two children were to occupy one cabin, Jeff, Allene, and their child another. The Crissmans, father, mother,

---

* In a 1971 interview with E. Victor and Judy Wolfenstein, Jeff Guthrie cast himself as the pivotal figure in the deal.

and two daughters, would take another cabin when they arrived. Matt Jennings, unable to find work as a butcher in Los Angeles and with nothing better to do, tagged along; he would flop with Woody—who had decided to throw Matt together with Maxine and hope that sparks ensued.

Things did not go well at the cavernous stone church converted to XELO's temporary studios in Tia Juana. They were on almost half the day, filling the long hours of airtime with songs, instrumentals, commercials, and more commercials. Woody and Lefty Lou had two shows to themselves, a half hour at noon and a fifteen-minute slot in the evenings. There were programs for the entire cast in the early afternoon, and then another after dinner that ran well into the night.

It was a big burden made worse because their shows were only roughly organized. Woody apparently presumed he or they could ad lib their way through the day as they had at KFVD. But in Mexico there were simply too many members of the cast.

In addition to the multiple Guthries, Horton had hired guitarist-singer Possum Trot Bruce; Jimmy Busby, a Texas-born fiddler off Los Angeles's Skid Row, who may or may not have been related by marriage to the sprawling Guthrie clan; and a talented fifteen-year-old singer-guitarist, Whitey McPherson. Collectively, they represented a hodgepodge of musical styles and temperaments. Fitting them together, with little or no rehearsal, was difficult enough, but Guthrie also had to contend with a scornful house band. Buck Evans and his boys played popular cowboy music, not the old-timey music of their grandfathers.

Then there were the commercials, long and loud, like Horton himself, peddling Peruna Tonic, Colorback hair dye, and half a dozen more of Consolidated Drug's products. Listeners often wrote to praise the music and damn the unrelenting hard-sell promotion.

Horton himself did not make things any easier. On weekends he turned up at the XELO studios, blustering about with inane suggestions, seeking to rein in one or another Guthrie. At one point he made Jeff so mad that the former policeman almost broke his beloved "panther" fiddle over his knee. At another he proposed that Maxine sing solo, a suggestion she sharply rejected.

"I don't like to sing solos."

When she persisted in her refusal, an exasperated Horton lashed out. "There's nothing keeping you here. I can play records." Maxine merely shrugged.

Undeterred, Horton was back with another idea, a fake radio romance between Maxine and Buck Evans. Maxine summarily scotched that notion.

Finally, Woody was as furious with Horton's meddling as Maxine had ever seen him. "Horton, why in *the* hell don't you stay at home and let me run the show?" he snapped.

They were getting mail praising the program, including an encouraging postcard from Woody's musical idols, the Carter family: A. P., his wife Sara, and sister-in-law Maybelle. Not long after, Woody and Maxine received a telegram from United Traders Drug Company, sponsor of WLS's *National Barn Dance*. United Traders wanted Woody and Maxine on its nationwide broadcast.

Horton was excited; other acts from XELO had gone on to WLS and had made it big.

The mail came from as far away as Indianapolis, Indiana, where Minnie Dittmeyer's father heard the nighttime program clearly enough to write in requests. A letter from Canada brought down humorless local authorities when Woody read the note on the air and casually remarked, "Looks like we smuggled some songs into Canada."

That afternoon as they were returning for the evening show, the *Federales* arrested Guthrie at the border. He was to be charged with smuggling. Or insulting Mexico. Something. The charges were never very clear.

"The rest of the evening was chaotic," Maxine remembered. First a frantic Mary wailed that the *Federales* were going to send her husband to Mexico City. Then Maxine and Allene were in tears.

Woody was in custody, and "we were stranded in a foreign land—without our 'leader.' We were very worried," Maxine commented later. "[We] had heard awful stories regarding Mexico City's jail."

Guthrie turned up hours later, in the middle of the program, bringing some order to that night's show. He had managed to talk himself out of trouble.

But not for long. Apparently at Horton's instigation, a squad of six armed soldiers marched into the XELO building and ordered Guthrie and his friends from the country. An army officer informed them in English that their visas did not have the necessary work permits to continue broadcasting. They would be arrested if they returned to work in the morning.

The show of force was intimidating. As the officer and his detail marched off, Guthrie heaved a big sigh. "*Damn*, I thought that old boy was going to lash us up against the wall and shoot us."

After three weeks, the Mexican adventure was over. Horton ducked out without paying the group's last two weeks' salary. The tantalizing WLS offer also mysteriously vanished.*

They were a chastened bunch returning to Los Angeles, the Crissmans now without a house and all of them broke. Without so much as a telephone call, on February 16, 1938, Woody and Maxine strode into KFVD, newly moved to studios on South Western Avenue near Wilshire, shortly before their formerly scheduled program time.

"We been looking for you," Frank Burke Jr. boomed. "Cross the hall and to your left."

As simply as that, they returned to KFVD.

The Woody and Lefty Lou Show resumed in the mornings as if they had never left. Burke Junior still had a contract with them, and his sales manager could peddle commercial time on their program. Moreover, Burke's mother was fond of the hymns and gospel songs Woody and Lefty Lou sang.

Still Guthrie was broke. Burke even loaned his star performer twenty dollars to pay his share of the rent—they had moved back in with cousin Amalee on Baywood—and to buy groceries. For some weeks three-year-old Teeny strutted about and announced to those within earshot that she had eaten "beans, bones and taters" for dinner.

With their return to KFVD, the stream of letters to Woody and Lefty Lou resumed. They were once again the most popular performers at the station, easily outdrawing even Stuart Hamblen, who had taken over KFVD's 1:00-to-2:00 A.M. time slot. Hamblen, Maxine recalled, was "Mr. Big" in country music in Los Angeles, long established and very popular; within two weeks of their arrival, the humbled Hamblen had moved his *Covered Wagon Jubilee* to another station.

Burke responded to the listeners' mail—eventually, Maxine would estimate, they received ten thousand pieces in a ten-month period—by moving the Woody and Lefty Lou program to a choice 1:00-to-1:30 P.M. slot, six days a week. They could easily be home for dinner, even after answering their mail.

The house on Baywood Street grew a bit more crowded when Guthrie's younger brother George turned up on the doorstep shortly after their

---

* Maxine was to learn later that Horton had used the work-permit dodge repeatedly on other musical groups. Seemingly, he never bothered with the permits, but bribed authorities when he wanted groups to stay. Apparently, he was happy to be rid of the fiercely independent Guthrie. Maxine also stated that she suspected Horton had secretly recorded their program for rebroadcast from Piedras Negras, Mexico; friends in the Midwest wrote later to say they had heard her on the air.

Ed Cray

return from Mexico. Woody was doing so well, George thought he might try his luck in California too.

Roy Crissman solved the cramped quarters of the Baywood house when he found a vacant three-bedroom home around the corner from Jeff and Allene. The Crissmans and Guthries would share the household expenses: Woody, Mary, and their two daughters would sleep in the rear bedroom; Roy and Georgia Crissman in the middle bedroom; Maxine, her sister Mary, and Mary's new baby boy in the front bedroom; and George on the couch in the front room.

When industrious George found a job as a box boy in a local market, Matt decided to return to Texas. Perhaps George could succeed in California, but Matt had had no luck there. Los Angeles had more than enough country fiddlers and too many good butchers. George replaced Matt as Maxine's *duenna* when she was with Woody. It was a happy task; George promptly developed a crush on the attractive Maxine.

Jeff and Allene were to follow Matt soon after. A foot of rain in the first week of March 1938 brought widespread flooding throughout Southern California. Streets became raging spillways, intersections flooded to cover wheel hubs. More than 130 people died in the floods; many of them were literally washed out to sea, their bodies never recovered.

From a concrete bridge hardly a mile from his house, Woody watched the muddy, torrential waters of the Los Angeles River churn under his feet and went home to write a lachrymose ballad about the storm and its victims.*

For Jeff, discouraged after the XELO debacle, it was a last blow. "You could see houses and automobiles and everything going down that river," he vividly recalled more than three decades later. "We were scared to death, afraid they were going to wash everybody right out to the ocean. I said, 'Just as soon as it dries enough, we're gettin' out of here.'"

Jeff bought an old Nash for thirty bucks, loaded everything he, Allene, and their child owned, and returned to Texas. California didn't need either a slick magician or a tricky fiddler, but there were always jobs in Texas for a good fingerprint man.

Through the spring of that year *The Woody and Lefty Lou Show* remained

---

* Farther north, weeks of winter rain flooded the transformed desert that was the San Joaquin Valley, leaving tens of thousands of migrants "hungry, sick, cold and wet. Newspapermen flocked to the scene of the natural disaster and everywhere discovered a human disaster. . . . The Okies had become an immediate visible problem, and the state's newspapers, urban and rural, hammered the migrant's misery into the public consciousness." See Walter J. Stein, *California and the Dust Bowl Migration,* (Westport, Conn.: Greenwood Press, 1973), p. 76.

the most popular one on KFVD. George worked in the mornings, then rushed home to join Woody and Maxine before they left for the station. Brother Woodrow meanwhile spent his mornings daubing at oil paintings in the Crissmans' garage; the crumbling Santa Barbara mission with its three arches was a repeated subject. Though he sold none of his oils, he swapped six of them to a neighborhood merchant for a Martin guitar; others he gave away as prizes to listeners who wrote from the farthest point from Los Angeles. (One winner wrote from West Virginia.)

Woody spent even more time at the typewriter in the first months of this rainy 1938. Increasingly, the songs he and Lefty Lou sang on the air fused humor with a growing social sensitivity.

The first of these was Guthrie's revision of a gospel song he learned from a Carter Family recording, "I Can't Feel at Home in This World Any More."

> *I ain't got no home, I'm just a-roaming round.*
> *Just a wandering worker, I go from town to town.*
> *The police make it hard wherever I may go,*
> *And I ain't got no home in this world any more.*

> *My brothers and my sisters are stranded on this road.*
> *It's a hot and dusty road, that a million feet have trod.*
> *Rich man took my home and drove me from my door,*
> *And I ain't got no home in this world any more.*

Guthrie was paying more attention to the newspapers, and from them acquiring a broader vision of the world. On his copy of "Chinese-Japs" he jotted a reminder, "Rewrite with better slant on the chinamen." Once a parochial young man from a small town in Oklahoma would have washed his hands of the entire war in China; now Guthrie could see that questions of right and wrong extended beyond the borders of his narrow world.

Sometime in the first months after returning to KFVD, he borrowed from *Grand Ole Opry*'s Robert Lunn the unusual talking blues form that Lunn had picked up from blacks in the South. To a simple walking bass line, Guthrie drawled:

> *The land around here's mighty poor,*
> *We don't own the place no more—*
> *You work all year on a place like this,*
> *And you ain't got change for fifteen cents.*

*This land is so poor that th' grasshoppers has got
to hop three times to break even. You couldn't
raise an argument on it.*

*I got a gal just through the slew,
Everybody calls her Shotgun Sue,
Shoots off at her mouth and full of wind,
She's a pretty good gal for the shape she's in.*

    *Her land is so rich that the fruit trees wear the
apples out waving them around in the air. Vines
wears the watermelons out a-draggin them around over
the patch. Grass grows so high on her place that
she goes in the hole 'cause she cain't find her
farm.*

It was droll. It hinted of social inequities, cloaking them in the cornpone humor of "On a Slow Train to Arkansas." The malleable talking blues form was to serve Guthrie repeatedly in years to come.

Beyond the hymns and gospel songs he and Maxine sang, Guthrie's songs often took on a moralistic or cautionary tone. A newspaper story inspired him to write "Reckless Drivers":

*You drunken drivers, come listen to my tale.
Your drinkin' and drivin's gonna get you in jail.
You can't drink likker and drive at the wheel,
You're bound to git lousy in Lincoln Heights jail.*

    **   *   *   **

*You lousy drivers, come listen to my tale.
Your smart-aleck drivin's gonna get you in jail;
One crack to the cop and you land in the cell;
And they all get lousy in Lincoln Heights jail.**

* In a tongue-in-cheek autobiographical sketch, Guthrie wrote, "I'm just a pore boy tryin' to get along. The dust run me out of Texas, and the Officers run me in at Lincoln Heights. But they was nice to me. They had bars fixed up over the windows so nobody could get in an steal my guitar." Guthrie may have been held overnight in the jail's drunk tank, or the song may have been inspired by cousin Jack Guthrie's arrest for failing to respond to various traffic citations. The quote is from "Woody and Lefty Lou's Favorite Collection [of] Old Time Hill Country Songs," (Gardena, Calif.: Institute Press, 1938 [?]).

Repeated listener requests for songs and for lyrics prompted Guthrie to compile a twenty-eight-page mimeographed songbook, "Woody and Lefty Lou's Favorite Collection [of] Old Time Hill Country Songs." The younger Burke's office was strewn with papers, ink, and mimeograph masters. Guthrie took the stacks of printed sheets home, where he, Mary, and Teeny assembled, then stapled them into booklet form.

Guthrie included in the songbook nineteenth-century parlor songs he had learned from his mother, songs and ballads he had picked up on the road somewhere between Oklahoma and California, and his own compositions. He filled the blank space at the foot of each page with medicine show jokes and romantic noodlings.

Ma never claimed to be an artist. She was a bit shy when the folks would ask her to play and sing. But she had a sort of a tender heart, made that way by suffering a lot of things, and by carrying big loads, and she went deeper, and tried to tell the "story" or the "thought" that is so rich in these old Hill Country songs. I was about six years old at that time, but I resolved in my heart to try to understand her singing inside her warm heart.

Writing about the original theme song he and Jack Guthrie sang, Woody attributed "Lonesome Road Blues" to "an old Colored Slave who was figgerin on runnin off from his master, cause his master was too much of a master." Then the young man who just six months before had peopled the "Santa Monica Examine 'Er" with "niggers," "coons," and "darkies" added:

I believe the Colored Slaves of old Dixie lived directly and closely in contact with an unseen Something or Other that we call Inspiration, a Something too many of us are too busy to pay any attention to.

Over time, the station mailed more than four hundred of the songbooks to listeners who requested copies. (Guthrie kept two hundred, which he sold at the infrequent personal appearances he and Maxine made.) When his supply of songbooks ran out, Guthrie reran the mimeograph stencils—an increasingly messy task—a second and perhaps a third time, according to Maxine Crissman.

Eventually Burke offered to underwrite publishing the songbooks at a printshop. If nothing else, it would remove the smudged mess from his office, once and for all.

But Burke's offer only inspired Guthrie's efforts. He began typing the manuscript for a new collection of 101 songs and ballads to be sold for a dollar.

With all their success, perhaps because it was *too* easy, Guthrie began to be restless. Maxine remembered dropping him on the edge of heavily traveled San Fernando Road after their midday broadcast. Even as he waved goodbye to her, "he would do a sort of Mississippi shuffle and I have seen three cars stop at once, wanting to pick him up."

The next morning he would be back, ready to go to the station, never offering an explanation of where he had been or an apology to Mary.

On the air, Guthrie became more headstrong, even contrary. When listeners wrote to complain that he talked too much—Maxine tended to agree—Guthrie deliberately spun longer tales. When Maxine, who seemed to grow more easily fatigued, wanted to go home, Guthrie would sail into long conversations with the night disc jockey, Jack Bell.

Maxine found it harder and harder to stay out late. She suffered from anemia, and the frantic pace since going on the air the previous August had taken its toll. She gave up trips with Woody to the Central Library and to used-book stores downtown or to the incongruous, Pleistocene La Brea Tar Pits on busy Wilshire Boulevard. She lost weight. Increasingly, she paused to catch her breath on the stairs in KFVD's studios. No longer did they playfully hold a note for twenty or thirty seconds, just to try to outdo the other. She was hardly able to finish a song now; Woody was necessarily carrying more and more of the show.

"It was time to take off," she concluded.

Burke Junior suggested they suspend the program for six weeks to three months, then return to finish out the year's contract. Maxine could rest up. In the meantime, his father had a proposal for Guthrie.

Burke Senior, the editor of the air, was serving as southern California chairman for the Democratic nominee for governor of California. Onetime Socialist Culbert Olson had come to the Golden State after a successful career in Utah and had plunged into local politics. In due course, he was elected Los Angeles County's sole state senator, and one of the few voices of liberalism in a reactionary state legislature comfortable in the bosom of railroads, oil companies, and corporate agriculture.

The month before, Burke had started a weekly newspaper, the *Light*. The eight-page paper doubled as Olson's campaign sheet and a platform for Burke's causes: group health plans, unions, and an end to exploitation of farm laborers. Since Guthrie was going off the air, Burke suggested that the songwriter might be interested in working on a series of stories covering the plight of the Okies in California.

Guthrie, with nothing better to do, agreed.

There was a small condition. As the capstone for the series, Burke proposed that Guthrie demonstrate incumbent Governor Frank Merriam's indifference to the wretched conditions of farm workers by getting himself arrested in the state capitol. No stranger to jails, Guthrie agreed.

As a writer for the *Light*, Guthrie came to politics. In an early "Cornbread Philosophy" column for the paper, Guthrie acknowledged he was a Democrat. What son of Charley Guthrie could be otherwise?

"I am trying to elect Olson for Governor. I heard he was for the Little Man. And I'm not but 5 ft. 6, and weigh a hundred and twenty with a bowl of chili."

He was still the droll country humorist, like the much-admired Will Rogers, vaudeville star, movie actor, and widely syndicated newspaper humorist. Radio performer Woody Guthrie sought to make the same leap, less visibly, but more the partisan.

On Saturday, June 18, 1938, some ten months after they first went on the air together, Woody and Lefty Lou from Old Mizzou broadcast together for the last time.

It was an emotional parting, for both performers and audience. After ten months and some ten thousand letters, they were like family, all of them striving to make a living in this strange, glorious country of California, yet yearning for distant homes. Woody was like their son, and Lefty Lou their daughter, doing whatever it took to get by. Other listeners fancied Woody and Lefty Lou a married couple from someplace "Back Home," young and hopeful in this land at the end of the West. Woody's self-deprecating descriptions of himself as a raggedy wanderer prompted concerned listeners to invite them to dinner. A casual mention of a birthday produced crushed-in-the-mail cakes and boxes of home-baked cookies.

On that last broadcast, Guthrie announced he would become the *Light*'s roving "hobo correspondent." First he planned to ride freights five hundred miles north to Chico, California, where hungry migrant farmworkers anxiously waited for the almonds and peaches to come in. From there, well, they could read the *Light* to find out.

To his surprise, Roy Crissman accepted Woody's casual invitation to come along. Crissman was toying with the idea of moving north and wanted to see the country before he made a decision.

On Sunday evening, the Crissmans drove the two men to the San Fernando yards of the Southern Pacific. There they heaved themselves into a slow-moving freight car—Roy hauling Woody up by the belt. As the train picked up speed, they could see in the twilight Jack Guthrie and Maxine singing to a small crowd at a San Fernando Road open-air market.

The way north was uneventful. Woody and Roy jumped off their freight car outside Chico and slept under a bridge the first night. (The next day they sent a postcard home from the "Greenleaf Hotel," Woody's sardonic reference to their outdoor accommodations.)

The two men spent a week together surveying the fields and orchards, the small towns and migrant camps before parting in the Tracy railyards. Roy was to return to Glendale; Woody was off to gather material for his newspaper articles. Roy had decided to move his family to Chico, which reminded him of his hometown, Creighton, Missouri. They agreed to rendezvous in the Chico town square a month later.

Guthrie hitchhiked to Sacramento with the idea of getting arrested. As he told the story to Maxine—it would be elaborated in later retellings—he walked into the capitol, unslung his guitar, and started singing in the marble rotunda. A crowd of secretaries and tourists applauded his impromptu serenade, and some good-naturedly threw coins for him. After a few songs, capitol police simply escorted Guthrie from the building—but not before he swept up and pocketed the change on the floor.

For a month he drifted from noisome Hoovervilles in the northern San Joaquin to smartly maintained farm labor camps run by the federal government. He slept in fetid ditches alongside country roads, covered only with cardboard, and in dismal hotels in the larger cities. He was on Stockton's skid row, then in Tracy, hanging around the railyard.

By prearrangement, on July 25 Guthrie was waiting when the entire Crissman family pulled into Chico's town square. Together they set up a tent among other migrant families camped in the oak groves on the banks of the Sacramento River. By day they looked for work. At night, Maxine and Woody sang by the campfire, entertaining folks who had listened to their radio program. A scant half hour was all the still anemic Maxine could manage.

For two weeks Woody and the Crissmans scraped by, living on fish they caught in the river, on wild rabbits they trapped, and on boxes of early peaches stolen from neighboring orchards. "It was peach-picking season," Guthrie wrote bitterly, "but a million carloads of good peaches were going to rot and nobody hiring to pick them." Bringing too much fruit to market would inevitably lower the price the big growers received.

The squalor and deprivation he saw this summer of 1938 rasped on him. He had seen hunger before, while tramping the Southwest, but armored in the self-absorption of the young, he had paid little heed.

In this fifth year of Franklin D. Roosevelt's New Deal, an older Woody Guthrie saw with a new understanding. These migrants were desperate amid plenty, proud folk trapped by the "crooked work and starvation going on all around."

The migrants were *his* people. They were the Okies who had listened to *The Woody and Lefty Lou Show*, who had written to him and Maxine at KFVD and had sent gifts, who had shared stories of their hard times and their abiding faith. He knew them; they were family.

Twenty-six-year-old Woody Guthrie was angry.

CHAPTER TEN

The Workhunters

*G*UITAR SLUNG OVER his back, a stained fedora clapped over his curly hair, Woody Guthrie left Chico and the migrants' riverfront encampment in the early summer of 1938. If he knew where he was going or when he would be back, he did not say. That was just Woody, Maxine Crissman said with a shrug. "He was always this way."

Just where he traveled in that restless summer and fall is not clear. In later writings he suggested he hopped a Union Pacific freight over the Sierra Nevada and dropped off in Reno. Arrested and booked for vagrancy, he spent a grim night in the Reno jail talking to a drug-addicted doctor charged with performing an illegal abortion.

Released the next day, Guthrie hitchhiked south to Carson City. He visited Virginia City and the Comstock Lode, then the dying mining town of Tonopah, all the while drifting southward in the scorched Nevada desert.

In early September the hitchhiking Guthrie was stranded for two days in Barstow, California. With hundreds of other sweating men, he stood on the sandy shoulder of the highway in 120-degree heat, waiting for a lift "and getting nowhere.

"These people are mostly the ones who have tired of marching with the starvation armies of wandering workers and grown weary of the smell of rotting fruit crops," he reported in the *Light* on September 9. "Bewildered and flat broke, they are trying to get back somewhere or other where the meals come oftener."

His telephoned reports to the paper's offices were restrained, perhaps because of editing, yet forceful:

Migration to California has no doubt slowed down, and it looks like the railroads and the city police officers have suddenly decided to detain all the migratory workers along the roads that they can in order to have free labor for their pea and bean patches.

The constant dread of the wandering worker is to be arrested by some city officer, charged with idleness or vagrancy and sent in almost chain gang style to the bean patch to work without pay.

Abandoning the highway in the Southern Pacific's Barstow yards, Guthrie swung aboard a freight headed east. He traveled as far as McAlester, Oklahoma, talking to migrants along the way. He apparently hitchhiked on his return trip to visit Okemah and boyhood friends there, then retraced the migrants' journey westward along the "Mother Road," Route 66.

At the foot of the Sierra Nevada, Guthrie turned northward, his intention to revisit Chico and persuade Maxine to return with him to KFVD. By train or by thumb, Guthrie found his way over the Tehachapis and down into Kern County, then roiled by a strike in the cotton fields.

No hand at picking cotton himself, and not one to take another man's job in any event, Guthrie watched from the edge of the road as the American Legion's vigilantes in their "black sedans with hot searchlights" scattered picket lines with flailing axe handles.

Guthrie was angered by the "vij-ees" and the grinning sheriff's deputies who watched benignly as the strikers fled. For the first time, Guthrie left the road to join the "several thousand cotton choppers, pickers, and field workers of every kind . . . [the] barefooted, with signs in their hands that said they was on a strike to get more money for their work, on a strike to get the mean cops booted out."

Dorothy Healey, a strike organizer, remembered Guthrie at the Kern County mass meetings, guitar over his shoulder, almost lost in a crowd of strikers gathered in a great empty field. But once he slipped the guitar from behind his back and began singing to the strikers, the skinny young man was transformed. The hobo correspondent and his audience shared a sense of understanding, even a kind of love. A half century later, Healey easily recalled the intensity, the understanding.

The November election looming, and with it the end of his assignment as the *Light*'s correspondent, Guthrie left the strike fields to rejoin the struggling Crissman family in Chico. He and Maxine sang one night for tips in a bar. They raked in six dollars over a two-hour period, but the performance left her exhausted.

It was the last time they would sing together. No matter how much Woody wanted her to resume singing on KFVD, Maxine simply lacked the stamina to continue with the program. Furthermore, she had met a young man in whom she was interested; his work was in the north. Her singing career was over.

The Woody Guthrie who returned alone to Los Angeles near the first of November 1938 was different from the wanderer who had left Pampa eighteen months earlier. His journeys from June through October had given the aimless radio singer a compelling sense of purpose.

The misery Guthrie saw that summer and fall struck him hard. For the first time, this man who masked his serious thoughts with deflecting humor spoke to his wife about what he had seen, "about people being hungry and not having a place to live." The plight of the migrants, "dust bowl refugees" he now called them, was pathetic. "His main object in life from then on was to help the poor man."

Her husband still cared nothing for money for himself or his family, Mary Guthrie added with a faint tone of exasperation. He agreed to return to KFVD as "Woody, the Lone Wolf," paid a dollar a day to cover transportation and lunch money. If he found sponsors as he had with Lefty Lou, he would split the fees.

Once again, he was not "doing the manly thing," Mary complained. As her brother Matt put it, Guthrie loved his family, "but had this idea of equality [that] all children are equal. 'Mine aren't better than anyone else's.' " Emotionally, the runny-nosed kids of the migrants playing in the fields were his children too.

The Okies and Arkies, the Texicans and Jayhawkers, had become Woody's people. They were rootless, ground down, stripped of farms and jobs back east, shorn of their dignity in California. Even the coined name "Okie" had become a snarled epithet, a euphemism for the shiftless and the unemployed. Yet as poor as they were, living in wretched hovels, in battered autos, and badly patched tents up and down the Golden State, they were hardly idle.

They were desperate. They "were running away from idleness and debt and a great natural calamity, the great and terrible dust storms . . . to look for work and more work. And fair and decent treatment and honest pay."

To the migrants and for their cause, Guthrie was singing "some new songs in the old way about the sights of people living hungrier than rats and dirtier than dogs in a land of the sun and a valley of night breezes."

The workhunters, as he called them, had somehow endured. They had traveled a thousand wearying miles and more on U.S. 66 before they crossed over the muddy Colorado River into California, that promised Garden of Eden. They filled canvas waterbags for steaming radiators, then pressed on until flagged down by state Department of Agriculture inspectors outside of Needles. Did they have any fresh fruit or vegetables? Nuts? Any cotton-picking sacks? Their meager food they would have to leave here in quarantine for two weeks—if they cared to come back for it. The cotton sacks would have to be boiled in large vats to kill any nesting boll weevils.

Some days the migrants made it through the inspection quickly. Other times they waited in slow-moving lines under the stifling desert sun while bored inspectors painstakingly picked through the luggage in overburdened automobiles. Finally past the barrier, they drove on, angry or frightened, but stigmatized as diseased, as outsiders, as "Okies."

Their crowded autos and sagging trucks lumbered west over the two-lane blacktop. Ahead lay Barstow, through 160 miles of parched Mojave Desert, through spring windstorms that could blow even heavy trucks from the road, through summer's radiator-bursting temperatures that hovered at 110 degrees in the dark of night.

In bedraggled Barstow, the muddy Fords and battered Chevrolets paused momentarily. Here was the parting of the ways. Those who turned north on 466, across the Tehachapi range, then down into the San Joaquin, toward Arvin, Earlimart, and Farmersville, would look for work in the valley's "factories in the fields." Those who continued west, toward Los Angeles, would take any job they could find, at whatever pay was offered.

Rumors of work in harvesting grapes, or topping sugar beets, or picking apricots and peaches drew the migrants northward. Whispers of jobs in Los Angeles warehouses and factories lured them westward. "Destinies were set by the decision to go right or straight," wrote historian Dan Morgan in chronicling the story of one Okie family.

The migrants came by the tens of thousands. They came even when there was no work to be had. They came, lured by handbills distributed from Oklahoma to Arizona by agricultural associations touting high wages in the Golden State. A labor surplus assured growers a supply of hungry people ready to work for a penny less than their neighbor.

At the behest of the politically powerful Associated Farmers of California, relief administrators purged their rolls of clients and ordered them to work in the fields. As Los Angeles County's relief administrator blandly explained, "We have to solve the farmers' problem, even if it does work hardships." He dispatched some hapless laborers 500 miles north to the peach orchards and others 250 miles easterly to the cotton fields of the Imperial Valley.

In reality, there was no labor shortage by the time Woody Guthrie first made his way to California in the spring of 1937, and no shortage in the summer of 1938 when he and Maxine went off the air.

The flow of migrants westward had steadily increased in inverse proportion to rainfall in the Great Plains. The drier the growing season "back home," the poorer the crop, and the harder it became for sharecropping families to hold on. Compounding the problem was the fact that southern-grown short-staple cotton could not compete with the higher-quality long-staple imports from India and, particularly, Egypt.

Contrary to the myth, the great majority of the people on the roads were neither blown out by windstorms nor tractored out by farm mechanization. In eastern Oklahoma, untouched by the dust storms, landlords and bankers were evicting tenant farmers in order to turn patchworks of small farms into vast cattle ranges. "For every farmer who was dusted out or tractored out," Guthrie came to understand, "another ten were chased out by bankers."

Landlords arbitrarily refused to renew sharecroppers' leases and razed the shacks in which they had lived. The displaced families moved on, first to ever poorer farms, then to Oklahoma City or Tulsa, later to the auto factories of Detroit and the beckoning cotton fields of Arizona and California.

As many as 1.25 million Americans were on the road in these last years of the 1930s. If some were the perpetually restless—the shabby hoboes and footsore tramps who hitchhiked the highways and humped the rail lines—most of the migrants moved only to find steady jobs somewhere and settle down. An estimated 350,000 of the dispossessed were to remain in California, more than half of them in the San Joaquin Valley, where they would provide an easily exploited pool of cheap labor.

When the seasons changed and the walnuts had been bagged, the last cotton, lettuce, and 'chokes shipped to market, the suddenly unemployable workers became "Okies." Texan Buck Owens, later to become a major country music figure, remembered the signs, "No Okies Allowed in Store," propped in the shop windows of his hometown Bakersfield. "Well, I knew I wasn't from Oklahoma, but I knew who they was talking about."

California's highways teemed with migrants looking for work, following rumors of work in the lemon orchards of Ventura or in the hops fields north of Marysville. The more fortunate slept in dismal auto courts, cooking outdoors. The rest slept where they found shelter, thousands camping out along the roadside in tents and cardboard boxes or crowding into fetid farm labor camps. Entire families crammed into a single room without running water or flush toilets, struggling to find a bit of privacy and preserve some shard of dignity.

The poorest among the migrants were stripped even of that. Wracked by ringworm, by influenza, deprived of milk, their infants died wasting deaths. Their toddlers walked about the scabrous campsites with swollen bellies that marked the malnourished. In this sixth year of the New Deal, child and adult alike fell victim to the diseases of poverty: typhoid, tuberculosis, and smallpox. Without cash, without credit, denied relief because they were not permanent residents, the migrants sold off their possessions, one by one, until, their spirits crushed, they were reduced to abject poverty.

The migrants camped where they could. Guthrie ruefully joked he had relatives living under every bridge in California. Hoovervilles or shacktowns sprang up everywhere as squatters pitched "cardboard, pasteboard and orange-crate houses, old rotten tents, dirty slick huts, furnished with old broke down furniture from the dumps."

Then, Guthrie added, his anger seeping through, sheriff's deputies periodically swept through the camps and forced the migrants to "hit the highway. . . .

"A drunk man dont like his own vomit. And a dizzy Profet System dont like it's own filth."

The best places to set down were in the federal government's thirteen labor camps scattered from Brawley in the Imperial Valley to the northernmost in Gridley, amid the peach orchards and hops fields. Run by the Farm Security Administration (FSA), these camps offered decent shelter, fresh running water, showers, and laundries. While the cabins were small, they were clean, and many had a nurse to tend the children's ailments. Compared to the filthy grounds run by farmers or labor contractors, life in the FSA compounds was living high off the hog, Guthrie's onetime schoolmate Bertha Bryan Edmoundson decided.

"We weren't used to having anything too much, so if we just had a decent living, food to eat, shelter, we thought we were living quite well," said Edmoundson, married, with the "two little ones" she and her husband Earl took to the fields with them each day in Arvin.

Alongside hundreds of other migrants, Bertha and Earl chopped cotton, laid irrigation pipes, spread eye-stinging sulfur to kill pests, picked table grapes for a cent and a half per thirty-five-pound tray, and celebrated the glorious day the two of them laid out 159 trays. Such good times came rarely, but at least they scratched out a living in Arvin.

For the Edmoundsons, and tens of thousands of Okies like them, there was one problem. The self-governing FSA camps could accommodate at most 3,500 families, perhaps 20,000 people in all. Meanwhile, as many as 250,000 just like Bertha and Earl were roaming the state's highways, looking for work.

Those who came were "hard workers, fine people for the most part," windworn and sunburned folks with a family to support, torn between homesickness and the knowledge that they could make a living in California, but not in Missouri, Arkansas, Oklahoma, or Texas. Some, like the Edmoundsons, never overcame the sense of loss; they would travel back and forth to Oklahoma again and again.

Woody Guthrie had grown up with these people. Like them he had come west in search of a new beginning. Like them he had been awed by the sheer grandeur of California, by the state's bountiful harvests, its "greener valleys where the rain drops are big and the wind is almost tender."

Some of the migrants managed to put down roots, to settle in the "Little Oklahoma" subdivisions that sprouted alongside the squatter camps. But most saw the promised blessings snatched from them, their lives reduced to disease, dashed hopes, and a dark future.

For the first time, in the summer of 1938, Woody Guthrie saw beyond his workaday world, beyond the unfulfilling psychology texts and books of eastern mysticism in the Pampa Public Library. He had found a social conscience and a cause worth fighting for.

Guthrie returned to Los Angeles just days before the gubernatorial election that would put a Democrat, a New Deal Democrat at that, in the governor's office for the first time in the twentieth century. He was effectively unemployed—the *Light* would fold before the end of the year—and had no prospects beyond what Frank Burke offered him at KFVD.

Without Maxine, Woody the Lone Wolf fared poorly; he urged his listeners to write the station, asking for Maxine to return to the air. Despite the letters, she refused.

To supplement his dollar a day, Guthrie sang for tips in the bars along "The Nickel," Los Angeles's Fifth Street Skid Row. Sometimes he made personal appearances at markets.

To fill his days, Guthrie hung about the station after his midday show, mimeographing songbooks he sold to listeners for a quarter, typing when he could cadge a typewriter, and listening to KFVD's programs.

In the hall one day he stopped Ed Robbin, who broadcast a nightly news commentary program with a decidedly leftward tilt. He had been listening to Robbin, Guthrie said, and liked what he heard. Guthrie suggested the two of them go out for a beer when Robbin went off the air at 6:45.

"There are a few things I'd like to just kind of talk over with you, if you don't mind," Guthrie offered.

Ed Robbin, like Guthrie, was another of the idiosyncratic J. Frank Burke's fliers. He was far too radical for the city's other stations. Burke, on the other hand, was unfazed by Robbin's commentary, which emphatically "slanted to the left, [and] talked about the struggles of workers and unions, [while standing] against war and fascism."

Like Guthrie, Ed Robbin had come to Los Angeles in search of opportunity. Born in Chicago in 1905 the son of Russian-Jewish immigrants—the family name was originally Rabinowitz—Robbin had graduated from the University of Chicago with his boyhood friend Meyer Levin. This was 1925; both were keen to become writers. Europe, particularly France, beckoned to the aspiring artists of that postwar generation.

Robbin and Levin, joined by the campus dramatic club's director, Bill Geer, set off in 1925. They hitchhiked to Montreal where they each paid fifteen dollars for the privilege of working their way to Great Britain on a rusting cattle boat.

Moving on to Paris, they hung about Left Bank cafés long enough for Robbin to meet, woo, and move in with "a little Sorbonne girl." Geer meanwhile disappeared into that city's flesh pots, not to be seen again.

Levin and Robbin bicycled from Paris to Vienna, where for the first time they saw a European ghetto. "We were shocked and frightened at the misery, the lack of dignity, the hopelessness of the inhabitants," Levin recalled in his memoirs a quarter century later. Out of curiosity, the two men traveled to Palestine, where they discovered the antidote to the hopelessness of Vienna's Jews. "Here were Jews like early Americans, riding guard at night in vigilance against hostile natives, pioneering in the malarial marshes, and living in communal groups," Levin wrote.

Robbin was to spend four years in Palestine, working on an English-language newspaper in Jerusalem, living on a kibbutz and soaking up the socialist politics of the kibbutzim. He married and fathered a child who died in infancy. The death of the infant shattered him and destroyed his marriage.

Robbin returned to the United States with a second wife, Clara, as tiny as Robbin was big, as quiet as he was brash, and as firm in her radical passions as he was in his. Depression-era Chicago offered no opportunity for a would-be writer, so Robbin moved to California. An uncle who ran a string of gambling parlors in beach cities offered Robbin a job.

Both Robbin and his wife plunged into radical politics in Los Angeles, supporting fledgling unions in a resolutely open-shop city, raising money—Robbin was good at that—in what he called "the struggle against fascism and Naziism," and eventually joining the Communist Party.

Ed joined out of idealism, Robbin's younger brother Morton said. A number of Ed's friends were black, and only the Communists seemed truly concerned with the plight of the Negro in America. Injustice and a feeling for the underdog impelled him ever leftward.

"The Left was his life," Mort concluded. The Robbin home on Preston Avenue in Los Angeles's Silver Lake District became a gathering place for leftists of all stripes. The spare bedroom was an added convenience.

By the time Woody Guthrie returned to KFVD late in 1938, Ed Robbin was bureau chief and sole reporter in Los Angeles for the party's newspaper in California, the *People's Daily World*. In his daily news commentary on KFVD, he railed against fascism in Europe and the German-American Bund at home, pointing out poverty amid plenty, arguing against Jim Crow laws in the South and de facto segregation in Los Angeles.

"I always listen to your program," Guthrie began. Robbin, assuming Guthrie was just another "hosses in the sunset" cowboy singer, could not return the compliment.

Guthrie had heard Robbin speaking about a guest scheduled to appear on his program. He wanted to know more about the framed-up Tom Mooney and why Robbin had invited Mooney to KFVD.

It was an old story retold, of decades-long, often bloody warfare between workers and the industrialists who employed them.

Shortly after his inauguration in January 1939, the newly elected governor of California, Culbert Olson, granted an unconditional pardon to onetime labor organizer and, more lately, labor martyr Tom Mooney. Convicted by perjurious testimony and sketchy identifications, Mooney had served twenty-two years and five months in San Quentin for bombing a 1916 San Francisco Preparedness Day parade in which ten people were killed and forty-four injured.

During that time, "Free Tom Mooney" had become an international slogan and an enduring cause for the Left. Under pressure from President Woodrow Wilson, the governor of California had commuted Mooney's death sentence to life; the first Democratic governor in the century had eventually pardoned him.

Robbin's interview with Mooney went badly. Each question triggered "fulminating oratory. Tom Mooney had become, for him, a cause that existed apart from himself." Despite that, an inspired Guthrie showed up at KFVD the next day with a new song:

Mr. Tom Mooney is FREE!
Mr. Tom Mooney is FREE!
Done got a pardon from the old jail house warden,
Mr. Culbert L. Olson's decree.

How does it feel to be FREE?
How does it feel to be FREE?
How does it feel to be out of jail
Since Olson has given you liberty?

Twenty-two years have gone by,
Twenty-two years have gone by,
And he spent the twenty-two for a crime he didn't do.
But now your cage is open, you can fly.

Pleased with the Mooney song, and the dust bowl ballads he sang that day, Robbin invited Guthrie home for dinner. Clara always cooked enough for the unexpected guest her husband tended to bring home.

"I'm bringing home a hillbilly, a cowboy. He's a real one," Robbin warned by telephone.

Clara was instantly taken with the bushy-haired "cowboy" with the delicately drawn face. At times Guthrie seemed almost childlike. At other times, he was quiet, almost withdrawn, with an enigmatic quality about him, she said later. "As much as you had of him—" she added, then broke off lamely.

At dinner Robbin abruptly invited Guthrie to sing his song at a Mooney victory rally in downtown Los Angeles that night.

"Sure, why not," Guthrie replied.

Well, for one thing, the meeting was sponsored by the Communist Party, "and it's a politically left-wing gathering."

Guthrie shrugged. "Left wing, right wing, chicken wing—it's the same thing to me. I sing my songs wherever I can sing 'em."

Robbin was gambling that Guthrie would be allowed to sing "since the Party was not too open to folk singers" and party rallies ran to speeches, not entertainment. He had difficulty persuading the party functionaries at first, but they eventually consented to fit the skinny Okie with his bushy hair into the program—only after a series of speeches and the obligatory collection.

As Robbin recalled the mass meeting in the Embassy Auditorium that night in January 1939, spokesmen for each section of the party—youth, Negro, labor, women—droned on. Even before the main speaker, doctrinaire national Communist Party leader Robert Minor, rose to speak, people in the once-full house had begun to slip away. Guthrie sat on stage, dozing through "the sloganeering, [the] wooden phony language that grew up in the party. . . . The ordinary person could sit through a meeting and not understand a goddamn thing that was going on because of the language," Robbin groused.

It was 11:00 P.M. when Mooney himself finished speaking. Guthrie, nudged awake by Robbin, shambled to the microphone, fiddled with the guitar, told stories about meeting Ed Robbin at the station, and said he had just written a song about Tom Mooney he wanted to sing.

> Way up in old Frisco town,
> Way up in old Frisco town,
> Mr. Mooney and Billings accused of a killin'
> And railroaded, jailhouse bound.
>
> But the truth can't be tied with a chain,
> O' the truth can't be tied with a chain.
> Mr. Olson said, "O' let Tom Mooney go!
> I'm a-breakin' that long, lonesome chain."
>
> Culbert L. Olson's decree!
> Culbert L. Olson's decree!
> He took the governor's chair, said, "I do declare
> I got to set this state of California FREE!"

"Well," Robbin wrote later, "the house came down." Guthrie then sang some of his dust bowl songs. It was for Guthrie, for Robbin, perhaps for some in the audience, a euphoric, even transforming moment.

For years, the Communist Party, and the radical Industrial Workers of the World before it, had supported efforts of farmworkers to organize into unions. A succession of Republican administrations, each more reactionary than the last, had beaten down their efforts. Just two months ear-

lier, the people in the auditorium had helped to elect Olson governor, and a
new day had dawned. What more proof than a free Tom Mooney, sitting
there on stage? Surely the farmworkers, "oppressed, beaten and exploited,"
were next.

And here was this skinny guy on the stage, the very embodiment of
these people, speaking their language in better humor and song,
with the dust of his traveling still on him, a troubadour, a balladeer,
a poet . . .

Guthrie slept that night on the Robbins' living room floor. The following
morning, Ed drove him home, to the dingy house in the rear of the lot.
Mary was waiting for him, Gwen and Sue at her side. It was the first inkling
Robbin had that Guthrie was married, and that he and Mary had come to
California to settle. As Guthrie put it, remembering "that dead sea of dust"
they had left behind, "I'd rather be in jail here, than settin' down on that
farm."

In the next months, Guthrie was to draw close to the Robbin family. The
two men spent time together at the station, talking about the news of the
day. Often as not, Robbin took his newfound friend home for dinner.

Guthrie played chess with ten-year-old Dan Robbin, feigning anger
when the boy beat him. While Woody was not good at chess, Dan recalled
a half century later, the lad "really liked him. I named my dog, a mutt from
the pound, after him." Guthrie pretended to be offended; still the name
stuck.

Guthrie was to spend hours in the backyard of the house on Preston
Avenue, picking his guitar, playing with Dan and his little sister Tammy,
while making up songs for them.

Robbin also introduced Guthrie to his father, mother, and brother Mort.
The senior Robbins, Russian-born, were at first "nonplussed on meeting
Woody, an alien kind of figure in boots," Mort recalled. "They couldn't figure him out." Mort, normally reticent, was instantly taken with Guthrie,
who showed him a series of card tricks. With card tricks, with his songs,
with fanciful stories of his travels, he charmed the family. "We were all
crazy about him."

The Robbin home offered another allure: a typewriter. Guthrie would
arrive early in the morning, then spend his days feverishly typing, pulling
page after page from the roller and throwing it on the floor until he had to
go to the station for his 2:15 broadcast. Ed was impressed with Guthrie's

writing, some of it autobiographical stories of his adventures on the road. Ed, who had long wanted to be a serious writer, told Mort he wanted to pick up and save the pages Guthrie was so casually throwing away.

Once again Woody had found a surrogate home. In Ed Robbin, he would also find a sorely needed source of income and a political mentor.

CHAPTER ELEVEN

Radical with a Twang

S O EASILY, SO QUICKLY, Woody Guthrie turned the Robbin home at 1961 Preston Avenue into a refuge and a booking office, "the place to reach Woody to have him come sing," Ed Robbin explained.

The bookings were sparse. As Robbin said later, the Okie world knew all about him; the Communists of Southern California knew nothing of him. Guthrie appeared whenever he was asked to sing, the size of the audience of no concern to him. Five dollars or ten, he took it.

Guthrie was cavalier about the fees. "If you're afraid I wouldn't go over in your lodge or party, you are possibly right. In such case, just mail me $15 and I won't come. When I perform, I cut it down to $10. When for a good cause, $5. When for a better cause, I come free. If you can think of a still better one, I'll give you my service, my guitar, my hat, and sixty-five cents cash money."

"He just loved to entertain on guitar," Robbin explained. "He never mapped out what he was going to sing. His repertoire was endless, and after the end of the endlessness he just made up new songs."

At times, Mary and the two girls joined Woody and the Robbin family on trips to the beach. Most of the time, Guthrie came alone to the Robbin home and stayed as long as he liked. So far as Ed Robbin could tell, Mary seemed to accept it; after all, she said, "that's what men did."

Others were not as tolerant. Norman Pierce, a Democratic Party worker responsible for organizing the unemployed, judged Guthrie talented, but "a cocksman" who used his music to seduce girls. "Woody was a great lover of humanity in the abstract, but was rough on people individually."

If Clara Robbin was also faintly disapproving, first of Guthrie leaving his wife and children for days at a time, then of the women who seemed to gravitate to him, Guthrie paid no heed. He needed Clara, reproving or not, in some way "as family. It was important that I be there," Clara reminisced years later.

At that, Clara's irritation rarely lasted long. Guthrie could always entice her to dance when he played. If she was especially angry, he would wander off to find someone else to amuse, particularly the Robbin children, or the folks who showed up for the backyard readings by actor Howard Da Silva or Ed himself.

In one such encounter, celebrated author Theodore Dreiser confessed, "Ed's been telling me about your songs, but I don't think I've ever caught you on the radio."

"Then we start even, Mr. Dreiser, 'cause I ain't read any of your books." At Dreiser's request, Guthrie sang some of his dust bowl–inspired songs. They swapped reminiscences of their boyhoods, the putative lyricist for "On the Banks of the Wabash" meeting the composer of "Oklahoma Hills."

Through Ed Robbin, Guthrie was also to meet a number of people in the film industry, including Robbin's college friend, Bill Geer. In Los Angeles to play the lead in a government-sponsored film to promote public health, Geer was every bit as committed in his radical political opinions as was Robbin. Robbin and the charismatic Geer were to sweep Woody Guthrie leftward into what they called "The Movement."

William Auge Geer stood over six feet tall, his head topped by a leonine mane. Born in tiny Frankfort, Indiana, in 1902, he had attended the University of Chicago, where he veered between acting and botany studies. The one would become his career, the other his enduring avocation.

Back from his European adventure with Meyer Levin and Robbin, Geer had enrolled in graduate school at Columbia University, studying botany by day and acting by night. Buoyed by his leading-man good looks, in 1927 he made his Broadway debut in Shakespeare's *The Merry Wives of Windsor*. Geer toured with tent shows and played riverboats along the Ohio River, honing his craft. He appeared in the last of the silent films and the first of the talkies. By the end of his apprenticeship he was considered a Shakespearean actor of note.

All the while, Geer drifted politically to the Left, radicalized by the impact of the depression and seeing in the Movement the only solution to the disparities of unrestrained capitalism. He became outspoken in his opposition to international fascism, so prominent an antifascist that in May 1935, Geer was briefly kidnapped at a Hollywood theater, beaten by four Nazi sympathizers, and dumped, bruised and half-conscious, in the hills under the Hollywoodland sign.

If anything, the unsolved beating only provoked Geer to greater involvement in the Left. Anxious to reach working-class audiences, he took to performing didactic sketches and singing his own topical ballads to unions and radical groups. By November 1935, he was a fully involved activist, credited with rallying weavers during a Paterson, New Jersey, strike. In January 1937, Geer was entertaining sit-in strikers at General Motors' Flint plant.

Meanwhile, he pursued his stage career. Six months after the Flint sit-in, Geer, as a member of Orson Welles's Federal Theater unit, defied a lock-out to present the premier of Marc Blitzstein's radical opera, *The Cradle Will Rock*. (Geer and his friend Howard Da Silva were later to join Welles when he organized the successor Mercury Theater, performing on stage and on radio.) In the fall of 1937, Geer, cast by John Steinbeck himself, would star in the stage adaptation of Steinbeck's novel *Of Mice and Men*.

Geer married within the faith. After a sporadic, five-year courtship, he wed budding actress Herta Ware, the granddaughter of the legendary Communist Party organizer Ella Reeve "Mother" Bloor. Together they moved to California early in the summer of 1939, Herta pregnant with their first child, Will to star in a motion picture, *The Fight for Life*.*

By now Geer's commitment was total. Even the new movie role reflected his concern for the poor. At the personal request of President Roosevelt, documentary filmmaker Pare Lorentz agreed to make a motion picture to promote passage in Congress of a comprehensive health care bill. Lorentz's script, written with the help of Steinbeck, dealt with the need for medical care during pregnancy. Geer not only took the key role, he typically and enthusiastically plunged into the project. "He was a big man in all respects," Herta Geer explained. "He loved people."

Both Will and Herta Geer were impressed with the slight young man with the unruly hair Ed Robbin brought to their Hollywood home one July afternoon in 1939.

"My God, he looks like Jesus Christ!" Herta blurted.

"He does!" Will agreed.

Guthrie was young, "and he had all this hair, and there was a purity about his face," Herta Geer said later. Yet despite Guthrie's youth, he seemed focused, perhaps more mature. "He knew who he was. He knew his power."

* Geer was homosexual by inclination and heterosexual by marriage. In the mid-1930s, Geer recruited his lover, Harry Hay, into the Party. Hay would later organize the Mattachine Society in Los Angeles following the model of Communist cells. The secret organization was dedicated to promoting Hay's belief in gay solidarity.

If the Robbin home was a magnet for leftists of all stripes, the Geer home on North Fuller Avenue in Hollywood was a gathering place for aspiring actors. Guthrie was to meet Burl Ives and Gilbert Houston there, the one a pudgy character actor who played a polished guitar and sang a few folk songs he had learned from his Illinois family, the other a black-browed, handsome youth whose acting career foundered on his extreme myopia.

Eddie Albert, fresh from Broadway and launched on a film career, judged Guthrie "a wonderful little fellow . . . loaded with songs. He was charming. He was very special. He had a connection with people." When Albert invited Ives and the four Guthries to a grand chicken dinner one evening, Guthrie repaid his host with the spontaneous gift of Guthrie's guitar. "That's the only thing he had," Albert explained.

If Guthrie was taken with Geer, the feeling was returned. "Will thought he had reached Mecca when Woody came along," Herta said. ". . . Woody was very much attracted to Will, because Will was charismatic. There was that about Will that everybody loved."

When Geer learned that Mary Guthrie was expecting their third child, he arranged for her to join Herta, who was herself due in August, as an extra on the film. Soon enough, Woody's pregnant cousin Amalee Harris joined them. Woody would portray an expectant father in the film—after makeup people literally ironed his unruly curls. The money, as long as it lasted, was welcome.

Geer also arranged medical care for Mary. A doctor with leftist sympathies agreed to provide prenatal care without charge. Geer "was the most loving man," a grateful Mary said long afterward. "He loved everybody."

In return, Mary added, "I just loved him. He was very kind, very understanding. He was just someone you liked."

In Geer and Robbin, Guthrie also found men who shared his newborn dedication to the people of the dust bowl migration. Geer and Robbin provided an embracing, extended family while their Marxist views offered a political and social explanation for the poverty Guthrie saw all about him. Guthrie reveled in their acceptance and he borrowed what he thought useful of their politics.

According to Ed Robbin, Guthrie cared nothing for political theory. He took what he wanted of doctrine and brushed aside the rest. Fundamentally he was "on the side of the poor . . . ever and always."

Like the Socialists of pre-statehood Oklahoma, Guthrie remained a bedrock Christian, unchurched, undisciplined, but certain of his faith. "I seldom worship in or around churches, but always had a deep love for people who go there," he explained.

If his writing now resonated with politics, Guthrie could still dash off an overtly gospel song:

The lepers cleansed, the dead were raised,
The halt and lame did walk.
Unto the lame he said the same
"Thy faith hath made thee whole."

"Thy faith hath made thee whole, my child;
Thy faith hath made thee whole.
Arise! cast out your fear and walk!
Thy faith hath made thee whole!"

Political or apolitical, Guthrie was intent upon succoring people. Those who met Guthrie casually thought him diffident, even retiring; those few like Robbin and Geer who knew him better realized their often quiet friend privately stoked evangelical fires. Even a newspaper article could inspire a cautionary ballad:

Then I watched from my window as he ran,
And thought what a big little man—
Little Billy had gone to the store,
And he never come back anymore.

He was struck by a car speeding past
And was still to his pennies holding fast.
The driver was drinking, they said,
And my little Billy was dead.

*   *   *   *

I guess God took away little Billy
As a lesson to all who remain—
That you must drive sober in the city:
There are so many children at play.

Hardly a simple man himself, Guthrie strove to solve complex social issues with solutions so simple they could be summed in a deliberately "folksy" aphorism: "If folks cood work for each other instead of aginst each other. If it was everbody for everbody, insted of ever man for his own little self—it would be okay."

For all his interest in communism, he remained his own man. When others praised the Soviet Union and the purported superiority of its economic system, Guthrie remained silent. According to brother George Guthrie, "He never did run the country down to me, or the way it was run, or anything like that."

To critics who dismissed communism as a "foreign," un-American philosophy, Guthrie replied, "Lots of folks say we dont want no european idees over here to help us thrash out our problems—well aint the bible from over there?"

As much as he found companionship among them, Guthrie was anything but a doctrinaire communist, George insisted. "He was independent. You can say that again. He liked things to go his way as much as possible, see. He had his own way of life and that's the way he was. And nobody could tell him different."

He continued to favor writer and Socialist Upton Sinclair's scheme of production for use, rather than for profit—the man and the plan the Communist Party in California had savagely scorned as a capitalist tool when Sinclair ran for governor as a Democrat in 1934. He also endorsed "Ham and Eggs," a California-based pension movement that promised thirty dollars every Thursday to the poor and the elderly. The Communist Party officially sneered at the scheme.

Such deviant thinking branded Guthrie as undisciplined in the eyes of local Communist Party leaders.

Certainly, doctrine of any sort bored Guthrie; Ed Robbin remembered his new friend dropping off to sleep during meetings at the Robbin home as the interminable discussions of the nuances of Marxist thought ground on. Guthrie instead picked up the slogans, if not the dialectic of the Communist Party U.S.A.

By the beginning of 1939, whether from tramping the San Joaquin Valley or musing in Glendale, Guthrie had formed a decided antipathy to banks and bankers—an unusual turn for the son of a real estate salesman who necessarily worked with the banks in and around Okemah. In March 1939, the broker's son draped the Robin Hood myth about the unworthy shoulders of bank robber Charles "Pretty Boy" Floyd, hounded

into a fugitive's life and sheltered by neighbors along Oklahoma's Canadian River.

> *There's many a starving farmer the same old story told*
> *How the outlaw paid their mortgage and saved their little home.*
> *Others tell you 'bout a stranger that come to beg a meal*
> *And, when the meal was finished, left a thousand-dollar bill.*

> *   *   *   *   *

> *Yes, as through this world I ramble, I see lots of funny men,*
> *Some will rob you with a six-gun, some with a fountain pen.*
> *But as through your life you'll travel, wherever you may*
> > *roam,*
> *You won't never see an outlaw drive a family from their home.*

Communist polemics offered Guthrie a convenient political shorthand.
The dust bowl bankers who capitalized on drought and low crop prices by
extension became the Communists' ever looming nemesis, Wall Street.

> *When them cards was dealt around*
> *Wall Street drawd the Aces down*
> *I'm looking for that New Deal now.*
> *When them cards was shuffled up*
> *The Workin' Folks they lost the Pot*
> *I'm a-lookin' for that New Deal now.*

> *   *   *   *

> *The Workin' Folks has got to all pitch in*
> *And play together if they hope to win*
> *I'm lookin' for that New Deal now.*
> *You got to stick with Mr. F.D.R.*
> *And Mr. Olson, your gover-nor.*
> *I'm a-lookin' for that New Deal now.*

In these first months of 1939, Guthrie's songs also took on a darker,
more bitter tone. His memories of poverty amid plenty in the San Joaquin
still rankled.

Twouda been better, better,
If we'da never, never, never,
Down that old 66 a-never went,
Cause we ain't got a dime,
We're broke all the time,
And we ain't never, never got a cent.

Sometimes those recollections ignited an anger new to Guthrie's lyrics:

From the Southland and the drouthland
Come the wife and kids and me,
And this old world is a hard world
For a Dustbowl Refugee.

*   *   *   *   *

Hard, it's always been that way,
Getting harder every day—
It's a long and weary journey
For a Dustbowl Refugee.

On reflection, Guthrie would rework the song at least twice in the next year so as to leach some of the anger from it. Optimistic Charley Guthrie's son also tagged on an upbeat last verse:

But this good land is a good land
For the true and brave and free—
I'm at home where e'er I roam
'Cause I'm a Dustbowl Refugee.

For all his conviction, Guthrie did not join the Communist Party—despite his later claim that "the best thing that I did in 1936, though, was to sign up with the Communist Party."

But in 1936, Guthrie was living in Pampa, Texas. He had not yet visited Sacramento, where he claimed he purchased a copy of the Constitution of the Union of Soviet Socialist Republics and fell under its sway.

His wife Mary insisted Guthrie did not join the Communist Party. They wouldn't have him, she added.

Brother George, then living with Woody, Mary, and the two girls in the woebegone cottage at 115 East Chestnut, concurred. "I never heard him being in any type of organization or anything like that."*

Ed Robbin, the first party member to take Guthrie in tow, deemed his friend a poor recruit. He was not asked to join.

Will Geer agreed. "Woody never was a party member, because he was always considered too eccentric by the party apparatus. . . . But he was a convinced socialist, positive that this country had to be socialist."

Guthrie instead served as what the party called a "fellow traveler," a nonmember who generally agreed with the Communist Party's platform but was not subject to party discipline. Guthrie did hang around the *People's World* office just off Los Angeles's Skid Row, said Dorothy Healey, a party member then assigned to organizing agricultural workers. "If he wasn't a member of the party, he was the closest thing to it."

At first indifferent to Guthrie—jazz rather than folk song was the music of choice among American liberals—the Communist Party in Southern California was to warm to him. Guthrie had fallen in with two members of the Communist Party, Ed Robbin and Will Geer, just as the party was coincidentally seeking to broaden its mass appeal, to become more American.

Though Karl Marx had theorized that all art was to be a weapon in the class struggle, and though the anarchist Industrial Workers of the World had used songs to encourage solidarity in the first decades of the century, the Communists were slow to make use of folk music. However pretty their tunes, many folk songs "are complacent, melancholy, defeatist, intended to make slaves endure their lot—pretty but not the stuff for a militant proletariat to feed upon," a *Daily Worker* critic insisted in 1934. Not until the summer of 1935 and the Soviet Union's proclamation of an international "Popular Front" did American Communists embrace the music of the very proletarians the party sought to enroll.

The Popular Front resulted from a radical shift in doctrine prompted by the Soviet Union's fear of a resurgent Germany. Moscow decreed that each Communist Party band with local liberals, regardless of their political affiliation, and join in a supranational effort to curb the spread of fascism. No matter that a united front against fascism required that Communists abandon their fundamental concept that revolution was imminent. Instead, each nation was theoretically to find its own way to communism—in the

---

* The Glendale cottage, more recently stuccoed over, still stands. The Chinese family that owned the house in front, at 113 East Chestnut, razed it and erected a grocery store instead.

United States by way of the ballot box. Communism, ran the freshly minted party slogan, "is Twentieth Century Americanism."

As a necessary corollary, the Communist Party was instructed to Americanize itself. Old Glory now led New York's May Day parade; party spokesmen extolled the American values of Jeffersonian agrarianism and Jacksonian Democracy, and American reformers, particularly Lincoln and Tom Paine. All were transformed into heralds of the proletarian or working class.

"Naturalization" was intended to submerge Moscow's influence on the Communist Party U.S.A.'s daily affairs and to mask the "foreign" origins of the party. (Party members, at least those with identifiably ethnic names, even went so far as to adopt American *noms de politique*.)

As part of the new strategy, art was to be enlisted to serve the needs of the masses, not the classes. The avant garde was to give way to glorification of the people's struggle against fascism in its economic and political forms. Folklore rather than the art of elites was to be celebrated, for in their folklore, people

recounted the democratic aspirations and revolutionary traditions of the past and present, thus lending a sense of hope and communal spirit to the people's existence. Popular traditions [according to the theory] were suffused with a class-conscious aura, it was implied, if for no other reason than that they were produced by the lower classes, not the bourgeoisie, though the latter might adapt or bowdlerize them on occasion.

The concept was romanticized beyond all proportion, and in that romance rendered unrecognizable by the folk themselves. Still, if his newfound associates wanted a "socially conscious" proletarian, a true man of the soil, Woody Guthrie stood ready to oblige.

Some months after introducing himself to Robbin at KFVD, Guthrie approached him with a proposal.

"Ed, I'd like to do a column for the paper—just little comments on things the way I see them."

Robbin was wary. While he realized Guthrie was prolific, easily inspired to song by anything from a news story to a whim, a newspaper column was different. Newspapers had deadlines. And producing a daily column, even a short one, could become a tedious chore.

Robbin suggested Guthrie write a few samples. Then he would see if Al Richmond, his editor at the *People's World*, was interested.

The next day, Robbin recalled, Guthrie was back with a sheaf of columns, as many as thirty short pieces on current events and the plight of the poor, as well as fanciful tales of his own adventures wandering the West. Guthrie's inspiration obviously sprang from Oklahoman Will Rogers's syndicated newspaper column. Unlike Rogers, Guthrie decorated his columns with small cartoon figures.

Robbin had little hope the political minders at the *People's World* would be interested in Guthrie's folksy musings. The overseers were two former Wobblies, longtime hardliners dispatched from New York, whose sense of humor did not extend to the struggle of the masses. He was happily surprised when Richmond, keen to broaden his paper's readership beyond the party faithful, agreed to use Guthrie's columns. "They were good . . . brief text, primitive drawings." Equally important, they were free.

Richmond took on the column despite his skepticism about Guthrie, the folksiness of his columns, and their deliberate misspellings. Unlike other writers for the paper, Guthrie underwent no "serious examination of his political credentials or antecedents, let alone an ideological screening test."

Guthrie introduced himself with an "Awtowbyografie" on Friday, May 12, 1939. From then until January 1940, he would write 174 four- or five-paragraph commentaries about current events or his own life. The format of "Woody Sez" was borrowed from Will Rogers, and the hill-country dialect from the patent medicine show joke books Guthrie had read as a boy. In addition, Guthrie contributed eighty-two cartoons, each drawn in a two-inch-square space, to run on page one with a caption that referred the reader to his column on page four. The cartoons were often no more than stick figures with faces, yet they were animated and distinctively Guthrie's.

"Woody Sez" was not expressly political. Nonetheless, Richmond later told Guthrie's would-be biographer, Richard Reuss, Guthrie was more aware of leftist thinking than he revealed. His understanding was bred in the bone, instinctual rather than intellectual.

Guthrie had a simple explanation of his own philosophy. "I never am overly attracted by anybody till everybody else goes to jumpin' on 'em. Strikes me they framed up a Carpenter that same way, back over in Jerusalem."

The daily column did not take much of Guthrie's time. He was busy during the summer of 1939, hanging around the *Fight for Life* film set by day, singing at leftist benefits or in Skid Row bars by night. When Lorentz suspended shooting to allow Herta to deliver—he needed her with babe in arms for the movie's last scene—Geer introduced Guthrie to writer John

Steinbeck. Steinbeck, in Hollywood to learn something about filmmaking from Lorentz, was living at the Garden of Allah apartments near the Sunset Strip, trying to preserve his privacy in the face of the surprising best-seller success of his novel *The Grapes of Wrath*. Guthrie, who otherwise paid no heed to celebrities, was impressed. "Once he heard about Steinbeck, he *had* to read *The Grapes of Wrath*," Ed Robbin stressed.

Grapes was to sell an unprecedented 420,000 copies in its first year of publication and win both the Pulitzer Prize and National Book Award. It ranked "very high in the category of the great angry books like *Uncle Tom's Cabin* that have roused a people to fight against intolerable wrongs," one critic concluded.

More important to Guthrie, Steinbeck, "trying to write history while it is happening," had captured in his eight-hundred-page novel the dust bowl migration and the lives of Woody's people. The book, Guthrie wrote in his own summary,

> is about us pullin' out of Oklahoma and Arkansas and down south and driftin' around over the state of California, busted, disgusted, down and out and lookin' for work. Shows you how come us got to be that way. Shows the damn bankers, men that broke us and the dust that choked us, and it comes right out in plain English and says what to do about it.

Steinbeck's characters were to make their way into Guthrie's songs as early as this summer of 1939. His angry "Vigilante Man" recalled *The Grapes of Wrath* without explanation, as if he were certain the reference would be understood by his left-wing audience:

> *Preacher Casey [sic] was just a working man,*
> *And he said, "Unite the Working Man."*
> *He was killed in the river by a Deputy Sheriff . . .*
> *Was that a Vigilante Man?**

After Darryl F. Zanuck purchased the film rights to *The Grapes of Wrath*, Steinbeck apparently arranged for his new acquaintance to serve as an uncredited "musical advisor" on the motion picture. Director John Ford

---

* Guthrie also started a ballad inspired by the odyssey of Tom Joad in Steinbeck's *The Grapes of Wrath*, but left it unfinished, Will Geer said in an interview with E. Victor and Judy Wolfenstein in 1970.

asked for a song that the majority of dust bowl migrants might know; Guthrie immediately suggested one he had first heard from his Uncle Jeff:

> *I'm going down the road feeling bad,*
> *I'm going down the road feeling bad,*
> *I'm going down the road feeling bad, oh, Lordy,*
> *And I ain't a-gonna be treated this a-way.*
>
> *They fed me on cornbread and beans,*
> *They fed me on cornbread and beans,*
> *They fed me on cornbread and beans, oh, Lordy,*
> *And I ain't a-gonna be treated this a-way.*

Ford fit the song, which Jeff Guthrie had learned as early as 1910 in Olive, Oklahoma, into the film. Woody was less than pleased because "they slowed it down and made it too doleful." He was still Charley Guthrie's son.*

With work on *Fight for Life* momentarily halted, Geer and Guthrie spent much of the summer working with a newly organized John Steinbeck Committee to Aid Farm Workers. "We went around to forum halls, rallies, picnics, meetings and all kinds of public places," Guthrie wrote later,

> back and forth over the mountains in old junk heap jalopies, playing, singing, making speeches, to the cotton strikers around Brawley, and around Indio, over the hump to Bakersfield, and we organized caravans of Hollywood people, Los Angeles people, to come and visit the feet walking barefooted with a picket sign, and we hauled the strikers and families into big Hollywood sets and studios, and staged a big country dance demonstration on the set of *The Lost Horizon* and *Hurricane*, as well as to house parties of naked vulgarity to win the passionate souls of Hollywood businessmen.

Bill Wheeler, a volunteer union organizer who saw Guthrie and Geer perform that summer, chuckled when he recalled the pair at the Weedpatch labor camp south of Bakersfield. Guthrie in outsized khaki shirt, denim pants, and a stained fedora "was a very colorful character." Guthrie played

---

* Steinbeck also arranged for Tom Collins, former director of the Farm Security Administration camp in Arvin, to serve as technical advisor on the film. Steinbeck biographer Jackson J. Benson credited Collins for much of the realism, the sense of authenticity in the completed picture. See Benson's *The True Adventures of John Steinbeck, Writer* (New York: Viking Press, 1984), p. 410.

and sang a new song, "So Long, It's Been Good to Know You," while Geer croaked along.

They were well liked by the migrants in the camp, Wheeler said. Guthrie "certainly had the interests of the people, agricultural workers in particular, at heart," and the unassuming Geer was "a very good, progressive guy, and a friend of the working man, that's for sure."

As the summer of 1939 wore on, Guthrie's reputation among Los Angeles's leftists grew. The editor of the avowedly liberal *Hollywood Tribune*, James Forester, compared one of Guthrie's mimeographed songbooks to *The Grapes of Wrath*.

"Steinbeck's book has a fine jacket and is well gotten up. Next to it Woody's book would look like a very poor cousin. But they are relatives just the same."

In this, the first review of Woody Guthrie's writing, Forester raved,

> For Woody is really one of them [the Joads] and at the same time he's a poet and a singer. He's the troubadour of those who are condemned to the other side of the fence. . . . He's full of the peculiar drawling humor and wisdom of that western country and every time he talks, a kind of folk wisdom comes out like something that has been long mellowing. . . . I think Woody is a new voice straight from the heart, a kind of Will Rogers, only still closer to the pain of his own folks than Rogers was.

Forester decided to hire this new voice to write an opinion piece for his "independent weekly." From now on, writing would take more of Guthrie's time and energy.

On Sunday, July 23, Guthrie, Geer, and Burl Ives entertained at a benefit in Los Angeles for the wounded veterans of the Abraham Lincoln battalion who had fought in the Spanish Civil War. Guthrie unintentionally provided the highlight of the afternoon program while clowning around with actor John Garfield. In a mock tussle with Garfield, the actor pulled down Guthrie's pants; in front of a fair number of Hollywood's elite, Woody Guthrie stood without underwear. "It was a howlin' success," Guthrie chortled.

Guthrie's popularity as a radio entertainer allowed him to aid the migrant workers scattered up and down the Central Valley. "The Old Wop"—the son of a migrant who insisted on no other identification—recalled that a telephone call to Guthrie at KFVD from stranded pickers near Bakersfield brought a man with "a full car load: three fifty-pound bags of flour, lots of suger, corn meal, cookies for the kids, powdered milk and a lot of canned goods. The car was setting on its springs till the people unloaded it, and Woody sent a message with it, saying if more was needed they were to just call anytime."

Over the Labor Day weekend, even as the first news of a German invasion of Poland broke, Woody and the visiting Jennings brothers, Matt, Fred, and Blue, drove to San Francisco. That weekend Woody was to meet Al Richmond, editor of the *People's World*, and perform at a benefit for the paper with Will Geer. War in Europe was no concern of theirs. Neither the United States nor the Soviet Union were involved—the one was too far away, the other had signed a nonaggression pact with Berlin just a week before. And just as suddenly, American communists were no longer speaking of "antifascist fronts."

Guthrie was also active in the fall of 1939 when the Steinbeck Committee twice brought to the Bakersfield cotton fields a busload of Hollywood figures enlisted by the married actors Helen Gahagan and Melvyn Douglas. Gahagan and Douglas were among the first such celebrities Guthrie was to meet. (Douglas had played Greta Garbo's leading man in *Ninotchka* and *As You Desire Me*; Gahagan had successfully sung in Europe's opera houses before turning to Hollywood and Democratic Party politics.)

Guthrie took celebrity in stride. On "Hollerwood Bolevard," he deadpanned in his weekly column,

> you see more wimmen, an more of each one, then enywhere else i know of. An they must be a clips of th sun 2 or 3 times a day, cause 1/2 th folks is a runnin a round with a set of smoked glasses on. i dont know how th world looks thrue a set of them black specks, but i hope you can see how to vote. i aint much of a radicle, but i wood shure like to increase th income tax, an help th blind

While she was able, the pregnant Herta Geer toured with them, performing in a dramatic version of Guthrie's "Philadelphia Lawyer." Guthrie played the cowboy hero, Herta the Hollywood sweetheart, and Geer the villain. The migrant audiences liked the performance, though Geer was dissatisfied with its lack of social content. More to his liking was a skit involving a tailor, a farmer, and middlemen. The farmer went without a suit, the tailor had nothing to eat, and the middlemen got the money. "It was very simple dialectic. They loved it," Geer said later.

There were no speeches, no overt political message, Herta said. "The songs were sufficient."

"It was amazing to hear Woody before his own people," she continued. "They adored him."

Guthrie seemed to blossom amid his Okies; it "was like going home," Geer noted. The man who was just another radio singer in Los Angeles was transformed in the cotton fields of Inyo and Bakersfield counties.

On one occasion, the Old Wop wrote, his father and Guthrie were camped along a state highway along with thirty migrants. Hungry, with no food, they gathered to bury an infant dead from some vaguely diagnosed fever. Guthrie stood alongside the tiny grave, picking out a hymn on his guitar as sheriff's deputies with long batons descended on the encampment.

Woody tried to explain that the people were burying a little girl and a man would come there within a few days to help the migrents move on with thier trucks.

But the deputies, acting on the sheriff's orders begun herding the people, about thirty or so, toward the highway.

A fight broke out and Guthrie waded into the melee. As the Old Wop remembered the clash, "My dad said people looking at Woody thought him a weakling as he was kinda short and pretty thin too. But Woody was a great fighter, had two good fists and knew how to use them. Besides he was a really good man. He stood up for the poor, homeless and beaten people."

That summer and fall of 1939, Geer and Guthrie lost themselves in their touring performances. Herta Geer, near term, was crushed when Bill went off in August on another trip to the Central Valley; she was certain her husband no longer loved her. Long-suffering Mary Guthrie took Woody's departure in stride. After all, he had not been present when Teeny was born either.

Even with his wife due to deliver their third child, Guthrie abruptly drove off with Will Geer to the Imperial Valley on a Friday night in October. Mary did not bother to protest; her husband did what he wanted.

Woody and Mary's son, Bill, was born the next day and named only after Guthrie asked his KFVD listeners for suggestions. "Will Rogers" was the favorite, but Mary put her foot down in a tiny bid for autonomy. She would agree to "Bill" but not "Will" Rogers. "And of course," she said with a chuckle, "Will Geer always said that Bill was named for him. He always said that, every concert."

Guthrie and Geer, meanwhile, were once again in the Imperial Valley, traveling with John Steinbeck. The Woody Guthrie that college student Sam Hinton met in the migratory labor camp outside Holtville that fall was subdued. At the same time, Guthrie seemed a churn of emotions. "He was like a pot about to boil over," Hinton said.

Hinton, an East Texas boy himself, came away with the impression that Guthrie was not comfortable. Hinton wondered if perhaps it was because of the presence of Steinbeck. Later, Hinton realized that Guthrie "was quite different among his compatriots." With them, he was a man among friends, easy-going and relaxed.

Guthrie returned to Los Angeles from the cotton fields of the Imperial Valley to learn that world affairs had overtaken his political opinions.

CHAPTER TWELVE

Talking Socialism

*T*HE TWO BURKES, the father a onetime Progressive, the son a Roosevelt man through and through, prided themselves as liberal New Dealers. But their liberalism was ever more strained in the fall of 1939 with the outbreak of war. It was one thing to allow a Communist airtime on KFVD when "antifascism" was the watchword among liberals everywhere. It was quite another when the Soviet Union not only signed a nonaggression pact with Germany, but also joined Hitler in carving up hapless Poland. The Burkes did not want lame excuses or strained explanations for Moscow's land grab, for its escalating threats on neighboring Finland. Ed Robbin, spinning apologia for the Soviet Union, would have to go.

As would Guthrie—if he persisted in singing his "purty dern left handed" songs on the air. "They was so left wing," he wrote in the Communist Party paper *People's World*, "I had to . . . sing em with my left tonsil, an string my gittar up backwards to git any harmony."

Independent Woody Guthrie, "The Lone Wolf," lasted a month longer than Robbin at KFVD. By early November 1939, he was adrift once more.

Without the daily program, Guthrie hardly had gas money and little opportunity to earn more. Will Geer had left for New York after he was cast on Broadway as Jeeter Lester in Erskine Caldwell's *Tobacco Road*. Without Geer, bookings at fund-raisers were fewer for a country singer who was overexposed in Los Angeles's leftist community. With the harvest all but completed, even trips to the fields to organize workers would be no more than brave but futile gestures.

Labor unions were in "the nickel and penny stages," Guthrie wrote later. "The Movement could not pay me enough money to keep up my eats, gas, oil, travel expenses, except five dollars here and three there, two and a quarter yonder, at places where I sung."

Mary was bitter. Her husband had gotten off on the wrong track. "He never should have been involved in politics; he had several job offers and ways to make money," she later insisted. But getting caught up in politics was "his downfall as an entertainer."

Given that his brother-in-law had a wife, three children, and no prospects, Matt Jennings wrote to suggest that Woody and his family return to Pampa. Business had picked up in the oil fields and, with the war in Europe, was sure to get better. The Jennings family would be able to help until Woody found something.

Mary was eager to go. Los Angeles just seemed too big for a girl from Pampa, a girl with too few friends and three little ones. As much as he liked Los Angeles, Woody had no pressing reason to stay; he could write his non-paying newspaper column anywhere. With "a new fresh start, things might run smoother." If they didn't, there was always the road.

Shortly before Thanksgiving 1939, the Guthries packed children, possessions, and food into a rattling 1929 Chevrolet sedan. They would limp seventeen hundred miles along U.S. 66 back to Pampa, choking on exhaust fumes spewing from a cracked engine block. They arrived in Pampa broke, but Mary and the children at least would enjoy the holidays with her family.

Beyond a letter in his pocket from Will Geer proposing Guthrie come to New York, Woody had as few job prospects in Pampa as when he left more than thirty months before. Neither newly married Matt nor Uncle Jeff, the one back behind the butcher's counter, the other back on the police force, could find time to play even local dances. When Mary insisted that Guthrie take a steady job, he reluctantly worked a few days for Shorty Harris in the drugstore. "I hated this worst than anything in the world," wrote the man who had boasted he was "born working, raised working." To Guthrie, soda-jerking once more for Shorty Harris was an acknowledgment of how little he had achieved.

Guthrie was near a low point. He dropped by the Pampa Public Library to visit with his old friend, Mrs. Evelyn Todd, limping in too-small shoes he said had been given to him by a motorist. His own were worn out.

He was still the Woody she remembered, full of stories about traveling in California and how beautiful it was there, about Hollywood, and meeting John Steinbeck. He had been offered a part in the movie they were making of *The Grapes of Wrath*, he told Mrs. Todd, but had left to tour migratory workers' camps and strikers' rallies. The movie role was gone by the time he returned to Los Angeles.

Guthrie was not to stay long in Pampa. Christmas passed, then the New Year, and Guthrie was off on a new venture. Charley Guthrie had invented an alarm that alerted gas station owners when a car drove in. Charley suggested they drive to Galveston on the Gulf Coast—if nothing else it was warmer than Pampa—and try to sell the device.

Father and son had no better luck than they had had years before peddling whetstones to barbers. "It was not the tourist season and nobody was driving cars into filling stations, and they didn't need no bell when one did come along," Woody decided.

From Galveston the two Guthries drove across the state, to Konawa, Oklahoma, where Woody's brother Roy was managing Streetman's Food Mart. The drive was perilous and the roads icy with the worst winter storms in memory. Guthrie drove bundled in an old rug, painting signs in exchange for gasoline. "I sold my spare tire for gas and oil. I sold my pump, jack, and pliers, and a couple of old wrenches, and a roll of paint brushes. I sold my guitar for $3.00 and pulled into Konawa, Oklahoma, frozen as stiff as a dead man."

On the last hill before town, the engine fan ripped through the radiator, spraying hot water on the broken windshield and the two Guthries huddled in the cab. The motor coughed, then died, and the doomed Chevrolet coasted its last mile to stop in front of the grocery store.

After a week with his brother and sister-in-law in their crowded second-floor flat, Woody showed Roy the invitation from Will Geer to join him in New York. In his letter, Geer suggested he might be able to get Guthrie a job with the *Tobacco Road* company. If that fell through, Geer reassured him, there were ample opportunities in New York for Guthrie to sing at fund-raisers and in progressive union halls.

Guthrie was anxious to go. Dissatisfied with Pampa, he had had no real intention of getting a permanent job and settling down. "I get more fun out of travelin' around, and seein' people, and doin' things and writin' my songs," he told his brother George.

Brother Woodrow "had his own way of life, and he had his mind made up, and you couldn't change it. I don't care if it was his father, his brother, or who." Since Woodrow was not going to change, George said, the family just accepted him for who he was.

With the twenty-five dollars Roy gave him for the hulk of the crippled Chevrolet, Guthrie bought a bus ticket for as far east as the money would take him, Pittsburgh. He was still three hundred miles from New York City when he set out to hitchhike the rest of the way amid a raging snowstorm.

He crossed the ice-jammed Susquehanna River at Harrisburg as the blizzard ripped along the river bottom "fully as hard as the winds we had in the high country out west."

His body numbed beyond pain, his hands and feet tingling, Guthrie "really froze stiff and died back yonder on that River Bridge." A passing forest ranger out to photograph hibernating animals saved Guthrie, who was stranded in the whiteout alongside the empty highway. The ranger plucked Guthrie from the snow bank along U.S. 22 and drove him to the nearby home of the ranger's parents. There the lady of the house fed Guthrie bowls of buttered clam chowder. "I will never forget how good that hot clam juice tasted as it slid down my throat. I had really given up all hopes of ever seeing any human beings alive on this planet any more."

The following morning, the ranger's parents gave a thawed-out Guthrie three dollars, and their son drove him to Philadelphia's Broad Street Station. From there, Guthrie rode a warm bus to New York City through what became a record winter storm so severe that people easily recalled it three decades later.

If sprawling Los Angeles had appeared boundless, New York, even muffled in snow on this February 16, 1940, seemed overwhelming. Los Angeles with a million and a half residents scattered far and wide never seemed crowded; New York, with five times that number jammed into half the space, teemed day and night with people.

"New York as a hole is okay," he wrote a week after his arrival. The city's skyscrapers and subways continually bemused him. "I been in New York long enough," he wrote seven months after arriving, "to notice that most everybody runs round either 19 stories above the ground or a couple or three below and so far since February I ain't found out just who's on the ground because I couldn't swear that I've seen it since I been here."

Guthrie found his way to Will and Herta Geer's apartment in the West 50s, a home befitting the star of a successful Broadway play. Guthrie was impressed, particularly when Geer told him the rent was $150. "I thought at first that was for a whole year."

Woody moved in with the Geers and their six-month-old daughter, Katie. He was wearing his winter underwear, Herta realized, and hadn't bathed properly in quite some time. Between Woody in his underwear and the baby's diapers, "it was pretty raunchy," Will agreed.

At Herta's insistence, Will fixed a pine soap bath in the tub.

Guthrie protested. "I'll catch cold."

Geer, six feet two inches tall and fifty pounds heavier than Guthrie, stripped off the ripening underwear and wrestled his guest into the tub. A sloe gin eventually mollified the outraged Guthrie.

Life with the Geers was pleasant. Woody would get up early and go into the bathroom with Herta's guitar, close the door, and sing. "If you had to use the pot," Will said, "then Woody would move over and sit on the edge of the bathtub. He loved to sing."

Two days after his arrival, Guthrie typed out a ballad written "in Will Geer's house, in the charge of his wine, and the shadow of his kindness":

I seen an apartment on 5th Avenue,
A penthouse, and garden, and skyscraper view;
A carpet so soft, with a hard-wood floor,
I don't feel at home on the Bowery no more.

I like my good whiskey, I like my good wine,
And good looking women to have a good time;
Cocktail parties, and a built-in bar,
So I don't feel at home on the Bowery no more.

*   *   *   *   *

I got disgusted and wrote this song,
I may be right, and I may be wrong;
But since I seen the difference 'tween the rich
     and the poor;
I don't feel at home on the Bowery no more.

Guthrie stayed with the Geers a week, sleeping on the couch, repaying his raids on the refrigerator with songs typed on Herta's portable and left on the kitchen table. In the evenings he borrowed Herta's prized rosewood Martin, a gift from her mother years before, and went off to play in bars along the Bowery.

"I won't beg nobody," he wrote in a notebook.

I won't go a begging.
I ain't that lost.
I'm still a man.

*   *   *   *   *

> *A feller might give me some help*
> *And I'd be much obliged*
> *But I'll not beg you*
> *I'll take it easy*
> *But I'll dang shore take it.*

When Guthrie had raised enough cash for a week's lodging, he moved to a grimy hotel at the corner of 43rd Street and Sixth Avenue. He took Herta's guitar with him.

She had loaned it to him, with "no question I would get it back." But when she asked Guthrie to put the guitar in its case because it was raining, he refused on the ground he never used a case. "I knew then I would never see that Martin again."

In his room at Hanover House, a long block from the New York Public Library, Guthrie spent the days reading newspapers and writing songs. One that he had mulled over for days he set down as an angry response to Irving Berlin's earnest, cloying "God Bless America." On a piece of lined three-holed notebook paper, Guthrie wrote:

> *This land is your land, this land is my land*
> *From the . . .*

He scratched out "the," and continued, " . . . California to the Staten Island." "Staten" he changed, so the line read "New York island."

> *From the Redwood Forest, to the Gulf Stream waters,*
> *God blessed America for me.*

He borrowed the tune from the Carter Family's "Little Darling, Pal of Mine," which had itself been inspired by a southern gospel hymn, "Oh, My Loving Brother."

If the written text is to be trusted, "God Blessed America" flowed quickly. As was his habit, Guthrie alternated between guitar and pen, fitting words to melody until he was satisfied. Only then did he write out the song, stanza by stanza.

> *As I went walking that ribbon of highway*
> *And saw above me that endless skyway,*
> *And saw below me the golden valley, I said:*
> *God blessed America for me.*

He would write six stanzas, the first of which would eventually become a chorus. At the end, he jotted an explanatory comment: "All you can write is what you see." He signed the page, "Woody G., N.Y., N.Y., N.Y."

While Guthrie shifted between his dingy room, the library, and the beery saloons along the Bowery, Will Geer was arranging the first of Guthrie's appearances in the city. As a benefit for Spanish Civil War refugees, the program on Sunday evening, February 25, 1940, at the Mecca Temple on West 56th Street offered the usual mixed bill, intended to attract the widest possible audience. Woody Guthrie, added at the last moment and introduced as just in from Oklahoma, was buried deep in the program, between the workers' chorus singing Russian folk songs and classically trained baritone Mordecai Bauman.

Guthrie sang two of his dust bowl songs and a newly composed political piece inspired a few days earlier by an article he had read in the liberal *New York Post*. "Why Do You Stand There in the Rain" was calculated to appeal to a largely left-wing audience that viewed Franklin Roosevelt as a warmonger.

Just days before, some six thousand delegates of the American Youth Congress (AYC) had gathered in Washington to advocate "Jobs and Peace." At the invitation of First Lady Eleanor Roosevelt, the delegates gathered in front of the south portico of the White House in a cold drizzle to listen to a half-hour speech by the president. FDR threw down the gauntlet, aware that the Young Communist League had taken firm grip on the once broadly based, Popular Front AYC:

> The Soviet Union, as everybody who has the courage to face the fact knows, is run by a dictatorship as absolute as any other dictatorship in the world. It has allied itself with another dictatorship and it has invaded a neighbor [Finland] so infinitesimally small that it could do no conceivable possible harm to the Soviet Union, a neighbor which seeks only to live at peace as a democracy, and a liberal, forward-looking democracy at that.

Roosevelt heard the boos and hisses spit through the cold rain. American Communists had once been friendly to Roosevelt, but the party now deemed him a capitalist tool; Moscow's diktat following the Stalin-Axis Pact of the previous August had placed president and fellow-traveling delegates on opposite sides.

People's World columnist Woody Guthrie knew where he stood. He chided the president in song:

> *Now the guns in Europe roar as they have so oft before,*
> *And the war lords play the same old game again,*
> *They butcher and they kill, Uncle Sam foots the bill,*
> *With his own dear children standing in the rain.*

> *Why do you stand there in the rain?*
> *Why do you stand there in the rain?*
> *These are strange carryings on*
> *On the White House Capitol lawn,*
> *Tell me, why do you stand there in the rain?*

> *Then the President's voice did ring; "Why this is the*
>   *silliest thing,*
> *I have heard in all my fifty-eight years of life.*
> *But it all just stands to reason as he passes another*
>   *season,*
> *He'll be smarter by the time he's fifty-nine.* *

In Los Angeles, he had sung "Tom Mooney" to a left-wing audience. A year later, he tapped into similar feelings with his antiwar song.

Guthrie made a great impression on the audience at the Mecca Temple. Almost sixty years later, Martha Garlin vividly recalled him: "A short man, slim, with a hat pushed back on his head, which looked big because of his curly hair. He was an original, an originator."

Mordecai Bauman, who was on the Mecca Temple program, was stunned by the laconic, earthy, seemingly unprepossessing Guthrie. "He was a talent we had never heard in New York. In a minute he had the audience in his hand."

Here was a triumph, repeated a week later at a "Grapes of Wrath" benefit for the decidedly left-wing Steinbeck Committee to Aid Farm Workers.

---

* During the twenty-one months of the Stalin-Axis Pact, Guthrie waved the "merchants of death" banner. "As long as the pore folks fights the rich folks wars, you'll keep havin' pore folks, rich folks, and wars. It's the rich folks thet makes the pore folks; it's the pore folks thet makes the rich folks; an' it's the two of 'em thet makes wars—rich folks ram-roddin' 'em, an pore folks a fighten' 'em." Quoted from Woody Guthrie, *Woody Sez* (New York: Grosset & Dunlap, 1975), pp. 63–64.

Will Geer had arranged with the producers of *Tobacco Road* to allow the committee use of the Forrest Theater for the midnight benefit. Guthrie, announced only as " 'Woody,' a real Dust Bowl refugee," was slotted into a long list of performers.

Guthrie ambled on stage and casually spoke into the microphone, Pete Seeger, another of the singers, recalled vividly.

Oklahoma, Guthrie drawled into the microphone, "is a very rich state. You want oil in Oklahoma, jus' go down a hole and get it. If you want coal, why, we've got coal in Oklahoma. Jus' go down a hole and get it. You want lead, we've got lead mines. Go down a hole and get you some lead. If you want food, groceries, just go in a hole . . . and stay there."

Composer Earl Robinson, in the audience that night, remembered the Oklahoman on stage, at ease, head cocked, chin up, his smile turned quizzical by a raised eyebrow. Guthrie stopped in the middle of an introduction to a song, Robinson said, to clean his fingernails with a guitar pick, all the while spinning a humorous story that ambled to no end. "It was an act, obviously, but it felt so fantastically real," Robinson marveled.

A classically trained composer, a lyricist, and performer in his own right, Robinson was struck by Guthrie's sense of timing. "Woody was a performer, a natural performer," Robinson continued. "It was terribly understated. It didn't look like much. But he made you look twice."

The slender singer with the borrowed guitar, wearing work clothes and a sweat-stained hat, carried about him "a heightened sense of reality," what a later generation would call charisma. His voice was nasal, raw, yet compelling. Later writers would scramble to describe the uninflected twang, comparing it to "tires on hot asphalt, the midnight howl of a coyote, the rhythm of a train clacking across the plains."

Robinson's friend and coworker at the Columbia Broadcasting System, Alan Lomax, was even more taken with Guthrie. Here was Will Rogers returned, without the rope tricks, Lomax said, but carrying a guitar. Guthrie had the same laconic speech; the same delivery of small jokes, then "a big popper at the end that brought down the house." He had the same mannerism of running his hand through his hair as Rogers had, and the same sympathy for working folk. More important to folk song collector Lomax, Guthrie wrote songs that captured the West that Lomax knew so well, "ballads . . . that will fool a folklore expert."

At twenty-four, gregarious Alan Lomax was an enthusiastic promoter of American folk music. The son of John Avery Lomax, a pioneering collector of folk songs in the West and Southeast, Alan had accompanied his father on lecture tours as early as age six. Later, father and son worked together, lugging a 350-pound Presto recording machine from school-house to mountain cabin, eventually to amass some ten thousand songs and ballads on three thousand aluminum discs.

Groomed to succeed his father, Alan had attended prep school at Choate, then the University of Texas for two years. He transferred to Harvard College and there, to his conservative father's disgust, became "hopelessly involved in the slimy toils of Communism." A friend of the elder Lomax, poet, Lincoln biographer, and sometime folk singer Carl Sandburg, laughingly waved off the young man's radical ideas. "Whatever jails he may land in, I am still for him as a character witness."

The old man prickly, the son volatile, Lomax senior and junior managed to put aside their political differences to edit two anthologies culled from the songs and ballads they had collected. Alan was just nineteen when the first was published; the second was due out as soon as music editor Ruth Crawford Seeger finished her transcriptions of the tunes.

Alan's own turn leftward had coincided with the Left's taking up folk music as a voice of the Popular Front. By March 1940, and the time of the Forrest Theater concert, Alan was a driving force in the burgeoning revival of American folk song in big cities. (His friend Pete Seeger would say the younger Lomax was *the* most important figure in that revival.) By then Lomax was carrying the title of "assistant in charge of the Archive of Folk-Song" at the Library of Congress in Washington—the core of which were the recordings Lomax father and son had made.

Beyond official Washington, the younger Lomax had promoted a succession of folk music programs broadcast nationally on the Columbia Broadcasting System. He had persuaded RCA, Columbia, and Decca Records to donate to the new Archive of American Folk-Song thousands of commercial recordings spawned by folk musicians. And he had picked the artists to perform for the Steinbeck Committee fund-raiser—all but Will Geer's friend from California, this bushy-haired Okie with the exaggerated drawl.

Lomax was overwhelmed. Guthrie was not only singing folk songs, he was writing his own, songs that reflected Lomax's own belief in a "New America," a nation in which the working people expressed themselves through folk culture. Never one to stifle his enthusiasms, Lomax was frankly excited.

After the concert, Lomax buttonholed Guthrie backstage. Guthrie initially was "somewhat skeptical" of him, Lomax recalled. Despite the familiar Texas accent, Lomax seemed too enthusiastic, too ingratiating, too much "the young cat" from the big city.

Off by themselves, the two men talked and swapped songs. Lomax came away ever more sure that Guthrie was an authentic voice of the underclass when Guthrie sang his outlaw ballad, "Pretty Boy Floyd."

> *Yes, he took to the river bottom along the river shore,*
> *And Pretty Boy found a welcome at every farmer's door.*
> *The papers said that Pretty Boy had robbed a bank each day,*
> *While he was setting in some farmhouse 300 miles away.*

To Lomax's ear, here was a protest song, a subtle, even sly protest song, that sprang from working class roots.

In Guthrie, Lomax heard "a real ballad maker," a man who wrote in "the people's idiom." Guthrie was "a natural genius," Lomax continued, "the kind of person who wrote the great ballads about Jesse James and Sam Bass. . . . That is your life's work," he insisted.

That night Lomax invited Guthrie to visit the Library of Congress and to record his songs. Whatever his reservations about this Texan with his toothy smile and wavy dark hair, Guthrie allowed as how he might go down to Washington and record some of his songs.

In the meantime, Guthrie fit himself into New York's radical circles— what Maxine Crissman, left behind in California, disdained as "the wrong crowd back there."

Guthrie resumed writing his "Woody Sez" column for the *People's World*, periodically sending a sheaf of columns to Al Richmond in San Francisco. The *Daily Worker* picked up the short commentaries—giving Guthrie a certain cachet among New York City's sectarian Left.

Once again, Guthrie played the country boy, remaking Okemah and his early life to appear an authentic proletarian.

> I was snatched up down in the Creek Indian Nation of what is now
> Okfuskee County in the town of Okemah . . . and the dust and the
> bankers and crooked politicians has run a lot of folks out of a
> mighty good stretch of country down in there. And sheriffs and
> deputies and city marshals and cops has done their part. She's a
> hard hit, hard hittin' place, Oklahoma.

Woody Guthrie was deliberately reshaping himself to the fantasies of the Communist Left: a voice of the people, unlettered yet intelligent, perceptive and droll. As Al Richmond described it, Woody "put on like he was less sophisticated than he really was. . . . He was not totally unsophisticated in terms of what might be called dogma."

His newspaper columns in these winter months before the invasion of France were more pointed than they had been: they caricatured Wall Street rather than "bankers" and were more firmly against the United States' involvement in the European war. "I ain't a gonna kill nobody. Plenty of rich folks wants to fight. Give them the guns," he suggested in a column.

In a handwritten draft of another column, Guthrie wrote, "I hate war. I hate anybody that goes into the war business just to make money. And that's all a big war is."

That apparently unpublished draft included a warning to his "dear rich cousin": "Just because I ain't got as much money as you got is a pretty good sign that you're crookeder than me. And it ain't to laugh about. It makes me do some pretty tall thinking how to get that money off of you and give it back to the folks that's broke." (Such sentiments did not prevent Guthrie from applauding the Soviet Union's attack and victory in the Russo-Finnish War.)

"Woody Sez" was hardly doctrine. Guthrie's most political statement was mild:

> I'm a Proletarian and proud of it. I've met some dern good folks that
> worked right handed and thought left. I should of said they worked
> 2 handed and got left. Anyway, if you go right you get left, and if you
> go right you go wrong . . .

The daily column, said *Daily Worker* feature editor Sender Garlin, was popular with readers. And though "it was not considered strategic or basic" to the Communist Party, Garlin added, the column was important to demonstrate the party's humanity, that it was "interested in people."*

When others compared Guthrie to Will Rogers, Garlin demurred. "I think he was better than Will Rogers." If Rogers said, "I never met a man I didn't like," Guthrie did not. "Woody wasn't that Christ-like," Garlin added.

In New York, Guthrie was to remake himself as an "untutored" spokesman for the underclass and an authentic voice of social protest. In a commentary he sent to Alan Lomax, the young man who had read his way

---

* On occasion, Garlin said in an interview, he ghosted the column for Guthrie "sometimes when he was sick." It was not difficult "because he didn't deal with any policy," and Garlin did not have to worry about "what they used to call 'deviations.'"

through the Okemah and Pampa public libraries wrote, "I've not read so many books. I doubt if I've read a dozen from back to back."

With a wash of such dissembling statements, Guthrie strewed confusion behind him.

Sender Garlin judged him "not educated, but very intelligent, with strong and good feelings." If he read anything at all, Garlin decided, it was "certified" party literature.

At the same time, Will Geer insisted, Guthrie "tried but he didn't get very far" in reading the *Communist Manifesto.* "He talked Marx but he talked socialism, even more than communism."

Because of that, Geer continued, "New York intellectuals distrusted him, I think. He was just a socialist, instead of being an extreme Marxist. He was more of a Eugene Debs type. He certainly wasn't a Stalinist."

Guthrie certainly remained more the romantic than doctrinaire in his Marxism, and he failed to grasp the scope of the New Deal's triumph in saving capitalism. He was, Geer averred, "quite sure that it [a bloodless revolution] was going to happen in our time. He was a great optimist on that score. We all were. . . . The revolution was going to happen in Chicago, then spread to the coasts."

He was wrong. Guthrie's revolution was to erupt in New York City.

CHAPTER THIRTEEN

Some Kind of Electricity

*A*LAN LOMAX'S ENDLESS enthusiasm and energy made him a passionate and influential evangelist for American folk music—whether it was the chain gang songs he had recorded with his father in southern prisons, the unaccompanied singing of North Carolina and Kentucky mountain people, the rowdy blues of Mississippi juke joints, or the western ballads his father had long championed. More than anything he wanted to teach America these songs, to return them to the people who had created them.

By dint of a toothy smile and overwhelming self-confidence, Lomax had persuaded the Columbia Broadcasting System (CBS) to produce a Tuesday-morning program devoted to folk song as part of the ongoing *American School of the Air* series. Even before leaving the Forrest Theater in the early hours of March 5, 1940, he had asked Woody Guthrie to appear on the half-hour program. He had also invited Guthrie to Washington.

Alternately put off by Lomax's gushing enthusiasms and swept up by them, Guthrie waited three weeks—meanwhile playing a handful of benefits in New York for five- and ten-dollar fees—before he appeared at the door of Lomax's basement cubbyhole at the Library of Congress in Washington.

An unconventional houseguest at best, Guthrie was to spend almost a month in Washington, living with Alan, his wife Elizabeth Harold, and their upstairs neighbor, Nicholas Ray. Early in his stay, Guthrie went to bed still wearing his muddy boots, provoking Lomax to scold his guest. He ought to behave himself and act like an adult, Lomax barked.

From then on, Guthrie slept on the floor, his heavy jacket serving as a blanket. As if he were asserting his independence, he insisted upon eating while he stood at the sink. "I don't want to get softened up. I'm a road man," he blandly explained.

Alan's younger sister Bess was unimpressed. "Woody was behaving kind of outrageously at that time," she snapped, "pretending he was such an ignorant country boy that he didn't know how to behave properly in public."

It was an act, "and it was very annoying actually. Everybody knew it was an act," Bess Lomax said. "It was perfectly obvious that he was quite a literate person, and he was writing up a storm all the time." He played the primitive when he was unsure of himself, she added. It was a test of their trust in him.

Lomax daily escorted Guthrie through the Archive of American Folk-Song's holdings, proudly playing field recording after field recording for him. Guthrie was particularly impressed with the Negro songs the Lomaxes had collected. It was at that point that he finally gained Guthrie's respect, Lomax said.

In the evenings, there was more music at the Lomax home: stacks of commercial "hillbilly" and "race" records sold in the South and unavailable elsewhere. Guthrie was to listen to these records repeatedly, at one point playing the Carter Family's "John Hardy" so many times that he wore the shellac from the record. Some nights they swapped songs into the early morning hours, challenging each other to see who knew the most songs about dogs, faithless women, or train wrecks.

At Alan's request, Guthrie spent a day typing an autobiography. The twenty-five single-spaced pages absorbed Lomax just as the first chapter of James Joyce's *Ulysses* had at Harvard, "except that what Woody had to say meant far more to me."

There was about Woody's language a "looping grace and originality of the prose masters," Lomax wrote later. Lomax in coming months was to urge Guthrie to contact magazine editors, to try freelancing articles, to become *a writer*.

Guthrie was a prize to be treasured, the one-in-ten-thousand informant who was close to his roots yet was supremely articulate. "Take care of Woody," Alan advised his younger sister Bess.

"It proved to be unnecessary," she said acidly.

Over a three-day period in late March 1940, Alan and Elizabeth—while her husband nursed a sore throat—recorded Guthrie singing, talking, and answering questions about his life. Lomax intended the sessions to result in a series of radio programs, perhaps to extend his *American School of the Air* contract. In any event, the discs were unusual among Library of Congress recordings in the amount of time Guthrie was allowed to speak rather than sing.

On seventeen 16-inch aluminum discs recorded in the sound studio of the Department of the Interior by engineer Jerome Wiesner, Guthrie set down forty songs and instrumental pieces.* More than half were Guthrie's own compositions, an unusual step for Lomax since the archive was specifically organized to preserve *traditional* folk music. If nothing else, that freedom suggested just how much Guthrie the songwriter had impressed his host.

Guthrie was relaxed during the afternoon-long sessions. He told tales of his boyhood in Okemah, of dust storms on the Panhandle, of hoboing to California. Some of it was fanciful or exaggerated, and some nakedly painful.

To begin with, he told Alan, he "wasn't in the class of people Steinbeck called the Okies because, to start with, my dad was worth $35,000 to $40,000, and he started having a little bit of bad luck. In fact my whole family started to have a little bit of it." He paused and took a breath. "I never do talk it much."

But talk he did, ever protective of the memory of his mother. Sister Clara's death, he choked, "was a little too much for her nerves, her something—Well, anyway, she died in the insane asylum at Norman, Oklahoma.

"My father, mysteriously, for some reason caught fire," Guthrie asserted, adding Charley's was a failed suicide attempt prompted by financial reverses. Charley, living still in Oklahoma City with his half-brother Claude, was to take the blame for mother Nora, dead for more than a decade.

The moment passed and Guthrie was again singing songs he had learned around Okemah as a boy. The songs came easily; once learned, they were never forgotten. Guthrie glibly explained later that "music is some kind of electricity that makes a radio out of a man and his dial is in his head and he just sings according to how he's a-feeling."

Normally the one to excite others, Lomax was fascinated by this Okie balladeer. Guthrie's voice, he wrote when the Library of Congress recordings were eventually released for commercial sale, "bit at the heart. A low, harsh voice with velvet at the edges, the syllables beautifully enunciated, the prose flowing with a professional writer's balance of sentence and the salt of a folk wit."

Sometime during Guthrie's three-week stay, Alan Lomax realized that

---

* Wiesner, who carried the lofty title of chief engineer for the Acoustical and Record Laboratory of the Library of Congress, went on to become presidential science advisor in the Kennedy Administration and later president of Massachusetts Institute of Technology.

Guthrie was more than a regional singer or even a writer. Guthrie *understood* the people of the dust bowl; his songs spoke to their fears and spoke for their anger. In Woody Guthrie, Lomax had found the man to complete a book project he had begun, then put aside for lack of time. It was a project, Lomax argued, that would expand the very definition of folk song.

Alan had amassed a thick file of social and political protest songs from field recordings of Alabama sharecroppers, Kentucky coal miners, and North Carolina mill hands, as well as from commercial hillbilly and "race" recordings. For five years he had gathered these songs with the hope that he could get some of them into the folk song anthologies his father and he were editing. But conservative John A. rejected his son's radical profferings; they offended him politically. Moreover, John argued, his publisher would be unwilling to handle such controversial material. Rebuffed but undiscouraged, son Alan decided to edit his own book.

Upon Guthrie's sudden arrival, Alan shifted his plan. Guthrie was "the logical person to write the commentary for my collection of topical folk songs," he stated in his postscript to the anthology. "We were both pretty young at the time. We were both angry about the social injustice rampant in our world. In different ways we were both children of the Depression and we wanted to tell the story of what it had done to the people we knew."

Lomax proposed to make a preliminary selection of the songs. Guthrie would write introductions to each while a young man Lomax had hired as an intern at the Archive of American Folk Song, Peter Seeger, would serve as the music editor.

Guthrie and Seeger, who would shoulder most of the burden of editing Lomax's book, were an unlikely pairing. The Seegers were patrician New Englanders, people of "old money" and older lineage. It was a heritage that twenty-one-year-old Peter Seeger both honored and hid. Though Seeger's father and mother were musicians, he a composer-conductor, she a concert violinist, their third son had declined formal musical training. A ukulele, a whistle, an Autoharp, anything would do for the boy—except the violin and compulsory lessons.

Fired instead by the American Indian romances of Ernest Thompson Seton, young Peter grew to adolescence "in a woodland tower," he later told his biographer. "I knew all about plants and could identify birds and snakes, but I didn't know that anti-Semitism existed or what a Jew was until I was fourteen years old. My contact with black people was literally nil."

Though money was tight in the Seeger household, Peter spent most of his youth at boarding schools, drawing closer to his father, Charles, and

eventually taking up his pacifist, leftist views. Together they attended meetings of the Pierre Degeyter Club in New York's Greenwich Village to hear
talks about music in a world cleansed by revolution.* Father and son
walked the streets of depression-era New York, attended May Day parades,
and heard for the first time a folk song from the South. Painter-muralist
Thomas Hart Benton's lusty singing of "John Henry" immediately set
young Peter's toe to tapping.

Seeger attended Spring Hill boarding school in Litchfield, Connecticut,
twigged out in the required uniform of Brooks Brothers suit and starched
wing collar for dinner. Though he was a scholarship student, his grades
were less important to him than playing a tenor banjo in a school jazz band
and editing the mimeographed newspaper he published. (Seeger was considering a career as a journalist, though he also weighed becoming a forest
ranger or a watercolor painter.)

In the summer of 1935, Charles and Peter Seeger traveled to Asheville,
North Carolina, to attend the Ninth Annual Folk Song and Dance Festival.
There for the first time Peter heard the uniquely American five-string
banjo, played not with the four-string's plectrum, but picked or strummed
with the fingers. He was riveted.

In "Aunt" Samantha Bumgarner's playing, young Seeger "discovered
there was some good music in my country which I never heard on the
radio. . . . I liked the strident vocal tone of the singers, the vigorous dancing. The words of the songs had all the meat of life in them. Their humor
had a bite, it was not trivial. Their tragedy was real, not sentimental."

Young Peter's discovery of folk music coincided with a leftward shift in
his politics. In father Charles Seeger, the patrician's *noblesse oblige* toward
those who were neither Seegers nor Seeger friends had grown to an
embracing concern for the working class. Once a university music professor at the University of California, the elder Seeger had come to Washington to work for the New Deal's Resettlement Administration. Son Peter
meanwhile settled on a simple credo: "No rich, no poor." Following that
commandment, he drifted into the orbit of the Young Communist League.

During visits home from Harvard College—the Seegers were expected to
attend that institution even if it meant Peter had to wash dishes—the

* Among those who were members of the Degeyter Club—named after the composer of the
  "International"—were Aaron Copland, Henry Cowell, Marc Blitzstein, Wallingford Riegger,
  Charles Seeger, and the woman he would take as his second wife, Ruth Crawford. Modernists
  all, they formed a splinter Composers Collective to produce music to accompany the workers'
  revolution.

young man had easy access to field recordings deposited in the Library of
Congress by John A. and Alan Lomax. His new stepmother, Ruth Crawford
Seeger, was meticulously transcribing the music for the second of the
Lomax anthologies of American folk song. Through her, Peter met the exu-
berant Alan Lomax.

Three years older than Seeger, Lomax was everything Pete Seeger was
not. He was brash. He was cocky. He was experienced if not sophisticated.
Seeger, on the other hand, was shy, and his shyness drew him to silent corners. He had grown to be more than six feet tall, but a severe case of acne
marked him the stripling still. "Most of what I knew about the rest of the
world I learned from reading," he said later. He had done little more than
pass out leaflets in front of Widener Library in support of Spanish War
Relief and cofound a short-lived radical newspaper. His boldest move was to
drop out of Harvard in the spring of 1938.

Lomax in late 1939 hired Seeger as an intern in the Archive of American Folk-Song—"$15 a week and overpaid at that"—after Seeger had
skipped from watercolor painting to puppeteering to singing in Manhattan's private schools. At the library, Seeger's job was to listen to the stacks
of 78-r.p.m. hillbilly and race records Lomax had cadged from RCA, Columbia, and Decca. It was a folklorist's form of higher education.

A few months later, Lomax insisted that Seeger appear on the benefit
program at the Forrest Theater. Seeger sang the outlaw ballad "John
Hardy" to a smattering of polite applause, and retired in confusion. Despite
that dismal showing, Woody Guthrie took a liking to the "long tall string
bean kid from up in New England."

Seeger was plainly flattered. He had heard of Guthrie a year before,
when Will Geer wrote from California to extol this Okie singer he had met,
and send along a copy of Guthrie's mimeographed "On a Slow Train
Through California."

By day Guthrie, Seeger, and Lomax worked at the Library of Congress.
At night the three of them, sometimes joined by Nicholas Ray, would swap
songs. Seeger, as musicians put it, "had a good ear." He could improvise on
a tune heard for the first time, picking an accompaniment on the banjo or
singing harmony in a reedy tenor. "I didn't try anything too fancy," he
acknowledged. "Woody didn't like a lot of fancy chords, so I stuck to the
chords he wanted."

Guthrie and Seeger got on well together. "He must have liked my banjo
picking, because everything else about me must have seemed strange,"
Seeger said later. "Didn't drink. Didn't smoke. Didn't chase girls." Woodrow

Wilson Guthrie certainly did all three. The unlikely pair, when Seeger's internship ended, moved back to New York City in April.

They stayed with Harold Ambellan and his fiancée, Elisabeth Higgins, friends of Seeger's with whom he had once shared a puppeteer's stage. There they worked sporadically on the protest song collection that Guthrie had titled "Hard Hitting Songs for Hard-Hit People."

The work was slow going. Guthrie had never written anything much longer than a night-long essay at the typewriter. While the introductions to the songs were short, the book had to have an overall message. It was a big project, and vexing, for Guthrie's headnotes had to convey the story of an American people striving for economic freedom—from the bosses, from the bankers, from all their oppressors.

"The biggest parts of our song collection are aimed at restoring the right among the people to the right amount of land and the right amount of houses and the right amount of groceries to the right amount of working folks," he eventually decided.

Unsatisfied with his work, Guthrie began to carry his typescript copy with him, uncharacteristically asking others to look it over, to advise him.

The anthology eventually grew to include 243 songs and ballads; twenty-eight of the entries were by Guthrie himself. It was never quite complete, and as it stood in the spring of 1940, the manuscript was unpublishable. It was a reflection of recent hard times—of labor strife, of economic crash, of boycotts and simple misery. The anthology neared completion just as the nation was pulling itself out of the Great Depression; it looked backward, not forward, and publishers, even those with Popular Front sympathies, deemed it unsaleable. Additionally, Seeger said in retrospect, "there are so many loose ends in that book it's silly. Words with no tune. [There were] rambling introductions that had no bearing on the song. Woody just sat down with a blank sheet of paper and put down what was on his mind whether it was apropos or not."

Though the book was important to him, perhaps more important than anything he had written so far, Guthrie was to put it aside in late April 1940 to take on another project arranged by entrepreneurial Alan Lomax.

RCA, the Victor Recording Company of old, had approached Lomax sometime earlier with the suggestion that he record an album of folk songs. Lomax, busy with the radio programs, managing the archive, and endlessly promoting singers and folk songs, had simply put it off.

Rather than do it himself, Lomax proposed that RCA record Guthrie. This new singer, an authentic chronicler of the dust bowl, was a man who "wrote and spoke the folk idiom of the Southwest with natural perfection." The company, apparently tantalized by the success of both the book and then the motion picture *The Grapes of Wrath*, agreed to record the unknown singer.

There is no record of an audition. RCA record producer Robert C. Wetherald apparently took the authoritative Lomax at his word. After all, Guthrie was "our best contemporary ballad composer," Lomax insisted.

According to Pete Seeger, Guthrie was somewhat reluctant to take on the project. Victor wanted twelve songs about the dust bowl to release in two six-song, three-record albums. Guthrie did not have that many even if he stretched some; he would have to write three or four more songs. As Pete Seeger would recount the story, Guthrie asked him if he had a typewriter in the apartment to which Seeger had moved.

"Yeah."

"Could I use it?"

"Well, I'm staying with a fellow in a six-floor walk-up on the East Side, but I guess he won't mind if you use it."

"Victor wants me to write a song about Tom Joad, about *The Grapes of Wrath*," Guthrie explained.

"Have you read the book?" Seeger asked.

"No, but I saw the movie," Guthrie replied. He was downwind from the truth.

Guthrie spent the evening at the typewriter in the walk-up rented by artist and sometime puppeteer Jerry Oberwager, picking out the ballad of "Tom Joad" verse by verse. He alternately shaped a verse in his head, tried it on the guitar, and when he was satisfied, typed the four lines.

One by one they dropped off. "And when we woke up in the morning, there was Woody curled up under the table with the finished song on the table."

Guthrie was immensely proud of the ballad, "the best thing I've done so far," he wrote in the *Daily Worker*. Its seventeen verses—set to the melody of the Carter Family's outlaw ballad "John Hardy"—condensed John Steinbeck's story into six minutes. "Half the job," Seeger estimated, "was done by [screenwriter] Nunnally Johnson. And Woody did the other half by boiling down an hour and one-half movie into a six-minute song."*

---

* The creation of "Tom Joad," unquestionably one of Guthrie's finest works, is swathed in a myth of Guthrie's making. *The Grapes of Wrath* opened at the Rivoli Theater in Manhattan on January 24, 1940, and closed its first run on March 21. In his column in the *Daily Worker* of March 30, 1940, Guthrie wrote, "Seen the pitcher last night, Grapes of Wrath, best cussed pitcher I ever seen." Assuming Seeger's memory is correct, then Guthrie's hint he was basing the ballad solely on the movie is disingenuous, a bit of his playing the unlettered country boy.

Guthrie recorded thirteen songs and ballads in the RCA studios on April 26 and May 3, 1940. He was assured and comfortable in front of the microphones; only one song, "Talking Dust Bowl Blues," required a second take. From these, Wetherald selected eleven titles ("Tom Joad" required two sides of the ten-inch 78-r.p.m. record). They would be released as Victor Records P-27 and P-28, the first commercial recordings Guthrie made. The albums also provided Guthrie with the biggest paycheck of his life: an advance against royalties of twenty-five dollars for each of the twelve masters. He promptly sent the three hundred dollars to Mary in Pampa.

Guthrie's notes to the "migratious" album were probably the most unusual RCA would ever publish. In the notes, Guthrie raked bankers, the police, and landlords. He slipped in a line sneering at "the wars in Europe." He urged "U.S. Government Camps for the Workin' Folks, with a nice clean place to live and cook and do your washin' and ironin' and cookin', and good beds to rest on, and so nobody couldn't herd you around like white-face cattle, and deputies beat you up, and run you out of town."

But most of the two-thousand-word essay was a defense of the "Okies, Arkies, Texies, Mexies, Chinees, Japees" who took to the road seeking "honest work at honest pay. We're hard hit, we're hard hitters, but it's a dern cinch, we ain't quitters."

The liner notes revealed a more polished, thoughtful writer than the author of the daily "Woody Sez." At Lomax's urging, Guthrie dropped the overdrawn dialect and the cornpone jokes of old. He was no longer just a radio entertainer; he was also a pamphleteer. Like his friend John Steinbeck, he was a spokesman and advocate for all the dust bowl refugees.

> You might be able to stand the dust, if it was dust alone, 'cause you're made out of dust, and can take a lot of it for a little while, or a little of it for a long time, but when things just sort of fly loose . . . and your land turns into a sand dune, and your barn is half covered up, and you see tractors covered under, and farm machinery, and

---

In a 1971 interview, Will Geer insisted, "He read *The Grapes of Wrath*. I'm quite positive he did. The picture wasn't out. He read *Grapes of Wrath*. He met John Steinbeck here at the Garden of Allah" in Los Angeles, the two men introduced by Geer. In Los Angeles too, Guthrie began a song based on the book, Geer stated, but apparently abandoned it, since Guthrie learned the "John Hardy" melody he eventually used for "Tom Joad" only in mid-March 1940. These comments are based in part on an interview with Geer by E. Victor and Judy Wolfenstein in December 1971. In an interview on February 26, 1978, Geer told Los Angeles writer Dick Russell that Steinbeck later groused, "That fuckin' little bastard! In 17 verses he got the entire story of a thing that took me two years to write!"

chicken houses dusted under, why, you scratch your head, and you pull your hair, and you walk the floor, and you think, and think, and think, but you just cant see your way out . . . you owe the bank money, you cant pay it, you cant get credit, you can't get fuel, coal, groceries nor a complete new set up of new stuff—so you hear of another place, say California, and you see herds and herds of people a pickin' up and leaving out—and you just sort say, "Well, I aint got nothin' to lose, so here goes."

The two albums, released in July 1940, received little critical notice. In the avowedly Democrat *Los Angeles Daily News*, critic Bruno David Ussher discounted the melodic and vocal aspects of "Dust Bowl Ballads," but praised the songs as "important and fascinating." While "the Woody Guthries are no Homers," Ussher continued, these "Dust Bowl Ballads" retold "an epic story." The Durham, North Carolina, *Herald*'s critic heard in the songs a "biting sagacity that is only faintly hidden behind a chuckle." A one-paragraph notice in the *Boston Post* credited the songs as proof of "the existence of true, rugged American pioneering spirit and indomitable will to survive."

The albums met a more earthy reception in Pampa, Texas. One of the Jennings brothers brought a set of the records to Shorty Harris's drugstore. Harris rigged a loudspeaker on the sidewalk and played Guthrie's dust bowl songs repeatedly. While Shorty liked them, oil field roustabouts working the night shift and trying to sleep by day in nearby rooming houses complained to the police. Harris shut down his broadcasts.

The two albums gained only limited distribution and scattered sales; fewer than a thousand copies were sold—and those largely among college intellectuals and members of the political Left. When Guthrie eventually asked Wetherald to reissue the two sets, he was turned down. The fuming Guthrie finally concluded that RCA refused to re-release the albums for political reasons "in order to silence him."

RCA's reluctance to promote the two albums hardly deterred Alan Lomax. Once begun on his campaign to raise Guthrie to national attention, he had no intention of stopping with just a book project or two record albums. He wrote his newly discovered dust bowl songmaker into the *American School of the Air* script devoted to "poor farmers' songs" broadcast over the CBS Network on Tuesday morning, April 2, 1940.

Lomax's program relied on Guthrie to read a dramatized script of a trip to the parched Southwest, and to follow music cues. In the half-hour program, Guthrie played "Freight Train Blues" on his harmonica, sang a duet with Lomax, acted a sketch with members of the all-black Golden Gate Quartet, sang his own "Do-Re-Mi" and "Talking Dust Bowl Blues," then closed the program with Lomax singing the Okie theme song, "Blowing Down the Road."

The show went well, Guthrie a professional before the microphone. Alan Lomax was elated—even if his father was not. The increasingly crotchety John A. Lomax grumbled that "the Oklahoma Dust Bowl man [was] an absolute zero on any program at any time."

The *American School of the Air* show was the first of a number of appearances on CBS that Guthrie was to make in the next months. Alone among the four national networks, CBS welcomed new ideas, its premier resident dramatist, Norman Corwin, explained. "It was open to suggestion. It was open to experimentation."

The experimentation at CBS burgeoned amid a newly regained national sense of optimism, Corwin recalled. "We were working together. It was a time when you could express yourself, openly, fully and affirmatively, pro-U.S., without it seeming you were waving a flag. It did not seem to us we were sentimentally, naively optimistic about America." Men like Corwin and the "forward-looking" coordinator of the network's Music Department, James Fassett, "understood the relevance and usefulness of the folk song" in expressing those feelings of patriotism.

Corwin took advantage of the adventurous spirit and used Guthrie repeatedly on his *Pursuit of Happiness* series in the next months. Whether singing or reading a script, the Oklahoman was the complete professional, standing out among the experienced actors and musicians with whom Corwin usually worked. He was colorful, yet, despite the accent, Corwin realized "you were conscious . . . there was a kind of worldliness, and he was not in awe of talent or big names. He had something to contribute that he thought was valuable and should be taken with respect."

For some months, CBS served as a playground for Guthrie. He hung about the studios, chatting with actors and directors, swapping stories. He flirted with receptionists and secretaries, unabashedly sexual, and often successful. "I think he worked his way through half the secretaries in the CBS building," Lomax said.

The dalliances came easily, according to Will Geer. At parties or fund-raisers, "Woody was a very sexy fellow and he wrote sexy ballads, the way he would sing them in a sexual manner. . . . He got a lot of the girls with charm.

"Woody would make love to them through the music and then the girls would do the courting," Geer concluded.

Guthrie supported himself with well-paying radio appearances, earning as much as eighty-three dollars for a sustaining show and even more if the program was sponsored. He sang "Do-Re-Mi" on Corwin's *Pursuit of Happiness* and earned fifty dollars for the one song, his best pay ever.

He spent time with a growing circle of friends: the black folksinger Huddie Ledbetter and his wife Martha, and three transplanted Kentuckians, Sarah Ogan, her brother Jim Garland, and their half-sister, "Aunt" Molly Jackson, singers all. When visitors from out of town, including John Steinbeck, would telephone, Guthrie went off to drink, to sing, and to tell stories into the early morning.

Other nights, he played saloons up and down the Bowery, or sang at benefits and union halls. By day he spent long hours typing, legs up on the table in front of him, often tapping out striking or touching pages on everyday subjects, according to Elisabeth Higgins. After she and Harold Ambellan married on May 4—Guthrie wryly provided the wedding song, "It Takes A Married Man to Sing a Worried Song"—Guthrie typed many of the thank-you notes for the gifts the couple received.

When he was not writing thank-you notes, Guthrie worked on the songbook. He prevailed upon Steinbeck to provide an introduction to the manuscript of the song collection "Hard Hitting Songs for Hard-Hit People." Steinbeck wrote of listening to the migrants' songs in the camps, and "while there was loneliness and trouble in their singing, there was also fierceness and the will to fight." Then he added a description of Guthrie linking him indelibly to the people they called Okies.

Woody is just Woody. Thousands of people do not know he has any other name. He is just a voice and a guitar. He sings the songs of a people and I suspect that he is, in a way, that people. Harsh voiced and nasal, his guitar hanging like a tire iron on a rusty rim, there is nothing sweet about Woody, and there is nothing sweet about the songs he sings. But there is something more important for those who will listen. There is the will of a people to endure and fight against oppression. I think we call this the American spirit.

For the first time in his adult life, Woody Guthrie had a bit of money to send to Mary and the children in Pampa. He was comfortable living with the Ambellans.

Too comfortable.

CHAPTER FOURTEEN

Sleeping under Money

WOODY GUTHRIE ADMIRED the almost new 1939 Plymouth he had just purchased on credit. Barefoot—the weather had turned warm after all—he proudly drove about New York City, heedless of signals, traffic, and pedestrians alike.

Guthrie owned the road. He took Sarah Ogan, the attractive young widow of a Kentucky miner and herself a fine singer, out for a spin, "to get acquainted," as she carefully put it. On another day he dashed up the Pulaski Skyway with a wide-eyed Liz Ambellan, then abruptly hung a U-turn to speed back to the city as fast as he had come. On another day his driving reduced the stolid Huddie Ledbetter to beseech "Mr. Woody" to drive more slowly.

Perhaps it was the new car, or his perpetual restlessness, or the announced desire to aid a radical running for Congress in his home state of Oklahoma. Perhaps it was a desire to see Mary and the three children or his relatives in Oklahoma. Whatever the reason, in mid-May 1940 Guthrie abruptly asked Pete Seeger, "Pete, you want to come out West with me?"

With nothing better to do, Seeger agreed to go along.

They left New York City to drive first to Washington, D.C. There they worked on the "Hard Hitting Songs" manuscript with Alan Lomax at his Arlington home and discussed a folk song program Lomax was going to propose to CBS, a program directed by Nick Ray that would feature Guthrie.

Guthrie and Seeger started westward in the last week of May 1940, traveling from Washington to Richmond, Virginia; on to Columbus, Ohio; then to Nashville, Tennessee, and St. Louis, Missouri. In Fort Smith, Arkansas, Seeger lost his portable typewriter to a thieving garage mechanic when they stopped to fix a flat tire.

They picked up hitchhikers along the way, including a legless itinerant, Brooklyn Speedy, working a grift and feeding an addiction. When Speedy learned Guthrie and Seeger intended to sing in saloons to earn gas money, he suggested instead, "Boys, you just let me off in front of a Woolworth's and in two hours I'll have enough cash to get to Oklahoma City."

Propped up in front of the five and dime, his crutches by his side, a fist-ful of pencils in a tin cup at his knee, Speedy proved his worth. Another short stint in Memphis produced enough for two ounces of paregoric, which he downed in a single long swallow.

Guthrie followed the roads by whim. In the Blue Ridge Mountains he boasted he almost got the Plymouth to climb a tree. In a riverbank town in Mississippi, Seeger swapped a song for a haircut; then the two of them wandered into a "little old rotty Low Levee cafe." The room was so dark they did not realize theirs were the only white faces in the diner.

The young black waitress, Guthrie later wrote, "edged up behind the counter and looked out the plate glass, and said partly down in a whisper, partly up in a headache, 'I'll just haf to ask you boys to please get up and go.'"

> *"Please. Please go now. They'll not say much while you're in here.*
> *They won't bust in an' tear this old place down long's*
>   *you're here.*
> *They won't do nothing that you two boys can see them do.*
> *They know, so do I know, you boys is come from somewheres*
>   *else.*
>
> *". . . I know you just dropt in here to eat some and be*
>   *friendly*
> *But I can't afford to let them see me being friends with*
>   *you boys*
> *'Cause it'll be after you boys gets on out and gone on*
>   *down the line*
> *They'll catch me an' give me a good fixin'."*

The trip with Guthrie through the Southeast was Seeger's first brush with poverty and with racial bigotry. It was his "coming out into the world," Seeger acknowledged.

They stopped in Konawa to visit father Charley, brother Roy, and sis-ter Mary Jo, now eighteen years old. It was brief and strained, Seeger recalled. "Charley didn't want to say too much in front of the stranger. He was obviously not too happy with his son. He sat in a rocking chair, kind of a lean, hardbitten guy, and we stayed there no more than a couple of hours, at most."

In Oklahoma City, they flopped for three days with the congressional candidate, Bob Wood, and his wife Ina, oil union organizers and members of the Communist Party. Guthrie came away with a new appreciation for unionization and worker solidarity. South of the city, across the Canadian River, an illegal shantytown had sprung up, governed by its own elected mayor and town council. "Woody was fascinated," Seeger said. " 'This is what people can do,' [Guthrie argued]. 'Give them some land and they can organize themselves.'"

In addition, as he would write in his *Daily Worker* column, the Workers Alliance in Oklahoma City and Tulsa had wrested from city officials a food stamp program that fed the unemployed. This was Guthrie's first real evidence—beyond the elections of Franklin D. Roosevelt—that united action by workers could achieve practical results.

> One thousand folks will get to eat today. By the looks of their faces, I'd say it will be a new venture for a lot of them. Oklahoma City and Tulsa has got the Plan, and next thing is to try like the devil to get it for all of the other counties. You can get just as hungry there as you can in Tulsa or Oklahoma City.

At Bob Wood's request, Guthrie and Seeger appeared at a nighttime meeting of the Tenant Farmers Union. Perhaps fifty or sixty people were in the hall, among them wives and children when the Woods began speaking. A line of American Legionnaires, self-styled patriots—"toughies," Guthrie called them—tramped into the room and, grim-faced, lined the back wall.

Wood leaned over to Seeger and Guthrie. "I'm not sure if these guys are going to try and break up this meeting or not. It's an open meeting and we can't kick them out. See if you can get the whole crowd singing."

Sing they did. The sluggers filed out without a fight, deterred by the presence of the women and children or by the singing. "Bob Wood told me that our good music actually tamed down this gang of thugs and kept a big fight from breaking out," Guthrie boasted.

The next day, Guthrie borrowed Ina Wood's portable typewriter. Inspired by the story of a Mrs. Merriweather, who had been stripped, beaten, and hung by a rope from the rafters of her farmhouse, Guthrie adopted the tune of a nineteenth-century sentimental song, "Redwing," "to tell all of you union busters how I felt about you and your gospel of hate":

There once was a union maid,
Who never was afraid
Of thugs, and ginks, and company finks
And cops that made the raids.
　　She knew that she was right.
　　She knew she'd have to fight
　　For beans and bread and they called her "Red,"
　　So this is what she said:

Chorus:
You have robbed my family and my people,
But the Holy Bible says we are equal;
Your money is the root of all your evil.
I know the poor man will win the world.

Now the rich man heard her speech
And he began to itch.
He hired his thugs to spill her blood
Along the city streets.
　　They whipped her till she bled.
　　They hung her up for dead
　　In her little shack one midnight black
　　For saying what she said:

The two travelers drove on to Pampa. Seeger was startled by the white-washed house on the corner of Russell and Craven, "not much better than a shack, and not much bigger than a trailer." Here was Guthrie, devoting himself to the plight of the unemployed and dispossessed, yet his own family hardly lived any better.

If he was uncomfortable, Seeger did not show it. Mary Guthrie took to the nice young man. So too Jeff and Allene Guthrie and Matt Jennings when they came over to make music together.

However different Oil Patch Pampa was from Brahmin New England, Seeger was taken aback only when Mary's mother, deciding he was trust-worthy, reached up to shake him by the shoulders. "You've got to make that man treat my daughter right," she earnestly insisted.

Seeger, an inexperienced twenty-one-year-old, could only shake his head. "Woody was 27. Not much I could do to help them," or to change Guthrie's ways, he said later.

Three days in Pampa playing with his children, now five, three, and fourteen months, were seemingly enough for the restless Guthrie. The two of them returned to Oklahoma City where they offered the Woods a ride to the national convention of the Communist Party U.S.A. in New York's Madison Square Garden.

Guthrie, Seeger, and the Woods left Oklahoma City for New York. Back in the city, Guthrie decided he did not need his somewhat battered Plymouth as much as the Woods did, so he simply gave them the automobile.

Guthrie attended the convention, applauding the nomination of General Secretary Earl Browder as the party's presidential candidate. Both Guthrie and Seeger thought of themselves as communists, Seeger stated. "We read the *Daily Worker*, and took it as our main guideline in what our politics should be."

"Guthrie was sympathetic" to the party's platform, said his editor at the *Daily Worker*, Sender Garlin, but "I don't think he was [a member] because he wasn't an organization guy. He wasn't the kind of a guy who would have liked to go to meetings and get assignments. I just don't believe that intrinsically he would be a useful member or a happy member."

Guthrie instead retained a skepticism unseemly in the Communist Party, an "organization [that] was very sectarian, divided between members of the party and the rest of the world," as Garlin described it.

"He kind of laughed at all the long words that the Marxists used," Seeger said. Henrietta Yurchenko, a musicologist and radio producer who met Guthrie at the time, agreed he was outspoken and critical of the "mossybacks who couldn't stand the authentic voices of the people."

Guthrie was drawn to communism by personal experience rather than theory: "I made ever thing except money," he wrote, "an lost ever thing but my debts. I aint a communist necessarily, but I have been in the red all my life."

In a letter to Alan Lomax written about the middle of September 1940, Guthrie dismissed charges that he was "a communist and a wild man and everything you can think of. . . . I ain't a member of any earthly organization."

Nonetheless, he *had* chosen sides, as he wrote in the notebooks he began keeping about this time. When Robert Wetherald at RCA deflected Guthrie's offer to record the antiwar song "Why Do You Stand There in the Rain," Guthrie decided the record company was politically "afraid." He would not be, he promised himself.

"The day will come when I will raise cain on the rich folks too much and they'll turn me every way but a-loose. But I don't care. You can't get afraid. You got to go on. Can't turn back."

Guthrie's foreboding came in the glowering summer of 1940 as public opinion began to shift from isolationism to lending aid to the western Allies. Hitler, Stalin's partner in the nonaggression pact of the year before, had abruptly sent the Wehrmacht into the Low Countries and France. The Phony War, no more than a deceptive lull before the storm of world war, had ended; France surrendered on June 21 as the tattered remnants of the Allied armies fled to England. By the end of the month, Great Britain—the Mother Country—stood alone against Hitler. On August 15, the Luftwaffe launched "The Battle of Britain," a battle portrayed by American news media as an unequal struggle between plucky British civilians and brutal German bombers.

The Communist Party's purblind support of Russian policy, its shrill screeds condemning the "Rich Man's War," its silence in the face of Hitler's continued aggression, all set the party and sympathizers like Woodrow Wilson Guthrie against a turning tide of American public opinion.

Meanwhile the last six months of the year were Guthrie's most lucrative as a performer. He sang at fund-raisers for worthy causes, and he worked steadily in radio. He appeared again on Norman Corwin's *Pursuit of Happiness*. When CBS broadcast the August 19 pilot for Alan Lomax's new program, *Back Where I Come From*, Guthrie was paid eighty-three dollars. Guthrie wrote Lomax a tongue-in-cheek report of the Nicholas Ray-directed show devoted to songs about the weather: "We just hearse and rehearse, dress and undress in this show business—and all of the boys and girls are having fun and hearsing around." The orchestra, he wrote, had "so many horns and fiddles . . . that you can't think—but on the radio you don't have to."*

While Lomax's script was deliberately didactic, simplistic, and painfully artificial, Guthrie held his own among the experienced cast members. If necessary, he cut verses to keep the show within the twenty-nine-minute-thirty-second frame. As both singer and actor in the brief sketches Lomax wrote to "enhance" the songs, Guthrie was the radio-wise professional. When the network decided to pick up the unsponsored *Back Where I Come*

---

* Nicholas Ray, born Raymond Nicholas Kienzle, was a veteran of the Works Progress Administration Group Theater, a onetime architecture student under Frank Lloyd Wright, later a collector of black folk songs for the Federal Arts Project working for John A. Lomax. He would eventually go to Hollywood to direct the films noir *They Live by Night* and *Knock on Any Door* (both released in 1949) and the celebrated *Rebel without a Cause* with James Dean in 1955.

From, Guthrie was set down as a featured performer; the prospect of a weekly check for $150 was truly tantalizing.

By the fall, Guthrie found himself in demand as a radio artist. For the princely sum of three hundred dollars he wrote a half-hour script on the career of Wild Bill Hickok, and tossed off a ballad to frame the narrative when it was broadcast on the National Broadcasting System's *Cavalcade of America.* The Model Tobacco Company, unhappy with its *Pipe Smoking Time* program, revised the format and added Guthrie to the show; the rehearsal alone was worth fifty dollars. He slipped in an appearance on CBS's *We the People,* sponsored by Sanka coffee, and appeared with his friends Huddie Ledbetter, Jim Garland, and Aunt Molly Jackson four times on WNYC's weekly folk music program, *Adventures in Music.*

In his first appearance on public radio station WNYC, Guthrie sang "Tom Joad," generating the most listener response Henrietta Yurchenko ever received for a show she produced. Guthrie's voice, his song, his message were galvanizing to folk music fans and leftists alike, she explained sixty years after. "We all thought the same thought: here was somebody who was talking about us, even though he was not from our part of the world, [and came] from a different class, a different kind of life. . . . Woody was talking to us."

He conveyed the same sense on Lomax's *Back Where I Come From.* The show was a loosely structured song swap, with each of the thrice-weekly programs devoted to a single subject. Guthrie, said occasional guest Earl Robinson, "was marvelous at certain times. He was at home with all these guys, even Burl Ives," an actor Guthrie came to scorn as "raised in lace drawers" because Ives had learned many of his songs from published folk song collections. While most of the performers, including Robinson, stood far to the Left politically, any effort to propagandize was limited to bland celebrations of the common man and unexceptional assumptions of racial equality. The Communist Party line was otherwise too antiwar, Robinson said. Particularly for a network proudly broadcasting Edward R. Murrow's reports of the London Blitz each night.

When he was not broadcasting, Woody was making music in the fifth-floor apartment of Martha and Huddie Ledbetter on East 10th Street. Despite the obvious differences of race, age, and even size, Guthrie and the burly man known as "Leadbelly" were unusually close. Guthrie "just *adored* Leadbelly," Yurchenko stressed, and "Leadbelly was just crazy about him. And Martha," said Ledbetter's niece, Queen Ollie "Tiny" Robinson.

Like Guthrie, Ledbetter was relatively new to the city. Born on a

Louisiana plantation in January 1888, he had acquired early on a large repertoire of field hollers, work songs, children's songs, and popular tunes of the day he played on his "windjammer," a small button accordion. At sixteen he was hanging around the sporting houses of nearby Shreveport; at eighteen he was on the road.

By 1908, he was married and living in Dallas, Texas. There he took up the twelve-string guitar and sought to adapt the stride piano of the whorehouse to the instrument. He became adept enough to spend seven years playing with the locally celebrated bluesman Blind Lemon Jefferson.

Ledbetter fell into a series of scrapes with the law, first sentenced to thirty days on a county road gang in East Texas, escaping, and eventually acquiring a reputation as "the baddest ass nigger." He was not yet thirty when he was convicted of murdering a cousin and sentenced to a term from seven to thirty years in prison.

After five years working on the state farm known as Sugarland, Ledbetter had acquired the nickname Leadbelly and a considerable reputation as a good field hand and a strong singer. That reputation won him a chance to entertain when Governor Pat Neff visited the prison in 1924.

Ledbetter had planned for this opportunity. In the course of the evening, he sang a song he had written to plead for a pardon:

> I put Mary in it, Jesus's mother, you know. I took a verse from the Bible, around about the twenty-second chapter of Proverbs, around the fourteenth verse; if you forgive a man his trespasses, the heavenly father will also forgive your trespasses.

On January 16, 1925, in one of his last acts as governor, Neff signed a full pardon for the songmaker. His was one of just five the governor granted during his entire term. Ledbetter, having sung his way to freedom, was now draped in legend.

For the next five years, Ledbetter worked as an entertainer around Shreveport, Louisiana, proclaiming himself "King of the Twelve-String Guitar." In 1930 he was arrested for knifing a white citizen who took exception to Ledbetter's foot tapping at a Salvation Army meeting. Dick Ellet survived, but Ledbetter was convicted of assault and sentenced to a six-to-ten-year term in Louisiana's infamous Angola State Penitentiary.

He was forty-three years old when he entered Angola's Camp A. Literally chained most of the day, the prisoners worked from sunup to sundown, through stifling heat and humidity, in the fertile fields along the banks of the Mississippi River. The discipline was harsh and arbitrary; at one point Ledbetter, a man who insisted on his dignity, suffered fifteen lashes for "impudence."

In the summer of 1933, crusty John Avery Lomax and his eighteen-year-old son, Alan, drove their Model T along the muddy road to Angola in search of "pure negro folk songs." On their fourth day of recording songs there, the guards brought prisoner 19469 around. Accompanying himself on his big Stella guitar, Ledbetter sang seven songs that Sunday afternoon, and fourteen a year later when the Lomaxes returned to Angola. A month after the second session, Ledbetter was paroled.

Broke, jobless, courting Martha Promise, Ledbetter wrote to John Lomax asking for work. He could drive automobiles, fix cars, cook, and wash clothes. Lomax wired back, "Come prepared to travel. Bring guitar."

Ledbetter drove, fetched, and carried. He broke the ice with convicts to help Lomax record songs in prisons throughout the Old South. When Alan, "Little Boss," joined them, Ledbetter gave him guitar lessons. Ledbetter sang in penitentiaries, passing the hat for prisoners' pennies, and, sponsored by the "Big Boss," at the annual meeting of the Modern Language Association in Philadelphia—where the collection was substantially greater.

On the last day of 1934, Ledbetter drove the Lomaxes through the Holland Tunnel into New York City. A professor at New York University, Mary Elizabeth Barnicle, arranged an impromptu party for the visitors on the evening of January 1. Among the guests was a reporter for the influential *New York Herald-Tribune*. He arranged an interview with the Lomaxes and Leadbelly that ignited a flash fire of publicity about the "sweet singer of the swamplands."

By March 1940, and the benefit concert for migrant workers at the Forrest Theater, Ledbetter was a fixture in left-wing New York. He had recorded some of his songs commercially and had seen a large part of his repertoire set down in a book by the Lomaxes. If there was a "star" in the nascent folk song movement, it was Leadbelly.

The apartment on East 10th Street he shared with his wife Martha and niece "Tiny" Robinson bulged from morning until late at night with singers and songs. "I don't know anybody who was playing the guitar in the 1940s had not been to Leadbelly's house," Ms. Robinson recalled.

Six decades later Jim Garland's daughter Margaret fondly recalled the Ledbetters—Huddie, who first intimidated the eight-year-old girl "because he was so huge, and I hadn't met many black people," and Martha, sweet and gracious, who made her feel so comfortable. Garland also remembered

the cobbled-together potluck dinners, "a way of feeding everybody"; playing on the floor of the apartment with Guthrie, "just a big kid"; and the
children falling off to sleep in the window wells as the evening wore on. The
Ledbetters' apartment was as much home as these migrants to New York
would know.

Guthrie was a frequent overnight guest. He would flop on the floor or on
the couch, contributing when he could to the community pot, spending his
days writing songs or making music with Ledbetter.

They were an odd pair, the taller one thick set, with arms "like big stove
pipes," the other slight and wiry; one glistening ebony, the other a faded
tan; one with impassive face, the other animated.

Despite their disparate musical backgrounds, the southern black songster and the essentially white songwriter from the West complemented one
another. "Leadbelly was teaching tradition," Henrietta Yurchenko said. "He
taught you exactly how to do things." Guthrie had another role; he was
inspiring young people interested in folk music to write their own songs
based on traditional models.

Guthrie and Leadbelly played well together, Ms. Robinson said. "I never
heard Huddie say, 'Woody, you're not playing that right,' or 'Woody, you
play this way,' and I never heard Woody say that to him. They just played
like they was born together." For hours on end, the two men would trade
songs and guitar licks, then go off to Harlem or Queens, to "darkly lit doorways where the key turned only because some eye looked out and seen our
gitboxes."

Decades later Ms. Robinson would chuckle in remembering the Woody
Guthrie of her youth. "He was funny all the time . . . in words and the way
he acted."

In Leadbelly and the woman he called "Mama," Guthrie found family.
"Aunt Martha would say, 'Woody, come in here. I'm gonna wash and comb
your hair right now.'

"And Woody would say, 'No, Mama.'

"And she would say, 'Get in here!' And she would wash and comb his
curls and they would look so pretty all on his head, and he would look so
much different."

As the Ledbetters had sheltered Guthrie, the Oklahoman returned their
loyalty that summer and fall. He worked with Leadbelly to shape a program
for WNYC—Guthrie to serve as the unpaid host-announcer. He appeared
with Leadbelly at the audition, then repeatedly pressed the station's managers to give the black songster his own show. Only after the programmers

relented and the sympathetic Yurchenko became the producer of the Wednesday evening show did Guthrie back away.

Guthrie's musical judgment and faith in his friend were validated. "Leadbelly on the air was just galvanizing," Yurchenko said.

But Nicholas Ray did not agree. As director of *Back Where I Come From*, the CBS-sustaining program broadcast three nights a week, Ray argued that Ledbetter's Louisiana-Texas singing was simply incomprehensible to a national audience. Furthermore, for all his being on time, being prepared with his songs, Ledbetter could not read the lines Lomax wrote for him. Ray insisted Lomax not book Ledbetter again.

Guthrie was furious. If they could do without Leadbelly, they could do without him too.

Prodded by Lomax, Ray offered a compromise. Leadbelly would continue to sing on the show when Lomax's script called for him, but actor-singer Josh White would read the lines. If the contrast between Leadbelly's rumbling bass and White's mellifluous baritone jarred the radio audience, the pairing kept Leadbelly as an occasional performer. Guthrie returned to the show.

Guthrie was increasingly busy. Liz Ambellan had secured a week's booking for him and newly arrived Gilbert, newly nicknamed "Cisco," Houston at a club in the Times Square area. Though Houston had never performed professionally as a musician—his days were spent as a barker for a 42nd Street burlesque house, his nights practicing guitar with Guthrie and Leadbelly—the booking went well until Guthrie told off a noisy patron. The gig at Jimmy Dwyer's Sawdust Trail ended before the week was out.

Still it had paid well, and there was the promise of similar bookings elsewhere, particularly after the *New York Sun* ran a pair of flattering articles on Guthrie by music critic Malcolm Johnson.[*]

Guthrie was busy with CBS's *Back Where I Come From* series. Increasingly, he served as the host or interlocutor, melding the disparate singing styles of polished Burl Ives, the close-harmony Golden Gate Quartet, and the rough-hewn Leadbelly.

---

[*] Guthrie apparently did not take the press seriously. He played the unlettered country boy when interviewed by Johnson of the centrist *New York Sun* (September 5, 1940). His farming family, he said, "never made much more than a living," and Guthrie himself went to school "only when it was raining and then I just went to torment the teacher." But when he was interviewed by a critic for the avowedly left-wing newspaper *PM* six days later (September 11, 1940), he acknowledged he was an Okie, but denied he was a fruit picker. "I never picked nothin' but my git-tar."

Guthrie on radio seemed to represent an American everyman, a quality that led the Model Tobacco Company in September to propose he join its revamped *Pipe Smoking Time* show as singer and host. (The tobacco company also hinted at Guthrie touring as its national spokesman.)

The offer was enticing—and lucrative. "They are giving me money so fast I use it to sleep under," he chortled in a letter to Alan Lomax after the first rehearsal for the program.

Just as he had while working on *Back Where I Come From*, Guthrie came to play a creative role on *Pipe Smoking Time*. Seeking a "country" sound, he invited Maxine Crissman in California to join him. "Hey Lefty Lou, we sure could use a soft southern voice here," he wrote.

"Folks back here, they just don't know how to sing country songs. Come show them how to do it." When Crissman, who was pregnant with her first child, turned him down, Guthrie recommended the producers hire Sarah Ogan. While she did not have the professional experience of Maxine Crissman, she was a fine singer, a niece recalled. Furthermore, Ogan needed the money.

The producers were uninterested. "They took us out to dinner, some of these big shots," Ogan told folklorist Ellen Stekert almost thirty years later. Guthrie was fuming as he waited in line at the cafeteria across from the CBS studios.

"Woody decided he's going to act the fool," Mrs. Ogan continued, "and he said to the girl behind the counter, 'Say, sis, give me a hunk of this and a slab of that,'" and jabbing his finger at the dish behind the glass.

Mrs. Ogan reproved him with a poke and a sharp "Woody."

"And he said, 'Well, they think we're goddamned fools. Let's not disappoint 'em.'"

Pipe Smoking Time's producers and advertising agency wanted Guthrie to sing "hillbilly" songs. Such songs were entertaining, they insisted. And made fun of folks, Guthrie retorted.

In a revealing letter to Alan Lomax, Guthrie tried to explain:

The best of all funny songs have got a mighty sincere backbone . . . People that laugh at songs laugh because it made them think of something and they want you to leave a good bit up to their guesswork and imagination and it takes on a friendly and warm atmosphere like you was thanking them for being good listeners and giving them credit for being able to guess the biggest part of the meaning. Lots of songs I make up when I'm laughing and celebrating make folks cry and songs I make up when I'm feeling down and out makes people laugh. These two upside down feelings has got to be in any song to make it take a hold and last.

The words and tunes of his songs Guthrie got "off of the hungry folks and they get the credit for all I pause to scribble down." And if those songs or his *Daily Worker* column branded him a communist, he was willing to live with it, he wrote to Lomax.

I've always knowed this was what I wanted to talk and sing about and I'm used to running into folks that complain but I don't ever intend to sell out or quit or talk or sing any different because when I do that drug store lemonade stuff I just open up my mouth and nothing comes out.

He would not sell out, but the salary of $180 per week "beats owning six farms in Oklahoma."* For the first time Guthrie was steadily sending money orders to Mary and his father. The *Pipe Smoking Time* program, even before it went on the air, "means so much not only to me but to my friends and relatives that I'll be able to help and my wife and three kids are feeling pretty good for the first time in a long time."

Through the fall of the year, Guthrie weighed his family responsibilities against his social consciousness. He particularly missed his three children. He had been absent so long "I have to set and study right real hard to think of being a dad," he confessed to Lomax in late September.

As if to explain his behavior, he added an exculpatory note: "I had to leave—couldn't take them with me down the road—so then I couldn't make a living for them there in the dust country, so I just lit out, and am still lit out."

Pipe Smoking Time went on the air on November 25, 1940, with Guthrie singing a theme song set to "So Long, It's Been Good to Know You":

Howdy, friend, well, it's sure good to know you.
Howdy, friend, well, it's sure good to know you.
Load up your pipe and take your life easy
With Model Tobacco to light up your way.
We're glad to be with you today.

* Guthrie's weekly salary of $180 in 1940 would be equivalent to $2,365 in 2003 dollars, or an annual salary of $123,000. When he also appeared on *Back Where I Come From*, he made as much as $350 a week, equivalent to $4,600 in 2003 dollars.

This was the first, and perhaps the easiest, of the small compromises Guthrie made over the next weeks in order to reunite his family. While he fretted about it—they wouldn't let him do anything he wanted, wouldn't let him sing his songs, he complained in a letter to Maxine Crissman—the weekly check salved his conscience. "These folks are paying me so much I have to back a truck up to the pay window to get my money," he wrote.

With that money, Guthrie bought a new Pontiac on credit; the registration listed his address as 115 East Chestnut Street, Glendale, the home he had abruptly left a year before. He sent for Mary and the three children, then hastily moved into a furnished apartment at 5 West 101st and Central Park West.*

Traveling by coach on the New York Central, Mary and the children arrived at Grand Central, no small feat with three young children and a changeover in Chicago. When Guthrie failed to meet them—he became distracted in the cavernous station and lost track of the time—Mary bundled the children into a taxi and rode to the new apartment.

To celebrate their arrival, Guthrie hosted a continuous party in the fourth-floor walk-up, interrupted only by his radio shows. The Guthries bought liquor by the half gallon, Mary said. She met Alan Lomax as well as Sarah Ogan, her brother Jim Garland, and half-sister Molly Jackson. Huddie and Martha Ledbetter were there often, Huddie flourishing a bottle of potent homebrew and booming offers to teach Teeny how to play the accordion.

New York was exciting, a twenty-four-hour-a-day city that swept up the wide-eyed Mary. There were parties virtually every night, all night; she even attended a burlesque show. Furthermore, their apartment was the best home they had ever had, complete with refrigerator and piano. She had a neighbor to watch the children when she and Woody went out. And she had money for the first time in her life, three $100 bills squirreled away in her wallet.

Mary chose to ignore the obvious evidence of her husband's dalliances with young women. After all, she was responsible for three children. Besides, Texas girls knew that was a man's way.

On New Year's Eve 1940, Will Geer arranged a booking for Guthrie at the country home of actress Katharine Cornell. Guthrie was irritable and

---

* Guthrie moved from the Ambellans' loft to the fourth-floor walk-up so abruptly he left behind a stack of papers, including a copy of the manuscript of the protest song collection he had been working on.

oblivious to Geer's efforts to placate him; Geer was unaware that the *Pipe Smoking Time* struggles had rubbed his friend raw.

"Well, I got Woody there to sing and he was just impossible," Geer said. The array of food, the expansive bar, the expensive formal dress both attracted and angered Guthrie in his everyday work clothes. The fact that the women in their gowns had shaved under the arms intrigued Guthrie. He did not sing so much as he "yawled" his outlaw ballads, his eyes closed or his head turned, refusing to look at the audience.

"Woody, sing your Dust Bowl ballads," Geer urged. The audience was sympathetic, liberal. "And why do you keep your eyes closed?"

"Their white shirts dazzle me. Get me outa here, Will."

Two nights later, Guthrie returned from the CBS studios and his seventh *Pipe Smoking Time* broadcast to instruct Mary, "Pack up the children. We're leaving."

CHAPTER FIFTEEN

The Leakingest Roof

*T*HEY DROVE FIRST TO Washington, leaving behind them Model Tobacco's *Pipe Smoking Time*. "They wanted to choose his songs and tell him what to say—and nobody told him that," Mary Guthrie explained three decades later.

"Besides," she added, "Woody had stayed put about as long as Woody wanted to stay put, and he wanted to do something else." No matter her husband had finally found a job to support them. No matter they were left homeless. No matter three-and-a-half-year-old Sue, when Alan Lomax asked where she lived, replied, "In the car."

The well-paying program cast aside, there was nothing to keep Guthrie in New York. A month earlier, he had discontinued writing his *Daily Worker* column. The parting, said Sender Garlin, came by mutual decision. Party theoreticians—and the American Communist Party was long on ortho-doxy—deemed the folksy columns beneath their dignity. No matter that "Woody Sez" was popular with subscribers and one of the few regular fea-tures to which readers turned. Guthrie's droll witticism was lost on the humorless party hierarchy in New York City.*

They stopped for two days in Washington—just long enough for Guthrie to mend fences with Alan Lomax for quitting *Back Where I Come From*, and to record seven more songs at the Library of Congress on January 4, 1941. Sometime during their stay, Lomax urged Guthrie to write a book about his wandering or about growing up in Okemah. Lomax considered Guthrie's autobiographical anecdotes, recorded during their marathon sessions of the previous March, some of the best accounts of an American childhood he had read. There was a book in those stories, Lomax insisted.

---

* In eighteen months, Guthrie had written more than 280 columns and drawn 80 cartoons for the *People's World* and the *Daily Worker*. In terms of duration, it was his longest "job."

Flattered, Guthrie allowed he would consider it.

With the idea that Woody might get his old job back on KFVD, the Guthries set out in the new Pontiac for Los Angeles. There was not much money in it, but Woody could sing the songs he wanted to sing, and say damn near whatever he pleased over J. Frank Burke's radio station.

They drove without stopping to El Paso, Texas, Woody and Mary alternating at the wheel. Mary's brother Matt had opened a flourishing butcher shop in El Paso; her other brothers had followed.

The visit lasted a week, long enough to change the children's clothes and air out the urine odor from the back seat. At 4:00 A.M. one Saturday morning, ill-equipped Guthrie and Fred Jennings dashed off to the nearby Chisos Mountains on yet another hunt for the lost mine of Jerry P. Guthrie. "We had one sandwich and about five jugs of tequila," Jennings said.

They also had a map Guthrie claimed would show them the exact location of the silver mine in Rough Run Canyon; his Uncle Claude, who had seen the mine as a boy, assured Guthrie the map would lead them to riches. Their alcohol-propelled adventure ended when Guthrie lost his car keys in the desert. Only after a long search did they manage to find them and return to town late that night.

More soberly, Guthrie purchased a portable typewriter from Matt Jennings for ten dollars. Lomax's suggestion that Guthrie write his autobiography appealed more and more. Then he, his wife, and three children crammed themselves into the Pontiac once more and set out for Los Angeles.

They pulled up in front of the Robbin home at 1961 Preston Avenue on a rainy night late in January. As Ed Robbin remembered the visitors, "They all looked miserable, tired and cold." The dusty Pontiac looked no better. The fenders were dented and the window on the driver's side broken out. "Woody had never been a respecter of property, particularly property that belonged to the finance company."

As suddenly as they arrived in Los Angeles, they left, on to the gold country and Sonora to visit Guthrie's Aunt Laura. Despite the pleasure Mary took in chatting with her old friend Amalee while their children played together, Mary was increasingly unhappy with her husband.

She had come to realize their marriage was over, she later explained. She had stayed with Guthrie more than seven years, half of that time living apart, while she nursed the hope their fortunes would improve.

But Mary had grown impatient with their gypsy life; this was no way to raise children. She scrapped with her restless husband, dismissing all of his promises of something better just over the horizon.

Guthrie, Mary, and the three children moved into a room in the forlorn City Hotel in Columbia, four miles from Sonora. He cut timber in the Sierra Nevada foothills one day, "and liked to work the tail off me," he wrote Alan Lomax. He and his cousin Jack went prospecting in the Stanislaus River, with no luck. He scrounged in the mine tailings, sometimes finding flecks of gold in the gravel deposits.

Guthrie was happy in the Mother Lode. The snow-swept and moonlit mountains, thick with pine and Douglas fir, were heart stopping in their beauty. Moreover, "a tramp musician is almost a welcome guest out here," he assured Lomax. The band in the dance hall across the street was not good; saloon keepers were quick to turn off their jukeboxes when Guthrie asked about "knocking off a few tunes to pick up a stake."

Keenly aware of all he had thrown over, Guthrie rationalized:

> The wife feels better out here but she likes New York City paychecks better than what I been able to carve out of the mountains so far. She just wasn't in New York long enough to get right good and sick of it. She never was around there when she was flat broke and she ain't got no idea of how far you can smell the garbage that folks throw out of their windows over there in that low-rent district. I ruther [sic] raise my kids like a herd of young antelope out here in the fresh air.

He missed both the cast and performing on *Back Where I Come From*, he wrote Lomax, "but the way it is it looks like it's got to be the road."

As if to explain himself, at the end of January Guthrie set down an allegory about "one certain old cricket back where I come from that used to sing me off to sleep of a night and wake me up right early next morning."

Two days later he expanded it, to insist "I wouldn't take a penny's tip for singing a song I didn't like."

Guthrie was once more "the singing cricket," hiding under rotten wood, "like houses that ain't painted and barns that's coming down. . . .

> Barns and toilets and old swayback farm buildings is a good place. Anywhere there's anything rotten. This is because, you might not believe it, but this is a warm place. This is good fertilizer for this kind of singing. Erosion, mold, rot, decay, damp, crooked work,

lies, broke promises, profit snatching, you will hear him sing around all of this. . . .

Somehow or another the best singing just naturally comes from under the leakingest roof. . . [Guthrie, the cricket,] didn't want to live nowheres else. He had to stay on the job and holler and sing that the house was rotting down. He had to stay. He couldn't sing nowheres else. There wasn't nothing to sing about nowheres else. So he stuck. He got blamed for all of the rotten work. But he stayed.

Finally one day over in the wood box behind the stove, or down in the barn by the manure pile in the sun—somebody thought that he was mean and hurting them, and squashed him under a shoe sole. But his relatives heard about it, and they sing about it. His brothers and his brothers' sisters heard about it and they sing about it. They stay around old rotten barns and houses and sing about it.

They sing the song called, The Song of the Singing Cricket.

Two weeks later Guthrie and his family were back in booming Los Angeles, living in a ramshackle tourist court. Los Angeles's expanding aircraft industry, the core of Franklin D. Roosevelt's "Arsenal of Democracy," offered well-paying jobs even to people without skills, but it left the city painfully short of housing. For Guthrie, it was just more evidence that the little people would suffer most as "War Shit Ton" edged the nation to world war.

When Guthrie grumbled that choosy landlords turned away families with kids, and even then demanded sky-high rents, Ed Robbin suggested the run-down house next to his was vacant.

The woman who had lived at 1965 Preston, a veteran of the Yiddish theater, had moved to Pasadena, Robbin explained. They could visit her and see if she'd rent it.

"You mean it's empty?"

"She's been out of there a couple of months."

"Well, let's get going."

Robbin thought they would drive to Pasadena. Instead, Guthrie pried open a window in the empty house and promptly moved his family in. (Some two months later, Guthrie finally met his unsuspecting landlord, charmed her with his singing, and settled on ten-dollars-a-month rent for the dilapidated house. He would never pay it.)

Mary did what she could to furnish the house with castoffs and scrounged furniture so as to make the dreary house livable in a February of pelting rain. It was difficult with so little money coming in. When too often there was no food in the house, Clara and Ed shared their table. "They were real good to me, good to Woody," Mary said later.

In mid-February, Frank Burke Jr. agreed to put Guthrie, "The Lone Wolf," back on the air—without pay. Guthrie saw the new program as an opportunity to collect material for Lomax, and asked him for a letter of recommendation on Library of Congress stationery. "Say anything you want to about me that will tell a prospective sponsor just what we done in Washington and also on CBS, etc. This will give me an introduction to sponsors at least."*

With his program unsponsored, the Guthries were broke once more—as Woody put it, "busted, disgusted, and not to be trusted." Behind on his car payments, Guthrie worried that the finance company would repossess "his wheels." In a fit of beer-born depression one Saturday afternoon, Guthrie began heaving empty beer bottles through the windows of the house. Amid the sound of breaking glass, Mary and the frightened children fled to the Robbins' home next door.

The drinking got worse, according to Ed Robbin. Guthrie spent more time in Skid Row bars, singing for pennies and nickels, drinking the night away. Meanwhile, bookings at fund-raisers grew fewer. Robbin suggested Guthrie had appeared so often before going to New York that he was devalued when he returned, but, in fact, significant numbers of leftists and liberals had deserted the Popular Front and the antiwar movement as Hitler consolidated his hold on the European continent.

Mary was miserable. "She didn't know what to do," Clara Robbin said. Mary and Woody argued more often, more heatedly. During one spat, Guthrie slapped Mary. "She was not looking for the kind of thing Woody was looking for," said Seema Weatherwax, who with her husband Jack befriended the Guthries during the first months of 1941. Mary was "very nice, but a rather simple woman." She wanted a home for her family yet her husband could not stay put.

---

* Lomax's undated "To Whom It May Concern" letter stated, "I hope he can stay on the air at least twelve hours a day, ten days a week. . . . Any radio station that puts him on is doing his listener audience and the U.S. a favor."

"My wife dont like to live too near the railroad tracks," Guthrie had acknowledged in a moment of self-awareness. "When that old, long, and lonesome 4-time highball whistles on the breeze, they aint no tellin' what an old Reckless Rambler like me will do."

Guthrie was often unhappy in these first months of 1941, Weatherwax added. "Woody was looking for solutions to his own pain, and the pain of the world, as far as I could see."

The spiritual no longer satisfied, he wrote in the midst of a month's despair. Even his bedrock belief in people, in "folks," was shattered.

In a poem dated February 27, 1941, he wrote:

Folks comes down to my house
In superstitious shoes.
They think a Psychic Reader
Can cure the Worried Blues;
They put their faith in Witchery
And confess to the Priest
And underneath their noses
Their life is lent and leased
To wars across the ocean
To murder o'er the sea—
To fight and die on foreign soil
To save-democracy(?)
The spiritualists gather a thousand times
To telephone the dead—!
And folks come to the Prophet
To have their profit read!
The working folks want to inquire
"When will I have to go?"
The moneyed man to find out
"Where to invest my dough?"
Yes, folks comes down to my house
To ask this every day—!
And most poor fools so broke
They can't afford a dime to pay!

Ed Robbin, who had known Guthrie longer than had Weatherwax, thought his friend "in the worst mood I had ever seen him in. He was very depressed, unhappy, angry and drinking." Ever moody, Guthrie had a short attention span, Robbin noted. "He was more like a child. When he brooded, he would sit in a corner, withdrawn" from the teeming household. "He would try and get away from people when he was depressed."

Just a few months before in New York, Guthrie had angrily stomped out of a New Year's party when he felt socially inadequate. In Los Angeles, Guthrie appeared restrained, said Sam Hinton.

Then a graduate student at UCLA, Hinton encountered Guthrie at parties of "high-powered people, intellectuals" in Los Angeles. "Maybe he was uncomfortable there," Hinton suggested. "I think they saw him as 'somebody different,' a child of nature on show. That's why I thought he might have been a little bit uncomfortable." Perhaps for the first time in his adult life, Woodrow Wilson Guthrie was too depressed to bother with the overbearing or pompous.

Only when he was at the Smith-Corona portable was he focused, hoping, he wrote Lomax, to interest an editor he had met in New York in his autobiography. An advance would "keep the wife and kids a-going till I can hack out the rest of it."

Writing came easily to him, even with the three children clamoring to sit in his lap or crawling underfoot. It was nothing so much as "a conversation with yourself . . . just a quiet way of talking to yourself." His prose was free-form, flowing and seamless, typed quickly, single-spaced and virtually without margins. "Its mighty seldom that I know what I'm a gonna . . . write till I read it back over to myself and the biggest part of the time its news to me."

If his writing flourished, his renewed radio career did not. Shortly after he returned to the air, his rival of old, country singer Stuart Hamblen, broadcast sneering references to the communist cowboy on KFVD. If Guthrie had hoped to find a sponsor for his program, Hamblen's attack made it all the more difficult. Guthrie's unsponsored show would last only a few weeks longer.

In April, Mary's brother Fred and his wife Franny dropped in for a visit. They had hardly settled in when, as Fred put it, "the sewer went bad."

With the sewage pipe backed up, and unable to pay a plumber, Woody suggested, "The thing to do is just to dig it up and knock a hole in it with a pick."

They borrowed a pick and began digging. When they found the pipe, they drove the pick blade into it.

"And turds were just floating out of it," Jennings said. The sewage from the broken pipe began to fill the hole and slosh over the crabgrass.

A neighbor man, as Jennings described Ed Robbin, said "This ain't gonna get it."

"So then we left."

As abruptly as that, Guthrie herded Mary, the children, and Fred and Franny Jennings through the dilapidated house. They packed their clothes, tossed the luggage into the trunk of the Pontiac, tied a mattress to the top, and set off for the High Sierras with Guthrie five months behind in the payments.

When the mattress inevitably burst its bounds, Guthrie and Jennings rolled it up and stuffed it in the front seat alongside Guthrie, Mary, and Franny. Four adults and three children drove north over the Grapevine, then into the Sierra foothills, back to the virtual ghost town of Columbia.

There they rented rear rooms behind a gift shop run by the state. Lacking electricity, Guthrie punched a hole in the wall separating the units, ran a drop cord through it, and bootlegged power.

Mary and Woody argued more; he felt trapped and she was weary of their nomadic life. Even if her husband seemed oblivious of the responsibility, they had three children, children who needed stability and a home.

Guthrie did what he could to earn a few dollars. He cut firewood, then hauled it in the Pontiac from the slopes to town. He painted window signs all over Calaveras County, promoting the celebrated jumping frog contest, pictures of "frogs shooting pooliards . . . drinking beer, riding broncs, roping steers." He sang in the saloons at night for the tourists who had come to the gold country. Life under the leakingest roof meant few dollars and faint hope.

In the first days of May, a forwarded letter unexpectedly offered Woody a job and lifted Mary's spirits. The Bonneville Power Administration (BPA), a division of the federal Department of the Interior, wanted Guthrie to narrate a documentary motion picture about the building of the Grand Coulee Dam on the Columbia River. Guthrie was also to appear in the film and sing songs he wrote for the soundtrack.*

The film project had begun the year before. The BPA's then-acting chief of its Information Division, Stephen Kahn, decided the agency needed

---

* In interviews Mary Guthrie Boyle insisted her husband had a firm job offer and was to receive travel expenses. However, the former Information Division director of the BPA, Stephen Kahn, stated in a 1983 interview with William Murlin of the agency that "Guthrie came up on his own." The documentation compiled by Murlin, as well as a Guthrie letter of March 1941 and his autobiographical "My Life," in *American Folksong* (New York: Disc, 1947), confirm Mrs. Boyle's account.

something more entertaining than the didactic, even ponderous documentary promoting public power and the Bonneville Dam they had produced earlier. Inspired by Pare Lorentz's use of snatches of folk song in his documentary *The River*, Kahn decided to employ a ballad singer as narrator. He asked Alan Lomax at the Archive of American Folk Song in the Library of Congress for suggestions. Lomax promptly recommended Guthrie.

At Kahn's behest, documentary film director Gunther Von Fritsch had visited Guthrie at the Preston Avenue house in March. Von Fritsch took pictures of the singer, Mary, and the children with a view to using them all in the film. Guthrie sang for him. Von Fritsch and Kahn were seeking a narrator "with a distinctive voice and style of delivery," what Kahn called the "common touch." Kahn also wanted Guthrie to add some of that common touch to Kahn's script as well as write "musical accompaniment." The job of "narrator actor" would last a year and pay $3,200.

Guthrie was eager for the work, as he wrote a friend in New York. Mary was ready to move; the job would mean a steady salary and some sense of permanence, if only for a year.

And there the matter rested, forgotten, until the BPA letter reached the Guthries in Columbia shortly after May 1.

As abruptly as they had left Los Angeles, the Guthries decamped from Columbia. Woody, who was still behind in his car payments, left unpaid a ticket for driving without a license. They drove north on Route 99, with a short detour to spend a day with Maxine Crissman in Chico, California.

Sporting a scraggly beard, sweat-stained khaki shirt and pants, and a guitar slung over his back, Guthrie presented himself to Steve Kahn at the Portland headquarters of the BPA on Northeast Oregon Street on May 12, 1941. He was so eager to work that by the end of the day he had written at least a portion of the first and one of the most memorable of his Columbia River songs:

> *Green Douglas firs where the waters cut through.*
> *Down the wild mountains and canyons she flew.*
> *Canadian Northwest to the ocean so blue,*
> *Roll on, Columbia, roll on!*

Despite Guthrie's enthusiasm, Kahn had second thoughts. He was worried about Guthrie's politics As Kahn later put it in an interview, "Guthrie's songs indicated he was in the class struggle pretty deep."

Nervous about scrutiny of Guthrie's job application by the Civil Service

Commission, Kahn instead opted for an "emergency appointment" of just one month. (Temporary jobs did not require Washington's approval.)

Kahn at the same time redefined Guthrie's responsibilities so as to eliminate the folksinger as an on-camera narrator. Guthrie, once to "appear in designated scenes," was deemed a month later "not very photogenic in the All-American sense." If Guthrie's voice was to be heard, it would only be on the sound track, singing songs Kahn had carefully sanitized. "I didn't want to film anything that would incriminate me," he acknowledged.

Additionally, Kahn decided his boss, Paul J. Raver, known as a political conservative, should approve Guthrie's temporary appointment as an "information consultant." Warning Guthrie to pick his songs carefully and certainly not to talk politics, Kahn sent him to see Raver.

Whatever his disappointment about losing a year's employment, an hour later Guthrie emerged from the office. "Put him on the payroll," Raver ordered.

Guthrie was to be paid at the rate of $3,200 per year, or $266 for the month he would work for the BPA. "Hiring Woody for $266 a month was the best investment the Department of the Interior ever made," Kahn crowed.

Kahn wanted Guthrie to put into song the problems an untamed Columbia posed to the people living along its twelve-hundred-mile course, what appropriately sited dams could achieve, and the government's role when private industry was unable or unwilling to take on the task.

Guthrie's job, Kahn told him, was to capture the "thoughts and ideals" behind the Bonneville and Grand Coulee Dams. "You're something of a poet. Put it in your songs."

"Okay, I'll try," Guthrie agreed.

Still Kahn wanted his new "consultant" to get some sense of the impact of the project, so he assigned a chauffeur to Guthrie. For the next week, Elmer Buehler drove Guthrie, strumming a guitar in a black 1940 Hudson, about the Columbia River Valley. There were more than a few telephone calls to the BPA complaining about lollygagging government workers.

Their first stop, at Kahn's suggestion, was the local Hooverville, Sullivan's Gulch, about five blocks from BPA headquarters. Guthrie was to think about how dam building would create jobs for the two hundred people squatting there under the Grand Avenue Bridge.

For almost a week, Buehler drove Guthrie through the Hood River Valley, then on to The Dalles, "and the whole time he just said, 'I can't believe it. I'm in paradise.'" Buehler guided him through apple orchards and wheat fields, along whitewater rivers with their silvery salmon runs, while Guthrie marveled at a terrain so different from dirt-dry Pampa.

In Spokane, the local chamber of commerce asked if Guthrie would provide background music for its meeting that afternoon. Guthrie declined. "I wouldn't play background music for any chamber of commerce, let alone in the foreground."

Buehler drove on to the bustling Grand Coulee Dam site, where contractor Henry Kaiser gave them a tour of the massive project. Everything about the Grand Coulee was beyond big in size. When completed, it would generate more electricity than any power plant in the world. The dam itself towered 550 feet, fifty-five stories from riverbed to rim road. Kaiser had constructed a gasoline-powered, five-mile-long beltline to move gravel to the construction site, where dozens of bulldozers and moveable cranes crawled like bugs far below their lookout point.

On the highway again, the Hudson overtook a string of aging automobiles piled with bedding and furniture. Migrants, Buehler pointed out, looking for a new start in land the Columbia River project would irrigate. "They are my people," Guthrie replied.

Guthrie immediately grasped the concept of the BPA in all its aspects, Buehler said. Controlling the river's periodic floods, irrigating the dry deserts in the rain shadow of the Cascade range, generating *public* power for farmers who would get electricity for the first time—the sheer sweep of the planners' dreams dazzled Guthrie.

"Guthrie was thrilled with the prospect," Kahn enthused. "He saw it was more than a power or a reclamation or a navigation project, but something that could touch the lives of the people of four or five states and set a pattern of how democracy could function in this country with the government doing something constructive to improve the conditions of the people."

Better still, Guthrie could put it in simple terms that told "a real story." It was a story Kahn intended to wring from Guthrie if he had to. "I didn't want him to soldier on the job."

Kahn put Guthrie in an office "and I kept whipping him to produce these songs." Guthrie was to type his lyrics double-spaced so Kahn could edit out "the bad stuff." He did not tell him what to write. "All I did was give him the opportunity to learn what the whole picture was and to come up with the songs."*

---

* While Guthrie was capable of writing a song a day, Kahn did not know that when he hired the singer. Rather than a year, Kahn had given Guthrie just one month to produce the songs they would need for the full-length documentary. Hence Kahn went to the whip—unnecessarily.

Inspired by the project, Guthrie's dampened creativity flickered anew. Eager to be a part of this vast enterprise, he allowed someone to edit his work for the first time in his life. Kahn wanted "hard-hitting stuff but not so hard hitting that it would be didactic. And Woody had the ability to realize that we had to have a meeting of minds on this thing and something that would go in a film, and convey an idea and yet would be easy to take," Kahn explained.

There lurked an additional concern, Mary Guthrie said. "They didn't want any politics." Kahn was to closely edit Guthrie's texts.

Whatever their political differences—Kahn was an ardent New Dealer—Kahn took a liking to Guthrie. When the BPA's newest consultant discovered his battered Pontiac had gone missing, Kahn suspected the truth.

"Is it paid for, Woody?" Kahn asked.

"Well, I made a down payment on it."

"Did you tell the finance company you're up here?"

"Yes, I told them I had a job with Bonneville."

Kahn offered to take Guthrie to the finance company to see if they could retrieve the automobile. First, he advised, Guthrie should shave off the beard.

To no avail. The finance company wanted full payment, something more than a thousand dollars.

Once again Guthrie was without wheels.

Guthrie spent his days in the Bonneville office, sitting at a typewriter, breaking off only to serenade the female clerks at their desks. In three weeks, he wrote twenty-six songs, nearly half of which were completely new, the balance being adaptations of songs he had written earlier.

Kahn remembered that Guthrie wrote "a lot of drafts and changes. . . . I was just amazed at the end of one month that we had as much material as we had that we could use."

Guthrie had rediscovered his voice. Of the twenty-six songs he eventually handed in, Kahn decided at least ten, perhaps twelve were worthy of recording for the film.

The songs crackled with the story of the Bonneville:

Uncle Sam took up the challenge in the year of '33
For the farmers and the workers and for all humanity.
Now river you can ramble where the sun sets in the sea,
But while you're rambling, river, you can do some work
    for me.

Some sparkled with the beauty Guthrie saw in the Northwest:

> *In the misty crystal glitter of the wild and windward*
> > *spray*
> *Men have fought the pounding waters, and met a wat'ry*
> > *grave,*
> *Well, she tore their boats to splinters and she gave men*
> > *dreams to dream*
> *Of the day the Coulee Dam would cross that wild and*
> > *wasted stream.*

In other songs he caught the confidence, the sheer exuberance of the men building the damn:

> *I clumb the rocky canyon where the Columbia River rolls,*
> *Seen the salmon leaping the rapids and the falls.*
> *The big Grand Coulee Dam in the State of Washington*
> *Is just about the biggest thing that man has ever done.*

Remembering the migrants he saw on the road, Guthrie wrote a most heartfelt tribute to "his people" and their faded dream:

> *It's a mighty hard row that my poor hands has hoed.*
> *My poor feet have travelled a hot dusty road.*
> *Out of the Dust Bowl and westward we rolled*
> *And your deserts are hot, and your mountains are*
> > *cold.*

> *   *   *   *   *   *

> *Look down in the canyon and there you will see*
> *The Grand Coulee showers her blessings on me;*
> *The lights for the city, for factory, and mill,*
> *Green Pastures of Plenty from dry barren hills.*

Despite the disappointment of a year's employment vanishing, Guthrie had broken the creative drought. In all, the month spent in Portland was probably the most productive of his life.*

---

* The projected film, *Columbia*, would not be completed until 1949, and then in much shortened form. In the spring of 1942 at Reeves Soundstudio in New York City, Steve Kahn

His optimism welling once again, when the Bonneville job ran out on June 11, 1941, Guthrie decided to return to New York and the promise of radio work. While CBS had canceled *Back Where I Come From*—leaving Guthrie to grumble that "this country's getting to where it can't hear its own voice"—there were other shows, other networks. Just as important, Pete Seeger had formed a singing group, the Almanac Singers, and had invited Guthrie to join.

When Guthrie announced they were leaving Portland, Mary suggested he go alone. She had finally wearied of Woody's restlessness; she refused to uproot the children once again. They were comfortably settled in a big frame house divided into four apartments at 6211 Northeast 92nd Street. The other tenants were young and friendly. It was a good place to stay for the while. Better to be on her own than to follow her husband once again to a city that was no place to raise children. If she went anywhere, she would take them back to Los Angeles or to El Paso.

There was no argument, not even tears as they parted, Mary recalled. "We didn't say we're not going to see each other again, but I knew within myself that that was it."

Guthrie "was looking for something," she added. "He was trying to prove something. He *was* for the down-trodden people, I know he was. There is no doubt about it. But as far as something for himself, even for his family, it didn't make that much difference."

She urged Guthrie to take up Seeger's offer. "She thinks its about the best thing that ever happened to me; a thing I always did hold out for, it's 'organizing me, damn it, organizing me!'" Guthrie wrote Seeger.

With cash still squirreled away in her wallet, Mary's independence was exhilarating. "After he left, I had a pretty good time. My girl friend

---

recorded on acetate discs Guthrie singing the dozen songs Kahn had selected for the documentary. But world war interfered with further production; there was no need to promote a project already providing vital electricity to shipyards on the coast, to aluminum plants in the Northwest, and to the atomic research facility at Hanford, Washington. Kahn belatedly turned back to the film project after floods in May 1948 all but wiped out the town of Vanport, Oregon. He recast his script as an argument not only for power generation and reclamation, but also for flood control on the upper reaches of the Columbia and Snake Rivers and their tributaries. He dropped the idea of an actor mouthing Guthrie's words, and used on the sound track portions of three songs Guthrie had recorded six years earlier: "Roll On, Columbia, Roll On," "The Biggest Thing That Man Has Ever Done," and "Pastures of Plenty." Ironically, the film did not contain "Roll On, Columbia, Roll On," which would become Washington State's official "folk song," or the often praised piece of Guthrie's Northwest poetry, "The Grand Coulee Dam" With its line "In the misty crystal glitter of the wild and windward spray,/Men have fought the pounding waters, and met a wat'ry grave . . ."

and I . . . we partied a lot. I was young," she said with a shrug. She went dancing at local bars, and once went to what she described as a "Chinese gambling den," secreted behind a locked door. "We had a helluva time getting out."

Meanwhile, Guthrie put up his thumb on the highway east of town.

CHAPTER SIXTEEN

Erratic Stew

A GUITAR SLUNG OVER his back by a leather thong, a brown paper bag containing a dirty shirt and the unfinished manuscript of his autobiography in his hand, Woody Guthrie climbed the five flights of the tenement on West 12th Street.

For two weeks he had hitchhiked his way across the country. He was still on the road on June 22, 1941, when he learned that Hitler had sent five great army columns eastward into the Soviet Union, a brazen stroke that sundered the Soviet-Axis Pact and drove the Red Armies into bloody retreat.

Guthrie had a wry grin as the fifth-floor door opened and he shook Pete Seeger's hand. "Well, I guess we're not going to be singing any more of them peace songs," he offered.

No, Seeger agreed. Against all reason, Hitler had opened a two-front war. The Soviet Union was now fighting alongside Great Britain.

Guthrie and Seeger could only shake their head at the irony of finding themselves with this new ally. "No one has been a more consistent opponent of Communism for the past twenty-five years," Britain's prime minister, Winston Churchill, had acknowledged. But the Russian danger in this wartime summer had become Britain's danger as well—"just as the cause of any Russian fighting for his hearth and home is the cause of free men and free peoples in every quarter of the globe."

As Guthrie put it, "Churchill's flip-flopped. We got to flip-flop too."

No group had been a more consistent foe of Franklin Roosevelt and his pro-British policies than the tenants in the fifth-floor flat. They had turned about with the Stalin-Axis agreement in August 1939; so they reversed themselves twenty-two months later.

"All of a sudden," explained Lee Hays, one of the most committed of the tenants of the 12th Street apartment, "it became one war, instead of two, and there was some chance of beating fascism on its own ground, which everybody was for. But it sure knocked hell out of our repertoire."

The Almanac Singers' peace songs, on which they had built a reputation as performers, would have to go—at the very moment that they were poised to begin a nationwide tour of union halls and picket lines. Their repertoire contained some union songs, borrowed or rewritten; they also had some folk songs they could spot between the stem-winders.

Guthrie had hardly set guitar and paper bag down when Seeger abruptly asked, "Woody, how would you like to go West?"

Guthrie scratched his head. "I just came in from the West, but I don't guess I mind if I join up with you."

As casually as that, Guthrie became a member of the loosely organized Almanac Singers, "the only group I've ever sung with that rehearses on the stage," Guthrie teased.

They were an odd collection, as Millard Lampell, one of the loft's residents, put it: Pete Seeger the rail-thin whooping crane; Lee Hays an Arkansas mule; Guthrie a gopher; and Lampell himself an alley cat. Three were musically talented; Lampell was a quick and clever versifier who filled in on choruses.

They had one thing in common. All of them had seen the worst of the Great Depression and the bread lines of shambling, watery-eyed men beaten past desperation to sullen anger. That experience had left them with a shared belief "that there are oppressed people and, therefore, oppressors," as Hays put it.

Moreover Guthrie had a special awareness, Hays added. "He was pretty sure in his own mind which was which, who was who," oppressor and oppressed.

Guthrie was to have a profound influence on the Almanacs. The Oklahoman spanned the distance between rural and urban. "There was the heart of America personified in Woody. . . . And for a New York Left that was primarily Jewish, first or second generation American, and was desperately trying to get Americanized, I think a figure like Woody was of great, great importance," said one man close to the group.

Hays took an immediate liking to Guthrie. The two had spent their boyhood years within one hundred miles of each other, the one in eastern Oklahoma, the other in western Arkansas. They knew many of the same fiddle and hymn tunes, the same medicine show jokes, the same tall tales. If Hays's church was more establishment than Guthrie's, Hays decided, they still shared a common southern background.

Nora Belle, Roy, Charley Edward (standing),

Clara (seated), in times of prosperity, ca. 1907–8.

Woody (seated, in the straw hat), Charley, a withdrawn Nora standing
on the porch, and George, in hard times, ca. 1924–25.

Maxine Crissman, "Lefty Lou from Old Mizzou," and Woody in a publicity picture for their twice-daily radio shows on KFVD, Los Angeles, about 1938.

Alan Lomax, about the time he first interviewed Guthrie in 1940.

Woody and Mary with Gwen, Sue, and Bill
on the steps of a temporary home at 1965 Preston Avenue, Los Angeles,
in the spring of 1941.

In the spring of 1941, Guthrie appeared anywhere he could pick up
a few dollars. The sign, which Guthrie might have painted himself,
was photographed by Seema Weatherwax a few blocks from Los
Angeles's skid row, Main Street.

One incarnation of the ever-changeable Almanac Singers, this in late 1941 or early 1942, features, from left to right, Guthrie, Millard Lampell, Bess Lomax, Pete Seeger, Arthur Stern, and Agnes "Sis" Cunningham.

Twelve-string guitarist Huddie Ledbetter, better known by his prison nickname, "Leadbelly," and his wife, Martha, repeatedly offered their home to the down-and-out Woody.

Guthrie in a publicity photo timed for the release of his
"autobiographical novel," *Bound for Glory*, in 1943,
shortly before he shipped on the first of
three merchant marine voyages during World War II.

Guthrie between voyages as a merchant mariner,
ca. 1943–44. The Gibson was one of three or four guitars
Guthrie owned to which he glued a sign proclaiming
"This Machine Kills Fascists."

Lee Hays, Burl Ives, Cisco Houston, and Woody Guthrie
in the spring of 1944 jamming in a corner of
the British Broadcasting Corporation's New York City studios.
Houston and Guthrie were within days of shipping out together
for a third time as merchant mariners.

Private Woodrow Wilson Guthrie and his new bride, Marjorie Greenblatt Mazia, on their honeymoon in November 1945.

Marjorie and Cathy Ann, the child Guthrie called "Stackabones," and the inspiration for most of Guthrie's children's songs.

Guthrie and Pete Seeger, performing at a Peoples' Songs benefit, about 1947.

Will Geer in 1951, testifying before the House of Representatives Committee on Un-American Activities. Because he refused to name others in the Communist Party, Geer would be blacklisted for a decade until hired to appear in the film *Advise and Consent*. Eventually he would portray Grandpa Walton on the television series *The Waltons*.

Anneke Van Kirk Marshall and Guthrie improvising together, probably in the winter of 1952–53 in New York.

Rambling Jack Elliott and Woody Guthrie sing in
New York's Washington Square Park in warmer weather in 1953.

Woody Guthrie accepts the cheers of the packed house at Pythian Hall in New York City after the March 17, 1956, benefit concert celebrating his life's work. From left, Al Addeo, Harold Leventhal, and Guthrie.

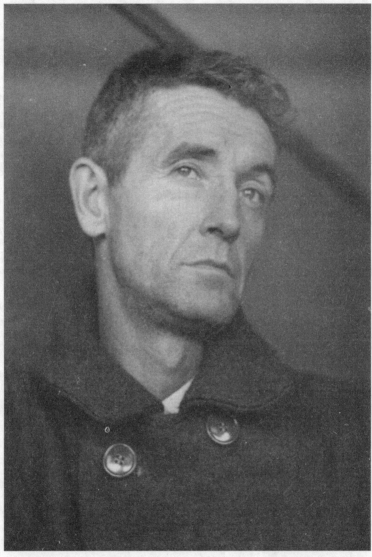

Woody Guthrie at Greystone Park Psychiatric Hospital; this previously unpublished portrait was probably taken in 1958. No picture of Guthrie quite captures his wisdom, his penetrating vision, or his sheer force of will as does this photograph taken by labor organizer and Guthrie Children's Fund trustee Lou Gordon.

Arlo Guthrie, Woody Guthrie, and Marjorie Mazia Guthrie at
Brooklyn State Hospital in 1966 after the presentation of a certificate
of appreciation from the federal Department of the Interior
commemorating Woody's Columbia River song cycle and
the naming of a power substation on the Columbia after him.

Like Guthrie, burly Lee Eldhart Hays was a child of middle-class parents; he was the son of a Methodist minister who took his Bible literally and venerated William Jennings Bryan for his victory in the Scopes case. Hays, born in 1914, was the youngest, and the biggest, of four children. All his life he would fret about his weight, often as much as three hundred pounds, while battling diabetes. The illness left him a confirmed hypochondriac, quick to take to bed, quicker still to swallow yet another pill of dubious origin or efficacy.

Hays grew up in Booneville, Arkansas, in the Ozark foothills near the Mississippi River. As a boy, he learned to sing bass from the hymn books, and, he told a interviewer, "once you get that bass line from the hymns planted in your consciousness, it never comes out."

Like Guthrie, Hays had watched his family disintegrate. The Reverend Hays died in an auto accident when his youngest son was thirteen. Within weeks Mother Hays suffered a nervous breakdown. His oldest brother arranged a job for Lee as a page in the Cleveland, Ohio, Public Library. He would spend almost four years there, reading widely and sundering a narrow fundamentalist upbringing. As the depression settled upon industrial Cleveland, Hays grew disenchanted with capitalism; by 1932, he was a confirmed socialist.

Two years later, Hays hitchhiked to Paris, Arkansas, not far from his former home in Booneville. In tiny Paris thundered the charismatic Presbyterian minister Claude Williams, whose fiery sermons excoriated the moneylenders and whose efforts to organize tenant farmers and lead miners had earned him the nickname "The Red Preacher."

For the next six years Williams stood as a surrogate father for Hays, first in Paris, later at Mena, Arkansas's Commonwealth Labor College. Sprung from a utopian socialist colony in Louisiana in 1925, Commonwealth boasted a student body composed of urban northerners drawn by ideology and rural southerners eager for education.

There were risks to those who followed Williams or organized unions— arrests by local sheriffs on specious charges, floggings by Ku Klux Klansmen, even the threat of kidnappings and murder. (Night riders would burn out the school's frame buildings in 1939.)

In spite of that, Commonwealth was one of Hays's "golden places." He left Mena early in 1940 for New York City with a fund of folksy stories and songs, a talent for writing the one and a sizeable bass voice for the other, all fired by a passion for organizing and a commitment to radical unionism. Just twenty-six years old, Hays looked older, in part because of his sober demeanor and rumpled black suit, in part because of his thinning chestnut hair.

In New York City, Hays moved in with another fledgling writer, Millard Lampell. (The two had earlier exchanged mutually admiring letters after reading articles each had written for the *New Republic*.) Within a month of occupying their Hell's Kitchen flat in October 1940, they met John Peter Hawes, a Mandarin-speaking Vermonter in overalls whose father was a curator of Boston's Fogg Museum, and Hawes's Harvard acquaintance, Pete Seeger. Seeger, earnest, intense, and eager for life's experiences, had recently returned to the city from a journey that took him from folk festivals in North Carolina to the steel mills of Birmingham, Alabama, and westward to the copper mines of Butte, Montana.

The idea of forming a singing group with Seeger, Hays, and Hawes evolved gradually. They sang folk songs Hays had learned from neighbors around Commonwealth College and hymns his father had boomed from the pulpit. They sang songs Seeger had plucked from the Library of Congress collections. But the majority of their songs were deliberately composed to protest any U.S. involvement in the threatening European war.

"We wrote a lot of pretty vicious songs," Hays said retrospectively, songs with clever rhymes and an avowed political message.

> *I don't want to be no bundle for Britain.*
> *I want to stay at home and stick to my knittin'.*

Seeger, using the stage name of "Pete Bowers" to protect his father's government employment from congressional scrutiny, arranged their first booking in January 1941. That fund-raising luncheon for Spanish Loyalist refugees at the Jade Mountain Chinese restaurant in Greenwich Village netted them $2.50.

As the bookings increased, Lampell began to join them. He was not much of a singer, but he could quickly turn a headline into an antiwar song in this year of the nation's first peacetime draft.

> *Do you want a silver medal, Billy Boy, Billy Boy?*
> *Do you want a silver medal, charming Billy?*
> *No desire do I feel to defend Republic Steel*
> *I'm a young boy and cannot leave my mother.*

Millard Lampell, born Milton, son of a Russian immigrant, had hoboed the country during the summer that he was sixteen, spent a night in a Georgia jail, and returned home to Paterson, New Jersey, long enough to finish high school and secure a football scholarship to West Virginia University. In his senior year, Lampell's roommate, the son of a coal miner, took Lampell into West Virginia's coal fields; there he met miners who had successfully organized locals of the radical National Miners Union. Their passion and commitment captured Lampell's considerable imagination and his loyalties. Eventually, degree in hand, intent on becoming a writer, Lampell moved to New York and talked himself into a job on a left-wing picture magazine, *Friday*.

Lampell was unhappy in his job, unsure of himself, his politics stifled until Seeger and Hays began singing for left-wing groups. Hawes and Lampell soon joined them. The quartet would become "The Almanac Singers," their name plucked from a letter Guthrie wrote to Seeger. "It was a good name which meant whatever anybody thought it meant," Hays concluded.

Now that they were singing together, they decided to live communally in a fifth-floor apartment on West 12th Street in Greenwich Village. "The Loft," as they called it, became a mecca for New York's intellectual and artistic Left; artist Rockwell Kent, writer Dashiell Hammett, poet Walter Lowenfels, and composer Marc Blitzstein, among others, sat at the twelve-foot-long pine table to eat Lee Hays's "erratic but interesting" stews. *Daily Worker* columnist Mike Gold brought the aging and revered Ella "Mother" Bloor; she brought with her a basket of produce from her farm in Pennsylvania. Into Hays's stew pot it went.

The Almanacs in these first months of 1941 were avowedly activist, antiwar, pro-union, and well left of center in their politics. (Even if they were not members of the Communist Party, they took their cues from the *Daily Worker*, Seeger acknowledged.) Their songs were topical, polemical, and blunt, propaganda set to music.

> *Franklin D., listen to me,*
> *You ain't a-gonna send me 'cross the sea,*
> *'Cross the sea, 'cross the sea,*
> *You ain't a-gonna send me 'cross the sea.*

*   *   *   *   *

> *Wendell Willkie and Franklin D.,*
> *Seems to me they both agree,*

Both agree, both agree,
They both agree on killin' me.

The Almanacs sparked varying reactions. Alan Lomax, never one to curb his enthusiasms, exclaimed, "You are the most important singing group in America right now because you are showing people in the cities the wealth of music that's in this country."

At an early booking, Lee Hays recalled, an even more exhilarated Theodore Dreiser, "a marvelous old tosspot, came up and kissed me, and he says, 'If we had six teams like this, we could save America.'"

Dreiser's theory would not be tested; there was only one such group, and as far as the Movement's organizers were concerned, the Almanacs were merely entertainers. "To most northern union officials, Communist leaders, and rank and file individuals under both, the left-wing interest in folk songs and other traditional genres had no further practical application." Guthrie, Seeger, and Lomax might see folk song as a bridge to working people; the Movement did not.

In March 1941, Eric Bernay, a former editor of the Communist monthly *New Masses* and the owner of a small recording company in New York City, agreed to record the Almanacs' clutch of peace songs. Once the six antiwar songs were recorded, however, Bernay became apprehensive. The Almanacs' antiwar posture uncomfortably aligned them with the strutting fascists of the German-American Bund and the bitter Roosevelt haters gathered into America First. Bernay decided to release the three-record album as *Songs for John Doe* on an expedient "Almanac" label.

If the Almanacs attributed Bernay's decision to fear of political reprisal, their faint distaste did not prevent them from recording a similar album of union songs for him in May 1941. That set, at Seeger's suggestion, included the first recording of Guthrie's revised "Union Maid," with a third verse by Lampell.*

The two albums, promoted largely in the Communist press, would have a comparatively limited sale through a handful of Left-oriented book and record stores. Despite that inauspicious introduction, the albums earned the Almanacs a sizeable reputation within the Movement.

At the end of May, while Guthrie was writing songs for the Bonneville Power Authority in Portland, the Almanacs sang at Madison Square Gar-

---

* The Almanacs collectively edited the second stanza, and Lampell added a third verse. Years later, Seeger, Hays, and Lampell would disclaim any credit so that undivided royalties might go to the Guthrie children.

den at a strike meeting of twenty thousand city transport workers. Their success and a seventy-five-dollar fee spurred Mill Lampell to plan a nationwide tour of Congress of Industrial Organizations (CIO) locals and a scattering of radical groups.

While Lampell completed arrangements for the summer tour, Guthrie slipped into the communal life of the loft. Once again he was in a welcoming "family." Only Mill Lampell had reservations about Guthrie, this "gopher" from Oklahoma, in part because Lampell envied Guthrie's gifts, in part because he yearned for the Oklahoman's self-assurance.

They were two bantam roosters. During Guthrie's first night in town, he tangled with Lampell.

Whose typewriter was that? Guthrie demanded.

Lampell claimed it.

Was he a writer?

Yes. Short stories.

The only real writing, Guthrie insisted, came from what a man had seen and done.

What if he imagined it? Lampell replied.

Guthrie bristled. No. You can't fake it, he stressed.

What about Stephen Crane's *The Red Badge of Courage?* Lampell asked. Best war book ever written—yet Crane was never a soldier, never on a battlefield before writing the book.

Guthrie glared at him, certain this college boy was insincere in his commitment to the working man. Their testy competition would never abate.

Guthrie spent a busy ten days in New York. With Seeger, he recorded for Bernay's Keystone label a favorite song of Guthrie's, "Babe o' Mine," written by his friend Sarah Ogan. It was Guthrie's first commercial recording since the RCA dust bowl sessions more than a year before.

Radio host Henrietta Yurchenko arranged for the Almanacs to record two albums of folk songs for a another small label, General Records. With virtually no rehearsal, on July 7 they recorded fourteen songs that would be released as *Sod Buster Ballads* and *Deep Sea Chanties and Whaling Ballads.* Guthrie played little guitar during the sessions, in deference to Peter Hawes, but added harmonica and wine-flavored vocals on the choruses.

With the $250 fee they earned for the day's work, Mill Lampell bought a 1932 midnight blue Buick from a New Jersey relative. Once owned by a thug nicknamed "Joey the Mouth," the armor-plated car got seven miles a gallon and burned a quart of oil with each tank of gas. It had one advantage; it was big enough for the five of them, their instruments, and luggage.

Shortly after the recording session, the Almanacs set out for Pittsburgh. Even before they got there, Peter Hawes fell ill with pneumonia and abruptly returned home. Five Almanacs became four.

Pittsburgh was daunting. Its steel mills lined the Monongahela River, their blast furnaces lighting the night sky a glowing red. On the Almanacs' first night in town, they sang in a grimy housing project for steel workers and spent the night in a cockroach-ridden hotel. The next day, performing at the United Steelworkers union hall for Jones and Laughlin employees, Guthrie began improvising:

> *Pittsburgh town is a smoky old town, Pittsburgh.*
> *Pittsburgh town is a smoky old town.*
> *Solid iron from McKeesport down*
> *In Pittsburgh, Lord God, Pittsburgh.*

The other Almanacs joined, Lampell contributing:

> *What did Jones and Laughlin steal in Pittsburgh?*
> *What did Jones and Laughlin steal?*
> *Up and down the river just as far as you can see*
> *In Pittsburgh, Lord God, Pittsburgh.*

In Cleveland, the Almanacs sang at a convention of National Maritime Union (NMU) members on the Great Lakes. Their performance of pro-union songs evoked a standing ovation from the delegates of the radical union and a handsome collection of $135. In Detroit they entertained a huge United Auto Workers' rally in Cadillac Square and went on to tour the newly organized Ford works at River Rouge—proudly wearing CIO buttons.

They were union singers, supporting a cause, bonded in brotherhood to the powerless who sought to organize. In the Chicago suburb of Cicero, the Almanacs met a sometime radio actor and union activist, "Studs" Terkel, on a fur workers' picket line. When he heard the Almanacs had no place to stay that night, Terkel took them home.

Almost four decades later, Terkel vividly remembered their stay. Hays slept on the sofa in the living room of the Terkels' 52nd Street flat, Guthrie, Seeger, and Lampell on the floor. For about a week they camped in the tiny apartment and shared their earnings with Terkel and his wife Ida.

Terkel was especially taken with Guthrie, "a good little bantamweight," and with "big, lumbering Lee Hays." Delighted by the teasing interplay between the two, Terkel decided, "They'd be a great act in a burlesque show."

Drunk or sober, "Woody was a lot of fun to be with," Hays agreed. "He did a lot of drinking." When they had money, Guthrie drank dark rum; when they were broke, he favored muscatel, the cheap, sweet wine sold in corner groceries.

At night Guthrie would make off to neighborhood saloons, to sing and play, then return to the Terkels' apartment to type away during the night. In the morning, while Guthrie slept curled on the floor, Terkel read the discarded pages with their scenes from Guthrie's youth or descriptions of the taverns he had visited. "It was Joycean, poetic and crazy and wild," he said. "It was sort of 'Ulysses in Nighttown,' with interior thoughts and everything."

Guthrie was "a hellion, an outlaw getting even with the big guys," Terkel concluded. He was like Terkel's friend Nelson Algren, "always fighting back against the System, the Bosses, the Interests."

Guthrie's rage against the Interests could be petty, even "unpardonably rude," as Alan Lomax's gently reared sister Bess put it. Invited with Lampell to the expansive home of a friend of Lampell's former girlfriend, Guthrie was uncomfortable and grew hostile. He brazenly tried to pocket a silver cigarette lighter, then silverware, and a cigarette box. Each time the hostess snatched them back. Guthrie finally went off—to the hostess's relief—with a wedge of cheese and a bottle of brandy stuffed in his pockets.

Guthrie's manners did not improve, Lampell wrote. At a picnic in Milwaukee for Allis-Chalmers workers, Guthrie got drunk on "Old Overcoat" and goosed the wife of the local's president. Lampell wrote that he hustled Guthrie away, hit him in the jaw, and threw him stunned into the back seat of the Buick to sleep it off.

Regardless of the actual truth of Lampell's report—Seeger wrote that Lampell "makes up stories"—there was a side of Guthrie many found off-putting, Lee Hays acknowledged. Guthrie's eating habits were offensive, out of either indifference or sheer perversity. "There were so many people who were turned off by Woody—his clothing, his hair, his whiskers, dirt in general, slovenliness." Even Pete Seeger, the most loyal of them, once conceded, "I can't stand him when he is around, but I miss him when he's gone."

The Almanacs drove on to Milwaukee through a fierce summer storm to join a restive picket line in front of the International Harvester plant. When trucks carrying strikebreakers drove up to the main gates, the angry strikers crowded into the roadway and pummeled trucks and scabs alike. Jammed against the gate, the frightened Almanacs bravely began to sing Guthrie's "Union Maid." They repeated the chorus again and again, "You can't scare me, I'm sticking to the union," all the while seeking to lead the angry workers out of the snarled fury.

National Guardsmen pressed into the melee, then lobbed tear-gas canisters at the retreating strikers. As Millard Lampell recounted the story, strikers and Almanacs scattered, the Almanacs to reassemble in a parking lot well down the street from the gate. Hays was retching while an ashen Guthrie leaned against the Buick, giddily laughing in relief.

After Milwaukee, Denver offered nothing more than a booking to earn enough money for gasoline and oil to take them to California. It was a long haul.

Hays seemed to be getting sicker. His face was yellowing, his appetite was gone, and all the while he complained of pains in his legs. His pill bottles were empty and he had no means of resupply. They drove through Reno—painfully familiar to Woody, who had spent a night in the local jail—then over the Sierras through Donner Pass, detouring only to see Lake Tahoe. They rode on to San Francisco, coasting downhill to save gas, arriving with less than a dollar among them. They had made it on brains and personality, Guthrie boasted.

Radical California north and south welcomed the Almanacs. The day after their arrival, the group sang for Harry Bridges's militant International Longshoremen's and Warehousemen's Union, a sharp thorn in the side of the Bay Area's dominant shipping interests. Facing a hostile membership disdainful of "hillbilly singers," Hays, Guthrie, Seeger, and Lampell won them over with their celebratory "Song for Bridges."

> Let me tell you of a sailor, Harry Bridges is his name,
> An honest union leader who the bosses tried to frame.
> He left home in Australia to sail the seas around.
> He sailed across the ocean to land in 'Frisco town.
>
> There was only a company union, the bosses had their way.
> A worker had to stand in line for a lousy dollar a day.
> When up spoke Harry Bridges, "Us workers got to get wise.
> Our wives and kids will starve to death if we don't get
>   organized."

Seven stanzas retold the triumph of Bridges and the International Longshoremen's and Warehousemen's Union over the waterfront bosses. When they finished, cheering dockworkers clapped the four of them on the back as they walked up the aisle to leave. Their triumph opened the Embarcadero to the Almanacs; wherever they sang for the next week—in bars, on the docks, in union halls—they were welcomed.

Hays, however, was exhausted. He was ill and needed weeks of rest, he pleaded; he could tour no more. He left for New York by bus.

From San Francisco, the remaining three Almanacs drove California's spectacular Highway 1 to Los Angeles, Guthrie acting as their tour guide during side trips through the garlic patches of Gilroy, the artichoke fields in Watsonville, and the Salinas lettuce rows.

Los Angeles welcomed the three remaining Almanac Singers. They stayed at the comfortable home of a steadily employed character actor, Elliot Sullivan, and his wife Glenda. They sang at picket lines in front of aircraft plants, at union halls, and fund-raisers. They played benefits for Spanish Civil War refugees, the International Labor Defense, and for Russian War Relief. Finally they marched in a Labor Day parade on September 1, singing "Union Maid" as Seeger coaxed the marchers to join the chorus.

For a brief moment the Almanacs were lions of Left-liberal Los Angeles society. They met Theodore Dreiser again. They sang at Salka Viertel's salon in west Los Angeles, mingling with movie stars and German émigrés, including Thomas Mann and Bertold Brecht. Lampell remembered the evening well; while he was talking with Brecht, Guthrie was off in a corner with a starlet.

Pining for an old girlfriend, Lampell announced that he was leaving the tour to return to New York. His future was as a writer, not a singer, and his conversation with Brecht had inspired him to start a novel. Guthrie encouraged him to go, over Seeger's protests. Neither Guthrie nor Lampell was unhappy when they parted.

With Lampell gone, Guthrie and Seeger drove over the Mexican border into Tia Juana. Guthrie led his friend around a town that was familiar from Guthrie's brief stay three and a half years earlier.

Once returned to Los Angeles, Seeger and Guthrie were intercepted by a lawyer, flourishing a legal writ. He demanded that Guthrie return what Seeger described as "a very good fiddle" borrowed earlier from a liberal lawyer in San Francisco. Somehow, Guthrie had forgotten to return the instrument. Back it went.*

---

* A few years later, Seeger met the owner of the instrument in San Francisco and sought to reassure him that "Woody meant to return the fiddle to you." The lawyer replied sternly, "No, he was going to take it and wasn't going to bring it back." Pete Seeger to Mill Lampell, October 1, 1987, courtesy of Ron Cohen.

Guthrie had one piece of personal business to attend to in Los Angeles before he and Seeger resumed the tour: Mary and their three children, who had also come back to Los Angeles.

Guthrie's meeting with Mary at the home of Ed and Clara Robbin was awkward. Guthrie told his wife that he had found his life's work, organizing unions, and that he expected to be on the road a lot. He suggested she and the children return to New York or stay in Los Angeles to wait for him.

Mary intended to do neither. She did not like New York, and beyond the Robbin family, she had no real friends in Los Angeles. Instead, she had decided to join her brothers Matt, Fred, and Blue in El Paso and to enroll Gwen in kindergarten when the school year began.

Though they said nothing about it, each accepted the fact that they would no longer live together, yet divorce for Mary, raised a Catholic, would be difficult. As Mary remembered their parting, Guthrie was indifferent. "Well, I don't think he could have cared less."

At Los Angeles's Union Station, Guthrie and Seeger shepherded Mary, the three children, and their luggage aboard the Southern Pacific train. Seeger was worried about her.

"I hope you've got your money to go on," he confided. Woody had nothing to give her, Seeger hinted. Mary, with money from Matt in her purse, assured him she did.

The couple's parting troubled Seeger. "Is that the price of genius? Is it worth paying?" he wondered. "Maybe it's easy for me to ask that. It wouldn't be as easy for poor Mary, who was trying to build a home and a family."

Seeger and Guthrie resumed the tour once scheduled for five Almanac Singers. They drove north on Highway 99, Guthrie once again traveling familiar roads. They sang for migratory workers at the federal government's Arvin Camp where Seeger "got a chance to see close up the scenes that had been put into the movie, *Grapes of Wrath*." They stopped to see Maxine Crissman in Chico, before continuing northward, through the redwood forests, and into Oregon's Willamette Valley. In Portland the two men sang for two or three unions, paid a visit to Steve Kahn at the Bonneville Power Authority, then moved on to Seattle and relative prosperity.

Long a radical stronghold—110 union locals in February 1919 had mounted the nation's first general strike in that city—Seattle and the Washington Commonwealth Federation welcomed the two remaining Almanacs. They were booked for a round of engagements at union halls, with old-age pensioners, and the unemployed. They made half a dozen concert appearances in the towns surrounding Seattle and were invited to join as many as one thousand people at a monthly "hootenanny" or fund-raising event for the Commonwealth Federation. It was the first time they heard that term for an informal potluck dinner in a hall, followed by swing and folk dancing or a movie, while, off in another room, others sang.*

Fired by the spirit of radicalism still alive in the city, Guthrie and Seeger left in late September to return to New York. They crossed the northern tier of states, first to Butte where they sang for mine workers, then on to Duluth and a lumber camp near the Canadian border, where fifty taciturn Scandinavian jacks listened to the men's songs in utter silence and then asked for encores—which they also greeted with silence.

From the Upper Michigan Peninsula, the Buick rumbled to Detroit, belching oily exhaust, then crossed to Windsor, Ontario, and continued on to Niagara Falls. For Seeger, these travels with Guthrie had taught him "a helluva lot. . . . The most valuable thing I learnt from Woody was his strong sense of right and wrong, good and bad, his frankness in speaking out, and his strong sense of identification with all the hard-working men and women of this world."

In early October 1941, Woody Guthrie braked the travel-stained Buick in front of a new Almanac house hard by a fire station in Greenwich Village. He had returned to New York with newfound resolve, a purpose, and a passion.

* According to Seeger, an organizer of senior citizens' groups, Terry Pettus, told them that *hootenanny* narrowly bested *wing-ding* in a vote on what to call these fund-raisers. Pettus explained that he had heard the word *hootenanny* as a youth in Indiana used to define "a loose, unplanned party." Pete Seeger to Mill Lampell, October 1, 1987, courtesy of Ron Cohen.

CHAPTER SEVENTEEN

A Desperate Little Man

*N*IGHT AFTER COLD WINTER night Woody Guthrie sat huddled in an army-surplus tunic at the kitchen table, typing on the Smith-Corona. The steady clatter of the keys paused only for Guthrie to make what he called "Oklahoma coffee," pouring hot water through used coffee grounds, before returning, cup in hand, to the typewriter.

In the morning, the four other residents of Almanac House often woke to find a sleeping Guthrie lying next to a cold stove and as many as thirty pages filled edge to edge, sometimes strewn on the floor, sometimes neatly stacked on the table. His autobiography, begun a year before, now consumed him.

Just as Alan Lomax had predicted, in Greenwich Village Guthrie received attention as a serious writer, a voice of working America. An editor at Viking Press recommended by Lomax had expressed interest in Guthrie's manuscript. Guthrie hoped that Viking might offer a sorely needed advance.

In November, Pete Seeger ran into a poet-friend from Harvard, Charles Olson, now a junior editor on the liberal-minded literary magazine *Common Ground*, and asked him to dinner. "Bowled over when he met Woody Guthrie," in Seeger's recollection, Olson asked Guthrie for an article. "Ear Players" in the Spring 1942 issue marked Guthrie's debut as a writer published and promising.*

With Olson's encouragement, the fitful autobiography—"binge writing," as newly recruited Almanac singer Bess Lomax put it—became an

---

* Funded by the Carnegie Foundation, the quarterly was dedicated to a multicultural, melting-pot America. Among others, its authors included a fair swath of the nation's intellectual elite, including Arthur Schlesinger Sr., Lin Yutang, Pearl Buck, Thomas Mann, Carey McWilliams, Langston Hughes, and Eleanor Roosevelt.

unpaying occupation. Perhaps Guthrie was implicitly challenging his rival, Mill Lampell. Perhaps it was the lure of success; Bess Lomax saw Guthrie in these first months of 1942 as " 'a desperate little man' . . . searching for some way to connect, some way to be a big, important person."

Guthrie slept by days, woke in the late afternoon, then sallied forth to scrounge dinner. He lived at Almanac House, went along on bookings with the Almanacs when he felt like it, and ignored the solemn organizational or financial meetings Seeger called.

Yet Guthrie remained vital to the group's existence; he was "our source, our wellspring," explained another new Almanac member, Peter Hawes's brother, Baldwin.

"He was so dominant because he was the authentic thing. For the rest of us, it was more or less something we adopted. For Woody, we assumed, it was authentic stuff," Hawes added.

"But he'd keep saying he's gonna go, he's gonna leave. He was never quite part of it."

"He had to remain independent, so he could pick up and go at any time," Bess Lomax decided.

Lomax—Alan Lomax's younger sister—had an additional explanation for the deference the Almanacs paid to Guthrie. As a musician, she said, "he was much more subtle than anybody ever gave him credit for. On rare occasions he would never change the chord all through the song. And you wondered, how did he get away with it? What he wanted was for people to listen to the words, and everything else could go by the board. He did not care. His solo runs stood out because they *were* so rare. But Woody had a lot more music to him than people think."

Because Lomax shared his musical sensibility, Guthrie was fond of her. She sang harmony, played guitar and mandolin, and she was spunky. While others deferred to Guthrie, Lomax was the one to sing "Great Hysterical Bum," when he seemed to swell in self-importance, to become "Woody, the general of the Free Oklahoma forces":

My name is Woody Guthrie, I'm a great hysterical bum.
I'm highly saturated with whiskey, rye and rum.
I've wrote a million pages and I've never read a one.
And that's about the biggest thing that I have ever done.

Like Lomax's, participation in the Almanacs was fluid. Organizations that booked them expecting Guthrie, Seeger, Lampell, and Lee Hays might get four entirely different singers. Other times, the Almanacs were over-booked, and a quartet might shuttle by subway from one fund-raiser to a second to a third in a single evening.* Seeger worked from a first-floor office to bring order to their organization—"a Protestant Ethic pricking him," in Lee Hays's phrase—but with marginal success.

Bess Lomax had drifted gradually into the Almanacs' orbit. While attending Bryn Mawr, she had visited and occasionally sung with the group. After her graduation in June 1941, she moved to New York, got a job at the New York Public Library, and gravitated to Almanac House. "I never joined. I was kind of absorbed."

At the same time, Peter Hawes was drifting away, to be replaced by his brother Baldwin in the fall of 1941. (Baldwin was looking for something to do after recovering from a bout of polio.) Baldwin "Butch" Hawes, Boston-raised like his brother, was so influenced by Guthrie that he would acquire a lifelong Oklahoma accent.

Shortly after Butch joined the Almanacs, Lee Hays fell into a depression and stopped singing; he was ill, he claimed, whenever they had a singing date. One winter night, as they were leaving for a fund-raiser, a skeptical Pete Seeger stood at Hays's bedside and played "Taps" on the recorder for their fallen friend.

Behind on their rent, the electricity and gas bills unpaid, Seeger grumbled that Hays the hypochondriac was malingering. Contrary to all social-ist doctrine, the Almanacs voted to ask him to leave the 10th Street house.

In Hays's place came Arthur Stern, an art teacher who sang bass, and Agnes "Sis" Cunningham, a raw-boned and square-jawed Oklahoman who played the accordion. Agnes and her husband, Gordon Friesen, a nonsing-ing member, brought a working-class sensibility to the Almanacs.

Cunningham and Friesen, radicals and union organizers, left Oklahoma after the state began cracking down on unions. Both felt a special affinity for Guthrie. Friesen, also a writer from Oklahoma, had first heard Guthrie on the *American School of the Air* and *Back Where I Come From*. "He looked almost exactly like I had pictured him; he just looked like a dust bowl refugee from Oklahoma: scrawny, underfed, uncut brambly hair, thin-faced, eyes that had learned to stay out of trouble, or at least not push trouble too far."

Agnes sensed in Guthrie "something that no one I ever heard had, a

---

* Bess Hawes recalled Guthrie bouncing his Gibson guitar, "tough as a board," on the subway platform. "It used to kill the rest of us. He was showing off its toughness as an instrument. We were playing more delicate Martins. He could play a *man's* guitar." Bess Lomax Hawes interview, January 23, 2002.

feeling," Cunningham said. "It seems he was expressing his whole life, a drifter and all that, in his music. . . . It was something that appeals to me and appealed to my husband. We were from Oklahoma, poverty-stricken."

Their working-class background offered them an insight into Guthrie; it also left them with no illusions about the real estate agent's son.

"He pretended to be something else," Cunningham explained years later. "He loved to have people think of him as a real working-class person and not as an intellectual.

"Gordon told Woody once, when Woody was boasting about how he had gone to work with the migratory workers, 'You never picked a grape in your life. You're an intellectual. You're a poet.'"

Both Bess Lomax and Butch Hawes also marveled at what she called Guthrie's "hyper-literacy" carefully hidden in an ill-kempt, often unwashed body. Guthrie born into the middle class, then fallen on hard times, was re-creating himself as a working-class figure, Hawes and Lomax agreed.

"He used to shave in cold water, no soap or anything else," Hawes said.

"It was terrible to watch him shave," Lomax added. "Woody would just hack himself to death."

"And nobody but me was watching him," Hawes continued. "It certainly wasn't done for the public. Smoking his butts down to the bare, last quarter-inch, this was all part of his image of himself as a great American hobo and hard-bitten person."

Either from a desire for independence or an unwillingness to get close to others—probably the same thing—Guthrie was frequently offputting, even rude. Camilla Adams, then a nineteen-year-old visitor to Almanac House, came away irritated by Guthrie's distance.

"You didn't converse with W. in the ordinary sense . . . ," she commented a quarter century later.

You either listened, or he took off, mentally and physically. He was always the entertainer, educator, telling you something you didn't know. And he wasn't about to waste himself listening unless you'd been somewhere he hadn't or seen something he hadn't, and that was pretty unlikely, considering all the places he'd been and all the things he'd seen.

Guthrie was self-engrossed, she added. "He seemed to feel that it was perfectly all right for other people to support him, to see that he had whatever he wanted, and furthermore, he did not see why he in return should assume any responsibility towards others."

Still, when Bess Lomax fell ill during that cold winter of 1941–42, Guthrie repeatedly clomped into her room in work boots to check on her. "It was very unlike his ordinary behavior," she recalled three decades later. "I was extremely moved by it."

Guthrie performing was another man, charismatic, appealing, a droll storyteller whose soft accent thickened to what Oklahomans called a "coon hunting" drawl. Seventeen-year-old Bernard Asbell saw the Guthrie of early 1942 as a "triangular faced bantamweight with a pointy chin and immense forehead topped by a thick brush of dark hair. . . . His Oklahoma Dust Bowl vowels and syllables, undisturbed by random human contact, were music enough even without the flow of his phrases and sentences that bubbled and sparkled like bursts of crystal, although made of the most ordinary words."

To raise rent money, on Sunday afternoons the Almanacs and invited friends entertained at hootenannies in the basement of Almanac House. They performed on a makeshift stage before audiences of as many as a hundred—at thirty-five cents a head, beer included. Within a short period the regulars came to include a fair number of Greenwich Village's artists with an active social conscience, including painters Jackson Pollock and Wilhelm de Kooning and actors Stella Adler and Franchot Tone.

Deferring musically only to his friend Huddie Ledbetter, Guthrie was the de facto featured performer at these hootenannies. At one Sunday afternoon session, Lee Hays recalled, "Woody was absolutely brilliant. He just had the whole audience absorbed with one of his eighteen-minute introductions to songs." Cisco Houston, left to shift uselessly from foot to foot while Guthrie rambled on, complained, "That little bastard pulled every little trick of the trade tonight. He pulled 'em all. And he sure knew how to make every one of them work."

By late fall 1941, the Almanacs collaboratively had begun to write war songs, rallying cries for a nation on the brink of the conflict. Their first, in early November, was Guthrie's "Reuben James," a memorial to 115 American sailors who lost their lives when their destroyer was sunk in the North Atlantic while protecting a convoy bound for Great Britain.

They agreed the first verses, set to the melody of the Carter Family's "Wildwood Flower," were good, but Guthrie's text included verse after verse listing the 115 names of those who died when the destroyer went down. "He put them into order so they'd rhyme, and he struggled and struggled and struggled with that list to make it come out. It was a tour de force.

"It was also unsingable and unlistenable," Bess Lomax said, yet Guthrie doggedly insisted the names be retained. They fiddled with the song for some weeks. Finally Seeger and Lampell came up with a new chorus to a tune Guthrie contributed:

> *Tell me, what were their names?*
> *Tell me, what were their names?*
> *Did you have a friend on the good Reuben James?*
> *Tell me, what were their names?*
> *Tell me, what were their names?*
> *Did you have a friend on the good Reuben James?*

With the new chorus to replace the impractical roll call, the lyrics transcended the subject of a lost destroyer and lent the song enduring value. "Its force," wrote Gordon Friesen, "came from its symbolism, in that the men on the *Reuben James* represented the thousands of Americans who were leaving home to fight the Nazis and the Japanese."

That same month, Guthrie wrote a second, unusual pro-war song, "Ship in the Sky." It was a subtle, seen-from-a-child's-eyes vision of FDR's Arsenal of Democracy.

> *A pug-nosed kid as he kicked up his heel*
> *Says, "My daddy works in the iron and steel.*
> *My dad makes planes so they fly through the sky*
> *And that's what keeps your daddy up there so high!*
>
> > *That's why your dad rides a ship in the sky.*
> > *That's why your dad rides a ship in the sky.*
> > *So if you ain't afraid, well, neither am I;*
> > *'Cause my dad keeps your daddy up in the sky!"*

The Almanacs' war songs were rarely so artful. With the December 7 attack on Pearl Harbor—they learned of it in the midst of their regular Sunday-afternoon hootenanny—patriotic fervor often overcame poetic sensibilities.* One of their most popular war songs, one they would sing at

---

* Patriotic fervor spurred them to classes in civil defense at the firehouse next door. Of all the Almanacs, only "Guthrie, by grim determination, . . . managed to drag his section of hose up a practice fire escape. None of the others made it." Gordon Friesen, "Winter and War Come to Almanac House," *Broadside*, June 30, 1962, p. 2.

least twice on national radio hook-ups, was set to the fiddle tune "Old Joe Clark":

Wish I had a bushel,
Wish I had a peck,
Wish I had old Hitler
With a rope around his neck.

Round and round Hitler's grave,
Round and round we go,
Gonna lay that po' boy down,
And he won't get up no mo'.

And then there was:

Adolph's a man of a super race,
A baboon head and jackass face.

Hirohito's flag is the rising sun,
But it'll set before we get done.

Guthrie was capable of similar lapses. His "Beat Mister Hitler Blues," written three weeks after Pearl Harbor, was as artificial as the Hollywood and Broadway songs he scorned:

I'll grab a cannon ball or two,
I'll drive an airplane through the blue,
I'll win this war, and when I'm through,
Wedding bells will ring for me and you.

Even writing these flag-waving stem-winders, Guthrie wanted to avoid "making it too much of a sermon." He liked to use humor, but disdained Mill Lampell's penchant for agitprop or jokes in verse form. "The best of all funny songs have got a mighty sincere backbone," he stressed in a letter to Alan Lomax.

Almost by way in illustration, he took time from his autobiography to toss off a satirical blues inspired by a cold winter and no heat in their building at 130 West 10th Street.

Oh, my name is Gordon Friesen, and I'm freezin' all the time.
I live here on West Tenth Street up above the timber line.
Hey, pretty mama, I got those Arctic Circle Blues.
Hey, pretty mama, I can't raise no heat on you.

I went into the bathroom and I pulled on the chain
Polar bears on icebergs came floating down the drain,
Hey, pretty mama, I got those Arctic Circle Blues.
Hey, pretty mama, I can't raise no heat on you.

Most of Guthrie's songs, good and bad, were inspired by everyday events; a drop in the temperature or a newspaper article would suffice. "Usually I set down and knock off a song in about 30 minutes or an hour," he explained, "but in most of them I've been going around humming and whistling it and a trying to get it all straight in my head what I want to say and why I want to say it."

Guthrie, said his friend, Pete Seeger, "was really a writer more than a performer. He'd write a song, and restlessly go on to write another song, and restlessly go on to write another song, and restlessly go on to write another song." He sang some of the songs a few times, "but more often than not, we wouldn't even hear them. He'd write it, and go and write another."

Seemingly in response to his perceived leadership, Guthrie criticized songs by others that he thought artificial, or that deviated from the folk or country style he knew so well. He protested when Seeger borrowed a calypso tune as a vehicle for a new song. "Woody was outraged," Seeger recalled. " 'This isn't our kind of music. Let's stick to what we know.' And he refused to have anything to do with that song."

They talked about songs all the time, Bess Lomax recalled. "We used to try to figure out what it took to make a great song, where were the 'great ones' to be found and what they might mean, and how you knew them when you found them, what kind of condition they might be in, and how they got there. It was kind of like an enormous Easter egg hunt . . . and just as much fun."

As the cold winter wore on, the Almanacs' bookings and income dwindled. They scraped by on Bess Lomax's twenty-five-dollar-per-week paycheck from the New York Public Library. (Guthrie would supplement Bess's pay with an occasional pound of butter, a loaf of bread, or a bunch of carrots shoplifted from a neighborhood market, Sis Cunningham said.) When the stewpot ran dry, they turned to cheap beer laced with Tabasco sauce; someone had told them the combination killed the appetite.

Early in January 1942, the Almanacs were evicted. Seeger found a new flat on Sixth Avenue, between 9th and 10th Streets, above Luigi's restaurant and a dance hall called the Dome. They moved in the dark of the night, skipping out on the rent due, with many people carrying furnishings down the street to the new tenement. Through it all, Guthrie sat at the kitchen table, seemingly oblivious, typing his manuscript. The last things moved from Almanac House were the table, typewriter, Guthrie, and the manuscript, Friesen noted.

Guthrie did pause long enough to commemorate the midnight move with a satirical poem in the style of James Whitcomb Riley:

> *Some piano players with time to spare,*
> *Artists just plain, and some long hairs,*
> *Professors, teachers, saints and nuns,*
> *And laundry men come on the run,*
> *All wanting the money for work they'd done;*
> *Yes, this is the house*
> *Where the Almanacs used to stay.*
>
> *There's lots more little things I could tell,*
> *But then I think, oh, what the hell . . .*
> *And thinking this, not long I'll dwell,*
> *Because we just can't pay the bill,*
> *So I'll take off over some old hill*
> *And leave the house*
> *Where the Almanacs used to stay.*

Two days after the midnight move, the Almanacs were invited to appear on *We the People*, a network radio show intended to boost public morale. Suddenly, surprisingly, they were in demand.

"As the Almanac singers," Seeger explained later, "we particularly didn't want to, much less expect to get popular." But when Ira Steiner, an agent with the powerful William Morris Agency, talked of recording contracts and national tours, the Almanacs agreed, "Let's see if he's serious, see what he's up to."

At a meeting in Steiner's plush office in midtown Manhattan, a wary Guthrie became uncomfortable with the negotiations. The enthusiastic

Steiner excitedly reported Decca Records' interest in recording them. He proposed a nationwide tour and raised the possibility of a weekly CBS radio program on which they might sing songs inspired by the news of the past week.

Guthrie grew increasingly angry as Millard Lampell, once again an Almanac singer, proposed one plan after another. The deal he seemed to be shaping with Steiner smacked of using the Almanacs to promote Mill Lampell's career.

Sitting across from Steiner in a deep leather chair, Guthrie slipped a Marine Band harmonica from his pocket and began to quietly play his "Train Blues." The more he played, the angrier Lampell became.

Lampell exploded. He jerked the harmonica from Guthrie's mouth and shouted, "We're talking big money here!"

Guthrie stormed out of the office. He was still furious when he returned to the Almanac's Sixth Avenue flat. He smashed a mandolin against a wall, then stomped on the broken body and neck. Barely cooled down, he described the meeting in Steiner's office to Friesen and Cunningham, then added, "Right then I started to hate Mill, I really started to hate him."

Did they have any money, Guthrie asked the couple. He needed two dollars. He was going to go over to New Jersey, buy a gun, and shoot Lampell.

"Fortunately or unfortunately," wrote Friesen, "we were as broke as he was."

Lampell would survive, to join the other Almanacs for an early February 1942 audition Steiner arranged at the Rainbow Room, in the upper reaches of Rockefeller Center. The Almanacs, Guthrie particularly, were uneasy in such opulent surroundings. "We were absolutely unprepared for success of any kind," Bess Lomax said later.

From the moment the six Almanacs—Guthrie, Seeger, Lampell, Cunningham, Lomax, and Arthur Stern—stepped off the elevator, Lomax sensed trouble. "I knew Woody was going to do something awful." He had played saloons across the country, but nothing like the posh Rainbow Room.

Moreover, "the people running the club," she continued, the people who would be auditioning them, *judging* them, "were sharp businessmen; they thought of us as an act, and treated us as one."

But the Almanacs were not an act. They were partisans, propagandists, and picket line agitators. They began with their most popular war song, "Round and Round Hitler's Grave."

Mussolini won't last long.
Tell you the reason why.
We're a-gonna salt his beef
And hang it up to dry.

The club's agents nodded approval. The Almanacs sang more songs, until one of the businessmen said, "Yes, I think I could use you. Of course, we'll want to put all the men in overalls, and we can put the girls in sun bonnets."

The suggestion was too much for Guthrie, who began the next song by improvising to the tune of Leadbelly's "New York City":

The Rainbow Room is mighty high.
You can see John D, a-flying by,
In New York City, in New York City
In New York City, you've got to know your line.

In the Rainbow Room the soup's on to boil.
They are stirring the salad with Standard Oil.
In New York City, in New York City
In New York City, you've got to know your line.

Lampell and Guthrie, the quickest of the group, began swapping ever more satirical verses.

It's sixty stories high, they say.
A long way back to the U.S.A.

The Rainbow Room is mighty fine.
You can spit from there to the Texas line.

Assuming the pointed insults were part of their act, the booking agent laughed off the jibes at the Rockefellers and Standard Oil Corporation. With the right costumes and a few hay bales as props, these kids would be fine. He offered them a two-week engagement.

The Almanacs were humiliated and confused. This was show business, and they were not an *act*, damn it; they were singers. They quickly packed their instruments and fled.

Guthrie was particularly angry. "He just didn't like people to tell him what he had to do," his friend Sarah Ogan said.

As Friesen and Bess Lomax remembered the aftermath of the audition, Guthrie refused to wear a costume—but then his everyday work clothes and scuffed boots might pass for one. It was Cunningham and Lomax who balked when a wardrobe woman turned up at their Sixth Avenue flat to fit them for gunny sack costumes.

Despite the group's stubborn refusal to become an *act*, Steiner would not give up. The more the agent worked to secure bookings, the more belligerent Guthrie became, and the more hostile to the values of the entertainment industry. "I noticed in New York and in Hollywood, and I stuck my head a good piece in both directions," he wrote later, "that the sissier, the smoother, the slicker, and the higher polished that you get, and the fartherest from the truth, that the higher wages you'll draw down."

To Guthrie, success in Steiner's world meant forsaking not only his carefully crafted identity as a hard-luck, hard-bitten hobo, but his soul as well. To reassert himself, at a well-attended reception for the Almanac Singers that Steiner mounted at the Hotel Weston, Guthrie yanked a drape from the wall, wrapped himself in a makeshift toga, and stalked from the room trailing yards of material. (A hotel manager reclaimed the wall-hanging, said to be worth nine hundred dollars, the following day from the Sixth Avenue apartment.)

Meanwhile, bookings continued to come in. CBS writer-director Norman Corwin had heard the group sing on *We the People* in January, and decided to use the Almanacs on the first of a six-part *This Is War* series. Their rollicking "Round and Round Hitler's Grave" became the recurring song that stitched together the show.

As many as 30 million people reportedly heard the Saturday-evening program broadcast over an unusual four-network hookup on February 14, 1942. No group of folk singers ever had a larger audience.

Under Corwin's direction, the Almanacs threw themselves into the task, professionally and patriotically. As Corwin put it,

It was a time when you could express yourself, openly, fully and affirmatively, pro-U.S., without it seeming you were waving a flag. It did not seem to us we were sentimentally, naively optimistic about America. We were, after all, the Arsenal of Democracy in the war, and we loved that man in the White House . . .

Then, as quickly as the Almanacs rocketed to national attention, they were to fall from grace. On Tuesday, February 17, the Scripps-Howard

World-Telegram trumpeted "Singers on New Morale Show Also Warbled for Communists." The article, which linked the Almanacs to the antiwar album *Songs for John Doe*, ignored the fact that Communist policy had changed in the year since its release. Once antiwar, the Almanacs were now militantly determined to beat the Axis. They were as "American" in their patriotism as any Legionnaire or Ku Kluxer.

The *New York Post*, a tabloid owned by New Dealer Dorothy Schiff, ran a similar story that day under the page 1 headline "Peace Choir Changes Tune." Reporter Robert J. Stephens not only linked the Almanacs to the antiwar *Songs for John Doe* of the year before, but implicitly criticized Corwin for hiring them.

The telephone abruptly fell silent. Despite Corwin's protests, the CBS network scratched future appearances by the Almanacs. Even sympathetic club owners opted to cancel their bookings. Decca Records tore up its proposed contract with the group. WCBS in New York City scrapped plans for the group to do a weekly program based on current events. Not long after, Seeger recalled, the William Morris Agency threw in the towel. "Our radical reputation was too much for them to handle—as well as Woody's unconventional ways in hotels."

Gordon Friesen summed their brief flirtation with popular success: "I think the Almanacs were deeply hurt," he wrote to folklorist-historian Richard Reuss.

> There was a sense of being unfairly treated, and very unfairly treated. After all, a lot of people changed their attitudes when the U.S. was dragged into the war. . . . There was also a deep hurt that Decca and William Morris reacted so quickly to the attack, dropping everything without the slightest defense of the Almanacs, or even of their own integrity.*

The Almanacs still had a fringe of the more radical CIO unions to count

---

* Complicating the Almanacs' situation, as early as May 21, 1941, a paid informant for the Special Committee on Un-American Activities of the House of Representatives testified in Washington, D.C., that "during the past three or four years Woodie [*sic*] Guthrie has become one of the outstanding entertainers in the Communist Party, Communist Party fronts, and other left-wing organization meetings. . . . And I have heard him on numerous occasions and it is always with this definite Communist Party tinge, and in his singing and his talk he has never tried to attempt to conceal the fact that he was the columnist for the *Daily Worker* or that he was a member of the Communist Party and represented it as such." Hazel Huffman's reliability as a witness could be called into question by her assertion that Guthrie was then a draftee at Camp Dix, New Jersey.

on, but even here they were hampered. Earl Browder, general secretary of the Communist Party U.S.A., had endorsed a "no-strike" pledge for the duration; what need is there for militant singers to entertain picket lines if there were no picket lines?

Never one for doctrine, Guthrie wryly commented on Browder's turn-about:

> I started out to sing a song
> To the entire population.
> But I ain't a-doing a thing tonight
> On account of this "new situation."

Bookings dwindled through the winter, and with them their fees. "This was the beginning of the end," Friesen concluded.*

Even the May 1942 release of a new Keystone album, *Dear Mr. President*, could not reverse the slide. An olive branch deliberately extended to the president they had so roundly scored a year before, the album contained six songs credited to the Almanac Singers. While Guthrie did not sing on the album, at least two of the six songs included in the set were his: "Reuben James," and another with Guthrie's thumbprints:

> Now me and my boss, we never did agree.
> If a thing helped him, then it didn't help me.
> But when a burglar tries to bust into your house
> You stop fighting with the landlord and throw him out.
>
> I got a new job and I'm working overtime,
> Turning out tanks on the assembly line.
> Gotta crank up the factories like the President said.
> Damn the torpedoes, full speed ahead.

·Guthrie missed the Keystone recording session. The autobiography commanded his days, and a woman was taking up his nights.

---

* In late 1942, according to Bert Alan Spector in "Wasn't That a Time," the Office of War Information (OWI) produced a series of morale-boosting programs, each featuring one of the forty-eight states. The third show, devoted to Michigan, included the Almanacs singing union songs in honor of the United Auto Workers. The show, broadcast in 1943, sparked another round of newspaper criticism of the Almanacs' Red-tinged politics. The newspaper fury culminated in the militantly conservative *Chicago Tribune*'s front-page editorial carping at the OWI's employment of "the American Communists' favorite ballad singers."

CHAPTER EIGHTEEN

Marjorie

*T*HE TWO YOUNG WOMEN took the stairs of the Sixth Avenue walk-up quickly, the unlikely basket of fruit that Sophie Maslow carried hardly slowing their dancers' light steps. Maslow was on a mission, or chasing a dream on this late January or early February day in 1942. Unsure just how her idea would be received, she had brought along not only a gift of fruit, but also a good friend and fellow member of the Martha Graham Dance Company for support.

Maslow had asked Marjorie Mazia to come with the vague explanation, "I want to do a couple of dances to folk music and Woody Guthrie's in town. I want to see if he will do the music."

"Good God, I've got to go and meet this man!" Marjorie exclaimed. She had heard Guthrie's album *Dust Bowl Ballads* at her sister's home in Columbia, Missouri. "Tom Joad" drew tears to her eyes. "I looked the album over from cover to cover and decided that this was a terribly moving experience in my life."

Listening to the album, she had pictured the singer as tall and thin, someone to tower over her five feet four inches—surely "Lincolnesque," she concluded—and wearing a cowboy hat. Instead, when a pompous Arthur Stern pointed Guthrie out to the two women, Marjorie saw "this little scrawny figure facing the windows," at the other end of the room.

His backlighted curls glowing, "this little boy turned around and looked at me, and I knew right then and there that I was going to marry him."

It was a stunning realization for the twenty-four-year-old woman born Marjorie Greenblatt in Atlantic City, New Jersey. She was already married, to Joseph Mazia, a metallurgist who worked on a classified job at the government's Frankfort Arsenal. She was an important member of the avant garde Martha Graham company, in Graham's grudging acknowledgment the dancer who best understood and taught the Graham method. She had built a secure and, to this moment, permanent life. While many of her radical friends were casual about their sexual liaisons, Marjorie Mazia was not.

But like her parents before her, Marjorie Greenblatt Mazia had a venturesome, daring spirit. Her mother, Aliza Waitzman, had illegally fled her native shtetl in Bessarabia while barely a teenager to finally settle in Philadelphia's Jewish quarter. There she met Isidore Greenblatt, a pushcart peddler, like her a refugee from Romania and a secular Jew; they shared a passion for learning and radical politics. In time they were married and raised five children. If the Greenblatt family shlepped about, first to Coney Island, then to Atlantic City, each pushcart, each store was bigger than the one before.

Marjorie, the next to youngest child, was twelve when her father, by then the owner of a factory, moved the family to a wealthy neighborhood in Philadelphia. Almost immediately, the crash of 1929 ruined Greenblatt's business and left them the "poorest family in the richest section of Philadelphia."

Rich or poor, the Greenblatts were a learned family. Mother Aliza was a Yiddish poet, published and respected. The three brothers would all attend college. Gertrude, a talented artist, and Marjorie, who played the piano and composed her own music, would become schoolteachers. Not unexpectedly, even the two Mazia brothers Gertrude and Marjorie brought home were said to be the smartest kids in their crowd.

After graduating from Overbrook High School, Marjorie was enrolled in college when she attended a recital by an early advocate of modern dance, Mary Wigman. The performance was galvanizing. That evening she determined to become a dancer.

In the following summer of 1935, Marjorie won a scholarship to study with Martha Graham at the Neighborhood Playhouse in New York City. Almost eighteen, she was starting late as a dancer.

That same year she eloped with Joe Mazia. She was starting married life early and hesitant about sex.

For the next six years, Marjorie commuted on the Penn Central from Philadelphia to New York, first as a scholarship student and rehearsal pianist for Graham, later as a member of her company. Eventually she took a room in Greenwich Village, where she stayed when Graham ordered more frequent rehearsals.

It was there Marjorie Mazia met Sophie Maslow, who danced with Graham whenever that imperious woman summoned her company to rehearsal or performance, and worked as a waitress at Schraft's to pay the bills. Understanding, supportive Marjorie Mazia was the one person Maslow sought out to accompany her to the Almanacs' walk-up on Sixth Avenue.

"Woody, we brought you some fruit," Maslow offered the figure at the far end of the room.

Guthrie turned and smiled.

Thirty years later, Marjorie Mazia recalled the moment when "this little boy" turned around and first smiled at her. He seemed frail, "a perfect foil for my motherly instinct. He was small; his clothes hung on him. He was the kind of person you could put your arms around and say, 'Woody, let me take care of you.'"

While the Almanacs stuffed envelopes with fliers announcing their next hootenanny, Maslow explained her idea. She had choreographed and danced to the recordings of two of Woody's dust bowl ballads; she now wanted Guthrie to sing on stage while she danced.

Guthrie was intrigued enough to mutter, "Yep." Despite all the nights playing for square dances in Pampa, he had never performed for ballet. And these were two good-looking women.

Well, they weren't exactly ballet dancers, Maslow explained. They were modern dancers. There was a difference—in training, in technique, in the very way they carried their bodies.

According to Graham's method, movement stemmed from muscular tension: the pelvis contracted, a leg locked or arm bent stiffly, all of which leant a harder, more assertive look to her dances. Graham sought flexibility in her dancers, the better to mold them into the stark and angular lines she favored. Ballet flowed; Graham exploded. Ballet dancers strained to fly; Graham's dancers might roll on the floor.

If she wasn't the first *modern* dancer in the United States—Isadora Duncan, Ruth St. Denis, or Ted Shawn might claim that honor—Graham was the first avowedly *American* modern dancer. Trained by St. Denis and Shawn, she had abandoned their mythic lyricism for leftist social realism by the mid-1930s.

Graham was as committed to the radical, reformist Popular Front and its stress on American themes as she was to her dance technique. In 1935 she created a six-minute ballet, *Frontier*, to depict the strength of those who had opened the western plains. The following year she declined an invitation to go to Berlin for the Olympics art festival; she would not dance in

Hitler's Germany. In the next years she would go on to create three dances plainly expressing her support of the Republican forces aligned against Francisco Franco's fascists in Spain.

Graham's was a relentless, demanding force. "There is no satisfaction whatever at any time," she confessed. "There is a queer, divine dissatisfaction, a blessed unrest that keeps us marching and makes us more alive than the others."

Marjorie Mazia fit comfortably into the Graham company. If she was not "a marvelous dancer, but a very good one," according to Sophie Maslow, the lithe Marjorie had mastered Graham's demanding technique. Equally important, she was attuned politically to Graham's vision of a socially concerned dance.

By 1942 and the first rehearsals for Maslow's dances, Marjorie, patient, firm, and understanding, was also Graham's best teacher.*

And she was about to confront her most difficult student.

The first rehearsal was confused, as Guthrie wryly reported. Maslow played two of Guthrie's recordings she had chosen from the RCA album, showing him the dances she had choreographed.

> I watched their pretty bodies and wished I was a dancer. I swore to quit whiskey and tobacco and start out taking physical exercise. I next tried to sing the same songs but I sung them all wrong. I sung them according to my old philosophy of "inspiration" and "feeling" but I sung the wrong counts, paused wrong, got the speed wrong and the time wrong.

When Maslow and Guthrie together tried "I Ain't Got No Home" or "Dusty Old Dust," the music was different. "So I stopped," Maslow recalled, "and I explained that he was singing it differently [from the records] . . . and dancers usually learn to do a dance after they have choreographed it, and they do it the same way each time."

They tried it once more, then again, with no better results. Maslow threw up her hands. The beats at the end of each line kept changing.

"Well, I'm a folk singer," Guthrie said with a shrug, "and if I want to clear my throat, I play a few chords and do it, and if I want to think of the

---

* Graham relied on Mazia to teach her unconventional technique. Two of Mazia's "pupils" were Merce Cunningham and Erick Hawkins, both of whom would later organize their own influential dance companies.

words for the next stanza, I play some more chords while I am thinking about it, and if I want to leave town, I get up and leave town."

Maslow understood the message. The rehearsal was over.

Still, Maslow was not easily discouraged. She had Guthrie's agreement to perform as an onstage musician. That would be musically exciting. The trick was to steady him.

Rather than back off, Maslow expanded her vision. She would dance to the RCA recordings of two dust bowl songs. In addition, she proposed Guthrie not only sing, but also with Earl Robinson read lines adapted from Carl Sandburg's poetic celebration of the American nation, *The People, Yes*. The set of eight dances Maslow titled *Folksay* was much more ambitious than the two solos she had first proposed, but Robinson, a well-trained musician, would be a steadying influence on Guthrie.

Guthrie was agreeable, even though he would not be singing his own compositions but four traditional songs Maslow had selected. He counted the talented Robinson a friend. Equally important, Robinson was a committed Communist and composer of a song Guthrie greatly admired, "Joe Hill."

Robinson was some help. But even when he sang and the two men played duets, Guthrie could be erratic; you played *with* Guthrie, or not at all. Bess Lomax, who stood at his shoulder counting beats during rehearsal, remembered, "He had a tendency to hold his notes, depending on if his voice was in good shape, and he felt like hanging on for five beats, and if he didn't, he'd leave it at two or something."

Everyone at Almanac House tutored Guthrie—"struggled" said Bess Lomax—to maintain the same rhythm and beats at the end of phrases. Frustrated, Maslow turned to Mazia, with a reputation among the Martha Graham dancers as a good teacher, to help out.

Mazia worked at Guthrie's side, counting beats into his ear. Eventually she typed up cue sheets, with the words in capital letters and the number of beats marked at the end of each line. Spread out on the floor in front of Guthrie were charts pasted to shirt cardboards, with everyone standing around counting for him. "It was a mess," Hawes said. One that only slowly resolved itself.

Rather soon after rehearsals began, both Maslow and Hawes noticed that Mazia and Guthrie were "together a lot. They would be off at one side, or they would disappear after a rehearsal." Earl Robinson was jealous; struck by Mazia's good looks, he had set his cap for her only to discover Guthrie was a step ahead of him.

A smile had evolved into an acquaintance and that to a cautious courtship. Guthrie, so brash with other attractive women, was suddenly shy in the presence of this poised and alluring dancer. Marjorie seemed different from the secretaries at CBS or the uptown society girls who turned up at fund-raisers for good causes. Quick to bed with so many others, he was skittish with Marjorie, apparently unsure of himself, of her, and of their feelings. The wrong word and she might bolt.

Common values drew them together. Unlike Mary or the other girls raised in the small towns of Guthrie's youth, Marjorie was politically sophisticated. Marjorie Mazia "had some of the spirit and the ideas that were going around at the time," Bess Lomax Hawes noted.

"It wasn't necessary to be a member of the Communist Party, or even know what the Communist Party was, to have strong feelings about the situation in the Pullman [porters'] strike or whatever was going on at the time. Most people in the country did, so we were not all that unusual in our interest in what was going on in this very basic conflict on unionization, and trying to get things going in the country in a more equitable manner."

A further attraction lay in the sheer romance of it all, the secret longings, the whispered conversations, even the "forbidden" nature of their relationship. It was captivating, Marjorie said. And it elicited feelings from Guthrie that he had never before acknowledged.

> I used to say I wasn't sentimental and said it for quite a long time—
> and then I wasn't emotional and said that for quite a spell—and
> next I said I wasn't ever lonesome and lied for a good long time—
> and then it seemed like when I met you I found out I was one of the
> world's worst at all of these.

They said nothing at the time, but nothing needed to be said, Mazia conceded. "We were very clear about our feelings."

Once again, as Cisco Houston admiringly put it, here was this scrawny guy who "was a little bit unwashed, but he always managed to get the beautiful women."

Guthrie was awed by how this woman of such coiled energy, of sheer power, and he "were built alike and visioned alike—could turn out work and fight alike." Sex was another matter; Guthrie, boasting he was "heavy hung" and experienced, sensed that Marjorie had yet to be awakened.

The premier of *Folksay* in March 1942 at the Humphrey-Weidman Studio Theater in New York City was a grand success. In two episodes, Robinson the none-too-smart city slicker and Guthrie the cagey countryman swapped snappy lines from Sandburg while the ten-member company continued to dance. Moreover, the four songs sung by Robinson and Guthrie, with the beats now written out on small pieces of paper taped to his guitar, came off without a hitch. Maslow had created an artistic fusion of dance, poetry, and music that reaffirmed the American spirit and patriotic resolve in these first anxious months of world war.

Consistent with the goals of the revolutionary dance movement, wrote dance historian Ellen Graff, Maslow had elevated

> the arts of rural and mostly poor folk. . . . The appeal of the folk movement to leftists at that time partly grew from the way in which folk art seemed to empower the ordinary man, and the extent to which Maslow blurred distinctions between her staged choreography and Guthrie's authentic rural voices is what had political implications. Guthrie may not have been an anonymous voice—and he probably was more calculated in his artistry than he was willing to admit—but he was a bona fide voice of the people.

Then and in successive presentations over the next years, Guthrie was to turn in reliable performances, Maslow said. While there was nothing showy about him, never any posturing, Guthrie "was a remarkable stage person," she marveled. "He had a natural, attractive quality about him, an ease of performing." (Even in rehearsal, he could draw a laugh with Sandburg's droll line "Not so cold, but pretty damn cold," though the ten dancers had heard the comment so many times before.)*

After the first performance of the *Folksay* program, Marjorie and Guthrie walked through the cold spring night to a cast party, holding hands, a single finger touching through a hole in her gloves. They were a couple. Later that evening they walked to her apartment at 148 West 14th Street where they talked the night through.

Facing a three-week tour with the Graham company, Marjorie offered Guthrie the use of her apartment. She had intended to give it up when she left town, she explained, but it would be quieter there than at Almanac House with all its comings and goings.

They spent her last night in Manhattan before the tour talking until

---

* *Folksay*, Maslow said in a 1998 interview, was to become her "most enduring dance." She taught it to numerous college dance companies, beginning with William Bales's at Bennington, and to a company in England. It was performed as recently as 1997 in Salt Lake City, she said.

dawn about their separate lives and their marriages, his sundered, hers nonfunctional. By this time, Marjorie told would-be Guthrie biographer Richard Reuss, they were very clear about their feelings for one another. Still, they hardly touched each other all night.

With Marjorie on tour, Guthrie spent his days working on the manuscript for his autobiography. He appeared on one or two radio programs, he occasionally sang with the Almanacs at night, and he might spend an evening playing on the deck of the Staten Island ferry when he needed cigarette money. Otherwise, he worked on the manuscript he had titled "The Boomchasers."*

By April 24, 1942, Guthrie felt confident enough about his writing that he read a selection from the manuscript at a works-in-progress meeting of the League of American Writers. The members of that Popular Front organization invited Guthrie to join as a representative of "proletarian regionalism"; the more he smacked of the soil and his book of the Okie migration, the better.

When her tour ended in late April, Marjorie returned to her tiny apartment on 14th Street and to Guthrie. Her hesitation swept away by desire, they fell into a passionate love affair. Meanwhile, she resumed her commute between the Graham company and Guthrie in New York City, and her husband in Philadelphia.

Their days—and nights—were intense. By day Marjorie watched over Guthrie, urging him to work regular hours, to be more disciplined. It was part of her nature, Sophie Maslow said. "I think Marjorie would enjoy the process of changing a person to what she thought was the right way to live."

While Guthrie might balk, Marjorie was not put off. "I lived with two great artists and they were both temperamental," her lover and Martha Graham. Both had "this stubbornness and tenacity about their creative efforts." Both worked on different projects at the same time, perfecting the best, discarding the rest. Guthrie "always rewrote his songs," Marjorie stressed. "Graham did the same thing, reworking it over and over again until she got it the way she wanted."

Marjorie, who understood Guthrie the artist, had no patience for his ill manners. "When you told him to wash his face or comb his hair prior to per-

---

* In February, around the time he met Marjorie, Guthrie and Pete Seeger had the same number of Almanac bookings. By June and the time of Seeger's induction into the army, Seeger was doing half of the bookings, his biographer noted. See David King Dunaway, *How Can I Keep from Singing: Pete Seeger* (New York: Da Capo Press, 1990), p. 103.

forming," recalled Bess Hawes, "he would take it as an insult to his class. The working class didn't fool with things like that, he said."

Marjorie would have none of it. "Margie simply took him in hand," Bess observed. She recalled that Mazia once reproved a shambling Guthrie with a drill sergeant's command: "All right, Woody, stand up straight and step out."

At night, Guthrie became the mentor, the one to lead Marjorie to discoveries of her own sexuality. The woman once timid about sex opened when her lover urged her to "kick your legs around in the air for me, and keep your womb clean for me."

> Spread your legs apart now and let me put this several inches of new life and lights into your plowed grounds, inside your hole and your nest, inside where you can bathe and warm it in all of your slick oils and salves. Let me come slow enough so as not to do you misery. Let me come in as slow as you want me. Let me hold you as you spread your knees nice and wide for me to lay my heavy load down here on your stomach. I will be so light and so easy that you will not even know that I am here in you. . . . Hunch your hips and your hairs against my belly and against my hairs. And I will stay here in you and through you and all here about you till your eyes have closed to the sights of both of us and see only yonder prettier lights which light up the plains and hills in the lands of creation. And let me be man enough to stay here in you till your whole spirit is satisfied and your soul comes down to rest again here where I'm holding you.

Guthrie would tape similar love letters to the furniture or the refrigerator where Marjorie would find them when she returned to their hideaway. The letters were an unexpected part of the romance that made these early years with Guthrie so "very, very good."

In public, they were discreet. When her older brother David, an engineering officer on a Sinclair Oil tanker, dropped by her flat during a twenty-day layover in New York harbor, Marjorie said nothing to him. Guthrie popped up on one of his visits, David Greenblatt recalled, but made no particular impression. "It was all very casual. I thought he was just a friend." (Guthrie was so unassuming or unprepossessing that Greenblatt, who had heard the dust bowl albums, did not connect them with the slight man sitting on the other chair in the room.)

The discretion was intended to protect Marjorie's husband, working at a sensitive position at the ordnance facility. Shortly after Marjorie had taken her husband to a Sunday hootenanny at Almanac House, a security officer at the arsenal had cautioned Joe Mazia. "I understand you are consorting with Communists," the officer warned Mazia. "They have a cell in Almanac House." It was the first and last time Joe Mazia visited the Sixth Avenue building.

As careful as Marjorie and Guthrie were, their affair could not remain secret for very long. Sometime in late May or early June 1942, Marjorie found a message waiting for her at the Graham rehearsal hall; her husband asked that she telephone him.

Joe Mazia was alternately angry and disbelieving. He had just had a visit from two agents from the Federal Bureau of Investigation who were conducting a security check on him. The agents asked him if he knew his wife "was having an affair with a Communist."

"Was it true?" he demanded.

Surprised, Marjorie confessed. But there was more to it: she was pregnant. She offered to take the next train to Philadelphia and explain.

Joe Mazia was hurt that his wife, who had been so sexually indifferent with him, was dallying with another man. "I felt betrayed"—by his wife, "so good looking . . . so warm," and by Guthrie as well, "a talented bum without any morals or scruples."

In hopes he might salvage his marriage, Mazia insisted that Marjorie return to Philadelphia, to stay with him. He would provide the best medical care to her and the baby, which just might be his, after all. At least the child need not be labeled "born out of wedlock." For the sake of her baby, Marjorie agreed to join him when she drew near her term.

Guthrie was furious, angry enough to ram his hand through a glass door in the apartment, when Marjorie told him her decision. The baby was due in early February; she promised she would leave Mazia and Philadelphia for good by April 15, 1943.

Over the next months Guthrie's rage alternated with depression and self-pity. Cisco Houston bore them through "a difficult and trying time," Marjorie acknowledged. "Cisco was a great comfort to me because when I would leave Woody he would be so distraught and Cisco would comfort him. They would play music all night long while I was gone and I always felt good because Cisco was there."

While Marjorie was living with Mazia, Houston would chide Guthrie for his "sob-sister act," his stories of Charley, Nora, and Clara; of fires, death, and insanity; his fear of losing Marjorie and his child. "You can't go through life just being sorry for yourself," Houston admonished.

Guthrie and Joe Mazia entered into a long correspondence over who should raise the baby. Mazia insisted he loved Marjorie, and so he would love her baby. Besides, how could they be sure that the child was not his? "There was a possibility, but not a probability that [the baby] was my child biologically," he explained many years later. Guthrie vacillated between boldness and self-effacement. First he insisted on *his* rights as a father and Marjorie's lover, then he conceded that he could not provide the child a truly stable home and asked they not forget him when he bowed out.

In mid-July 1942, while Marjorie was at Bennington with the Graham company, Guthrie returned to Almanac House, now moved to 647 Hudson Street. Pete Seeger had been drafted into the army; Guthrie and Sis Cunningham were virtually the only Almanacs left in New York City.*

These were productive months for Guthrie. Fired by patriotism, he turned out one war song after another, most of them little more than quickly forgotten doggerel:

> *Now, I am just a soldier, I've traveled all around;*
> *I've been to Fort McClellan and other camps around.*
> *My uniform is spotless, my shoes are shining too;*
> *I'm proud to wear the uniform of the old Red, White and*
> > *Blue.*

Relying on the *Daily Worker* for his war news, he parroted Moscow-inspired propaganda. His "Open up That Second Front Today" was a strident call to sacrifice untrained American troops by prematurely invading France and ease Wehrmacht pressure on a beleaguered Soviet Union.

> *We don't care what Hitler don't 'low,*
> *Gonna open up on him anyhow.*
> *Open up that second front today.*

> *   *   *   *   *   *

> *The Yanks are tough and the Reds are brave,*
> *Gonna shake hands over Hitler's grave.*
> *Open up that second front today.*

---

* Bess Lomax, Baldwin Hawes, Arthur Stern, and new Almanac Charles Polacheck had moved to Detroit in June, lured by the promise of bookings in that heavily unionized city.

* * * * * *

Cross that channel in one big jump,
Stick a bayonet in Hitler's rump.
Open up that second front today.

Guthrie could be bloodthirsty when it came to fighting fascism with song. He heralded a Red Army sniper, Lyudmilla Pavlachenko, who had killed 257 German soldiers and was to tour the United States as a hero.

Miss Pavlachenko is well known to fame.
From Russia's fair land and sniping's her game;
We always will love you for all time to come;
More than three hundred Nazis have fell by your gun.

Marjorie's return to the city in August prompted them to move to an apartment at 74 Charles Street in the West Village, a flat they took to calling "the rancho" or "the ranchhouse" for no reason other than silliness. There Guthrie wrote what Marjorie called "fabulous stories" about the child Guthrie had dubbed "Railroad Pete," a child whose goodness they were certain would change the world, a child so tough "that he could sit in one corner of the room and spit and never miss a spittoon in the other corner."

Onto the pages of a day-by-day appointment calendar, Guthrie told both the unborn child and himself about Marjorie, a "hoper," a planner, a dreamer. "Every detail of her life is not only a plan, but it is a dream, and the whole plan of a better world is one that she dreams about always."

Marjorie and Guthrie continually surprised each other, perhaps "because we come from such opposite ends of life. I have let myself wonder at times if this wouldn't cause a distance to grow between us, but it works like a magnet every day and what one end says, the other end knows."

Days for Marjorie, then four and a half months into her pregnancy, were difficult "because her dreams are so bright and things are so unsettled." But things would settle down and Marjorie would take them both in hand, Guthrie promised himself and the child. "She will see to it that your walking and breathing, eating, celebrating and sleeping, fits in with the higher aims of the people's struggles to live better lives."

Toward the end of August, Marjorie wrote Guthrie from Philadelphia hinting she would sooner or later stop commuting to New York City. Gra-

ham was to begin rehearsals for a fall tour and Marjorie could no longer
dance. If she could not be a part of it, she would prefer not to come.

"And that was the part," Guthrie confided to Railroad Pete, "that was
just a shade rough—not too rough but pretty damn rough."

A pair of patricians, the sort of people Guthrie had once disdained,
would carry him through these months of anxiety and self-pity.

CHAPTER NINETEEN

Breaking New Land

WILLIAM DOERFLINGER WAS in a quandary. As an acquisitions editor for the publishing house of E. P. Dutton, he was keenly interested in the stack of wrinkled and stained pages Woody Guthrie called his autobiography. The problem was wresting a book out of the hundreds of typed pages.

Doerflinger, who was himself collecting sea songs from old sailors living in a retirement home, had earlier asked Lomax if he had a book in mind. Lomax himself did not, but wondered if Doerflinger knew Guthrie was working on his autobiography.

Intrigued, Doerflinger visited Almanac House in late February 1942 and asked Guthrie if he had anything Doerflinger might read. Guthrie rather diffidently showed Doerflinger a short section from the autobiography and the newly published article in *Common Sense*.

Doerflinger was impressed. "Woody wrote vividly and with great originality and spirit . . . a good, graphic writer," Doerflinger commented. "He was interested in the world, and people, and describing it." While there did not seem to be a completed manuscript, Doerflinger arranged a contract for the book Guthrie had entitled "Boomchasers."

For the first time since leaving Model Tobacco's radio show, Guthrie had a steady income. He was to get an advance against royalties of $250; a similar amount would go to Mary in El Paso in five monthly installments.

Encouraged by Doerflinger and by Dutton's money, Guthrie plunged into the book. He worked steadily through the spring of 1942 at Marjorie's apartment on 14th Street, hardly bothering to return to his bed at Almanac House on Hudson Street. It was one way to forget that she was not at his side. "I have already found out," he wrote her, "that the only thing that keeps me from going completely screwball is just to keep at work every minute of the night and day, and maybe this is a good thing, maybe the best thing that can

happen to anybody. To keep at work. If I can think that I'm somehow helping others, I can forget my own little personal troubles."

The pace Guthrie set was telling, Gordon Friesen recalled. "He was so
skinny you couldn't tell by looking at him if he had anything to eat in
weeks."

Guthrie wrote a ten-page, single-space synopsis of the book for Doerflinger and Dutton, essentially a summary of his youth, the years before he
arrived in New York City. But as the pile of pages mounted steadily, the book
seemed to lose focus. The manuscript, Friesen concluded, like Guthrie's
wanderings, set off in one direction and turned to another, without plan or
even destination.

Marjorie Mazia, returned to New York from Philadelphia in the early
summer of 1942, brought some order to the stacks of paper Guthrie had
piled about her apartment. In a letter to Railroad Pete, Guthrie later confessed, "I will always believe that this book was a symbol of my whole life—
the mess and mixup of the past."

Guthrie needed a secretary, someone to organize him and the ever-
growing manuscript. "And that is where your mama came in. She jumped
in and took about three or four flying leaps, and sailed handfuls of loose
papers all over Fourteenth Street—and when the air got clear again, I was
surprised to see all the notes, and papers, and papers stacked in their proper
order and labelled and naturalized—all meaning something."

While *he* was now organized, his manuscript was not. According to
Gordon Friesen, himself a published novelist, the twelve-hundred-page,
single-spaced manuscript did not have an acceptable conclusion. "There
was a beginning, a middle, but then the story just went on and on."

Guthrie had intended a proper ending, a scene of "Oakies getting
together" in a dirt-floor church. There a preacher in overalls was to deliver
a sermon reminding a congregation in overalls

that Jesus Christ was a carpenter, that he said the best thing that you
can do is to get together, work together, and learn more about each
other, don't say that you own this or you own that, but everybody
own everything that he needs, a job you like to do, and a job for you
all of the time; because that's why you've drug yourself across the
continent three or four times, that's why you'd do it again if you
thought this country needed you to work; you've built your shacks
and left them a dozen times, broke the new land and left it a dozen
times, you've seen the boom towns come and the boom towns go;

and you don't know anything but work, your life has been work, you, yourself are just your work.

That last chapter remained unwritten while Guthrie's manuscript rumbled on, episode after episode extolling the value of union organizing and radical politics, while raking the bosses, the banks, and their law enforcement toadies.

To shape the book, and to provide the missing conclusion, Doerflinger turned to his wife, Joy.

They were an odd pairing. Joy Doerflinger was poised, elegant, well dressed—a two-lapdogs-on-leashes New Yorker Woody Guthrie might normally have disdained. But the twenty-seven-year-old daughter of opera singer Louise Homer had worked as a medical relief worker in China, trekked some fifteen thousand miles through that war-scarred land, and come home to write a powerful book condemning Japan's aggression, *Dawn Watch in China.* Woody Guthrie deemed her a woman to be respected.*

Because she was acting as both his uncredited tutor and his agent, Guthrie agreed that Doerflinger was to receive 20 percent of future royalties. She would earn her fee.

Former Almanac singer Lee Hays was present when Joy Doerflinger came to pick up Guthrie's manuscript at Almanac House. Hays helped her carry the bulk of papers while Doerflinger was busy with her dogs. "I kept wondering how she was going to get a manuscript out of that mess," Hays said later.

For six weeks during July and August they worked together, Joy Doerflinger hacking out hunks of the manuscript while Guthrie wrote connective transitions. The two of them met virtually daily at the Doerflinger's West 27th Street apartment, working "to make the manuscript readable," her husband recalled.

Inspired by the Doerflingers' support, Guthrie burst with renewed creative energy. One night, Marjorie recalled, Guthrie wrote thirty-eight typewritten pages to fill a gap in the story. The next day, an incredulous Joy Doerflinger sat in disbelief when Guthrie handed over the copy.

Guthrie apparently saw ahead of him a new career as a serious writer like Thomas Wolfe, whose books Guthrie had seen at Alan Lomax's home. Guthrie worked hard at writing, careful to follow the advice Joy offered. He was a good worker, William said, and "we were very good friends."

---

* Guthrie had once written about "The Chinese and the Japanese," but in doing so violated his own insistence that one had to write what he knew.

In the end, as much as three-quarters of the published book was as Guthrie had originally set it down, William Doerflinger later estimated. Only the last portion, Gordon Friesen said, was substantially "rewritten, changed, faked even, to round out a conclusion."*

The manuscript, completed in late September 1942, was a weave of Guthrie's imagination in full flower and biographical incident. He changed the names of characters, though the faintly disguised family members would later scold him for telling tales best left at home. He scrambled events in the interest of drama; he confused his childhood homes in Okemah. While the narrative extended to Guthrie's initial success in New York City, he recast the Rainbow Room audition with himself as the sole singer. He omitted his younger brother and sister, his marriage, his three children, the Almanac Singers, Marjorie and Railroad Pete, all in the interests of dramatic urgency.

Most of all, the manuscript idealized Guthrie's parents. Even the worst of events—the horror of Clara's death, his father's mutilation, the fire that burned the house on Ninth Street—were covered over:

> Mama got up with the match in her hand. She struck the match on the floor and held it up between her eyes and mine, and it lit up both of our thoughts and reflected in both of our minds, and struck a million memories and ten million secrets that fire had turned into ashes between us.

Aware of the protective fictions he had crafted and the heroic yarns he spun, Guthrie invariably called his book "an autobiographical novel." Others were to assume Guthrie's fantasies were true; there lay the seeds of myth.

With the manuscript completed in September—retitled *Bound for Glory* from a gospel song the fictional Guthrie sang in the first and last chapters of the book—Guthrie promptly began a second novel. He was soon in trouble, Gordon Friesen said. Guthrie's convoluted story centered on a band of beggars, masquerading as the blind or legless, who brought their daily pluckings from subway and street to give to a Fagin-like ring leader. The plotting was mechanical and contrived, the writing lifeless, Friesen said.

---

* Guthrie would later claim that the Doerflingers censored his political statements, an assertion he did not make in 1942. If true, it would be odd for William Doerflinger and Guthrie to exchange social visits as late as 1960, when Doerflinger attended the bar mitzvah of Guthrie's son Arlo. Friesen also discounted Guthrie's censorship complaint.

Guthrie would abandon it in favor of all-night jam sessions with Huddie Ledbetter and two new friends, Sonny Terry and Brownie McGhee.

At the suggestion of Alan Lomax, Terry and McGhee had come to New York from Memphis, their bus fares paid by the Almanacs, in the early spring of 1942. Terry, blind since a pair of boyhood accidents, had first come to New York with his blues harmonica in the late 1930s. Sponsored by Alan Lomax, he had provided the music for Martha Graham dancer Jane Dudley's *Harmonica Breakdown* in 1938 and participated in a historic "Spirituals to Swing" concert at Carnegie Hall in 1939.

Unable to make a living in New York, Terry returned to North Carolina where he paired with Piedmont blues guitarist Brownie McGhee. Together they played Durham's juke joints and street corners for what they could pry from drunks and passersby. The Almanacs' offer of bus fare and bookings was all the urging they needed to move to New York City.

As Guthrie completed the manuscript for his "autobiography" in the fall of 1942—he had only to finish the drawings that would be scattered through the book—he began to think about performing once again. The Almanacs were scattered, their organizer, Pete Seeger, drafted into the army. Cisco Houston had joined the merchant marine. "Sis" Cunningham and Gordon Friesen had moved to Detroit to work in a war plant. Lee Hays had returned, but bookings for the group had drained away, replaced by interminable organizational meetings.

Guthrie discounted the Marxist dialectic. "Musical ability," he wrote to Marjorie in November, "should be the first requirement, not how good a Marxist or Leninist [you are]." Around this time, he wrote in his date book:

LENIN: "Where three balalaika players meet, the fourth one ought to be a communist."

ME: "Where three communists meet, the fourth one ought to be a guitar player."

The Almanacs had outlived their times. Even the quartet in bustling Detroit booked fewer and fewer engagements; taking a no-strike pledge for the duration, unions had put the war effort ahead of further organizing. Bookings in New York too dried up; the radical causes of the Popular Front had given way to winning the war.

The *New York Times* drove the stake through the heart on January 5, 1943:

The Office of War Information admitted yesterday that it had made a mistake. The Almanac Singers—a hillbilly group that once made a specialty of a number called "Plow Every Fourth American Boy," and has been periodically praised in the Communist organ "The Daily Worker"—were hired to do short wave broadcasts in the propaganda service. The mistake, the OWI said, has been corrected. The Almanac Singers are no longer thumping out their alleged folk songs for the short wave propaganda service.

Virtually the last Almanac in the fall of 1942, Guthrie wrote long appeals to Maxine Crissman in California, one day imploring her to reunite "Lefty Lou from Old Mizzou" and the "Lone Wolf," the next praising Marjorie. "He was truly in love with that woman," Crissman concluded.

When Crissman rebuffed him, Guthrie set off in another direction. The disintegration of the Almanacs had left Sonny Terry and Brownie McGhee floundering. When Terry applied for welfare, state officials proposed putting him in the Lighthouse for the Blind.

Guthrie suggested instead they join him and Huddie Leadbetter as the Headline Singers. They would be a singing newspaper, writing songs based on the news, supporting the war effort. Alan Lomax reportedly had first suggested the name, but by the beginning of 1943 he had second thoughts. The hour of the fist-shaking radical had passed; now was the time of the soldier with a rifle or the worker with a rivet gun.

"Hurry up and change your name," Lomax urged, "and for heaven's sake make it a good old countrified name like 'Oklahoma Rangers' or something of that sort. Your chief point of contact in America is that of the background of the American soil and American folk songs. Don't become 'Headline Singers,' even though you may be singing 'the headlines.'"

Leadbelly's involvement in the Headline Singers was minimal even though he commanded a luxurious fee of $10 for a half-hour performance. (The other three got $7.50.) Instead, Leadbelly and his wife, Martha, looked on Guthrie in a parental way. Their apartment "was always a place where Woody could go and did go often for food and a place to sleep and probably gave Martha, Huddie's wife, fits, . . . considering some of his personal habits, because Martha had one of the best kept houses I've ever seen," Lee Hays commented.*

---

* Guthrie also sought to boost Leadbelly's career. Guthrie wrote to Max Gordon, owner of the Village Vanguard nightclub, a thoughtful letter criticizing the presentation of Josh White and Huddie Ledbetter. Trying to help two friends, Guthrie abandoned his pose of unlettered regionalism:

The Headline Singers was Guthrie's modest contribution to the war effort. Still married to Mary and the ostensible supporter of three young children, Guthrie was exempt from the draft. He had earlier proposed recording some of his pro-war songs but was turned down by both RCA and its major rival, Columbia. He had pasted a hand-lettered sign on the face of his guitar proclaiming, "This Machine Kills Fascists." More practically, the Headline Singers would seek to sell war bonds.

One such performance in Baltimore, as Pete Seeger later told the story, seems to have been the high point of the group's short career. When Guthrie, Terry, and McGhee finished singing, the sponsor invited Guthrie to eat.

"Mr. Guthrie, we have a chair for you at the table, and we have some food for your friends out in the kitchen."

Guthrie frowned. "What's going on here. You heard us singing together. Why can't we eat together?"

"Well, Mr. Guthrie, this is Baltimore, remember."

As Seeger told the story, "Woody just shouted out, 'This fight against fascism has got to start right here and now!' And he grabbed the tablecloth and ripped it off, scattering chinaware and silver and glasses all over the floor. He started tipping over tables and shouting; and they finally hustled him out before anybody got arrested."

The last months of 1942 were hard. With Marjorie once again in Philadelphia, "the ranch" offered little comfort. Guthrie spent afternoons at the nearby communist bookstore, reading Marx and Engels.

All the while Marjorie wavered between her duty to her faithful husband and her love for Guthrie. On December 20, 1942, she finally found a compromise, and a decision. She would stay in Philadelphia with Joseph until he received his security clearance from the FBI in April. Only then would she leave her husband for Guthrie. While neither man was happy, both agreed to abide by her decision.

Patriotism fused with responsibility determined her decision.

I shall stay here in Philadelphia and give Joseph the courage he needs to fight a battle that is not only his but all of us [*sic*] who suffer the tortures of fascism. . . .

The guitar to Leadbelly is just another way to get people to set still and listen to what he's got to say to them. He's dead serious. He's a great speaker in his own right. He tells you of life as it's hit him, and tells you how to take it easier, and miss the hard spots that he's been through, and how to have as much fun as he's had.

The guitar to Leadbelly: Woody Guthrie to "Dear Max and Everybody," November 27, 1941, courtesy of Barry Ollman.

Hitler's kind must be swept away and those of us who see this must work together to accomplish this. . . . Let's all help each other—you to write the songs that give our people courage, Joseph to give our boys the physical weapons with which to do the job and me to add Pete to this world to do his part and give all of us the strength and courage it takes to win such battles.

Fearful of Joseph Mazia's security clearance, Marjorie reminded herself—and Guthrie—"We must be careful because the whole purpose of my being here is to settle this 'political issue' and we must be successful!" They would not see each other, so as to allow the FBI to believe their affair ended with her pregnancy. Eventually they would be able to be together and proclaim their love to the world. They had nothing to hide.

The following day, Marjorie began a diary with the intention of later sharing it with Guthrie. Seven months pregnant, her decision made, the baby felt lighter, his kicks fainter, she wrote:

Maybe he's saying that I've passed over the fire and he's leading me on to a very beautiful soviet world where love and courage and good work are there a-plenty for all. . . . Of course maybe Pete is becoming a girl and that's why the kicking is a bit lighter today—but I'd so much rather it was the other reason.

Even here, in a diary Guthrie would not read until months later, Marjorie was the proper housewife. Fix the sink and the fireplace, she wrote. Dust the bookshelves.

"Keep your desk in order. Build the extra table. Give out laundry when you should (there were three dish towels that really need it). Keep the cash account clear. Write something *everyday*."

Guthrie could have all the company he wanted, but he was not to stay up too late. "Form some healthy eating habits," she admonished, and "drink moderately!"

Violating their rule against direct communication, Marjorie telephoned Guthrie on Tuesday, December 22. "I had to hear him speak and tell him again how much I love him and to tell him how we *will* be all together soon!"

Guthrie told her he had completed the drawings for his autobiography, scheduled for publication in March, and was working on the cover. This was just the beginning, he promised. He would work so hard to be worthy of her.

Marjorie was stunned, she confided in her diary. "Him being worried about being worthy! I don't know anybody in this whole wide world who's been gypped out of so much. . . . Well, by God, I'll just have to impress upon that fellow just how deserving he is of everything good that's coming his way!"

She was full of plans for their future. He should edit a collection of his songs, with their music. "They've got to get out where others can sing them. That's when these songs really do their part toward winning the war."

On Christmas Eve, Guthrie invited Cisco Houston, who was laying over after a coastal run as a merchant mariner, and Joy Doerflinger to celebrate the completion of the book. Her husband overseas with the Office of War Information, Doerflinger accepted and was swept up in a gay tramp through Greenwich Village. First they ate, then the two men unslung their guitars and played as they marched through the narrow streets to a subway entrance.

In the Dutton in-house newsletter, Doerflinger described the two men boarding the subway to the Battery, a clutch of delighted celebrants following the two pied guitarists:

> They began to sing a song Woody had made up: "You're bound to LOSE, You Fascists, bound to LOSE!" There were many reasons given as to exactly why You Fascists are bound to lose, and each reason was better and funnier than the last. It was a good song. It went on for seven stations. In the last hop, between Rector Street and South Ferry, every single human being in that subway car was singing that song.

It was a grand way to close out one year and usher in the next.

On February 6, 1943, Marjorie Mazia delivered a daughter, whom she had decided was to be named Cathy. While she was hardly the whip-any-man-standing Railway Pete he had imagined, Guthrie was instantly enchanted with his five-pound fourteen-ounce daughter.

Two days after Cathy was born, Guthrie barged into the Philadelphia hospital, pulled his guitar from his back, and began serenading the staff. "That was Guthrie," marveled the incredulous Joseph Mazia, alerted by Marjorie's doctor, George Weinstein. "It was a nice thing to do."

It was also appropriate. Marjorie had told Weinstein the newborn was Guthrie's, not Mazia's.

A new daughter—whom Guthrie dubbed "Stackabones," because like all newborns, she lacked muscle tension—and a new book were to turn Guthrie's world upside down. Marjorie was suddenly, unexpectedly unsure of her parents' acceptance of Guthrie or his daughter. When she suggested she might move with her newborn to Seagate in Brooklyn to be near her parents' home, Guthrie lashed out. He petulantly questioned Cathy's paternity. He complained that she had chosen to sleep beside Joseph Mazia night after night, then needled her, "I haven't exactly been alone." He could not resist a lecture:

> In my mind you don't seem to understand the first simple principles of "love" and I guess to you I appear the same. To me people that are in love wrap their little babies up in a rug or blanket and cross deserts, wade swamps, cross icebergs, wade snow, do anything to be together, but it seems that you have always put a hamburger or an orange juice or your belly before any thoughts of love.

Marjorie responded with a pointed reminder that she needed no man's financial swaddling.

> I am self-sufficient and can stand on my own two feet. I wasn't coming to New York only for you. There is something else in my life and by God it's something that won't call me names and it's something I can always live for and with. I'm still coming to New York when and how I choose. You were never much help anyway in seeing to it that I got there. You only cried that you were helpless . . . that you were lost . . . that you were insane . . . that you were lonely . . . always you and you and you . . . Well, Mr. YOU, I hope you find that there are some other things in this world and they don't all begin with YOU.

Because Guthrie would not, or could not "provide a decent home in these days for yourself or your family . . . I knew I could never really count on you and that's why I planned to be alone." Guthrie had admitted as much in a radio interview with Henrietta Yurchenko. "You don't think you could ever settle down and you'd been in New York long enough."

Finally, after bathing Cathy, Marjorie returned to her typewriter for a parting shot:

"Take and give and try living like the real masses. . . . You have to live like they do to understand them and maybe you did in the past but you certainly didn't since I['ve] known you. . . . There is such a thing as home and family and budgets and jobs and that's what people are really thinking about and doing."

Guthrie wilted. If Marjorie wished to live in Coney Island with their daughter, he would accept her decision. He celebrated their arrival on April 13 by purchasing Maxim Gorky's *Culture and the People*, inscribing on an endpaper, "To Mama and Cathy Coming Home."

The first of the 150 reviews of *Bound for Glory* began to trickle in. The reviewers were captivated with Guthrie's use of language and the sheer verve of the narrative. Guthrie scholar Guy Logsdon described the volume as written "with a strong realistic base of Oklahoma parlance . . . in what Oklahomans refer to as coon-hunter's style, that is, fact and a foundation of truth are essential to the story but the greatness of the teller of the tale lies in his ability to elaborate and embroider."

The reviewers were almost uniformly caught up with the book. In the influential *New York Times Book Review*, Horace Reynolds rhapsodized, "Like [Sean] O'Casey, Guthrie likes violence and sentiment. Like O'Casey, he is verbally sportive; he plays with words, makes 'em dance, makes 'em cry, makes 'em sing. Like O'Casey, too, Woody is on fire inside, a natural born poet trying to make prose do the big job of verse."

"Woody writes well," Reynolds enthused.

Clifton Fadiman, a doyen of the Book-of-the-Month Club, wrote in *The New Yorker* that *Bound for Glory* "will never rank among the classic autobiographies, for it lacks entirely that element of egotism, even of pomposity, that all the great confessions seem to me to have." At the same time, Fadiman—who had appeared on radio with Guthrie—predicted, "Someday people are going to wake up to the fact that Woody Guthrie and the ten thousand songs that leap and tumble off of the strings of his music box are a national possession, like Yellowstone and Yosemite."

In the well-read *Saturday Review of Literature*, Louis Adamic, Guthrie's editor at *Common Ground*, described Guthrie as a "born artist, whether he is singing songs or making pictures or putting down words in a story." Guthrie was like Walt Whitman in his belief in people, Adamic added.

The reviewer in Massachusetts's staunchly conservative *Springfield Republican* unknowingly acknowledged Joy Doerflinger's contribution: "Guthrie writes (at times with touches of sheer poetry) from the heart and not from economic perspective." His book, the reviewer continued, would be far more stirring for some readers than even John Steinbeck's *The Grapes of Wrath.**

---

* Of the more than 150 reviews that *Bound for Glory* would amass, perhaps the most foresighted was Edith Roberts's in *Book Week* for April 4, 1943: "I want to start right off with a prediction that Woody Guthrie is going to walk straight into the hearts of a million readers."

Despite the critical enthusiasm, some of those who knew Guthrie were dissatisfied with the book, Lee Hays said. The Guthrie portrayed in *Bound for Glory* seemed one-dimensional, ever the wide-eyed innocent. "It was a neat job of editing but it had nowhere near the imagination, the fantasy that Woody had, which was sensational."

Bound for Glory certainly tamed Guthrie's political views to a tepid back-the-underdog populism. "I never did make up many songs about the cow trails or the moon skipping through the sky, but at first it was funny songs of what's all wrong, and how it turned out good or bad. Then I got a little braver and made up songs telling what I thought was wrong and how to make it right, songs that said what everybody in the country was thinking."

(The book implicitly criticized President Roosevelt for Executive Order 9066 authorizing the military evacuation of 110,000 Japanese nationals and citizens of Japanese descent a year earlier. In a fictionalized episode, Cisco Houston and Guthrie stood with "sailors and working men" against a mob of "pool-hall gamblers and horse-race bookies" intent on attacking Japanese-American store owners shortly after the December 7 attack on Pearl Harbor.)

Guthrie was immensely proud of the book. He sent copies to members of his family, inscribing Charley Guthrie's copy: "To my papa, as good a dad as a kid ever had. I wrote this book wishing I had more of the stuff that made my dad the best fist fighter in Okfuskee County."

To Mary he inscribed, improbably, generously: "Anything good I ever do will be because of you, Mary."

In return, Mary mailed Guthrie a copy of the divorce papers she had signed in El Paso on March 23, 1943. She was doing well, working her way up from a three-dollars-a-day waitress to manager of the Welcome Inn, with a staff as large as thirty-five people. The twenty-four-hour restaurant was "a gold mine," crowded with troops from the five military posts in the El Paso area. She was twenty-six years old, making "damn good money at this," and she wanted her freedom. Even if it meant offending her father, an observant Catholic.*

Guthrie was unfazed. He said only, "She was right from her side and I was right from my side."

While Mary sought no alimony, at Marjorie's prompting, Guthrie made

---

* In a December 28, 1971, interview with E. Victor and Judy Wolfenstein, Mary Boyle stated that while on tour with the Martha Graham company, Marjorie took a side trip to visit Mary in El Paso. Marjorie reportedly asked Mary to divorce Guthrie so that he and Marjorie could marry.

an effort to provide some child support. He arranged with his publisher to take twenty-five dollars a week from his royalty account and send the money for the next six months to Mary. Guthrie's contribution would more than pay the parochial school tuition for seven-year-old Gwendolyn.

In May 1943, Guthrie learned that he had been granted a $1,800 Julius Rosenwald Fellowship, his name earlier submitted by Alan Lomax. The fellowship, to allow him to "write books, ballads, songs, and novels that will help people to know each other's work better," was to be paid in monthly installments of $150. Again at Marjorie's urging, Mary was to receive $100 from each check.

Guthrie would not need the money. While bookings had dried up, Joy Doerflinger, acting as his agent, had arranged a busy writing schedule. Dutton extended a three-book contract on April 7. The first book, tentatively entitled *I Want to Be Right*, was to be based on Guthrie's quest for the lost silver mine in the Chisos Mountain. (Because much of it was already written—hewed by Joy from Guthrie's original manuscript for *Bound for Glory*—he agreed to an early deadline of October 1.) Guthrie would receive a five-hundred-dollar advance.

He was now launched as a professional writer, honored with reviews on one book, awarded a contract for a second. Cisco Houston, when he was not at sea, chided him for growing soft, an Okie too comfortable in New York's honeyed luxury. There was a war to be won, and Guthrie was not doing his part.

If Houston's comments were a goad, Guthrie's draft board was a prod. He was divorced, and though the father of four—three legitimatized by marriage, the fourth acknowledged by birth certificate—he *was* legally single and therefore subject to induction. Men between the ages of eighteen and thirty-eight were eligible for the draft; Guthrie was still shy of his thirty-first birthday.

If he had to go, Guthrie preferred to do it on his own terms.

CHAPTER TWENTY

Seamen Three

*J*UST AT MIDNIGHT, the Liberty ship slipped its mooring at the New Jersey docks and edged downstream into Buttermilk Channel. On deck watching the shore recede in the darkness, Woody Guthrie stood with Cisco Houston and Jim Longhi, three messmen aboard the S.S. *William B. Travis*, bound eastward on this night in June 1943 toward the submarine killing grounds of the North Atlantic.

A sense of patriotism stoked by Houston's chiding had persuaded Guthrie to follow Houston to the union hiring hall on 17th Street. Guthrie would be doing his share, sacrificing the Rosenwald fellowship intended to support his writing. He could hardly do less. His younger brother George was in the navy; older brother Roy and his wife Ann had moved to Phoenix, Arizona, where Roy worked at the Douglas Aircraft plant. Mary Jo's new husband was in the army.

Like Cisco, many of the Almanacs and those who had sung at their Sunday hootenannies were now scattered. Pete Seeger was stationed in Mississippi. Jim and Hazel Garland were in Vancouver, Washington, building Liberty ships on the Columbia River. Jim's sister Sara and her new husband, Joe Gunning, were working in defense plants in Detroit. Marjorie's two older brothers were engineers in the merchant marine. (David Greenblatt wondered if he was the example that had inspired Guthrie to join the radical National Maritime Union and go to sea. They could build a strong union and help defeat Hitler at the same time.)

Cisco Houston's presence aboard the "Willy B." went far to ease Marjorie's apprehensions. "There was something marvelous about Cisco's temperament," she explained some years later. Ashore, Houston often stifled his disagreements with Guthrie, as if he believed "if Woody said it, well, it's OK. I'm not going to argue with Woody." At sea, however, Cisco was the experienced one and their leader. Two voyages as a merchant seaman steaming through the wolf packs of the North Atlantic granted him a veteran's wisdom.

Guthrie himself was inclined to agree. Houston, Guthrie wrote later, was "one of our manliest and best of our living crop of ballad and folksong singers. . . . I like Cisco as a man. I like him as a person, and as a funhaving, warmhearted, and likable human being."

Born in Wilmington, Delaware, in 1918, Gilbert Vandine Houston had moved with his mother, two brothers, and a sister to the Los Angeles suburb of Eagle Rock. His father abandoned the family, leaving young Gilbert to turn to his year-older brother "Slim" as the man in the house.

The depression struck the Houston family hard. They lived over the store that provided them a scant livelihood selling groceries to their hardhit neighbors. First Slim and then Gilbert sought some explication in radical politics for their hard times. Growing up in Los Angeles, the strikingly handsome Gilbert studied acting at the Pasadena Playhouse. He took small parts in little theater productions, found work as an extra in Hollywood, and eventually fell in with actor Will Geer.

Despite his good looks, Houston was hampered as an actor. Like his brothers, he suffered from an inherited eye disease that left him so nearsighted as to be legally blind. He could perform on stage by hitting his marks; film, particularly the action and cowboy movies for which he seemed best suited, was out of the question.

Through Geer, Houston met Guthrie in 1939. The three like-minded men were keen to aid California's migrant farmworkers. It was Guthrie who first showed Houston a handful of guitar chords, and it was with Guthrie that Houston first sang in labor camps and bars. Gil Houston, the actor, took the western nickname "Cisco" as more appropriate for a union organizer and Skid Row familiar.

Singing with Woody, Cisco deferred to his partner. He recast his natural baritone into a high tenor to better harmonize with Guthrie's gravely lead. Over time Houston's guitar playing became more secure and subtle. His playing and singing never called attention to himself; he understood his role.

"Cisco was so good at the guitar and so good at adapting himself with others. Woody could do whatever he wanted to do without having to worry what the next guy was doing because Cisco covered up. All of this was spontaneous, unrehearsed," a mutual friend commented.

Shortly after the war began, Slim Houston shipped out as an engine room wiper on a tanker. When a U-boat torpedoed his ship off the coast of

Maine, he reportedly drowned as he sought to escape a flooded engine room. Cisco immediately followed the example of his idealized brother. He joined the Communist-dominated National Maritime Union (NMU) and then the merchant marine as a messman.

Houston eventually persuaded Guthrie to join. Typically, Guthrie minimized the decision; he wrote Maxine Crissman in California that he signed on because "I want to sail across the sea, and walk across foreign lands."

A week before they were to ship out, Houston met law student Jim Longhi at a party and enlisted him too. Longhi, like Guthrie, faced the draft; joining the merchant marine as an alternative was not only helping to win the war, it was building a bigger, stronger NMU.

Houston was their leader, in part because of his prior voyages, in part because of his "spirituality," Longhi explained. Cisco inspired in them "courage, tolerance and idealism in a quiet way."

Shipping was vital to the Allied war effort, particularly on the dangerous North Atlantic and Murmansk runs. By mid-1943, when Guthrie shipped out on the Willy B., more than six thousand merchant mariners had lost their lives at sea, Longhi recalled. Sailors signed on to vessels unaware of the destination or the cargo they might carry.

"It was not a safe thing to ship out," Longhi said emphatically. "And that certainly increased Woody's determination."

Once committed, Guthrie threw himself into the task at hand. So careless of his dress ashore, he was immaculate at sea. "Woody had a *zest* for doing things *happily*, the way things *should* be done," Longhi emphasized. "'If you're going to do a job, do it right,' Woody would say."

Assigned to wash dishes, Guthrie ripped into the task. "With every rinse and wipe it was a slap in the face of Hitler. . . . He was a phenomenon. When he made a menu board, it was the greatest menu board God ever [saw]. There would be little angels all over it, and newts." With the intensity Guthrie brought to the galley, Longhi concluded, "he seemed like a zen person."

From the portside deck of the Willy B., Guthrie watched a darkened Coney Island slide by. Somewhere out there on Mermaid Avenue, Marjorie and Cathy lay sleeping.

With the dawn, they could see their ship, one of a hundred formed up in a convoy, ten lines of gray and black vessels shepherded by nervous corvettes and destroyers. The *William B. Travis*, with its mixed cargo of food and ammunition, stood second from the end, in an outside line. Houston solemnly informed Guthrie and Longhi their ship held down the "Coffin Corner"; German U-boats tended to pick off the last vessels in line.

For two weeks the convoy sailed eastward, Guthrie washing dishes, then taking part in gun and boat drills. Off duty, he played a new guitar and his fiddle, read Charles Darwin's *On the Origin of Species*, and wrote songs.

A week out, their convoy came under attack. A submarine torpedoed a cargo ship in the middle of the convoy, then cunningly evaded the frantic destroyers to track its next victim. That night, Guthrie lay on his bunk, staring into the darkness.

"No, I wasn't scared," he announced to no one in particular. The thing he feared most was fire, he continued. Fire had taken a childhood home. Fire had killed his sister and crippled his father. Fire had taken away his mother after his father agreed to commit her to the state asylum.

"But I'm sure that she was not insane. I'm sure she had a physical illness of some kind. The talk in our family is that she inherited it." Guthrie paused to light a cigarette. "And the fact is that I'm beginning to suspect that I have it too." He sometimes "felt woozy," but "Meyers's black Jamaican rum fixed him up good."

It was a rare moment of candor, an autobiography recounted without emotion. As open as he seemed to be with Houston and Longhi—"three guys living together in a foc'sle, under fire, you get pretty close"—still "there were things inside Guthrie that didn't come out."

The next day, Guthrie began construction of his "wind machine," a creaking, spinning device whittled and sawed from wooden crates, with pulleys and a whirling propeller all fastened to a midship rail of the slow-moving Willy B. Its purpose, Guthrie told credulous crew members, was to generate "a flow of thermo-propulsion airwaves which pass over the ship's typography, creating an aerovacuum force behind the stern, which squeezes the ship forward, thus increasing its velocity." Because the ship was at the rear of the convoy, "the wind caused by the machine will propel the entire convoy, however imperceptibly, just a little bit faster" and cause torpedoes to miss their targets, he deadpanned.*

Guthrie's "Anticyclone and Ship Speeder-Upper Aerodynamic Wind Machine" lasted only as long as the first storm, which also protected the convoy from lurking submarines. Fifteen days after leaving New York, the *William B. Travis* passed through the Straits of Gibraltar, one half of the convoy proceeding to North Africa, one half, including the Willy B., left to

---

* This seems to be the earliest report of what would later become a Guthrie hobby, fashioning *objets trouvés*.

anchor off shore. The following day, they learned that British and American troops had invaded Sicily.

They would wait at anchor for more than two weeks, celebrating Guthrie's thirty-first birthday aboard ship with drinks from a hidden stash of whiskey. Only with the capture of Palermo and the opening of the docks there did the remaining ships weigh anchor.

The three-day run to Sicily was a welter of general alarms, a submarine attack that left a transport and a tanker burning, a dash through the sea of burning oil from the sinking tanker, and a near collision with another vessel. Despite the dangers, Messman Guthrie remained coolly at his gun post.

The Willy B. spent three weeks tied up to the Palermo docks while longshoremen unloaded its deadly cargo. With Longhi to interpret, Guthrie and Cisco spent days exploring the island, meanwhile fending off the children begging for candy and cigarettes, the ten-year-old boy pimping his little sister, and the ex-fascists and Mafiosa maneuvering for political power. Guthrie worked on the manuscript of a new book—he had written his father that he intended to write "a spy story"—and a number of songs. Their deadly cargo finally unloaded, the idle ship lay moored in the middle of the bay for another three weeks.

Finally, they took aboard a platoon of military police and received orders to ferry them to Tunis. The Willy B. was in the middle of the overnight run when a torpedo struck the number three hold. With his ship taking water forward, the second officer ordered the bos'n to take three men and search for casualties below.

Houston stepped forward. "I've got to get my guitar anyway," he explained. Guthrie and Longhi followed. As Guthrie's song went, "Cisco, Jimmy and me; if you ever saw one, you'd see all three."

Below decks, the empty hold taking water, they found a badly wounded soldier and managed to carry him to the waiting lifeboats. Once more they ducked down the ladder, this time to retrieve their instruments.

The captain ordered the engines restarted and the Willy B. limped toward the safety of the Tunisian shore. On deck, Guthrie began singing, warding off fear that the submarine would finish off the job. They sang through the night until by first light they could see the shoreline, and a pilot boat coming to meet them. Within hours the fatally wounded *William B. Travis* lay sinking in the shallows of the Lake of Tunis.

They returned to New York in the middle of October, Guthrie whooping as they steamed past Coney Island, "I'm a-comin' Momma Marjorie! I'm a-comin' Missie Stackabones!"

Guthrie moved in with Marjorie and Cathy in the drab one-bedroom apartment Marjorie had rented at 3520 Mermaid Avenue. For a month they were a family. (Guthrie had promised to stay, "books and all, as a resident at 3520 Mermaid Avenue, first floor rear, for a period of six months.") Guthrie would mind Cathy while Marjorie taught dance lessons during the day. He pushed Cathy in her stroller along the boardwalk, prepared her bottle, and diapered her, all chores he had avoided with his first three children. When Marjorie came home, he massaged her aching legs and dutifully washed the dishes and tidied up after dinner.

This was a different, chastened Guthrie, a man raised up or cast down, no longer the grand lover of anonymous mankind, but a man truly in love with Marjorie and their daughter. "Just how much I love them I know I will never be able to make plain," he came to realize.

The Mermaid Avenue idyll ended on November 14, when Guthrie received yet another draft notice. His plea for a deferment—he had served in the merchant marine and he had to finish an overdue book for E. P. Dutton— was to no avail. He could choose between the draft or a return to the sea.

He chose the merchant marine, signing on for a short run along the eastern coast. He was home with Marjorie and Cathy for Christmas, a holiday they shared with Jimmy Longhi, Longhi's new wife, and Cisco, who brought along a new girlfriend, Bina Rosenbaum.

Shortly after his return, Guthrie crafted a long letter to the *Daily Worker* describing his trip to Sicily. It was a letter full of regrets for the past: "Oh, had we only joined our hands and destroyed Hitlerism on the young battlefields of Spain, France, Poland, then the wreckage [of war] would have been ten times less." It was also a letter of hope: "Here in Palermo, I think I breathed the real spirit of socialism more clearly, more plainly than ever. Books take you so far and no farther. Here, your mind joins, unites, hopes and plans with several hundred thousand others, and everybody knows that the next step is out of the slavage [sic], and into the new daylight of a worker's world."*

Like so many others in the Movement, Guthrie foresaw a postwar world as single-minded as the wartime, where competitive philosophies would give way to a cooperative fight against poverty. News of the Teheran conference at the end of November excited him; here was proof of his beliefs:

---

* The *Daily Worker* rejected his article on Sicily, on the grounds that it did not square with party doctrine. Here the man who refused to let corporate sponsors dictate what songs he might sing, or costumes he might wear, meekly accepted discipline. In the spirit of winning the war, Guthrie yielded to the collective wisdom of the Communist Party.

> *Well, a union sun was shining*
> *And November it was ending*
> *And the year was Nineteen Hundred Forty Three*
> *They shook hands across the table*
> *In the city of Teheran.*
> *Joe Stalin! Churchill! and Franklin D!*
>> *Joe Stalin! Churchill! and Franklin D!*
>> *Joe Stalin! Churchill! and Franklin D!*
>> *And our new union world was born on that spot.*

It was a new world for Guthrie as well; 3520 Mermaid Avenue was more and more like home. In an optimistic letter to his father on December 10, 1943, he allowed, "Well, this is as good a place as any to drive down a homestead claim."

The three messmen were to ship out together on January 12, 1944, on another Liberty ship, the S.S. *William Floyd*, which Guthrie promptly dubbed the "Floy Floy." Guthrie spent most of his off-duty time writing during the uneventful transatlantic run to the Mediterranean in a convoy of twenty vessels. He wrote as many as three songs a week, songs sung once and forgotten. He worked on a novel, "Ship Story," inspired by his first voyage on the *William B. Travis*; a former CBS production vice president, Bill Lewis, had expressed some interest in adapting it as a radio tribute to the merchant marine.

Inspired by Carl Sandburg's *The People, Yes*, Guthrie wrote free verse, stretching his voice, turning surely and permanently from the "swimmy waters" of Walt Whitman.

> *. . . They are around a table playing cards*
> *They chant home made words*
> *Odd rhymes, and tease one another*
> *For pastime as they try to pull*
> *All of the tricks there are in the game . . .*
>
> *You take all. It ain't fair, Shorty.*
> *Go by the rules, boy.*
> *That gunnery school shore did waste a lot*
> *Of educating on a guy like you.*
> *Here I go again. Might win.*
> *Quit looking at my hand, man.*

You'll stick out your neck
And draw back a stub.
You boys can't outlie me;
I'm the biggest liar on this tub . . .

While the crossing was uneventful—their stay in the harbor beneath the heights of Oran memorable only for a trip to the fabled casbah—Guthrie was incensed about the refusal of the former Vichy authorities to allow Joe Curran, the Communist president of the NMU, to disembark from another vessel. Here was further proof that "the fascists," French and American alike, were out to destroy unions.

For three nights on the return voyage, the "Floy Floy" and its small convoy endured submarine attacks. The ships docked in late March in Newport News, Virginia, an overnight train ride to Penn station in New York.

Immediately picking up where they had left off, Guthrie and Houston joined the large radio cast of a folk-inspired "ballad opera" written for the British Broadcasting Corporation (BBC) by Elizabeth Lomax, Alan's wife. (Lomax selected the music.) *The Martins and the Coys: A Contemporary Folk Tale* resolved the long-running feud of the two families in the interests of fighting fascism, adding a Romeo and Juliet subplot for good measure. "The fabulous Woody Guthrie," in BBC producer D. G. Bridson's phrase, played one of the leads with professional aplomb; Houston sang in the chorus. The program was recorded at Decca Records' studio in Manhattan near the end of March for the BBC.

At this recording session either Alan Lomax or Pete Seeger, on leave prior to going overseas, told Guthrie about a small record company on West 46th Street interested in recording folk music. Seeger had already recorded six mostly southern mountain songs for Moses Asch; whether they would ever be released on record in this period of wartime shortages of shellac was another matter.

Craggy Moe Asch—brusque when he wasn't irascible—professed Seeger to be a mystery to him. "We understood nothing of each other right from the start," he snapped. It was Asch's effort to protect those he most loved from even friendly inquiry.

Similarly, Asch's biographer noted, Woody Guthrie turned up one afternoon unannounced at Asch Records' tiny studio. "Asch later concocted a half dozen different versions of this first encounter," wrote his biographer Peter D. Goldsmith, "but they all went something like this:

" 'Hi. I'm Woody Guthrie.' Sits down on floor.

" 'So what?' Asch said with a shrug."

Guthrie wanted to record. Asch later claimed ignorance of the Oklahoman's reputation, an unlikely story since Asch, a longtime member of the Movement, subscribed to the *Daily Worker*. In any event, Asch was not put off by Guthrie's bald assertion, "I'm a communist, y'know."

As they talked, Guthrie's country-boy accent faded. They discussed folk music, their shared passion for the working man, and left-wing politics. (Asch, said longtime associate Irwin Silber, was not a member of the Communist Party. A curmudgeon of the first rank, "he would never affiliate with anything.") Still, whatever his initial skepticism of this man sitting on the floor of his studio, Asch on April 16, 1944, decided to record acetate masters of Guthrie singing "Hard, Ain't It Hard" and "More Pretty Gals Than One."

Despite Asch's seeming indifference, these were the first of more than three hundred different songs, ballads, and fiddle and harmonica tunes Guthrie was to record for him over the next eight years. Asch, whose early catalogue leaned heavily toward Jewish liturgical music, had become keenly interested in folk music, the more authentic the better. He had recorded Leadbelly three years before and Pete Seeger earlier that year. During wartime, when the major labels used shellac only for their most popular singers and bands, Asch was an striking exception. He believed in his little-known artists—jazz, liturgical, and folk alike—and gave them free reign in his tiny studio.

Born in Warsaw, Moe Asch was the son of the successful Yiddish writer Sholem Asch. The four children of Sholem and Frances were raised in a cosmopolitan setting, first in Paris and later in New York City after the family emigrated in 1915. Socialist politics and intellectual inquiry were the stuff of dinner table conversations and parlor arguments in the Asch home. Having grown up in a family that knew the great Jewish intellectuals of the time, including Albert Einstein, Asch ever after "looked upon himself as a worldly man."

To escape the long shadow of his father, Moe Asch trained in Germany as an engineer in the new technology of radio and sound recording. His musical tastes were unconventional; thirty-nine years old when he recorded Guthrie, Asch skated on the edge of bankruptcy

Woody Guthrie, at once a folk artist and an increasingly well-read intellectual, intrigued Asch. Three days after recording the first two songs, Guthrie was back in the Asch studio with Cisco Houston. In a day-long session they recorded fifty-six songs and ballads. They returned the next day—

probably with Sonny Terry—to cut seventeen more masters. On April 24 and 25, the pair recorded another fifty songs.

> We tried hilltop and sunny mountain harmonies and wilder yells and whoops of the dead sea deserts, and all of the swampy southland and buggy mud bottom sounds that we could make. We sung to the mossy trees and to the standing moon, and Moe Asch and Marian Distler [Asch's secretary and alter ego] worked through their plate glass there in the recording studio.

The 125 individual songs and tunes recorded in these marathon sessions surveyed Guthrie's repertoire. He played guitar and harmonica on some cuts, fiddle on others. With Houston adding "those high sour tenor notes" and a steadying guitar, he sang the songs learned as a boy from his Uncle Jeff. He recorded English ballads learned from his mother, including "Gypsy Davy"; songs learned from Lomax field recordings like "Ranger's Command" and "Po' Lazarus"; his own compositions, ranging from early ("Philadelphia Lawyer") to the newly autobiographical ("Talking Merchant Marine," so unfamiliar that it required five takes before Guthrie could get the words right).

> *This convoy's the biggest I ever did see*
> *Stretches all the way out across the sea.*
> *And the ships blow the whistles and a-rang her bells*
> *Going to blow them fascists all to hell!*
> *Win some freedom, liberty, stuff like that.*

> *Walked to the tail, stood on the stern,*
> *Lookin' at the big brass screw blade turn.*
> *Listen to the sound of the engine pound*
> *Gained sixteen feet every time it went around.*
> *Gettin' closer and closer. Look out you fascists!*

> *I'm just one of the merchant crew*
> *I belong to the union called the N.M.U.*
> *I'm a union man from head to toe*
> *And U.S.A. and C.I.O.*
> *Fightin' out here on the waters,*
> *Win some freedom on the land.*

It was a bravura marathon, yet it hardly tapped a quarter of Guthrie's repertoire.*

Guthrie was impressed with Asch. Reviewing Asch's album *Songs for Victory*, Guthrie enthused, "Main reason why this is the best of our union albums is because the Asch Record folks treat you so honest that you just naturally got to sing and play your best. . . . There's a real honest to God union feeling here at Asch's and I only pray and hope that it will all last."

With their month's leave up in mid-May, the seamen three shipped out again, this time on a spanking bright C-3 troopship, the S.S. *Sea Porpoise*. As the convoy assembled, they realized their transport, carrying as many as three thousand troops, was just one of a number in what appeared to be an invasion fleet. Their excitement was palpable; they were to take part in opening the long-awaited second front.

In mid-Atlantic, destroyers guarding the convoy picked up the pinging sonar of lurking submarines. The convoy commander ordered his ships to general quarters, an order that confined the frightened army troops to their fetid holds below deck.

Depth charges launched by the destroyers boomed below the surface, the sound louder below decks than topside, and far more frightening, Jim Longhi recalled. In their crowded cabin, Guthrie picked up his guitar and mandolin, then shoved a harmonica into his pocket.

"Where are you going?" Longhi asked.

"I think the soldiers could use a little music," Guthrie said over the resounding boom of the depth charges.

"Are you crazy? If we get hit while we're down there—"

"I'm going down below. I'll see you."

Sighing, Houston and Longhi picked up their guitars, dragged along "by guilt—cords that're stronger than steel."

Decades later, Longhi could only marvel at what he saw as Guthrie's "saintly" quality. "That's what a saint does: puts the lives of his brothers and sisters ahead of him. He was saintly. Believe me," Longhi insisted.

"When you're under submarine attack, 3,000 men below, and only six

---

* The last session, sometime after April 25, 1944, included a song Guthrie had written more than three years earlier but was still reworking. Asch set the title down as "This Land Is My Land." He would not commit the recording to long-playing record until 1951. Details of the recording sessions are in Peter D. Goldsmith, *Making People's Music: Moe Asch and Folkways Records* (Washington: Smithsonian Institution Press, 1998); in Guy Logsdon's notes to Woody Guthrie, "This Land Is Your Land" (Smithsonian Folkways 40100); and in Logsdon's "Woody Guthrie: A Biblio-Discography" (Washington: Smithsonian Institution, 1998). Logsdon credits Jim Kweskin for his early discography of the Asch recordings.

lifeboats on the ship, the first thing you want to do is climb up a mast . . . or stand next to a life boat. The last thing you want to do is go down below, 'cause if you are hit, there is no way out.

"And Woody went down below, to entertain the troops."

The fear in number three hold was palpable, the frightened soldiers curled in their five-high bunks. Even as another barrage of depth charges thundered in the waters off the transport, Guthrie calmly tuned his guitar, and launched into "The Sinking of the *Reuben James.*"

> *Tell me, what were their names?*
> *Tell me, what were their names?*
> *Did you have a friend on the good Reuben James?*

Soon the troops were singing the chorus with the seamen three. "Verse after verse, depth charge after depth charge, Woody sang out the whole song," Longhi wrote in his autobiographical account of their days in the merchant marine. Southern boys who played fiddle and mandolin picked up the spare instruments and joined in. For an hour and a half, until the depth charges faded off, Guthrie, Houston, and Longhi sang through the general quarters alarm.

As the three made their way out of number three hold, they heard the singing voices of black men coming from one of the toilets. Festooned with instruments, Guthrie stood in the doorway. "That's about the best darn singing I ever heard," Guthrie told the staff sergeant who seemed to be the leader. He invited the fifty men to join them in number three hold.

"That is kind of you. But we can't do that." An army segregated in peacetime would go to war segregated.

Guthrie decided they would sing here, in the toilet.

Can't. "This here is the colored toilet."

Guthrie would hear none of it. His guitar cocked across his chest, he struck a loud chord. "John Henry-y-y-y-y—"

Back and forth Guthrie, Longhi, and Houston traded songs with the black chorus. The depth charges resumed, closer than before, yet they sang on.

When a white sergeant that protested they were singing in a "Nigra toilet," Guthrie waved him off. "We love singing in toilets. Good acoustics."

The depth charges boomed off the riveted plates of the "Sea Pussy." If the six hundred white soldiers wanted them to sing, Guthrie insisted the black troops would have to come along.

The sergeant reported to the captain and the captain to a flummoxed colonel. Since Guthrie, Houston, and Longhi were civilians, and not subject to military orders, the army was stymied. The colonel relented. Fifty black soldiers shifted to number three hold, a laughing Guthrie, Houston, and Longhi marching among them, Guthrie holding aloft his guitar with its hand-lettered slogan: "This machine kills fascists."

The convoy was at sea when the *Sea Porpoise*'s loudspeakers announced that Allied forces had landed on the Normandy coast. The troops aboard the vessel were replacements, to be put ashore in France as they were needed.

For the next four weeks, the convoy lay moored, first in Liverpool harbor, then across the Irish Sea in Belfast Lough. Guthrie, Houston, and Longhi managed to slip ashore for two unauthorized nights. Ever fearful of venereal disease, Guthrie avoided the prostitutes who were eager to sell favors for cigarettes. Finally, on July 4, 1944, the turbines hissed to life, and the Sea Pussy edged into the Irish Sea, southbound through Saint George's Channel for the Normandy coast.

Escorted by minesweepers, the convoy stood off Omaha Beach on July 5. From the deck of their transport, they could see in the early morning darkness what Longhi described as a red glow. As they drew inshore, the red turned to bright orange along a twenty-mile front, and they could hear the distant clump of artillery.

The three thousand troops aboard the vessel began to disembark as occasional German shells whistled overhead. Landing craft pulled alongside to collect the troops clambering down nets, then loaded and churned away toward shore. Back and forth they ran until only the eighty-five crew members remained aboard.

Two hours later, the three messmen were off duty. In their cabin, Guthrie extolled the beauties of Jane Dudley dancing *Harmonica Breakdown* to the music of Sonny Terry. "And then the ship rocked."

The *Sea Porpoise* rose from the water, stricken, then slammed down into the sea. Guthrie was thrown first to the overhead, then to the deck. Longhi tumbled from his bunk and struck his head on the deck. Only Cisco escaped unharmed.

"Our ship is shaking, trembling, rising and falling. She leans, she slips to one side, the waters rush and foam and slosh around her with such a big noise that my ears hurt," Guthrie wrote. "She is twisted and hurt and she shakes like she is nervous. . . . This nervous shaking hurts the men, runs through your blood like electricity and makes you sick at your belly." Their first thought was they had taken a torpedo; surely a second would follow and finish them off.

Guthrie, momentarily rattled, and cool Cisco Houston made their way topside, then realized that Longhi was not with them. Back down the companionways they scrambled, steadying themselves against the severe list. Together Guthrie and Houston pulled a stunned Longhi to his feet. Quickly they explained they had been on deck before they realized he was not with them.

"You mean you guys came back for me?"

"Hell no, we came back for the guitars," Guthrie drawled.

Finally on the boat deck together, they shifted nervously, waiting for the captain to order them to abandon ship. When a member of the engine gang frantically reported that one of the crew was trapped there in the darkness, Houston bolted for the ladder. Longhi and Guthrie followed.

Two decks below, they found the seaman, screaming that he couldn't see. They sought to calm the terrified sailor, then carried him back the way they had come. Once more Guthrie ducked below decks, emerging with their guitars and his fiddle and mandolin.

They reassembled on deck while the captain sought to assess the damage to his gravely broken ship. They had been struck by a mine, not a torpedo. The explosion had destroyed the engine room amidships and left the *Sea Porpoise* with a pronounced list, but still afloat.

Tugs from Southampton came alongside, attached lines, and towed the stricken ship to comparative safety in the roadstead. For the next three nights, Guthrie watched V-1 "Buzz Bombs" drilling down on the harbor or flying high overhead toward London. The pilotless weapon emitted "a ghostly, awful, spooky moan," but it was the silence once the engine turned off that was most terrifying. Then the flying bomb, Hitler's Reprisal Weapon-1, would nose over and mindlessly hurtle into row houses and shops, schools and offices.

After three days watching the buzz bombs whistle over Southampton, the crew of the disabled troopship was ordered home. A five-hour layover in London allowed Guthrie to visit the BBC studios, to shake hands with a friend he had met earlier that year while recording *The Martins and the Coys* in New York, and to sing three songs on *The Children's Hour*.

On July 13, 1944, at Euston Station, they boarded the Royal Scot for Glasgow, the first leg of the trip home. The seamen three had sailed together for a last time.

CHAPTER TWENTY-ONE

Shackled

*T*HE APARTMENT ON Mermaid Avenue in Coney Island was small, but Woody Guthrie prided himself on needing little space. His clothes hardly filled a drawer, his instruments hung on a wall, just above Cathy's reach. A triangular piece of wood Marjorie had nailed into a corner of their bedroom created a "desk" just large enough to hold the Smith-Corona portable. The hobo in Guthrie was content.

Guthrie and Marjorie's entire relationship was by turns passionate and strained. Twice stung by Guthrie, she was wary and insisted on her financial independence. She essentially supported the household by giving dance lessons. Guthrie contributed, particularly when he returned from voyages with his accumulated pay, doubled for the time spent in combat zones. Still, by Christmas 1944, with the last gifts sent off to the three children in El Paso, Guthrie was again broke—and facing another draft notice.

Proud holder of NMU Book No. 86716, Guthrie had remained draft-exempt so long as he served in the merchant marine. But as he told Jim Longhi, the FBI had lifted Guthrie's seaman's papers because of an article he had written for the *Sunday Worker*. He would regain his papers, he promised, and sail with Jim Longhi on the next voyage.

Guthrie's appeal failed. A self-important officer from Naval Intelligence now sat screening seamen in the NMU hiring hall off Eighth Avenue. Guthrie's name was on a blacklist.

How long had he been a member of the Communist Party? the officer demanded.

He wasn't, Guthrie replied. Nor was he ashamed to be described as a communist.

Despite his denial, "Woodrow Wilson Guthrie" appeared on the lieutenant's list. The officer refused to stamp Guthrie's seaman's papers. Guthrie was stranded ashore.

He was defiant. "I thank my God in heaven that I'm on these black lists," he snapped. "If my name wasn't on these lists of Hoover and Dewey and Dies, I don't guess I could enjoy a decent night's sleep."*

Hoover, Dewey, and Dies were antiunion, Guthrie insisted, particularly unions led by avowed Communists. In contrast, Guthrie thundered, "I live union. I eat union. I think union. I see union. I walk it and I talk it. I sing it and I preach it."

In October 1944, Guthrie, Cisco Houston, and Will Geer had joined a pro-Roosevelt "Bandwagon" tour sponsored by the newly organized Communist Political Association (CPA). The chairman of the Communist Party U.S.A., Earl Browder, had dissolved the party in May in favor of wartime coalition and postwar cooperation. As Browder put it, the revolutionaries of old "must help to remove from the American ruling class the fear of a socialist revolution in the United States in the post-war period."

When Browder's new CPA praised President Roosevelt for cooperating with Soviet Premier Joseph Stalin to win the war, Woody Guthrie was ready to switch his vote and join the tour. Four years earlier he had sharply criticized Roosevelt for leading the nation to war; now, like Browder, he viewed Republicans as "appeasers and defeatists" eager "to bring about a compromise peace with Nazism-Fascism."

Guthrie's about-face was understandable only in terms of his compelling need to defeat fascism and win the war. In 1940, he insisted, "the average elections are about as useful as a slop jar without a bottom in it." In 1944 he was campaigning for Roosevelt as the only politician in the country who would preserve the cooperative spirit of the Big Three at the Teheran conference.

The abrupt reversal was heartfelt, Cisco Houston later explained. Guthrie's politics, Houston insisted, "were about as honest as anything about him. They may have been confused and erratic, and they might have blown with the wind a little bit—like everyone else's—but he made no bones about it."

While Guthrie had read the basic tracts of communism, if he had anything approaching a coherent political philosophy, it might have been described as patriotic socialism. Guthrie certainly shared the Movement's mandate that "the highest social priority must go to the needs of the least fortunate."

* J. Edgar Hoover was director of the FBI. Thomas E. Dewey, governor of New York, was the Republican Party nominee for the presidency in 1944. Representative Martin Dies (Democrat, Texas) was chairman from 1938 until the end of 1944 of the House of Representatives Special Committee on Un-American Activities.

But his was an intensely personal synthesis of primitive Christianity and nondoctrinaire communism, shaped as early as the spring of 1941:

> Every single human being is looking for a better way . . . when there shall be no want among you, because you'll own everything in Common. When the Rich will give their goods unto the poor. I believe in this Way. I just can't believe in any other Way. This is the Christian Way and it is already on a big part of the earth and it will come. To own everything in Common. That's what the bible [*sic*] says. Common means all of us. This is pure old Commonism.

Browder was now asking Guthrie to apply his belief in Christian socialism, in an effort to find a better way. Guthrie joined the Roosevelt tour.

Quickly tagged by the press as "Communist-sponsored," the Roosevelt Bandwagon enjoyed only modest success. A large "People's Rally for Victory and Unity" in Chicago was followed by a stink bomb attack in Boston's Symphony Hall. Things deteriorated from there. Even the unionized cities of the industrial east, Buffalo, Akron, Cleveland, and Indianapolis, turned out scattered audiences.

Well before the end of the tour, Guthrie was yearning for Marjorie. "You see what Akron done to me," he wrote on the train between that city and Chicago. "How broke and lonesome that a man can be."

Hours later, he was writing a plea to an absent Marjorie: "You and me have got union of a wild kind that boils like melted metal and runs like greasy fat. . . . Staying apart, separate, distinct, afraid to mix, [is] the mistake of our world."

Professing his love and apologizing for his shortcomings, Guthrie wrote her constantly from the road. His letters grew more and more passionate:

> You make me the luckiest and happiest man in the world when you move your body with mine, when you close your eyes and open your mouth and roll your belly and hips, when you spread your legs apart slow and easy and let me put my mouth and tongue on the hairs of your womb. There is a smell that goes through me finer than the prettiest morning and the skin and hair of your belly and womb are my whole life's desire. To touch your lips with my lips and lick my tongue in your hole of your vagina absolutely boils every drop of blood in my whole body.

Roosevelt was reelected for a fourth term, and Guthrie wrangled a return to radio on WNEW in New York City. Offered a fifteen-minute program on Sunday afternoons at 4:45, Guthrie began his first show on December 3, 1944, with a long plea to listeners. "A little old fifteen minutes here on the radio, well, it cramps me just a little bit." But if enough listeners wrote to him, "the men that run this radio station told me that they'd stretch my time out and make it thirty minutes."

Unlike the free-and-easy KFVD days, Guthrie was careful to type a script at least part of which he would read on the air to explain why he sang the songs he sang.

I hate a song that makes you think you're not any good. I hate a song makes you think you are just born to lose. Bound to lose. No good to nobody. No good for nothing. . . . Songs that run you down or songs that poke fun at you on account of your bad luck or your hard traveling.

I am out to fight those kind of songs to my very last breath of air and my very last drop of blood.

I am out to sing songs that'll prove to you that this is your world and that if it's hit you pretty hard and knocked you for a dozen loops, no matter how hard it's run you down or rolled over you, no matter what color, what size you are, how you are built, I am out to sing the songs that make you take pride in yourself and in your work.

Even edited drastically, his plea ran long. He had time for only three songs in the fifteen-minute show, a *Variety* reviewer grumbled. Still the reviewer concluded, "Folk ballad fans should go for this one. It's as authentic as a cook shack."

If New York's folk ballad fans did tune in, it made no impression on the station's managers. Guthrie's *Ballad Gazette* remained a fifteen-minute program, canceled after twelve weeks on the air. It came, it went, and left only a vestigial trace: a twenty-five-cent mimeographed songbook containing ten songs that Marjorie and Guthrie assembled in their Mermaid Avenue apartment.

Guthrie's career, if so meandering a course could be called a career, was faltering. He appeared on an experimental CBS television broadcast. With Earl Robinson, he provided the music once more for Sophie Maslow's *Folksay* during the winter of 1944–45. He found a few writing assignments, including a prize-winning NBC program, "America for Christmas," broadcast on December 25, 1944, that used four of his songs arranged by Robinson.

Guthrie worked sporadically on his book, promised to E. P. Dutton long since, but his "Ship Story" manuscript was unfocused and unfinished; both Joy Doerflinger, working for the Office of War Information, and her husband William, with the army in Italy, were unavailable to him. "I write like the Montgomery Ward catalog," Guthrie grumbled, "and sell very little material."

In the first months of 1945, he slipped into uncharacteristic gloom. "I believe I could be a better poet than Walt Whitman, if only I didn't have to make enough money to support four children," Guthrie wrote in a disingenuous essay probably intended for no one but himself. (Mary, who was soon to be remarried, supported Guthrie's three children. Marjorie continued to maintain the apartment in Coney Island.)

The task of supporting himself and contributing to the household budget was more difficult than ever. Guthrie found few bookings at union halls, where fully employed, complacent war workers honored no-strike pledges, and he refused to sing for unions that hampered the war effort by striking.

Guthrie's steadiest work was for Moses Asch—most of it unpaid. Guthrie wrote the liner notes for the first release of some of the songs he had recorded with Cisco Houston during the April 1944 marathon in the Asch studio.*

Guthrie's notes for the album Asch had unimaginatively dubbed *Folksay* were a howling against the wind. "Hollywood songs don't last," Guthrie insisted.

> Broadway songs are sprayed with a hundred thousand dollars to get them going, and they last, we'll say, a few months at most. The Monopoly on Music pays a few pet writers to go screwy trying to write and rewrite the same old notes under the same old formulas and the same old patterns. Every band on the radio sounds exactly alike. . . . Do the big bands and the orgasm gals sing a word about our real fighting history? Not a croak.

---

* The four-record *Folksay* album—Guthrie appeared on six of the eight sides—was released both on Moe Asch's eponymous label and on Stinson. (Each numbered it "Album 432.") The set was the offspring of a marriage of convenience between Asch, who owned the master recordings made earlier that year, and Stinson's Robert Harris, who had the shellac necessary for 78-r.p.m. recordings in this fourth year of war.

Tin Pan Alley was intent on amusing the public and making money. Guthrie, on the other hand, sought songs that sparked "the spirit of work, fight, sacrifice." Yet this first release on Asch/Stinson contained nothing that could be interpreted as political, or even as pro-union; Moe Asch sensed the times, even if Guthrie refused to.

While the album was well reviewed—Guthrie "is a folk singer of more than casual interest," a *Billboard* writer decided—the set sold poorly. Asch was a crafty businessman, but more interested in recording music than marketing it. "We never balanced books," he conceded in a 1972 interview; he preferred instead to work on an off-the-books basis. Guthrie would often write Asch, urging him to send records to the usually small, independent record stores Guthrie scouted out when he traveled. As often as not, Asch ignored these requests.

Guthrie's recordings, on Stinson or on Asch, did not sell much beyond stalwart unionists and members of the Popular Front. Still, Guthrie was optimistic enough to propose that Asch release no fewer than four albums from material already recorded. Two sets, cowboy ballads and fiddle tunes, would be drawn from Guthrie's own life; two others, pioneer songs and sea songs and shanties, were Guthrie's re-creations of field recordings in the Archive of American Folk-Song. Asch agreed to begin with the fiddle tunes, for no other reason than he lacked an album of traditional dance tunes, and he anticipated sales to square-dance groups.

Asch *was* more enthusiastic about another of Guthrie's suggestions of "a kind of musical newspaper" the Almanacs had put forward four years before. Guthrie proposed to re-create major news events in topical songs each month; Asch committed his company to release this *American Documentary* album periodically.

However, when Guthrie turned up at the Asch studios in the early spring of 1945 to record the first album, he had recast the concept of *American Documentary*. As Asch described it, each album would depict "the struggle of working people in bringing to light their fight for a place in the America that they envisioned."

The result was Guthrie's "pet album . . . six songs and ballads in that album I've always been my proudest of. They sound to me like I hope I sound to other folks."

Two of the songs Guthrie had prepared for the recording session were inspired by his recent reading of the autobiography of legendary Communist labor organizer Ella Reeves Bloor, *We Are Many*. "Ludlow Massacre" recounted the deaths of thirteen women and children at the hands of the

Colorado National Guard during a strike against John D. Rockefeller's Colorado Fuel and Iron Company. The second, which Guthrie originally titled "Copper Miner Christmas," would be one of his most powerful indictments of corporate America in ballad form.

"They had a Christmas Ball at Calumet, Michigan, to raise money for strikers and union families," Guthrie explained in his notes to the album. "Copper boss thugs yelled 'Fire!' in the door and seventy-three children smothered to death on the stairs."

> *Take a trip with me in Nineteen-thirteen,*
> *To Calumet, Michigan, in the copper country.*
> *I will take you to a place called Italian Hall,*
> *And the miners are having their big Christmas Ball.*

The combination of text and tune, a three-quarters time melody adapted from a southern mountain love lament, was vivid and immediate. The ten-stanza ballad concluded:

> *Such a terrible sight I never did see.*
> *We carried our children back up to their tree.*
> *The scabs outside still laughed at their spree,*
> *And the children that died there were seventy-three.*

> *The piano played a slow funeral tune,*
> *And the town was lit up by a cold Christmas moon.*
> *The parents they cried and the miners they moaned,*
> *"See what your greed for money has done."*

The Bloor autobiography was but one of a clutch of political books Guthrie read in the first months of 1945. After reading V. I. Lenin's *Theory of the Agrarian Question*, Guthrie, ever the eager student, wrote on the flyleaf: "I wish I knew what I could do to make all the thoughts of Marx and Engels and Lenin and Stalin and Willkie and Roosevelt and Earl Browder fly down and roost in my brain."

A week later, on March 4, he bought the first volume of Karl Marx's *Das Kapital*, promising in a note on the flyleaf to memorize the contents in a week or so. "The man that writes our best ballad will read this book from cover to cover. . . . I'd like to try and write all of these things down in short words."

In March 1945, Guthrie finally received his induction notice. An appeal to his draft board failed, as did an audition for Special Services, the army's entertainment branch. Despite a left arm slightly shorter than the right (the result of the badly reset broken bone), she passed his physical on April 9. He was inducted, ironically enough, on May 7, 1945, the day the embattled Third Reich surrendered.

Marjorie was frankly worried about her undisciplined lover melding into a disciplined army. "How was he going to stand in line, and march and do what they told him, at that moment?" How could this man, whom she had to remind to bathe and brush his teeth, get up with a bugle call and dress in the proper uniform? The merchant marine was so different, so much less rigid than the army. She could only grit her teeth. "When he went into the army, I thought I'd die."

Assigned arbitrarily to the Army Air Force, Guthrie was sent to Sheppard Field, Texas, for basic training. There Private Woodrow Wilson Guthrie, Army Serial Number 422 346 34, threw himself into the task. "Like everything else, he went way overboard, and was just enamored of the idea of winning this war and doing his bit," Marjorie said. Ordered to pick up litter, Guthrie determined to police the area in one day rather than the three the other men on his detail proposed. They were slackers. "What kind of a war effort is this?" he demanded.

His thirty-one days of basic training were no more than close order drill alternating with police details. Mary Guthrie drove her three children 750 miles across the state in her Chevrolet sedan to visit their father. While he had written, and sometimes sent a few dollars or toys, Guthrie had not seen Gwen, Sue, and Billy in almost four years.

By mid-August and the surrender of Japan, Guthrie's fight against fascism had come to an end. He was succumbing instead to "the big lazy spirit that come over us all since VJ Day."

After basic training, teletype school at Scott Field, outside East St. Louis, Illinois, seemed a waste of time now that fascism had been defeated. Like millions of other GIs, Guthrie cared only about his discharge.

Marjorie's visit during that summer of 1945 renewed their courtship. Between sweet moments of love and sex in the musty hotel room Guthrie had booked, they talked of Cathy, of Marjorie's pending divorce, of their lives together. Finally, tentatively, warily they talked again about marriage and more children.

Nothing settled between them, Marjorie left at the end of July. In a funk, Guthrie tried out again for Special Services as a musician and again was turned down. He was marked AWOL, absent without leave, for staying too long in the post library and failing to report for a roll call. He was confined to the barracks when an instructor in class caught him reading "non-technical literature"—a report about the Potsdam Conference. "Then I decided that I would just set through every class and fail all of the tests . . . and get thrown out of the window with my guitar," he wrote to Sophie Maslow and her husband, Max Blatt.

Guthrie had miscalculated. He had been sent to Scott Field to become a teletype operator, his commanding officer insisted, and by God, Private Guthrie *would* become a teletype operator. He offered Guthrie a choice: take the course again, and pass it, or face the guardhouse for deliberately malingering.

Guthrie chose to pass the test. He scored a 92, he boasted, when a grade of merely 70 was passing.

Shortly after Marjorie left for New York, Guthrie was in the Scott Field Post Exchange when he heard a familiar voice singing an equally familiar song on the jukebox. Cousin Leon "Jack" Guthrie, the one they called "Oak" or "Okie," had recorded Woody's song "Oklahoma Hills." Now a big hit, here was the Capitol recording on the jukebox of the Post Exchange at Camp Scott, Illinois; Jack Guthrie's record would eventually spend ten weeks as the best-selling "western" song in the nation and sell more than 150,000 copies.

Woody Guthrie was initially pleased, even flattered, upon hearing the recording. He changed his mind when he learned that cousin Jack had put the copyright in *his* name. Jack had changed a few words to smooth the meter and he had eliminated the names of Oklahoma's Indian tribes, what Guthrie deemed "the best part of the whole song." While Jack had "jazzed up the rhythm and clowned up the chorus," the changes were hardly enough to claim even a coauthorship, let alone the composer's credit. Woody Guthrie promptly wrote to Capitol Records, demanding that the song be credited to him and that he receive royalties. He sought no damages. Jack, after all, "is not a vicious or mean guy, just vastly adventurous and romantically inconsiderate," Guthrie explained in a letter to Marjorie.*

---

* Despite his assertions that he welcomed people singing his songs, earlier Guthrie was not so kind to Jack's larceny. Writing Alan Lomax in March 1941, Guthrie pointed out that Jack had had most of Guthrie's songbook retyped "and I had the pleasure of seeing that each of his copies said at the bottom—'Orig. by Leon J. Guthrie, The Oklahoma Yodeling Cowboy.' Well,

After completing his teletype course in September, Guthrie found himself idling in an army intent on demobilization. He was painting signs and pulling duty as a barracks guard; the undemanding work details left him with hours to play his guitar and to write songs. And all the while he waited for the Army Air Force to decide what to do with this thirty-three-year-old private.

Guthrie's letters to Marjorie in these autumn months were full of sexual yearning. He was simultaneously ardent and pleading, boasting that since high school he had masturbated often, even when they lived together. Marjorie, after all, did not relish sex as he did, he rationalized. "I could see that in spite of your good trying, the business of sex for sex's sake wasn't felt very strongly in you. To me it was the center of everything." Still, he assured her in another letter, he had steadfastly avoided the women of the town. Instead, he wrote to Marjorie, "There's a little New York dancing gal that I want to snuggle up with and shackle onto." He was once more the yearning lad from Okemah. "I'm more of a shackler than a fighter. Or even a traveller. I would quit anything to build my days up around yours."

After more than a month of near idleness, the restless Guthrie received a two-week furlough. He made his way by train to New York, where, on November 13, 1945, Woodrow Wilson Guthrie and Marjorie Greenblatt Mazia were married. The ceremony was hastily arranged, witness Sophie Maslow recalled; the wedding party, including dancers Sasha Liebich and Zoe Williams, scrambled to make it to the Manhattan City Clerk's office before it closed. They were the last couple to be married that day, five minutes after the office closed.

The honeymoon, if five days in the Mermaid Avenue apartment with Cathy could be called a honeymoon, went too quickly for Private Guthrie. The marriage had not only bound Guthrie to Marjorie, but it served to free him from the service. As a married man, he could now claim Cathy as a dependent. The father of four children, Guthrie had enough points under the army's complicated system to qualify for a discharge.

---

no hard feelings amongst us. Cousins is cousins, you know." WGA Notebooks 1, Folder 4. According to Guthrie scholar Guy Logsdon, Jack Guthrie insisted in his defense that "Oklahoma Hills" would never have been known had he not buffed the lyrics and recorded the song. Eventually Woody agreed to share the copyright as: "By Jack Guthrie and Woody Guthrie." Much recorded, particularly by Hank Williams and Gene Autry, who sang it in the film *Sioux City Sue*, Jack's recording has since become a country and western standard; it was also cousin Woody's first commercial success.

He dutifully reported before Thanksgiving to his new station outside Las Vegas, Nevada. There he reported his new marital status and dependents.

He would spend a dreary month in the desert, marking time. Ticketed for an early discharge—under political pressure the army was now rushing to demobilize—Guthrie idled his days playing guitar and tormenting his new wife with long, tortuous, and convoluted letters. In one, he taunted Marjorie with his unfulfilled sexual fantasies for other women, then obsequiously apologized in a letter mailed an hour later.

On December 21, 1945, two days later, Private First Class Guthrie was released from active duty. Like millions of other ex-GIs, he returned home to hang his dress uniform with its "ruptured duck" in the far corner of a dark closet; it had never fit his slender frame anyway. He was honorably discharged on January 13, 1946.

Woodrow Wilson Guthrie's great war against fascism was over.

A second was about to begin.

CHAPTER TWENTY-TWO

The Running Man

*T*HE ORIGINAL IDEA was Pete Seeger's, conceived while he was in the Pacific, waiting to be shipped home and discharged from the army. As he wrote Lee Hays, there was a need for a group of union-minded singers, banded together, who would write and distribute songs to progressive organizations. Hays agreed, adding that this new group might publish a newsletter to bring together "people like us," regardless of where they lived. From there the concept grew.

Seeger, discharged in December 1945, and Hays assembled a small group of friends in New York City on the last day of the year. "Thinking along terms of the Communist movement," Seeger explained later, he drafted the opening statement: "People are on the march, and must have songs to sing. . . . It is clear there must be an organization to make and send songs of labor and the American people through the land."*

The organization's program would be based "largely in the rich and democratic traditions of American folk music. We feel that the whole American folk tradition is a progressive people's tradition. For that reason our comments, our new songs, our activities are, in great measure, rooted in the fertile soil of American folk music."

Seeger envisioned a broadly based organization, a renewal of the pre-war Popular Front. He personally recruited an impressive array of "sponsors" including composer-conductors Leonard Bernstein, Aaron Copland, and Marc Blitzstein; lyricists Oscar Hammerstein and E. Y. Harburg; actors

---

* Three of the five people at the first meeting were members of the Communist Party: Seeger, Earl Robinson, and Herbert Haufrecht. Robinson and Haufrecht were well schooled as classical composers. The other two attending, Hays and Alan Lomax, had been aligned with the Popular Front of the 1930s.

Sam Wanamaker, Paul Robeson, Judy Holliday, and Gene Kelly; and entertainer Lena Horne.*

Discharged from the Army Air Force, Guthrie promptly joined People's
Songs. How could he not, when the organization's goal was to "circumvent
. . . the music monopoly of Broadway and Hollywood"?

While he spent a good deal of time hanging about the People's Songs
office, Guthrie was uninterested in the organizational meetings; he came to
sing. He was particularly enthusiastic about its functioning as a booking
agency, a one-stop source of entertainers for unions, liberal groups, and old
Popular Front organizations.

Guthrie, said the man charged with running the day-to-day operations,
"was a unique figure. He was *Woody*, one of a kind in personality and what
he did." He had roots in the country but wrote contemporary political
songs in a style that was at once folk and sophisticated. "And he was absolutely
amazing," Irwin Silber added.

Guthrie was not a universal success, Silber conceded. "A lot of the audiences around New York had a hard time understanding him, especially the
older Jewish left audiences. It was something about the style, the manner of
singing." The distance between Pampa and the shtetl of the Lower East Side
was too great.

At the same time, younger audiences, the "New York, Northeastern
Jewish kids who largely created the folk revolution," were attracted to
Guthrie, his "lemon juice voice" and a guitar slightly out of tune, the editor
of the People's Songs newsletter, Bernard Asbell, noted. "They had never
seen anyone like that."

They were called "Woody's children," said one of them, then-eighteen-
year-old Joe Jaffee. They made what Jaffee called "the pilgrimage" to Mermaid Avenue, often to baby-sit Cathy, other times to sit with Guthrie and
play for hours on end.

To Jaffee, who was just learning to play the guitar, Guthrie the performer seemed casual but "always in control. . . . It was almost like he did-
n't want to appear too organized. . . . He was obsessed with the idea of
being as natural as possible. He dreaded the idea of sounding commercial
in any way."

Here seemingly was an American voice, authentic as these first- and
second-generation young people could not be. The more Guthrie laid on

---

* People's Songs would eventually enlist some three thousand members organized into chapters
across the country. New York, Chicago, and Los Angeles were the main centers of activity.

his accent, the more he drawled long introductions to his songs, the more he appeared artless, and the more they celebrated him.

"I was sitting there like at the feet of a guru with somebody who has gone through working class struggles and all the romance of it," said actors' agent Harvey Matusow, a People's Songs volunteer. "I had a great deal of love, honor and respect for the guy."

For all their admiration, or the time spent with Guthrie, he kept his distance, Jaffee said. "It was almost as if he were standing on the outside watching himself converse with you."

Fred Hellerman, recently discharged from the Coast Guard and teaching himself to play guitar while he studied music, also considered Guthrie remote, a man apart. "Woody lived in his own world. You could look in and see what you saw, but he's not going to show you."

Guthrie apparently understood. In a composition book he kept about this time he wrote, "There ain't no one little certain self that is you. I'm not some certain self. I'm a lot of selfs. A lot of minds and changes of minds. Moods by the wagon loads and changes of moods."

There were skeptics among the young as well. Hellerman decided "Woody was not a really good performer." He had heard Guthrie's RCA albums of dust bowl ballads some years before and thought, "Oh, my god, this is astounding." It was simple and clean, even if the musical style was taken from the Carter Family, he noted. But Hellerman "never heard Woody perform anywhere that well again."

While Asbell, like Hellerman, personally preferred Guthrie the song-poet to Guthrie the singer, as editor, Asbell did not use much of Guthrie's material. The first Guthrie song he published in the monthly newsletter of People's Songs was far more folk than it was sophisticated. With a few simple word changes, Guthrie had turned a gospel hymn into a union-organizing anthem:

You got to go down and join the union.
You got to join it for yourself.
There ain't nobody can join it for you.
You got to go down and join the union by yourself.

Succeeding verses ranged through the members of the family: sister, mama, brother, papa. Sung "with some good old-fashioned harmony," Guthrie assured his readers, "each verse seems to sound a little bit better than the last."

Two of Guthrie's songs appeared in the July 1946 issue, one newly written, the other from 1944. Another, "Hard Traveling," rewritten since he fashioned it during his Columbia River stint in 1941, was printed in the first issue of 1947.

As a singer, however, Guthrie "was one of the favorites, always asked for," recalled Jackie Alper, who volunteered to work in the People's Songs office. The fees were nominal, fifteen dollars was the maximum, she added. Much of the time, a half hour of entertainment might net them five dollars. With Marjorie's income from dance lessons, it was enough to get by.

In a pinch, Moe Asch was good for a few bucks out of petty cash. "It was very loose," Asch conceded. "They didn't usually come up there to record; they came up because they needed a couple of bucks."*

With the end of the war, Asch had dissolved Asch Records and his ties with Stinson to form the new and independent Disc label. He had big plans, including more jazz releases, which did not interest Guthrie. But none of the Disc sets would sell as well, or leave so lasting an imprint as the songs inspired by Guthrie's not-yet-three-year-old daughter, Cathy Ann.

Stackabones was an almost cherubic infant with tumbles of dark curly hair. Sometimes she was also "Cathy Rooney," or "Catharooney," or "Miss Stack" or "Stacky." Always she was a happy child, inquisitive, intelligent, with a child's understanding of the woolly-headed man who made up funny songs for her. Woody doted on her.

With Cathy Ann's birth he had kept a diary, a record of coos, burps, and bowel movements, interrupted by his merchant marine voyages and army service, then faithfully resumed whenever he returned to Mermaid Avenue. He played with his daughter for hours, frolicking in the fantasy world he shared with this miraculous creature Marjorie and he had made.

Cathy somehow tickled all that was childlike in her father, the man who still played marbles with neighborhood kids, who glued together seashell and popsicle-stick flowers, or slathered watercolors on pages with a three-year-old's careless freedom. Guthrie, who took dozens of children to the nearby beach to build sand castles, "was so much fun as a father, because he loved kids. He was a big kid, in that sense," Marjorie Guthrie reminisced. "Everything was a game; even I played games with him. We played games with the children and without the children."

---

* According to Guy Logsdon, Guthrie cashed his first check for royalties from his cousin's "Oklahoma Hills" recording and took home 1,156 one-dollar bills in a shoebox. As he entered the door, he started throwing dollar bills in the air and yelling, "We're rich! We're rich!" A week later, Marjorie was still finding dollar bills under the furniture. See Logsdon's "Woody Guthrie and His Oklahoma Hills," *Mid-America Folklore* 19 (1991), p. 70.

Fascinated by Cathy's fanciful wordplay, Guthrie sometimes typed out the charming illogic of her poetry, as if he were learning a new language:

Sam, Sam, how did you grow?
How did you grow? I don't know.
I don't know.
I don't know.
I don't know.
Sam, Sam, I don't know.

King of the sailors, clean off the ceiling.
Wear the navy blue, wear the navy blue.

The zebra fell down,
Hurt his self on the finger.
I picked them up.
They weren't dead no more.

Inevitably, he would write songs for Cathy and her friends, simple songs spun from the stuff of a children's world:

Mamma, o, mamma, come wash my face,
Wash my face, come wash my face,
Mamma, o, mamma, come wash my face,
And make me nice and clean-o.

Daddy, o, daddy, come fix my shoe,
Fix my shoe, fix my shoe,
Daddy, o, daddy, come fix my shoe,
And polish it nice and clean-o.

Many of the songs were directly inspired by the little girl with the curly hair:

Why can't a dish break a hammer?
Why, oh why, oh why?
'Cause a hammer's got a hard head.
Goodbye. Goodbye. Goodbye.

Chorus:
Why, oh why, oh why-o,
Why, oh why, oh why?
Because, because, because, because, because.
Goodbye. Goodbye. Goodbye.

Why can't a mouse eat a streetcar?
Why, oh why, oh why?
'Cause a mouse's stomach could never get big enough to
*   hold a streetcar.*
Goodbye. Goodbye. Goodbye.

Others were fashioned from their playing together:

Take my little hoe,
Dig a hole in the ground.
Take my little seed
And I plant it down.
Took-y, took-y, took-y,
Took-y, ti-dal-o.
Let's all dance around
And see my little seed grow.

Guthrie tried out the songs on Cathy's friends; she seemed to make play-mates out of everyone who ambled along Mermaid Avenue to the board-walk. He sang them for and with the children of Alan and Elizabeth Lomax, and friends John Henry and Hally Faulk, adding verses, fixing lyrics, making certain these were songs for children, not songs directed to children.*

Unlike most of his recordings, Guthrie took special care when he showed up in February 1946 at Moe Asch's tiny studio to record the first group of six children's songs. Marjorie was there to offer advice, "smart enough to slow me down, to get me to take it greasy, easy, and to say my words plain."

A month later, Guthrie recorded a second album of six songs. This sec-ond set was "a speck better" than the first, though he was "not real sure" this "second batch [was] quite as bubbly" as the first. The unusual self-criti-

---

* Radio writer and humorist John Henry Faulk would later successfully sue blacklisters who prevented him from working in the broadcasting industry.

cism was a mark of the importance Guthrie placed on these songs for Cathy.

Not everyone agreed. Pete Seeger, for one, confessed he did not immediately appreciate the children's songs. As he explained later, "some of [Guthrie's] greatest songs are so deceptively simple that your eye will pass right over them and you will comment to yourself, 'Well, I guess this was one of his lesser efforts.' Years later you will find the song has grown on you and become part of your life."

The children's songs were an immediate success in left-wing book and record stores, and with the Montessori-influenced nursery schools that catered to "Red-diaper" babies. The *Daily Worker* predictably praised the first set on Disc as "some of the most delightful children's songs ever recorded." By July 1947, Asch's Disc Records ad in the People's Songs newsletter—with only a bit of hyperbole—referred to the first set, *Songs to Grow on: Nursery Days*, as "famous."*

A second project, proposed by Asch himself, did not go as well.

Keen to complete a second "documentary" album, Guthrie was casting about for a topic, Asch explained in a 1972 interview with E. Victor and Judy Wolfenstein.

In early January 1946, Asch suggested Guthrie look at "one of the great historical events of their time," the case of Italian immigrants Nicola Sacco and Bartolomeo Vanzetti. They had died as martyrs to the cause of labor, left-wing doctrine held, executed on flimsy evidence by the State of Massachusetts. Asch wanted "documentation, what actually happened, not the bullshit in the papers."

Guthrie reviewed pamphlets on the case Asch had forwarded and decided, "There is plenty here for a good album." There could be ballads about each of the two anarchists convicted of a murderous payroll robbery in 1921, and others detailing the holdup and killing, the arrest and what Guthrie described as the "foney trial."

The Sacco and Vanzetti project did not go well. The more intense the Cold War, the more Guthrie's lyrics became polemics. Poetry gave way to political speeches in verse.

Guthrie was conscious of the problem. Unhappy with his work, unable

---

* Exact sales figures for Asch, Disc, and, later, Folkways Records would be hard to assess. According to Irwin Silber, who worked with Moses Asch for twenty years, the books were poorly kept, and sales were often on an off-the-books cash basis. Further, record-pressing plant orders were thrown out. Still, it is possible, even likely, that the two Guthrie collections of children's songs that Asch released in 1947 and 1948 were his best-selling records. Literally tens of thousands of nursery school and kindergarten teachers considered them basic to any music library.

to rewrite what he had written, Guthrie missed one deadline after another. At one point, his frustration burst upon a letter to Asch: "I refuse to write these songs while I'm drunk and looks like I'll be drunk for a long time."

It would take Guthrie a year to complete the song cycle in late January 1947. Twice Asch gave Guthrie money to travel to Boston, to do research or soak up the atmosphere before writing what Guthrie deemed "the most important dozen songs I have ever worked on." Still the resulting eleven songs were labored, not as well conceived as the earlier dust bowl cycle. They seemed to run on too long, to lack the economic terseness that marked Guthrie's best work. As Pete Seeger said, they lacked direction.

The writerly discipline Guthrie had demonstrated in ballads such as "Pretty Boy Floyd" and "Tom Joad" was missing in much of his work in these postwar months. With the children's songs, the formlessness did not matter as much, Seeger concluded. With the Sacco-Vanzetti ballads, with three similarly flawed miner's songs inspired by the Centralia mine disaster in 1947, and the long-winded ballad recounting the blinding by police of a black veteran, Isaac Woodward, it did.

The spare voice and wry comment were gone, replaced by a tone of preachy rectitude. Guthrie was no longer writing about people, *his* people, but about great issues of the day.

Every dollar in the world, it rolled and it rolled,
And it rolled into Uncle Sammy's door;
A few they got richer and richer and richer,
But the poor folks kept but getting poor.

Well, the workers did fight a revolution
To chase out the gamblers from their land;
The farmers, the peasants, the workers in the city
Fought together on their five-year plans.

The soul and the spirit of the workers' revolution
Spread across every nation in this world;
From Italy to China, to Europe and to India,
And the blood of the workers it did spill.

His "serious" autobiographical novel, "Ship Story," had become a burden. Inspired by Guthrie's experiences in the merchant marine and his relationship with Marjorie, "Ship Story" seemed to have no climax or an appropriate ending. It was *Bound for Glory* once more, and a seriously ill Joy Doerflinger was no longer available to winkle a narrative from the pages and pages of manuscript.

Guthrie seemed unable to concentrate. He wrote a great deal, but no two days' work fit together coherently. On visits to Lee Hays's apartment, Guthrie would spend hours at the typewriter, then walk away without a thought for what he had written.

"I used to find pages tucked in my dictionaries, and my encyclopedia," Hays said.

> [Guthrie] didn't care what happened to it. The important thing was writing. I used to compare him to Thomas Wolfe. I read a description of Wolfe writing standing up, on the top of a dresser, and just dumping the pages into a big trunk he had, and Maxwell Perkins coming along and sorting the pages out into some manuscript form. And Woody always reminded me of water over a dam, just an unstoppable creation.

While Guthrie was struggling as both a novelist and a poet or song maker, he remained a popular entertainer. With Pete Seeger and Lee Hays, in March 1946 he flew to Pittsburgh to entertain ten thousand striking Westinghouse Electric workers. "We sang 'Solidarity Forever,'" Guthrie wrote in his notebook, "and the papers said the rally started off with a communist song. Oh. Well. Any song that fights for the cause of the workhand is a communist song to the rich folks." The song-writing spark might be missing, but the spirit was still there.

The ten-dollar bookings through People's Songs continued to come in, Jackie Alper recalled, "but Woody started to get very cantankerous." Guthrie would accept a date, then later insist that Alper, herself a singer, sing with him. If she refused, he threatened not to fulfill the engagement.

"He liked singing with people, and we sang well together," she suggested. "I think he just wanted me to go."

Guthrie had another reason. He was eager to bed the wary Alper. "He had lots and lots of affairs," she knew, "whenever and wherever he could."*

---

* While he avoided prostitutes for fear of venereal disease, Guthrie apparently dallied with some. On April 25, 1946, he wrote, "I seen a whore today with a PH degree and a good brain and a big set of books, and a nice apartment and a friendly way about her and I asked her how she ever did turn out to be a whore and she told me, 'Oh it was just a lucky break.'" Courtesy of Barry Ollman.

Almost by accident they would fall into a "really stupid" affair. Guthrie now had a low tolerance for liquor—one and a half drinks transformed him into a loud drunk, Alper said. After a Pete Seeger concert, Toshi Seeger urged Guthrie to stay with them rather than risk the long ride home to Coney Island. Alper yielded when Guthrie insisted she stay too.

Their intermittent affair would stretch over five years. Throughout, Guthrie acted no differently around her, Alper noted. "He certainly felt no guilt about the fact that he had this perfectly wonderful, caring woman, Marjorie, who really gave him love and devotion and so much of her life. He did an awful lot that wound up hurting her."

He hurt others as well. When one woman he impregnated asked him for money to help pay for an abortion, Guthrie refused. His seed, his "creation ore," was too precious to be squandered; the woman found a cooperative doctor without his help, and ended their affair.*

"He was an extraordinary genius, a gifted guy. He was also a little weasel," said one woman who crossed Guthrie's path during this time. He seemed to think "women are kind of cute and not much to think about except as sexual partners. . . . He gave me the creeps, but I must say it wasn't true for most of the girls around him."

Marjorie was aware of Guthrie's dalliances and comforted herself with the assurance that she "was the chosen one." Guthrie would leave, sometimes for weeks, then return, pledging his love as he walked in the door. "I had learned that he was not running away from me. He was going away to *be* something."

Each time Marjorie would take him back. "I knew that Woody loved me," she explained. "There is no question about that."

At the same time he desperately needed this self-possessed woman with the long, black hair. He yearned for her when she toured with the Martha Graham company for five weeks in the early spring of 1946, then sulked when she announced she was going to the theater on her second night in New York.

"No man," he whined, "should be this lonesome nor this lone."

---

* Though Guthrie was often careless with numbers, there is some hint in his papers that he may have fathered at least one more child out of wedlock. On October 9, 1948, Guthrie wrote, "Arlo is here today around my same old feet where *six* sprouts now have played." At the time, Guthrie was known to have fathered *five*: Gwen, Sue, and Bill with Mary; Cathy and Arlo with Marjorie. See Woody Guthrie Archives, "Old Goodbye," Manuscripts Box 7, Folder 15.

No man should say he's lonesome in his poem.
No man should stay this solitaire for long.
No man should sing this empty table song.
I hope no man will live so dry as I
I hope no man will sit down here and write
These sad and sorry words of ache and pain . . .

Guthrie was floundering—personally, professionally, and politically.

A fellow traveler, as the dialectic of the times had it, Guthrie faithfully hewed to the Communist Party's mandates. From the Popular Front to the cooperative Teheran sentiment, from antiwar to enthusiastic supporter of the war effort, he was first the American patriot, then the party loyalist.

During the war, Guthrie had no difficulty reconciling the two; American patriot and American communist were one and the same.

But as the Red Army on the east and the Allied armies on the west closed on Hitler's Germany, President Franklin D. Roosevelt died; in his place was Harry S. Truman, as reflexively anticommunist as Roosevelt was instinctively a negotiator. Truman was of no mind to compromise when the second in command of the French Communist Party fired the first shot of the Cold War.

Under the by-line of Jacques Duclos—his article was at least partially inspired by the Kremlin—the May 1945 issue of *Cahiers du Communisme* sharply criticized Earl Browder's cooperative wartime position. According to Duclos, Browder had usurped classical Marxism, first by predicting class peace, then by ensuring it when he dissolved the only "independent political party of the working class in the U.S."

The national committee of the Communist Political Association—the CPUSA in war paint—took the hint. Browder, his "Americanization" policy, and the cooperative spirit of Teheran were all to be purged; Browder, the deviationist, was to be replaced by an orthodox Marxist more to the liking of Moscow, William Z. Foster.

The shift from Browder to Foster was necessary, as dedicated party member Earl Robinson wrote from Los Angeles, if they were "to beat back the native fascists and keep America out of [a] new war that sure won't be a people's war."

By mid-June 1945, the transformation was complete. Loyal Communists across the country were hastily retracting support of Browder, of "Teheranism," of what now was officially termed "revisionism."

The party's rank and file shuddered under the impact. At its peak strength of a hundred thousand in 1944, it began to bleed members and fellow travelers.

Though not a member of the Communist Party, according to Marjorie, Guthrie thought of himself as "a full blood Marxican." He dutifully followed this abrupt change of leadership from Browder to Foster. (About this time, on the flyleaf of Foster's prewar *Pages from a Worker's Life*, Guthrie wrote, "If Willy Zee hadn't of done any more than to live and to write this book, he'd be the highboy for my dough.")

At the same time, Guthrie's adherence came with a skeptically raised eyebrow. He commented favorably about Comrade Browder during a performance—only to be reproached by a party functionary: "Don't you know Browder is a diversionist?"

Guthrie, never a sycophant, slyly replied, "What's wrong with a little diversion?"

In time, Guthrie would fall into line. Criticizing "the two best papers in the country, the *People's World* and the *Daily Worker*," Guthrie recommended the editors sweep out the remnants of Browderism "so as to make the D.W. and the Sunday Worker less of a thing of private enterprise."

(Guthrie also suggested that the papers' columnists write in simple English, avoiding even "longhandled Marxist phrases." The papers needed less dialectic, and more stories about "actual things that happen to working folks, more human experiences." Even the poetry, he complained another time, was "museum smelling, bookshelf tasting" stuff that had "scared away the calloused hands of thousands.")

The Duclos letter, the intensified scrutiny by FBI agents, the increased tension of a new and unfamiliar "cold war," all took their toll on the Movement.

For party faithful and fellow traveler alike, the optimism of the Roosevelt years seemed to have evaporated. Roosevelt, they insisted, would never have let international affairs grow so chilly; they laid the blame on the inexperienced Harry S. Truman. Meanwhile, Communist East and Capitalist West settled into a stalemate frozen by mutual mistrust.

In Berlin, the Soviet Union faced off against an equally adamant United States, Great Britain, and France over the reunification of Germany. Ever wary of western intentions, the Soviet Union established its own *cordon sanitaire*, a barrier of puppet governments that ran from the Baltic states, through East Germany and Poland, southerly to include Czechoslovakia, Romania, Bulgaria, and Hungary, finally to link with the independent Communist state of Marshal Tito's Yugoslavia on the Mediterranean. "An iron curtain is drawn down upon their front," British Prime Minister Winston Churchill cautioned President Truman in a secret cable.

Policies East and West hardened. The Second World War won, on February 9, 1946, Joseph Stalin publicly reaffirmed the fundamental Marxist position that communism and capitalism were incompatible, and war between the two was inevitable. The Soviet would rearm for that future conflict.

Leftist optimism in the United States and the bright promise of international cooperation gave way to gray disillusionment for the radical Left. Union organizing, dampened by high wartime wages and full employment, had lost its fervor. Returning veterans, many of them onetime blue-collar workers who might have aided the cause, instead used the GI Bill to buy homes in new suburban tracts or attend college in pursuit of dreams beyond fancy.

Still many of the prewar problems remained—southern racism and northern bigotry especially rankled the old Left—but those issues seemed lost in the great rush to convert from war to peacetime production, from rationing to prosperity, from winning the war to defeating the Communists.

A sense of impending threat crept up on the Left as 1946 wore on. The off-year elections in November produced a resounding victory for a reenergized Republican Party. With the opening of a new and receptive Congress, the National Association of Manufacturers began lobbying for a harsh antiunion measure under the guise of curbing communist influence in the labor movement.

The gains of the New Deal years seemed to be in peril. Guthrie himself complained that "the war is so far from won that you can nearly say that we've lost outright to the fascists."

For all the pessimism, on May Day 1946, Guthrie and his friend Stetson Kennedy marched among the writers' contingent in the May Day parade down Eighth Avenue and over to Union Square. There Guthrie clambered onto a stone sill of a bank building, in order to better see the speakers' platform. A burly policeman waving a billy club bellowed, "Get offa that bank!"

With all the dignity he could muster, Guthrie dropped to the sidewalk and looked up at the policeman. "Very well, officer, but a little courtesy if you please. Don't forget, I help pay your salary."

It was a faint protest in the face of growing disillusionment on the Left. The members of People's Songs felt an increasing alienation in New York City as 1946 wore on. Lee Hays abruptly decamped to Philadelphia to live with his longtime friend Walter Lowenfels. Bess Lomax and Butch Hawes, now married, also talked of leaving. Housing was tight in the city; twice they and their newborn daughter were legally evicted from apartments in favor of returning veterans. "There was nothing more to be done in New York," she explained.

"Woody, Leadbelly, Cisco, they all felt it," Moe Asch said. "They thought everything was going to be better, and it was worse.

"It was a terrible letdown," he continued. "Woody and Cisco had nothing to do. They borrowed money; they were not interested in anything."

Guthrie grumbled more. He wanted to see more "slum pictures" but "the movies are sewed up too tight by our bankers these days to fight or to ridicule our landlords." Aside from classical music, which Marjorie tuned in "when our radio is not on the buzz and the blink," Guthrie listened "just out of habit once in a while." He read little beyond what he bought at the Communist Party bookstore, complaining that friend John Steinbeck's latest novels had lost their social relevance.

Almost as a refuge, Guthrie in mid-1946 spent days typing hundreds of pages of his wartime essays and songs, papers that had been damaged by sea spray and salt water. Some would later appear with songs Guthrie wrote in the years before and after the war in a slender collection underwritten by Asch's Disc Records. The songs and ballads were uneven, but the fifty-four-page book contained a five-page celebration of Leadbelly, Jim Garland, and sisters Sarah Ogan and Molly Jackson that evoked warm memories of the prewar years of promise.

So much had changed since then. Guthrie's own songwriting suffered in quantity and quality in these first postwar years. Seemingly, the longer the Cold War wore on, the more his lyrics hardened into polemic. Only rarely did he equal his earlier poetry.

A radio news report inspired Guthrie to keen a lament for the twenty-eight nameless migratory workers being deported to Mexico who died in an airplane crash in Los Gatos, California. Like his earlier "Reuben James," the song sought to identify the nameless, the anonymous workers, *his* people.*

The sky plane caught fire over Los Gatos Canyon,
A fireball of lightning [that] shook all our hills.

---

* About this time Guthrie typed an aphorism in his manuscript: "I cannot help/But learn my most/From you who count yourself least/And cannot help/But feel my best when/You that need me most/Ask me to help/You/And I never did know exactly why this was/That is just/The way/We are built." Woody Guthrie Archives, Manuscript Series 2, Box 1, File 30.

Who are all these friends all scattered like dry leaves?
The radio says they are just deportees.

Is this the best way we can grow our big orchards?
Is this the best way we can grow our good fruit?
To fall like dry leaves to rot on my top soil
And be called by no name except deportees?

Refrain:
Goodbye to my Juan, Goodbye Rosalita;
Adios muy amigo, Jesus and Maria.
You won't have a name when you ride the big airplane
All they will call you will be deportees.

Floundering through much of 1946 and 1947, in search of something familiar, something safe, Guthrie sought to return to the past. On a visit with Marjorie to the Seegers, Guthrie suggested restarting the Almanacs and opening a new Almanac House. Seeger was frankly skeptical. "You've got a family and I've got a family," he reminded his friend.

The Almanacs, Seeger argued, "were something unique for that period of history." Five years and more had passed; their lives had inexorably changed. It just wouldn't work now.

The stress took a toll on Guthrie, and his dalliances on his marriage. During a two-week separation from Marjorie, Guthrie wrote Maxine Crissman, in August 1946, to suggest the two of them return to KFVD. He was fed up with New York, he wrote. Crissman, living now in the San Fernando Valley, was momentarily intrigued, at least interested enough to visit J. Frank Burke Jr., the station manager.

Burke Junior was cool to the idea. Maxine was welcome to return to KFVD, he offered, but without the Lone Wolf. Guthrie was too radical, too controversial, and too easily associated with Communists, Burke insisted. Crissman wrote Guthrie to explain, and provoked a blistering reply, "mostly preaching about the finest people he ever met were Communists."*

Guthrie found refuge in a new project suggested by Popular Front film critic and sometime director Irving Lerner. When Lerner suggested adapt-

---

* Guthrie in these years was quick to defend Marxism. At Guthrie's mention of the *Daily Worker*, someone within earshot sneered, "I have a stack I keep in the outhouse." Guthrie snapped, "Some people can't absorb knowledge any other way." Lee Hays interview by E. Victor and Judy Wolfenstein, March 11, 1972.

ing *Bound for Glory* as a motion picture, Guthrie saw it as an intriguing possibility. Guthrie, fancying his book in the movie palaces he so loved, agreed in July 1946 to give Lerner an option on *Bound for Glory*.

Then or shortly after, an eager Guthrie pitched the story of the abortive search for Jerry P. Guthrie's lost gold mine. Guthrie wanted to revive it and, at Lerner's suggestion, set out to turn a single chapter into another "autobiographical novel."

Within days, on no more than a handshake, Guthrie was a writer once more. He hoped to keep the story short, he wrote Lerner, "but when I set down to a typing machine it seems like everything in the world gets bigger and wider and longer."

He was escaping a gray world of disappointment into a romantic past that had never existed.

CHAPTER TWENTY-THREE

Worried Man Blues

"*D*ON'T CRY, WOODBLOCK*,*" Clara had instructed him. Don't cry.

Woodrow Wilson Guthrie, age six, promised. He would not cry. Never again.

"Don't cry," Clara had said.

Guthrie would not, even now.

"No matter what happens," Marjorie, four months pregnant, insisted, "we've got to hold onto ourselves and to do things the way that Cathy would like to see us do."

Guthrie would not cry. Even as Cathy of the thousand songs and dances, the adored child, lay swathed in gauze in Coney Island Hospital. Even as she shrieked when nurses peeled off bandages caked with blood and charred skin.

She lingered for almost a day, burned over most of her body, long after the doctors at Coney Island Hospital had told her father that Cathy would not live.

Marjorie had been gone only a few minutes, five at the most, just across the street to the neighborhood market for a few oranges and some milk. It was hardly any time at all. Woody had left that morning for Elizabeth, New Jersey, where he was to sing at an afternoon rally for the victorious Phelps Dodge Electric strikers, and Cathy needed the milk for her supper.

A short circuit in the electrical cord of the newly rebuilt Stromberg radio, firemen said, had started a fire in the mattress of the folding bed. Perhaps Cathy, just three days past her fourth birthday, had tried to put the fire out. Arthur Young, the sixteen-year-old kid who lived upstairs, saw the smoke seeping under the front door and heard the child scream.

The neighbor children doused the flames and saved the contents of the small apartment on Mermaid Avenue. Only the sodden mattress, later tossed by the firemen into the yard, marked the fire.

It was Arthur who wrapped Cathy in the gray wool blanket and handed the whimpering child to her mother. The pharmacist across the street administered first aid until the ambulance arrived.

Cathy was brave, even gay as she rode to the hospital, Marjorie calmly reported. The child could only say, "Mommy, I burnt up my new pink dress."

From three in the afternoon until ten that night when she slipped into a coma, Cathy laughed and babbled about her nursery school friends and teachers. She sang songs. She spoke the few words of Yiddish her *bubbe* had taught her. She drawled children's jokes in her father's Oklahoma accent.

When he returned home at 11:30 that night, Guthrie found the note stuck to the front door of the apartment: "Come to the Coney Island Hospital at Once." Mrs. Shapiro in the front apartment told him what had happened.

Through the coldest night of the year and into the gray, windy day, friends and relatives turned up at the hospital to spell the parents. Marjorie's sister-in-law, steady Clara, the one who had been an ambulance driver during the London blitz, held Cathy's leg when the doctor sought a vein that had not been burned. The ex-sailor Woody called "Carrot Top," a boyfriend of Cathy's first baby-sitter and a self-appointed guardian of the four-year-old, stood by the child's bed through the night. Socialist grandmother Eliza Greenblatt came to *daven* in her own way in the hallway.

Delirious, Cathy died about 11:30 the morning of February 10, 1947, "calling off in funny ways all of the names of folks and friends, kids, teachers, etc. that she had seen in her four big years."

There would be no funeral. Marjorie and Woody had the body cremated with the intention of scattering Cathy's ashes along the Coney Island beach she loved. A day or two after Cathy's death, Cisco Houston and Jim Longhi silently walked along that dark beach with Guthrie, the seamen three bonded in grief. Guthrie suddenly threw himself on the sand, his arms and legs in the air, raging into the dark sky. "He screamed for thirty seconds," Longhi recalled. "And then he got up. And it was over."

Marjorie sought to keep her composure for the sake of their unborn child, younger daughter Nora later said. "I think that, if she wasn't pregnant, she would have fallen apart. . . . Every time she talked about Cathy for the rest of her life she cried."

They gave the child's clothes and toys to needy families, then carefully put away her drawings and scribbles. Woody would often take them from the closet to look at. He could not let go of the sprightly daughter he so cherished. For weeks afterward, he signed his letters, "Us Guthries: Cathy, Marjorie, Pete [the unborn child], Woody."

However well he and Marjorie stoically soldiered on—the two of them at her insistence performing a program at a nursery school just days after Cathy's death—Guthrie suffered the loss of this golden child.

There has been made in me an open place and an empty spot now, a spot lots emptier than I ever felt it before, a spot so sinking and so empty that I reach around a thousand times a day and grab onto things, old letters, signs, faces, people, pictures, and things, and I try to use all of these things in some way to fill up this hungry and thirsty empty place.

Guthrie added a pledge and a prophecy: "Cathy's works in her four short years will echo from iron to brick for some long seasons to come, and maybe always keep on living and growing."*

"We told all of them"—those who wrote condolences, Cathy's teachers at the nursery school, those who visited the small apartment on Mermaid Avenue—"that we had no intention of letting such a wild accident get us down nor to keep us down in spirit, that we aimed to go right on and to have our next several babies in the same progressive and social-minded ways which we raised Cathy on."

Cathy's death was "a wrenching experience" for the entire family, said Marjorie's first husband, Joe Mazia. Both Earl Robinson and Sophie Maslow thought Marjorie and her husband never entirely surmounted a sense of guilt. Jackie Alper, in the midst of an on-again, off-again affair with Guthrie, insisted that her sometime lover "was destroyed . . . absolutely wiped out" by his daughter's death.

Just weeks after Cathy's death, Guthrie fled Coney Island, bound for Spokane, Washington, and the convention of the National Association of Rural Electric Cooperatives. Bonneville Power Authority information specialist Ralph Bennett, introduced to folk music as a Harvard undergraduate

---

* In an interview in November 1998, Pete Seeger stated that after "This Land Is Your Land," the children's songs will most likely survive. "Woody was temporarily at least a real family man, and this wonderful little girl Cathy, who died so tragically and so young, inspired him to write just one song after another. Living out there on Coney Island and watching her grow, he just turned out one great song after another, truly great songs."

prior to the war and "the number one Guthrie fan in town," couched the invitation in a promise:

> Good chance your [Columbia River] songs might come into their own out here where they were meant to be sung. Might arrange other appearances.

Guthrie promptly accepted, then cashed in the plane ticket Bennett sent and exchanged it for a train ticket. He would travel to Spokane following his own path, to seek solace in familiar towns along the way, among old friends and family.

In Pampa, Guthrie dropped off the Southern Pacific train, his new Spanish guitar, a gift from Marjorie, slung over his shoulder. The town was little changed—the same joints, the same Coney Island Hot Dog shop on Broadway, his friend Lillian Snow still working in the library in the basement of City Hall. Guthrie told his old friend John Gikas that he had no plans; he was heading for the coast. Gikas, like Guthrie a veteran of the merchant marine during the war, offered to put Guthrie up.

In the next two weeks, Guthrie "spent a lot of time" at the home of Kate Heiskel on West Foster, Gikas recalled. While Mrs. Heiskel was a fan of Guthrie's, one of the few in town with his RCA records, Guthrie was more interested in daughter Deaun.

"Deaun was a runaround girl." She was single and she had a car. She had also been a runner-up for Miss Texas a while back, Gikas said. And if Deaun was busy, there were the "raunchy" waitresses at the Empire Cafe just below Gikas's apartment. "Guthrie would chase anything."

For two weeks, Guthrie was like a sailor ashore, Gikas said. And suddenly Guthrie was gone, traveling by bus northwesterly toward Spokane.

The Spokane date did not go well. Ralph Bennett termed it "something of a disaster." None of the conventioneers seemed to care one whit.

When Bennett arrived at Spokane's fanciest hotel, Guthrie was nowhere to be found. He had stayed only long enough to discard his traveling shirt for a new one, leave the toilet unflushed, then hit a bar on Spokane's grimy Main Street. He returned in time for his first appearance at a luncheon.

"Things went from bad to worse," Bennett recalled. He had the feeling that Guthrie had been drinking. "He was pretty disgraceful." At the opening luncheon, the delegates ignored him, the clatter of forks and knives drowning out Guthrie's songs. An angry Guthrie "took the old runout powder."

At Bennett's behest, Guthrie tried twice more to sing for the unheeding delegates in different settings, and twice failed. "He was not a performer really. He was a poet. He'd forget his music, and make mistakes," said Bennett.

After the conference ended, Guthrie joined Bennett at the Bonneville Power Authority headquarters in Portland. There Bennett tried to re-record the Columbia River songs Guthrie had written six years earlier. "We didn't get anywhere because he couldn't remember the songs very well. He couldn't remember the words, and he couldn't remember the music either. The result was about a complete zero."

Guthrie hung around Portland for a week, visiting acquaintances of years before and giving a concert at Reed College. "The kids loved him, but I was greatly troubled," said Michael Loring, an ex-New York leftist who arranged the Reed concert. "He was having a great deal of difficulty remembering the words and carrying it off." Later, Guthrie seemed agitated. Unable to sleep, he paced the floor of his room all night, strumming his guitar.

Guthrie told Bennett that he was considering moving to the Pacific Northwest, some of the prettiest country he had ever seen. Bennett thought the lure might have been the radical temper of Seattle. Portland, by comparison, was a "good fifty years behind," Guthrie insisted.

On May 1 Guthrie marched in San Francisco's May Day parade, and spent the next day in Oakland singing for striking telephone operators.

From the Bay Area, Guthrie drifted south to Los Angeles, his visit forecast by a worried Marjorie.

She had reason to be concerned. Driven by his brother George, Guthrie unexpectedly turned up at the San Fernando Valley home of his former singing partner, Maxine Crissman. Woody seemed changed, smaller, insecure, his eyes dull, she recalled. Even his voice was rather high-pitched, with a hint of a New York accent. "He wasn't Woody. He looked very, very bad. I didn't know him at all."

When Crissman's three-year-old daughter, Patricia, ran into the room, Guthrie impulsively reached out for her. The frightened child scampered out of reach.

"I had one like her," Guthrie said sadly.

Guthrie proposed that he and Maxine record some of their songs in Los Angeles "before it's too late." So long out of a studio, no longer a singer but a housewife and mother, Crissman was hesitant.

The conversation lagged. "Guess you're doin' all right," Guthrie concluded.

She nodded. Yes, she was.

"You've got to sing," he advised. The silence hung between them.

The Guthrie brothers stayed little more than an hour. As he was getting into George's automobile, Woody turned to her a final time. "Well, Lefty Lou, keep singing. Don't ever stop singing. That's all that matters."

When George drove off, Woody turned in the seat to look back at Lefty Lou waving goodbye. Woody did not wave back.

She would not see him again.

Guthrie stayed for two weeks at the Silver Lake home of Clara and Ed Robbin. The once lighthearted Guthrie was morose, Clara remembered.

The death of his daughter preyed upon Guthrie. "He talked about Cathy all the time," Clara said. "He was talking about the child, and how beautiful she was. He had that terrific feeling for that child."

Guthrie seemed more than distraught, she stated. He talked about himself and his sometimes strained marriage with Marjorie. He talked about possible illnesses descending upon him, in the same way that madness had seized his mother after the death of Clara Guthrie.

And then he would talk no more about it. He spent evenings sipping cheap wine and, Tokay stoked, became indifferent to the audiences at the fund-raisers Ed arranged. His singing and guitar playing lapsed.

As suddenly as he had turned up, Guthrie disappeared. Ed and Clara grieved for their friend, so plainly a man adrift. In the end she decided, "He wasn't coming anywhere; he was just running somewheres."

This time he was drawn back to Marjorie, seven months pregnant with the child Guthrie had nicknamed "Pete." Only Marjorie, he confessed, "makes Woody Guthrie feel like a lost man getting found."

From her he drew sustenance, from her a renewed confidence. Marjorie, "a beautiful, talented lady," wrote Guthrie's sister-in-law Ann, "saw in Woody the gifted talent that we, his next of kin, failed to recognize."

Guthrie, so quick in years past to assert his independence, now clung to his wife. "Life is pretty tough," he had once quipped. "You're lucky if you live through it."

With Marjorie's guidance, he might.

The picture that you paint with your common and everyday words is much better to me than anything I'll ever write down, because I say that your spoken word is lots and lots better than my written word. . . . This is the main reason why you mustn't think you can come to a book of mine and learn as much from me as I learn from you.... [I]t is you who inspires me more than I will ever inspire you. I come to your pillow and door for my inspiration. You'll not find in my book what I see in your face and hear in your voice. That is the whole truth, the honest truth and nothing but the truth, so help us, God.

Without Cathy, Guthrie and Marjorie could not fill the three-room apartment on Mermaid Avenue. Late in June, they invited Guthrie's eleven-year-old daughter, Gwendolyn, to visit.

"You'll find out that Marjorie is just a kid in ways and actions. You'll find out that I'm just a kid, too. You might be the most grown uppest one in this whole bunch. We'll run this house here like you say it ought to be run."

Marjorie added her own plea: "I'm sure your sweet Daddy would feel very, very sad if he didn't help you grow up at least a little bit here and there.... About clothes and stuff: This is Coney Island and all; we wear our bathing suits most all of the day."

Gwen's arrival and the birth of a baby boy on July 10, 1947, at Brooklyn Jewish Hospital eased some of the pain in "this rough year." There were children's things and children's noise about the house once more. Guthrie entertained his daughter by day and wrote by night. Marjorie meanwhile lost herself in six-day-a-week teaching and caring for the newborn Arlo. "The kids make me feel like Cathy used to make me feel," she wrote Mary Jo.

Arlo—named after the hero of a book Marjorie had read as a child—was a pleasure. Even before the infant was four months old, Guthrie was writing songs for "Arlikins." Arlo could not replace Cathy, but he helped to fill the loss; the Guthries promptly resolved to have another child.

Slowly, their optimism rekindled. In July, Moe Asch printed a collection of twenty-eight Guthrie songs. The songbook contained a none-too-factual autobiography and an essay celebrating his singing friends from prewar New York City: Leadbelly, Molly Jackson, Jim Garland, and Sarah Ogan.

Guthrie was proud of the fifty-three-page book, though the most radical song in the collection heralded Joe Hill, the Industrial Workers of the World organizer executed in 1914. (Asch, in the current political climate, was less fearful of old leftist causes than of new.)

While he and his father disagreed politically, Woody sent a copy to Charley in Oklahoma City with an inscription crediting him for putting

this little spark of fight and fire somewhere in me same as I hope to pass a little speck of this same fire onto whichever offsprings come to roost with me and to dance here with Marjorie. . . . You are just about my favorite man in the human species.

Guthrie stopped work on the autobiographical "Ship Story" in favor of his newly renamed novel about the search for the lost gold mine, "Study Butte." He found it too hard going; for the first time his typewriter sat silent for long periods.

Unable to write, yet driven to speak out, Guthrie was both burdened and irritated by critics' comparisons of his writing to that of Pushkin, Whitman, Rogers, or Sandburg:

> . . . *If I did think that Whitman did talk my lingo and thoughts*
> *If I did think that Will spoke my dialect and feelings*
> *If I even felt that Mr. Pushkin had said my plainest feelings*
> *Or if Carl Sandburg had told my folkiest tale*
> *Or if any truck driver or trip hammer man or diesel driver woman*
> *Anywhere on this planet had said what I say*
> *Well, then, I wouldn't even knock my fingernails off ten hours a day*
> *Trying to cut out some old and newer thoughts and feelings to get said . . .*

As if to emphasize his written comments, his observations of the city, his rambling essays about love, politics, and sex, Guthrie took to slashing purple watercolor brush strokes down his typewritten pages. Sometimes he swirled broad, faceless cartoon figures on the pages; sometimes he merely seemed to add graffiti announcing, Woody Guthrie was here, alive, still alive.

Guthrie was scattered and easily distracted. He could not concentrate on the manuscript for "Study Butte." In 1947 he wrote a draft of "another lifebound novel real and unreal . . . ," "House of Earth," inspired by his long-held fancy to build a home from adobe brick. Then he abandoned it after writing 160 pages that Alan Lomax deemed "the best material I'd ever seen written about that section of the country," the windy caprock country of the Texas Panhandle. Guthrie instead began other autobiographically inspired short stories or chapters, then left them unfinished as well.

By mid-June he was grumbling, "There is something too slow and too plowy and ploddy for me to spend my time at fooling around with long novels when I'd rather to hear a room full of my comrades and friends sing out real loud on one of my songs which I've wrote."

Guthrie picked up "Study Butte" where he had left off. He had 375 pages of manuscript completed, he wrote movie director Irving Lerner in Los Angeles, "and it is getting better every page, I think. I'm just not sure how good the whole thing is."

Where once he would have fled, some sense of obligation or mission now drove him to continue. Lerner's interest in the gold mine story as a possible film—as well as vague queries from publishers—suggested that "Study Butte" might be the best way for Guthrie to bring in money. His singing dates dwindled, while from the West Coast Lerner wrote to say the studios had lost interest in filming *Bound for Glory*. Guthrie seemingly took the disappointment in stride. "My heart beats a different rhythm lots of times than you hear the heart of Hollywood beat," he wrote Lerner in reply.

In the first week of November Guthrie finished "Study Butte," toying with the notion of retitling it "Foolish Gold." He was acutely aware that the manuscript needed to be edited, and he fretted that Will Geer—whom Guthrie recommended for the part of Woody's father—thought it slow moving. (Guthrie would blow hot and cold about his Hollywood acquaintance Eddie Albert playing Woody's alter ego in the proposed film.)*

If most of Guthrie's novels, however autobiographical they might have been, were more fiction than not, Guthrie occasionally allowed himself a painful truth. He had assiduously protected the memory of his mother since her death; he had dismissed her part in the death of Clara, in the scarification of Charley Guthrie's torso, in the suspicious home fires. In the manuscript for "Study Butte," he finally acknowledged his mother was "having regular fits and spasms and a-cussin' out at Papa all day long so loud that everybody along our whole block'd get out onto their porches jist to stand there 'n' listen to 'er." As the bewildered Charley put it, "I don't know why, and I never will know why—she just turned mean and hateful towards every good thing I tried to do for her."

Pete Seeger said Guthrie became dissatisfied with himself as he worked to complete the manuscript. "He said quite plainly, 'I'd rather have one song which is sung by a whole lot of people than a book which is printed and sits on the shelf most of the time.'"

Though the Seegers and Guthries visited less often than before, Pete thought that his friend of old drank more after Cathy's death. In fact, Guthrie drank "too much," in his opinion. Marjorie was also worried; her husband just seemed to be deteriorating, she confessed to Seeger.

---

* Guthrie was ambivalent about the motion picture industry. According to Bernard Asbell, he resented Burl Ives leaving New York, "our world," and sneered at him "in Hollywood and all that powdered pussy he likes." Asbell interview, July 25, 1998.

On his occasional visits, Jim Longhi too sensed a difference in his old shipmate. Longhi could not identify it precisely—"a little bit in the way Woody walked, he shook his head, the way he drank from the bottle [of Myers's black rum] and the swipe of his hand on his mouth." Guthrie's drinking did not surprise Longhi; because of a shipboard confidence, Longhi knew of Guthrie's fear of the madness that had swept away Nora in 1925. "The rum made him feel good."

Guthrie escaped the drudgery of the typewriter to spend hours fashioning bizarre assemblages he later dubbed "hoodis."* To satisfy a "cravery to make something out of nothing," Guthrie glued together found objects—a lemon juicer purchased at the five and dime, a broken prune-juice bottle and a discarded mop from the trash, Marjorie's "bright twinklers" from her button collection, a cracked seashell or a broken yo-yo.

Compulsively he began to glue together his "jinkers," his "thingamabobblers," his "gluejiggers," his "Woodygrams." Marjorie fell to interpreting the *objets trouvés*, spending as long as an hour describing to friends the shape, the feeling, the sheer artistic exuberance of these hoodis.

The art work, Guthrie hinted, had an underlying political, even autobiographical message. A hoodis "goes to show you that you can take all of your ugliest things, your brokest and your worn outtest things, and stick them together the ways mama nature does her leaves and her stems and her weeds and her grassblades, and make out of your trashiest things your very nicest and prettiest of flowers."

Unexpectedly, 1947 provided Guthrie with an odd form of public recognition—in a Broadway show, no less, just the sort of vehicle he most despised for its insincerity. But *Finian's Rainbow* was a different musical, a satirical fable about southern racism and politics, and boom-and-bust economics. Co-written by E. Y. Harburg, a Popular Front friend of Earl Robinson, *Finian's Rainbow* featured "Woody Mahoney." He first appears, as the script put it, "in the navy-blue garb of a merchant seaman, is back from fighting fascism and fleas in the South Pacific and is no pushover for people who like to push other people around."

Guthrie, who resisted seeing the musical for six months before spending $1.40 to stand at the rear of the balcony, claimed proudly, "I'm the real brother which they copied your union seaman after, the Woody everybody sings and dances about." Even before his army discharge in December 1945, Guthrie asserted, he had told Earl Robinson "about how I wanted to

---

* The name came from toddler Arlo's question "Who dis?" sister Nora Guthrie explained.

see some kind of a play done about a guy that gets the pregnant idea into his head of bumming around . . . to sing . . . for workers in inspiring trade union halls." Robinson had passed the idea on to Harburg, with whom he was working at the time; the idea germinated for a year before the character "Woody" became the romantic lead in the new musical by Harburg and Fred Saidy.

The problem with the story, Guthrie snorted, is that the Woody of the musical abandons his wanderings in favor of settling down with the female lead. In an essay addressed to Pearl Lang, a former member of the Martha Graham company who had taken a leading role in *Finian's Rainbow*, Guthrie wrote:

> Me nor my gitbox wouldn't look a second time at no shemale that
> said she didn't like for us to sing, play, and to dance in our union
> hall. . . . The union is my religion, the strike is my way of praying,
> and my picket line is my walking true believers feeling the true spirit
> of the holy ghost of world union in their breasts. . . . I'm Woody the
> union man. Woody, the union worker, and my guitar is my factory
> machine, my machine that kills fascists.

This was empty boasting, as Lang must have known. She was a close friend of Marjorie, close enough to have spent the night before Arlo was born with Marjorie and a homebound Woody in Coney Island. Guthrie also dedicated Hoodis No. 6 to Lang.

As 1947 wound down, some of Guthrie's optimism and resulting energy returned. In November, he flew to Chicago for the first national convention of the People's Songs organization. He traveled a month later to Winston-Salem, North Carolina, to sing at a rally for the black strikers of the Tobacco Workers Union. Then Sophie Maslow booked Guthrie once again for a tour in February and March 1948, with her evening of dance, *Folksay*.

Though the Guthries were in debt, having borrowed money from Marjorie's parents, Woody was once again doing the sort of work he most cared about.

He and Marjorie planned a joint tour of folk songs and dance. Unaware that Moe Asch's Disc Records was near bankruptcy, Guthrie continued to propose thematic albums he might record; he was especially keen to sing some of his new children's songs for Asch's microphone. With the apparent expectation that an acquaintance might introduce him to television,

Guthrie also wrote a script featuring Marjorie's dances to a half dozen of his "Songs to Grow On."

Christmas 1947 "wasn't exactly easy for me or for Woody," Marjorie wrote to Guthrie's sister, Mary Jo. Their pain lingered. "Arlo isn't quite big enough to count and so we didn't really do much except talk about our last one which was really so wonderful."

The next year, she hoped, would be better.

CHAPTER TWENTY-FOUR

The Noise of Roaches

*T*HESE WERE THE dark years, the time of the toad, in blacklisted screenwriter Dalton Trumbo's phrase. This was the hour of the informer, the blacklist, and the loyalty oath, the time of headline—hunting congressional committees and the long night of civil liberties.

Communists, shrilled the attorney general of the United States, "are everywhere—in factories, offices, butcher stores, on street corners, and private business. And each carries in himself the death of our society."

A fervid hunt for "subversives" spread across the nation, with publicity-seeking members of Congress and the director of the FBI, J. Edgar Hoover, leading the hounds. Mere sympathy with a political position once endorsed by the Communist Party was enough to put a job in jeopardy. Outspoken advocacy often provoked government surveillance of trade unionists, schoolteachers, political dissenters, or anyone the investigators deemed "suspect."

A pall of anxiety fell upon the nation, even as membership in the Communist Party plummeted. Wartime patriotism became fearful conformity and timid silence. And all the while, as Scots folklorist Hamish Henderson put it, "The Communist Party [was] being pursued through the petrified forest of Stalinism by nightmarish trolls."

The trolls sniffed after Woody Guthrie, the avowed antifascist and pro-union agitator. As early as June 9, 1941, the FBI opened a closely held "internal security" file on Guthrie, because "a confidential informant" had advised that Guthrie was a Communist. That first report also noted that General Motors Acceptance Corporation was looking for Guthrie because of his failure to make car payments; that Guthrie had been cited for driving with expired license plates while crossing from California to Oregon; and, perhaps hardest to believe, "subject said to be traveling about the country making a motion picture for the Department of Interior."

Guthrie's file was spotty; from 1941 through the war his record was marked only by two clips from the *Daily Worker* and a *William B. Travis* shipmate's charge that Guthrie, Cisco Houston, and Jim Longhi "followed the Communist Party line in that they were very pro-Russian, and advocated racial intermarriage."

The entries in the FBI file for the postwar years largely noted the occasional articles Guthrie wrote for the *Daily Worker*. Additionally, a secret informant reported that Guthrie on April 11, 1947, sang at a benefit for the Spanish Refugee Appeal; an FBI agent duly noted that the attorney general had labeled that organization a Communist front.

Not until June 1948, with the publication of the fourth biennial report of the California state senate's Fact-finding Committee on Un-American Activities was Guthrie publicly labeled a Communist. The report named Guthrie as a contributor to "Joe Stalin's California mouthpiece," and listed him among "the following Communists" who write "for the *People's Daily World*."

The document also listed Guthrie as a member of the board of directors of People's Songs. "Needless to say," the report continued, "all of the productions of People's Songs, Inc., follow the Communist Party line as assiduously as do the people behind the organization."*

In fact, the FBI's file was no more than a garbled assortment of guilt by association charges and misinterpreted facts—one informant identified Guthrie as a member of the "Factionalist Sabotage Group," waiting for Moscow's signal to wage war by sabotage. Guthrie was certainly a communist in spirit, but never a member of the party or a terrorist group.

Marjorie Guthrie, herself quite politically astute, insisted, "I don't know what happened prior to my time, but from my time, in Coney Island, he was not welcomed by the party because he did not want to follow a party line. . . . You couldn't tell Woody what to think. And so we were not members of the party in Coney Island."

Husband and wife were both registered as American Labor Party (ALP) voters in 1948 and 1949, five years after the ALP was cited as a Commu-

---

* Among those on the board of directors or board of sponsors were composers Leonard Bernstein, Marc Blitzstein, Aaron Copland, and Alec Wilder; balletomane Lincoln Kirstein; lyricists Oscar Hammerstein II and E. Y. Harburg; director John Houseman; entertainers Judy Holliday, Lena Horne, Paul Robeson, and Sam Wanamaker; as well as writers Alain Locke and Dorothy Parker.

nist front by the special Committee on Un-American Activities in March 1944. The FBI also considered their membership—for its inexpensive medical care program—in the International Workers Order to be suspicious.

Guthrie was, in the coinage of the times, a fellow traveler. He often quipped, coyly, evasively, "Some people say I'm a Communist. That ain't necessarily so, but it is true that I've always been in the red."

Among members of the Movement, the commitment to orthodox Marxism varied. "Some were intellectual about it, and some were emotional. It was what was happening in those days," said Bess Lomax. Whatever their inspiration, they were idealistic and patriotic; in the words of music critic Harold Clurman, "They were all on the side of the good."

A pure heart, however, was not enough to spare one from the pursuing hounds. Though he was not specifically blacklisted, the anti-Communist crusade sideswiped Guthrie.

The Hollywood studios once interested in Guthrie had cooled, their ardor dampened by the hearings on Hollywood held by the House of Representatives Committee on Un-American Activities during the last two weeks of October 1947. The studios abruptly turned away from films of social relevance and possible controversy in favor of simple-minded entertainment. Director Irving Lerner shelved *Bound for Glory*, with its raw depiction of depression America, in favor of Guthrie's "Study Butte."

But the "hot deal" Lerner seemed to have for "Study Butte," retitled "Foolish Gold," evaporated over the next months.* While the publishing house of Duell, Sloan and Pearce had expressed interest in the 748-page manuscript, a movie sale would be difficult. Guthrie insisted on being hired as a consultant and codirector, with approval of locations, actors, musicians, and script. "I demand these rights because I wish the motion picture to contain the best balance possible of realism, truth, history, and fiction," he wrote Lerner.

Even more problematic, Guthrie wanted the film "snortier, hornier, and more fornicational than the book itself is. I have not been able to breathe as much pure scenes of nakedness in here as I feel the novel really and truly needs."

* The change of title suggests Guthrie himself had lost faith in the existence of the chimerical mine, despite his Uncle Jeff's assurance it was still to be found. In 1944, Jeff wrote Woody, the brothers Gid, Claude, and Jeff returned to the Chisos Mountains to search for the mine. "We found the old doby house my mother, father and all of us kids lived in. . . . We found an old Dutch oven hanging in a tree that my father left it there about 42 years before." Gid and Claude spotted the mine's location but could not reach it without horses. Jeff Guthrie to Woody Guthrie, November 3, 1948.

Just as dreams of a Hollywood film disappeared, RCA Victor, claiming slow sales, discontinued *Dust Bowl Ballads* on July 2, 1948. Asch took it as an excuse in October to reissue Guthrie's *Ballads from the Dust Bowl* on his new Folkways label, but Asch could not match Victor's distribution system or its sales promotion force.

Meanwhile, the union bookings Guthrie had long relied upon for his income dwindled. Fearful of the new antilabor Taft-Hartley Act, which required union officials to sign anti-Communist oaths, even the avowedly radical unions grew more conservative, less confrontational in dealings with management, fearful of being tagged as "communist sympathizers."

Guthrie raged against the repressive congressmen, the blustering senators, and especially J. Edgar Hoover's FBI.

The roaches
crawl
acrost my page
tonight
and make
a noise
that makes
more sense
than all
that Hoover
writes.

He intended to stand against the Hoovers large and small. "The job to be done is to get this thing called socialism nailed and hammered up just as quick as we can. I believe this just as much as I believe my own name, and lots more." (Though "socialism" here meant Marxist communism, Guthrie *was* independent enough to praise the former chairman of the Socialist Party, Eugene Debs, as "a pure cross between Jesus Christ and Abe Lincoln." Party dogmaticians would have condemned this as deviationism.)

Not to hold high the Red Flag when his politics were under fire would be to succumb to fear.

On June 7, 1948, Guthrie wrote, "Fascism is being afraid. Fascism is fear bossing you. Fascism is worse than all of these things, and fascism is more closer to you than I can make you see. I'm trying to wake you up to tell you that you're sleeping with something ten times more dangerous than a poison fang snake in your bed. . . .

"If fascism does come and if it does kill me, well, when you add me alone onto the hundreds of millions which fascism has already dusted under, it don't scare me so very much."

Nine days later, he was sure of his martyrdom.

Yeahp, I know.

You're out to get me.

And I guess I'm out to get you, too.

Who's gonna get who first?

That's what I wanta know.

Well, if you do get me, boss, all I can say is you'll get a good 'un.

You'll get one that you never did get before. . . .

You're going to get me one day. Or one night, I guess. You've done in several mil-
lion like me, already.

I talked against you. I sung out against you.

I never did fight nor talk for the violent overthrow of our U.S. form of govern-
ment, but I sure do believe in the violent overthrow of these crooks and gang-
sters in the places of our government.

Goodbye all. Drink up. Sing a loud one, yell a ripper, shoot a windy, tell a tall
salty for me when I get gone on along.

You'll not find me where the landlord has gone.

Daily the headlines tracked the twisted congressional testimony of Whittaker Chambers and Alger Hiss, while editorials thundered accusations of Communist spies in high government offices. In a burst of wishful thinking Guthrie wrote, "These Un-American Committee boys are causing more folks to love us communists than to hate us."

Guthrie's "martyrdom" at the hands of the fascists was more accidental than deliberate. With fewer calls for his songs, money at 3520 Mermaid Avenue was tight. Pregnant once more, Marjorie taught dance six days a week, including two well-paying days at the Newark Young Men's and Young Women's Hebrew Association, often leaving Guthrie responsible for Arlo before and after the baby-sitter showed up. At times Guthrie felt neglected, even inadequate.

Where once they had communicated so easily, Woody and Marjorie now quarreled, each feeling they shouldered the greater burden. Presumed slights bruised Guthrie's pride. Disagreements sent Guthrie off to sulk.

"When I don't try to make love to my wife," he wrote near the end of winter 1948, she always wants me to try. And when I do try it's always at the wrong time or the wrong hour. And the wrong way. Outside of using the wrong words at the wrong time and never knowing what move to make next, and flunking out from the very start, we do pretty good.

Despite increasing tension in the household, Guthrie managed to finish the revisions on the "true fictitious vicious novel" retitled "Foolish Gold" and impatiently waited Irving Lerner's response. He mailed an audition tape of six children's "Grow Big" songs to Capitol Records, where he hoped Jack Guthrie's great success with "Oklahoma Hills" might open a door or two. Finally, with Marjorie's assistance, in November 1948, he completed brightly colored artwork for the dummy of a children's songbook, "Twenty Songs to Grow Big On," and sent it to Viking Press.*

"My maw," Guthrie wrote to Earl and Helen Robinson in the voice of fourteen-month-old Arlo, "takes the Mailbox Watching Fever, too, but, some way or another, she never does let it get the upper hand on her as much as it does on my pawpaw."

Marjorie added to the packet her own letter in which she hinted of the difficulty of her husband "waiting, waiting to hear what the fruits of his labor will be and waiting to get his energy to begin pounding the keys again, and this little period might be called '*a taste of hell*,' fiery, seeing red like a bull, hot, sticky and all."

Marjorie, in a frank letter to Guthrie's sister Mary Jo, confessed the waiting was "pretty awful if you need the money." Woody had written more that year, and earned less, than in any previous year. "So it's a good thing Woody and I love each other so much. We live on love these days."

"As a provider for the family," Marjorie's brother David summarized with a laugh, "Guthrie wasn't worth a damn."

In debt three thousand dollars to Marjorie's parents, Guthrie took refuge in a last hurrah for what remained of the Movement, the presidential election of 1948. A Democratic Party splintered into party regulars, southern States' Righters, and old New Dealers had grudgingly backed the "accidental" president, Harry S. Truman. The Republicans, savoring victory, had nominated New York Governor Thomas E. Dewey.

---

* Rejected by Viking Press, the manuscript and artwork were returned to Guthrie. Marjorie sent it to Sophie Maslow and eventually forgot about it. When the manuscript was rediscovered, it was published in 1992 by HarperCollins. The lively watercolor and ink illustrations are among Guthrie's best.

Leftists, Guthrie included, viewed Truman with suspicion, as a stout foe of Joseph Stalin's Soviet Union and as antilabor for his opposition to strikes in critical industries. Rather than support Truman, leftists of all stripes and disaffected New Dealers turned to Henry Wallace. Here was Roosevelt's rightful heir, the vice president who would now be president if FDR had not bowed to party bosses and dumped Wallace from the ticket in favor of Truman. Wallace, later sacked by Truman as secretary of commerce, was an avowed New Dealer. He advocated détente with the Soviet Union. His prounion record was impeccable.

Wallace's campaign on the Progressive Party ticket was a forlorn thing, long on enthusiasm but underfunded and doomed from the start. Truman tagged Wallace early and often as "soft on communism." Labor, particularly the CIO, voted to back Truman rather than the tainted Wallace. So too prominent liberals such as Eleanor Roosevelt, the late president's widow; Protestant churchman Reinhold Neibuhr; public intellectuals like Arthur Schlesinger Jr. and John Kenneth Galbraith; and the United Auto Workers' president, Walter Reuther.

Wallace's campaign, said one man active in it, "would not have gotten very far without the Communist Party's role in it." In virtually every major city, an experienced cadre of party members managed the local campaign.

"Henry Wallace was a great catch for the Communist movement," Irwin Silber, then executive director of People's Songs, continued. Wallace argued for an end to the anti-Communist hysteria at home and the anti-Soviet stance abroad. He provided a political visibility the Communist Party could not have achieved on its own. Party theoreticians argued a Wallace campaign would launch a permanent third-party movement "which the Communists would control outright or at least be enormously influential."

To further the cause, there was to be politically conscious music wherever Wallace campaigned. Alan Lomax staffed a "musical desk" responsible for assuring this would be truly a singing campaign—and signed up E. Y. Harburg, Pete Seeger, Lee Hays, Guthrie, and others to write campaign songs.

Guthrie was an early recruit. "President Truman has proved to me that he don't like my trade unions, don't like organized labor, don't like the Communist Party, don't like the human race."

Guthrie and Cisco Houston sang together at rallies for Wallace from June 1948 until election day, but Guthrie was increasingly unhappy. In keeping with the Communist influence on the direction of the campaign, the songs turned out by Lomax's squad were heavy-handed and grated on Guthrie.

He was "wildly opposed to agit-prop," Bess Lomax Hawes recalled. "He felt artistically it was very inferior." According to Guthrie, songs had to be about people to be interesting, to be art. "A song was a different kind of thing than a speech. . . . A song had to have some staying power."

With or without music, Wallace would poll only a million votes nationally, half of them in New York State, where the Communist Party was best organized. His bare 2.4 percent of the 48 million votes cast left the Communist Party howling bootless in the wind. Two months later, People's Songs, strapped for cash and cut off from most unions, closed its doors. With that, Guthrie lost even more bookings.

Guthrie was undaunted. In an election postmortem, he pledged "to get a good deal louder from now on, because I am slowly commencing to think that I've forgotten more about writing progressive songs of social protest than the rest of our entire staff combined."

He would no longer bow to the "third and fourth raters in our midsts," people who cloaked propaganda in popular music garb. Instead, he argued for more hootenannies, with "cowboy-hillbilly-spiritual performers . . . badly exploited and hijacked by reactionary agents, promoters, and handlers, [who] live a miserable half paralyzed life under the thumb of robber producers."

California was the place to begin, he argued. "The people in California who worship and follow the oldtime traditional protest songs of the Wobblies are alive in big numbers. . . . Even in bad and lousy weather, these hoots of a Cowboy, Hillbilly, & Religious nature could outgrow in a few short years anything yet seen on the Eastern Seaboard."

Guthrie judged West Coast people to be more migratory, more pushed and pulled by thugs, vigilantes, and cops, simply tougher. "The hobo spirit is more prevalent on the west coast than in New York. The west coast rank and filer has missed and begged more meals than the average New Yorker."

Guthrie closed his argument typed at "Coney on the Lowland Sea" with a terse aphorism:

All of my words
If not well put
Nor well taken
Are well meant.

But if Guthrie sneered at popular music forms, at sequined cowboys, at jazzy orchestrations, he was not himself above casting about for a new, more entertaining way to reach large audiences with his songs. He sold recording rights to a few of his compositions, including "The Philadelphia Lawyer," to the Maddox Brothers and Rose, "the best hill country string band in these 48 states of ours."

At one point he pondered forming a quartet, something less formal than the group Pete Seeger was forming. As Guthrie envisioned it, his quartet would have a less polished sound, an earthy tone provided by a young black woman, Hope Foye, whose voice he liked. Guthrie pictured "Jolly" Smollens, the onetime secretary at People's Songs, and Cisco Houston as the other members.*

The quartet notion fizzled quickly. Cisco Houston, for the moment, was not interested. He had returned to Los Angeles, was living with a new girlfriend, and still chasing an elusive career in Hollywood.

As an alternative, Guthrie reached back to the prewar years at KFVD. He wrote Maxine Crissman once again, and again she turned him down. That prompted Guthrie to lash out in one of the "bitterest letters I have ever read in my life," Crissman recalled. "Oh, my God, it was filthy. Porno. It was absolutely unbelievable," so uncharacteristic of the Woody she remembered.

If Maxine would not sing with him, Guthrie would find someone else: People's Songs office assistant Jackie Gibson perhaps; or Hally Faulk, separated from her husband; or Jolly Smollens. None agreed.

At least one of the women suspected Guthrie was more interested in her sexually than musically. "He was pursuing me as a woman he was obsessed with," Smollens said. "I figured that one woman may not be enough. He wanted to spread it around. I think he had this fantasy of reproducing himself. I honestly do."

As much as he loved "sweet Marjy," Guthrie was driven to other women. The women he met, "all my girls and wifes and women . . . like to play me, all you puntas like to lay me, oh, a week, but then no longer, or a month, but never more. Why I'm born so, I can tell you only this, folks, I don't know."

---

* Apparently with the idea of blending in rather than dominating, Guthrie decided to switch from the steel-string Gibson he had carried since the recording sessions with Asch in April 1944. He pawned the Gibson with its hand-lettered sign "This Machine Kills Fascists," and casually gave the ticket to young Joe Jaffee, an acquaintance. In its place, Guthrie picked up a fine nylon-string guitar made by Carlos Barquero. (The Barquero might sing sweetly, but it could never shout over the hubbub of a skid row bar.) A year later, Jaffee saw Guthrie strolling the boardwalk, the Barquero slung by a leather thong across his back. "I felt sorry for the guitar," Jaffee said in a December 27, 1969, interview with E. Victor and Judy Wolfenstein. (Three decades later Jaffee still owned the Gibson.)

Guthrie's marriage by mid-1948 was a "shambles," said Bernard
Asbell, to whom Guthrie had taken a liking when Asbell was managing the
People's Songs office. While visiting Chicago for a People's Songs convention, the two men spent an afternoon walking around the Loop, each con-
fiding in the other about their marital difficulties.

Still Guthrie clung to home and "Mama," Marjorie, and to his son Arlo
Davy, playfully nicknamed first "Davy Dybbuk," after the Yiddish for an evil
spirit or soul, and later "Zibberzee."

Like Cathy had before him, Arlo Davy "broke his way into my inside
place and pushed his head into my heart and feelings," Guthrie wrote at the
end of September 1948. He was again inspired. "And now my old life moves
in such ways that set my old world breathing and wiggling with a rhyming
that I feel in very word I say now."

Arlo and his new baby brother, Joady Ben, born on Christmas night
1948 at Brooklyn Jewish Hospital, held Woody and Marjorie together.*
"We have not had any too placid nor peacefully blessed marriage at all of its
odd seasons," Guthrie acknowledged. "We have seriously considered trying
a divorce on several occasions; the kids have usually succeeded in being the
cause of us coming back and trying it again."

During one separation in early 1948, Guthrie went so far as to move to
a rented room in nearby Seagate. From there he began writing to Maxine
Crissman's twenty-eight-year-old sister, Mary Ruth, in northern California.
Since she had divorced her husband and he intended to divorce Marjorie in
Reno—he had even given away his few clothes before hitting the road west—
Guthrie suggested the two of them get together as singers and as lovers.†

There were as many as twelve rambling letters, typed on legal-sized
foolscap, filled with handwritten comments in the margins. Guthrie wrote
in passionate detail how he would make love to Mary Ruth, going on for
pages. Into the envelopes Guthrie stuffed pages torn from New York's
tabloids with muddy magenta circles slathered around stories of grisly
murders.

---

* Their second son was named after the two traditions from which he sprang, "Joady" after
John Steinbeck's Joad family, and "Ben," Hebrew for "son of." He was, Guthrie wrote to the
Earl Robinson family, "the son of all the poor folks on the roads."
† According to Maxine Crissman, Guthrie's proposal came without warning. Until then, he
had looked upon Mary Ruth as Maxine's kid sister, not yet out of her teens when Guthrie left
for New York in early 1940. For her part, Mary Ruth was smitten with Guthrie's cousin and
sometime singing partner, Jack Guthrie, who succumbed to tuberculosis at Livermore Veterans Hospital on January 15, 1948. Word of "Cowboy Jack's" death apparently launched
Woody in Mary Ruth's direction.

The packets, sometimes two or three a week, frightened Mary Ruth by their intensity, the sexual proposals, and the suggestion of violence. She drove to Los Angeles to show them to her sister, who knew Guthrie best of all.

"You have no idea how horrible it was," her older sister Maxine said. She, in turn, called the police.

A deputy district attorney visited the Crissman sisters to warn them Guthrie might be in Los Angeles. A police psychiatrist had advised they watch Woody carefully and not be alone with him under any circumstances. "He could chop you to pieces and sit right there by you and watch you bleed to death," Maxine recalled.

A family friend who worked as a Los Angeles Police Department sergeant dropped by with grisly pictures of the disemboweled body of Elizabeth Short, the so-called Black Dahlia. They wanted to question Guthrie about the murder. "That was the kind of thing this man would be capable of," the officer told the Crissmans.

Apparently exonerating Guthrie as a possible suspect in the Black Dahlia murder, Los Angeles police turned his letters over to postal inspectors. The letters, as grisly, as obsessive as they were, violated no state law. But Guthrie might be in violation of the nineteenth-century Comstock Act, which prohibited sending obscene material through the mail.

Guthrie was personally offended to learn he was under investigation. "Since I did not write this pile of letters to rob this girl, to hijack her, to blackmail her, to hurt her in any possible way, since I did not write to her in hate, then I must have written her those words in friendship and in all the states of mind we call love.

"And no earthly human can pass laws, rules, regulations, nor build any mud walls around the words and feelings and actions that grow up in love."

Guthrie protested he had no intention of harming Mary Ruth.

I told her that she did not have to accept my (friendly) romantic offers of a matrimonial classification; I did not try to frighten her nor to blackmail her, nor, in the least way to bring violence nor destruction to her property nor her person. My words may have been too hotly writ in the verbiage of a life-rafting seaman; but she can accuse me at the most . . . of loving her (in my own way) too much.

"Woody was having an absolutely platonic thing with her through the mail," insisted Jim Longhi, now a successful lawyer whose office was defending Guthrie. "Woody being Woody, a love letter has no inhibitions, sexual restrictions or anything."

Guthrie surrendered on August 2, 1949, in New York City on an indictment that charged him with mailing three letters containing material so obscene they could not be spread upon the court records. He was freed on a thousand dollars bail posted by Marjorie and her brother David.

Seeking dismissal of the indictment, Guthrie solicited letters from prominent individuals with whom he had worked.* With Alan Lomax he visited the deputy federal attorney, who pointedly left the three offending letters on his desk and excused himself from the office. The invitation was clear: take the letters, the evidence, and the case would disappear. Guthrie declined, Lomax told his sister Bess.

Guthrie took the looming prospect of jail time in stride. "There was no tragic, oh-my-God banging his head against the wall," Longhi said. Guthrie had willingly washed dishes in the merchant marine. He had served in the Army Air Force "for a lousy eight months" even with the war won. He would do the prison time as well.

Marjorie, reunited with her husband and pregnant for the fourth time, also seemed calm. According to Guthrie, she told him, "Well, Woody, if they do lock you away for writing these letters off to your old friend, I'll just imagine that you've gone off to the wars again, and wait for your ship to dock."

In a plea bargain arranged by Longhi, Guthrie pled guilty on October 5, 1949, to a single count of mailing "an obscene, lewd and lascivious letter." Longhi spent the next seven weeks, with the aid of four continuances, getting Guthrie into a pioneering psychiatric counseling program—and keeping him there.

A therapist at the clinic, Quaker Emergency Services Readjustment Center, saw Guthrie as many as twelve times for treatment of "sexual behavior disorder." Guthrie was evasive during their sessions, his Oklahoma coon-hunting drawl so thickly laid on that the therapist had to ask him to repeat statements. "There was something of the con about him, telling a long, funny story to avoid a problem," the therapist commented.

Guthrie was charismatic. He spun tales of his month on the Columbia

---

* In a September 20, 1949, letter to Norman Corwin, Guthrie wrote as proof of his good citizenship, "I have never been convicted of any crime in any court room." Any nights spent in local jails, Los Angeles and Reno among them, were solely on police authority.

River; of narrow escapes from the Pinkertons, who he said had placed him on a "most wanted list"; of songwriting and singing on picket lines. "He portrayed himself as a hero who had cunning, was idealistic, class-conscious and pro-union. It was self-advertisement."

The therapist, who had heard Guthrie sing at Almanac hootenannies, was put off. Guthrie was remote and completely self-absorbed during the sessions. "I realized that just because he was a great folk singer did not mean necessarily he was a great person."

On two or three occasions Marjorie accompanied her husband to the clinic in downtown Manhattan. "She was worried about him, and what she called his 'wandering all over the face of the United States,'" the therapist recalled.

"He was crazy about Arlo," she told the therapist, "so I can't understand how he can just go off like he does."

She worried too about the possibility of a long jail term. Her husband "doesn't have evil intentions," she stressed. "It is just who he is."

Guthrie attributed his current legal problem to alcohol. Because he was partially Native American, even the smallest amount of alcohol could produce bizarre behavior. "He drank whiskey and went out of control," the therapist quoted Guthrie.

Guthrie added that he wrote the letters to Mary Ruth Crissman while drunk on a beer. He promised not to touch alcohol again.

It was all too glib for the therapist, who concluded that Guthrie exploited the people close to him and that a succession of losses of dear ones—first Clara, then his mother, then Cathy—would lead him to shut down. "He really didn't have any respect for me," the therapist added. Guthrie abruptly decided not to return to the clinic, even though it meant possible jail time.

The agreement broken, on November 30, 1949, federal District Judge Harold M. Kennedy sentenced Guthrie to six months' imprisonment. Twelve days later Guthrie surrendered and was ordered confined to the Federal Detention Headquarters at the foot of Manhattan.*

Longhi scrambled to free his former shipmate. "The sentence was long

---

* Also known as the "West Street Jail," the facility had earlier housed Murder, Inc. capo Louis "Lepke" Buchalter and Catholic conscientious objector and poet Robert Lowell, the one imprisoned for murder, the other for refusing to kill—as Lowell noted. In his poem "Memories of West Street and Lepke," Lowell wrote that the best thing about the prison was its rooftop view of the Hudson River "through sooty clothesline entanglements." Courtesy of Jon Connolly.

enough to go over Christmas, and I didn't like that," he explained. "I did a little talking around, and got him out before Christmas. The irony is that some of my right-wing friends got him out."

Ten days after entering the detention center, Guthrie was free once more. Longhi's "talking around" had persuaded Judge Kennedy to reduce Guthrie's sentence to the time served "upon reflection and upon consideration of other cases of similar pattern together with the defendant's record of service in the war."

Guthrie, who had decided to arrange a Christmas Eve program for the inmates, was miffed that he would not participate in the show. But a pregnant wife and two sons offered a cheerier Christmas at home on Mermaid Avenue.

CHAPTER TWENTY-FIVE

The Compass-Pointer Man

*S*PRING, AND THE RETURN of warmer weather, invariably impelled Woody Guthrie to eye the road outside his front door, anxious to loosen the tethers that bound him to Mermaid Avenue, wanting more than ever to escape his arguments with Marjorie.

There were three children now, with the addition of Nora, the child he dubbed "Puffy," born on a January night while Guthrie was in jail on a vagrancy charge.* Still as much as he loved the children—and Guthrie played with them endlessly—when spring came, the restlessness stole over him.

In February, Guthrie had enrolled under the GI Bill at Brooklyn College, signing up for philosophy, English, Spanish, and classical civilization classes. The $120-per-month subsidy the federal government paid returning veterans to go to school helped the Guthrie family budget.

Money or no, the first warm day of 1950 produced an itch to try the road once more. On a whim, he dropped out of classes and set out for California.

On the way, Guthrie unexpectedly stopped at the home of Roy and Ann Guthrie, who had newly moved to Pampa, Texas. "He looked thin, down and out, and he did not have his guitar or his paint brushes," his sister-in-law recalled. Though Woody assured them he was all right, Ann realized that "there was a very noticeable change about him. He was not

---

* According to Nora, when Guthrie called, her mother asked police to hold him, "because at least she knew where he was and that he was being taken care of." Nora Guthrie interview, March 10, 2000.

so lively, didn't talk very much and showed some signs of jerky movements in his body."

Woody explained he was on his way to California and had run out of cash somewhere along the road. Roy dug into his pocket for bus fare to Los Angeles, but Woody apparently got off the bus to hitchhike along busy Route 66. He made it as far as Barstow, in California's high desert, where he literally collapsed in front of a restaurant.

A telephone call from authorities in Barstow summoned George Guthrie from his home in Long Beach, California. Woody was waiting outside the restaurant when George finally arrived. "The dadgum proprietor wouldn't let him inside. He was dehydrated and frankly looked like a bum."

George took his older brother home to Long Beach, fed him for two days, bought him new clothes, and talked a reluctant barber into cutting "that bum's hair."

Over the next two weeks, Woody regained strength and began to fill pages of notebook paper with his thoughts. The pages that Guthrie scattered about the couch he slept on, the cigarette-filled coffee cups he left about the neat apartment—as well as his casual attitude toward personal cleanliness—offended George's wife, Emily. She said nothing, but Guthrie sensed her disapproval and abruptly announced that he was leaving.

George insisted on telephoning Marjorie, and the two of them decided to buy Woody an airline ticket back to New York. That way, he could not decide to hitchhike in midjourney.

On the plane, Guthrie was seated next to an acquaintance, folklorist John Greenway, "a coincidence that would pale the most egregious of Thomas Hardy's into insignificance," Greenway wrote. As they flew over Oklahoma, Greenway woke Guthrie and pointed out the window. "There's your old home."

Guthrie peered at the cloud cover below, then asked Greenway if he had a pen. "I handed him a particularly fluid ball-pointer and in a matter of seconds he had written a song beginning, 'I want to lay my head tonight on a bed of Oklahoma clouds.'"

Surprised, Greenway asked, "Do you always write a song that fast?"

"No," Guthrie replied in a long drawl, "only when I got a good pen."

Such moments of inspiration came less often. He had finished the manuscript for "Foolish Gold," retitled "Seeds of Man," and presented it to an editor at Duell, Sloan and Pearce whom Alan Lomax had recommended.

The editor was enthusiastic, Lomax reported, but the manuscript was unpublishable in its now 840-page form. According to Lomax, the editor had lavishly praised Guthrie as a writer "as good as Melville, but it would cost me $25,000 to prove it and I can't afford that."

While Lomax was unsure about Melville, he did add, "I do know about Mark Twain and Whitman and you're cut out of the same material."

Lomax encouraged Guthrie to cut the manuscript. He believed Guthrie's was an authentic voice, one that needed to be heard, "the one who corresponded most closely to what kind of poet and writer I felt belong in the United States. . . . You write closer to the American bone than anybody else—well, better say the southwestern bone."

Not everyone agreed with Lomax. In September 1950, Guthrie wrote to Duncan Emrich, Lomax's successor as head of the Archive of American Folk-Song at the Library of Congress, offering to pick up where he had left off in 1941. "I'd love to record a few hundred more of my tales, travels, jokes, songs, ballads, and such to finish up the other 99/100ths of my legend on your wax."

Emrich turned him down, vaguely citing budgetary woes. It was a feeble excuse, according to Pete Seeger. Emrich's refusal was actually based on his fear of the archive being tainted as Communist.

Guthrie muddled through the year, singing where he found paying engagements and caring for the three children while Marjorie taught dance. The stress on Marjorie was grueling, said Judith Mazia, her niece and sometime baby-sitter. "She was manic." Marjorie slept as little as four hours a night. "She could not take a vacation, or stop to take a deep breath."

Relief came from an unexpected quarter. Late in 1949, Pete Seeger, Guthrie's prewar traveling companion, and Lee Hays had joined with two younger veterans of the bankrupt People's Songs to form a quartet that would perform folk songs. Though there were serious doubts among them about "going commercial," these newly named Weavers parlayed a holiday engagement at the Village Vanguard into a recording contract with Decca Records, a stunning succession of hits, and sold-out nightclub appearances.

Unlike their earlier People's Songs performances, the Weavers worked out careful arrangements, their recordings backed by the Gordon Jenkins Orchestra and a chorus in the studio. If the Weavers were uncomfortable amid the record industry's crass pandering, they nonetheless kept an ear cocked to artists and repertoire men, to what disc jockeys would play, and to the requirements of the commercial market. They compromised, rationalized, and popularized folk music. If they adapted Leadbelly's "Irene" to omit a reference to morphine and a whisper of sexual inference, they could comfort themselves with the thought they *were* singing a friend's song.*

In the summer of 1950, Seeger suggested that the Weavers record Guthrie's dust bowl ballad of 1941, "Dusty Old Dust." (Coincidentally, Guthrie had refashioned Leadbelly's tune for "Irene" to set the text of "Dusty Old Dust.")

Guthrie was excited. He spent an afternoon in a midtown hotel room rewriting the lyrics of "Dusty Old Dust," changing a protest song into a comic song. He expected the "Weavery folks'" record, retitled "So Long, It's Been Good to Know You," to "sell up into the blue jillions," he wrote his sister Mary Jo.

He would not be disappointed. In October, he received an advance of ten thousand dollars against royalties, a princely sum to the cash-strapped Guthrie family. He turned the money over to Marjorie.

Marjorie immediately began looking to rent a new apartment large enough to accommodate three children as well as provide a work space for her husband. She bought "Totsy III," a new 1950 Pontiac, discounted after the 1951 models had come out the month before. The automobile would halve the time she spent twice each week commuting to New Jersey to teach dance classes. More important, she repaid her parents the thousands of dollars she and Guthrie had borrowed over the years.

On December 5, 1950, the Guthries moved from Mermaid Avenue to a new apartment building at 49 Murdock Court in Brighton Beach, Brooklyn. Apartment 1J in the Beach Haven development offered a bedroom for the three children, another for Guthrie and his wife, a work area for Guthrie's desk and typewriter, and two balconies facing Ocean Parkway and Coney Island Hospital.

Best of all, Marjorie purchased an upright piano. She would play chords while Guthrie stood behind her and brushed her long black hair—as he had with his mother so many years before.

The remaining $2,400 of the advance Marjorie banked with the intention of opening her own dance studio. Guthrie himself took little of the money. He bought a three-speed record player to play the imported albums of classical music Moe Asch had given him in lieu of royalties. (Prokofiev's "Romeo and Juliet" was a Guthrie favorite; he would put it on when Mar-

---

* Retitled "Goodnight, Irene," the record would sell some two million copies and eventually generate thirty thousand dollars in royalties. His portion of money would come too late to help Huddie Ledbetter, who died penniless in December 1949, but it did free his widow, Martha, from her job as a laundress.

jorie left for work in the morning and play it repeatedly until she returned in the evening. He also listened to the piano music of modernist John Cage, "who overhauls the family piano in his own way.")

With the turn of the new year, Guthrie was optimistic. The sale of "So Long" to Decca had led to him acquire co-managers, Pete Kameron and Harold Leventhal, and a publisher, Howard Richmond. (Kameron was also helping to manage the Weavers while working for Richmond's publishing company.) A recording contract seemed at hand.

"So it looks like I've got the good news to rolling at long and last on this money front," he chortled. He anticipated that royalties on the Weavers' recording, on sheet music sales, and on foreign rights would be worth as much as forty thousand dollars during the next two or three years.

Despite the prospect of financial security, Woody and Marjorie fought more than ever. In earlier years, Marjorie had attributed their quarrels to the notion that her husband was a temperamental artist like Martha Graham. "I don't think it is possible for a person to be a great artist and a great human being," she confided to friends. Certainly Guthrie could be cruel, as cruel as was the driven Martha Graham.

They fought, Guthrie lashing with a wicked, cutting tongue, while Marjorie berated him for being self-destructive and hard on the family.

"We were fighters and great make-er uppers," Marjorie explained. "I would get sore and argue back and I was as stubborn as he was, and very vocal and he would say one or two mean, bad words, and that's all it would take.

"I'd fly off the handle and say, 'Get out!' And he'd pick up the guitar and walk. I wouldn't see him for three or four days, and I would cry the whole time. Then he would come back in the door. Of course, I wouldn't say a word, and we would kiss and make up and start again."

The arguments and the wandering continued. Guthrie would stay in Beach Haven a few weeks, then disappear for a month. On more than one occasion, he failed to show up for bookings, and left his new singing companion, Tom Paley, to perform alone. Once Marjorie told Paley she hadn't seen her husband in several days and had no idea where he was. Another time, she said Guthrie had gone out a few days before to buy cigarettes "and would probably be back in a week or two."

Something about Guthrie seemed different. He could be abusive, even violent, said Lee Hays, who had laid a bed on the floor for Guthrie more than once. "You were aware of this sense of doom hanging around him."

In rare moments, Guthrie saw himself clearly. The arguments with

Marjorie would send him falling down among his songs and papers, "dog-drunk deaddrunk and so mad and messed up in general. . . . I'm not the greatgreatgreat hero of the masses that many minds have drempt me to be; but I'm sure not the rubbout deadlygone failure that these many others say I am," he wrote after one bitter argument with Marjorie.

Their fights grew more stormy through the year. Friends, fearing for her safety, advised Marjorie to get a divorce, if not for her safety, at least for the three children: Arlo, almost three and one-half; Joady, two; and year-old Nora.

When Marjorie suggested a divorce, Guthrie wavered. They were not "mortal deadly enemies," he insisted, just "all wrong for one another most times." They hung on for the sake of the children.

Guthrie waffled. "I'm against it and then I'm for it, then I shift over again and I'm all for it and then all cold and deadset against it." For most of their years together, Marjorie had been the one "to really work and earn money and support me and to keep me sheltered and fed and gee-strung and nose-haltered."

With the success of "So Long," Marjorie again proposed they separate, pointing out he could get more good work done if he were living alone. She extended generous visitation with the children, and the comforts of her bed on occasion. He was willing to accept her offer; after all, he was "well and keenly aware of the clear fact that I've not made her any kind of a model mate nor exemplary husband since we've tied the kink in the old cow's tail."

Furthermore, Marjorie had told Guthrie she wanted no more children. For Guthrie, this was "surely no fun and in reality a very blinding kind of pain." Guthrie, for his part, deemed it his mission to bring forth a vast number of children—of "every known size and shape and color skin." To do so, he imagined he might next marry "the sweetest negroid girl which and whom will also have and also try me out."

Without Marjorie, Guthrie strained to clasp to a woman, any woman. His momentary fascination was with Jolly Smollens, who had moved to Philadelphia. She possessed a voice he admired; consequently she was a woman whose body he immediately coveted "in my hottest and my most passionate ways ever since I met you."

In Guthrie's eyes, Jolly Smollens became all that Marjorie was not. Marjorie did not march in May Day parades, join picket lines, or sign petitions promoted in the pages of the *Daily Worker*. Jolly did all of that, and more.

As much as she wanted to sing with Guthrie, Smollens said she was cool to his sexual advances. Years earlier, driving to a People's Songs booking, "he was drunk, very sloppy. . . . It was repulsive when he made a pass," she insisted. "He was very impulsive, and when he drank, he was much worse."

The courtship by correspondence between Guthrie and Smollens was interrupted on February 9, 1951, when Guthrie shambled across the parkway to Coney Island Hospital, complaining of a persistent stomachache. Doctors examined him, then rushed him to surgery for an emergency appendectomy.

It was a close call. The doctors told him "that if I'd got to that operation table thirty minutes later or one year sooner they couldn't have saved me." Thirty minutes later and his appendix would have burst "and in my rundown shape I couldn't have outran the gravedigger very far." A year before a new form of streptomycin doctors used during the operation would not have been available to them.

Guthrie's near call sobered both him and Marjorie regarding a possible divorce. "It showed us once more how bad and sad are the visitations of ills even onto our three innocent kids when either one of us, the mama or the papa, or both, get gone too far." He and Marjorie would try once more.

While in the hospital, Guthrie was visited by a twenty-year-old college dropout who called himself "Buck" Elliott. Born Elliot Charles Adnopoz, the son of a successful Brooklyn surgeon, young Elliott was fascinated by horses, cowboys, and the mythical West. He had run away from home at fourteen to join a rodeo, changed his name to something more *American*, scraped through high school between journeys westward, and taken up the guitar as the suitable instrument for a would-be cowboy from Brooklyn.

Guthrie's *Documentary Struggle* album, loaned by a friend, snared the teenage Elliott's imagination just as the rodeo had earlier. He listened to the record steadily for a month, copying as he could the guitar runs, learning the songs, and singing in a gravelly voice much like Guthrie's own.

For three days in a row, Elliott stayed through visiting hours in Guthrie's room to play guitar, sing, and talk. He was in many ways a younger version of Guthrie, stocky where Guthrie was wiry, but like Guthrie a man to guard his feelings behind a weather-worn face.

On the third day, Guthrie pointed out the window to the new apartment building across the highway. Elliott could see two children playing on a balcony. "Go over there and introduce yourself," Guthrie instructed.

Elliott spent a half hour visiting with Marjorie, then set off on an impromptu trip to Arizona and California. Three months later, he returned, no longer "Buck" but "Jack." He called Guthrie and was invited to a party.

"We started playing music, and one day led to another," Elliott explained. "I ended up staying there for about a year and one-half." There was never a formal invitation to move in, "but they didn't kick me out and I became like a member of the family."

The two men managed to play together daily, sometimes for hours on end, Nora recalled. Her father would sometimes spike the children's morning orange juice with rum so they would be quiet while he and Elliott played guitar. (To save time, he also fed them hot dogs for breakfast and bribed them with candy during the day.)

Elliott was, as he put it, the "perfect mimic." For years after, he "did Woody Guthrie songs exactly the way that Woody did." He played guitar the same way; he sang in the same rusty voice so well that people often mistook one for the other.

Guthrie was amused, then flattered by Elliott's doting attention. Though he refused to teach Elliott directly, he quoted Huddie Ledbetter's graceful sanction, "I ain't gonna show it to ya, but you're welcome to steal it if ya like it."

Weekdays at Murdock Court fell into a routine. With the children fed and off playing by themselves, the two men played guitar together. At lunchtime, they frolicked with the children. Guthrie, as Nora put it, "wasn't as good a father as most fathers that I know. . . . He was more like a big brother." At the same time, she added, "he was a good father because he really loved us and he loved to play with us."

Early in the afternoons, they would take the children for a ride in the new Pontiac—unless Guthrie had one of his periodic dizzy spells. Then he would retreat to the bedroom he shared with Marjorie and nap for a couple of hours.

Despite their resolve to stay together for the sake of the children, Woody and Marjorie bickered continually. Marjorie's long days left her husband to grouse he was "a kind of nursemaid to our kids all of my hours till we all get to feeling like we've got no mammy a tall."

They would fight and Guthrie would storm out, with Elliott in tow. But as often as he disappeared—perhaps for days at a time—he returned, sheepish this time, defiant the next. Marjorie would ask him to stay, just for a few days, until she could make arrangements for a baby-sitter. And one day would stretch to weeks while they fell into old habits just to get by. As husband and wife, their marriage had ended months before. Still they could not let go of each other.

By the end of October 1951, Marjorie was again weighing a divorce.

She was finally weary of Guthrie's disappearances, his increasingly odd behavior when he was home, and his drinking. Alcohol had become a problem when Guthrie took to rifling Marjorie's purse for change or emptying the envelopes of small bills she had set out for rent, for food, or for utilities.

The divorce would be friendly, Guthrie assured a friend, Stetson Kennedy. They merely had to settle on "an airtight story to fix for the purposes of getting my divorce. . . .

"She knows I am a compass-pointer man and that I have to always be free to wing and wander."

Conveniently, Kennedy, an author and outspoken Ku Klux Klan foe, invited Guthrie to north Florida and the acreage Kennedy had inherited from his father near the town of Green Cove Springs. Kennedy had dreams of transforming his property—dubbed "Beluthahatchee" after a mythical land of forgiveness in Florida Negro folklore—into a writers' colony or resort for weary leftists.*

Guthrie was quick to accept. "I feel like Florida needs me and my talents a good deal more than New York City needs me." The local klavern of the KKK had threatened to run Kennedy off his land; another defender would be useful. Meanwhile, Guthrie could help Kennedy dam a stream and convert a bog into a lake stocked with government-supplied fish.

In November 1951, Guthrie left Beach Haven, telling Marjorie he would send for his papers later. When Kennedy arrived to pick him up at the Greyhound bus station, Guthrie was sleeping on the sidewalk, his head on his guitar.

"Woody, where is your baggage?"

Guthrie pulled open his jacket. Underneath, he wore five shirts. "It was not so cold, but pretty damn cold," he explained.

Guthrie had arrived in Florida in time to reinforce a motley platoon of neighbors Kennedy had assembled to defend Beluthahatchee. Anticipating a raid by the local klavern, Guthrie visited a local gunshop and had made cartridges for Kennedy's rifle, a World War I vintage Springfield '03. With some practice, former Private First Class Guthrie became a crack shot, even though they had agreed only to shoot into the trees over the heads of raiders.

When the klan finally roared up in a convoy of pickup trucks, Kennedy's impromptu platoon was at the ready. Guthrie, at the first alarm, tumbled

---

* Kennedy learned the name from Zora Neale Hurston when the two worked on the Federal Writers Program collecting folklore in Florida during the 1930s.

from his hammock. In his excitement he dashed across the hot coals in the barbeque pit, Springfield in hand, to blaze away at the marauding night riders. Amid the gunfire and a hail of falling twigs and leaves, the panicked klansmen circled the driveway in front of Kennedy's home and sped off, never to return.

After the excitement passed, Guthrie moped about Beluthahatchee. He wrote Marjorie on November 16, 1951, a letter both pleading and longing:

> What's wrong with us, Mommy? What's wrong between us? Can't we ever fix it, whatever it is? Are our kids bound and destined to live the lives of little orphans in another one of those crazy, insane, broken homes, broken by a divorce and a couple of loud, nervous, raving, ranting parents?

Yet in the next paragraph, Guthrie appeared almost resigned to a divorce. There had been no letter from Marjorie, who was dating other men. "I know in an odd sort of way that there's just not going to be for me any kind of a friendly word from you."

Then he was defiant: "No matter how far this divorce between us has gone . . . I never will sign my signature of agreement to it. I'll stop it every possible way I can. For the sake of all our kids, and for the sakes of all of us as a family."

Whatever his mood, Marjorie remained a lodestone to her compass-pointer man. Three days after writing her, he was back in New York City, closer to Beach Haven, to his wife and the three children. For weeks he had no fixed address. He moved from flophouse to flophouse along the Bowery. He sponged off friends. Drifting and rootless, Guthrie finally rented a room in the dreary building at 148 West 14th Street where he and Marjorie had first made love seven years earlier.

There he sat, feeling sorry for himself, grieving until his agent, Pete Kameron, arranged an audition for Guthrie with Decca Records on January 7, 1952. Guthrie recorded two songs, "This Land Is Your Land" and a denatured bawdy song he called "Kissin' On." (It was intended to be sold as yet another of the then-popular humorous novelty songs.) Guthrie judged the audition a failure, but Decca, to everyone's surprise, offered him a recording contract.

Moses Asch at Folkways was unconcerned with Guthrie's threatened defection to a major label and its commercial machinery. "With the audience I was trying to reach, I couldn't do it with him," Asch told interviewers E. Victor and Judy Wolfenstein in 1972. "Woody to me at that time was lost. And I felt he was not interested."

Guthrie, once so passionate, once so articulate, now "wrote incoherent letters, [and sent] incoherent abstract drawings, nothing like before." Asch was no longer interested in Guthrie the songwriter or Guthrie the artist. "I felt it wasn't worth while. I felt it wasn't my function" to take care of Guthrie.

Then, as if daring contradiction, he added, "I was not his nursemaid."

Guthrie decided to sign with Decca, but at the same time he boldly offered to appear on a program with blacklisted composer-guitarist Earl Robinson. "Just don't think that the Decca Recording Company has got me wrapped up around any of their little fingers; I was born to be a reddical and the life and death of a reddical is the only kind of a life and a death I'd sign up with."

Guthrie's defiance was a gesture of friendship and integrity. A movie composer, Robinson suddenly found himself without work in Hollywood, banned for his Communist Party membership. His career aborted, he had eventually taken a marginal job teaching music in a Left-oriented private school in New York City, appearing where he could to supplement his meager salary.

A number of Guthrie's other friends and acquaintances in these months also fell victim to the insidious blacklist, not only in Hollywood but also in New York, where the bulk of nationally broadcast television and radio was produced. After CBS writer-producer-director Norman Corwin was termed a "fellow traveler" by the FBI in a confidential report leaked to the press in June 1949, Corwin found it difficult to get work. So too John Henry Faulk.

The Washington Commonwealth Federation, which had hosted Guthrie and Seeger in 1941, was formally labeled a "subversive organization" by Tom Clark, the attorney general of the United States; any former member seeking employment with the government, by law, would have to reveal his membership, thus assuring he would not be hired.

In 1950, once successful radio and motion picture writer Millard Lampell began keeping a grim diary of the sudden dearth of writing assignments. A year later, the House Committee on Un-American Activities subpoenaed Guthrie's friends Will Geer and John Garfield, director Lewis Milestone, and playwright-director Abe Burrows, a member of People's Songs board of directors, who once jibed, "Is Woody growing as a musician." All would find themselves graylisted or blacklisted.

No one was immune, as Corwin pointed out. "Suddenly men of good standing and repute and honor like Ed Murrow, and artists like Leonard Bernstein and Orson Wells were objects of suspicion."

The blacklist operated covertly, haphazardly, and carelessly. Burl Ives, once Guthrie's singing companion, secretly testified before the committee; to save his acting career, Ives identified as many as a hundred former associates as Communists or fellow travelers. The business of naming names was indiscriminate, a matter of feeding the hungry maw that was the House Committee. "If you *knew* somebody who *knew* somebody, you got blacklisted," Seeger said years later.

Both Seeger and Guthrie certainly knew people within the declining party and the moribund Popular Front. If Ives had failed to name them in secret testimony, Harvey Matusow did so publicly on February 6, 1952.

Matusow, a former volunteer for People's Songs, testified before the Un-American Activities Committee, then holding hearings on "Communist Activities Among Youth Groups," that

> we in the youth movement had the task of making sure that young people who were not already in the Young Progressives of America or the Labor Youth League, became interested in the organization by using people such as the Weavers . . . using their appeal to the young people as a means of getting the young people down to the meetings of the Communist fronts and indoctrinating them with the party line and later recruiting them.

Guthrie—"a name I didn't mention before" in closed testimony—was part of the plan in that he wrote one of the Weavers' big hits, "So Long It's Been Good to Know You." According to Matusow, Guthrie "was a member of the cultural division of the Communist Party, and he had also been a member of the Brighton section of the party in Brooklyn."*

Whether it was Matusow's testimony, or Ives's, or the earlier citations by the California senate's Un-American Activities Committee, the blacklist

---

* Matusow's testimony was cast into question by his admission that he had repeatedly perjured himself. In an interview shortly before his death on January 28, 2002, Matusow conceded, "No, I didn't know Woody was a dues-paying, card-carrying member of the Party." The Weavers, because of their celebrity, were the committee's intended target; Guthrie "was a sideline, a throwaway name." Matusow eventually served four years in federal prison, convicted "for saying that [Senator Joseph McCarthy's staff counsel] Roy Cohn when he was an assistant U.S. attorney had suborned perjury. They never prosecuted me for any of my lies; I went to prison for something that was true."

snared Guthrie in early 1952. Decca dropped the Weavers, its number one act. At the same time, the company cast aside the hapless Woody Guthrie, just as the Weavers' recording of "So Long" reached number four on the hit parade.

Guthrie apparently shrugged off the dismissal. It was spring again, and once more he was on the road, visiting his scattered family. In El Paso, Guthrie told Jack Elliott, he attempted to cross the border into Mexico, only to be turned back by the Border Patrol because his name was on a list of "political suspects." He hitchhiked instead to the arid Chisos Mountains, and from there to Oklahoma City to visit his father.

Guthrie returned to New York by bus, arriving to find that a sailor's heavy seabag thrown on top of Guthrie's nylon-string Barquero had broken the neck from the body. Guthrie, who "was hard on guitars" and changed them so readily, took this one to be repaired at New York City's premier guitar shop. Keeping the guitar was one way to hold onto something of Marjorie.

There was little else he might cling to in the gloomy fourth-floor room on 14th Street. His world was shrinking into a bottle. Once or twice, a drunken Guthrie threatened suicide, Jack Elliott recalled. "I was kind of herding him around like a brother," Elliott added.

The changes in Guthrie were stark, according to Henrietta Yurchenko. Returned to New York City after a long trip collecting Mexican folk music, she was surprised by Guthrie's shabby appearance, his strange gait, and his moods. When she inquired, friends told her Guthrie had been drinking.

Pete Seeger also noted a difference. Guthrie simply wasn't the same. He was no longer turning out great songs, one after another. He seemed to be drinking too much and even embarrassing himself with poor performances.

Without Marjorie, Guthrie had foundered. His letters to her alternated between anger and pleas, raging one moment, despairing the next. He wrote on May 9, 1952, to insist he did not want to see her again. "No dates, no movies. No nothing more between us. . . . No Marjorie. No Marjorie. Thank God."

He would seek solace elsewhere. "Life owes me one more wife and three more kids and you'd might as well prepare yourself to hear the news."

Three days later, he wrote from 148 West 14th Street to ask that she read his last letter "just backwards and you'll be seeing the real truth of how I feel." He pleaded, "Please don't let me die again."

In a second letter that day, he offered to return to the hospital to dry out.

"I want my body and my brain to forever be freed and cleared from my terrible time-wasting and life-wasting alcoholic habit."

He could not do it without her. "Please help me," he begged. "I know how many, many times I didn't help you; but don't sign my death warrant for that; Marjorie, please believe, please believe."

He signed the letter: "My last chance. Can you spare it? Woody, Sinking Down."

He was swallowed in despair. That night Guthrie weaved his way to Beach Haven and pleaded with Marjorie to take him back. When their conversation was interrupted by a telephone call from Marjorie's current beau, Anthony Marra, Guthrie exploded in violence.

The next morning he was contrite, and wrote in a bold, slashing hand to apologize for "that last fight we had in which I treated you too rough." He blamed his drinking, which "came in an inch last night of destroying me and everybody I love first and most, you and our kiddys."

A day later, Guthrie's letter to Marjorie was at first angry, then brashly impenitent. Cisco Houston had assured him he was "not an alcoholic or anything very close to an alcoholic," Guthrie wrote to Marjorie. Houston, he rationalized,

> has got a way of talking to me that clears my head up quicker and better than anybody else I've ever known. He helped me to undo, and to wash out, and to get rid of several thousand destructive, deadening suggestions you've so truly shot at me, oh, about being a psycho case, and an alky case, and every other poison kind of a sting you tried to shoot into me.

He blamed Marjorie for his violence. His love letters had failed, Guthrie proclaimed in crisply printed characters, so Marjorie

> just had to be treated that rough just once, just one time, in your life and I thought because I've lost you, anyway, that I got forced by all circumstances to be picked to do that one night of violent fighting which I hated to see come ten times more than you did.

If Marjorie wanted a divorce, she could have it. He would make no claims on her and would sign over the deed of ownership on the dance studio. "Marjorie, I love you for the mommy you've tried so hard to be to this world's wildest and stormyest son."

On May 15, 1952, Guthrie took the subway to the Beach Haven apartments. He camped on the steps, chain-smoking, waiting for Marjorie to return from a date with Tony Marra. As he waited, his jealous rage simmered.

Marjorie paid the baby-sitter then turned, apologetic, to her husband. Perhaps she should not have gone out with Tony, she conceded, but she thought their marriage was over.

Guthrie was not to be placated. In a flash of anger, he struck Marjorie—"He beat the hell out of me," she later acknowledged—cut the telephone cord, then threatened her with the scissors.

Terrified, Marjorie went limp. Her passivity momentarily deflated Guthrie. "Why don't you fight back?" he demanded.

Marjorie cautiously eased herself from the bed, warily eyeing the exhausted stranger standing across the room with his eyes dilated and spittle rising on his lips.

"It was like Woody wasn't there," she later told her daughter Nora. "The man she knew was not there."

At that moment, Marjorie realized her husband was sick, beyond alcoholism, stricken with some unknown illness.

Marjorie excused herself, asserting she had to go to the bathroom. Guthrie followed her, to watch as she washed her reddened face. She then checked on the three children sleeping in the next room, with Guthrie trailing close behind.

Marjorie suddenly bolted. She dashed for the front door, flung it open, and ran down the hallway, screaming for help. She finally roused a sleeping neighbor—it was two o'clock in the morning—who called the police.

When the police arrived, Marjorie explained her husband was desperately sick and needed to be hospitalized. The responding officer eventually calmed Guthrie, who lay on the bed smoking the policeman's cigarettes.

After a while, Marjorie returned to the bedroom and told Guthrie he was sick. He balked, then hesitantly agreed to commit himself to Kings County Hospital. It was that or jail, where he would get no help at all.

Guthrie was, as Jack Elliott said, "struck with fear." Guthrie feared he had his mother's disease, the madness that had sent her off to die in the asylum, "but he was afraid to admit it to himself. He was kind of hoping that it was just alcoholism."

Marjorie made tea and then called Earl Robinson. About six in the morning, Robinson arrived, and he and Marjorie took the subdued Guthrie to the detoxification ward at Kings County Hospital.

At the hospital, Guthrie told the doctors that he suffered dizzy spells and blackouts. The doctors responded with an unsurprising diagnosis of alcoholism.

Three weeks later, a temporarily sober Guthrie left the hospital and returned to his apartment on 14th Street in Manhattan. There he spent days reading about alcoholism, and growing more and more despondent.

A performance of *Spoon River* choreographed by Marjorie for her dance students plunged Guthrie into remorse for what his "drinking bottle has caused me to lose.

"I don't want our kids to have a drunkard sot for a daddy any more than you do," he wrote in anguished embarrassment. His rambling letter wound through praise of Tony Marra and advice to Marra to stay sober; to understanding why Marjorie had rejected him sexually; and finally to regrets for his drinking. "Alcohol numbed me and killed me so nearly dead . . . that I died twenty deaths. And when I saw how that bottle robbed me of Marjy and our kids I died twenty more."

Hours after mailing the letter, Guthrie telephoned Marjorie at her dance studio. He was drunk once again, and repeatedly threatened to kill himself by jumping off a building. The threat grew more ominous when he refused to tell her where he was. Alarmed, Marjorie telephoned police precinct after precinct seeking help. Finally she found a desk sergeant willing to send a patrol car; on a hunch, she gave the officer the 14th Street address. Guthrie was there.

That night Marjorie beseeched her husband to seek help. Despite his fear of what doctors might learn if he returned to a hospital, he finally agreed to a voluntary commitment at Bellevue on June 14, 1952.

He stayed for observation in what inmates on the seventh floor called "the raving ward." He was docile, as if accepting his fate, and spent his days assisting the staff where he could, making beds and feeding other inmates.

For the first two weeks, he was miserable drying out. "The pain I feel," he wrote to Marjorie in early July, "is something no pill nor powder nor needle can help nor ease much." The withdrawal was worse than the addiction. Then came reality, which was worse still.

Guthrie spent a month in Bellevue, first wringing the alcohol from his guts, then undergoing the repair of a hernia by Jack Elliott's surgeon father, Abraham Adnopoz.

Released on July 15, a day after his fortieth birthday, Guthrie gingerly found his way to Beach Haven. He was carrying two three-quarter-size Gibson guitars when he rang the buzzer. One guitar was a present for Arlo's fifth birthday, the other was for a neighbor's daughter.

Marjorie was at first dismayed, then angry. Just out of the hospital, Woody was unsteady on his feet. Apparently he had been drinking. Worse still, he had spent scarce money on the two birthday gifts.

Guthrie was defensively insistent. "He said that if you got the kid a toy he would abandon it in a few weeks, and that would be the end of it," Arlo recalled. "But if you bought a real thing he would play it all his life."

The birthday visit ended badly. Apparently angry that the children were up late, Guthrie lost control. He struck at least one of the children, then hit Marjorie.

Unbidden, a remorseful Guthrie checked himself back into the raving ward the next morning. He would stay there a week while Marjorie sought help.

She badgered the doctors who had earlier treated Guthrie at Bellevue. "Is it possible that you have released my husband without a diagnosis, without even letting me know?"

The doctors were distant, conciliatory, but not very helpful. "Mrs. Guthrie, your husband is a very sick man, and we don't know what to do with him," said one.

Eventually, Earl Robinson's brother-in-law, a doctor, suggested Guthrie transfer to Brooklyn State Hospital. The staff there was experimenting with insulin shock therapy to treat alcoholism.

Accompanied by Marjorie, Guthrie entered Brooklyn State on July 22, 1952. While he was prepared to undergo further tests, a tearful Marjorie pleaded with doctors not to let him out until they could provide a diagnosis beyond simple alcoholism.

In a letter addressed to his family, but intended particularly for Marjorie, Guthrie begged forgiveness for his behavior:

In and through all of my walkouts and disappearances, I loved you. I felt like I had failed you so bad that I didn't deserve your companionship and healing hand and constant love. I tried to leave you because I hated myself. I hated myself because I felt like I'd failed you. I felt like I failed you politically, socially, musically, husbandly, fatherly, manfully, and in every other way a man can or ever could fail a woman.

For almost six weeks doctors at Brooklyn State Hospital fumbled for the definitive diagnosis Marjorie had demanded. Their patient, doctors noted, was a "scrawny looking white male, looking somewhat older than his 40-odd years, because of his lined face and weather-beaten features."

Guthrie, the medical records continued, was cooperative but withdrawn. He showed little or no emotion. He constantly fidgeted, unable to sit still for even a few minutes. His movements were spasmodic and random, his speech hesitant with awkward pauses. He grimaced, twitched, sniffed, and shifted about in his chair during interviews.

Reviewing his life story for the doctor, Guthrie suggested he had "hit the skids" since his army discharge and had tried to blot out his failure with alcohol. He described himself as often depressed and irritable; more recently he conceded his explosions of anger had left Marjorie physically bruised.

The doctors were perplexed. "This is one of those cases which stubbornly defies classification," one wrote in Guthrie's medical record. The patient presented "elements of schizophrenia, psychopathy and a psychoneurotic anxiety state, not to mention the personality changes occurring in Huntington's chorea." The diagnosis would be deferred.

Then, on September 3, 1952—a family story has it that Guthrie was on a gurney, prepared for his first insulin shock treatment—a young doctor looked at the medical record and noted Guthrie's mother had been institutionalized with an undiagnosed illness. The doctor asked, "How come no one has said this guy has Huntington's chorea?"

Perhaps it required a young doctor, a man fresh from medical school, to recall a passing mention in one of his textbooks of a rare hereditary disease of the nervous system first described by a Long Island physician, Dr. George Huntington, in 1872. Huntington's chorea—"chorea," or dance, for the spontaneous muscular contractions that wracked the limbs—was an inherited degenerative disease. It struck most often when the victim was between thirty and fifty years old; the physical, emotional, and cognitive symptoms appeared gradually, but inexorably worsened.

There was no cure.

Eventually the signature staggering walk of chorea's victims would be mistaken for a drunk's stumbling gait. But there was no simple explanation for the mumbled speech, the inability to concentrate or to think through a problem.

In the end the helpless victim died, limbs twitching or grown rigid and unmoving. As often as not, death came from choking, or infection, or starvation, not from the disease itself. Huntington's chorea was a sentence of death by slow degrees.

Later they all would wonder just when the disease began. Guthrie himself stated it was shortly after he got out of the Army Air Force. Marjorie attributed the onset to Cathy's death, convinced there was a psychological trigger. However it began, alcohol seemed to exaggerate, if not exacerbate, Guthrie's condition.

Sixty days after he entered Brooklyn State Hospital, the attending physicians had settled on a diagnosis: Guthrie was suffering from Huntington's chorea. There was nothing they could do to help him.

Guthrie was released on September 24, 1952, bravely dissembling, doubtful of the prognosis. "There are lots of kinds of chorea and nobody is plumb sure about what kind I'll most likely have, if any," he wrote to Pete Seeger. "They say it ain't deadly nor fatal, so, my days in yonders hospital weren't quite wasted if they got me off my bottle."

At the same time, Guthrie wrote to Seeger, his doctors had advised Marjorie to get a divorce for the safety of the children. She would not file immediately; she might later even consider a reconciliation. The reprieve gave him some hope.

But for now, Marjorie suggested, Guthrie should leave New York. She suggested he go to California. He loved the state, he had friends there, and in the warmer climate he just might get better.

Pliant and confused, the compass-pointer man looked westward.

CHAPTER TWENTY-SIX

Anneke Anni

*P*ACIFIC COAST HIGHWAY clung to the shoreline, an asphalt divider between beach sand and eroded palisades. Four lanes wide, it ran four miles north from the end of Route 66 in Santa Monica to the boxcar-red trading post where Topanga Creek trickled into the bay.

From the coast it was another five miles up Topanga Canyon Boulevard—a brave name for a two-lane, winding highway—to the little community where Will and Herta Geer had bought land.

The town of Topanga clustered around a bar, a community store, and an elementary school. Half the residents worked in town, many in the motion picture industry; half scuffled as best they could, artisans of various sorts who sold the odd canvas or ceramic pot. Working or not, all saw themselves as social or political adventurers, deliberately, even defiantly unconventional.

Will and Herta Geer had come the year before to join a clutch of liberal friends already established in the sparsely settled town. Herta had found the tract with its rustic house in Topanga Canyon and insisted they buy it. Will, blacklisted for his politics, could not appear in films, on radio, or the disdained medium of television. Instead they would build a hillside amphitheater with help from other blacklisted actors and writers, and present plays. They would get by, Herta insisted.

Geer, a botanist by training and avocation, "would be happy if there was a place he could work with his plants. As soon as he saw it," Herta added, "he jumped right in and started digging."

The first performances, readings before small audiences, began the following spring under a large sycamore tree. Rex Ingram, Norman Corwin, Earl Robinson, and Carl Sandburg were among the early performers. They took up collections to pay for the actors' meals. Presiding was Geer, full of bonhomie, "a marvelous entertainer," said Sam Hinton, who attended performances at Geer's Theatricum Botanicum.

Herta was expecting Guthrie when he suddenly showed up in October 1952 and bluntly announced, "Well, I've got it. I've got Huntington's chorea; I'm done for."

Marjorie, remorseful and mourning, had telephoned earlier to say that she and Guthrie had parted. "You know, Herta," she insisted, "I wouldn't have let him go," but the doctors had cautioned that there was nothing she could do. "The illness was taking over."

At Marjorie's suggestion Guthrie was making his way west. As she told the children, he "was fixing himself in the warm sunshine." To Arlo, she explained, "We want Woody to be well and the sun is so good for him. Maybe it is better for us to miss him and for him to be well than for him to stay with us and be sick."

Guthrie moved into a one-room stone hut—a converted storage shed for garden tools—a hundred yards from the Geers' home. The shed became "Woody's House" by the simple act of placing a snapshot of Marjorie and the three children on the table. His hours were as irregular as his habits— singing and acting in Will's Theatricum; writing three or more unproduced, droll, thoroughly "pornographic" plays; or strolling naked about the yard in front of the Geers' two daughters, Kate, thirteen, and Ellen, eleven. Red-haired Kate, who had physically matured, remembered Guthrie was always staring at her. She, in turn, ignored him. "Woody was just part of an irritation that wouldn't go away."

Herta was upset with her antic guest but said nothing for the moment. "I never thought there would be any use in scolding Woody for anything. I let him alone. I let Will alone. You have to let certain people alone. They'll do it anyway, and the more you bug them, the worse it is going to be for you. You're only going to hurt yourself."*

Guthrie seemed unaware of or indifferent to his impact on the people around him, a young visitor, Frank Hamilton, said. "Woody didn't know that he was a burden on people. He probably didn't realize that he left a

---

* Herta Geer would eventually insist Guthrie move on after he wrote an explicit love letter to thirteen-year-old daughter Kate. While Herta declined to say what was in the since-destroyed letter, Kate confirmed that she read it.

mess or a glass to clean up, got in the way or walked naked in front of little girls. He was a child in that way."

At the same time, it was hard to be angry with him. "He was a very loveable guy. He was so honest, trying and sincere."

Hamilton, a junior college student at the time, had made his way to Topanga when he learned Guthrie had turned up. Hamilton had auditioned for the part of harmonica-playing Sonny in his school production of *Finian's Rainbow*, got the part, then decided it would be useful to learn how to play a blues harmonica. Guthrie could teach him.

"Woody had no problem with time," Hamilton recalled. The days were free of obligation and Guthrie welcomed company. The two would spend long days singing and talking.

Young Hamilton was impressed initially with Guthrie's honesty and lack of pretense, then with the straightforward musicianship he demonstrated. "He played straight from the heart without any artifice and he was kind of mesmerizing in his playing. He never allowed his accompaniment to get in the way of his words."

California seemingly *had* restored Guthrie. Once again he was the natural performer who "just drew people in," Hamilton said. "He was a natural."

At the same time, said Hamilton—who would later enjoy a career as a professional musician—"Guthrie was the kind of performer who probably would not have held an audience in Carnegie Hall."

The days Guthrie and Hamilton shared were relaxed, their evenings built around hootenannies and paying gigs. Guthrie drank sparingly around Hamilton. Still, he left the younger musician with the impression that Guthrie was an alcoholic. Momentarily Guthrie would seem to lose concentration, to disappear. "I felt like he wasn't there and then he would come back. He seemed preoccupied."

When he was not noodling on the guitar, Guthrie worked with Will Geer moving rocks to shore up the stream bridge leading to his theater, or cultivating a vegetable garden. He had found bookings, enough to support himself, and was playing better than ever, he assured Marjorie. "It sure is plenty fun getting to feel that I'm not quite as gone and hopeless and useless and unneeded as I was around your neighborhood."

Signs of the illness came and went. He suffered "disssy sppells," though not as badly as he had in New York City, he wrote Marjorie in October 1952. A month later, he reported that the attacks were worse:

My chorea sure isn't kidding these days. I feel it as a nervous fluttery heart condition along with a slight lack of control over my body at times. I feel it sort of steady now at all times and a bit more so sometimes than at other times. I don't [get] entirely lost nor entirely gone but partly so part of the time. I'm pretty sure that I do need companionship like you say but I'm not any too posolutely certain about who'd be foolish enough to shack up with me when it gets down to bare facts.

In repeated letters to Marjorie, Guthrie attempted a brave face. "I feel every day less like I've been hurt and more like I've been helped by this whole business of our separation and our divorce. . . . I don't see the least earthly chance now that we can ever be able to get back together anymore on anykind of a longtime basis."

Something was wrong within him, Guthrie realized, something that snarled his marriage. Whatever it might be, he stared it down.

This world it's hit me in my face.
It's hit me over my head.
It's beat me black and blue and green,
But still tho' I ain't dead.

I ain't dead! I ain't dead!
I ain't dead! I ain't dead!
I ain't dead, folks.
I ain't dead! I ain't dead!

I stumble an' I fall and roll and crawl
In thornybushes like I said.
I'm all bawl'd up and all fowled up
But still folks, I ain't dead.

I ain't dead! I ain't dead!
I ain't dead! I ain't dead!
I ain't dead, folks.
I ain't dead! I ain't dead!

For all his bravado, Guthrie lay wounded in pride and love. After a telephone call in early November from Marjorie, he wrote angrily:

> I cant ever quite forget how you refused your love to me and gave it oh so freely to Tony because you said you were already for all practical purposes and reasons his wife; and that you and I could remain, ohh, such good friends forever and ever if only none of this old love and life reared its head; how you said this to me such a short spell ago, and then, how, now, and all at once, you call up to ask me do I love you and to tell me again that you love me (still).

His chorea was now under control, he added dismissively, "and, well, to be real truthful, I've heard the last word I want to hear about this whole chorea mess."

Guthrie assured Marjorie he was not drinking; a glass of wine at dinner was more than enough for him. He had nursed a bottle of bonded whiskey, he wrote to Marjorie about November 1952, just enough to get sick and "decide my bottling days are all out and all over with."

Topanga was invigorating. He brimmed with ideas. He would record an album of songs opposing Spain's fascist generalissimo, Francisco Franco, for Stinson Records; Stinson's Bob Harris, an ardent Stalinist, "was freer politically about censoring our recordsong ideas," Guthrie wrote Pete Seeger. He intended to add a hundred pages to his "Foolish Gold" ("Seeds of Man") manuscript and ask advice about it from blacklisted screenwriter Ben Maddow. He might even tour England if Alan Lomax could arrange some dates.

California, where Guthrie was seemingly better known than in New York, just might prove to be a permanent home. It seemed a sensible choice. He had friends here: the Geers; Bess and Butch Hawes; Cisco Houston, perfecting a system to beat the blackjack dealers in "Lost Wages"; and even a boyhood pal from Okemah, John "Smokey" Woods. ("Smokey" Woods's father, Zach, had passed out Socialist literature on the indifferent streets of Okemah, Guthrie recalled with admiration.)

Meanwhile, a local real estate agent, Bob DeWitt, had touted Guthrie about a piece of canyon property up the road from the Geers that DeWitt could sell cheaply. Guthrie and Frank Hamilton made their slow way up to the hillside plot; Guthrie looked over the vista and decided he would build an adobe home overlooking the land, *his* land, that he dubbed Pretty Polly Canyon. (To buy the eight-acre site—the progressive-minded DeWitt was going to sell it for just $1,250—Guthrie asked Marjorie to send the down payment of $250 from his "So Long" royalties.)*

"Frankie" Hamilton, as Guthrie called him, had his doubts about Pretty Polly Canyon. "This is sure one perfect spot for a sex crime," Hamilton decided.

"It's a perfecter spot for sex without the crime," Guthrie retorted. With the help of his brother George and young Hamilton, in the next days Guthrie hauled up a Dutch oven and a tarpaulin, which he lashed into a teepee-like tent. He was eager to move in.

One thing was missing. He yearned for female companionship, Guthrie wrote to Marjorie late in November. "I'm rusting out and cankering over for some lady companion to fill up this bottomless pit hole of lonesomeness I feel too much grando."

He was still "foolishly" in love with Marjorie, he confessed, "now more so than I ever was. Now more needful of you than I've ever been. Now more passionately than ever before. . . . In love with you beyond all reason and all sense."

If his marriage with Marjorie was over, Guthrie was not discouraged about marriage itself. "I kid and joke around here with the Geers about getting out and finding me my Wife Number Three . . . ," he once more wrote Marjorie, adding, "She must be darkskinned. She can't be blonde nor light-colored."

Guthrie would not long remain alone. As Herta Geer noted, he needed the company of women. He had even made a pass at her, an advance she rejected. "It was always very hard for the women he got involved with."

In the end, the female companionship Guthrie found was neither dark skinned nor blonde.

Brown-haired Anneke Van Kirk Marshall was Pennsylvania Dutch by extraction; her family was said to be wealthy, she herself something of a renegade for her liberal politics and obvious sensuousness. She had met and married David Marshall, when both were working at the Provincetown Playhouse. With Marshall intent on breaking into the movies, they made their way west, eventually to end in Topanga. There Anneke laid out a two-thousand-dollar down payment on a small hilltop house with sweeping views of the Santa Monica Mountains. Marshall sought work as an actor

---

* Guthrie had long dreamed of owning a home "except I am stubborn as the devil, want to build it my own self, with my own hands and my own labors out of pisse de terra sod, soil, and rock and clay, and want it to be bug proof, fire proof, wind proof and termite proof." Quoted from Woody Guthrie to Harry St. Amand, January 14, 1947, courtesy of Barry Ollman.

when he could, or doubled as a carpenter and tile layer in their still unfinished home when theater and motion picture work was unavailable.

By all accounts, Anneke—"Anni" to her friends—was a lush beauty at twenty-one, a broad-hipped woman with a long braid falling down the middle of her back. Amid the relaxed atmosphere of Topanga, she stood out, a married woman who was generous with her sexual favors, an "earth mother," as one put it, "a very luscious, young girl who liked to play music and have a good time," in the words of another. Physically strong—she would move good-sized rocks to help Geer construct his open-air amphitheater on the hill—she gravitated to men she could nurture.

"She was a nice person—generous, talented, open," said Bob DeWitt, who had sold the house to the Marshalls. "She was the first hippie that I ever knew . . . a free-spirited person in 1952 and that was unheard of at the time."

The Marshalls had been married just six months by the time Guthrie sauntered up Topanga Canyon Boulevard with his guitar slung over his shoulder, shirts, dirty socks, and book manuscript in a brown paper bag. Anneke, who had never before heard of Guthrie, saw him at a hootenanny and came away unimpressed. "I didn't like Woody at first," she later wrote. "He was unlike anyone I had ever known. So quiet and seeming not to care about anything much."

Early in December, Anneke wandered down to the DeWitt barn where Bob had set up a potter's wheel. She was intently turning a pot when Guthrie, who was then staying with the DeWitts, walked in.

They said no more than hello before Anneke turned back to her wheel and Guthrie unwrapped the wet towel from the figurine he was sculpting. "We worked there for at least an hour and didn't say one word to each other. But there was a warm feeling in the air, as though we didn't really need to say anything much."

Guthrie, "so lowly sunk down in my own worst kind of a lonesomeness," invited Marshall to climb Pretty Polly Canyon with him. They clambered up the steep arroyo to the grass-covered peak, where they spent hours talking about politics, religion, people, movies, and folk song.

By the time they parted, Marshall was smitten. "I felt that I wanted to see him again. I enjoyed being with him. I felt happy and peaceful, as though there were no one else I would rather have been with."

Sometime after the first of the year, Anneke asked her husband if they could put Guthrie up for a while. When he agreed, Guthrie packed his few belongings and the boxes of papers Marjorie had sent him and moved in. In

retrospect, Anneke acknowledged, she should never have invited Guthrie-
"at least not feeling about Woody the way I was starting to."

Anneke spent her days as a telephone operator thinking about Guthrie
and her evenings playing five-string banjo accompaniments to his guitar.
"She sung harmony of that very special extemporaneous antifascist kind
right along with me, hitting all of them ruff tricky turns and twistings that
me & Cisco Frisco used to be so damnable good at." Guthrie determined to
stick to "one certain particular female sheemale girlygal that somebody
someplace named by that name of Anneke."

For her part, Anneke wrote later, "I didn't stop to think how jealous my
husband would be in this strange set-up. As a matter of fact, I really didn't
care what he felt. I just wished he would go away, and leave me alone."
Guthrie, continued Anneke, "did nothing to encourage this situation, but I
knew he did care for me."

"I think she was star-struck with Woody," Frank Hamilton said. In
Anneke's eyes, Guthrie seemingly symbolized the romantic wanderer ever
seeking a better America, an almost mythological figure sprung in equal
parts from Jack London's socialism, Carl Sandburg's patriotism, and John
Steinbeck's passion. (In reality, Hamilton realized, Guthrie was an intellectual. "I didn't get the feeling that he was really a laborer in the proletarian
sense of the word.")

Guthrie had lived with the Marshalls for two or more weeks when, in
late January 1953, he announced he was leaving. He intended to camp out
on top of Pretty Polly. Two men could not love the same girl, he explained.

With Guthrie gone, Anneke's house seemed lonely and empty, "and so
terribly cold without him, even in bright sunlight." That evening she told
her husband she was leaving him. At his insistence, she agreed to recon-
sider for a few days.

After a day or two, Anneke decided. "I couldn't be happy without
Woody." She made her way to Guthrie's campsite, where the two of them
talked. Guthrie was frank; he couldn't guarantee any girl security or happiness.

Swept up in the sheer romance, as she would later admit, Anneke waved
his caution aside. "The happiness was in me, just in being with him. No one
can guarantee happiness for another."

Herb Cohen, like Guthrie a sometime merchant mariner with whom he
swapped "bullshit stories," shrugged off the escapade. "She was living with
Woody because he's Woody. . . . Everybody in the community worshipped
him or idolized him. That's the reason she loved him."

Still the liaison between Woody Guthrie and Anneke Marshall, a girl half his age, stunned the tight-knit community. Some, like Frank Hamilton, realized that Anneke was not happy with her husband; at the same time, it seemed that Guthrie never "even thought about how he was hurting people."

Bob and Doreen DeWitt also described the Marshalls' marriage as "strained," but for this they blamed Guthrie. "He was just a bum with a lot of talent," Bob snapped. "Nobody had talent like him."

Even a year later, Jack Elliott learned, close-knit Topanga still resonated with the news of Anneke's flight from her marriage. "Everybody was kind of down on Woody for running off with Dave Marshall's wife," Elliott recalled.*

When a winter rainstorm washed away Guthrie's campsite, he and Anneke decided to leave by bus for New York City. With no place to stay, they camped temporarily with Martha Ledbetter and her niece, Tiny Robinson, on East 10th Street. A visitor, Fred Gerlach, invited Guthrie and Anneke—now using Guthrie's last name—to stay with him; he had plenty of room.

Gerlach played a twelve-string guitar in the style of Leadbelly, which irritated Guthrie. "Guthrie didn't like imitators. He didn't like people imitating him. He was not much for fans," Gerlach noted. Guthrie advised Gerlach to find his own way of playing the unwieldy twelve-string.

Guthrie was broke, Gerlach said, until "Oscar Brand paid him something like $300 or $400 to come up and record a program" for Brand's weekly radio show devoted to folk music. Guthrie "took $200 and bought a

---

* The end of the Marshall's marriage would have unusual consequences. Left to himself, David Marshall worked as a member of the crew shooting pick-up shots in Topanga for the avowedly radical, pro-union film *Salt of the Earth*. When the filmmakers found Hollywood's facilities closed to them, Marshall allowed them to edit the film in the home he had once shared with Anneke. (*Salt of the Earth* was written by blacklisted Communist Party members Paul Jarrico and Michael Wilson, and directed by Herbert Biberman, one of the original Hollywood Ten. The film, which starred Biberman's wife, Academy Award winner Gail Sondergaard, told the story of a failed strike by radical Mine, Mill, and Smelter Workers' locals at a New Mexican zinc mine. Completed against great odds, the film never found a distributor and was seen by relatively few people. Details may be found in Ellen Schrecker's history of the blacklist, *Many Are the Crimes: McCarthyism in America*.) Meanwhile, Herta Geer discovered her husband was conducting a homosexual alliance, perhaps more than one. "A lot of young men were attracted to him," she said in a 1998 interview. Wounded emotionally, Herta instructed him "to keep his life separate from me." Eventually, she left with her three children to live with Marshall. They would have a child together before they separated; Herta and the children returned to the Theatricum Botanicum.

Martin guitar, bought some groceries, gave me a few dollars, and never showed up."

With the balance of the money, Guthrie, Anneke, and Jack Elliott set off for the warm weather of Beluthahatchee, Florida, in a Ford Model A that Elliott had purchased for twenty-five dollars in a junkyard. The trip would take five days, with stops for repeated repairs that Guthrie paid for.

They arrived in Florida on March 12, 1953, to find Stetson Kennedy and his wife gone, on an extended stay in Europe, the better to escape the anti-Communist hysteria. Guthrie, Anneke, and Elliott moved into a disused bus and a shed on the property.*

Within a week the triangular relationship became strained, Elliott said. "Woody seemed to be a little uncomfortable with young me around. See, I was twenty-one, and Anneke was twenty-one, and Woody was forty-one." Since Guthrie had put up the money for repairs on the Model A, Elliott decided to give him the car and to hitchhike to Texas. Guthrie, in turn, would eventually pass the car on to Kennedy's poor neighbors with the explanation they could keep it in repair better than he could.

After Elliott left, Guthrie purchased a typewriter and began revising the manuscript for "Foolish Gold," retitled "Seeds of Man." "This would cover the mornings down there, and in the afternoons we would go for a swim or a walk," Anneke remembered. (Apparently they were unusually casual in their dress. A pair of dignified black church elders were offended when they paid a Sunday visit—only to be greeted by a "buck naked" white couple. "What kind of people do you call that?" they huffed when Kennedy next met them. "I don't know," Kennedy shrugged. "Just Woody Guthrie.")

For three months, they lived in what Anneke described as "this haven of peace," amid trees draped with Spanish moss. They carried water from a neighbor's well—the electricity at Beluthahatchee was turned off—and cooked over a campfire. In the evenings, Anneke pecked out letters by candlelight while Guthrie played his guitar or mandolin. Anneke wrote amicable letters to Marjorie and sent well-done ink sketches of local birds and bugs to the children.

Grateful that Anneke was caring for Guthrie, Marjorie apparently

---

* Agents for the FBI tracked Guthrie and the woman calling herself Anneke Guthrie to Beluthahatchee in the spring of 1953. Agents asked attorney Gerald Hart, a Kennedy neighbor, if they knew of any disloyal activity by Guthrie and showed him a photograph of Guthrie and his guitar inscribed "This Machine Kills Fascists." Meanwhile, doctors at Brooklyn State told the FBI on April 10, 1953, that Guthrie was suffering "a chronic neurological condition with occasional psychotic manifestations" that was inherited and incurable.

reached out to Anneke, a gesture that Anneke rejected. "We are only poor lone individuals, struggling along our separate ways. . . . So I think I would be happier, far, far happier if we remained in our separate corners of the earth."

Their idyll in Beluthahatchee's wetlands ended in a flash of kerosene-fed flames on June 10. In an attempt to quickly start the morning's fire by dousing the previous night's cold logs with kerosene, Guthrie accidentally splashed fuel on his sleeve. A match tossed toward the blackened logs ignited his sleeve in a burst of flame. Guthrie rolled on the ground to snuff the flames, but not before the skin from his right shoulder to his fingers had "blistered and dropped off, rather slid off, as skin does."

A neighbor drove them to a doctor's home, he was not there, then to Jacksonville where the neighbor left them at a police station. A squad car ferried Guthrie, first in shock, then stoically bearing the pain, to Duval Medical Center.

The hospital's intake card filled out that morning noted:

> Pt threw gasoline on an open fire; blazed and burn his arm. Pt says he plays stringed instruments, receives $100 a mo royalty on songs he has written. This Pt is a peculiar case. This couple are drifters—came down here several mos ago. Pt is supposed to be a musician—folk music. Has quite a history in [neighboring] St. Johns County. Allowed one visit *only*. Says will make own arr[angement]s for further care. He wears shaggy hair and beard which he says is to keep mosquitos away.

Guthrie suffered silently through a three-hour return journey by bus to Beluthahatchee. The pain would come later, when the hospital-administered drugs wore off; it would last for weeks as the sweet-sour flesh on his arm turned an array of frightening colors. A local doctor assumed Guthrie's treatment, stanched an infection, and saved Guthrie from blood poisoning. A hundred-dollar check from Marjorie paid the doctor when Anneke, who picked rutabagas for fifty cents a day, could not pay the bill.

Through June and much of July Guthrie was unable to bend his right arm as the scarred tissue drew taut over the elbow. With each day the couple grew more restive.

There was an urgency now. Anneke learned that she was pregnant, the child due in February. They decided to return to California where they could escape Florida's humidity, and live in the home Anneke had bought with her husband in Topanga.

On four hundred dollars borrowed from a friend of Anneke's, they left in July for California, once more traveling by bus. They stopped in El Paso to visit Mary and the children, as well as Matt Jennings, then crossed the Rio Grande to Ciudad Juarez on July 28, 1953. There Guthrie filed for a divorce with a lawyer arranged by Jimmy Longhi; Guthrie's complaint alleged he and Marjorie were incompatible.

The day Guthrie and Anneke arrived in Los Angeles, they purchased a 1937 Hudson Terraplane for $115. Anneke was weary, coping now with morning sickness as well as Guthrie's slow recovery. When they visited George and Emily Guthrie in Long Beach, Emily realized "Anneke just couldn't move anymore," and put her to bed. The visitors would be house guests for two weeks.

Despite the rigid arm, which hung stiffly from his side, Guthrie himself seemed fine, George said. There was no sign of the tremors or the weaving walk that were the mark of Huntington's chorea. "He just acted like he did when I knew him before."*

Eventually, Guthrie and his new wife made their way back to Topanga. While they waited for David Marshall to move out of the home he had shared with Anneke, they stayed in the canyon with former Almanac Singer Bess Lomax Hawes and her husband, Baldwin.

"We had a little shack up there, with three little kids and no money," "Butch" Hawes remembered. "Woody was hanging around the house with his burned arm hanging out." He was lethargic, drained of his familiar vitality.

For Bess, who had known Guthrie since 1940, "it was just more than you could take in a way. He'd stick his arm out . . . and he wouldn't ever try to move it. And it meant he couldn't play. He tried to type and he couldn't type. You'd urge him to move it, to take some exercises, and he wouldn't. He was just falling on you, in effect, emotionally, and it was really just more than you could bear.

"At the same time, you had the feeling that he needed something desperately, and you didn't know what it was or how to give it to him.

"Woody was more of an emotional burden than anybody else would have been," she added with a laughing snort. "It was too much emotion in one small house." Finally, they asked Guthrie and Anneke to leave.

---

* Guthrie apparently told differing stories about his fire-scarred right arm. As sister-in-law Emily Guthrie recounted the story in a 1971 interview with E. Victor and Judy Wolfenstein, when Guthrie eventually got to a hospital, the admitting nurse asked his religion. "Everything," Guthrie replied. He was refused treatment.

Anneke found a job at the telephone company, earning forty-five dollars a week. It was enough to pay the mortgage on the house she had shared with David Marshall and buy potatoes and beans to live on. Perhaps when his arm improved, Guthrie could make money as a performer once more; or they could sell pots, Anneke suggested.

At night, Anneke retyped portions of the manuscript for "Seeds of Man" while Guthrie dictated corrections. But that task ended temporarily before the end of August as "wild and wooly Woody, unshaven, hair like a matted halo," slipped into lethargy. Anneke fretted about "unhappy Woody with his stiffening arm, frustrated Woody without the smallest audience, a Woody with dizzy spells, Woody with such a hunger for people, for sound, movement, a 'cause.'"*

Before the end of the year, a very pregnant and very nervous Anneke wrote a despairing "private note" to Marjorie beseeching her for royalty monies. They were "just skimming through" on her salary at the telephone company, and she expected to quit her job in late January to await delivery of her baby. "We really need some help badly."

His Mexican divorce granted on October 22, 1953, Guthrie was free to remarry. With Marjorie's encouragement—she argued it best that the child Anneke was carrying be legitimatized—Guthrie and Anneke Van Kirk Marshall were married. A momentarily revived and exuberant Guthrie wrote to his second wife, "Me & Annye went off down here to my hall of justice a few days ago and had our sexylives made legal & binding."†

Hardly a month later, they left for New York City in the road-weary Hudson. Eight months pregnant, Anneke did the driving while her silent husband huddled, eyes closed, in the seat beside her. California had not panned out, but Guthrie had friends in New York who would help, including a bruised but resilient Will Geer, who had returned to the city earlier.

They stayed for a few days with Huddie Ledbetter's niece, Tiny Robin-

---

* The manuscript for "Seeds of Man" was complete, ready for an editor's eye, if not father Charley Guthrie's, Anneke wrote to the old man in August 1953. She suspected Charley, living in the moldering Crystal Hotel on West California Avenue in Oklahoma City, would find the book vulgar, but defended it as true-to-life. In an effort to reach out to him, Anneke asked seventy-four-year-old Charley his definition of a successful person. He replied, "My definition of a Successful Person: One who is least like me." C. E. Guthrie to Anneke Guthrie, August 14, 1953, in Woody Guthrie Archives.

† Just how Anneke secured her divorce from David Marshall was not clear. She suggested in a letter to Marjorie that divorcing Marshall would be difficult—presumably because of California's interlocutory period of one year. Apparently Marshall obtained a divorce in Nevada, which required only a six-week residency.

son, who shared what little she had. Anneke was in the last weeks of her pregnancy, perpetually tired, and Guthrie was subdued. They did not argue, but it was clear to Robinson that something was wrong.

Guthrie found a dreary fifth-floor walk-up apartment on East 5th Street in the Lower East Side. He spent long days nursing bottles of Ballantine ale in the chilly apartment. Occasionally he would shamble out to cadge five or ten dollars from his music publisher Howie Richmond, or from Stinson Records' Bob Harris or Folkways' Moe Asch. On January 18, 1954, Guthrie joined Jack Elliott, Brownie McGhee, and Sonny Terry in Asch's small recording studio for an ill-fated session. Whether it was a result of Huntington's or alcohol, Guthrie had trouble remembering the words to even his most familiar songs. His guitar playing had slowed; his right arm, hardly bending, could only strum the strings up the neck of the Martin. Fred Gerlach, who a year earlier had opened his home to Woody and Anneke, described Guthrie's playing as "just a bunch of noise. It was really sad."

Perhaps aware of his physical condition, Guthrie firmly rejected an invitation to visit Marjorie and the three children in their new house in Howard Beach, Queens. "I decided against it," he managed to type in his characteristic capitalized style, "on account of because I don't firmly think that my presence around there can make matters a bit better than they are when I stay gone. . . . You'll grow lots healthier if you just quit ever expecting me to visit your sweet cemetery. Not in fifty lifetimes. Leave me be. Leave me alone."

Then, as if the effort had been too great, Guthrie slipped into an ale-induced fog. Three weeks later, he was unable to accompany his wife to Bellevue Hospital on a city bus after her water broke. Alone in the hospital, Anneke delivered a baby girl, named Lorina Lynn at Guthrie's insistence, on Washington's Birthday in 1954.*

With Guthrie unable to work, Anneke found a job as a telephone operator at Bellevue. Of necessity, each day she left Lorina with Guthrie, laying out instructions to feed and change her, only to return in the afternoon to find the "baby naked and pissed, Woody filthy, all gas jets flaming for heat."

"Sad, sad, sad," Anneke wrote later. "No glory here. Not even bound for. Just bound. Bound by illness and the passing of time."

Guthrie was bound as well by memories. Of touring with Will and Herta Geer in the San Joaquin. Of telling simple stories spun by ballads. He tried to write those kinds of stories for Geer, who was presenting blacklisted actors

---

* The child's name, Lorina, was similar to that of the heroine of Guthrie's newly finished manuscript, Riorina. Guthrie nicknamed the baby "Rina Nevady."

and singers under the omnibus title of "Folksay." Guthrie's scripts were unpresentable, Geer said, the writing both cumbersome and pornographic.

Guthrie would occasionally show up at the evening performances in Geer's studio apartment above a Greenwich Village pizza parlor, Anneke and the infant in tow, where he was waved through by acting doorman Harold Leventhal.

"Guthrie would come up from time to time," said Fred Hellerman, one of the four Weavers blacklisted earlier. "He was pretty bad by now. . . . He was tottering and it was just Woody drunk again. So Woody would come around and there was this silence, like, 'Oh, shit! here's Woody again.'"

Woody had aged. He could neither play guitar nor sing. It was difficult for him to talk, though his mind seemed clear. "The old gaiety was gone, and he seemed desperate," a visiting Ed Robbin recalled.

So too was Anneke, said Henrietta Yurchenko. "As he got worse and worse, Anneke called Marge because she was young, because she didn't know what to do, because Woody was violent at times." Concerned—for Anneke, the baby, and for Woody—Marjorie did what little she could to help.

The violence erupted on a spring night in 1954. A tired Anneke snapped at Guthrie for using freshly laundered diapers to wipe up a puddle of spilled ale. He pushed her. She slapped him. Then they were tangled on the floor, her hands squeezing his neck. She abruptly broke away, Guthrie left gasping.

The marriage was over.

Within days, Guthrie invited Jack Elliott to accompany him to California. The folks in Topanga were holding a beard-growing contest; Guthrie, with his wiry beard well underway, intended to compete for the prize, a case of beer. They could ride with a friend who had agreed to deliver a new car to a buyer in San Diego. Their transportation would be free.

Elliott and Guthrie together made eleven dollars performing in Washington Square, Elliott playing slowly for Guthrie's benefit, Guthrie hacking chords on the neck of his Martin. The money was enough to pay for sandwiches on the four-day drive west.

The two men eventually made their way to Topanga Canyon and the home of Bess and Butch Hawes. Walking along the highway, Guthrie suddenly pointed across the road and whooped, "There's my land!" Elliott saw only a forty-foot cliff rising straight up on the other side of the creek.

Guthrie insisted they climb to the top of Pretty Polly. There Elliott found a tent, folded neatly six months before and placed under a rock.

They spent their days at the Hawes home sunbathing in the nude and playing guitar. Hearing him play from another room, Bess often mistook Elliott, with his uncanny ability to mimic Guthrie's guitar playing and singing, for Woody.

Guthrie relied increasingly on Elliott, who took odd jobs to help pay their way. Guthrie's every gesture, every step was exaggerated, "overdone," in Elliott's phrase, "because Woody had lost control."

Topanga did not seem as welcoming. Elliott suggested Guthrie "might have been aware of the fact that people there were not real in love with him on account of the way he took off with Anneke."

One morning Guthrie disappeared. He and Elliott had shared a last fifty-cent bottle of Olympia ale atop Pretty Polly. Elliott left to find Frank Hamilton, and Guthrie lay down to sleep. When Elliott returned, Guthrie was gone.

Guthrie had no plan. David Zeitlin, who had met Guthrie the year before, encountered "this little guy walking towards me on the beach. He was carrying a guitar on his back and he had a shopping bag in his hand. He was dirty, disheveled."

Zeitlin invited Guthrie to dinner at the beach house his father and mother had rented where Topanga Creek ran into the Pacific.

"We fed him. After dinner, we talked, played guitar a bit and sang and eventually Woody curled up on the couch and went to sleep.

"I got up the next morning, and Woody was gone and so was our silverware. I imagine he pawned it for a bottle."

Guthrie was hitchhiking northward along Pacific Coast Highway. From Santa Barbara, ninety miles north of Los Angeles, he sent Anneke a postcard telling her he was on his way to San Francisco to ship out as a merchant seaman. That notion passed as quickly as it had come.

From Olympia, Washington, home of his momentarily favored ale, Guthrie sent a postcard to Elliott, who was scraping by as a 'tween acts ballad singer at Geer's theater. Guthrie had spent a night in the Olympia jail, picked up on a vagrancy charge.

He crossed into British Columbia, was jailed overnight, and again in Montana, Elliott learned later. Then Guthrie wandered his way to Denver and the home of his fidddle-playing Uncle Jeff. He turned up at four in the morning, so ragged and bearded and wet from a rainstorm that he seemed a "haunting apparition."

Guthrie, according to his FBI file, next "appeared" in El Paso on the night of August 6, 1954, to see Mary and the children and Matt. He "appears beat up and has grey hair," the FBI agent noted.

Guthrie spent a night sleeping on the couch in the living room of the home Mary shared with her new husband, Percy Bailey. After he urinated on the couch, an embarrassed Guthrie confessed he was having trouble with his bowels and bladder.

He visited Matt, now the owner of a meat-packing company, steady Matt, the stay-at-home who had given up thoughts of a musical career to care for his family. According to Jennings, Guthrie was wearing tattered clothes and carrying a bottle of tequila to "cover up" his illness. (Jennings noted that Guthrie's walk was unsteady, yet the bottle was full.)

Guthrie left El Paso by Greyhound bus for Tulsa on August 9, 1954, FBI agents trailing after him. He intended to visit his uncle, Claude Guthrie, who owned a machine shop there, and locate Jeff Guthrie's married daughter, Patricia Berry. "Claude saw a raggedy, dirty, unkempt Woody and was disgusted." He repeatedly refused to tell Guthrie where the woman lived. Finally Guthrie shambled off.

Guthrie had told Matt he was returning to New York, but the route seemed to change by whim. On August 29, 1954, the Columbus, Ohio, *Citizen,* reported that "Woodrow Wilson Guthrie, citizen of New York City and the world at large" was an overnight guest in the city jail. This was his twelfth arrest in the last six weeks, he told the *Citizen*'s police reporter, Eugene Grove.

Guthrie was philosophical about it, Grove wrote. The arrests "give me a chance to get a shower and couple of meals." He had been arrested for trespassing in the freight yards, nabbed while sleeping. "Before the officer hauled me off, the brakeman slipped me a dollar. Something like that always happens just when you get to starving. I can safely say that Americans will let you get awful hungry but they never quite let you starve."

Then he was on his way, carrying with him his sole possession, a book entitled *Yogi Philosophy and Oriental Occultism.*

Guthrie eventually found his way to New York City and the East 5th Street flat he had shared with Anneke and the baby. On his rare good days, he daydreamed about records he might make or of finding a new singing partner. On the bad days, he merely sat huddled on a kitchen chair. He was lost, of no good to anyone, barely able to care for himself.

On Thursday, September 16, 1954, Guthrie put a pad of writing paper, a shirt, and the manuscript for "Seeds of Man" into a paper bag. Bag in hand, he checked himself into Brooklyn State Hospital, surrendering finally to the doctors' diagnosis.

CHAPTER TWENTY-SEVEN

Adversity Guthrie

"MY NAME IS WOODY adversity guthrie," he typed in December 1954 while a voluntary patient in Brooklyn State Hospital. "Adversity, adversity, I've held ye too close. I knew ye and know ye too well."

He was frightened. He was alone; his third wife and eighth child had vanished from his life. In their place loomed a vision:

> *Christ is my choice,*
> *Christ, your cross is here.*
> *Christ, I hear your word run clear up here across all my old crazy, sickly, lost*
> *   centuries.*
> *Jesus Christ, you're my best doctor.*
> *All my songs flow out of Christ.*
> *All my factories run by powers of Christ in God.*
> *Jesus didn't die,*
> *Christ shows me how to die and live on.*

Still, Guthrie remained fiercely independent. "I've just not seen any church that can save my soul. . . . God is the only political party I believe in."

In the end, he sang a hymn learned long before:

> *Death is my best friend*
> *Death is my best day*
> *I pray every little passing minute to die die die.*
> *Death O death O deathless death.*

Confronted with Huntington's chorea, Guthrie became compliant. The struggle had become too hard—better to take the easier route, to surrender to the doctors.

He was "halfways knocked out," he conceded in a letter from Brooklyn State Hospital to newly married Jolly Smollens Robinson, and left with little hope. "Chorea gets worser and dizzier by slow slow sure degrees, and nobody but God alone knows of any cure for it or any kind of a treatment."

He was left with faith—"God, be my preachy teacher and I couldn't ever ask You for no other favors"—and memory. If he could no longer march in Labor Day parades because of his "damd damd old chorea stuff," Guthrie wrote in a last letter to Robinson in June 1955, still his heart was with "my . . . bestest union men and my union maides . . . the only people that I love on this earth, my union hearted army."

When he learned that seven-year-old Naomi Hawes, daughter of one-time Almanac Singers Bess Lomax and Butch Hawes, had been badly burned in a kitchen accident, Guthrie wrote her parents a grief-stricken letter. "The entire letter, a single page, simply repeated the question, 'What can I do? What can I do? What can I do?' " Bess Hawes recalled.

If he could not help Naomi, he could work in the hospital wards, even writing about "my patients"; hospital authorities counted him "cooperative" in his behavior. "I'm lots better off in here than outside," Guthrie confided to an acquaintance, the Communist Party's chairman in Pennsylvania, Steve Nelson. "My chorea has chopped me down too dern dissy to navigate or to walk my long crossytie any more."*

Moreover, Guthrie bragged, he was receiving a sixty-six-dollar-a-month government pension for his "service-connected" disability, his chorea. The monthly stipend helped Anneke and "my gal Reno" to live.

The money alone was not enough to hold their marriage together.

Overwhelmed, Anneke felt unable to cope with Guthrie's illness, and care for a child. And then there loomed Marjorie in Sheepshead Bay, strong, capable Marjorie ready to take up the burden, Marjorie, once more with a man who seemingly understood the unbroken bond between her

---

* The FBI, still doggedly tracking Guthrie, spoke with doctors at Brooklyn State Hospital and learned Guthrie was suffering from "Huntington's Chorea, a chronic neurological condition with occasional psychotic manifestations. It is a deteriorating disease with no known cure." Considering his health and "the lack of reliable firsthand [sic] information reflecting Communist Party membership in the last five years," the special agent in charge of the New York City office recommended to FBI Director J. Edgar Hoover that Guthrie be removed from their watch list. See SAC New York City to the director, J. Edgar Hoover, May 18, 1955; and SAC, New York to Director, FBI, June 3, 1955, both in Guthrie's FBI file.

and her second husband. Wearily, Anneke in October of 1955 would file for divorce.

With Guthrie hospitalized, Marjorie took command, said Henrietta Yurchenko. "I never did see her as a big boss lady taking charge of Woody, but I suppose she did. I *know* she did."

They were bound together, Marjorie and Woody, so much alike that people had mistaken them for brother and sister, daughter Nora Guthrie said. Her eighteen-month courtship with Tony Marra ended, Marjorie made it clear Guthrie was a member of her family when she linked with a new suitor, Al Addeo. She was frank, Nora noted. "She said that he was marrying both of them, and that she came with a 'husband,' that she came with Woody."

As strong as she might be, and as independent, Marjorie said that "in the big city you just can't get around by yourself and you need somebody to help with the children," Mary Jo Edgmon recalled. The new beaus, Edgmon quoted Marjorie, were momentary surrogates for Woody, with whom she had shared a life. "She said, 'Woody was real smart and we could talk, and play together, and create together and these other men, they just weren't men.'"

Attached as she was, Marjorie and the children visited Guthrie virtually every week. In warm weather, they would take Guthrie for a drive or sometimes bring him to the beach. The Sunday visits offered a semblance of a normal family life.

There were other visitors as well: Jack Elliott and his new wife June; Harold Leventhal, the former manager of the Weavers; and a trickle of younger people from Washington Square who came to sing for him.

Leventhal was to be the most important. Born in the South Bronx in 1919, raised in an Orthodox Jewish home by a widowed mother, Leventhal had waffled between the rabbinate and the political Left as a youth. At fifteen, he joined the Young Communist League's Helen Lynch Club, the largest YCL organization in the country. "It was the depression," he explained a lifetime later. "I wanted a solution to the problems. I found socialism and communism at that point as being the hope for the future."

The youngest of five children, Leventhal never forgot about living in a tenement with fetid hallway bathrooms that his mother had cleaned in lieu of rent. He joined the Movement to improve the life of the least. In doing so, this once *yeshiva bocher* decided, "You live by that. . . . I've always felt I've got to be totally honest, to do the best with people I'm working with, and maintain integrity."

An older brother eventually got Leventhal a job as a song plugger for Irving Berlin. When world war intervened, Private Leventhal found himself in the Signal Corps and sent overseas to India.

He joined the Communist Party after the war and was assigned to a New York City branch devoted to music and entertainment professionals. In joining the party, he said, "We never thought the Communist Party would take over the government. But we could influence social security, unions, discrimination, and other issues."

Almost by accident, Leventhal shifted from song plugger to artists' manager. In 1949, he saw the Weavers perform at the Village Vanguard and went backstage to say hello to Pete Seeger, whom he knew through the Communist Party. Seeger, who knew of Leventhal's professional career, promptly asked him if he would manage the Weavers. The newly organized quartet was on the brink of major success and needed someone to watch over their careers and financial interests.

Leventhal agreed. He realized, "The Weavers needed somebody politically aligned with them, because that was so much of the values they were dealing with in their performances."

Shortly after, Leventhal met Guthrie and quickly recognized the improbable bond between the unkempt Oklahoman and the upright New Englander. Guthrie, Leventhal learned, was "already admired for being a songwriter, although certainly not a popular one."

Beginning with their first meeting—when at Seeger's behest, Leventhal gave Guthrie carfare home—Leventhal would assume ever more financial responsibility for Guthrie. "I would ask if he needed anything and would get it," Leventhal explained.

While Guthrie's needs were minimal, something more than the generosity of fellow travelers was necessary to provide for his children. Leventhal conceived the idea of mounting a concert of Guthrie songs "to make some money for the children, and publicize what's happening to Woody."

The concert would be a last gesture of the Old Left to the singer-songwriter who had captured so many of its causes in verse. Leventhal persuaded Millard Lampell to write a script that would link the songs to Guthrie's life. Seeger tapped Lee Hays and Earl Robinson as narrators, then fit singers and songs to Lampell's script. Irwin Silber, formerly with People's Songs, now editing a folk music monthly, *Sing Out!*, suggested a onetime boxing forum, Pythian Hall, on West 70th Street just off Central Park. It was clean, it was convenient, and it was available; as Pete Seeger recalled, "Back in those days, not everybody would rent to us."

Pythian Hall's twelve hundred seats were filled well before curtain time. Silber could sense an excitement, an anticipation running through the audience. Guthrie's illness and hospitalization had transformed him; he was no longer a living presence, Silber said, but a shadowy, almost legendary figure.

In a dark sport jacket, tended by Marjorie's new husband, Al Addeo, Guthrie sat watching the performance that Saturday night, March 17, 1956. Through the evening, Leventhal nervously shuttled from backstage to the Guthrie family's box at stage right, asking, "Are you all right?"

Yes, he was fine, Guthrie repeatedly assured him. The shaking was not too bad.

As the cast repeated the chorus of "This Land Is Your Land" to end the program, Seeger pointed from the stage to Guthrie sitting in the box with his three children and his ex-wife's new husband.

"From the redwood forests to the Gulf Stream waters, this land was made for you and me."

The applause swelled. Prodded by Addeo, Guthrie slowly rose, then stood blinking and swaying, his head cocked to one side. He waved first in tentative gesture to the singers on stage and to the audience, then ever more confidently, and smiling.

"That was the best he'd been," Leventhal said in recollection, "and from there his condition went down."

As the applause ran on, the legend of Woody Guthrie—the banty, brilliant songmaker who had stood for the underdog and downtrodden—crystallized, Silber decided.

The house lights blinked repeatedly. Fearing they would run late, at a cost of five hundred dollars in overtime pay, Leventhal sought to end the concert. Slowly, as if reluctant to end not only an evening but an era, in which all things progressive seemed possible, the audience filed out onto 70th Street.

Shortly after, Marjorie called a meeting at the home of Earl Robinson to decide how to protect the proceeds of the concert, a net of $1,698.50, and Woody's future royalties. Seeger, Hays, Leventhal, Alan Lomax, and Abraham Lincoln Brigade veteran and union organizer Lou Gordon opted to establish a trust fund for Arlo, Joady Ben, and Nora. Seeger, Gordon, and Leventhal were the trustees; Leventhal offered to contribute his time to manage the fund.*

---

* That sum would be equal to approximately $11,118 in 2003 dollars.

Guthrie, hospitalized but alert, reviewed the agreement that turned over to the trust all rights to his songs and publications. Any future income was to be used to pay medical and educational expenses for Arlo, Joady Ben, and Nora. (Creation of the trust also served to prevent state authorities from seizing the income from royalties to pay for Guthrie's hospitalization.)*

Guthrie meanwhile was growing restless. It was spring once more, and he had been confined in Brooklyn State Hospital since September 16, 1954, twenty idle months of no improvement, no relief. Brooklyn State, once his safe haven, had become the "Buller Shitting Housery." As a voluntary patient, Guthrie was free to leave when he wished.

In late May 1956, a scruffy Guthrie made his way to the Central Park West apartment of Harold and Natalie Leventhal. Hours later—Leventhal was never quite certain how long Guthrie had waited—the Leventhals returned to find him slumped outside their door. Invited in, Guthrie sat on the living room couch, heedless when his cigarette fell and burned a hole in the seat cover. He was broke, he told Leventhal.

What else could Leventhal do? He shrugged. "So you give him whatever you've got in your pocket."

Leventhal's ten or twenty dollars did not go far.

On May 28, 1956, Morristown, New Jersey, police arrested Guthrie for trespassing, the local interpretation of "wandering aimlessly on a highway" in a dazed condition. Guthrie sought to explain he was on his way to visit a friend, the poet Walter Lowenfels in Philadelphia, and had missed his bus.†

Guthrie explained to the arresting officers that he was ill and should be taken to a hospital. When the officers called Harold Leventhal at Guthrie's suggestion, Leventhal concurred.

Guthrie spent the night in the Morris County jail. The next morning, after a perfunctory medical examination, Dr. George Comeau determined that Guthrie needed to be restrained "for the welfare of patient and safety

---

* With his agreement, Guthrie effectively denied any benefits to his three children by Mary, whom he erroneously believed had been adopted by Mary's second husband. His youngest child, Lorina Lynn, meanwhile, was to be put up for adoption by Anneke, with Guthrie's blessing. Still there were ties. Marjorie somewhat later contacted the adoptive parents to tell them of the threat of Huntington's disease. As Harold Leventhal put it, "They seemed to want to ignore that, and apparently did not want to have any connection with Woody for this kid."

† There is a tantalizing hint in Guthrie's FBI file that Guthrie may instead have been in New Jersey seeking to visit his daughter Gwen, who had married and moved east. The FBI's often inaccurate field reports noted that Gwen's husband, Frank Lackey, in early 1954 or 1955, sent the unkempt Guthrie away without seeing his daughter.

of others." Judge Nelson K. Mintz committed Guthrie to the New Jersey State Hospital at Greystone Park.

In the mental hospital's reception room, Guthrie was "quiet, cooperative, partly oriented for time and place, [and] delusional." He was cogent enough to repeatedly tell doctors and nurses that he suffered from Huntington's chorea.

"This is just the same way my mother walked. This is just the way my mother acted," he insisted. He also explained that he had been in Brooklyn State Hospital until a few days earlier.

Why did he leave New York? the intake doctor asked.

His third wife had filed for divorce, Guthrie replied. "I thought it would be better for all concerned if I sort of left New York City because I didn't want to cause her too much trouble."

Did he hear voices? the doctor asked. Yes. Jesus and Maria.

Did they accuse you of doing anything wrong? No.

Do you think people are against you? No.

Do you think people talk behind your back? No.

Do you think people stare at you in a funny way? No.

The doctors heard what they wanted to hear:

Mental examination showed patient to be overproductive, circumstantial, rambling and his answers were only partially relevant. He was manneristic and gesturing in a grandiose way and had a silly smile on his face at times. His affect was inappropriate. He stated that he was hearing voices and saw Jesus and Maria talking to him and giving him advise [*sic*] as to what to do. He said he has special abilities in music and has made some ten thousand dollars writing songs.

Doctor M. A. Dolinsky's diagnosis was "Schizophrenic Reaction, Paranoid Type."*

Shortly after Guthrie was committed to Greystone, Fred Hellerman and Harold Leventhal paid a visit. At the asylum, they met first with a staff doctor to learn about Guthrie's condition. The doctor looked through Guthrie's medical record, then began chuckling to himself.

---

* It would take more than six months before doctors took Guthrie at his word and changed their diagnosis to "chronic brain syndrome associated with diseases of unknown or uncertain cause . . . Huntington's Chorea with psychotic reaction."

"This is a very sick man," the doctor offered. "He is delusional. He says he wrote a thousand songs and says he was in movies." The staff had concurred in a diagnosis of schizophrenia.

It was a lovely spring day, Hellerman recalled, so the two visitors took Guthrie for a walk on Greystone's greening lawns. Guthrie was shaky, but otherwise seemingly in good health.

"Are they treating you all right?" Hellerman asked.

"Oh, yeah, the food is swell. People are kind of nice."

"Well, do you need any money?" Hellerman and Leventhal were keen to help.

"You don't have to worry about me. I'm worried about how *you* boys are doing. Out there, if you guys say you're communists, they'll put you in jail.

"But in here, I can get up there and say I'm a communist and all they say is 'Ah, he's crazy.' You know, this is the last free place in America."

Guthrie received a "second run peaceable lease on life" when Marjorie and the children sent him birthday greetings. He was especially grateful for six-year-old "Norydee's own personal hand drawn card to lift up my olde lost sunken sunken down feelings a good ways back up higher than just plain olde normal." His life was in Marjorie's hands, Guthrie wrote.

Anneke had not visited. A month after Guthrie was committed to Greystone, the attending doctors agreed he was competent to agree to put Lorina Lynn up for adoption. Marjorie advised the doctors that Anneke had taken up with a new suitor and was to live in Japan with him.

Though it was a lockdown facility, Guthrie was not entombed at Greystone. He granted interviews to the newspaper reporters who occasionally called. He had fan mail, which first Marjorie and then Nora answered for him. (The best were the letters, particularly from children who wrote to tell him they were singing his songs in school.)

Sunday became Woody's day. Marjorie and her three children would travel to faraway Greystone virtually every Sunday. "It was part of our life and that's what we did," Arlo recalled, "It was just routine." While hospital rules barred youngsters from entering the buildings, growing Arlo sometimes snuck in. Other times, the three children stood on the lawn and waved to mother and father in the window of the ward.

On pleasant days, Nora recalled, she and her two brothers would climb "The Magic Tree" while their parents sat far below. "We were literally able to transcend and go higher than the disease. We were up in the tree this whole time looking down at our parents hugging, kissing and sharing. . . . They had such an intimacy that it almost didn't allow us in."

Arlo, then nine, would connect with his father through music. He counted his favorite moment as the day Woody taught him the heartfelt verses he had cut from "This Land Is Your Land." As Nora put it, "Arlo was really given the torch to continue his guitar playing."

Joady was less taken with the music, she continued, and more with his father's talent for graphic arts. Nora took after her mother, a "Little Marjorie," as she put it, even going so far as to become a dancer in her own right.

Photographer John Cohen, later a member of the influential New Lost City Ramblers string band, on one occasion ferried Guthrie to New York City to attend a folksong festival. When they stopped at Cohen's loft in Greenwich Village, Guthrie ate most of a jar of Cohen's peanut butter. Others took him to Washington Square, where folk singers and musicians gathered on Sunday afternoons for extended jam sessions.

At Marjorie's urging, sister Mary Jo Edgmon traveled by bus for three days to visit in late 1956. "Woody was doing all this walking crazy and stumbling around; he was exactly the way Mama was," she recalled.

There were other visitors: Lee Hays, Hally Wood, and Harold Leventhal, all from his activist days. Additionally, a steady stream of younger singers made the pilgrimage to Greystone, the more faithful among them Ellen and Irene Kossoy, who had sung at the Pythian Hall concert.

For all that, Guthrie yearned to see Marjorie and the children in the summer of 1956, though Marjorie was working at a girls' camp upstate, in Racquette, New York. "Being in here away from you and our kids is absolutely causing me to hurt more here than I can stand." He pleaded with Marjorie to take him from the hospital, "to come get me." He enclosed a printed letter to "Arlo Barlow" in which he asked the nine-year-old to intercede with his mother. "I love alla you so much I want to come out of this old goody hospital and to be your best daddy . . . and to be just as closey to you as I possibly can all the rest of the days of my life time."

Even with daily doses of 100 milligrams of the antianxiety drug Thorazine, Guthrie's moods grew increasingly mercurial. When Marjorie did not come, he petulantly wrote: "No more meetings. No more letters. No more favors. No more helps. No more car rides. No more baths. No more fites. Anneke gets my $. You don't getta penny." Marjorie ignored the letter.

Barely weeks later, he recanted:

"God bless you.

"God help you.

"God save us all.

"Love me, Woody."

For her part, Marjorie felt responsible for her former husband, she wrote to Mary Jo.

> I know from years of living—I am almost 39—that there is no one, not anybody who would take on this responsibility if I don't. And I feel that I cannot really live a happy life unless I know that Woody is being attended to and more than that, that he must feel that he is still a part of life and living.

Guthrie turned inward. News of his father's death in July sparked a prayerful meditation in which he urged Mary Jo to join him "and all of us struggle our best to live such a godlyful kind of earthy life here we will each and all and everyone one of us here enter on into gods great eternal glory at the day of our deathy. Amen Amen."

This was virtually the last legible letter Guthrie would write. The marriage of his oldest daughter, Gwen, and the later birth of a daughter, Guthrie's first grandchild, passed without notice.

He asked for a typewriter, then discovered "I'm just ajerkin here a little too bad, I know, to type up no more good readable goody books anyhow." He asked for a guitar and left it untouched. Harold Leventhal retrieved both.

Greystone became Guthrie's world as his "twitchey chorea [grew] lots more twitchedy than ever before." Case number 65935 slept in Ward 40 at Greystone Park with thirty other men. He spent his days once again as a messman, helping to serve meals and sweeping the floors. Between chores he read aloud from the Bible or from Christian Science literature; his sermons earned him the nicknames "Rabbi" or "Reverend."

He took to thinking of the others in the ward as his patients. He worried that one had a high fever, that another was dying of syphilis; he took pleasure when his "very sickest patient [made] a comeback mentally and bodily and soulful and all."

Guthrie became proprietary about Ward 40. When two "hemosexual" lovers embraced in the bed next to his, Guthrie "pointed out the pair of unnatural lovers" to the ward attendant. The lovers were placed in separate wards.

He advised Marjorie and the children he would have to stay in goody Greystone "to help my doctors all ta make alla my several thousands of sicky people here all feel a little bit better."

Confinement at Greystone was in one way a blessing, he wrote Marjorie in a second letter. "I asked God alla my life to please make me a kind of a divine healer and God put me in a perfect spot here to be an awful busy healer."

Over time, the Sunday visits grew more difficult. Guthrie lost the ability to communicate normally, Arlo said. Though he was cogent, his speech became less intelligible. As father and son, "we never sat down and talked about things important. There was none of that. It was all intuition on my part; my relationship to him is as much in my mind as anything else."*

It fell to the boy to watch over his father, to take him to the bathroom if they were on an outing, to light his cigarettes, and thus to begin smoking himself. Arlo was his father's caretaker. "He always looked like he was going to fall over. He looked like he was going to get burned. He always looked like there was some disaster pending."

Late in 1959 or early the following year, two former Californians, Robert and Sidsel Gleason, learned that Guthrie was confined to Greystone, just a forty-minute drive from their home in East Orange, New Jersey. Twenty and more years earlier, Sidsel Gleason had listened to the Woody and Lefty Lou morning program on KFVD. While she was attracted to Maxine Crissman's voice, she realized it was Woody Guthrie—singing with Maxine or as the Lone Wolf—who was the Okies' favorite. "He was one of those people that just mesmerized you," she said six decades later.

With Marjorie's concurrence, the Gleasons arranged to take Guthrie each Sunday to their home on Arlington Avenue. At least there, the children could see their father. So each Sunday when the Gleasons arrived, "He would get into the car, summer or winter, roll down the windows, and he would say, 'How about a smoke?'"

Once at the Gleasons' fourth-floor apartment, Guthrie would take a long bath while Marjorie and the children, as well as fans of Guthrie, gathered. "A lot of people would come by and would sing and play guitar," so many they eventually had to limit the number to five or six. "Too many people excited Woody," Sidsel explained.

She might give Guthrie a haircut, no more than a trim, or they would answer some of the fan letters he had stuffed into his shirt pockets or his

---

* Marjorie did seek to impart to their children some of her former husband's values. Shortly after he was confined at Greystone, she asked Guthrie to set down his opinions about social conformity. He replied, "I do just try to go by my own God-given voice of my best conscience more than I ever try to listen to hear or to try to always please or to satisfy any word from any man." The undated letter is in Woody Guthrie Archives, Correspondence Series 1, Box 3, Folder 12.

socks. Guthrie dubbed her "Sidewall," because "if it wasn't for his sidewall the wheel wouldn't go around."

Bob Gleason, a carpenter by trade, knew where to shop for the blue chambray work shirts and khaki pants Guthrie liked to wear, clothes he bought with money Oscar Brand sent. (Brand's checks also bought the postage stamps Guthrie used to answer his growing fan mail.) Sidsel cooked Sunday afternoon dinners, especially Guthrie's favorite, a "cowboy stew" of beef heart, liver, kidney, garlic, onion, and canned tomatoes served with hot biscuits.

Guthrie was grateful and uncomplaining, Sidsel told a reporter. He seemingly accepted the disease and his inevitable death. "I have never met a human being that has the courage that he has."

Arlo remembered the weekly visits with affection. "The Gleasons were wonderful. . . . As a kid I would love going to the Gleasons' house. I was always playing my guitar, the three-quarter size Gibson my Dad had bought for me.

"We would sit around playing music while he and my Mom talked and me and my brother and sister would just run around and create havoc."

On warm days, they spent the afternoon outdoors in the garden the Gleasons had created. In cooler weather, they stayed indoors, Guthrie seated in a special chair that Bob had fashioned for him, with cigarettes and a root beer—doctors had forbidden alcohol—within easy reach. Gathered at his feet, the younger singers played Guthrie songs and ballads while he tried to beat time to the music.

There were increasingly more of these acolytes, including a nineteen-year-old dropout from the University of Minnesota, Robert Zimmerman, who arrived amid a New York City snowstorm almost twenty years to the day after Guthrie. In late January or early February 1961, Bob Dylan, as Zimmerman had taken to calling himself, knocked on the door of the home Marjorie had bought in Howard Beach. One of Marjorie's teenage dance students, hired to keep watch over the children, took one look at the young man's work boots and mismatched attire, then politely suggested he come back another time.

Arlo, not yet fourteen, took a liking to Dylan and invited him in. Dylan explained he was from Hibbing, Minnesota, and was looking for Woody.

"I was there as a servant, to sing him his songs," Dylan later explained. "That's all I did. I was a Woody Guthrie jukebox."

Between harmonica tunes, Arlo told him Guthrie was in Greystone but visited the Gleasons on Sunday. The following Sunday, Dylan found his way to East Orange and the Gleason home. Dylan, according to his authoritative biographer, Robert Shelton, found Guthrie "a suffering shell. Guthrie's hands quivered, his shoulders shook involuntarily, and he spoke only in thin, unintelligible rasps."

As Dylan apparently recounted the story, he was at the Gleasons' when Cisco Houston came to say goodbye to his old shipmate. Diagnosed with inoperable stomach cancer, Houston was returning to California to die.

He was forty-two and, with Harold Leventhal's help, on the brink of a solo career. He had recorded his first long-playing record and had just returned from a concert tour of India under the auspices of the Department of State.

Still, Houston was fatalistic. "The situation I'm in," he told Lee Hays,

is much more difficult for friends of mine, people that I know, and people that find out, than it is for me. I don't say this out of bravado. A particular sort of calm comes over you. I don't consider my case nearly as bad as some. When I go out to see Woody, and I see this broken man going in and out, back and forth from his hospital room trembling and shaking . . . the way he faces all this is with tremendous courage.

Now if I were placed in that position, where I had to struggle on for years and years, knowing that there was no hope, it would remain to be seen just how good I would be at it. Perhaps I wouldn't be as good as he is.

When you see someone like that, you just try to be as pleasant as you can. There's nothing you can really say, although it just breaks my heart to look at the guy, and it's tough, it's really tough.

Dylan sat in silent awe among such personal heroes. He came away from this first meeting stunned. That night, in a drugstore on 8th Street in New York City, he wrote a "Song to Woody" set to the tune of Guthrie's "1913 Massacre":

Hey, hey, Woody Guthrie, I wrote you a song
'Bout a funny ol' world that's a-comin' along.
Seems sick an' it's hungry, it's tired an' it's torn,
It looks like it's a-dyin' an' it's hardly been born.

Hey, Woody Guthrie, but I know that you know
All the things that I'm a-sayin' an' many times more.
I'm a-singing' you the song, but I can't sing enough,
'Cause there's not many men that done the things that
    you've done.

Here's to Cisco an' Sonny an' Leadbelly too,
An' to all the good people that traveled with you.
Here's to the hearts and the hands of the men
That come with the dust and are gone with the wind.

In later visits to the Gleason home, Dylan fastened on Jack Elliott, who had returned from a six-year stay in Great Britain, where he had introduced Guthrie's songs to a host of young musicians. Elliott, as he acknowledged in a newspaper interview, "did Woody Guthrie songs exactly the way that Woody did," and was criticized for "being a perfect mimic, aping Woody Guthrie down to the very last movement and gesture and facial expression."

Years before, Guthrie had drawled, "Jack sounds more like me than I do." Now, watching Elliott—whose two made-in-Britain recordings Dylan had repeatedly listened to in Minneapolis—Dylan copied appearance, manner, and gesture.

John Cohen had known Guthrie for as long as eight years and had seen the creeping pace of Huntington's chorea. Later, watching Dylan sing in a Greenwich Village club, "jerking around, tilting his head this way, and making these moves—I'd never seen anything like that except in Woody. When I first saw him, I said, 'Oh, my God, he's mimicking Woody's disease.'"*

Guthrie himself could no longer sing or play an instrument, Sidsel recalled. The involuntary muscular spasms had grown worse over time, particularly in his right arm. "He would hit his forehead with his thumb," she said, "and actually it would be all red and would have scabs on the places where his thumbnail had made holes on his forehead." She learned to stop the spasms by hooking his right thumb in his belt loop.

The weekly visits to the Gleason home ended abruptly when Marjorie moved Guthrie from Greystone back to Brooklyn State Hospital. Forty years

* According to her daughter Nora, Marjorie was furious when Elliott, Dylan, and others imitated Guthrie after the disease had set in. "They heard Huntington's, the slur when singing, talking. In Elliott, Dylan, you hear early Huntington's. Dylan didn't even know the real person. Woody was mythology in his own mind." Nora Guthrie interview, March 10, 2000.

later, Sidsel Gleason still smarted at the loss; she blamed Marjorie for being jealous of the attachment the Gleasons had formed with Guthrie. In truth, Marjorie had sought to transfer Guthrie for more than two years so as to shorten their weekly commute.

Guthrie had spent four years, ten months, and five days at Greystone. In that span, his third wife had put their daughter up for adoption, had divorced him, remarried, and fled the country. Greystone dentists had removed eight of his teeth. Surgeons had repaired hernias on both his left and right sides and performed a hemorrhoidectomy on him. An occupational therapist had put him to work sanding bookends to "help keep him stimulated, afford him an opportunity for approval and recognition and help develop his ego strength." In the next two years Guthrie—described as "neat, quiet and socializes with other patients"—would complete two belts and start work on a potholder.

On April 4, 1961, Woodrow Adversity Guthrie shuffled from the New Jersey State Hospital at Greystone, discharged as "improved."

CHAPTER TWENTY-EIGHT

I Ain't Dead Yet

*T*HE DYING DID not come easily.

"He is failing all the time," Marjorie wrote to Guthrie's sister July 1962. Woody no longer walked, he staggered. While Marjorie and the children continued to take him home to Howard Beach in Queens each Sunday, the visits grew shorter and shorter. "After a few hours he really can't take all the noise, and gets overly excited," Marjorie explained.

The other outings dwindled as well. In the winter of 1961–62, Marjorie and her friend Shirley Fuchs drove Guthrie to visit Arlo in Stockbridge, Massachusetts, where the boy was going to school. Woody dropped a cigarette, which set fire to the back seat of Marjorie's car, and, carsick, he threw up once on the side of the road. She deemed the three-hundred-mile, day-long trip a grand success.

Emboldened without reason by that venture, Marjorie accepted Pete Seeger's invitation to take Guthrie to a cocktail party welcoming Frank Hamilton to the reunited Weavers in the spring of 1962. It would be a small gathering of old friends at a steakhouse on Manhattan's West Side, Seeger assured her. More than that Guthrie could not take.

Guthrie spent the evening slumped in a wheelchair while Seeger tenderly hovered about his former mentor. Guthrie was alert, though speech came only with great effort. When Frank Hamilton, Guthrie's acquaintance from Topanga Canyon, approached, Guthrie's head snapped up, and he croaked with as much excitement as he could summon, "California!"

Henrietta Yurchenko, who had often invited Guthrie to her radio program two decades before, did not immediately recognize Guthrie. His face was drawn, his wiry hair had turned gray. Someone was holding a cigarette to Guthrie's lips, someone else was feeding him slowly.

When Yurchenko approached, Marjorie asked Guthrie if he remembered her. Guthrie could not shape an answer. "Just blink your eyes if you remember her," Marjorie instructed. Guthrie blinked.

"I walked away. And sobbed," Yurchenko said later. "I couldn't help myself, remembering this absolutely marvelous creature who turned words into poetry . . . the life, the sense of justice, I mean, the whole way he expressed himself, with such tenderness and such expressiveness. And there he was, unable to speak.

"My heart was absolutely broken."

Talking became difficult, then impossible for Guthrie by the beginning of 1964. To communicate, Marjorie drew three cards: "YES," "NO," and a question mark. She would pose questions that Guthrie would answer by pointing at a card. At first she used the cards to test his coherence, to prove to the hospital staff Guthrie retained his sanity. Soon the cards became their only means of communication.

Eventually, Guthrie was unable to control his arms, unable to halt the involuntary spasms. The cards no longer worked so Marjorie devised a simple system of one or two eye blinks for yes and no.

"I changed the number occasionally," she wrote in a later pamphlet,

to be sure we were still communicating. In this way I learned that there was a whole man locked up inside this shell of a person. I learned that he had no physical pain, although his nervous system was deteriorating and affected him in many ways. He could not feel or taste, which was why he wanted more seasoned foods, candy, and strong coffee.

Marjorie continued to take Guthrie home on Sunday afternoons until the summer of 1965. "It was pretty tough during that year just to carry him over my arm, but he liked coming home and listening to records or just lying in the sun in the yard or drinking gobs of milk and munching hotdogs," she wrote Stetson Kennedy in Florida.

For all he ate—at a sitting he might down six of Nathan's finest franks without the buns—he continued to lose weight. Osteomyelitis from a bone chip in his elbow took grueling months to heal during the summer of 1965 and left him severely weakened. Bedridden or physically tied into his wheelchair, he was barely able to stand after that dark summer.

Because of his condition, Guthrie could no longer leave the hospital. Marjorie invented exercises to build up his thigh muscles and enable him to walk. Weeks later he was able to take a few steps away from the wheelchair, turn, and shuffle back. It was a momentary triumph.

By early 1966, Guthrie weighed no more than 100 pounds, down from the 125 pounds he had weighed when he was confined to Greystone nine years earlier.

Matt Jennings, Guthrie's friend from Pampa and onetime member of the Corncob Trio, visited Guthrie in Brooklyn State while on his way from El Paso to a vacation in Europe. More than thirty years later, the memory of that visit was vivid, and painful.

> When I walked in—and I'm not a person who shocks real easy—he was layin' in that bed, shaking all over, and he was just skin and bones. He was just like these pictures from Germany, starved people, all skin and bones. And his arms and hands were moving, and his feet. I lit a cigarette and held it to his lips 'cause he had even lost control of his lips, and can't take a drag on it. But he didn't want me to take it away. I could see he was inhaling through his nostrils and suckin' that smoke up just as hard as he could. . . . I went over to the window and said my silent goodbyes.

Despite his condition, Guthrie remained Charley's optimistic son. Marjorie would periodically ask, "Do you want to live?" Guthrie would answer that he did.

"I guessed his desire was to see what was going to happen next," Marjorie explained.

When she asked, "What do you do here all day, think about the past?," he would nod.

"Do you worry about the future?"

Guthrie would smile and shake his head. Memories, she guessed, were enough to keep him going—that and "his stubborn sense of pride," Marjorie told a reporter for the *New York Post*.

Guthrie had good days and bad in Brooklyn State, unresponsive one day, alert the next. "I find no pattern to his responses, sometimes good, sometimes not so good, and thus it goes from one week to another. It is heartbreaking to see him this way," Marjorie acknowledged.

In April 1966, Stewart Udall, the secretary of the Department of the Interior, presented Guthrie a citation for the twenty-six songs he had written in May 1941 for the Bonneville Power Administration. Udall announced at the same time the BPA was to name a small power distribution station along the Columbia River after Guthrie. In a letter to Guthrie, he wrote that the double honor was "in recognition of the fine work you have done to make our people aware of their heritage and the land."

The Washington ceremony was symbolic. Though Guthrie hardly suffered for his politics—the FBI and its handmaiden Un-American Activities Committee had dismissed him as terminally ill and therefore of no great consequence—Udall's presence at the ceremony and the certificate itself marked Guthrie's rehabilitation.*

While Moe Asch termed the ceremony in Washington "a great occasion," some of the more militant survivors of the Movement were angered by the award. The former People's Songs functionary Irwin Silber complained, "They're taking a revolutionary, and turning him into a conservationist."

Some of the anger may have stemmed from the fact that the militants were themselves unable to resume their careers.

Though Senator Joseph McCarthy was discredited by a Senate censure in December 1954—his name would be permanently attached to the baseless political smear and to the era in which it flourished—the blacklist lived on.

Even the September 1956 perjury conviction of Harvey Matusow did not lift the ban on those Matusow had falsely named as Communists. (Matusow himself was to serve four years in prison, then readily secure jobs in publishing and broadcasting; meanwhile, those he had accused, many falsely, continued to find meaningful work hard to come by. As far as Guthrie was concerned, Matusow maintained, "his illness negated the impact of the blacklist.")†

---

* At the first annual Woody Guthrie Festival in Okemah on July 18, 1998, Arlo, by then a long-experienced performer, commented on the release two weeks before of a postage stamp honoring Guthrie: "For a man who fought all his life against being respectable, this comes as a stunning defeat."

† Guthrie's friends who were either radicals or Communists endured blacklisting for a decade or more. Otto Preminger cast Will Geer in 1961 in the film *Advise and Consent*, Geer's first motion picture in nine years. He would go on to play Grandpa Walton on television's *The Waltons*. Similarly, Millard Lampell and Earl Robinson found their way back to Hollywood, the one as a scriptwriter, the other as a composer. Yet even as their fortunes improved, Pete Seeger's fell. Blacklisted since 1952, Seeger was hailed before the House Committee on Un-American Activities ostensibly investigating subversive activities in the entertainment industry. Questioned about the songs he sang, for whom he sang, and his political beliefs, Seeger declined to answer on principle. Seeger might have shielded himself behind the Fifth Amendment's guarantee against self-incrimination, but chose instead to assert a First Amendment right of free speech and free association. He was cited in 1956 for contempt of Congress and convicted on ten counts the same day Guthrie left Greystone for Brooklyn State Hospital. Facing a year in prison, Seeger appealed, and in 1962 a three-judge panel of the U.S. Court of Appeals reversed the conviction on procedural grounds. Even then, he found himself barred from lucrative television appearances; not until February 1968, with an invitation from the Smothers Brothers to appear on their television show, did Seeger prevail.

Guthrie was a radical of the 1940s. He had sought no revolution, no violent overthrow of the government. Yet the Red hunters of the 1960s, gripped by fear or blinded by ideology, saw no more in the man than "Guthrie the radical." (As late as 1967, the American Legion managed to kill a proposed Woody Guthrie Day in his hometown of Okemah, Oklahoma, on the grounds that Guthrie was a Communist.)*

By 1966 Guthrie was no longer a threat. He was bedridden in his forty-man ward, ever more weakened, often unable to swallow. Marjorie arranged to have him moved to Creedmore State Hospital in Queens in July at the suggestion of a doctor who was studying Huntington's chorea patients there. Dr. John Whittier could offer no hope of a cure at Creedmore, only somewhat more private quarters.

Marjorie and Shirley Fuchs continued to visit. They would dole out bits of family gossip and news of the neighbors or the children. Guthrie could only smile and nod his appreciation.

For a while Guthrie seemed to improve slightly, Marjorie wrote to his younger brother George in California. George took it as an omen: didn't folks get better before they died?

In the last week of September, Guthrie came down with pneumonia for the second or third time. When Marjorie and Shirley visited on October 2, "he heard us come into his room, opened his eyes, and made a grunting sound when I asked him if he would like some water. I fed him a spoon of water to wet his dry lips. He was still a whole person, but this person was dying and he knew it."

At her request, a hospital chaplain recited the Lord's Prayer while Guthrie and Marjorie looked at each other.

"The Lord is my shepherd. I shall not want."

Guthrie listened with his eyes shut, then opened them again when Marjorie stroked his forehead. She kissed him goodbye. When she left the room, Marjorie wrote later, she knew it was for the last time.

---

* David A. Noebel, a professor of biblical studies at American Christian College and a trustee of the militantly anti-Communist Christian Crusade, saw a sinister link between the Communists' use of folk music through Guthrie and Seeger, the coming of the Beatles, and the rise of rock and roll as late as 1974. "The combination of the dangerous beat of rock 'n' roll with the potentially dangerous lyrics of folk music . . . alone could spell the doom of the United States of America, for no nation can long endure with its younger generation singing itself into defeatism, pessimism, a peace-at-any-price mentality, disarmament, appeasement, surrender, fear of death, hatred toward the South, atheism, immorality, drugs, revolution and negation of patriotism." Of Guthrie he wrote, "The feeling was that what Marx wrote and Lenin did, Woody sings!" See Noebel's *The Marxist Minstrels: A Handbook on Communist Subversion of Music* (Tulsa, Okla.: American Christian College Press, 1974), pp. 139, 196.

Guthrie died at 7:20 A.M. the next morning, Tuesday, October 3, 1967. He was fifty-five years old. He had spent the last thirteen years and seventeen days in state mental hospitals, essentially untreated, wasting away slowly.

Following Harold Leventhal's directions, Guthrie's daughter Sue, legally of age and next of kin, ordered the body removed to Greenwood Cemetery in Brooklyn, where it was cremated the following day. Meanwhile Leventhal was calling Pete Seeger on tour in Japan, Mary in El Paso, Guthrie's sister Mary Jo, Will Geer, Millard Lampell—"whoever's number I had." He also alerted the wire services and the *New York Times*.

The response was overwhelming. Within two hours of Guthrie's death, top-of-the-hour news broadcasts over the country reported it. All three television network news broadcasts that evening carried the story, CBS and NBC showing photographs of Guthrie and playing his music. The *Times* ran a thousand-word obituary, crediting Guthrie's "profound influence on American folk singing."

Leventhal was stunned by the outpouring. "I guess none of us ever really knew the great influence that Woody had," he wrote to Seeger.

As Guthrie had instructed, there was to be no funeral, no solemn service. After all, what church did this reader of world religions belong to? What service would be appropriate for a man who jokingly wrote "All" when asked his religious preference?

The family grieved privately. Nora, the youngest of Guthrie's children with Marjorie, recalled they were stoic. Nora returned to college the day after her father's death. "There was a long period of time where I felt that I wasn't allowed to cry. I think my brothers felt the same way," she said.

Her mother, said Nora, was conflicted about their father's death. "I could tell that she was really relieved, because he was in bad shape at the end." At the same time, Marjorie felt Woody's absence. "She really missed him in her waking life."

Though Guthrie and Marjorie were long divorced, "she never stopped loving him," Marjorie's friend and sometime coworker Irma Bauman said. Marjorie acknowledged as much in a letter to Anneke shortly after she met Guthrie. "To this day Woody knows that I do love him very much and maybe more just because I know that we can not be together. . . . I think Woody knows even now that loving his children and, yes, even me is a part of his life forever after."

There remained for Marjorie and the three children one task. Greenwood Cemetery delivered Guthrie's ashes in a container more like a coffee can than an urn. As she had promised, she intended to strew his ashes into the ocean along Coney Island.

On a blustery fall day, the family picked its way along the jetty that marked a fanciful boundary between Seagate and Coney Island. First was the problem of opening the can, solved when Marjorie used a bottle opener to puncture the sealed tin. But when they tried to shake the ashes into the ocean, the small holes clogged.

Frustrated, Arlo finally cocked his arm and threw can and ashes as far as he could into the surf. The container bobbed momentarily before it sank.

All they could do was shrug. As Nora put it, smiling, "Woody did not go gently; he went humorously into that good night."

Months later, Mary Josephine and sister-in-law Ann Guthrie, Roy's widow, designed a memorial marker for Woody that was later laid in the family plot in the cemetery just outside the northeast limits of Okemah. On the bronze plaque facing west, set in the hillside next to Clara, 1904–1918, was a reproduction of a cartoon Guthrie had drawn of himself, legs crossed, playing the guitar. The plaque read:

Woodrow Wilson "Woody" Guthrie
1912–1967
BOUND FOR GLORY

CHAPTER TWENTY-NINE

Woody's Children

"WE BROKE DOWN IN TEARS after the memorial concert," Harold Leventhal acknowledged later, "realizing this was *it*." Woody Guthrie, hospitalized for the last thirteen years of his life, dying by inches, was finally gone.

Leventhal had arranged the concert in Guthrie's memory at Carnegie Hall in January 1968. The performers represented some of the major figures in the burgeoning folk music revival: Guthrie's friends of old—Pete Seeger, Brownie McGhee, and Sonny Terry—and younger singers Guthrie had inspired, including Judy Collins, Bob Dylan—in his first performance since a near fatal motorcycle accident—Richie Havens, Odetta, Tom Paxton, and Arlo Guthrie, launched on a singing career of his own. Actors Will Geer and Robert Ryan narrated the script adapted by Millard Lampell from his earlier "California to the New York Island." Their stature was a reflection of Guthrie's importance to the revival.

The proceeds from that concert and a later one in the Hollywood Bowl went to a committee organized by Marjorie to combat Huntington's disease. Distressed by Woody's treatment and the sheer lack of knowledge about the disease, she had first located six other families nursing Huntington's victims, and then enlisted Creedmore's Dr. John Whittier as medical advisor. Here was a cause to which she could devote herself.

"Everything she did from that day on was in relationship to Huntington's," Nora said. "She couldn't just be a mom," Nora noted. "She couldn't be known as Nora's mother. She was *Marjorie*, Woody's wife."

Supported by successive husbands, Lou Cooper and Martin Stein, Marjorie gave up her dance studio and devoted herself to the Committee to Combat Huntington's Disease. She was dynamic, bright, charming, and persuasive.

With all the determination she had demonstrated as a dancer and a teacher, Marjorie lobbied legislators for increased funding for research about all neurogenetic diseases. (To get through secretarial barriers or to reach possible donors, Marjorie would ask resisting secretaries how old they were. "If they're under thirty, I say I'm Arlo's mother. If they're over thirty, I say I'm Woody's wife.") Marjorie argued for social services and physical and speech therapy for the thirty thousand Americans who had the disease. She traveled on money raised by Leventhal to England, Germany, and Australia to set up similar organizations.

Eventually, researchers supported by the committee would locate the gene for Huntington's and develop a blood test for determining if a person is at risk. While doctors have found some drugs that alleviate both the psychiatric and the physical symptoms of the disease, there has been no cure. The Huntington's Disease Society, a much bigger successor to Marjorie's committee, continues to sponsor research into the causes and amelioration of the disease.

The work with the Committee to Combat Huntington's Disease consumed Marjorie until her death in 1983 at age sixty-five. All the while, she was terrified her children would inherit the disease, daughter Nora said. Marjorie insisted they were to dance and do physical activities so that they would be in good shape if they were ever afflicted.

As it happened, none of her three surviving children would contract the disease.*

Mary Guthrie, Woody's first wife, was not so fortunate. She would care for Gwendolyn, the oldest daughter, who suffered a shattering mental breakdown in 1966 and was diagnosed with Huntington's two years later. Gwen's younger sister, Sue, was stricken with Huntington's in 1972. Sue was eventually unable to care for either herself or her young son. She gave the boy to her husband and moved in with a man willing to attend her. Gwen died in 1976, Sue in 1978. Both were just forty-one.

Decades later, Mary still mourned her daughters and her son Bill, killed at age twenty-three in an auto-train accident in Pomona, California. Bill died literally within hailing distance of the Route 66 his father had first traveled to California in 1937.

Tragedy stalked the children of Woody Guthrie. Cathy, the child he had nicknamed "Stackabones," was dead, fatally burned in a fire twenty years earlier. Her death had seemingly drained her father of creative energy; cer-

---

* Arlo and Nora declined to take the test developed to determine if an individual is carrying the gene for Huntington's. Joady Ben, who did, came up negative. At this writing, Arlo is fifty-six and Nora fifty-three; both are well beyond the usual onset of the disease.

tainly there were few notable works from him after that. Marjorie too grieved. "Every time she talked about Cathy for the rest of her life she cried," said daughter Nora.

Lorina Lynn, Guthrie's last born, put up for adoption by Anneke as an infant, in 1973 also died in an auto accident. She was just nineteen. Only Arlo, Joady Ben, and Nora escaped premature deaths.

Under Harold Leventhal's management, the Guthrie Children's Trust Fund and the later Woody Guthrie Publications prospered. In late 1964, Elektra Records issued an edited version of Guthrie's 1941 Library of Congress interview with Alan Lomax. The following year, Robert Shelton edited a collection of Guthrie's *Daily Worker* columns and unpublished essays under the title *Born to Win*. Buoyed by the folk music revival among college students—and particularly by Pete Seeger's unflagging advocacy of Woody the songwriter—Guthrie's reputation spread steadily beyond the parochial confines of the Old Left.

Canny promotion of Guthrie's songs by music publisher Howie Richmond added steadily to the total. (In a business hardly celebrated for upstanding ethics, Richmond treated Guthrie honestly, Leventhal said in a 1998 interview.) Richmond essentially allowed free use of Guthrie's works in school texts—including the increasingly popular "This Land Is Your Land." He was effectively building a fan base; sixty years after they were made, Guthrie's recordings of the 1940s continue to sell; in turn, they too perpetuate Guthrie's memory.

As early as 1963 there were plans to make a film of *Bound for Glory*. Not until 1975 did Leventhal, acting as the producer, get a script he considered workable, and even then the resulting motion picture seemed inadequate to the subject. Despite that, the film was nominated for five Academy Awards, including Best Picture, and won two: for Haskell Wexler's cinematography and Leonard Rosenman's adaptations of Guthrie's songs.

When Nora, the last of Marjorie's children, turned twenty-one, the trust fund was dissolved and its copyrights turned over to a new Woody Guthrie Publications. Marjorie owned the bulk of the stock, the children owned most of the rest. Leventhal, who had never taken a fee for managing the earlier trust fund on the grounds "it wasn't something that kept me busy every day," received a 5 percent interest and a manager's fee.

In a 1999 interview, Leventhal said with some pride, "Guthrie hasn't written since 1952, yet for forty-eight years, the royalties have increased every year." In the first years, the annual income ranged between $10,000 and $15,000, most of it from the Weavers' record sales. Annual income from royalties topped $100,000 in 1999—that to a man who Leventhal estimated had never made more than $50,000 in his entire working life.

Guthrie might have made much more if wealth had been his goal, Leventhal noted. "He never strayed in his lifetime from the social consciousness of what he stood for. Woody, like Pete Seeger, would not have abandoned his social conscience to get to the charts."

Ironically, his very lack of financial success would prove to be a part of the legend of Woody Guthrie.

Thirty-five years after his death, Guthrie's reputation has grown to mythic proportions, and as with all myths, the unpleasant, the inconvenient, the less-than-heroic has been shorn from the image. As early as 1972, Millard Lampell pointed out, "The problem is to keep the mass media from turning Woody into a precious folk hero."

It would be an impossible task. "The more urban we become," folklorist Archie Green argued, "the more we have to worship a rural past."

His own generation fast dying, Guthrie's reputation as a poet-songwriter seems secure. Newspapers commonly refer to him without an identifying tag like "Okie balladeer" or even "folk singer"; readers are expected to know who this unidentified "Woody" was.

By nature, legends are spare. By the time of his death, Guthrie had been refashioned in the popular press as "a good and simple man who brightly sang his sound of music through the agonies of the Dust Bowl Exodus and the Great Depression like an unwanted child of the Trapp Family," grumbled folklorist John Greenway.

However, the elevation of Woodrow Wilson Guthrie began well before his death. In 1960, an adoring Robert Shelton, later to herald the coming of Bob Dylan, wrote of Guthrie:

He really is too short to be a giant. He's almost too lean and delicate-faced to be a hero. He is terribly ungrammatical for a poet. He's got too flat and inconsequential a voice to be considered a great singer.

Despite all the inconsistencies, Woodrow Wilson Guthrie is all these things: a giant of a humanist, a hero of the American little man, a poet of major proportions and a singer and composer of some of our greatest songs.

Noting that Guthrie's music was popular throughout Western Europe and in as unlikely a place as India, Shelton's rhapsody continues:

A little hero-worship of him might be in order in the United States today. It can only serve to restore him to the proper place he deserves. . . . The name and work of Guthrie need to be touted today as never before. For he represents the best of an honest, creative tradition, a stunningly positive pride in nation and people that he best expressed in "This Land Is Your Land," which might be called America's folk national anthem.

For every critical action, there is an equally critical reaction. Feminist critic and folklorist Ellen Stekert scored Robert Shelton, who "waxed enthusiastic to the absurd point of calling Guthrie 'a major American literary figure.' The sad fact is that Guthrie produced reams of abominable prose and ditties, only the smallest fraction of which is aesthetically worth anything either in the folk culture from which he came or in the urban culture to which he wanted at times to belong."*

Stekert, relentless in her assessment of both Shelton and Guthrie, fails to see the humor, the self-mockery, the dry wit in Guthrie's poetry. In her opinion, he is simplistic in his politics. "Like a child he often wished for the 'one word' which would make everything right," she argued.

Why not? Guthrie believed that a singular evil, unbridled capitalism, was responsible for the plight of the Okies and the boomers and the 'croppers, *his* people. Why not a singular cure?

"His writings," Stekert continued, "reflect his time, not his art; his works are social documents, not literature."

Others would disagree. Newspaper columnist and social critic Murray Kempton argued, "He had the range of talents that intimate the possibility of genius without any of them being transcendent enough to quite realize it. He belongs less to music than to literature."

Much of Guthrie's output was agitprop, stultifying *pièces d'occasion*, sung once, if at all, and probably forgotten. Most of the extant poetry is tuneless; he recorded fewer than half of the estimated twelve hundred songs in the Guthrie archive; the melodies are lost for the balance.

At the same time, a good deal of Guthrie's writing, particularly the overnight essays he tapped out on his Smith-Corona portable, is worthy

---

* Shelton's anthology of Guthrie essays and poems, *Born to Win*, also brought forth the first harsh criticism of Guthrie the writer. Stekert, of Wayne State University, dismissed the book as "a shoddy conglomeration of rambling, repetitious, often incoherent, and incredibly poor prose and poetry. . . . [Guthrie] is clearly not a great literary figure," she concluded. *Western Folklore* 25 (1966), pp. 274-276.

stuff. It is literate, it is often humorous, it can be gripping, but because the pieces are short, they do not go far to enhance his *literary reputation*.

Perhaps Guthrie's works are both literature and social documents at the same time. His best work, singer-songwriter Bruce Springsteen noted, "had a spiritual center amidst the sense of fun, the tough optimism." Speaking at a 1996 concert on the occasion of Guthrie's induction into the Rock and Roll Hall of Fame, Springsteen continued, "He took you out of yourself and got you thinking about the next guy, thinking about your neighbor." Stekert notwithstanding, that is exactly what literature does.

There is less dispute about Guthrie's role in shaping American popular music. Critic Nat Hentoff equated Guthrie's influence on popular music with that of the equally fabled saxophonist Charlie Parker on jazz. Hentoff argued that after Parker and Guthrie, contemporary jazz and urban folk music were not the same.

Guthrie's achievement as a magnetic force is all the more remarkable because of his musical limitations, Hentoff argued. "No instrumental virtuoso by any means, and a singer of limited range and color, Woody nonetheless was his own most compelling interpreter, there being no way to separate the music from the man who mined the American experience so widely and deeply."

Guthrie's impact on successive singers and songwriters was profound. As one of them, Tom Paxton, put it, "The most important thing Woody gave us was courage to stand up and say the things we believe."

Among those who have acknowledged their debt to Guthrie were not only Dylan, The Band, Joan Baez, and Judy Collins, but Phil Ochs, Jerry Garcia, Country Joe McDonald, David Crosby, and Graham Nash. Guthrie also influenced country musicians as well; "outlaws" like Willie Nelson shared his fierce independence. In Great Britain, probably through Jack Elliott's recordings, a pair of Liverpudlians, John Lennon and Paul McCartney, were influenced by Guthrie. "I love Woody Guthrie and really admire the kind of songs he writes," McCartney told Harold Leventhal.

Dylan remains the most influential of Woody's "children." "He was the artist who singlehandedly introduced the works of Woody Guthrie to rock. From Dylan flowed Guthrie's social and political consciousness and his penchant for writing topical songs," rock and roll historian Robert Santelli noted.*

---

* Over a forty-year career, Dylan has recorded more than thirty of Guthrie's songs, according to Matthew Zuckerman (zook@globalnet.co.uk). As late as July 2000, having gone through a series of personal musical mutations, Dylan recalled the young man he once was and sang in concert his "Song to Woody."

A generation later, a handful of singers continues to follow Guthrie's lead, though the social concerns that he expressed in song have been generally replaced by younger artists awash in angst. Still, there are significant performers who readily acknowledge a debt to Guthrie and share his vision of social responsibility: Bruce Springsteen, Tom Waits, the Indigo Girls, Bob Geldof (who named his band "The Boomtown Rats" after reading *Bound for Glory*), and more recently, Ani DeFranco and Billy Bragg.

If Guthrie, Alan Lomax, Pete Seeger, and the Almanacs failed to create a workers' music, they did succeed in bringing folk music to a wider audience. Subsequent generations would interweave "folk songs and the folk idiom into the entire fabric of American music and cultural life." Guthrie played a major role in that grand accomplishment.

An important figure in that revival, Guthrie has become an iconic figure. He is the subject of academic theses and conference papers; details of his early life and songs are woven into studies of the Great Depression, of the politics of the 1930s, and the American Left. Even there the mythic intrudes, when Guthrie is termed "a bardic voice" who seems "in the context of the vastness of the American experience to have transmitted, adapted, and created bodies of song which capture and thus 'represent' the voice of the folk."

In doing so, one young scholar argued, Guthrie continued the transcendental idealism stretching from Emerson and Thoreau to Whitman. He reflected their argument "for an American culture which is independent from that of Europe and reflects the ideals of democratic brotherhood." If his stature as a transcendentalist was unrecognized, it was because Guthrie couched his philosophy in the words of a common man rather than of scholarly discourse.

His literary reputation seems less secure, grounded as it is almost entirely on his inventive autobiography, *Bound for Glory*. World war, Cathy's death in 1947, the onset of Huntington's before 1950, all conspired to thwart a career as a significant American writer. Guthrie had a great ear for the authentic voice—as his daughter Nora said, "He made himself invisible so that he could catch everything that was going 'round." Yet the unrelieved dialect that marks his only other published novel, *Seeds of Man*, is tedious and the book slow going.

It is in his songs and poems, that is, songs without music, that Guthrie's genius glistens. In those works are the passion and compassion, the anger and the humor that make him a significant poet.

His achievement was to capture a part of the American experience, the lives of people who had previously been excluded from public view, and he did so in as honest a telling as he could fashion. If he sometimes offended those who fancied the United States a perfect union, for perhaps ten years, from 1937 to 1947, he never wavered.*

His later traveling companion Jack Elliott understood Guthrie's singular strength. "Woody was too honest, too real, for people to tolerate. They wanted things sugared-up. Woody wouldn't do that."

Guthrie, praised for his authenticity, was inauthentic himself. Perhaps it is in the nature of performers to adopt a stage persona; Jack Elliott, Bob Dylan, and Guthrie's son Arlo—born like Elliott "on a 5,000-acre cattle ranch" in Brooklyn, later given speech lessons to lose the local accent, bar mitzvahed on the Lower East Side of Manhattan—all would end up on stage with a generic Western drawl.

Guthrie posed early on as the untutored Okie, the old settler who verbally bested the city slicker in "The Arkansas Traveler" routine; it worked in Los Angeles on KFVD. But listeners were in on the joke, which made it all the more appealing.

If later the Movement—party members and fellow travelers alike— wanted proletarians, Guthrie would be a prol. His drawl thickened. He dropped the final d's and t's in his otherwise careful speech. On stage, he told long, sly stories in the manner of his idol, Will Rogers. Offstage he was monosyllabic, relying on a fey smile, a snicker, or a droll comment.

Born into the middle class, Guthrie turned his back on the very values that drove his go-getter father, Charley. The cause was not merely the breakup of his family with the hospitalization of his mother and his father's long recuperation. After all, brothers Roy and George and sister Mary Jo settled into solid middle-class lives. Instead, brother Woodrow deliberately chose to roam the countryside, finding honest men to emulate in Hoovervilles and farm labor camps, in Skid Row bars and union hiring halls. He had to become one of them, before he could become their champion.

In the cotton rows of California's Imperial Valley, in the fields and orchards of the Central Valley, twenty-five-year-old Woody Guthrie first recognized the social and economic inequities that burdened the migrants.

---

* Anthropologist and folk singer John Greenway, the first to accord Guthrie serious scholarly attention, noted, "The literary men tell us that every poet has his ten years. Guthrie had his decade; before 1939 he was not yet Woody Guthrie; after 1948 he was no longer Woody Guthrie." Greenway, "The Anatomy of a Genius: Woody Guthrie." _Hootenanny Magazine_ 1, No. 3 (May 1964), p. 17. Courtesy of Ron Cohen.

Only later, in early 1939, did he adopt the Socialist credo: "The highest social priority must go to the least fortunate."

The adult Woody Guthrie straddled two social classes, two political camps. "Given the fact that Guthrie was at least as much a middle-class leftist intellectual as he was a rural folk bard," wrote critic H. R. Stoneback, "we might christen his manner and mode 'Marxist Local Color.'"

Here was more irony, sometime factory worker and later folklorist Archie Green pointed out. "Guthrie is remade into an archetonic wanderer, a hobo, a blithe spirit.

"If he is remembered, he will be remembered that way. The irony is that so many of those values are so antithetical to the rigid, puritanical Communist Party values that he espoused."

According to Green, Guthrie *needed* the Communist Party's structure as something firm to hold onto. At the same time, "in terms of the party's Popular Front strategy, discovering Guthrie was worth ten million dollars, a hundred million."

Guthrie represented a synthesis of populism, religious values, and a fierce love of country, overlaid with Marxist concepts of the dictatorship of the proletariat and Communist Party leadership as infallible. While he was less disciplined than members of the party, he nonetheless followed the party line, even to the extent of endorsing Communist North Korea's invasion of autocratic South Korea.

There were those who could not forgive Guthrie either his politics or his lifestyle. Not until 1971 did the city of Okemah finally honor the most famous of its native sons, and then it did so almost furtively. On Guthrie's birthday, Marjorie and Arlo presented the Okemah library with a collection of Guthrie's long-playing albums, as well as a selection of his books. According to the organizer, Mrs. V. K. Chowning, "Details of the program were kept secret so as not to gain undue publicity which might attract hordes of people to flood Okemah."

A wire service story reported the unwanted hordes as "hippies."

Four years after his death, Guthrie could still stir a tiny tempest.

The 1971 event was the second attempt to gift the library with the material. The first, four years earlier, fell afoul of the militantly anti-Communist American Security Council's vigilance against all things labeled "Un-American." Guthrie's Communist affiliations marked him as a man "who betrayed the conservatism of rural, east-central Oklahoma."

Guthrie's fans in Okemah did manage in 1972 to persuade the city council to adorn the third of the three town water towers with the legend:

"Okemah, Home of Woody Guthrie." (The other two towers, in a fit of local humor, read "Hot" and "Cold.")

The State of Oklahoma relented enough in April 1997 to name Guthrie to a new Oklahoma Music Hall of Fame. Finally, in July 1998, Okemah mounted the first annual Woody Guthrie Festival, a three-day array of concerts by musicians paying homage to Okemah's most celebrated citizen, capped by the unveiling of a bronze bust of Guthrie.*

It is in the nature of myth and legendry to inflate the hero's importance. So too with Guthrie, who has been called "unquestionably the most important American folk singer of the Twentieth Century." He is not. He can be described as unquestionably the most important writer-performer of songs that expressed a personal political view. With the exception of "Hard, Ain't It Hard," Guthrie's most popular, most often recorded songs are not traditional songs at all, but songs and ballads of his own composition. Those works inspired dozens of young musicians to follow his lead, to take up the cause for social justice at home and peace abroad.

Neither can it be said that he "did more than any other single musician to launch a tradition of American folk music." That might describe Peter Seeger, who, blacklisted, spent more than a decade playing before growing audiences at colleges, churches, and gatherings of 1960s activists. He encouraged the notion that anyone could play an instrument and sing songs for their own enjoyment without regard to professional standards. In doing so, he transformed tens, perhaps hundreds of thousands of music consumers into music makers. Seeger is aware of that achievement; he himself described it as his most important work in an interview in 1998.

The image of Woody Guthrie Remembered is composed of his legendary wanderings, his songs and autobiography, and the looming tragedy of Huntington's. Had he not been stricken with the disease, just what he would have written, what he would have become can only be conjecture. Gordon Friesen, himself an avowed activist *cum* Communist, maintained that by the 1960s his old friend "would have been more of a poet. I think he sidetracked his poetic creativity because of his strong sense of the need

---

* Not everyone could put aside Guthrie's politics. In the early 1980s, the University of Tulsa scotched plans for a Woody Guthrie show when confronted with Guthrie's radical past. As late as 1999, a decade after the end of the Cold War, Oklahoma City's Cowboy Museum declined to open a Smithsonian Institution touring exhibition devoted to Guthrie's life and music. (Guthrie's political beliefs reportedly offended the museum's primary benefactor, Edward K. Gaylord, the very conservative publisher of the *Daily Oklahoman*.) The Autry Museum of Western Heritage, just two miles from Guthrie's first home in California, inaugurated the show on June 24, 1999. It was still touring cities large and small two years later.

for immediate communication to the masses of the people, not only in his songs but in his other writings."

Perhaps. By the 1960s, the Communist Party was shattered, its authority over members and fellow travelers discredited. The spirit of American radicalism had passed to a new generation with largely new issues: civil rights, environmental protection, feminism, and perhaps most of all, an end to the bloody war in Vietnam. Guthrie would have been comfortable in any of those causes.

His record on civil rights is clear; so too his opposition to wars he judged imperial. Though Guthrie deemed it his mission to propagate freely and widely, Marjorie taught him "the women are equal and they may be ahead of the men." Similarly, Guthrie in 1941 sang the praises of the massive Columbia River project because it offered the promise of economic prosperity—cheap electricity, irrigation, and jobs for the unemployed. Six decades later, the Army Corps of Engineers was studying a proposal to remove four of the dams built along the Snake River to allow depleted salmon stocks to recover. At the same time, "to boost environmental awareness," Target Stores was using "This Land Is Your Land" as the music for radio commercials. It would be ironic if Guthrie's songs were to outlast the concrete that inspired them.

Predictions of immortality tend to be fallible, yet Guthrie's songs continue to resonate even in an era of videos and celebrity flash.

"This Land," virtually the unofficial national anthem, will surely persevere. "Roll on, Columbia, Roll on," Washington State's official "folk" song, is routinely taught in its public schools. Guthrie's marvelously silly children's songs, which offer a kid's-eye view of the world, are a nursery school fixture. "Philadelphia Lawyer" and "Oklahoma Hills" remain country-and-western standards. Some of the dust bowl ballads—"Pretty Boy Floyd," "Do-Re-Mi," and "So Long" among them—endure. "Pastures of Plenty" and "Union Maid" persist, and perhaps "Reuben James," though its patriotic message has been overtaken by its great melody in recent years.

As long as Guthrie's lyrics can be adapted to contemporary issues, his songs will be sung. As long as there remain social inequities against which he protested, his songs will be sung.

So the songs live.

So too does Woody Guthrie, American.

*T*HE SMALL HOUSE on First Street clung to the side of Okemah's lone hill, its windows sightless, punched out, the door slamming open and closed in the winds that blew across the green rills and sandy lands of central Oklahoma.

From the front porch and the small balcony above, the little boy once could see the tracks of the Fort Smith and Western Railroad just before they crossed Division Street. From there he could watch the plodding farm wagons, the heavy trucks from the oil fields, and the Model-T's flitting to and from the stores on Broadway. When he was bigger, he would walk to those shops, perhaps for a peewee jawbreaker at the drugstore or a hot dog at the Coney Island Grill.

The old London house was empty now. Its porch was rotting, its balcony bowed under the years. The paint was parched, cracked, and peeling. Ragged shrubs and stubborn vines grew against the pilings of the foundation, as if to clutch the joists and pull down the house, inch by inch.

The boy had long since left—for Texas, for California, for New York, for half a hundred homes scattered across the country. The train tracks were abandoned, rusted. The oil boom too had come and gone. The weathered frame house on First Street abided.

Now and again, giggling high school kids made their way up the broken steps with a blanket to adventure in a dark corner of the house. Sometimes they brought cans of spray paint and stroked obscenities across the dirty walls.

Occasionally, pilgrims made their way to the waiting house. Some came with guitars, some with only the clothes on their back. They came in awe, as strangers in a holy place, and they left their messages of reverence among the graffiti.

"Woody, they never care until it's too late," one wrote in pencil.

"Woody," another began, "I've come here just to sing a song that you wrote. My heart is filling just to see that what you left us is going to remain in some of our hearts."

One night, a careless stranger trying to light a cigarette or a heedless kid rasped by some vague rage set fire to the old London place. Parched boards crisped in moments. Porch and balcony collapsed. The frame house, a neighborhood nuisance, an eyesore, was gone even before firemen arrived.

Year by year, the shrubs crept closer, covering the tumbled bricks of the foundation and the blackened timbers. Finally, only the most determined were able to pick out the remains of the holy place.

And the legend grew.

Unattributed interviews are by the author.
I have used a handful of abbreviations throughout the notes, including

BJO—The Collection of Barry and Judy Ollman.
RRP—Richard Reuss Papers, Indiana University Archives. Material from
      this collection is cited by box and file number.
EV&JW—Victor and Judy Wolfenstein Collection, Los Angeles.
INT—interview.
LC—Library of Congress, Washington, D.C.
WG—Woody Guthrie.
WGA—Woody Guthrie Archives, New York City. Material in the
      archives is cited by box and file number.

INTRODUCTION

Material for the introduction was drawn from interviews with Irene Kossoy Sale-
tan and Ellen Kossoy Christenson, Pete Seeger, Irwin Silber, and Harold Leventhal; from the program notes for "Bound for Glory," March 17, 1956; and the
sources cited below.

xxi   Over that 66: WGA, Manuscript Series 2, Box 1, H-I file; also in Alan Lomax,
       Woody Guthrie, and Pete Seeger, *Hard Hitting Songs for Hard-Hit People* (Lin-
       coln: University of Nebraska Press, 1999), p. 61.
xxi   His name: Script written by Millard Lampell, *California to the New York Island*
       (New York: Guthrie Children's Trust Fund, 1958), p. 7.
xxi   I don't know: *Ibid.*, p. 41. In fact, this was not Guthrie's but Lampell's inspira-
       tion.
xxiii   Sing the last chorus: Pete Seeger, *The Incompleat Folksinger*, edited by Jo Met-
       calf Schwartz (Lincoln: University of Nebraska Press, 1992), p. 173.

CHAPTER ONE

3   Irreproachable private life: *Okemah Ledger*, April 5, 1907, courtesy of EV&JW.
4   A pretty good hitter: "Notes on Claude Guthrie Interview," Tulsa, Oklahoma,
       June 1968, in RRP, Box 8, Folder 3. Additional information about the Tanner
       and Guthrie families is from "Genealogy of the Family of Woody Guthrie Com-
       piled by Dick Reuss," January 1968, in RRP, Box 7, Folder 7.

5   He had a lot of pride: Int with Mary Josephine Guthrie Edgmon, July 24, 1998.

5   Partly western: Robert Allen Rutland, *A Boyhood in the Dust Bowl* (Niwot: University Press of Colorado, 1995), p. 4.

5   Our house was full: Woody Guthrie, "My Life," in *American Folksong* (New York: Disc, 1947), p. 1, reprinted in Woody Guthrie, *Pastures of Plenty: A Self-Portrait*, edited by Dave Marsh and Harold Leventhal (New York: Harper-Perennial, 1992), pp. 1–14. Guthrie's often contradictory autobiographical writings, including his "autobiography," *Bound for Glory*, cannot be wholly relied on. He tended to embroider incidents and to rearrange events for dramatic purposes; Guthrie deliberately and repeatedly called *Bound for Glory* "my novel."

6   The greatest wheat country: Worth Robert Miller, *Oklahoma Populism: A History of the People's Party in the Oklahoma Territory* (Norman: University of Oklahoma Press, 1987), p. 29.

6   The earthly paradise: Garin Burbank, *When Farmers Voted Red: The Gospel of Socialism in the Oklahoma Countryside, 1910–1924* (Westport, Conn.: Greenwood Press, 1976), p. 18.

6   Tooth-and-claw: Miller, *Oklahoma Populism*, p. 8.

7   I am a small farmer: John Thompson, *Closing the Frontier* (Norman: University of Oklahoma Press, 1986), p. 107.

7   Farm ladder: *Ibid.*

7   The $25.00 a bale: Burbank, *When Farmers Voted Red*, p. 17.

7   Robbery business: *Ibid.*, p. 141.

7   Hard hittin': Woody Guthrie, *The Library of Congress Recordings*, Rounder 1041/42/43. The recordings were made by Alan Lomax in March 1940 and eventually issued commercially on Elektra, before reappearing on Rounder in 1988.

8   Leaving him: The unidentified newspaper is quoted in Joe Klein, *Woody Guthrie: A Life* (New York: Alfred A. Knopf, 1980), p. 12.

8   One of the most: *Ibid.*, p. 12.

8   The equal of: Murray is quoted in Jimmie L. Franklin, "Black Oklahomans and Sense of Place," in Davis D. Joyce, *An Oklahoma I Had Never Seen* (Norman: University of Oklahoma Press, 1994), p. 267.

8   Hot headed Democrat: Int with Claude Guthrie, in RRP, Box 8, Folder 3.

9   An enveloping: Burbank, *When Farmers Voted Red*, p. 15.

9   Leviticus: The biblical citation is noted in *ibid.*, p. 61.

9   The primitive gospel: *Ibid.*, p. 21.

9   There is only: *Ibid.*, p. 27.

9   Under socialism: *Ibid.*, p. 37.

10 A political tool: *Ibid.*, p. 18, quoting a 1914 edition of the *Boswell Submarine*.

10 Free Love: The headlines are quoted in Klein, *Woody Guthrie*, p. 15.

10 While charging free love: *Ibid.*, p. 15.

10 Once hit a guy: Int with Claude Guthrie, in RRP, Box 8, Folder 3.

10 Been an earnest: Charley Edward Guthrie, "Kumrids: A Discussion of Scientific Socialism" (Okemah: Ledger Print, 1912) in EV&JW. Charley was well enough read to cite, among other sources, works by Sidney Webb, John Stuart Mill, Karl Marx, Friedrich Engels, and H. G. Wells.

11 The less industrious: A copy of the booklet is in RRP, Box 7, Folder 8.

11 He wants the rate: Klein, *Woody Guthrie*, p. 16.

11   As happy as a lobster: *Okemah Ledger*, July 18, 1912, in RRP, Box 2, Folder 1.

11   Bubbly and bouncy: Int with Mary Josephine Guthrie Edgmon, July 17, 1998.

11   Negro minstrel: Woody Guthrie "High Balladry," typescript, p. 3, dated February 1948, in WGA, Manuscripts Box 7, Folder 4.

12   She had a sort: "Woody and Lefty Lou's Favorite Collection of Old Time Hillbilly Songs," mimeographed, Los Angeles, ca. 1937, p. 8, in WGA, Notebooks 1, Folder 4.

12   The weeks and days: "A Story I Know Too Well," in WGA, Notebooks 1, Folder 5.

12   It was late: "The Gypsy Davy" (Child 200) is quoted in Guthrie, "High Balladry," p. 5.

12   Worked out pretty fair: Guthrie, "High Balladry," p. 3.

13   Mean ol' house: Quoted by David Dick on the *CBS Evening News*, March 11, 1971, in WGA.

13   The drinkingest: Guthrie, *Pastures of Plenty*, p. 3.

13   Papa was: Guthrie, *Library of Congress Recordings*, Rounder 1041.

13   Deep devotion: Harry Menig, "Woody Guthrie: The Oklahoma Years, 1912–1929," in Joyce, *An Oklahoman*, p. 164.

13   The hurt songs: Guthrie, *Pastures of Plenty*, p. 4.

14   Fat men were few: Nigel Anthony Sellars, *Oil, Wheat and Wobblies* (Norman: University of Oklahoma Press, 1998), p. 38.

15   In most towns: Guthrie, *Library of Congress Recordings*, Rounder 1041/42/43.

15   Rich man's war: Sellars, *Oil, Wheat and Wobblies*, p. 86.

15   Had been set on fire: *Okemah Ledger*, October 5, 1916, courtesy of EV&JW.

16   Our big new black buggy: Guthrie, "High Balladry," p. 7.

16   That ripe and tender time: Guthrie, *Ibid.*, p. 8.

16   Papa went to town: Woody Guthrie, *Bound for Glory*, new ed. (New York: E. P. Dutton, 1976), p. 23.

16   The children always had: Quoted in Menig, "Woody Guthrie: The Oklahoma Years," p. 174.

16   One day: Mrs. V. K. Chowning of Okemah is quoted in *ibid.*, p. 165.

17   He will want: *Okemah Ledger*, July 25, 1918, in EV&JW.

17   First indication: *Okemah Ledger*, August 22, 1918, in EV&JW.

18   I put the coal oil: *Okemah Ledger*, May 29, 1919, in EV&JW.

18   Why are you crying: Guthrie, "High Balladry," pp. 10–11 and p. B.

19   Oh, papa: Int of Mrs. R. G. Potter by Rosan A. Jordan, August 16, 1966, in RRP, Box 7, Folder 11.

19   Laugh like me: Guthrie, "High Balladry," pp. 10–11 and p. B.

CHAPTER TWO

In addition to the sources cited for this chapter, I drew material from Guy Logsdon's article, "Woody's Roots," in *Music Journal* 14 (December 1976), pp. 18–21; and letters from Gladys Moore Gordon to WG on April 26, 1966; and to Richard Reuss, February 17, 1969, both in RRP, Box 1, Folder 23. Joe Klein and Mrs. Gordon provided the description of WG's visit to the state asylum.

20   If I'd not kept: Guthrie, "High Balladry," p. C.

20   A coal oil stove: *Ibid.*, p. 11.

20   Ironing on an oil stove: "A Synopsis of the Book, 'Boomchasers,'" p. 3, in WGA Manuscripts Box 1, Folder 15. This was WG's proposal for the book that became *Bound for Glory*.

20   To spite: Menig, "Woody Guthrie: The Oklahoma Years," p. 173.

20   Did she do it: Guthrie, "High Balladry," p. 9.

21   Crooked gamblers: Guthrie, *Bound for Glory*, pp. 85–86.

21   Get Out the Hemp: Thompson, *Closing the Frontier*, p. 192.

21   An extralegal arm: Sellars, *Oil, Wheat and Wobblies*, p. 164.

22   Equal terms: Guthrie, *Library of Congress Recordings*, Rounder 1041/42/43.

22   Were almost as many: Guthrie, "A Synopsis of the Book, 'Boomchasers,' " p. 2.

22   Just a little bit wrong: Int of R. E. Boydstun by Sylvia Grider, June 7, 1968, in RRP, Box 8, Folder 2.

22   The finest game: Edward Earl Purinton, "Big Ideas from Big Business," *Independent*, April 16, 1921, p. 395.

23   I'm the only: Guthrie, "High Balladry," p. 12.

23   Mr. Guthrie: *Okemah Ledger*, August 26, 1920, in EV&JW.

23   Short speeches: Guthrie, "A Synopsis of the Book, 'Boomchasers,'" p. 2.

24   Had played: *Ibid.*

24   When he lost: Guthrie, "High Balladry," p. 12.

24   He had to have: Guthrie, "A Synopsis of the Book, 'Boomchasers,'" p. 2.

24   The doctor: Guthrie, "High Balladry," p. 12.

24   We got the grease: Guthrie, *Library of Congress Recordings*, Rounder 1041/42/43.

24   The shackiest house: Guthrie, "High Balladry," p. 13.

25   We never did get: *Ibid.*

25   Lots of fistfights: Guthrie, "A Synopsis of the Book, 'Boomchasers,'" p. 3.

25   The rottenest: Guthrie, "High Balladry," p. 13.

25   Too poor: Rutland, *A Boyhood in the Dust Bowl*, p. 13.

25   A little fellow: "Woody Guthrie, By Nelle E. Bras, Former Teacher," in RRP, Box 7, Folder 11.

26   But never got a new toehold: Woody Guthrie, "My Life," in Guthrie, *Pastures of Plenty*, p. 4.

26   Maybe you don't: Guthrie, *Bound for Glory*, p. 144.

26   She would be: *Ibid.*, pp. 128–129.

27   Mama would throw: Int with Mary Josephine Guthrie Edgmon, July 24, 1998.

27   Hard on her children: Int of Mrs. R. G. Potter by Richard Reuss, August 16, 1966, in RPP, Box 7, Folder 11.

27   A case of nerves: Int with Mary Josephine Guthrie Edgmon, November 23, 1999.

27   Was incapable of being: *Ibid.*

27   Mama was not safe: Int with Mary Josephine Guthrie Edgmon, February 16, 1999.

27   Big, old, loveable: Int with Mary Josephine Guthrie Edgemon, January 29, 1999.

27   Our little farm town: Guthrie, "My Life," in Guthrie, *Pastures of Plenty*, p. 3.

28   That's undoubtedly: Guthrie, *Library of Congress Recordings*, Rounder 1041/42/43. Fourteen years after recording this interview, WG wrote in a letter that he first learned to play a railroad blues from his boyhood chum John "Smokey" Woods, and not from "George."

28   I'm a-walkin' down the track: "900 Miles," Woody Guthrie, *Muleskinner Blues: The Asch Recordings, Vol. 2*, Smithsonian Folkways 40101. See also John A. and Alan Lomax, *Folk Song U.S.A.* (New York: New American Library, 1975), p. 311.

28 That's a big bird: Woody Guthrie, "Ear Players," *Common Ground*, Spring 1942, p. 34.

28 Missed a lunch: *Ibid.*

29 To be full: Guthrie, *Library of Congress Recordings*, Rounder 1041/42/43.

29 Where the oil flows: Guy Logsdon, "Woody Guthrie and His Oklahoma Hills," *Mid-America Folklore*, 19 (1991), p. 61.

29 He was a little showman: Menig, "Woody Guthrie: The Oklahoma Years," p. 179.

30 The teacher never: Int with Bertha Bryan Edmoundson, August 6, 1998.

30 I jig danced: Woody Guthrie, "Woody Guthrie, By Me," manuscript in the archives of TRO Richmond Music, quoted by Guy Logsdon, in his notes accompanying Guthrie, *Muleskinner Blues*, p. 4.

30 An accident: Charley Guthrie's Works Progress Administration application, quoted by Richard Reuss, in RRP, Box 7, Folder 7.

30 He wanted: Guthrie, "High Balladry," p. 14.

31 My mother and father: Guthrie, "Woody Guthrie, By Me," p. 4.

31 Papa went: Guthrie, "High Balladry," p. 13. In an interview with Alan Lomax recorded for the Library of Congress Archive of American Folk Song, Guthrie said, "My father mysteriously burned himself. . . . I always thought he done it on purpose because he lost all his money." See Rounder CD 1041, Track 5. In the purportedly autobiographical "My Life," he simply noted, "Our shack house caught on fire. Dad was hurt in it." In *Bound for Glory*, p. 151, Guthrie allows himself to cast some doubt on the "oil-stove-exploded" account. His sister Mary Jo said Charley denied his Nora had deliberately burned him, but added in an interview, "And I never did know the truth."

31 Way over yonder: Guthrie, "High Balladry," p. 13.

31 Hit rock bottom: Int with Geneva Boydstun Adkins by Sylvia Grider, June 9, 1968, in RRP, Box 8, Folder 2.

31 Only the few: Guthrie, "Washing Dishes," in WGA, Manuscripts Box 4, Folder 3.

31 Hard liquor: Guthrie, *Pastures of Plenty*, p. 107.

32 Brief period: Int with Mary Josephine Guthrie Edgmon, July 24, 1999.

32 So long: Int with Colonel Martin by Richard Reuss, August 18, 1966, in RRP, Box 8, Folder 2.

32 Woody was a mess: Menig, "Woody Guthrie: The Oklahoma Years," p. 178.

32 A beautiful tenor: Gladys Moore Gordon to Richard Reuss, February 17, 1969, p. 4, in RRP, Box 1, Folder 23.

32 Buy you some underwear: Gladys Moore Gordon to WG, April 26, 1966, p. 6, in RRP, Box 1, Folder 23.

32 Woody had different ways: Nora Moore is quoted in Gladys Moore Gordon to Richard Reuss, February 17, 1969.

33 You're Woody: Int with Matt Jennings, January 1972, in EV&JW.

33 And every time: Int of Colonel Martin by David Dick on the *CBS Evening News*, March 17, 1971, in WGA.

34 This old gal house song: Guthrie, "High Balladry," p. 2a.

34 It's hard and it's hard: As printed in Alan Lomax, *The Folk Songs of North America* (Garden City, N.Y.: Doubleday, 1960), p. 439.

34 Ear music: Guthrie, "Ear Players," p. 38.

34 I followed: Guthrie, "High Balladry," p. 2a. Guthrie's deliberate spelling errors have been silently corrected.

34 All caused: *Ibid.*, p. 2b.

34 Some are supposed: Guthrie, *Library of Congress Recordings*, Rounder 1041/42/43.

35   With the wind: Guthrie, "Ear Players," p. 38.

35   My harmonica: *Ibid.*, p. 34.

35   A clown: Int with Bertha Bryan Edmoundson, August 6, 1998.

35   A little wiry haired: Menig, "Woody Guthrie: The Oklahoma Years," p. 179. Smith was not a member of the family with which Guthrie lived.

35   He didn't look: Int with Bertha Bryan Edmoundson, August 6, 1998.

36   I don't think: Int of Colonel Martin by David Dick on the *CBS Evening News*, March 11, 1971, in WGA.

36   Big money: Guthrie, "Woody Guthrie, By Me," p. 4.

CHAPTER THREE

37   Staked Plain: Legend has it the name, translated from the Spanish *Llano Estacado*, comes from the Coronado Expedition of 1541, which left piles of buffalo bones to mark its way across the trackless barrens.

37   There wasn't much: Int with Carl "Shorty" Harris by E. Victor and Judy Wolfenstein, September 26, 1971, courtesy of EV&JW.

38   So bad: Int of Jess Turner by Richard Reuss, June 8, 1968, in RRP, Box 8, Folder 2.

38   Three things: Guthrie, "High Balladry," p. 2b.

38   See to it: Guthrie "Woody Guthrie, By Me," pp. 4–5.

38   The beds: Guthrie, *Bound for Glory*, p. 160.

38   In a rough part of town: Undated int of Jeff Guthrie by Richard Reuss, in RPP, Box 8, Folder 2. Jeff, a Pampa policeman, was in a position to know.

39   Cowhands: Guthrie, "High Balladry," p. 2c.

39   Wages were cheap: Int with Carl T. "Shorty" Harris by Richard Reuss, June 8, 1968, in RRP, Box 8, Folder 2.

39   Better than anybody: Int with Carl "Shorty" Harris by E. Victor and Judy Wolfenstein, September 26, 1971.

40   I thought: Guthrie, *Library of Congress Recordings*, Rounder 1041/42/43.

40   When I pulled: Int of Jeff Guthrie by Richard Reuss, June 28, 1967, in RRP, Box 8, Folder 4. Jeff was indicted, pro forma, for murder on December 15, 1928, and quickly acquitted by a jury on April 10, 1929.

40   I had to go through: Int of Jeff Guthrie by E. Victor and Judy Wolfenstein, September 28, 1971, courtesy of EV&JW.

41   High-headed: Woody Guthrie, *Seeds of Man* (Lincoln: University of Nebraska Press, 1995), p. 15.

41   A natural musician: Int of Nat Lunsford by Sylvia Grider, June 5, 1968, in RRP, Box 8, Folder 2.

41   After a while: Guthrie, "My Life," in Guthrie, *Pastures of Plenty*, p. 5.

42   Not a leader: Richard B. Hughes, "Been Good to Know You," *Texas Observer*, July 24, 1992.

42   Wills her store: Int with Mrs. Winifred Crinklaw by Richard Reuss, in RRP, Box 8, Folder 2.

42   He didn't seem: Hughes, "Been Good to Know You."

42   Come easy: Int of Mrs. Hattie Holt Harmon by Sylvia Grider, in RRP, Box 8, Folder 2.

42   I wasn't very much: Int with Matt Jennings, August 21, 1998.

42   Probably done: *Ibid.*

43   Things like: *Ibid.*

43   Had learned: Int with Matt Jennings, December 29, 1998. Jennings stated
     Guthrie, like himself, "used the 'N-word.' "
43   He wanted: *Ibid.*
43   The scene of a gambler: "A Picture from Life's Other Side" is taken from the
     unpublished "Alonzo Zilch Songbook" in WGA, Notebooks 1, Folder 4.
44   Just fine people: Int of Jeff Guthrie by Richard Reuss, June 28, 1967, in RRP,
     Box 8, Folder 4.
44   Old champ fiddlers: "Kords and Disskords," quoted in the program notes to "A
     Musical Tribute to Woody Guthrie," (New York: 1957), courtesy of EV&JW.
44   We'd go: Int with Jennings, August 21, 1998.
44   He just wanted: *Ibid.*
45   If he had had: Int of Mrs. Evelyn Todd of Clarendon, Texas, by Sylvia Grider,
     June 6, 1968, in RRP, Box 8, Folder 4.
45   A good picture: *Ibid.* Mrs. Todd left the two-foot-by-one-foot portrait hanging
     in the library when she resigned in the 1940s. It has since disappeared.
45   A lot: Int with Matt Jennings, December 29, 1998.
45   Had a letter: Int with Jennings, August 21, 1998. Jennings also recalled this
     night in more detail during an interview with E. Victor and Judy Wolfenstein
     on January 9, 1972.
45   No way: Int with Matt Jennings by E. Victor and Judy Wolfenstein, January 9,
     1972, courtesy of EV&JW.
46   Papa, Roy, Woody: Int with Mary Jo Guthrie Edgmon, January 19, 1999.
     Charley was unable to pay for a gravestone. Nora's unmarked plot was redis-
     covered by Ms. Evelyn Parker, chairwoman of the Cleveland (Oklahoma)
     Genealogical Society's research committee, who combed the records of the
     Norman, Oklahoma, International Order of Oddfellows Cemetery in January
     2002.
46   Ologies of all sorts: Int with Matt Jennings by E. Victor and Judy Wolfenstein,
     January 9, 1972.
46   The tough end: Guthrie, "A Synopsis of the Book, 'Boomchasers.'"
46   You always had: Int of Rufus Jordan by Richard Reuss, June 5, 1968, in RRP,
     Box 8, Folder 2.
46   A go-easy guy: Charlie Pipes to Sylvia Grider, June 7, 1968, in RRP, Box 8,
     Folder 2.
47   Woody would visit: Hughes, "Been Good to Know You."
47   Forced by the fun: "Dear Prostitute," in Woody Guthrie, *Born to Win* (New
     York: Macmillan, 1965), pp. 99–100.

CHAPTER FOUR

48   Pretty heavy stuff: Int with Matt Jennings by E. Victor and Judy Wolfenstein,
     January 9, 1972, courtesy of EV&JW.
49   I wouldn't claim: Int with Matt Jennings, August 21, 1998.
49   Some people: Int with Matt Jennings, January 9, 1972, by E. Victor and Judy
     Wolfenstein.
49   Who could really: *Ibid.*
49   Woody loved: *Ibid.*
49   Sleep out every night: Menig, "Woody Guthrie; The Oklahoma Years," p. 182,
     points out the Rodgers song.
49   Goodbye to the Stepstone: As recalled by Matt Jennings in an int with E. Vic-

tor and Judy Wolfenstein, March 1972. Guthrie probably picked it off a 1928 recording by the popular Stoneman family, "Goodbye Dear Old Stepstone." The song was written by J. O. Webster in 1880.

50   He hoped: Int with Matt Jennings, August 21, 1998.

50   I was in a buckboard: "Old Gray Team Hosses" in WGA, Notebooks 1, Folder 6, p. 185. At the foot of the page, he carefully noted: "This is the first song I ever wrote—WG."

51   About sixteen years: Guthrie, *Born to Win*, p. 23. The unusually popular "Talking Blues" form he learned from Albert Lund, on the *Grand Ole Opry* radio program, Matt Jennings said.

51   One night: Int with James King by Richard Reuss, June 7, 1968, in RRP, Box 8, Folder 2.

51   Everybody suffered: Int with Matt Jennings, by E. Victor and Judy Wolfenstein, January 9, 1972.

51   It was only: Int of Minnie Dittmeyer Barrett by Sylvia Grider, June 9, 1969, in RRP, Box 8, Folder 2.

51   Let's get this panther: Int with Jeff Guthrie, June 27, 1967, in RRP, Box 8, Folder 3. Woody would later make reference to Jeff's "panther" fiddle, suggesting his uncle's aggressive fiddle style.

51   Played a real sweet: George Hamlin to Sylvia Grider, June 6, 1968, in RRP, Box 8, Folder 4.

52   A clamper fiend: Guthrie, *Seeds of Man*, p. 50.

52   But we didn't make: Guthrie, "High Balladry," p. 2b.

52   Woody was so sick: Int with Matt Jennings, August 21, 1998. Both Pete Seeger and Baldwin Hawes as members of the Almanac Singers would later use the name as a pseudonym.

52   One of his rubbish: Woody Guthrie, "News Expose," Vol. 1, No. 1, dated December 24, 1935, courtesy of BJO.

53   A favorite there: Int John Gikas, March 14, 1999.

53   Born natural: Charlie Pipes to Sylvia Grider, June 7, 1968, in RRP, Box 8, Folder 2.

53   Give him: Int with Shorty Harris by Sylvia Grider, June 8, 1968, in RRP, Box 8, Folder 2.

53   Woody would play: George Hamlin to Sylvia Grider, June 6, 1968, in RRP, Box 8, Folder 2.

53   Once you had: *Ibid.*

54   He would get: Int of James King by Richard Reuss, June 7, 1968, in RRP, Box 8, Folder 2.

54   He never did worsen: George Hamlin to Sylvia Grider, June 6, 1968, in RRP, Box 8, Folder 2.

55   Any piece: Int of Jeff Guthrie by E. Victor and Judy Wolfenstein, September 28, 29, 1971, courtesy of EV&JW.

55   Yankee farmer wig: Guthrie, "A Synopsis of the Book, 'Boomchasers.'" Details of the tent show adventure are from Klein, *Woody Guthrie*, pp. 63–64.

55   Comical: Int of Robert Boydstun by Sylvia Grider, June 7, 1968, in RRP, Box 8, Folder 2.

55   I stopped: Thomas W. Jackson, *On a Slow Train through Arkansaw*, edited by W. K. McNeil (Lexington: University Press of Kentucky, 1985), p. 48. This is a reprint of the 1903 first edition. The jokebook was continually reprinted for the next three decades.

55 I used to play: Thomas W. Jackson, "I'm from Texas: You Can't Steer Me" (Chicago: Thos. W. Jackson Publishing, 1948), p. 42.

55 There is a section: *Ibid.*, p. 56.

56 They have raised: *Ibid.*, p. 77.

56 Our show folded: Guthrie "A Synopsis of the Book, 'Boomchasers.'"

56 'Cause he stayed: Int of Jeff Guthrie by E. Victor and Judy Wolfenstein, September 28, 29, 1971.

57 When times was good: WGA, Manuscripts Box 1, Folder 14.3, p. 48. This account of the Guthrie silver mine is supplemented by a June 1968 interview with Claude Guthrie by Richard Reuss and Guy Logsdon, in RRP, Box 8, Folder 2.

57 Who was always: Int with Matt Jennings, by E. Victor and Judy Wolfenstein, January 9, 1972.

57 I wanted: Woody Guthrie to "Dear Lerners," September 28, 1947, in EV&JW.

57 This was a sandyland: Guthrie, *Seeds of Man*, p. 122.

58 Has done my soul: *Ibid.*, p. 195. Details about the treasure hunt were drawn from a letter from Jeff to WG, probably written November 3, 1948. Jeff returned in 1944 to look for the mine and learned that even if they had found Jerry P.'s claim, they would not have been able to exploit it. The mine, the entire mountain range, had been incorporated into the Big Bend National Park; federal officials would not let them haul ore out even if they found the mine.

58 Fleshy: Int of Robert Boydstun by Richard Reuss, June 7, 1968, in RRP, Box 8, Folder 2.

58 A big, squareheaded: Guthrie, *Seeds of Man*, p. 49.

58 We didn't ask: WGA, Manuscripts Box 1, Folder 14.3, p. 60.

59 All of a sudden: Int with Geneva Boydstun Adkins by Sylvia Grider, June 9, 1968, in RRP, Box 8, Folder 2.

59 She was a very: Int with Mary Josephine Guthrie Edgmon, July 24, 1998.

59 Charley was pretty: Int with George Guthrie by Richard Reuss, December 12, 1967, in RRP, Box 8, Folder 3.

59 Religious Faith: Guthrie, *Seeds of Man*, p. 49.

59 Life was: WGA, Manuscripts 1, Folder 14.3, p. 61.

59 They were crazy: Int with Shorty Harris by Sylvia Grider, June 8, 1968, in RRP, Box 8, Folder 4. Hazel later appears in various Guthrie manuscripts as "Helen" and "Harriet."

60 A funny couple: Int with Minnie Dittmeyer Barrett by Sylvia Grider, June 9, 1968, in RRP, Box 8, Folder 2.

60 What in the world: Int of Minnie Dittmeyer Barrett by Richard Reuss, June 8, 1968, in RRP, Box 8, Folder 2.

60 My dad: Int with Matt Jennings by E. Victor and Judy Wolfenstein, January 9, 1972.

61 A nice girl: Int with Violet Pipes by Richard Reuss, June 9, 1968, in RRP, Box 8, Folder 2.

61 Just didn't have: Int with Jeff Guthrie by E. Victor and Judy Wolfenstein, September 28 and 29, 1971.

61 I was a young girl: Int with Mary Jennings Guthrie Boyle, August 19, 1998.

61 The Jennings: Int with Jeff Guthrie, in RRP, Box 8, Folder 4.

61 Was so damned: Int with Mary Jennings Guthrie Boyle by E. Victor and Judy Wolfenstein, December 28, 1971, courtesy of EV&JW.

61   Woody had: Int with John Gikas, March 14, 1999.
61   Sort of paired off: Int with Mary Jennings Guthrie Boyle by E. Victor and Judy Wolfenstein, December 28, 1971.
61   Woody said: *Ibid.*
61   Before we were married: Int with Mary Jennings Guthrie Boyle, August 19, 1998.
62   I was stunned: Int with Matt Jennings, August 21, 1998.
62   Woody not having: Int with Matt Jennings by E. Victor and Judy Wolfenstein, January 9, 1972.
62   That he wouldn't speak: Int with Mary Jennings Guthrie Boyle, August 19, 1998. Matt Jennings recalled their parents opposed the marriage because "Woody didn't have a steady job."
63   Drank up: *Ibid.* Other details of the wedding are from an interview with Matt Jennings by Richard Reuss; and from Klein's *Woody Guthrie.* According to Richard Reuss, the Guthries' wedding license was not on file at the Gray County courthouse.
63   Bad, very, very bad: Int with Mary Jennings Guthrie Boyle, August 19, 1998.

CHAPTER FIVE

In addition to the sources cited, I relied on a research paper written by Savoie Lottinville, forwarded by Guy Logsdon.

64   Day of national: *New York Times,* March 5, 1933.
65   Didn't know: Int with Anna Gideon Guthrie, July 24, 1998. Seeking "a better way of life," she explained, ". . . I picked my way out of the cotton patch."
65   Honk-honk hoboes: Sellars, *Oil, Wheat and Wobblies,* p. 181.
65   Oil was being: Int with Rufus Jordan by E. Victor and Judy Wolfenstein, September 26, 1971, courtesy of EV&JW.
65   Five dollars: Rufus Jordan to Sylvia Grider, June 5, 1968, in RRP, Box 8, Folder 2.
65   The big swappers: "Handsome Old Times," in WGA, Manuscripts Box 7, Folder 11.
66   You talked: Guthrie, *Pastures of Plenty,* pp. 185–186. The manuscript is dated August 11, 1947, by which time FDR had been dead more than two years. There would be no more elections. More likely, this was written some years earlier and rewritten in 1947.
66   Halfway made: Int with Matt Jennings, August 21, 1999.
66   A good, easy girl: Typescript in WGA, Notebooks 1, Folder 4, p. 201.
66   She very seldom: Woody Guthrie, "About Woody," in Lomax, Guthrie, and Seeger, *Hard Hitting Songs,* p. 21.
66   The ricketiest: *Ibid.*
66   But we got by: *Ibid.*
66   It was good times: Int with Mary Jennings Guthrie Boyle, August 19, 1998.
67   The least adapted: Hughes, "Been Good to Know You."
67   Until he lost: Int with Mary Jennings Guthrie Boyle, August 19, 1998.
67   Wushy-headed: Int of Violet Pipes by Richard Reuss, June 9, 1968, in RRP, Box 8, Folder 2.
67   At first: Int with Hattie Hamlin by Sylvia Grider, July 12, 1966, Pampa, Texas, in RRP, Box 8, Folder 2.

67   Woody wasn't: Int of Mary Boyle by E. Victor and Judy Wolfenstein, December 28, 1971, courtesy of EV&JW.

67   And that child: Int with Mary Jennings Guthrie Boyle, August 19, 1998.

68   Mary was desperately: Int of Violet Pipes by Richard Reuss, June 9, 1968, in RRP, Box 8, Folder 2.

68   There was nothing: Elizabeth Wupperman, Cedar Park, Texas, 1999, to Cray. The phrase "Dust Bowl" was coined by Associated Press reporter Robert Geiger in a story filed on April 15, 1935, from Guymon, Oklahoma. It is reprinted in Frank Luther Mott, *Headlining America* (Boston: Houghton Mifflin, 1937), pp. 157-160, accidentally misdated to 1936.

68   A cloud: Int with Bertha Bryan Edmoundson, August 6, 1998.

69   So dark: Quoted by Guy Logsdon, "The Dust Bowl and the Migrant," *American Scene* 12, No. 1 (Tulsa, Okla.: Thomas Gilcrease Institute of American History and Art, 1971).

69   We were too scared: Sylvia Grider, "Black Easter-April 14, 1935," paper delivered to the Texas Folklore Society, March 1970, in RRP, Box 8, Folder 2.

69   You couldn't see: Int of Robert Boydstun by Richard Reuss, June 7, 1968, in RRP, Box 8, Folder 2.

69   Like the Red Sea: Guthrie, *Library of Congress Recordings*, Rounder 1041/42/43.

70   Lord amercy: Int of Jess Turner by Richard Reuss, June 9, 1968, in RRP, Box 8, Folder 2.

70   Everybody was: Carl "Shorty" Harris to Sylvia Grider, June 8, 1968, in RRP, Box 8, Folder 4.

70   They thought: Int with John Gikas, March 14, 1999.

70   Coming down the street: Sylvia Grider's notes of int with Violet Pipes, June 8, 1968, in RRP, Box 8, Folder 2. The author's int of John Gikas took place on March 14, 1999.

70   It was a year: Int with John Gikas, March 14, 1999.

70   Where the wheat: Grider, "Black Easter," p. 10.

70   This Panhandle: Guthrie, "High Balladry," p. 2c.

71   Damper spots: Untitled typescript, probably written for Folkways Records, December 1, 1953, courtesy of BJO. Pampa seems to have had more than its share of good musicians at the time. Among others, the brothers Jimmie and Leon Short, who reportedly sat in with Guthrie, later recorded with the celebrated Ernest Tubb.

71   He was a better: Int with James King by Richard Reuss, June 7, 1968, in RRP, Box 8, Folder 2.

71   Most of the time: Int with Mary Josephine Guthrie Edgmon, July 24, 1998.

71   It always seemed: Int with George Hamlin by Sylvia Grider, June 6, 1968, in RRP, Box 8, Folder 2.

71   He modeled: Int with Matt Jennings, August 21, 1998.

72   He loved: Int with Matt Jennings, December 29, 1998.

72   On the fourteenth day: As "Dust Storm Disaster," this is printed in Lomax, Guthrie, and Seeger, *Hard Hitting Songs*, pp. 218–219. Writing about contemporary events, Guthrie was actually following an old tradition. He had already learned "The Sherman Cyclone," an older ballad inspired by a natural disaster in 1896, and half a dozen railroad songs based on train wrecks.

72   Here, Minnie: Int of Minnie Dittmeyer Barrett by Sylvia Grider, June 9, 1968, in RRP, Box 8, Folder 2.

73   Woody was a wonderful: Int with Mary Geneva Adkins by Richard Reuss, June 10, 1968, in RRP, Box 8, Folder 2.

73   You have to learn: Int of Jeff Guthrie by E. Victor and Judy Wolfenstein, September 29, 1971, courtesy of EV&JW.

73   Secret of all power: Robert Collier, *The Secret of the Ages* (New York: Robert Collier Publisher, c. 1926), vol. II, p. 72. This summary of the book is drawn from notes by E. Victor and Judy Wolfenstein, courtesy of EV&JW.

73   Prayer is: *Ibid.*, vol. II, pp. 99, 103.

73   Time and again: *Ibid.*, vol. V, p. 385.

73   To treat: *Ibid.*, vol. VII, pp. 608–609.

74   Let me quote: *Ibid.*, vol. II, pp. 138–139. The italics are the author's.

74   Never [to] let: *Ibid.*, vol. IV, p. 335.

74   God Almighty: Int of Jeff Guthrie by E. Victor and Judy Wolfenstein, September 29, 1971.

74   She had quite a few: Int with Roy Fritz Buzbee, November 17, 1999.

75   I still figured: Guthrie, "About Woody," p. 22.

75   The superstition business: WG to Alan Lomax, February 20, 1941, in LC.

75   Hundreds of people: Guthrie, "Synopsis of the Book, 'Boomchasers,'" p. 6.

75   Alonzo M. Zilch: Woody Guthrie, "News Expose," Vol. 1, No. 1, dated December 24, 1935, courtesy of BJO. It seems to have had a "run" of only two issues. Mary Jennings Guthrie Boyle recalled that her then husband also wrote stories for the women's confession magazine, *True Stories*. If they were published, they would have been printed with a woman's byline.

75   Strange powers: *Pampa Daily News*, November 19, 1935, courtesy of EV&JW.

76   Helped many: *Pampa Daily News*, January 1, 1936, courtesy of EV&JW.

76   A lot of people: Int of Minnie Dittmeyer Barrett by Sylvia Grider, June 9, 1968, in RRP, Box 8, Folder 2.

76   Most everybody: Guthrie, "About Woody," p. 23.

76   Woody felt: Int with Matt Jennings by E. Victor and Judy Wolfenstein, January 9, 1972, courtesy of EV&JW.

76   People thought: Int of Robert E. Boydstun by Richard Reuss, June 7, 1968, in RRP, Box 8, Folder 2

76   Said that if: Int of Minnie Dittmeyer Barrett by Sylvia Grider, June 9, 1968, in RRP, Box 8, Folder 2.

77   On a visit: Richard Reuss's int with Frank Streetman is in RRP, Box 7, Folder 11. The longer WG's hair, groused barber Jess Turner, "the harder it was to shape. He had to be more particular with it." Int with Jess Turner by Sylvia Grider, June 8, 1968, in RRP, Box 8, Folder 2.

CHAPTER SIX

78   Was not one: Int with Mary Jennings Guthrie Boyle, August 19, 1998.

78   From what I know: WG to "Dear Ann," April 16, 1936, courtesy Anna Gideon Guthrie. He attached to the letter two long meditations on marriage by Khalil Gibran.

78   But the more: Typescript in WGA, Notebooks 1, Folder 4, p. 200.

79   Mr. Tom: Gladys Moore Gordon to Richard Reuss, February 17, 1969, in RRP, Box 1, Folder 23.

79   And a quick tongue: *Ibid.*

79   Just until: *Ibid.*

79   Odd and curious: WG to "Dear Lerners," September 28, 1947, courtesy of EV&JW.

80   I slept in jails: Guthrie, "Ear Players," p. 38.

80   I walked up: Guthrie, "Synopsis of the Book, 'Boomchasers,'" p. 6.

81   So stove up: *Ibid.*

81   My stepmother: Int with Mary Josephine Guthrie Edgmon, July 24, 1998.

81   I was spanked: Int with Roy Fritz Buzbee, November 17, 1999.

81   Betty Jean had: George Guthrie to E. Victor and Judy Wolfenstein, undated interview prior to December 28, 1971, courtesy of EV&JW.

81   To make us kids: Guthrie, "Synopsis of the Book, 'Boomchasers,'" p. 5. By 1931 and Betty Jean's appearance in Pampa, Woody was 19; this is yet another example of his adapting the history of others (siblings George and Mary Jo, in this case) into his own biography.

81   He made us respect: Int with Mary Jo Guthrie Edgmon by E. Victor and Judy Wolfenstein, September 25, 1971, courtesy of EV&JW.

81   I never seen: Int with Roy Fritz Buzbee, November 17, 1999.

82   I'm an iceman: *Ibid.* Buzbee's portfolio was apparently lost when he enlisted in the navy during World War II.

82   There wasn't very much: Guthrie, *Seeds of Man,* p. 49.

82   Papa was shirking: Int of Mary Jo Edgmon by E. Victor and Judy Wolfenstein, September 25, 1971.

83   Fighting Betty Jean: Int with George Guthrie by Richard Reuss, December 12, 1967, in RRP, Box 8, Folder 3.

83   Left its scars: Int of Mary Jennings Guthrie Boyle by E. Victor and Judy Wolfenstein, February 28, 1971, courtesy of EV&JW.

83   At Thanksgiving: Int with Matt Jennings, August 21, 1998.

84   If there is a spirit: Int with Roy Fritz Buzbee, November 17, 1999.

84   Was always: Int with Ann Gideon Guthrie, July 24, 1998.

84   He was just: Int of George and Emily Guthrie by E. Victor and Judy Wolfenstein, ca. December 1971, courtesy of EV&JW.

85   We adults: "A Few Kind Words Prepared for Miss Mary Ann Guthrie by Her Uncle, Woody Guthrie, 2-5-37," courtesy of Ann Guthrie.

85   Was not affiliated: Int with Mary Josephine Guthrie Edgmon, January 19, 1999.

85   A great guy: Int with Matt Jennings by E. Victor and Judy Wolfenstein, January 9, 1972, courtesy of EV&JW.

85   We're all offbeats: Int of George Hamlin by Sylvia Grider, June 5, 1968, in RRP, Box 8, Folder 2.

86   Woody felt: Int with Geneva Boydstun Adkins by Sylvia Grider, in RRP, Box 8, Folder 2.

86   To find himself: Richard Reuss to Heidi Press, February 16, 1974, in RRP, Box 2, Folder 1. Other details are in Richard Reuss to E. C. McKenzie, March 14, 1969, in RRP, Box 2, Folder 1.

86   If I was President: "If I Was Everything on Earth," in "Alonzo Zilch's Own Collection of Original Songs and Ballads," typescript, American Folklife Center, LC, courtesy of Judith Gray. The songs were all set to "some good old, family style tune that hath already gained a reputation as being liked by the people."

87   A little teed off: Int with Matt Jennings by E. Victor and Judy Wolfenstein, January 9, 1972.

87   Something you get rid of: Int with Matt Jennings, August 21, 1998.

87   Woody was far: Int with Matt Jennings by E. Victor and Judy Wolfenstein, January 9, 1972.

87   Always serious: Int of Evelyn Todd by Richard Reuss, June 6, 1968, in RRP, Box 8, Folder 4.

87   Republicans were: Int with Matt Jennings by E. Victor and Judy Wolfenstein, January 9, 1972.

87   He was always: Int with Roy Fritz Buzbee, November 17, 1999.

87   Sour: Int with Mary Jennings Guthrie Boyle, August 19, 1998. Almost six decades after their divorce, Mrs. Boyle added, "And I look back and I'm glad, I'm glad I didn't get stuck in a rut with somebody who would go to work at eight o'clock and they would come home at five, and that's all they did in their lives."

87   An old lady: Mary Jo Edgmon scrapbook, Seminole, Oklahoma. Guthrie was to paint at least one oil painting of a pueblo when he returned to Pampa.

88   I knew: Typescript in WGA, Notebooks 1, Folder 4, p. 201.

88   To be somebody: Int witz Buzbee, November 17, 1999.

88   It's a pretty tough thing: Int with Mary Jennings Guthrie Boyle, August 19, 1998.

88   To have no: Guthrie, "My Life," in *American Folksong* (New York: Oak Publications, 1961), p. 3.

88   That if he could: Int with Mary Jennings Guthrie Boyle, August 19, 1998.

88   He was going: *Ibid.* Minnie Dittmeyer provided details of the living arrangement in an interview with Richard Reuss.

CHAPTER SEVEN

90   Colder: Guthrie, "About Woody," p. 23.

90   A nice little town: Guthrie, *Bound for Glory*, p. 196. This often fanciful "autobiography" must be read with caution.

90   You hate: Lomax, Guthrie, and Seeger, *Hard Hitting Songs*, p. 23.

90   Offering to do: *Ibid.* Guthrie elaborates a bit on this experience in *Bound for Glory*, pp. 203–213.

91   This was my first time: Lomax, Guthrie, and Seeger, *Hard Hitting Songs*, p. 24.

91   Coming out: Guthrie, *Bound for Glory*, pp. 225–226.

91   West of the West: Quoted in Carey McWilliams, *Southern California Country* (New York: Duell, Sloan & Pearce, 1946), p. 313.

91   Japanese boy: Guthrie, *Bound for Glory*, p. 225.

92   Here's something extra: *Ibid.*, p. 228.

93   That was the closest: *Ibid.*, p. 230. While Guthrie considerably embroidered his purported autobiography, the details there agree generally with other sources. See "Synopsis of the Book, 'Boomchasers,'" and the headnote for "Vigilante Man," in Lomax, Guthrie, and Seeger, *Hard Hitting Songs*, p. 234.

93   Sweet as could be: Guthrie, *Bound for Glory*, p. 234.

93   You might: *Ibid.*, p. 236.

94   Come here, you: *Ibid.*, p. 240.

94   Don't you know: *Ibid.*, p. 243.

95   I didn't pass: Guthrie, "A Synopsis for the Book, 'Boomchasers,'" p. 7.

95   I can't tell you: Guthrie, "High Balladry."

96   I know it upset: Int with Mary Jennings Guthrie Boyle, August 18, 1998.

97   All kinds: WG, "High Balladry."

97   And it was immediate: Int with Maxine Crissman, July 25, 1998.

98   A low, tomboy-sounding: Woody Guthrie, "Songs, People, Papers," in WGA, Manuscripts Box 4, Folder 31.

98   Southern E-chord: Guthrie, "My Life," in *American Folksong*, p. 4.

98   The crossnote: Int with Maxine Crissman by Richard Reuss, June 14–18, 1968, in RRP, Box 8, Folder 6.

98   That was my start: Int with Maxine Crissman, July 25, 1998.

99   How do you get: WG, "High Balladry."

100   You see: *Ibid.*

100   Could sell: Int with Maxine Crissman, July 25, 1998.

101   An exciting eight years: *Orange County Register*, August 4, 1966.

CHAPTER EIGHT

103   I'm a-going down this road: This text is from WG's untitled 200-page songbook, a copy of which is in the American Folklife Center, LC.

104   The run-of-the-mill: Int with Maxine Crissman by Richard Reuss, June 14–18, 1968, in RRP, Box 8, Folder 6. This interview and that of the author with Crissman are the main source for Guthrie's radio career in Los Angeles.

105   Hilarious: Int with Maxine Crissman by Richard Reuss, June 14–18, 1968, in RRP, Box 8, Folder 6.

105   She's my curly-headed baby: "Woody and Lefty Lou's Favorite Collection [of] Old Time Hill Country Songs" (Gardena, Calif.: Institute Press, 1938[?]), n.p., courtesy of Peter LaChapelle. Guthrie's wife Mary stated he was inspired to write the song by the birth of their daughter Gwendolyn.

106   O' the Chinese: *Ibid.*, p. 3.

107   I thought: Guthrie, "Synopsis of the Book, 'Boomchasers,'" p. 8.

107   Sweet singers: Int with Maxine Crissman, July 25, 1998.

107   Buckaroo ballads: Gerald Haslam, *Working Man Blues* (Berkeley: University of California Press, 1999), pp. 29 *ff.*, distinguishes the various genres of traditional, country, hillbilly, and western music.

108   We would set: Int. with Maxine Crissman, July 25, 1998.

108   Santa Monica Social Register: Int with Maxine Crissman by Richard Reuss, June 14–18, 1968, in RRP, Box 8, Folder 6.

109   I am a Negro: *Ibid.*

109   Thousands of folks: "Woody and Lefty Lou's Favorite Collection."

110   Lefty Lou and me: *Ibid.*

110   Way out in Reno: *Ibid.* Guthrie's typescript dates it to August 1937.

111   On all that wealth: Int with Maxine Crissman, July 25, 1998.

111   Where you from: *Ibid.*

111   Many years: "Woody and Lefty Lou's Favorite Collection."

112   Woody had relatives: Int with Maxine Crissman by Richard Reuss, June 14–18, 1968, in RRP, Box 8, Folder 6.

112   You're selfish: Int with Maxine Crissman, July 25, 1998.

112   You're out of your mind: Int with Maxine Crissman by Richard Reuss, June 14–18, 1968, in RRP, Box 8, Folder 6.

113   How much mail: *Ibid.*

114   Sail the seas: *Ibid.*

114   He just wasn't: Int with Maxine Crissman, July 25, 1998.

115   Me, my dad: *Ibid.*
115   Wouldn't open the door: Int with Maxine Crissman, July 27, 1998.
116   He was a master: *Ibid.*
116   That was the last: *Ibid.*
116   I was the top: *Ibid.*

CHAPTER NINE

Details of the trip to California on Route 66 were drawn from a letter by Bertha Bryan Edmoundson of Bakersfield, California, September 29, 1998. The migrants' living conditions are reported by John Steinbeck in "Their Blood Is Strong" (San Francisco: Simon J. Lubin Society of California, 1938). Clifford J. Ocheltree in an email letter fixed Whitey McPherson's age. McPherson was apparently not related to Betty Jean McPherson.

117   He listen: Int with Maxine Crissman, July 25, 1998. That interview and one conducted by Richard Reuss in June 1968 retold the story of the Mexican adventure.
117   Nobody spoke: Int of Maxine Crissman by Richard Reuss, June 14–18, 1968, p. 26, in RRP, Box 8, Folder 6.
118   If one could endure: Bill C. Malone, *Country Music, U.S.A.* (Austin: University of Texas Press, 1970), p. 113.
118   Okay, come back: Int with Maxine Crissman, July 25, 1998.
119   I don't like: *Ibid.*
120   Horton, why in *the* hell: *Ibid.*
120   Looks like we smuggled: Int with Maxine Crissman by Richard Reuss, June 14–18, 1968, in RRP, Box 8, Folder 6.
121   We been looking: Int with Maxine Crissman, July 25, 1998.
121   Beans, bones: *Ibid.*
122   You could see: Int with Jeff Guthrie by E. Victor and Judy Wolfenstein, Golden, Colorado, September 28, 29, 1971, courtesy of EV&JW.
123   I ain't got no home: These are the first two stanzas from "Songs of Woody Guthrie," typescript in the American Folklife Center, LC, p. 82. A revised version is in Lomax, Guthrie, and Seeger, *Hard Hitting Songs,* p. 64.
123   Rewrite with better: "Chinese-Japs," in WGA, Notebooks 1, Folder 6.
123   The land around here's: "The Talking Blues" typescript, courtesy of BJO. Guthrie carefully typed at the bottom: "Except for the first 2 stanzas this is an original composition by W (Woody) Guthrie."
124   You drunken drivers: "Songs of Woody Guthrie," p. 82. A revised version is in Lomax, Guthrie, and Seeger, *Hard Hitting Songs,* pp. 74–75.
125   Ma never claimed: Typescript in WGA, Notebooks 1, Folder 4, p. 8.
125   I believe: Typescript in WGA, Notebooks 1, Folder 4.
126   He would do: Int with Maxine Crissman, July 25, 1998.
126   It was time: *Ibid.*
127   I am trying to elect: Undated clip from the *Light,* ca. June 1938, courtesy of Peter LaChapelle.
128   It was peach-picking: Guthrie, "A Synopsis of the Book, 'Boomchasers.' "
129   Crooked work: Guthrie, "Woody Guthrie," in WGA, Manuscripts 2, Box 1, Folder 34, p. 6.

CHAPTER TEN

130 He was always: Int of Maxine Crissman by Richard Reuss, June 14–18, 1968, in RRP, Box 8, Folder 6.

130 And getting nowhere: "Desert Sun, RR. 'Bulls' Harass Workers," *Light*, September 9, 1938, p. 1. Courtesy Peter LaChapelle.

130 Migration to California: *Ibid.* Guthrie was clearly following the news. In an editorial column in that same issue of the *Light*, Guthrie suggested "the Jews are too brilliant folks to live in Great Ripped and War-Torn Europe." War looming, "the most intelligent dwellers will rest very uncomfortably or try to pack and git out."

131 Black sedans: Guthrie, "Songs, People, Papers," p. 5.

132 About people: Int with Mary Jennings Guthrie Boyle by E. Victor and Judy Wolfenstein, December 28, 1971, courtesy of EV&JW.

132 Doing the manly thing: Int with Mary Jennings Guthrie Boyle, August 19, 1998.

132 But had this idea: Int of Matt Jennings by E. Victor and Judy Wolfenstein, January 9, 1972, courtesy of EV&JW.

132 Were running away: Untitled, signed "W.G. 1940," in WGA, Manuscripts Box 1, Folder 2.

132 Some new songs: WG, "Songs, People, Papers."

133 Factories in the fields: The phrase was coined by writer-lawyer-advocate-for-the-migrants Carey McWilliams for an article in the *Nation*, and later used as the title of his classic book published in 1939.

133 Destinies were set: Dan Morgan, *Rising in the West* (New York: Alfred A. Knopf, 1992), p. 57.

133 We have to solve: Carey McWilliams, *Factories in the Fields* (Boston: Little, Brown, 1939), p. 289.

134 For every farmer: Quoted in Thompson, *Closing the Frontier*, p. 218.

134 No Okies Allowed: Haslam, *Working Man Blues*, p. 68. The population statistics are from Walter J. Stein, *California and the Dust Bowl Migration* (Westport, Conn.: Greenwood Press, 1973), p. 46; and the unsigned "Preface" in Steinbeck, "Their Blood is Strong."

135 Cardboard, pasteboard: "On a Slow Train Through California, By Woody, Th' Dustiest of th' Dustbowl Refugees," mimeographed songbook, undated, but April 1939, in WGA. Guthrie was not exaggerating. See the "Report of Carey McWilliams, Chief, State Division of Immigration and Housing," in United States Senate Subcommittee of the Committee on Education and Labor, *Violations of Free Speech and Rights of Labor* (Washington, D.C.: Government Printing Office, 1940), Part 59, p. 21892.

135 We weren't used: Int with Bertha Bryan Edmoundson, August 6, 1998.

136 Hard workers: *Ibid.*

136 Greener valleys: Woody Guthrie, untitled 1940 manuscript, in WGA, Manuscripts Box 1, Folder 2.

136 Little Oklahoma: Drawn from Carey McWilliams's testimony before the United States Senate Subcommittee of the Committee on Education and Labor, *Violations of Free Speech and Rights of Labor*, Part 59, p. 21773.

137 There are a few things: Ed Robbin, *Woody Guthrie and Me* (Berkeley, Calif.: Lancaster-Miller, 1979), p. 27.

137 A little Sorbonne girl: Meyer Levin, *In Search* (New York: Horizon, 1950), p. 30.

137 We were shocked: *Ibid.*, p. 33.

138   The struggle: Robbin, *Woody Guthrie and Me*, p. 19.
138   The Left was: Int with Morton Robbin, October 10, 2000.
138   I always listen: Robbin, *Woody Guthrie and Me*, p. 28.
139   Fulminating: Robbin, *Ibid.*, p. 30.
139   Mr. Tom Mooney: Typescript in WGA, Notebooks Box 1, Folder 4. The manu-
       script is dated in Guthrie's writing January 15, 1939.
139   I'm bringing home: Int of Clara Robbin by E. Victor and Judy Wolfenstein,
       December 28, 1969, courtesy of EV&JW.
139   As much as you had: *Ibid.*
139   Sure, why not: Robbin, *Woody Guthrie and Me*, p. 32.
139   Since the Party: Int of Ed Robbin by E. Victor and Judy Wolfenstein, December
       28, 1969, courtesy of EV&JW.
140   The sloganeering: *Ibid.*
140   Way up in old Frisco: "Mr. Tom Mooney Is Free," in Guthrie "On a Slow Train
       Through California."
140   The house came down: Robbin, *Woody Guthrie and Me*, p. 33.
141   That dead sea: Guthrie, *Library of Congress Recordings*, Rounder CD
       1041/42/43.
141   Really liked him: Int with Dan Robbin, October 25, 2000.
141   Nonplussed: Int with Morton Robbin, October 10, 2000.

CHAPTER ELEVEN

143   The place: Int with Ed Robbin by E. Victor and Judy Wolfenstein, December
       28, 1969, courtesy of EV&JW.
143   If you're afraid: Robbin, *Woody Guthrie and Me*, pp. 35–36, quoting Guthrie's
       first column for the *People's World*.
143   He just loved: Int with Ed Robbin by E. Victor and Judy Wolfenstein, December
       28, 1969.
143   A cocksman: Int with Norman Pierce by Richard Reuss, July 8, 1967, in RRP,
       Box 8, Folder 3.
144   As family: Int of Clara Robbin by E. Victor and Judy Wolfenstein, December
       28, 1969, courtesy of EV&JW.
144   Ed's been telling: Robbin, *Woody Guthrie and Me*, pp. 46–47.
145   He was a big: Int with Herta Geer Ware, August 11, 1998.
145   My God: *Ibid.*
146   A wonderful little fellow: Int with Eddie Albert, August 1, 2001.
146   Will thought: Int with Herta Geer Ware, August 11, 1998.
146   Was the most loving: Int with Mary Jennings Guthrie Boyle, August 19,
       1998.
146   On the side: Richard Reuss's notes of conversation with Ed Robbin, July 5,
       1967, in RRP, Box 8, Folder 3.
146   I seldom worship: Woody Guthrie, "Thirty Bucks Wood Help," *Hollywood Tri-
       bune*, July 24, 1939.
147   The lepers cleansed: Woody Guthrie, "Thy Faith Will Make Thee Whole," in
       WGA, Notebooks Box 1, Folder 4, dated "3/4/39 KFVD." The song apparently
       was inspired by Luke 7:22 and Mark 5:34.
147   Then I watched: Woody Guthrie, "Little Billy," in WGA, Notebooks Box 1,
       Folder 6, dated March 1939. He must have liked the song; some years later,
       Guthrie wrote on the typescript, "needs a record done./W.G."
148   If folks: Guthrie, "Thirty Bucks Wood Help." The misspellings are deliberate.

148   He never did run: Int with George Guthrie by E. Victor and Judy Wolfenstein, after September 1971, prior to December 28, 1971, courtesy of EV&JW.

148   Lots of folks: Guthrie, "Thirty Bucks Wood Help." The misspellings are deliberate.

149   There's many: "Pretty Boy Floyd" was to become one of Guthrie's most popular songs. A text is in Lomax, Guthrie, and Seeger, *Hard Hitting Songs*, p. 115. Though Floyd was killed by law enforcement officers in 1934, Charlie Pipes, Jeff Guthrie's partner on the night patrol, recalled that Pretty Boy Floyd had "been through Pampa lots of times," holing up with an uncle in the area. Pipes and Guthrie left Floyd alone—apparently there were no Texas warrants out for him—until they picked him up for disturbing the peace: drinking beer in a restaurant. Richard Reuss's interview of Pipes is in RRP, Box 8, Folder 2.

149   When them cards: Woody Guthrie, "Looking for the New Deal Now," in "On a Slow Train Through California."

150   Twouda been better, better: *Ibid.*

150   From the Southland: "Songs of Woody Guthrie," p. 100. A slightly different version is on p. 1 with a note that it was written in 1939 while living at 115 East Chestnut Street, Glendale.

150   But this good land: Undated text of "Dustbowl Refugee" written prior to 1942, in "Songs of Woody Guthrie," p. 145.

150   The best thing: Woody Guthrie, "My Constitution and Me," in WGA, Manuscripts Box 7, Folder 23.1. The undated manuscript was probably written in 1949 in New York City. The date of 1936 is repeated in the manuscript; hence it is probably not a typographical error.

151   I never heard: Int with George Guthrie by E. Victor and Judy Wolfenstein, after September 1971, prior to December 28, 1971.

151   Woody never was: Int with Will Geer by E. Victor and Judy Wolfenstein, December 1971, courtesy of EV&JW.

151   If he wasn't: Telephone conversation with Dorothy Healey, May 18, 1998.

151   Are complacent: Charles Seeger, writing as Carl Sands, quoted by Richard Reuss, "Folk Music and Social Conscience: The Musical Odyssey of Charles Seeger," *Western Folklore* 38 (1979), p. 229.

152   Recounted the democratic: Richard Reuss, "American Folklore and Left-Wing Politics: 1927–1957," unpublished Ph.D. dissertation, Indiana University, 1971, p. 70.

152   Ed, I'd like: Robbin, *Woody Guthrie and Me*, p. 36.

153   They were good: Al Richmond, *A Long View from the Left* (Boston: Houghton Mifflin, 1973), p. 280.

153   I never am: Guthrie, "On a Slow Train Through California."

154   Once he heard: Int with Ed Robbin by E. Victor and Judy Wolfenstein, December 28, 1969.

154   Very high: Critic Malcolm Cowley is quoted in Jay Parini, *John Steinbeck: A Biography* (New York: Henry Holt, 1995), p. 220.

154   Trying to write: Jackson J. Benson, *The True Adventures of John Steinbeck, Writer* (New York: Viking Press, 1984), p. 375.

154   Is about us: Robbin, *Woody Guthrie and Me*, p. 31.

154   Preacher Casey: "Songs of Woody Guthrie," p. 4. Guthrie set it to a melody, "Candy Man Blues," learned from the black guitar player and blues singer in Pampa he nicknamed "Spider-fingers."

155   I'm goin down the road: WG's version is in Lomax, Guthrie, and Seeger, *Hard Hitting Songs*, pp. 215 *ff.*

155   They slowed: Ben Crisler, "Critic at Large," *PM*, September 11, 1940, p. 10.

155   We went around: Guthrie, "Songs, People, Papers," internally dated to 1946.
155   Was a very colorful: Int with Bill Wheeler, July 29, 1998.
156   Steinbeck's book: James Forester, "Slow Train Thru California," *Hollywood Tribune*, July 3, 1939. Guthrie would republish his *Hollywood Tribune* articles and selected commentaries from his songbooks in an eighty-page pamphlet produced in the East 5th Street printshop of Saul Marks, a friend of Ed Robbin. He sold "$30 Wood Help!" for 25 cents. Significantly, it contained only one song: "I'm Looking for that New Deal Now."
156   It was a howlin': Guthrie, "$30 Bucks Wood Help."
157   A full car load: "The Old Wop" to Nora Guthrie, n.d., but 2002, in WGA.
157   You see more wimmen: Woody, the Dustiest of th' Dustbowlers, "Hollerwood Bolevard," *Hollywood Tribune*, July 31, 1939, p. 7.
157   It was very simple: Int of Will Geer by E. Victor and Judy Wolfenstein, December 1971.
158   The songs were sufficient: Int with Herta Geer Ware, August 11, 1998.
158   Was like going: Int with Will Geer by E. Victor and Judy Wolfenstein, December 1971.
158   Woody tried: "The Old Wop" to Nora Guthrie, n.d., but 2002 in WGA.
158   And of course: Int with Mary Jennings Guthrie Boyle, August 19, 1998.
159   He was like: Int with Sam Hinton, July 27, 1998.

CHAPTER TWELVE

160   Purty dern: *People's World*, September 13, 1939.
160   The nickel and penny: Guthrie, "My Life," in *American Folksong*, p. 4.
161   He never should: Int of Mary Jennings Guthrie Boyle by E. Victor and Judy Wolfenstein, December 28, 1971, courtesy of EV&JW.
161   A new fresh start: Guthrie, "My Life," in *American Folksong*, p. 4.
161   I hated: "Woody Guthrie by Me," p. 7, in WGA, Manuscripts 2, Box 1, File 34. Other details of the Pampa trip are from Sylvia Grider's notes of an interview with Mrs. Evelyn Todd, in Clarendon, Texas, June 6, 1968, in RRP, Box 8, Folder 4.
161   Born working: Guthrie, *Bound for Glory*, p. 159.
162   It was not: "Woody Guthrie by Me," p. 7.
162   I sold: *Ibid.*
162   I get: Undated int with George Guthrie by E. Victor and Judy Wolfenstein, post September 1971, prior to December 28, 1971, courtesy of EV&JW.
163   Fully as hard: "Woody Guthrie by Me," p. 8.
163   New York: "The Government Road," in WGA, Notebooks 1, Folder 4.
163   I been in New York: WG to Alan Lomax, September 20, 1940, in American Folklife Center, LC.
163   I thought: Guthrie, "My Life," in *American Folksong*, p. 5.
163   It was pretty: Int with Will Geer by E. Victor and Judy Wolfenstein, December 1971, courtesy of EV&JW, and with Herta Geer Ware, August 11, 1998.
164   If you had: Int with Will Geer by E. Victor and Judy Wolfenstein, December 1971.
164   In Will Geer's house: "I Don't Feel at Home in the Bowery No More," written February 18, 1940, in WGA, Notebooks 1, Folder 4.
164   I seen an apartment: *Ibid.*
164   I won't beg: Guthrie, *Born to Win*, pp. 235–236.
165   No question: Int with Herta Geer Ware, August 11, 1998.

165   This land: The holograph is hung in the Woody Guthrie Archives. A copy is in Pete Seeger, *Where Have All the Flowers Gone* (Bethlehem, Pa.: Sing Out, 1997), p. 142.

166   The Soviet Union: Robert E. Sherwood, *Roosevelt and Hopkins* (New York: Harper & Brothers, 1948), p. 138.

167   Now the guns in Europe: "Why Do You Stand There in the Rain," in Lomax, Guthrie, and Seeger, *Hard Hitting Songs*, p. 363.

167   A short man: Int with Martha Garlin, July 23, 1998.

167   He was a talent: Int with Mordecai Bauman, July 14, 1998.

168   "Woody," a real Dust Bowl refugee: *Daily Worker*, March 1, 1940.

168   Is a very rich state: Pete Seeger with Robert Santelli, "Hobo's Lullaby" in Robert Santelli and Emily Davidson, eds., *Hard Travelin': The Life and Legacy of Woody Guthrie* (Hanover, N.H.: Wesleyan University Press, 1999), p. 23.

168   It was an act: Int with Earl Robinson by E. Victor and Judy Wolfenstein, June 9, 1971, courtesy of EV&JW.

168   Tires on hot asphalt: Dunaway, *How Can I Keep from Singing*, p. 63.

168   A big popper: Int of Alan Lomax by Richard Reuss, August 29, 1966, in RRP, Box 8, Folder 3.

168   Ballads . . . that will fool a folklore expert: Undated letter of recommendation for WG by Alan Lomax, probably written in 1941.

169   Hopelessly involved: Nolan Porterfield, *Last Cavalier: the Life and Times of John A. Lomax* (Urbana: University of Illinois Press, 1996), p. 427.

169   Whatever jails: Porterfield, *Last Cavalier*, p. 339.

169   Somewhat skeptical: Int of Alan Lomax by Richard Reuss, August 29, 1966, in RRP, Box 8, Folder 3.

170   Yes, he took: Lomax, Guthrie, and Seeger, *Hard Hitting Songs*, p. 115.

170   A real ballad-maker: Int of Alan Lomax by Richard Reuss, August 29, 1966, in RRP, Box 8, Folder 3.

170   The kind of person: Int of Pete Seeger, November 19, 1998.

170   The wrong crowd: Int with Maxine Crissman, July 25, 1998.

170   I was snatched: WG to Alan Lomax, September 20, 1940, in the American Folklife Center, LC, courtesy of Judith Gray.

171   Put on like: Int of Al Richmond by Richard Reuss, July 10, 1967, in RRP, Box 8, Folder 3.

171   I ain't: Woody Guthrie, *Woody Sez* (New York: Grosset & Dunlap, 1975), p. 71.

171   I hate war: Untitled entry in WGA, Notebooks 1, Folder 7.

171   I'm a Proletarian: *Daily Worker*, April 11, 1940.

171   It was not: Int with Sender Garlin, July 26, 1998.

172   I've not read: Untitled essay, dated September 25, 1940, in the American Folklife Center, LC.

172   Not educated: Int with Sender Garlin, July 26, 1998.

172   Tried but he didn't get: Int with Will Geer by E. Victor and Judy Wolfenstein, December 1971.

CHAPTER THIRTEEN

173   I don't want: Liner notes to *Library of Congress Recordings*, Rounder CD 1041/42/43. The notes were originally written for the first commercial release of these recordings on Elektra Records in 1964.

173   Woody was behaving: Int of Bess Lomax Hawes and Baldwin "Butch" Hawes by E. Victor and Judy Wolfenstein, December 11, 1971, courtesy of EV&JW.

174   Except that what: Liner notes to *Library of Congress Recordings*, Rounder CD 1041/42/43. Details of Guthrie's visit to Washington are taken from an Alan Lomax interview by Richard Reuss on August 29, 1966, in RRP, Box 8, Folder 3.

174   Take care of Woody: Int of Bess Lomax Hawes and Baldwin "Butch" Hawes by E. Victor and Judy Wolfenstein, December 11, 1971.

175   Wasn't in the class: Guthrie, *Library of Congress Recordings*, Rounder CD 1041/42/43, Track 5.

175   Music is some kind: WG to Alan Lomax, ca. September 19, 1940, in the American Folklife Center, LC.

175   Bit at the heart: Liner notes to *Library of Congress Recordings*, Rounder CD 1041/42/43.

176   The logical: Lomax, Guthrie, and Seeger, *Hard Hitting Songs*, p. 366. The postscript was written in 1966, for the first publication of the book.

177   In a woodland: Dunaway, *How Can I Keep from Singing*, p. 38.

177   Discovered: *Ibid.*, p. 49.

178   No rich: Int with Pete Seeger, November 19, 1998.

178   Most of what: *Ibid.*

178   $15 a week: Pete Seeger, "Afterword 1999," in Lomax, Guthrie, and Seeger, *Hard Hitting Songs*, p. 369.

178   Long tall: Guthrie, *Pastures of Plenty*, p. 9; originally written for "My Life," in *American Folksong*, p. 5.

178   I didn't try: Seeger with Santelli, "Hobo's Lullaby," p. 25. In fact, Seeger the untutored was to become an accomplished, if ever dissembling, musician.

178   He must have liked: Seeger, *Where Have All the Flowers Gone*, p. 17.

179   The biggest parts: George Lewis, "America Is in Their Songs," *Daily Worker*, March 24, 1941, p. 7.

179   There are so many: Int with Pete Seeger, November 19, 1998. The manuscript would not be published until 1967, and then only by a publisher seemingly more interested in it as a historical than a political document.

179   Wrote and spoke: Lomax, Guthrie, and Seeger, *Hard Hitting Songs*, p. 366.

180   Our best: Alan Lomax's notes to Archive of American Folk Song record No. 1, released in 1942.

180   Yeah: Int with Pete Seeger, November 19, 1998. Information about the RCA recording sessions was drawn from Guy Logsdon, compiler, "Woody Guthrie: A Biblio-Discography," unpublished research paper, National Endowment for the Humanities and the Smithsonian Institution, May 15, 1998.

180   The best thing: *Daily Worker*, undated clip, in WGA, Scrapbooks Box 3.

180   Half the job: Int with Pete Seeger, November 19, 1998. Johnson's script was so well crafted that critic Edmund Wilson concluded the novel "went on the screen as easily as if it had been written in the studios, and was probably the only serious story on record that seemed equally effective as a film and as a book." See Parini, *John Steinbeck*, p. 225.

181   Migratious: "Dust Bowl Ballads, by Woody Guthrie, 'The Dustiest of the Dust Bowlers,'" RCA record album P-27.

181   You might be able: *Ibid.*

182   Important and fascinating: WGA, Scrapbooks Box 3 contains the three reviews.

182   In order to silence: Int with Marjorie Guthrie by Richard Reuss, January 2, 1969, in RRP, Box 8, Folder 3.

183   The Oklahoma Dust Bowl man: Nolan Porterfield, *Last Cavalier*, p. 421. Lomax

Senior also dismissed the Golden Gate Quartet as too slick for a folk music program.

183   It was open: Int with Norman Corwin, August 8, 1998.

183   I think he worked: Klein, *Woody Guthrie*, p. 157.

183   Woody was a very sexy fellow: Int with Will Geer by E. Victor and Judy Wolfenstein, December 1971.

184   While there was loneliness: John Steinbeck, "Foreword" to Lomax, Guthrie, and Seeger, *Hard Hitting Songs*, pp. 8-9.

CHAPTER FOURTEEN

185   To get acquainted: Int of Sara Ogan Gunning by Ellen Stekert and Archie Green, Detroit, Michigan, March 3, 1964. Ambellan's adventure is recounted in an interview with Richard Reuss, June 27, 1969, in RRP, Box 8, Folder 3. Ledbetter's ride was set down by Reuss during a 1969 interview with Marjorie Guthrie and Henrietta Yurchenko, in RRP, Box 8, Folder 3.

185   Pete, you want: Int with Pete Seeger, November 19, 1998.

186   Boys, you just let me off: *Ibid.*

186   Little old rotty: "Low Levee Cafe," in WGA, Manuscripts Box 4, Folder 55. Other details of the trip are in Seeger, *The Incompleat Folksinger*, p. 43.

186   Coming out: Int with Pete Seeger, November 19, 1998.

187   Woody was fascinated: *Ibid.*

187   One thousand: *Daily Worker*, June 6, 1940, p. 7.

187   I'm not sure: Seeger, *Incompleat Folksinger*, p. 43. Seeger said it was a meeting of oil workers; Guthrie twice described it as the small Tenant Farmers Union.

187   Bob Wood told: Untitled document in WGA, Manuscripts Box 7, Folder 6.

188   There once was a union maid: This original version, later edited, with new stanzas added by the Almanac Singers, is in WGA, Notebooks 1, Folder 7. The Almanacs added the chorus by which the song is best known: "Oh, you can't scare me, I'm sticking to the union/I'm sticking to the union I'm sticking to the union,/Oh, you can't scare me, I'm sticking to the union/I'm sticking to the union 'til the day I die."

188   Not much better: Pete Seeger to Richard Reuss, January 30, 1969, in RRP, Box 2, Folder 25.

188   You've got to make: Int with Pete Seeger, November 19, 1998.

189   We read: *Ibid.*

189   Guthrie was sympathetic: Int with Sender Garlin, July 26, 1998. Seeger used the same phrase in a separate interview.

189   He kind of laughed: Int with Pete Seeger, November 19, 1998.

189   Mossybacks: Int with Henrietta Yurchenko, June 16, 1999.

189   I made ever thing: WG, *Woody Sez*, p. 153.

189   A communist: WG to "Dear Alan," ca. September 19, 1940, in American Folklife Center, LC.

189   Afraid: WG to "Dear Allan [sic] and Elizabeth," n.d., in American Folklife Center, LC.

189   The day will come: Untitled in WGA, Notebooks 1, Folder 7.

190   We just hearse: WG to Alan Lomax, undated, but fall 1940, in American Folklife Center, LC.

191   We all thought: Int with Henrietta Yurchenko, June 16, 1999.

191   Was marvelous: Int of Earl Robinson by E. Victor and Judy Wolfenstein, June 17, 1971, courtesy of EV&JW.

191 Raised in lace: Alan Lomax to Richard Reuss, August 29, 1966, in RRP, Box 8, Folder 4.

191 Just *adored*: Int with Henrietta Yurchenko, June 16, 1999.

191 Leadbelly was just: Int with Queen Ollie Robinson, August 8, 1998. According to Ms. Robinson, the original spelling of her uncle's name was "Lead Belly." Careless usage in the press led to the combined form.

192 Windjammer: Charles Wolfe and Kip Lornell, *The Life and Legend of Leadbelly* (New York: HarperCollins, 1992), p. 16.

192 Baddest ass: *Ibid.*, p. xiv.

192 I put Mary: *Ibid.*, p. 86.

193 Impudence: *Ibid.*, p. 103.

193 Pure negro: John A. Lomax, *Negro Folk Songs as Sung by Leadbelly* (New York: Macmillan, 1936), p. ix.

193 Come prepared: Wolfe and Lornell, *Life and Legend of Leadbelly*, p. 124.

193 Sweet singer: *New York Herald-Tribune*, January 3, 1935.

193 I don't know: Int with Queen Ollie Robinson, August 8, 1998.

193 Because he was: Int with Margaret Garland Harrington, January 30, 2002.

194 Like big stove pipes: Woody Guthrie, "The Singing Cricket," in WGA, Manuscripts Box 1, Folder 3.1.

194 Leadbelly was teaching: Int with Henrietta Yurchenko, June 16, 1999.

194 I never heard: Int with Queen Ollie Robinson, August 8, 1998.

194 Darkly lit doorways: Woody Guthrie, notes to *Leadbelly: Bourgeois Blues*, Smithsonian Folkways, SF CD 40045.

194 He was funny: Int with Queen Ollie Robinson, August 8, 1998.

195 Leadbelly on the air: Wolfe and Lornell, *Life and Legend of Leadbelly*, p. 220.

196 They are giving: WG to "Brother Lomax," September 17, 1940, in American Folklife Center, LC.

196 Hey, Lefty Lou: Int with Maxine Crissman, July 25, 1998.

196 They took: Int with Sarah Ogan Gunning by Ellen Stekert, August 11, 1968, in RRP, Box 8, Folder 3.

197 The best: WG to "Dear Alan," ca. September 19, 1940, in American Folklife Center, LC.

197 I have to set: WG to Lomax, undated but September 25, 1940, in American Folklore Center, LC.

197 Howdy, friend: As quoted in Klein, *Woody Guthrie*, p. 171.

198 These folks: Int with Maxine Crissman, July 25, 1998.

199 Well, I got: Robbin, *Woody Guthrie and Me*, p. 119.

199 Pack up: Int with Mary Jennings Guthrie Boyle, August 19, 1998.

CHAPTER FIFTEEN

200 They wanted: Int of Mary Boyle by E. Victor and Judy Wolfenstein, December 28, 1971, courtesy of EV&JW.

200 In the car: Int with Mary Jennings Guthrie Boyle, August 19, 1998.

201 We had one sandwich: Int with Fred Jennings by E. Victor and Judy Wolfenstein, March 25, 1972, courtesy of EV&JW.

201 They all looked: Robbin, *Woody Guthrie and Me*, p. 58.

202 And liked to work: WG to Alan Lomax, January 22, 1941, in American Folklife Center, LC. Courtesy of Judith Gray.

202 The wife feels: *Ibid.*

202 One certain old cricket: "The Railroad Cricket," January 30, 1941, in American Folklife Center, LC. Courtesy of Judith Gray.

202 I wouldn't take: "The Singing Cricket," February 2, 1941, in WGA, Manuscripts Box 1, Folder 3.1. It is reprinted in Guthrie, *Born to Win*, pp. 145 *ff*.

203 War Shit Ton: WG to Alan Lomax, n.d., in American Folklife Center, LC. Courtesy of Judith Gray.

203 You mean: Robbin, *Woody Guthrie and Me*, p. 59.

204 They were real good: Int with Mary Jennings Guthrie Boyle, August 19, 1998.

204 Say anything: WG to Alan Lomax, February 15, 1941, in American Folklife Center, LC. Courtesy of Judith Gray.

204 Busted: WG letter to Alan Lomax, ca. March 1941, in American Folklife Center, LC. Courtesy of Judith Gray.

204 His wheels: Int with Ed Robbin and Marjorie Guthrie by Robbie Osman, Radio Station KPFA, Berkeley, Calif., prior to July 17, 1979. Tape courtesy of Mort Robbin. Details of Guthrie's drinking are included in the interview.

204 She didn't know: Int with Clara Robbin by E. Victor and Judy Wolfenstein, December 28, 1969, courtesy of EV&JW.

204 She was not: Int with Seema Weatherwax, October 27, 1998.

205 My wife: "On a Slow Train Through California."

205 Woody was looking: Int with Seema Weatherwax, October 27, 1998.

205 Folks comes down: Untitled manuscript in WGA, Manuscripts Box 1, Folder 10. The poem, of course, contains a deft reference to the Lend Lease Act to aid Great Britain, passed by the House of Representatives and under debate in the Senate when Guthrie wrote the poem. The parenthetical question mark is in the original.

205 In the worst mood: Int with Ed Robbin by E. Victor and Judy Wolfenstein, December 28, 1969, courtesy of EV&JW.

206 He was more: Int of Ed Robbin by Richard Reuss, in RRP, Box 8, Folder 3.

206 High-powered people: Int of Sam Hinton, July 27, 1998.

206 Keep the wife: WG to Alan Lomax, February 20, 1941, in American Folklife Center, LC.

206 A conversation: Untitled in WGA, Notebooks 1, Folder 7, emphasis added. Note the dialect and contractions; Guthrie is writing for an unidentified audience.

206 The sewer went bad: Fred Jennings during the interview with Matt and Loma Jennings by E. Victor and Judy Wolfenstein, January 1972, courtesy of EV&JW.

207 Frogs shooting: Woody Guthrie, "Jump the Frog," in WGA, Manuscripts Box 1, Folder 10.

208 With a distinctive voice: "Memorandum for the Administrator, The Bonneville Project, Personnel Action," April 23, 1941, in file number 14X1225.004 801.1, a copy of which Bill Murlin provided the author.

208 Common touch: Int with Stephen Kahn, August 6, 2001.

208 Green Douglas firs: "Roll on, Columbia, Roll on," is set to the melody of Huddie Ledbetter's "Irene."

208 Guthrie's songs: Int with Stephen Kahn, August 6, 2001.

209 Emergency appointment: "Memorandum for the Administrator, The Bonneville Project, Personnel Action," May 13, 1941, in file number 14X1225.004 801.1, courtesy of Bill Murlin.

209 Appear in designated: *Ibid.*

209   Not very photogenic: Int of Stephen Kahn by Michael Majdic, June 21, 1998. The interviews by Majdic are courtesy of Michael Majdic, University of Oregon.

209   I didn't want to film: Int with Stephen Kahn, August 6, 2001.

209   Put him on the payroll: Int with Stephen Kahn by William Murlin and Bob Jones, Bonneville Power Administration, October 5, 1983. The interviews cited here by Murlin are courtesy of Murlin and the Bonneville Power Administration.

209   Hiring Woody: Int with Stephen Kahn by Michael Majdic, June 21, 1998.

209   Thoughts and ideals: *Ibid.*

209   And the whole time: Int with Elmer Buehler by William Murlin, September 6, 1984.

210   I wouldn't play: *Ibid.*

210   They are my: Int with Elmer Buehler by Michael Majdic, ca. June 1998.

210   Guthrie was thrilled: Int with Stephen Kahn by Michael Majdic, June 21, 1998.

211   Hard-hitting: Int with Stephen Kahn, August 6, 2001.

211   They didn't want: Int with Mary Jennings Guthrie Boyle by William Murlin, ca. 1983.

211   Is it paid for: Int with Stephen Kahn by Michael Majdic, June 21, 1998.

211   A lot of drafts: *Ibid.*

211   Uncle Sam: "Roll, Columbia, Roll," in Woody Guthrie, *Roll on Columbia* (Portland, Ore.: Bonneville Power Administration, 1988), p. 5.

212   In the misty crystal glitter: "Ballad of the Great Grand Coulee," in Guthrie, *Roll on Columbia*, p. 31.

212   I clumb: "The Biggest Thing that Man Has Ever Done," in Guthrie, *Roll on Columbia*, p. 29.

212   It's a mighty hard row: "Pastures of Plenty," in Guthrie, *Roll on Columbia*, p. 10. The second stanza here is from an alternate version "from the collection of Woody Guthrie, Professional Oakie [sic], just a passin' through," a typescript courtesy of Barry Ollman.

213   This country's getting: WG to Alan Lomax, February 20, 1941, in American Folklife Center, LC.

213   We didn't say: Int with Mary Jennings Guthrie Boyle, August 19, 1998.

213   Was looking: Int with Mary Jennings Guthrie Boyle by William Murlin, ca. 1983.

213   She thinks: WG to Almanacs, n.d., in WGA, Correspondence Series 1, Box 1, Folder 3.

213   After he left: Int with Mary Jennings Guthrie Boyle by William Murlin, ca. 1983.

CHAPTER SIXTEEN

215   Well, I guess: Pete Seeger to Millard Lampell, October 1, 1987, courtesy of Ronald Cohen.

215   No one has been: Martin Gilbert, *Churchill: A Life* (New York: Henry Holt, 1991), p. 701.

215   Churchill's flip-flopped: Lomax, Guthrie, and Seeger, *Hard Hitting Songs*, p. 371.

215   All of a sudden: Doris Willens, *Lonesome Traveler: The Life of Lee Hays* (Lincoln: University of Nebraska Press, 1993), p. 69.

216   Woody, how would: Seeger, *Incompleat Folksinger*, p. 15.

216   The only group: Int with Pete Seeger by E. Victor and Judy Wolfenstein, May 3, 1972, courtesy of EV&JW.

216   That there are: Lee Hays, "On Woody" manuscript, p. 174, Lee Hays Papers, Ralph Rinzler Folklife Archives and Collections, Smithsonian Institution, Washington, D.C.

216   There was the heart: Int with Irwin Silber, August 13, 1998.

217   Once you get: Int with Lee Hays by E. Victor and Judy Wolfenstein, March 11, 1972, courtesy of EV&JW.

217   Golden places: Willens, *Lonesome Traveler*, p. 59.

218   We wrote a lot: Int with Lee Hays by E. Victor and Judy Wolfenstein, March 11, 1972.

218   I don't want: *Ibid.*

218   Do you want: "Billy Boy," as printed in Ronald D. Cohen and Dave Samuelson, *Songs for Political Action* (Hamburg, Germany: Bear Family Records, 1996), p. 84.

219   It was a good: R. Serge Denisoff, *Great Day Coming: Folk Music and the American Left* (Baltimore: Penguin Books, 1973), p. 77. According to Hays, the explanation for the name—though Seeger attributed it to him—was Guthrie's: "There are two things every farmer has in his house, a family bible and the almanac. One takes care of you in the next world and one takes care of you in this." Int of Lee Hayes by E. Victor and Judy Wolfenstein, March 11, 1972.

219   Erratic but interesting: Quoted by Reuss, "American Folklore and Left-Wing Politics," p. 205.

219   Franklin D.: "Washington Breakdown," as printed in Cohen and Samuelson, *Songs for Political Action*, p. 84. The song is credited to Seeger, Hays, and Lampell.

220   You are the most: Alan Lomax quoted by Pete Seeger in an interview on November 19, 1998.

220   A marvelous: Int of Lee Hays by E. Victor and Judy Wolfenstein, March 11, 1972.

220   To most northern: Reuss, "American Folklore and Left-Wing Politics," p. 142. Seeger later acknowledged that "except for a few unions, there never was as much singing as some people now suppose. . . . [That] the United States was full of class conscious harmonizing in those days, 'taint true." Pete Seeger, "Whatever Happened to Singing in the Unions," *Sing Out!* (May 1965), p. 29.

221   Whose typewriter: Paraphrased from Lampell's unpublished autobiography, "Home before Morning," p. 81. Courtesy of Ron Cohen.

222   Pittsburgh town: Willens, *Lonesome Traveler*, p. 70.

222   A good little bantamweight: Int with Studs Terkel, August 8, 1998.

223   Woody was: Int of Lee Hays by E. Victor and Judy Wolfenstein, March 11, 1972.

223   It was Joycean: Int with Studs Terkel, August 8, 1998.

223   Unpardonably rude: Int with Bess Lomax Hawes, August 27, 1998.

223   Makes up stories: Pete Seeger, personal communication to Cray, March 17, 2003.

223   There were so many: Int of Lee Hays by E. Victor and Judy Wolfenstein, March 11, 1972.

223   I can't stand: Hays, "On Woody." Hays repeated the quote in an interview by E. Victor and Judy Wolfenstein, March 11, 1972.

224   Hillbilly singers: Pete Seeger to Millard Lampell, October 1, 1987, courtesy of Ron Cohen. This letter and Lampell's reply of December 19, 1987, provided many of the details of the tour and life in Almanac House.

224   Let me tell you: Cohen and Samuelson, *Songs for Political Action*, p. 86.

225   A very good fiddle: Pete Seeger to Millard Lampell, October 1, 1987, courtesy of Ron Cohen.

226   Well, I don't: Int with Mary Jennings Guthrie Boyle, August 19, 1998.

226   I hope: Pete Seeger, "Remembering Woody," *Mainstream* (August 1963), p. 29.

226   Got a chance: Pete Seeger to Millard Lampell, October 1, 1987, courtesy of Ron Cohen.

227   A helluva lot: Seeger, "Remembering Woody," p. 29.

CHAPTER SEVENTEEN

228   Bowled over: Pete Seeger to Millard Lampell, October 1, 1987, courtesy of Ronald Cohen. "Ear Players," perhaps because of excellent editing, led to two further articles in the magazine that year.

228   Binge writing: Int with Bess Lomax Hawes, August 27, 1998. "A desperate little man" comes from the first line of the American ballad "John Hardy."

229   Our source: Int with Bess Lomax Hawes and Baldwin "Butch" Hawes by E. Victor and Judy Wolfenstein, December 11, 1971, courtesy of EV&JW.

229   He was much: Int with Bess Lomax Hawes, August 27, 1998.

229   My name is Woody Guthrie: *Ibid.* Bess Lomax Hawes credits Lee Hays for this parody of Guthrie's own "The Biggest Thing That Man Has Ever Done," written on the Bonneville Dam project. She described "Woody, the general" in an interview with E. Victor and Judy Wolfenstein on December 11, 1971.

230   A Protestant Ethic: Int with Lee Hays by E. Victor and Judy Wolfenstein, March 11, 1972, courtesy of EV&JW.

230   I never joined: Int with Bess Lomax Hawes, August 27, 1998.

230   He looked: Gordon Friesen to Richard Reuss, Novmber 1, 1965, in RRP, Box 1, Folder 20.

230   Something that no one: Int with Agnes Cunningham, July 13, 1998. As evidence of his intellectual achievements, she noted that Guthrie is credited in the foreward to *The Cup and the Sword* by Alice Tisdale Hobart, published in 1942.

231   Hyper-literacy: Int with Bess Lomax Hawes and Baldwin "Butch" Hawes by E. Victor and Judy Wolfenstein, December 11, 1971.

231   It was terrible: Int with Bess Lomax Hawes, January 23, 2002.

231   And nobody: Int with Bess Lomax Hawes and Baldwin "Butch" Hawes by E. Victor and Judy Wolfenstein, December 11, 1971.

231   You didn't converse: Camilla Adams, "Woody Guthrie in the Days of the Almanac Singers," *Broadside*, 71 (June 1966).

232   It was very unlike: Int with Bess Lomax Hawes and Baldwin "Butch" Hawes by E. Victor and Judy Wolfenstein, December 11, 1971.

232   Triangular: Bernard Asbell, "Storyteller," unpublished manuscript, p. 73, courtesy of Asbell.

232   Woody was absolutely: Int with Lee Hays by E. Victor and Judy Wolfenstein, March 11, 1972.

232   He put them: Int with Bess Lomax Hawes, January 23, 2002.

233   Tell me: Waldemar Hille, ed., *The People's Song Book* (New York: People's Artists, 1948), p. 60. Just who wrote the chorus is unclear. Seeger, in a letter

written in October 1987, credited Guthrie—for the words as well as the music. Lampell believed he and Seeger were responsible. Bess Hawes in a 1971 interview specifically attributed the key line, "What were their names?" to Seeger. This vague attribution suggests why the Almanacs yielded copyright to Guthrie's heirs after a later recording by the Limelighters generated sizeable royalties. See Gordon Freisen to Richard Reuss, November 18, 1965, in RRP, Box 1, Folder 20.

233 Its force: Gordon Friesen to Richard Reuss, December 1, 1965, in RRP, Box 1, Folder 20.

233 A pug-nosed kid: Stanza 2 of "Ship in the Sky," in WGA Notebooks 1, Folder 3. The tune is a variant of "Hard, Ain't It Hard."

234 Wish I had a bushel: "Round and Round Hitler's Grave," *That's Why We're Marching: World War II and the American Folk Song Movement*, Smithsonian Folkways CD 40021. In early 1942, Bob Miller, a Tin Pan Alley publisher, brought out a folio of Almanac war songs. Once a stalwart of the Popular Front, Miller wrote the widely sung country lament of the depression era, "Eleven Cent Cotton, Forty Cent Meat (How in the World Can a Poor Man Eat)."

234 Adolph's a man: "Ain't that a Pity," attributed to Guthrie, but the second verse was probably by Gordon Friesen. Friesen to Richard Reuss, February 18, 1967, in RRP, Box 1, Folder 20.

234 I'll grab: WGA, Notebooks 1, Box 3. For Guthrie on popular songs, see Woody Guthrie, "Guest Article," *Broadside*, 5 (July 1962), p. 10.

234 Making it too much: WG to Alan Lomax, September 19, 1940, American Folklife Center, LC.

235 Oh, my name: The first stanza of "Arctic Circle Blues" was quoted in a letter from Pete Seeger to Millard Lampell on October 1, 1987; the second by Gordon Friesen in "Winter and War Come to Almanac House," *Broadside*, 8 (June 30, 1962), p. 2.

235 Usually I set down: WG to Alan Lomax, September 19, 1940, American Folklife Center, LC.

235 Was really a writer: Int with Pete Seeger, November 19, 1998.

235 Woody was outraged: Pete Seeger to Millard Lampell, October 1, 1987, courtesy of Ronald Cohen. But then Guthrie would do the same: "Matthew Kimes" was set to the calypso tune of "It Was Love, and Love Alone, That Caused King Edward to Leave His Throne."

235 We used to try: Bess Lomax Hawes, "Ruth Crawford Seeger Talk," presented in New York City, October 2001.

236 Some piano players: Untitled, but dated November 19, 1941, in WGA, Notebooks 1, Folder 3.

236 As the Almanac: Int with Pete Seeger, November 19, 1998.

237 We're talking: Int with Agnes Cunningham, July 13, 1998.

237 Fortunately: Gordon Friesen to Richard Reuss, October 19, 1970, in RRP, Box 1, Folder 20.

237 We were absolutely: Dunaway, *How Can I Keep from Singing*, p. 100.

237 I knew Woody: Klein, *Woody Guthrie*, p. 219.

237 The people running: Dunaway, *How Can I Keep from Singing*, p. 100.

238 Mussolini: Cohen and Samuelson, *Songs for Political Action*, p. 104.

238 Yes, I think: Pete Seeger to Millard Lampell, October 1, 1987, courtesy of Ronald Cohen. Other details of this audition are from Gordon Friesen to Richard Reuss, July 20, 1965, in RRP, Box 1, Folder 20; and in an interview with Bess Lomax Hawes, January 23, 2002.

238   The Rainbow Room: Reconstructed from Guthrie, *Bound for Glory*, pp. 301–302; Dunaway, *How Can I Keep from Singing*, pp. 100–101; and an interview with Bess Lomax Hawes, January 23, 2002.

238   He just didn't: Int with Sarah Ogan Gunning by Ellen Stekert and Archie Green, August 11, 1968, in RRP, Box 8, Folder 3.

239   I noticed: Woody Guthrie, "Union Show Troupe," in WGA, Manuscripts Box 1, Folder 12.

239   It was a time: Int with Norman Corwin, August 8, 1998.

240   Our radical: Pete Seeger to Millard Lampell, October 1, 1987, courtesy of Ronald Cohen.

240   I think: Gordon Friesen to Richard Reuss, February 12, 1968, in RRP, Box 1, Folder 20.

241   I started out to sing: Quoted by Reuss in his "American Folklore and Left-Wing Politics," p. 229. According to Bess Lomax Hawes in an interview on January 23, 2002, Guthrie sometimes sharpened the satire by referring to a Lenin pamphlet then in the Communist bookstore: "But I 'Anti-Duhring' a thing tonight/On account of my bad reputation."

241   This was the beginning: *Broadside* (November 1962), p. 9.

241   Now me and my boss: "Deliver the Goods," as printed in Cohen and Samuelson, *Songs for Political Action*, p. 105. Alan Lomax reported that a copy of *Dear Mr. President* made its way to the White House, where Franklin and Eleanor Roosevelt heard and approved of it.

CHAPTER EIGHTEEN

242   I want to do: Int of Marjorie Guthrie by Richard Reuss, January 2, 1969, in RRP, Box 8, Folder 3.

243   Poorest family: Quoted by E. Victor and Judy Wolfenstein in conversation with Marjorie Guthrie, April 18, 1972. Marjorie Greenblatt Mazia Guthrie's life is reconstructed from that conversation and an entry in the *Encyclopedia of Jewish Women*.

244   Woody, we brought: Int of Marjorie Guthrie by Richard Reuss, January 2, 1969, in RRP, Box 8, Folder 3.

244   A perfect foil: Marjorie Guthrie interviewed by Robbie Osman on KPFA, Berkeley, prior to July 17, 1979, courtesy of Mort Robbin.

245   There is no: http://www.cybernation.com/victory/quotations/authors/quotes_graham_martha. Accessed June 1, 2003.

245   A marvelous dancer: Int with Sophie Maslow, October 6, 1998.

245   I watched: Woody Guthrie, "Singing, Dancing and Teamwork," originally commissioned in 1942 by *Dance Magazine*, and reprinted in Guthrie, *Pastures of Plenty*, p. 73. Maslow had successfully premiered the two dust bowl ballads in May 1941; she hoped to add live music when she approached Guthrie.

245   So I stopped: Int with Sophie Maslow, October 6, 1998.

245   Well, I'm a folk singer: *Ibid.*

246   He had a tendency: Int with Bess Lomax Hawes by E. Victor and Judy Wolfenstein, December 11, 1971, courtesy of EV&JW.

246   It was a mess: *Ibid.*

246   Together a lot: Int with Sophie Maslow, October 6, 1998. Details of their courtship are from an interview of Joseph Mazia by E. Victor and Judy Wolfenstein on May 3, 1972, courtesy of EV&JW.

247   Had some of the spirit: Int with Bess Lomax Hawes, August 27, 1998.

247 I used to say: Guthrie, *Pastures of Plenty*, pp. 107–108.

247 We were very clear: Int of Marjorie Guthrie by Richard Reuss, January 2, 1969, in RRP, Box 8, Folder 3.

247 Was a little bit: Hays, "On Woody," p. 174.

247 Were built alike: "Motor Idling about Women," in WGA, Manuscripts Box 1, Folder 14.2.

247 Heavy hung: Manuscript for the autobiographical "Study Butte," p. 263, courtesy of EV & JW. Guthrie added, "I took sech good cyare of myne th't I dun growed 'um up ta be seven an' a half inchez awreddy."

248 The arts of rural: Ellen Graff, *Stepping Left: Dance and Politics in New York City, 1938–1942* (Durham, N. C.: Duke University Press, 1997), p. 150.

248 Was a remarkable: Int with Sophie Maslow, October 6, 1998.

249 Proletarian: Folklorist Benjamin Botkin is quoted by Michael Denning, *The Cultural Front* (New York: Verso, 1997), p. 133.

249 I think Marjorie: Int with Sophie Maslow, October 6, 1998.

249 I lived with two: Int of Marjorie Guthrie by Richard Reuss, January 1, 1969, in RRP, Box 8, Folder 3.

249 When you told: Int with Bess Lomax Hawes, August 27, 1998.

250 Kick your legs: "Untitled," published in *Sing Out!* (December 1967–January 1968), p. 7.

250 Very, very good: Int of Marjorie Guthrie by Robbie Osman on KPFA, Berkeley, prior to July 17, 1979, courtesy of Mort Robbin.

250 It was all very casual: Int with David Greenblatt, April 5, 2001.

251 I understand: Int with Joseph Mazia, October 6, 1998.

251 Was having an affair: Int of Marjorie Guthrie by Richard Reuss, January 2, 1969, in RRP, Box 8, Folder 3.

251 I felt betrayed: Int with Joseph Mazia, October 6, 1998.

251 A difficult: Int of Marjorie Guthrie by Richard Reuss, January 2, 1969, in RRP, Box 8, Folder 3.

251 Sob-sister: Quoted in an int of Lee Hays by E. Victor and Judy Wolfenstein, March 11, 1972, courtesy of EV&JW.

252 There was a possibility: Int with Joseph Mazia, October 6, 1998.

252 Now, I am just: "I'll Fight for the U.S.A.," in WGA, Notebooks 1, Folder 3.

252 We don't care: WGA, Notebooks 1, Folder 3. The tune is from the jug band song "Mama Don't 'Low."

253 Miss Pavlachenko: WGA, Notebooks 1, Folder 3. (Guthrie spells her name so; others write it "Pavlichenko.") This is one of the few war songs Guthrie actually recorded. The song is set to the banjo tune "Roll on the Ground."

253 Fabulous stories: Int of Marjorie Guthrie by Richard Reuss, January 2, 1969, in RRP, Box 8, Folder 3.

253 Hoper: A portion of the "Railroad Pete" letters is reprinted in Guthrie, *Pastures of Plenty*, pp. 95 *ff.* Though written on the printed pages for January 19 et seq., the entries were actually set down in August.

254 And that was the part: Guthrie, *Pastures of Plenty*, p. 107.

CHAPTER NINETEEN

255 Woody wrote vividly: William Doerflinger to Cray, August 27, 1999.

255 A good, graphic writer: Int with William Doerflinger, September 29, 1998.

255 I have already: WG to Marjorie, November 17, 1942, in WGA, Correspondence Box 1, Folder 44.

256   He was so: Gordon Friesen, "Woody Works on His Book," *Broadside*, 9 (July 1962), p. 9.

256   I will always believe: Guthrie, *Pastures of Plenty*, pp. 103–104.

256   There was a beginning: Gordon Friesen to Richard Reuss, April 19, 1966, in RRP, Box 1, Folder 20.

256   Oakies getting together: "A Synopsis of the Book, 'Boomchasers.'"

257   I kept wondering: Int of Lee Hays by E. Victor and Judy Wolfenstein, March 17, 1972, courtesy of EV&JW.

257   To make the manuscript: Int with William Doerflinger, September 25, 1998.

257   We were: *Ibid.*

258   Rewritten: Gordon Friesen to Richard Reuss, April 19, 1966, in RRP, Box 1, Folder 20.

258   Mama got up: Guthrie, *Bound for Glory*, pp. 161–162.

258   An autobiographical: See WGA, Box 4, Folder 55, for an example.

259   Musical ability: Quoted by Klein, *Woody Guthrie*, p. 244.

259   Lenin: Guthrie, *Pastures of Plenty*, p. 89.

260   The Office of War Information: Quoted by Cohen and Samuelson, *Songs for Political Action*, p. 20.

260   He was truly: Int with Maxine Crissman, July 25, 1998.

260   Hurry up: Alan Lomax to WG, January 21, 1943; other details about the Headline Singers' short career are in Gordon Friesen to Richard Reuss, July 16, 1965, in RRP, Box 1, Folder 20.

260   Was always a place: Lee Hays, "On Woody," p. 174.

261   Mr. Guthrie: Pete Seeger to Millard Lampell, October 1, 1987, courtesy of Ron Cohen.

261   I shall stay: WGA, Notebooks Box 1, Folder 90.

262   We must be careful: *Ibid.*

262   Maybe he's saying: *Ibid.*

262   Keep your desk: *Ibid.*

262   I had to hear: *Ibid.*

263   They began to sing: *News* (Publication of E. P. Dutton), Vol. 3, No. 1, pp. 1 *ff.*

263   That was Guthrie: Int with Joseph Mazia, October 6, 1998.

264   I haven't exactly: WG to "Dear Mrs. M. Mazia," in WGA, Correspondence Series 1, Box 1, Folder 46.

264   I am self-sufficient: Marjorie Mazia to WG, in WGA, Correspondence Series 2, Box 2, Folder 30.

264   You don't think: *Ibid.*

264   Take and give: *Ibid.*

265   With a strong: Guy Logsdon, "Woody's Roots," *Music Journal*, 14 (December 1976), p. 21. A reviewer in *Library Journal*'s issue of March 15, 1943, grumbled, "Too careful reproduction of illiterate speech through most of the book makes slow reading."

265   Like [Sean] O'Casey: *New York Times Book Review*, March 21, 1943, p. 7.

265   Will never rank: *The New Yorker*, March 20, 1943, p. 68.

265   Born artist: *Saturday Review of Literature*, April 17, 1943, p. 14.

265   Guthrie writes: *Springfield Republican*, March 28, 1943, p. 7e.

266   It was a neat job: Int of Lee Hays by E. Victor and Judy Wolfenstein, March 17, 1972.

266   I never did make up: Guthrie, *Bound for Glory*, pp. 175–176.

266   Sailors and working men: Guthrie, *Bound for Glory*, p. 290.

266   To my papa: Quoted in Klein, *Woody Guthrie*, p. 255.

266 Anything good: Int of Mary Jennings Guthrie Boyle, August 19, 1998. Mrs. Boyle's second husband made her throw out the book, at least two of Guthrie's oil paintings, and a number of letters he had written to her and the children, she said.

266 A gold mine: *Ibid.*

266 She was right: Guthrie, "My Life," in *American Folksong*, p. 6.

267 Write books: *New York Times*, May 10, 1943. The Chicago foundation granted $65,000 in fellowships to thirty-eight others selected for their creative talent or scholarship.

CHAPTER TWENTY

268 There was something: Int of Marjorie Guthrie by Richard Reuss, January 2, 1969, in RRP, Box 8, Folder 3.

269 One of our manliest: Guthrie is quoted by Guy Logsdon in the liner notes to *Cisco Houston: The Folkways Years 1944–1961*, Smithsonian Folkways SF 40059.

269 Cisco was so good: Folkways Records' Moses Asch is quoted by Logsdon in *ibid.*

270 I want to sail: Int with Maxine Crissman, July 25, 1998.

270 Spirituality: Int with Jim Longhi, September 17, 1998.

271 No, I wasn't: "Talking Merchant Marine," printed in Jim Longhi, *Woody, Cisco, and Me: Seamen Three in the Merchant Marine* (Urbana: University of Illinois Press, 1997), p. 62.

271 Felt woozy: Int with Jim Longhi, March 11, 1999.

271 Three guys: Int with Jim Longhi, September 17, 1998.

271 A flow of thermo-propulsion: Longhi, *Woody, Cisco, and Me*, p. 62.

272 I've got to get: *Ibid.*, p. 111.

272 Cisco, Jimmy: Guthrie, *Pastures of Plenty*, pp. 134–135.

272 I'm a-comin': Longhi, *Woody, Cisco, and Me*, p. 113.

273 Books and all: Klein, *Woody Guthrie*, p. 272.

273 Oh, had we only: WGA, Manuscripts Box 4, Folder 1.

274 Well, a union sun: Quoted in Maurice Isserman, *Which Side Were You On?* (Urbana: University of Illinois Press, 1993), p. 157.

274 Well, this is as good: WG to "Dear Papa," December 10, 1943, courtesy of Mary Jo Guthrie Edgmon.

274 Swimmy waters: Woody Guthrie, "From Cathy to Pete," August 10, 1947. Guthrie added, "He didn't find a woman/In all of his/Leaves of Grass."

274 They are around: "Gunners' Card Game," in WGA, Manuscripts Box 4, Folder 4.

275 The fabulous: D. G. Bridson, *Prospero and Ariel* (London: Victor Gollancz, 1971), p. 115, cited by Sally Osborne Norton, "A Historical Study of Actor Will Geer, His Life and Work in the Context of Twentieth-Century American Social, Political and Theatrical History," p. 416, unpublished Ph.D. dissertation, University of Southern California, 1980.

275 We understood nothing: Peter D. Goldsmith, *Making People's Music: Moe Asch and Folkways Records* (Washington: Smithsonian Institution Press, 1998), p. 126.

275 Hi. I'm Woody: *Ibid.*, p. 135.

276 I'm a communist: Klein, *Woody Guthrie*, p. 273.

276 He would never: Int with Irwin Silber, August 13, 1998.

276 Looked upon himself: *Ibid.*

277 We tried hilltop: Guthrie, "My Life," in Guthrie, *Pastures of Plenty*, p.11.

277   Those high sour tenor: Woody Guthrie, "Songs for Victory: Music for Political Action," in WGA, Manuscripts Box 4, Folder 8.

277   This convoy's: "Talking Sailor" as printed in Cohen and Samuelson, *Songs for Political Action*, p. 123.

278   Main reason: Guthrie, "Songs for Victory: Music for Political Action."

278   Where are you going: Longhi, *Woody, Cisco, and Me*, p. 227.

278   By guilt—cords: Int with Jim Longhi, March 11, 1999.

279   That's about the best: Longhi, *Woody, Cisco, and Me*, p. 231. Additional details are from interviews with Longhi.

280   And then the ship: Woody Guthrie, "Write It Right," in WGA, Manuscripts Box 4, Folder 15.

281   You mean you guys: Longhi, *Woody, Cisco, and Me*, p. 259.

281   A ghostly, awful: Guthrie, "Write It Right."

CHAPTER TWENTY-ONE

283   I thank: Woody Guthrie, "Union Labor or Slave Labor," in WGA, Manuscripts Box 4, Folder 16.

283   Must help: Isserman, *Which Side Were You On?*, p. 208.

283   Appeasers: *Ibid.*, p. 186.

283   The average elections: WG to Alan Lomax, September 20, 1940, in American Folklife Center, LC.

283   Were about as honest: Int of Lee Hays by E. Victor and Judy Wolfenstein, March 11, 1972, courtesy of EV&JW.

283   The highest social priority: As stated by Martin Duberman in the *Nation*, July 16, 2001, p. 36.

284   Every single human: Added in handwriting by Guthrie to his 1935 typewritten songbook, "Alonzo M. Zilch's Own Collection of Original Songs and Ballads," a copy of which is in American Folklife Center, LC; another copy is in WGA, Manuscripts Box 1, Folder 3.2.

284   You see what Akron: WGA, Manuscripts Box 4, Folder 11, p. 4.

284   You and me: *Ibid.*, p. 7.

284   You make me: Klein, *Woody Guthrie*, p. 284.

285   A little old: Untitled script, "WNEW 1st Program," December 3, 1944, in WGA, Manuscripts Box 4, Folder 14.

285   I hate a song: *Ibid.*

285   Folk ballad fans: Klein, *Woody Guthrie*, p. 287.

286   I write: Woody Guthrie, "Union Show Troupe," in WGA, Manuscripts Box 1, Folder 12.

286   I believe: WGA, Box 4, Folder 11, written approximately November 1944. Guthrie also rejected the label of "the second Will Rogers. My curse of my life has always been that I was just born in Will's home state, Oklahoma."

286   Hollywood songs: Goldsmith, *Making People's Music*, p. 147.

287   Is a folk singer: *Ibid.*, p. 157.

287   We never balanced: Int of Moses Asch by E. Victor and Judy Wolfenstein, April 24, 1972, courtesy of EV&JW.

287   A kind of musical newspaper: Quoted in Goldsmith, *Making People's Music*, p. 159.

287   The struggle: Asch's notes to *Struggle: Documentary #1* are reproduced in *Struggle* (Smithsonian Folkways, 1990).

287   Pet album: WG to Harry St. Ammand, July 10, 1947, courtesy of Barry Oll-
      man.
288   They had a Christmas: WG's notes to *Struggle: Documentary #1* are repro-
      duced in *Struggle* (Smithsonian Folkways, 1990).
288   Take a trip: *Ibid.* Paul Stamler identified the source of Guthrie's tune. Guthrie
      also called the song "The Miners' Christmas" before settling on "1913 Mas-
      sacre."
288   I wish: Quoted by Richard Reuss in "Political Books Owned by Woody
      Guthrie," in RRP, Box 6, Folder 26.
289   How was he: Int with Henrietta Yurchenko and Marjorie Guthrie by Richard
      Reuss, January 2, 1969, in RRP, Box 8, Folder 3.
289   Like everything else: *Ibid.*
289   The big lazy spirit: WG to Moe Asch, September 14, 1945, Smithsonian/Folk-
      ways, courtesy of Jeff Place.
290   Non-technical literature: WG to Earl and Helen Robinson, August 31, 1945,
      courtesy of EV&JW.
290   Then I decided: Guthrie to the Blatts, August 21, 1945, courtesy of Barry Oll-
      man.
290   The best part: WG writing in March 1951, courtesy of Barry Ollman.
290   Is not a vicious: Klein, *Woody Guthrie*, p. 297.
291   I could see: *Ibid.*, p. 301.
291   There's a little: Guthrie, *Pastures of Plenty*, p. 145.

CHAPTER TWENTY-TWO

In addition to the sources cited, a May 3, 1972, interview of Pete Seeger by
E. Victor and Judy Wolfenstein proved of value in writing this chapter.

293   People like us: Int with Pete Seeger, November 19, 1998.
293   People are on the march: Quoted from *People's Songs*, Vol. 1, No. 1, dated Feb-
      ruary 1945 but actually 1946.
293   Largely in the rich: Anonymous mimeograph quoted in Richard A. Reuss,
      "American Folksongs and Left-Wing Politics," *Journal of the Folklore Institute*,
      12 (1975), p. 96.
294   Circumvent: Pete Seeger, "People's Songs and Singers," *New Masses* (July 16,
      1946), p. 9.
294   Was a unique figure: Int with Irwin Silber, August 13, 1998.
294   A lot of the audiences: *Ibid.*
294   New York: Int with Bernard Asbell, October 22, 1998.
294   Lemon juice voice: *Ibid.*
294   Woody's children: Int of Joe Jaffee by E. Victor and Judy Wolfenstein, Decem-
      ber 27, 1969, courtesy of EV&JW.
295   I was sitting: Int with Harvey Matusow, July 13, 1999.
295   It was almost: Int of Joe Jaffee by E. Victor and Judy Wolfenstein, December
      27, 1969.
295   Woody lived: Int with Fred Hellerman, August 6, 1998.
295   There ain't no one: "Acting and Dancing," an undated essay courtesy of Barry
      Ollman.
295   Woody was not: Int with Fred Hellerman, August 6, 1998. In a separate inter-
      view by E. Victor and Judy Wolfenstein on December 27, 1969, Joe Jaffee

agreed with Hellerman's estimate. As time passed, Guthrie's guitar playing "just seemed to get sloppier."

295   You got to go down: *People's Songs*, Vol. 1, No. 1, dated February 1945 but actually 1946, p. 6.

296   Was one of the favorites: Int with Jackie Leiserowitz Alper, July 26, 1998.

296   It was very loose: Int with Moses Asch by E. Victor and Judy Wolfenstein, April 24, 1972, courtesy of EV&JW.

296   Was so much fun: Int with Marjorie Guthrie by Robbie Osman on KPFA, Berkeley, prior to July 17, 1979, courtesy of Mort Robbin.

297   Sam, Sam: From the files of Folkways Records, now at the Smithsonian Library. Writing to a family friend, Guthrie acknowledged he was learning much from his daughter. "I made lots of pretty sad mistakes in raising up Cathy, but Cathy did not ever make a mistake in raising me up that I can clearly remember. She had a way of always being right." WG to Marcia Kagno Copel, in WGA, Correspondence, Box 5, Folder 1.

297   Mamma, o, mamma: "Clean-o," as printed in the notes to Woody Guthrie, *Nursery Days*, Smithsonian Folkways SF 45036.

297   Why can't a dish: "Why, Oh Why?," as printed in the notes to Woody Guthrie, *Songs to Grow on for Mother and Child*, Smithsonian Folkways SF 45035.

298   Take my little hoe: "Little Seed," No. 17 in Guthrie and Guthrie, *Woody's 20 Grow Big Songs*.

298   Smart enough: From WG's draft notes for the second children's album, *Work Songs for Nursery Days*, as printed in Guthrie, *Pastures of Plenty*, p. 175.

299   Some of [Guthrie's] greatest: Guthrie, *Roll on Columbia*, p. 17. In a November 1998 interview, Seeger allowed that the children's songs as a group were the most likely of Guthrie's songs after "This Land Is Your Land" to be remembered and sung by later generations.

299   Some of the most: The August 21, 1946, review is quoted in Goldsmith, *Making People's Music*, p. 181.

299   One of the great: Int of Moses Asch by E. Victor and Judy Wolfenstein, April 24, 1972.

299   There is plenty: Goldsmith, *Making People's Music*, p. 182.

300   I refuse: WG to Moses Asch, November 4, 1946, quoted in Goldsmith, *Making People's Music*, p. 185.

300   The most important: *Ibid.* Additional information was drawn from an interview of Pete Seeger by E. Victor and Judy Wolfenstein, May 3, 1972, courtesy of EV&JW.

301   Every dollar in the world: "The Flood and the Storm," the opening song in the *Ballads of Sacco and Vanzetti*, Smithsonian Folkways SF 40060.

301   I used to find: Int of Lee Hays by E. Victor and Judy Wolfenstein, Croton-on-Hudson, March 11, 1972, courtesy of EV&JW.

301   We sang "Solidarity Forever": Guthrie, *Pastures of Plenty*, p. 174. The rallying song dates from the first decades of the century, prior to the formation of a Communist Party. It was written by Ralph Chaplin to the Civil War tune of "John Brown's Body" for the Industrial Workers of the World, "the one big union." As late as the mid-1950s it was still included in the official "AFL-CIO Songbook."

301   But Woody started: Int with Jackie Leiserowitz Alper, July 26, 1998.

302   Creation ore: *Sing Out!* (December 1967–January 1968), p. 11. A friend of Marjorie's, Irma Bauman, claimed in a July 14, 1998, interview that "Marjorie knew that Woody had bastards during their marriage."

302   He was an extraordinary: Int with Ronnie Gilbert, September 17, 1998.

302   Was the chosen one: Int with Marjorie Guthrie by Robbie Osman on KPFA, Berkeley, prior to July 17, 1979, courtesy of Mort Robbin. Fred Hellerman, later a member of the Weavers singing group, described Marjorie in an interview on August 6, 1998, as "a survivor. She never knew the word 'self-pity.' . . . She was a nourisher. . . . She was really a very special person."

303   No man: WGA, Manuscripts Box 4, Folder 28.

303   Independent political: Maurice Isserman, *Which Side Were You On?: The American Communist Party during the Second World War* (Urbana: University of Illinois Press, 1993), p. 217.

303   To beat back: Robinson to WG, December 17, 1945, courtesy of EV&JW. Robinson wrote to tell Guthrie that Yip Harburg and Fred Saidy had written the book and lyrics for a projected Broadway musical—Robinson was to do the music—in which the main character was a union organizer-singer named "Woody." The Woody of the play, wrote Robinson, was a composite of Guthrie, Pete Seeger, CIO President Philip Murray, and Michael Quill, president of the Transit Workers Union. That character of "Woody" faintly survived in the later, hugely successful musical *Finian's Rainbow*, for which Harburg wrote the words.

304   A full blood: Written October 28, 1946, on the flyleaf of the third volume of Marx's *Das Kapital*, and quoted in "Political Books Owned by Woody Guthrie," in RRP, Box 6, Folder 26.

304   If Willy Zee: "Political Books Owned by Woody Guthrie," in RRP, Box 6, Folder 26.

304   Don't you know: The anecdote is much retold, by Lee Hays in an interview with E. Victor and Judy Wolfenstein, March 11, 1972, and in an interview with Pete Seeger, November 19, 1998.

304   The two best: "Dear 'What's Wrong Column,'" November 14, 1946, in WGA, Manuscripts Box 4, Folder 32.

304   Museum smelling: Guthrie, "Songs, People, Papers."

304   An iron curtain: Quoted in David McCullough, *Truman* (New York: Simon and Schuster, 1992), p. 383. Churchill, by then out of office, would use the phrase publicly in a speech at tiny Westminster College in Missouri in March 1946.

305   The war: WG to Harry St. Ammand, July 10, 1947, courtesy of Barry Ollman.

305   Get offa that bank: Int with Stetson Kennedy, January 9, 1999.

306   There was nothing: Int with Bess Lomax Hawes, January 23, 2002.

306   Woody, Leadbelly: Int of Moses Asch by E. Victor and Judy Wolfenstein, April 24, 1972. Asch added that he had suggested the Sacco-Vanzetti project to boost their morale. Asked if there was an audience for the album, he snapped, "I didn't give a good God damn."

306   Slum pictures: Woody Guthrie, "Ingrid and Me," *Daily Worker*, January 12, 1947, as noted in WG's Federal Bureau of Investigation file, NY 100-87247.

306   When our radio: WG to Harry St. Ammand, January 14, 1947, courtesy of Barry Ollman.

306   The sky plane: "Plane Wreck at Los Gatos" is printed in John Greenway, *American Folksongs of Protest* (Philadelphia: University of Pennsylvania Press, 1953), pp. 294–295. The plane crashed in January 1948; Guthrie dated the song February 3, 1948. Guthrie did not record the song and left no tune. Set to music by Martin Hoffman in the early 1950s, it was so popularized by Pete Seeger that "Deportees" remains one of Guthrie's best-known works.

307   You've got a family: Int with Pete Seeger, November 19, 1998.

307   Mostly preaching: Int with Maxine Crissman, July 25, 1998.
308   But when I set: WG to Irving Lerner, August 3, 1946, courtesy of EV&JW.

CHAPTER TWENTY-THREE

Beyond the sources cited below, a letter from WG to Harry St. Ammand and an interview with David Greenblatt proved useful.

309   No matter what happens: Woody Guthrie, "Cathy Ann Guthrie," n.d. but February 1947 in WGA, Manuscripts Box 4, Folder 57. It is reprinted in Guthrie, *Born to Win*, pp. 198 *ff.*
310   Mommy: *Ibid.*
310   He screamed: Int with Jim Longhi, March 11, 1999.
310   I think that: Int with Nora Guthrie, March 10, 2000.
311   There has been made: WG to "Dear Toddy," February 27, 1947, in WGA, Correspondence Series 1, Box 1.
311   We told all: Guthrie, "Cathy Ann Guthrie," n.d. but February 1947 in WGA, Manuscripts Box 4, Folder 57.
311   A wrenching: Int with Joseph Mazia, October 6, 1998.
311   Was destroyed: Int with Jackie Leiserowitz Alper, July 26, 1998.
312   The number one: Ralph Bennett to Bill Murlin, October 9, 1983, courtesy of Bennett.
312   Good chance: Eric Scigliano, "Travels with Woody," *Weekly: Seattle's Newsmagazine*, June 27, 1984, pp. 26 *ff.*, courtesy of Ralph Bennett.
312   Spent a lot: Int with John Gikas, March 14, 1999.
312   Something: Scigliano, "Travels with Woody," p. 30.
312   He was pretty: Int with Ralph Bennett, August 28, 2001.
312   Took the old: Woody Guthrie, "Woody Guthrie is Back to Sing about People," *People's World*, April 28, 1947, p. 5.
313   He was not: Scigliano, "Travels with Woody," p. 30.
313   We didn't get: Int with Ralph Bennett, August 29, 2001. The abortive effort led Guthrie to write Moe Asch from Seattle with the suggestion that Asch record the Columbia River songs. Asch would eventually release *Ballads from the Dust Bowl* combining three songs written in California in the late 1930s and three from the Columbia River cycle.
313   The kids loved: Scigliano, "Travels with Woody," p. 32.
313   Good fifty years: Woody Guthrie, "Portland Is OK Except for . . . ," *People's World*, May 5, 1947, p. 5.
313   He wasn't Woody: Int with Maxine Crissman, July 25, 1998. Details are in Richard Reuss's int of Crissman, June 12–14, 1968, in RRP, Box 8, Folder 6.
314   He talked: Int with Clara Robbin by E. Victor and Judy Wolfenstein, December 28, 1969.
314   Makes Woody: Woody Guthrie, "My Best Songs," dated February 6, 1947, in WGA, Box 4, Folder 49.
314   A beautiful: Ann Guthrie, "The Woody Guthrie I Knew," courtesy of Ann Guthrie, July 29, 1998.
314   Life is pretty tough: WG quoted by Gordon Friesen, *Mainstream* (August 1963), p. 2.
314   The picture: Woody Guthrie, "I'm Not the Man," written February 8, 1947, in WGA, Box 4, Folder 50.

315 You'll find out: WG to "Dear Gwendolyn Teeny Gal Guthrie," June 23, 1947, courtesy of Barry Ollman.

315 This rough year: WG to Natanya Neuman, n.d., but July 1947, courtesy of Barry Ollman. Neuman, Cathy's baby-sitter and a dance student of Marjorie's, went on to have a successful career as a dancer.

315 The kids: Marjorie Guthrie to Mary Jo Guthrie Edgmon, October 11, 1947. Courtesy of Mary Jo Edgmon.

315 This little spark: *Ibid.*

316 If I did think: Woody Guthrie, "Me and the Others," June 6, 1947, in WGA, Box 4, Folder 55.

316 Another lifebound novel: Woody Guthrie, "Bound for Glory," in WGA, Manuscripts Box 4, Folder 55.

316 The best material: Klein, *Woody Guthrie*, p. 333.

316 There is something: Guthrie, "Bound for Glory," in WGA, Manuscripts Box 4, Folder 55.

317 And it is getting: WG to "Dear Irving, and All Your Folks," October 31, 1947, courtesy of EV&JW.

317 My heart beats: *Ibid.*

317 Having regular fits: Guthrie, *Seeds of Man*, p. 47. Guthrie eventually settled on this title for the manuscript edited by William Doerflinger, the husband of the late Joy Doerflinger.

317 He said quite: Int with Pete Seeger, November 19, 1998.

318 A little bit: Int with Jim Longhi, March 11, 1999.

318 A cravery: Guthrie, "Hoodis," in WGA, Manuscripts Box 4, Folder 36.

318 In the navy-blue: E. Y. Harburg and Fred Saidy, *Finian's Rainbow: A Musical Satire* (New York: Random House, 1946), p. 21. The script states that when Woody speaks, he does so "in a 'Talking Union Blues' rhythm" (p. 22). He is a union organizer who is going to take guitar lessons from a New York City "folklore teacher" (pp. 39–40).

318 I'm the real: Woody Guthrie, "Ranian's Finbow and Me," in WGA, Manuscripts Box 4, Folder 60. This undated essay was probably written in early 1948.

319 Me nor my gitbox: *Ibid.*

320 Wasn't exactly: WG to "Dear Tinkin," December 29, 1947, courtesy of Mary Jo Guthrie Edgmon.

CHAPTER TWENTY-FOUR

321 Are everywhere: President Truman's attorney general, J. Howard McGrath, is quoted in William H. Chafe, *The Unfinished Journey* (New York: Oxford University Press, 1986), p. 99.

321 The Communist: Hamish Henderson, *Alias MacAlias* (Edinburgh: Polygon, 1993), p. 13.

321 A confidential informant: WGA, Personal Papers, Box 2, Folder 48. Guthrie's FBI file, at least the portion released under the Freedom of Information Act, is a scant twelve pages long. Guthrie would undoubtedly have been miffed; according to Pete Seeger biographer David Dunaway, the FBI files on folk musicians bulk ten feet high.

322 Joe Stalin's: *Fourth Report of the Senate Fact-Finding Committee on Un-American Activities, 1948: Communist Front Organizations* (Published by the California

State Senate, 1948), pp. 342–343. Ironically, the chairman of the committee, State Senator Jack Tenney was the composer of the hit song "Mexicali Rose." He showed no favoritism to his fellow songwriters. Actually, the first to "out" People's Songs was a May 1947 United States Army's "Weekly Domestic Intelligence Summary," which cited the organization as a communist front.

322 Factionalist: The June 2, 1952, entry is in WGA, Box 2, Folder 48.

322 I don't know: Int with Marjorie Mazia by Robbie Osman, KPFA, Berkeley, prior to July 17, 1979, courtesy of Mort Robbin. In an interview with the author on January 23, 2002, Bess Lomax Hawes stated that Guthrie specifically told her he had never been a member of the party. Gordon Friesen, on the other hand, maintained that Guthrie *was* a member of the Communist Party briefly in 1942. It ended sometime in the summer months, Friesen wrote, after Guthrie was summoned by "his organizer" to "a branch meeting" in Greenwich Village. Guthrie was "to answer charges of lack of discipline. . . . He had pledged to appear at a certain Village street corner to sell *Daily Workers* and then had failed to show up." Friesen to Richard Reuss, October 19, 1970, in RRP, Box 1, Folder 20. Friesen and his wife, Agnes "Sis" Cunningham, are the only people to assert Guthrie was actually a member of the party. According to Pete Seeger, Sis Cunningham claimed Guthrie was a member of the Greenwich Village branch, briefly, sometime between December 1941 and June 1942. "She saw his membership card." Int with Pete Seeger, November 19, 1998.

323 Some people: Marjorie Guthrie is quoted in Edward Robbin, *Woody Guthrie and Me* (Berkeley: Lancaster-Miller Publishers, 1979), p. 133. In April 1949, Guthrie and "his spiritual brother" Lee Hays, who was a member of the Communist Party, planned a benefit for twelve leaders of the party who had been charged with conspiring to overthrow the government. There is no indication the fund-raiser was actually held.

323 Some were: Int with Bess Lomax Hawes by E. Victor and Judy Wolfenstein, December 11, 1971, courtesy of EV&JW.

323 They were all: Harold Clurman, speaking of the members of the Composers Collective, is quoted in Aaron Copland and Vivian Perlis, *Copland: Since 1943* (New York: St. Martin's, 1989), p. 191. Copland and Marc Blitzstein are probably the best known of the Composers Collective; both were sponsors of People's Songs.

323 Hot deal: WG to "Dear Irving," September 26, 1947, courtesy of EV&JW.

323 I demand: WG to "Dear Mr. Lerner," December 16, 1948, courtesy of EV&JW.

323 Snortier: WG to Lerner, September 24, 1948, courtesy of EV&JW. He added, "I've tried to write each page so highly truthful that the Hays Office can chew it for a year and I'll still have plenty of book."

324 The roaches: WGA, Manuscripts Box 7, Folder 7, written March 15, 1948.

324 The job: "Thing Called Socialism," n.d., but 1948, in WGA, Manuscripts Box 7, Folder 12.

324 A pure cross: "Gene Debs," August 4, 1948, in WGA, Manuscripts Box 7, Folder 15.

324 Fascism is: Woody Guthrie, "Bloody Run," June 7, 1948, in WGA, Manuscripts Box 7, Folder 9.

325 Yeahp: Woody Guthrie, "Dear Sir Lord and Bosser," June 16, 1948, in WGA, Manuscripts Box 7, Folder 11.

325 These Un-American: Woody Guthrie, "Picture Change," August 3, 1948, in WGA, Manuscripts Box 7, Folder 15.

325 When I don't: Woody Guthrie, March 15, 1948, in WGA, Manuscripts Box 7,

Folder 7. See too Woody Guthrie, "Nite of Love," January 26, 1948, in WGA, Manuscripts Box 7, Folder 3.

326   True fictitious: WG to "You Robinsons," November 20, 1948.

326   My maw: *Ibid.*

326   Waiting, waiting: Marjorie Guthrie to "Dear Robinsons," dated "Tuesday night" (November 23, 1948), courtesy of EV&JW.

326   Pretty awful: Marjorie Guthrie to Mary Jo Guthrie Edgmon, January 11, 1949, in WGA, Correspondence Series 3, Box 1, Folder 3.

326   As a provider: Int with David Greenblatt, April 5, 2001.

327   Would not have gotten: Int with Irwin Silber, August 13, 1998.

327   President Truman: Guthrie, *Pastures of Plenty*, p. 173.

328   Wildly opposed: Interview with Bess Lomax Hawes and Baldwin "Butch" Hawes by E. Victor and Judy Wolfenstein, December 11, 1971.

328   To get: Woody Guthrie, "My Ideas about the Use of Peoples Songs in the Progressive Party Movement . . . ," January 9, 1949, in WGA, Manuscripts Box 7, Folder 17.

329   The best hill country: Woody Guthrie, "The Maddox Brothers and Rose," May 20, 1949, in WGA, Manuscripts Box 7, Folder 22. "Philadelphia Lawyer" on 4 Star Records was a great hit for the band and singer, but apparently did not produce royalties for Guthrie. Guthrie took a flat fee for his songs, generous enough so that he could fly from Los Angeles to New York rather than return by Greyhound bus as he had come west.

329   Bitterest letters: Int with Maxine Crissman, July 25, 1998.

329   He was pursuing: Int with Marianne "Jolly" Smollens Robinson, May 10, 2001.

329   All my girls: WG, "I Don't Know," July 16, 1948, in WGA, Manuscripts Box 7, Folder 12.

330   Shambles: Int with Bernard Asbell, October 22, 1998.

330   Broke his way: Woody Guthrie, "Circle of Life, Septembre [*sic*] last, 1948," in WGA, Manuscripts Box 7, Folder 15.

330   We have not had: Woody Guthrie, "A Statement of the Facts," July 6, 1949, in WGA, Manuscripts Box 7, Folder 24.

331   You have no: Int with Maxine Crissman, July 25, 1998.

331   He could chop: Int with Maxine Crissman by E. Victor and Judy Wolfenstein, June 14–18, 1968, courtesy of EV&JW.

331   Since I did not: Woody Guthrie, "Love Letters," February 25, 1948, in WGA, Manuscripts Box 7, Folder 3.1.

331   I told her: Guthrie, "A Statement of the Facts," July 6, 1949, in WGA, Manuscripts Box 7, Folder 24.

331   Woody was having: Int with Jim Longhi, March 11, 1999.

332   There was no: *Ibid.*

332   For a lousy: WG to "Jolly Again" [Marianne "Jolly" Smollens], January 15, 1951, courtesy of Marianne Robinson.

332   Well, Woody: Guthrie, "A Statement of the Facts," July 6, 1949, in WGA, Manuscripts Box 7, Folder 24.

332   An obscene, lewd: Count One, Grand Jury Indictment, *United States v. Woodrow Wilson Guthrie*, United States District Court, Eastern District of New York, Cr. No. 42202.

332   Sexual behavior disorder: Quoted from an interview conducted in 2000 with Guthrie's therapist, who asked for anonymity. The quotes that follow are from two interviews with that therapist.

333   The sentence: Int with Jim Longhi, March 11, 1999.

334   Upon reflection: *United States v. Woodrow Wilson Guthrie*, United States District Court, Eastern District of New York, Cr. No. 42202, Transcript of December 22, 1949.

CHAPTER TWENTY-FIVE

In addition to the sources cited, I relied on Richard Reuss's interview of Marjorie Guthrie and Henrietta Yurchenko, January 2, 1969, in RRP, Box 8, Folder 3; interviews with Henrietta Yurchenko, June 16 and November 18, 1999; and an interview with Nora Guthrie on March 10, 2000.

335   He looked thin: Ann Guthrie, "The Woody Guthrie I Knew," post-1967, courtesy of Ann Guthrie.

336   The dadgum: Int with George and Emily Guthrie, undated, but recorded between September 1971 and December, 28, 1971, by E. Victor and Judy Wolfenstein, courtesy of EV&JW.

336   That bum's hair: Int with George Guthrie by Richard Reuss, December 12, 1967, in RRP, Box 8, Folder 3.

336   A coincidence: Greenway, *American Folksongs of Protest*, p. 288.

337   As good as Melville: Alan Lomax to WG, December 5, 1952, courtesy of Anna Lomax Chairetakis and Matt Barton, Alan Lomax Archive, New York City.

337   I'd love: WG to Duncan Emrich, September 12, 1950, in American Folklife Center, LC.

337   She was manic: Int with Judith Mazia, October 1, 1998.

338   Weavery folks': WG to Mary Jo Edgmon, December 1, 1950, courtesy of Mary Jo Guthrie Edgmon. Agnes Cunningham deemed Guthrie's rewrite a "contemptible garblization," and refused to believe Guthrie himself was responsible. See Cunningham to Richard Reuss, August 22, 1971, in RRP, Box 1, Folder 20.

339   Who overhauls: Guthrie, *Pastures of Plenty*, p. 205.

339   So it looks: WG to "Dear Sweet Perty Jollygal" [Marianne "Jolly" Smollens], January 12, 1951, courtesy of Marianne Robinson.

339   I don't think: Int with Jack Elliott, September 15, 2002.

339   We were fighters: Transcript of int of Henrietta Yurchenko and Marjorie Guthrie by Richard Reuss, January 2, 1969, in RRP, Box 8, Folder 3.

339   And would probably: Email from Tom Paley, August 24, 2002.

339   You were aware: Int of Lee Hays by E. Victor and Judy Wolfenstein, March 11, 1972, courtesy of EV&JW.

340   Dogdrunk: WG to "Jolly Again" [Marianne "Jolly" Smollens], January 16, 1951, courtesy of Marianne Robinson.

340   Mortal deadly enemies: *Ibid.*

340   I'm against it: WG to "Dear Sweet Perty Jollygal" [Marianne "Jolly" Smollens], January 12, 1951, courtesy of Marianne Robinson.

340   Well and keenly: *Ibid.*

340   Surely no fun: *Ibid.*

340   In my hottest: WG to Marianne Robinson, January 12, 1951, typed on the reverse of the dust jacket of a gift copy of *Bound for Glory*, courtesy of Marianne Robinson.

341   He was drunk: Int with Marianne Robinson (the former "Jolly" Smollens), June 24, 2001.

341 That if I'd got: WG to "Hey Jolly" [Marianne "Jolly" Smollens], March 22, 1951, courtesy of Marianne Robinson.

341 It showed: *Ibid.*

341 Go over there: Int with Jack Elliott, August 19, 2002.

342 We started: *Ibid.*

342 Perfect mimic: Jeff Stark, "Hard Travelin': Ramblin' Jack Elliott Has a Few More Stories to Tell," *Dallas Observer*, April 9, 1998.

342 Wasn't as good: Int with Nora Guthrie, March 10, 2000.

342 A kind of nursemaid: WG to "Dear Stetzlyne" [Stetson Kennedy], November 5, 1951, in WGA, Stetson Kennedy Papers.

343 An airtight: *Ibid.* Apparently they were contemplating filing for divorce in New York, which granted divorces at the time only for adultery.

343 I feel: *Ibid.*

343 Woody, where: Int with Stetson Kennedy, January 9, 1999

344 What's wrong: WG to "Dear Mommy and All," November 16, 1951, in WGA, Correspondence File 1, Box 3, Folder 2.

344 With the audience: Int of Moses Asch by E. Victor and Judy Wolfenstein, April 24, 1972, courtesy of EV&JW.

345 Just don't think: WG to "Dear Robinsons," September 8, 1951, courtesy of EV&JW. See too Pete Seeger, "Remembering Woody," *Mainstream* (August 1963), p. 31.

345 Is Woody growing: Int of Lee Hays by E. Victor and Judy Wolfenstein, n.d.

345 Suddenly men: Int with Norman Corwin, August 8, 1998.

346 If you *knew*: Griffin Fariello, *Red Scare: Memories of the American Inquisition* (New York: W. W. Norton, 1995), p. 363.

346 We in the youth movement: Matusow's testimony is printed in "Communist Activities Among Youth Groups," United States House of Representatives, Subcommittee of the Committee on Un-American Activities," February 6, 1952, pp. 3273 *ff.* Matusow would name 244 people as members of the Communist Party.

347 Political suspects: Int with Jack Elliott, August 19, 2002.

347 Was hard on guitars: *Ibid.*

347 I was kind: Steven Stolder, "Traveling Back with Ramblin' Jack Elliott," *NARAS Journal* 6, No. 2 (1995), p. 19.

347 No dates: WG to "Dear Marjorie," May 9, 1952, in WGA, Correspondence File 1, Box 3, Folder 3.

347 Just backwards: WG to "Deary Marjery Dear!," May 12, 1952, in WGA, Correspondence File 1, Box 3, Folder 3.

348 I want my body: WG to "Dear Marjy Once More," May 12, 1952, in WGA, Correspondence File 1, Box 3, Folder 3.

348 That last fight: WG to "Dear Marjy," May 13, 1952, in WGA, Correspondence File 1, Box 3, Folder 3.

348 Not an alcoholic: WG to "Dearest Marjorie," May 14, 1952, in WGA, Correspondence File 1, Box 3, Folder 3.

349 He beat: Int of Marjorie Guthrie and Henrietta Yurchenko by Richard Reuss, January 2, 1969, in RRP, Box 8, Folder 3.

349 It was like: Int with Nora Guthrie, March 10, 2000.

349 Struck with fear: Stolder, "Traveling Back with Ramblin' Jack Elliott," p. 17. Other details are from an interview with Jack Elliott, August 19, 2002.

350 Drinking bottle: WG to "Dear Marjorie," June 14, 1952, in WGA, Correspondence File 1, Box 3, Folder 3.

350   The raving ward: WG to "Dear Margy," "Letter No. Two," dated July 1952, in WGA, Correspondence File 1, Box 3, Folder 1.

350   The pain: *Ibid.*

351   He said: Int with Arlo Guthrie, February 3, 2002. A half century later, both Arlo and the neighbor's daughter still play Woody's childhood gifts.

351   Is it possible: Henrietta Yurchenko with Marjorie Guthrie, *A Mighty Hard Road* (New York: McGraw-Hill, 1970), p. 141.

351   In and through: Undated letter from WG to "Margery," in WGA, Correspondence Series 1, Box 3, Folder 3.

352   Scrawny looking: Klein, *Woody Guthrie*, p. 373.

352   How come no one: Int with Nora Guthrie, March 10, 2000.

353   There are lots: WG to "Dear Pete" Seeger, September 27, 1952, in WGA, Correspondence Series 1, Box 3, Folder 24.

CHAPTER TWENTY-SIX

In addition to the sources cited, Sally Osborne Norton's dissertation on Will Geer proved useful in this chapter.

354   Would be happy: Int with Herta Ware [Geer], August 11, 1998.

355   A marvelous: Int with Sam Hinton, July 27, 1998. Fifty years later, the Theatricum Botanicum is a permanent institution, successfully managed by Kate and Ellen Geer.

355   Well, I've got it: Int of Clara Robbin by E. Victor and Judy Wolfenstein, December 28, 1969, courtesy of EV&JW.

355   You know, Herta: Int with Herta Ware [Geer], August 11, 1998.

355   Was fixing himself: Marjorie Guthrie to "Dear Anneke," April 1, 1953, in WGA, Correspondence Series 3, Box 3, Folder 9.

355   Woody was just: Int with Kate Geer, September 11, 1998.

355   I never thought: Int with Herta Ware [Geer], August 11, 1998.

355   Woody didn't know: Int with Frank Hamilton, August 27, 1998.

356   Woody had no problem: *Ibid.*

356   It sure is plenty: WG to "Dear Marjorie & Cetera," October 13, 1952, in WGA, Correspondence Series 1, Box 3, Folder 4.

356   Disssy sppells: *Ibid.*

357   My chorea: WG to "Dear Marjy," November 1952, in WGA, Correspondence Series 1, Box 4, Folder 4.

357   I feel every day: WG to Dear Marjorie & Cetera," October 13, 1952, in WGA, Correspondence Series 1, Box 3, Folder 4.

357   This world it's hit me: "I Ain't Dead," dated October 1952, in WGA.

358   I cant ever quite: WG to "You All Bayshead Sheep," ca. November 9, 1952, in WGA, Correspondence Series 1, Box 3, Folder 4. Marjorie, the three children, and Tony Marra had moved to a larger house in the Sheepshead Bay section of Brooklyn.

358   Decide my bottling: Undated letter to Marjorie, in WGA, Correspondence Series 1, Box 4, Folder 4.

358   Was freer: WG to Seeger, n.d., in WGA, Folder 24, Number 485.

359   This is sure: WG to Pete Seeger, November 19, 1952, in WGA.

359   I'm rusting out: WG to Marjorie, November 24, 1952, in WGA, Correspondence Series 1, Box 3, Folder 4.

359   Foolishly: WG to "You All Bayshead Sheep," ca. November 9, 1952, in WGA, Correspondence Series 1, Box 3, Folder 4.

359   I kid: WG to "Dear Margy Again," written in "Curly" part of October 1952, in WGA, Correspondence Series 1, Box 3, Folder 4.

359   It was always: Int with Herta Ware [Geer], August 11, 1998.

360   Earth mother: Int with Frank Hamilton, August 27, 1998, and with Matt Miller, April 7, 2001.

360   A very luscious: Int with Bob and Doreen DeWitt, August 13, 1998.

360   I didn't like: Anneke Van Kirk Guthrie to Mary Jo Guthrie Edgmon, October 30, 1954, in WGA, Correspondence Series 3, Box 1, Folder 30.

360   We worked: *Ibid.*

360   So lowly sunk: WG to "Dyear Tribe & Herd . . . ," March 20, 1953, in WGA, Correspondence Series 1, Box 3, Folder 5.

360   I felt that I wanted: Anneke Van Kirk Guthrie to Mary Jo Guthrie Edgmon, October 30, 1954, in WGA, Correspondence Series 3, Box 1, Folder 30.

361   She sung harmony: WG to "Dyear Tribe & Herd . . . ," March 20, 1953, in WGA, Correspondence Series 1, Box 3, Folder 5.

361   I didn't stop: Anneke Van Kirk Guthrie to Mary Jo Guthrie Edgmon, October 30, 1954, in WGA, Correspondence Series 3, Box 1, Folder 30.

361   I think she was: Int with Frank Hamilton, August 27, 1998.

361   And so terribly: Anneke Van Kirk Guthrie to Mary Jo Guthrie Edgmon, October 30, 1954, in WGA, Correspondence Series 3, Box 1, Folder 30.

361   Bullshit stories: Int with Herb Cohen, August 20, 27, 1998.

362   Even thought: Int with Frank Hamilton, August 27, 1998.

362   Strained: Int with Bob and Doreen DeWitt, August 21, 1998.

362   He was just: Int with Bob DeWitt, August 21, 1998.

362   Everybody: Stolder, "Traveling Back with Ramblin' Jack Elliott," p. 19.

362   Guthrie didn't like: Int with Fred Gerlach, April 4, 2002.

363   Woody seemed: Int with Jack Elliott, August 19, 2002.

363   This would cover: Anneke Van Kirk Guthrie to Mary Jo Guthrie Edgmon, October 30, 1954, in WGA, Correspondence Series 3, Box 1, Folder 30.

363   Buck naked: Int with Stetson Kennedy, January 9, 1999.

363   This haven: Anneke Marshall to "Dear Marjorie," March 12, 1953, in WGA, Correspondence Series 3, Box 1, Folder 17.

364   We are only: Anneke Marshall to "Dear Marjorie," March 30, 1953, in WGA, Correspondence Series 3, Box 1, Folder 17.

364   Blistered: Anneke Marshall to "Dear MGM" [Marjorie Guthrie Marra], n.d., but probably June 10, 1953, in WGA, Correspondence Series 3, Box 1, Folder 17.

364   Pt threw: "Interview Card," Duval Medical Center, Jacksonville, Florida, June 10, 1953, in WGA, Correspondence Series 3, Box 1, Folder 17.

365   Anneke just couldn't: Int with George and Emily Guthrie by E. Victor and Judy Wolfenstein, n.d., but recorded between September 1971 and December 28, 1971, courtesy of EV&JW.

365   We had a little: Int of Bess Lomax Hawes and Baldwin "Butch" Hawes by E. Victor and Judy Wolfenstein, December 11, 1971, courtesy of EV&JW.

366   Wild and wooly: Anneke Guthrie to "Dear Marjorie," October 17, 1960, in WGA, Correspondence Series 3, Box 1, Folder 17.

366   Private note: Undated letter from Anneke Guthrie to "dear Marjorie," in WGA, Correspondence Series 3, Box 1, Folder 17.

366   Me & Annye: Guthrie to "Dear Marjorie," December 7/8, 1953, in WGA, Correspondence Series 3, Box 1, Folder 17.

367   Just a bunch of noise: Int with Fred Gerlach, April 4, 2001.

367   I decided: WG to "Dear MGM," February 3, 1954, in WGA, Correspondence Series 1, Box 3, Folder 6.

367   Baby naked: Anneke to "Dear Marjorie," October 17, 1960, in WGA, Correspondence Series 3, Box 1, Folder 18.

368   Guthrie would: Int with Fred Hellerman, August 6, 1998.

368   The old gaiety: Int of Ed Robbin by Richard Reuss, n.d., but 1968, in RRP, Box 8, Folder 3.

368   As he got: Int with Henrietta Yurchenko, June 16, November 18, 1999.

368   There's my land: Int with Jack Elliott, August 19, 2002. In fact, Guthrie had defaulted on the payments.

369   This little guy: Int with David Zeitlin, September 1, 1998. Zeitlin's father, Jake, and mother, Jacqueline Ver Brugge, were rare-book dealers and prominent figures in Los Angeles's literary circles, friends of a number of Guthrie acquaintances.

369   Haunting: Notes of an int with Jeff Guthrie by Richard Reuss, June 27–29, 1967, in RRP, Box 3, Folder 3.

369   Appeared: A copy of the agent's report, dated September 14, 1954, is in WGA, Personal Papers, Box 2, Folder 48.

370   Claude saw: Notes of an int with Jeff Guthrie by Richard Reuss, June 27–29, 1967, in RRP, Box 3, Folder 3.

CHAPTER TWENTY-SEVEN

371   My name: Untitled typescript internally dated to December 1954, while Guthrie was a patient at Brooklyn State Hospital, courtesy of BJO.

372   Halfways: WG to "Dearest Jolly," June 15, 1955, courtesy of Marianne Robinson.

372   God, be my preachy: Untitled typescript internally dated to December 1954, courtesy of BJO.

372   Damd damd: Quoted in Gordon Friesen, "The Man Woody Guthrie," *Broadside*, 57 (April 10, 1965).

372   The entire letter: Int of Bess Lomax Hawes and Baldwin "Butch" Hawes by E. Victor and Judy Wolfenstein, December 11, 1971; int of Bess Lomax Hawes, January 23, 2002.

372   I'm lots better: WG to Steve Nelson, from Brooklyn State Hospital, June 1955, courtesy of BJO. Nelson, embattled by investigating committees and government prosecutions, seems to have been a sympathetic acquaintance of Guthrie's.

373   I never did see: Int with Henrietta Yurchenko, June 16 and November 18, 1999.

373   In the big city: Int of Mary Jo Guthrie Edgmon by E. Victor and Judy Wolfenstein, September 25, 1971, courtesy of EV&JW.

373   It was the depression: Int with Harold Leventhal, February 15, 2001.

373   You live: Int with Harold Leventhal, January 14, 1999.

374   We never thought: Int with Harold Leventhal, February 15, 2001.

374   The Weavers needed: Int with Harold Leventhal, January 14, 1999.

374   Already admired: Int with Harold Leventhal, July 30, 1998.

374   Back in those days: Int with Pete Seeger, February 24, 2001.

375   Are you all right: Int with Harold Leventhal, February 15, 2001, and January 14, 1999. In recalling that concert, Leventhal noted, "I've often been accused

of making him into a myth, a hero. That wasn't a consideration. The consideration was things had to be taken care of, particularly how do we collect his royalties, how do we protect his writings that have not been protected [with copyrights]? How do we get more recordings so we can make more money? But I was doing that only as a manager and a music publisher."

375 That was the best: Int with Harold Leventhal, February 15, 2001.

376 Buller Shitting: Written on a paper towel, April 1956, in WGA.

376 So you give: Int with Harold Leventhal, January 14, 1999.

376 Wandering aimlessly: "Nurse's Notes on Admission," The New Jersey State Hospital at Greystone Park, May 29, 1956, in WGA, Personal Papers, Box 2, Folder 9.

376 For the welfare: WGA, Personal Papers, Box 2, Folder 8.

377 Quiet, cooperative: "Physician's Admission Notes," The New Jersey State Hospital at Greystone Park, May 29, 1956, in WGA, Personal Papers, Box 2, Folder 9.

377 This is just the same way: Int with Mary Jo Guthrie Edgmon, November 23, 1999.

377 I thought: "Mental Examination," June 1, 1956, in Case No. 65935 (Summary), in The New Jersey State Hospital at Greystone Park, May 29, 1956, in WGA, Personal Papers, Box 2, Folder 9.

377 Mental examination: M. A. Dolinsky, M.D., "Diagnostic Summary," Case No. 65935 (Summary), in The New Jersey State Hospital at Greystone Park, May 29, 1956, in WGA, Personal Papers, Box 2, Folder 9.

378 This is a very sick man: Int with Fred Hellerman, August 6, 1998.

378 You don't have to worry: Dave Marsh quotes Hellerman in "This Machine Kills Preconceptions," http://www.addict.com/html/hifi/Columns/American _Grandstand/407/index.html. Accessed December 2002.

378 Second run peaceable: WG to "Deary MGM," in WGA, Correspondence Series 1, Box 3, Folder 9.

378 It was part of our life: Int with Arlo Guthrie, February 3, 2002.

378 The Magic Tree: Int with Nora Guthrie, March 10, 2000.

379 Woody was doing: Int with Mary Jo Guthrie Edgmon, July 17, 1998.

379 Being in here: WG to "Marjory," n.d., but written on a letter to WG dated July 25, 1956, in WGA, Correspondence Series 1, Box 3, Folder 12.

379 No more: WG to Marjorie Guthrie Addeo, n.d., but probably August 1956, in WGA, Correspondence Series 1, Box 3, Folder 12.

379 God bless: WG to Marjorie and the children, September 6, 1956, in WGA, Correspondence Series 1, Box 3, Folder 9.

380 I know from years: Marjorie to Mary Jo, July 22, 1956, WGA, Correspondence Series 1, Box 3, Folder 10.

380 And all of us struggle: *Ibid.*

380 I'm just ajerkin: WGA, Correspondence Series 1, Box 3, Folder 11.

380 Twitchey chorea: WG to "Deary Ally," August 18, 1956, in WGA, Correspondence Series 1, Box 1, Folder 1.

380 Very sickest: WG to "Guthrie Tribe," December 4, 1956, in WGA, Correspondence Series 1, Box 3, Folder 11.

380 To help my doctors: WG to Marjorie, October 2, 1956, in WGA, Correspondence Series 1, Box 3, Folder 10.

381 I asked God: WG to "Dear Marjy," n.d., but late 1956, in WGA, Correspondence Series 1, Box 3, Folder 12.

381 He was one: Int with Sidsel Mari Gleason, March 9, 1999.

382   I have never met: Robert Shelton, "A Man to Remember: Woody Guthrie," reprint (New York: Guthrie Children's Trust Fund, 1967).

382   The Gleasons were: Int with Arlo Guthrie, February 3, 2002.

382   I was there: Dylan is quoted in Colin Irwin, "The Dust Brother," *Mojo* (November 1997), p. 75, courtesy of Larry Pryor.

383   A suffering shell: Robert Shelton, *No Direction Home: The Life and Music of Bob Dylan* (New York: William Morrow, 1986), p. 101.

383   The situation I'm in: "Woody," *Sing Out!* (December1967–January 1968), p. 3. Cisco Houston died in Los Angeles on April 28, 1961.

383   Hey, hey: Bob Dylan, *Lyrics 1962–1985* (New York: Alfred A. Knopf, 1998), p. 6. The song is recorded on Dylan's first eponymous long-playing record, released in 1962.

384   Did Woody Guthrie songs: Stark, "Hard Travelin': Ramblin' Jack Elliott Has a Few More Stories to Tell."

384   Jack sounds: Int with Jack Elliott, September 15, 2002.

384   Jerking around: David Hajdu, "Bound for Glory," *Vanity Fair* (May 2001), p. 218.

384   He would hit: Int with Sidsel Mari Gleason, March 9, 1999.

385   Help keep him stimulated: Entry dated August 14, 1957, in Case No. 65935 (Summary), in The New Jersey State Hospital at Greystone Park, May 29, 1956, in WGA, Personal Papers, Box 2, Folder 9.

CHAPTER TWENTY-EIGHT

386   He is failing: Marjorie to Mary Jo Guthrie Edgmon, July 1, 1962, in WGA.

386   California: Frank Hamilton to Cray, email, November 3, 1998.

386   Just blink: Reconstructed from int with Henrietta Yurchenko, June 16 and November 18, 1999.

387   I changed the number: Marjorie Guthrie, "Finding Our Way" (New York: Huntington's Disease Society of America, 1979), p. 22.

387   It was pretty tough: Marjorie [Guthrie Addeo] to Stetson Kennedy, February 2, 1966, courtesy of Kennedy.

388   When I walked in: Int with Matt Jennings, August 21, 1998.

388   Do you want: Marjorie Guthrie, "Finding Our Way," p. 31.

388   His stubborn sense: Alfred T. Hendricks, "Woody Guthrie in Hospital for 10 Years," *New York Post*, March 4, 1963.

388   I find no pattern: Marjorie [Guthrie Addeo] to Stetson Kennedy, February 2, 1966, courtesy of Kennedy.

388   In recognition: "The Woody Guthrie Newsletter," June 1966, p. 1.

389   A great occasion: Robert B. Semple Jr., "U.S. Award Given to Woody Guthrie," *New York Times*, April 7, 1966.

389   They're taking: Silber is quoted in Klein, *Woody Guthrie*, p. 434.

389   His illness: Int with Harvey Matusow, July 13, 1999. Ironically, Matusow described Guthrie in the interview as "a folk hero for me. . . . There was a purity about him. There was a simplicity. He could cut through the garbage and the end result was a simple solution."

390   He heard us: Marjorie Guthrie, "Finding Our Way," p. 23.

391   Whoever's number: Int with Harold Leventhal, July 30, 1998.

391   Profound influence: *New York Times*, October 4, 1967.

391   I guess none of us: Harold Leventhal to Pete Seeger, October 10, 1967, in WGA, Personal Papers, Box 2, Folder 31.3.

391   There was a long period: Int with Nora Guthrie, March 10, 2000.
391   She never stopped: Int with Irma Bauman, July 14, 1998.
391   To this day: Marjorie to "Dear Anneke," April 1, 1953. She added, "I didn't have any choice. It was just a simple medical decision that told me. Woody cannot live 24 hours a day within this family unit. The strains and stresses that he was beginning to feel was [sic] not good for his children."
392   Woody did not go: Int with Nora Guthrie, March 10, 2000.

CHAPTER TWENTY-NINE

In addition to the sources cited, the following provided information for this chapter: Colin Irwin, "The Dust Brother," *Mojo* (November 1997), pp. 77 *ff.*

393   We broke down: Int with Harold Leventhal, July 30, 1998.
393   Everything she did: Int with Nora Guthrie, March 10, 2000.
394   If they're under thirty: "Tribute," *The New Yorker*, January 29, 1972, p. 32.
395   Every time she talked: Int with Nora Guthrie, March 10, 2000.
395   It wasn't something: Int with Harold Leventhal, January 14, 1999. With Marjorie's concurrence, the Guthrie Children's Trust Fund gave some money to Bill Rogers Guthrie, to attend college. The fund also paid for funeral expenses for both Gwen and Sue when they died, Leventhal said. In an interview on August 19, 1998, Mary Jennings Guthrie Boyle credited Leventhal: "Harold is like an old mother hen when it comes to family. If it hadn't been for Harold, my kids would never have gotten any money."
396   The problem is: "Tribute," *The New Yorker*, January 29, 1972, p. 32.
396   The more urban: Int with Archie Green, October 16, 1998.
396   A good and simple man: John Greenway, "Woodrow Wilson Guthrie (1912–1967)," *Journal of American Folklore*, 81 (1968), p. 62. Greenway too does a bit of myth-making by discounting Guthrie's dedication to the Movement and asserting Guthrie was duped "by others far more sophisticated and intelligent."
396   He really is too short: Robert Shelton, "A Man to Remember: Woody Guthrie," uncredited article reprinted by Guthrie Children's Trust Fund, ca. 1967, courtesy of EV&JW.
397   Waxed enthusiastic: Ellen Stekert, "Cents and Nonsense in the Urban Folksong Movement," in Bruce Jackson, ed., *Folklore and Society: Essays in Honor of Benj. A. Botkin* (Hatboro, Pa.: Folklore Associates, 1966), pp. 162–163. Similarly, one Frederick E. Danker, at a meeting of the Popular Culture Association in 1973, commented, "Today many of Guthrie's later songs and political prose seems [sic] simplistic or simply dull drum-beating for partisan causes whose time has passed. . . . He had, perhaps, moved just too far from his roots." ("Voices of the Bard: The Songs of Guthrie, Haggard and Cash," a paper read before the Popular Culture Association, April 13–15, 1973, p. 10.)
397   He had the range: Murray Kempton, "The Curse of the Guthries," *New York Review of Books*, February 14, 1981, p. 9. Courtesy of Bill Deverell.
398   Had a spiritual center: Bill Eichenberger, "Today's Artists Evoke Spirit of Woody Guthrie in Tribute," *Columbus Dispatch*, September 30, 1996. Guthrie's induction into the Rock and Roll Hall of Fame came a year after that institution named three of his songs among the 500 most influential in rock history: "Pastures of Plenty," "Pretty Boy Floyd," and "This Land." In 2000, National Public Radio settled on a list of the 100 "most important" American

musical works of the twentieth century, classical, popular, folk; "This Land" was included, along with Huddie Ledbetter's "Goodnight, Irene." The next year, a panel created by the Recording Industry of America Association, the National Endowment for the Arts, *Scholastic* magazine, and an arm of AOL ranked "This Land Is Your Land" the second most historically important song of the twentieth century. ("Over the Rainbow," with lyrics by People's Songs sponsor E. Y. "Yip" Harburg, was first.) Guthrie surely would have been pleased to know that Kate Smith's recording of "God Bless America" came in nineteenth, seventeen spots behind him.

398   No instrumental virtuoso: Nat Hentoff, "Woody Guthrie Still Prowls Our Memories," *New York Times*, April 16, 1972.

398   The most important: Paxton is quoted in Yurchenko with Marjorie Guthrie, *A Mighty Hard Road*, p. 153.

398   I love Woody Guthrie: Harold Leventhal is quoted in Robert Santelli, "Beyond Folk: Woody Guthrie's Impact on Rock and Roll," in Santelli and Davidson, *Hard Travelin'*, p. 48.

398   He was the artist: *Ibid.*, p. 49.

399   Folk songs and the folk idiom: Reuss, "American Folklore and Left-Wing Politics," p. 172.

399   A bardic voice: Frederick E. Danker, "Voices of the Bard: The Songs of Guthrie, Haggard and Cash," a paper read before the Popular Culture Association, April 13–15, 1973, p. 1. "Bardic" seems just a little less pretentious than University of North Carolina Professor Robert Cantwell's pompous assertion that Guthrie was a "Druidic figure . . . who tapped into subconscious racial memories." Cantwell is quoted in Michael Sangiacomo, "Woody's Words Unwound as Talk Takes the Stage," *Cleveland Plain Dealer*, September 29, 1996. On the same panel, Fred Hellerman, who knew Guthrie personally , retorted, "Woody was an iconoclast, and it's amusing to see him being treated here as an icon."

399   For an American culture: Paul Goodnature, "Woody Guthrie: Folk Music Transcendentalist," M.S. thesis, Mankato State College, Mankato, Minn., March 1975. Caleb Hellerman, a television writer and producer, also saw in Guthrie's work a "transcendental philosophy." See "Bound for (More) Glory," *Nation*, April 24, 2000, p. 40.

399   He made himself: Int with Nora Guthrie, March 10, 2000.

400   Woody was too honest: Rick Mitchell, "Ramblin' Jack Still Rustles Up Gems," *Houston Chronicle*, April 9, 1998.

400   On a 5,000-acre: Int with Jack Elliott, August 19, 2002.

401   The highest: Quoted by Martin Duberman, "A Fellow Traveling," *Nation*, July 16, 2001, p. 36.

401   Given the fact: H. R. Stoneback, "Woody Sez: Woody Guthrie and 'The Grapes of Wrath,'" *Steinbeck Newsletter*, Summer 1989, p. 8.

401   Guthrie is remade: Int with Archie Green, October 16, 1998.

401   Details of the program: "City Salutes Woody Guthrie at Secluded Meet," *Okemah News Leader*, July 15, 1971.

401   Hippies: *Los Angeles Times*, July 12, 1971.

401   Who betrayed: B. Drummond Ayres Jr., "Woody Guthrie's Home Town Is Divided on Paying Him Homage," *New York Times*, December 14, 1972.

402   Unquestionably: Neal Walters and Brian Mansfield, eds., *MusicHound Folk: The Essential Album Guide* (Detroit: Visible Ink, 1998), p. 336.

402   Did more than any other: Felicia Hardison Londré, "A Voice of the People," in

the program notes for "Woody Guthrie's American Song," presented by the Berkeley [California] Repertory Theater, n.d., but probably July–August 1992. Courtesy of Bill Deverell.

402   Would have been more: Gordon Friesen to "Dear Dick," January 6, 1971, in RRP, Box 1, Folder 20.

403   To boost environmental: *Discount Store News*, June 21, 1993, p. 14. Guthrie's opinions of the Bonneville Power Authority are in his *American Folksong*, p. 44.

AFTERWORD

404   Woody, they never care: Quoted from the *Daily Oklahoman*, October 14, 1974.

Allsop, Kenneth. *Hard Travellin'* (London: Penguin Books, 1971).

Benson, Jackson J. *The True Adventures of John Steinbeck, Writer* (New York: Viking Press, 1984).

Bernstein, Irving. *The Turbulent Years* (Boston: Houghton Mifflin, 1969).

Burbank, Garin. *When Farmers Voted Red: The Gospel of Socialism in the Oklahoma Countryside, 1910–1924* (Westport, Conn.: Greenwood Press, 1976).

Carman, Bryan K. *A Race of Singers* (Chapel Hill: University of North Carolina Press, 2000).

Cohen, Edwin. "Woody Guthrie and the American Folk Song." Unpublished Ph.D dissertation, University of Southern California, 1971.

Collier, Robert. *The Secret of the Ages* (New York: Robert Collier Publisher, ca. 1926), Vols. I–VII.

Columbia, The. Written and directed by Stephen B. Kahn (Portland, Ore: Bonneville Power Authority, 1949).

"Communist Activities Among Youth Groups." United States House of Representatives, Subcommittee of the Committee on Un-American Activities," February 6, 1952, pp. 3273 *ff.*

Corwin, Norman. *Norman Corwin's Letters,* edited by A. J. Langguth (New York: Barricade Books, 1994).

Curtis, James R. "Woody Guthrie and the Dust Bowl," in George O. Carney, ed., *The Sounds of People and Places,* 3rd ed. (Lanham, Md.: Rowman and Littlefield, 1994), pp. 253–62.

Dawidoff, Nicholas. *In the Country of Country* (New York: Pantheon Books, 1997).

Denisoff, R. Serge. *Great Day Coming: Folk Music and the American Left* (Baltimore: Penguin Books, 1973).

Denisoff, Ronald Teague. "Folk Consciousness: People's Music and American Communism." Unpublished Ph.D. dissertation, Simon Fraser University, Canada, 1970.

———. "The Proletarian Renascence." *Journal of American Folklore* 82 (1969), pp. 51–65.

——. "Songs of Persuasion." *Journal of American Folklore* 79 (1966), pp. 581–89.

——. "Take It Easy, But Take It." *Journal of American Folklore* 83 (1970), pp. 21 *ff*.

——. "Urban Folk 'Movement' Research: Value Free?" *Western Folklore* 28 (1969), pp. 183–97.

Denning, Michael. *The Cultural Front* (New York: Verso, 1997).

Dillsaver, Jon. "Woody Guthrie's Depression: A Study of Situation." Unpublished Ph.D. dissertation, University of Missouri, 1975.

Dunaway, David King. *How Can I Keep from Singing: Pete Seeger* (New York: Da Capo Press, 1990).

Dunbar-Ortiz, Roxanne. *Red Dirt: Growing Up Okie* (New York: Verso, 1997).

Fariello, Griffin. *Red Scare: Memories of the American Inquisition* (New York: W. W. Norton, 1995).

Goldsmith, Peter D. *Making People's Music: Moe Asch and Folkways Records* (Washington: Smithsonian Institution Press, 1998).

Goodnature, Paul. "Woody Guthrie: Folk Music Transcendentalist." M.S. thesis, Mankato State College, Mankato, Minn., 1975.

Green, Archie. "Notes to 'Girl of Constant Sorrow'"(Huntington, Vt.: Folk-Legacy Records, FSA-26, 1965).

——. *Songs about Work: Essays in Occupational Culture for Richard A. Reuss* (Bloomington: Folklore Institute, Indiana University, 1993).

Greenway, John. *American Folksongs of Protest* (Philadelphia: University of Pennsylvania Press, 1953).

Gregory, James N. *American Exodus* (New York: Oxford University Press, 1989).

Guthrie, Charley Edward. "Kumrids: A Discussion of Scientific Socialism" (Okemah: Ledger Print, 1912).

——. "Procrastination Is the Thief of Time" (Okemah: Ledger Print, 1912).

Guthrie, Woody. *American Folksong* (New York: Oak Publications, 1961).

——. *Born to Win* (New York: Macmillan, 1965).

——. *Bound for Glory*, new ed. (New York: E. P. Dutton, 1976).

——. "Ear Players." *Common Ground*, Spring 1942, pp. 32–43.

——. "My Life," in *American Folksong* (New York: Oak Publications, 1961).

——. "Old Time Hill Country Songs Being Sung for Ages, Still Growing Strong" (Gardena, Calif.: Spanish American Institute, 1938 [?]).

——. "On a Slow Train Through California." Mimeographed songbook, Los Angeles, 1939.

——. *Pastures of Plenty*, edited by Dave Marsh and Harold Leventhal (New York: HarperPerennial, 1992).

——. *Roll on Columbia* (Portland, Ore.: Bonneville Power Administration, 1988).

——. *Seeds of Man* (Lincoln: University of Nebraska Press, 1995).

——. "Woody and Lefty Lou's Favorite Collection [of] Old Time Hill Country Songs" (Gardena, Calif.: Institute Press, 1938[?]).

——. "Woody and Lefty Lou's Favorite Collection of Old Time Hillbilly Songs." Mimeographed, Los Angeles, ca. 1937.

——. *Woody Sez* (New York: Grosset and Dunlap, 1975).

Guthrie, Woody, and Marjorie Mazia Guthrie. *Woody's 20 Grow Big Songs* (New York: HarperCollins, 1992).

Haslam, Gerald. *Working Man Blues* (Berkeley: University of California Press, 1999).

Hurston, Zora Neal. *Go Gator and Muddy the Water*, edited by Pamela Bordelon (New York: W. W. Norton, 1999).

Isserman, Maurice. *Which Side Were You On?* (Urbana: University of Illinois Press, 1993).

——. "Peat Bog Soldiers: The American Communist Party during the Second World War, 1939–1945." Unpublished Ph.D. dissertation, University of Rochester, 1979.

Jackson, Bruce. *Folklore and Society: Essays in Honor of Benj. A. Botkin* (Hatboro, Pa.: Folklore Associates, 1966).

Jackson, Thomas W. "I'm from Texas: You Can't Steer Me" (Chicago: Thos. W. Jackson Publishing, 1948).

——. *On a Slow Train through Arkansaw*, edited by W. K. McNeil (Lexington: University Press of Kentucky, 1985).

Joyce, Davis D. *An Oklahoma I Had Never Seen* (Norman: University of Oklahoma Press, 1994).

Kagan, Sheldon S. " 'Goin' Down the Road Feelin' Bad': John Steinbeck's *The Grapes of Wrath* and Migrant Folklore." Unpublished Ph.D. dissertation, University of Pennsylvania, 1971.

Klein, Joe. *Woody Guthrie: A Life* (New York: Alfred A. Knopf, 1980).

Leader, Leonard. *Los Angeles and the Great Depression* (New York: Garland, 1991).

Levin, Meyer. *In Search* (New York: Horizon, 1950).

Logsdon, Guy. "The Dust Bowl and the Migrant." *American Scene* 12, No. 1 (Tulsa, Okla.: Thomas Gilcrease Institute of American History and Art, 1971).

——. "Woody Guthrie and His Oklahoma Hills." *Mid-America Folklore*, 19 (1991).

——, compiler. "Woody Guthrie: A Biblio-Discography." Unpublished research paper, National Endowment for the Humanities and the Smithsonian Institution, May 15, 1998.

Lomax, Alan. *The Folk Songs of North America* (Garden City, N.Y.: Doubleday, 1960).

Lomax, Alan, Woody Guthrie, and Pete Seeger. *Hard Hitting Songs for Hard-Hit People* (Lincoln: University of Nebraska Press, 1999).

Longhi, Jim. *Woody, Cisco, and Me: Seamen Three in the Merchant Marine* (Urbana: University of Illinois Press, 1997).

Majdic, Michael, and Denise Matthews, producers and directors. *Roll on Columbia*. Videotape production of the University of Oregon Knight Library Media Services and School of Journalism and Communication, 1999.

Malone, Bill C. *Country Music, U.S.A.* (Austin: University of Texas Press, 1970).

McWilliams, Carey. *Factories in the Fields* (Boston: Little, Brown, 1939).

——. *Southern California Country* (New York: Duell, Sloan & Pearce, 1946).

Menig, Harry. "Woody Guthrie: The Oklahoma Years, 1912–1929," in Davis D. Joyce, *An Oklahoma I Had Never Seen Before* (Norman: University of Oklahoma Press, 1994).

Miller, Worth Robert. *Oklahoma Populism: A History of the People's Party in the Oklahoma Territory* (Norman: University of Oklahoma Press, 1987).

Mitchell, Don. *The Lie of the Land: Migrant Workers and the California Landscape* (Minneapolis: University of Minnesota Press, 1996).

Morgan, Dan. *Rising in the West* (New York: Alfred A. Knopf, 1992).

Mott, Frank Luther. *Headlining America* (Boston: Houghton Mifflin, 1937).

Noebel, David A. *The Marxist Minstrels: A Handbook on Communist Subversion of Music* (Tulsa, Okla.: American Christian College Press, 1974).

Norton, Sally Osborne. "A Historical Study of Actor Will Geer, His Life and Work in the Context of Twentieth-Century American Social, Political and Theatrical History." Unpublished Ph.D. dissertation, University of Southern California, 1980.

Parini, Jay. *John Steinbeck: A Biography* (New York: Henry Holt, 1995).

Porterfield, Nolan. *Jimmie Rodgers* (Urbana: University of Illinois Press, 1979).

Purinton, Edward Earl. "Big Ideas from Big Business." *Independent*, April 16, 1921.

Reuss, Richard A. "American Folklore and Left-Wing Politics: 1927–1957." Unpublished Ph.D. dissertation, Indiana University, 1971.

——, compiler. "Woody Guthrie Bibliography" (New York: Guthrie Children's Trust Fund, 1968).

Robbin, Ed. *Woody Guthrie and Me* (Berkeley, Calif.: Lancaster-Miller, 1979).

Robinson, Earl, with Eric A. Gordon. *Ballad of an American* (Lanham, Md.: Scarecrow Press, 1998).

Rutland, Robert Allen. *A Boyhood in the Dust Bowl* (Niwot: University Press of Colorado, 1995).

Sandburg, Carl. *Complete Poems* (New York: Harcourt, Brace, 1950).

Santelli, Robert, and Emily Davidson, eds. *Hard Travelin': The Life and Legacy of Woody Guthrie* (Hanover, N.H.: Wesleyan University Press, 1999).

Schreker, Ellen. *Many Are the Crimes* (New York: Little, Brown, 1998).

Seeger, Peter. *The Incompleat Folksinger*, edited by Jo Metcalf Schwartz (Lincoln: University of Nebraska Press, 1992).

———. *Where Have All the Flowers Gone* (Bethlehem, Pa.: Sing Out!, 1998).

Sellars, Nigel Anthony. *Oil, Wheat and Wobblies* (Norman: University of Oklahoma Press, 1998).

Shelton, Robert. *No Direction Home: The Life and Music of Bob Dylan* (New York: William Morrow, 1986).

Shindo, Charles J. *Dust Bowl Migrants in the American Imagination* (Lawrence: University of Kansas Press, 1997).

Spector, Bert Alan. "Wasn't That a Time: Pete Seeger and the Anti-Communist Crusade." Unpublished Ph.D. dissertation, University of Missouri-Columbia, 1977.

Spitzer, Nick, producer. *American Routes*. "Labor Day" segment, broadcast September 2000, distributed by Public Radio International, Minneapolis.

Stark, Jeff. "Hard Travelin': Ramblin' Jack Elliott Has a Few More Stories to Tell," *Dallas Observer*, April 9, 1998.

Stein, Walter J. *California and the Dust Bowl Migration* (Westport, Conn.: Greenwood Press, 1973).

Steinbeck, John. "Their Blood Is Strong" (San Francisco: Simon J. Lubin Society, 1938).

Steinhaus, Kathleen Milligan. "The Life and Times of Woody Guthrie." M.A. project presented to the faculty of California State University, Chico, Fall 1978.

Stolder, Steven. "Traveling Back with Ramblin' Jack Elliott," *NARAS Journal* 6, No. 2 (Winter 1995–96), pp. 7–33.

Thompson, John. *Closing the Frontier* (Norman: University of Oklahoma Press, 1986).

Tick, Judith. *Ruth Crawford Seeger: A Composer's Search for American Music* (New York: Oxford University Press, 1997).

Townsend, Bob. "Ramblin' Jack Elliott," *Atlanta Journal*, May 17, 1996.

Violations of Free Speech and Rights of Labor. Hearings Before a Subcommittee of the Committee on Education and Labor, United States Senate, 76th Congress, Part 59, San Francisco, January 25, 1940 (Washington, D.C.: Government Printing Office, 1940).

Violations of Free Speech and Rights of Labor. Report of the Committee on Education and Labor, Pursuant to S. Res. 266 (Washington, D.C.: Government Printing Office, 1942).

Ward, Stephen. "Talking Blues." National Public Radio, March 23, 2001.

Willens, Doris. *Lonesome Traveler: The Life of Lee Hays* (Lincoln: University of Nebraska Press, 1988).

Wolfe, Charles, and Kip Lornell. *The Life and Legend of Leadbelly* (New York: HarperCollins, 1992).

Yurchenko, Henrietta, with Marjorie Guthrie. *A Mighty Hard Row* (New York: McGraw-Hill, 1970).

The Almanac Singers. *Their Complete General Recordings.* MCA Records, MCAD 11499, 1996.

Guthrie, Woody. *Ballads of Sacco and Vanzetti.* Smithsonian Folkways SF CD 40060, 1996.

——. *Buffalo Skinners.* The Asch Recordings, Vol 4. Smithsonian Folkways SFW CD 40103, 1999.

——. *Columbia River Collection.* Rounder CD 1036, 1987.

——. *Dust Bowl Ballads.* Rounder CD 1040, 1988.

——. *Hard Travelin': The Asch Recordings,* Vol. 3. Smithsonian Folkways SF CD 40102, 1998.

——. *The Library of Congress Recordings.* Rounder 1041/42/43, 1988.

——. *Long Ways to Travel.* Smithsonian Folkways SF CD 40046, 1994.

——. *Muleskinner Blues: The Asch Recordings,* Vol. 2. Smithsonian Folkways 40101, 1997.

——. *Nursery Days.* Smithsonian Folkways SF 45036, 1992.

——. *Sings Folk Songs with Leadbelly, Cisco Houston, Sonny Terry, Bess Hawes.* Smithsonian Folkways SF 40007, 1989.

——. *Songs to Grow on for Mother and Child.* Smithsonian Folkways SF 45035, 1991.

——. *Struggle.* Smithsonian Folkways SF 40025, 1990.

——. *That's Why We're Marching: World War II and the American Folk Song Movement.* Smithsonian Folkways SF CD 40021, 1996.

——. *This Land Is Your Land: The Asch Recordings,* Vol. 1. Smithsonian Folkways SF CD 40100, 1997.

Maddox, Rose. *Rose of the West Coast Country.* Arhoolie CD 314, 1990.

The Martins and the Coys. Rounder 11661–1819-2, 2000.

in Pampa, Tex., 36, 37–41, 46–47, 62,
65, 66–70, 77, 78, 79–89, 161–62,
188–89, 312, 335–36
as performer, 29–32, 34, 36, 51–56, 61,
67, 71–72, 97–116, 125, 131–32,
136, 140, 143, 155–56, 160–61,
166–68, 198–99, 229, 232, 235,
247–48, 259, 269, 283–84,
294–95, 312–13, 317, 324, 325,
327–28, 339, 356, 366, 367, 400
personality of, xxii, 11, 32–33, 46,
48–49, 59, 79, 81–82, 95–96, 116,
145–46, 161, 170–71, 194, 205–6,
230–32, 251, 332–33, 339,
355–56, 400
personal philosophy of, xxii, 34, 44–45, 48,
79, 84–85, 136, 146–48, 152–53
photographs of, iv, 62
physical appearance of, xvii, xx, xxi, xxiii,
11, 25, 35–36, 38, 60, 155, 167,
194, 208, 209, 211, 242, 244, 247,
347, 352, 364, 366, 369, 370, 381,
383, 386–87, 388
physical decline of, 314, 356, 369–90,
394–95
physical stamina of, 92–93, 158,
233n–34n
plays written by, 355
political views of, 34, 66, 86–87, 109–10,
123, 127, 159, 160–61, 170–72,
189–90, 200, 208–9, 211, 266,
273, 282–84, 288, 322–25, 397
postage stamp for, 389n
press coverage of, 182, 195, 239–40,
265–66, 285, 287, 299, 370, 378,
382, 388, 391, 396
Pretty Polly Canyon property of, 358–59,
360, 368, 369
psychiatric evaluation of, 332–33,
376–78, 385
Pythian Hall concert for (1956), xix–xxiii,
374–75, 379
in radio broadcasts, 52, 53, 67, 86,
101–23, 182–84, 185, 190–91,
195–99, 200, 201, 206, 239–40,
255, 275, 281, 285–86, 329,
362–63, 381, 400
radio contracts of, 113, 117–18, 120–21,
191
radio programs of, 101–27, 128, 129,
132, 136, 156, 158, 191, 195–99,
200, 202, 236, 239, 255, 285, 307,
381, 400
"Railroad Pete" stories of, 253, 254, 256,
263
reading by, 36, 44, 46, 48, 84–85, 86, 87,
136, 165, 171–72, 271, 288, 306,
370
religious beliefs of, 85–86, 90–91,

146–47, 283–84, 365n, 371, 380,
390, 391
reputation of, xvii–xviii, xx, xxii–xxiii,
108, 112–13, 116, 117, 120, 121,
139, 156–57, 158, 166–77,
182–84, 195–99, 265–66, 285–86,
287, 294, 299, 318–19, 358, 361,
389–90, 395, 396–403
restlessness of, 77, 78–80, 84, 87–88,
126, 130, 162, 184, 185, 189,
198–99, 201–2, 205, 207, 213,
264, 291, 335, 364
at rodeo, 104–5
rudeness of, 173–74, 198–99, 223,
231–32, 237, 238, 249–50,
312–13, 336, 339
sculptures of, 271n, 318, 319, 360
sense of humor of, 30, 35, 42, 48, 54,
71–72, 84, 107, 123–24, 127, 132,
168, 196–97, 232, 234–35, 400
sexuality of, 35, 250, 284, 292, 302,
330–34, 340–41, 355, 359
as sign painter, 40, 47, 48, 66, 71, 80, 84,
90, 95, 162, 207, 291
in silver mine expeditions, 56–58, 201,
267, 308, 323n, 347, 415n
singing by, 43, 44, 54, 90, 97–98, 103,
107–8, 164, 168, 175, 221, 294,
314, 368, 369, 384
"singing cricket" story of, 202–3
in singing duos, 96–116, 117, 118,
119–20, 121, 122–23, 125–26,
127, 128, 129, 131–32, 136,
178–79, 182–83, 185–89, 225–27,
259, 263, 266, 267, 268–72,
278–81, 307, 313–14, 322, 339,
381
social life of, 42, 50, 141–42, 184, 262,
355–56, 358, 368, 379, 386–87
speech loss of, xx, 381, 384n, 386–87
as spokesman for dust bowl migrants,
xvii–xviii, 126–32, 148–50, 154–59,
168–72, 175–76, 179–82, 184,
397, 400–401
string bass played by, 54, 71
as teletype operator, 289, 290, 291
"This Machine Kills Fascists" slogan of,
319, 329n, 363n
tobacco habit of, 31, 48, 376, 381, 386,
388
in Topanga, Calif., 354–62, 364–66,
368–69
travels of, xxi, 33–34, 77, 78–80, 87–96,
127–32, 158, 162–63, 185–89,
221–27, 256, 267, 268–71,
335–36, 354–70, 402
typing ability of, xviii, 36, 111, 115, 141,
164, 184, 201, 206, 211, 223, 282,
301, 306, 308, 316, 363, 365, 380

"WORdy" Gutherie